Applied Operations Research and Management Science

W. J. Fabrycky
P. M. Ghare
P. E. Torgersen
all of
Virginia Polytechnic Institute
and State University

PRENTICE-HALL, INC., Englewood Cliffs, N.J. 07632

Library of Congress Cataloging in Publication Data

FABRYCKY, W. J. (Wolter J.). (date)
  Applied operations research and management science.

  Bibliography: p.
  Includes index.
  1. Operations research. 2. Management science.
I. Ghare, P. M. II. Torgersen,
Paul E. III. Title.
T57.6.F3 1984   658.4'03'4   83-3445
ISBN 0-13-041459-X

Editorial/production supervision
  and interior design: **Karen Skrable**
Manufacturing buyer: **Anthony Caruso**
Cover design: **Debra Watson**

© 1984, 1972, 1966 by Prentice-Hall, Inc., Englewood Cliffs, N.J. 07632
Previous edition published under the title *Industrial Operations Research*.

*All rights reserved. No part of this book
may be reproduced in any form or
by any means without permission in writing
from the publisher.*

Printed in the United States of America

10 9 8 7 6 5 4 3 2 1

ISBN 0-13-041459-X

Prentice-Hall International, Inc., *London*
Prentice-Hall of Australia Pty. Limited, *Sydney*
Editora Prentice-Hall do Brasil, Ltda., *Rio de Janeiro*
Prentice-Hall Canada Inc., *Toronto*
Prentice-Hall of India Private Limited, *New Delhi*
Prentice-Hall of Japan, Inc., *Tokyo*
Prentice-Hall of Southeast Asia Pte. Ltd., *Singapore*
Whitehall Books Limited, *Wellington, New Zealand*

Contents

Preface ix

I INTRODUCTION TO OR/MS *1*

1 OR/MS and Scientific Management *3*
    1.1 The Scientific Approach to Operations *4*
    1.2 Human Want Satisfaction *8*
    1.3 Objectives and Alternatives *10*
    1.4 Effectiveness and Efficiency *12*
    1.5 A Plan for Applying OR/MS *14*

2 Models and Simulation in OR/MS *19*
    2.1 A Classification of Models *20*
    2.2 Experimentation Through Simulation *22*
    2.3 Model Formulation and Optimization *23*
    2.4 Control of the Model Solution *26*
    2.5 The Application of Models *27*

II MATHEMATICAL PROGRAMMING MODELS *31*

3 General Linear Programming Models *33*
3.1 Mathematical Model Formulation *34*
3.2 Graphical Optimization Methods *34*
3.3 Maximizing by the Simplex Method *42*
3.4 Minimizing by the Simplex Method *46*
3.5 Matrix Formulation of Linear Programming *47*
3.6 The Revised Simplex Method *52*
3.7 Duality in Linear Programming *58*
3.8 Related Linear Programming Topics *60*

4 Distribution Models of Linear Programming *66*
4.1 The Transportation Model *67*
4.2 Vogel's Approximation Method *75*
4.3 The Assignment Model *77*
4.4 The Traveling Salesman Problem *84*

5 Goal Linear Programming Models *95*
5.1 Goal Programming Model Formulation *96*
5.2 Formulations for Multiple Goals *97*
5.3 Graphical Optimization Method *100*
5.4 Modified Simplex Optimization Method *102*

6 Dynamic Programming Models *108*
6.1 Dynamic Programming Model Formulation *109*
6.2 Some Computational Procedures *110*
6.3 Capital Allocation Problem *113*
6.4 Shipping or "Knapsack" Problem *117*

III MODELS FOR DECISION ALTERNATIVES *123*

7 Decision and Game Models *125*
7.1 The Payoff Matrix Model *126*
7.2 Decisions Under Assumed Certainty *127*
7.3 Decisions Under Risk *129*
7.4 Decisions Under Uncertainty *132*
7.5 Game Decision Models *138*

8 Models for Production Operations *148*
8.1 The Production System *149*
8.2 Classification of Production Cost *151*
8.3 Production Quantity Decisions *154*
8.4 Linear Break-Even Models *158*
8.5 The Production Function *163*

9 Models for Economic Equivalence 175
    9.1   The Time Value of Money 176
    9.2   Interest and Interest Formulas 178
    9.3   The Calculation of Equivalence 183
    9.4   Evaluating a Single Alternative 187
    9.5   Comparing Multiple Alternatives 190

10 Depreciation and Replacement Models 195
    10.1   The Concept of Depreciation 196
    10.2   Some Depreciation Models 198
    10.3   The Basic Replacement Model 207
    10.4   The Optimum Replacement Interval 212
    10.5   A Dynamic Replacement Model 215
    10.6   Replacement of Units That Fail 219

IV MODELS FOR PRODUCTION AND OPERATIONS CONTROL 229

11 Production Progress Models 231
    11.1   Production Time Improvements 232
    11.2   The Graphical Progress Function 235
    11.3   The Mathematical Progress Model 239
    11.4   Defining the Progress Model 242
    11.5   Applications of the Progress Model 245

12 Models for Production Sequencing 253
    12.1   Flow-Shop Sequencing for Two Machines 254
    12.2   Flow-Shop Sequencing for Several Machines 256
    12.3   The Job-Shop Sequencing Problem 262
    12.4   Comparison of Job-Shop Sequencing Rules 266

13 Project Planning and Control Models 279
    13.1   Deterministic Project Control—CPM 280
    13.2   An Example of Project Control with CPM 282
    13.3   Probabilistic Project Control—PERT 286
    13.4   An Example of Project Control with PERT 287
    13.5   Economic Aspects of Project Control 290

14 Statistical Control Models for Operations 297
    14.1   The Concept of Statistical Control 298
    14.2   Control Models for Variables 301
    14.3   Operating Characteristics of $\bar{X}$ Charts 306
    14.4   Control Models for Attributes 310
    14.5   Acceptance Sampling Models 316

V PROCUREMENT AND INVENTORY MODELS 329

15 Deterministic Procurement and Inventory Models 331
- 15.1 The Procurement and Inventory System 332
- 15.2 The Decision Environment 334
- 15.3 The Purchase Alternative 337
- 15.4 The Manufacture Alternative 340
- 15.5 Making the Source Decision 343
- 15.6 Models for Variable Item Cost 345
- 15.7 Models for Finite Shortage Cost 348
- 15.8 Procurement to Meet Variable Demand 355
- 15.9 Procurement Based Only on Item Cost 359

16 Probabilistic Inventory Models 366
- 16.1 Simulation of Inventory Flow 367
- 16.2 Expressions for Expected Values 373
- 16.3 The Distribution of Lead Time Demand 375
- 16.4 Expressions for Shortage Condition 378
- 16.5 The Minimum Cost Inventory Policies 382
- 16.6 Minimum Cost Policies for a Simplified System 386
- 16.7 A Single-Period Inventory Model 388

VI MODELS FOR QUEUING OPERATIONS 393

17 Deterministic Queuing Models 395
- 17.1 The Queuing System 396
- 17.2 The Decision Environment 398
- 17.3 Models for No Initial Waiting Line 400
- 17.4 A Model with an Initial Waiting Line 403
- 17.5 An Approximation for Total Waiting Time 407
- 17.6 A General Numerical Solution Method 409

18 Probabilistic Queuing Models 414
- 18.1 Simulation of Waiting Lines 415
- 18.2 Single Channel Queuing Derivations 418
- 18.3 The Distribution of Waiting Time 424
- 18.4 Multiple-Channel Waiting-Line Derivations 427
- 18.5 Poisson Arrivals with Nonexponential Service 429
- 18.6 Finite Population Models 432
- 18.7 Finite Population Models and Maintenance 436

APPENDICES *445*

- A   Linear and Matrix Algebra *447*
- B   Classical Optimization Methods *455*
- C   Probability and Simulated Sampling *463*
- D   Statistical Tables *482*
- E   Interest Factor Tables *492*
- F   Progress Function Tables *506*
- G   Finite Queuing Tables *510*

Selected References *518*
Index *521*

Preface

Operations research and management science (OR/MS) have much in common: Both were developed from an interest in applying the scientific method to problems faced by managers. Continued progress in this endeavor may be expected to extend and refine the quantitative approach to decision making. Anyone who aspires to a managerial position, or who is part of the management process as a decision maker or staff member, will find an understanding of OR/MS to be very helpful.

This text is applied in its orientation. We have elected to minimize abstract material and have avoided complex mathematical explanations. Necessary mathematical derivations are accompanied by numerical examples. Simulated sampling is used to provide insight into probabilistic operations prior to model derivation. A general decision model structure is utilized to illustrate the similarity of decision situations and to facilitate decision model development.

Part I presents prerequisite concepts. The viewpoint that OR/MS should not be an end in itself, but should be a means for improving the want satisfying capacity of organizational activity, is emphasized in the first chapter. The second chapter presents the decision model as a simulation device for achieving optimum operating effectiveness.

Parts II through VI cover a wide range of topics associated with business and industrial operations, with an emphasis on economic criteria. Mathematical programming is presented first and encompasses the general linear programing model, distribution models of linear programming, goal linear programming, and dynamic programming. Next, models for decision alternatives are presented in general terms and then with applications to competitive game situations, production operations, economic equivalence, and asset replacement. The important area of production and operations control is covered by production progress models, models for production sequencing, project planning and control models, and statistical control models. Both deterministic and probabilistic procurement and inventory models are then presented. Waiting-line operations are treated by both deterministic and probabilistic queuing models, including the finite population case.

We have treated each topic in a concise manner to make this text reasonably complete in presenting the popular quantitative methods applicable to operations. Each topic is organized within chapters so that the more advanced may be omitted without loss of continuity. The text contains sufficient material and an organization that allows considerable flexibility in the design of a course. A complete set of questions and problems is included at the end of each chapter to facilitate the learning and application of OR/MS.

The ABCs of the mathematical background essential to an understanding of OR/MS are presented for review in Appendices A, B, and C. These concise reviews encompass linear and matrix algebra, classical optimization techniques, and probability and simulated sampling. Statistical tables, interest factor tables, progress function tables, and finite queuing tables are found in Appendices D through G.

This text first appeared in 1966 under the title of *Operations Economy: Industrial Applications of Operations Research*. Then, in 1972, it was revised under the title of *Industrial Operations Research* and received the Institute of Industrial Engineers book of the year award. The current revision has been broadened to encompass business and industrial operations generally, while retaining the technological orientation of the prior editions.

We are grateful to the many students and practicing professionals who helped us to refine and organize this material in the most useful way. Special thanks are due Mrs. Joy Compton for her patience and skill in typing this edition.

Blacksburg, Virginia

W. J. Fabrycky
P. M. Ghare
P. E. Torgersen

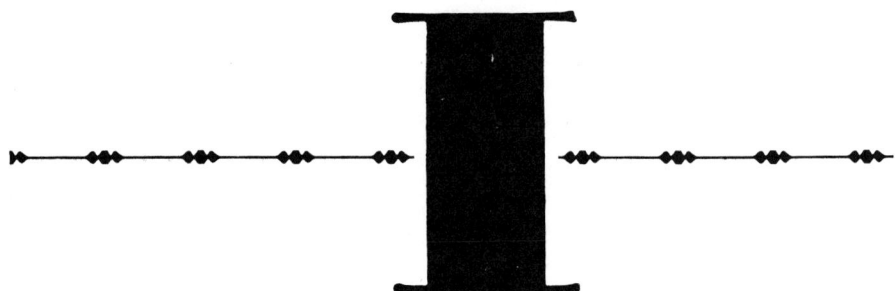

Introduction to OR/MS

1

OR/MS and Scientific Management

In dealing with physical phenomena, human beings have accumulated an expanding body of physical laws upon which to base their reasoning. With every advance in the physical sciences, new relationships are discovered which provide further understanding of the physical environment. Although much less is known about the science of the management of operations, this important area is now receiving considerable attention. The increasing difficulty of rational decision making has been followed by numerous efforts to put this process on a more quantitative, objective, and routine basis.

This chapter begins with a description of the scientific approach to operations through operations research and management science (OR/MS). The maximization of human want satisfaction is highlighted as the ultimate objective of organized human activity. Effectiveness and efficiency are defined in relation to alternative courses of managerial action. Thus, this chapter emphasizes that OR/MS are not ends in themselves, but are means for improving operational activity.

1.1 THE SCIENTIFIC APPROACH TO OPERATIONS

The management process involves numerous decisions that determine the present and future status of the organization. These decisions deal with many levels of operational activity. They may range from routine recurrent decisions required in finance, production, marketing, or distribution, through top-level policy determination for the firm as a whole. Scientific approaches to management have the objective of developing and recommending logical bases for choosing from among operational alternatives. Although intuition, experience, and subjective judgment are still the predominant ingredients in top-level decisions and in most operating-level decisions, considerable progress has been made in adopting scientific decision aids.

To accept the OR/MS viewpoint, management must first accept the scientific method as being relevant to many management decisions. The scientific method is a process of inquiry that calls for the formulation and systematic test of a hypothesis, and the acceptance or rejection of that hypothesis based on empirical evidence. The method is assumed to be free of subjective elements so that the facts may speak for themselves.

Operations Research. Research applied to operations was practically unknown prior to World War II. The first record of a modern operations research effort is that of the Anti-Aircraft Command Research Group organized in 1940 in the United Kingdom to study problems arising from the interaction of radar equipment and antiaircraft guns. The problem was that new radar equipment did not appear to perform at field sites as well as it did at the testing stations. This discrepancy called for on site scientific observation during actual operation. P.M.S. Blackett of the University of Manchester, a Nobel laureate, was asked to study the problem. So that several perspectives could be examined, Blackett assembled a team composed of an astrophysicist, two mathematical physicists, a general physicist, two mathematicians, three physiologists, a surveyor, and an Army officer. "Blackett's circus," as the group was called, successfully demonstrated the value of the scientific approach to an operational problem of considerable military importance.

In the United States, similar operations research groups were organized within the military branches. These groups were attached to operational commands at various levels to recommend policies that would improve military effectiveness. Mathematicians, engineers, physicists, psychologists, and others were recruited to assist in the complex task of military decision making. Besides radar operational improvements, studies included such activities as antisubmarine operations, aerial mining of the sea, merchant convoy size determination, ship maneuvers under aerial attack, and statistical analysis of bomb damage.

Although the military retained its capability in operations research after the war, many military operations researchers found a strong demand for their talent in civilian operations research. Large corporations and civil governmental agencies created research activities dealing with operational problems similar to the research efforts directed to product development and marketing. In this role, operations research may be described as the application of scientific methods to problems arising from operations involving integrated systems of people, machines, and materials. It normally utilizes the knowledge and skill of an interdisciplinary research team to provide the managers of such systems with optimum operating solutions.

Organizations of professional operations researchers were formed early in the postwar period. An operational research club, which came into being in the late 1940s in the United Kingdom, was renamed the Operational Research Society. The Operations Research Society of America (ORSA)[1] was organized in the United States in 1952. With the advent of a number of other societies throughout the world, the International Federation of Operational Research Societies was established. Almost two dozen nations were represented at the first international conference at Oxford in 1957.

The attractiveness and importance of operations research in business, industry, and government led to the development of course work and degree programs at many leading univeristies. With roots in the mathematical and physical sciences, operations research has evolved toward a discipline, while retaining many of its interdisciplinary characteristics. Some academic units within which course work and degree programs may be found are applied mathematics, industrial engineering, systems engineering, and statistics. In the quantitatively oriented schools of business and management, the more frequently used designation is management science.

Management Science. Like operations research, management science traces it origin to the period during and immediately following World War II. The Institute of Management Sciences (TIMS)[2] was organized in 1953, just one year after ORSA. Both ORSA and TIMS belong to the International Federation of Operational Research Societies. In 1973 these two societies began sharing their journals and professional functions to serve better the large overlap in membership.

Management science is often indistinguishable from operations research. While operations research tends to focus on the formulation and manipulation of mathematical models for common operational processes, management science tends to focus on the use of models in the practice of management.

Operations research and management science are bound together by a common intellectual interest. They share a philosophy of method stimulated by the need for more complete analyses of the complicated problems facing man-

---

[1] ORSA has as its purposes "the advancement of operations research through exchange of information, the establishment and maintenance of professional standards of competence for work known as operations research, the improvement of the methods and techniques of operations research, the encouragement and development of students of operations research, and the useful application of operations research."

[2] TIMS has as its purpose "to identify, extend, and unify scientific knowledge that contributes to the understanding and practice of management."

agers. This need can often be satisfied by the use of mathematical and statistical methods and/or by carefully constructed experimentation and observation.

The scientific method, which has been so successful in advancing humankind's understanding of physical phenomena, has not yet met with equal success in dealing with management problems. These are some explanations. It is certainly more difficult to conduct a "scientific experiment" in business or industry. Decision situations are not easily replicated in dynamic and competitive business operations. However, to the extent that an effectiveness function can be established that relates the variables under direct control of the decision maker to those not subject to direct control, a decision can be made or an operating policy can be selected that optimizes some measure of effectiveness.

Management science is a relatively new but increasingly accepted area of study in academic programs of business administration and management. Many of the quantitative techniques currently encompassed by management science were taught almost exclusively in engineering or applied mathematics. Increased emphasis on developing the quantitative skills of business and management students has led to the inclusion of management science as an integral component of business and management degree programs at most colleges and universities.

Scientific Management. From one viewpoint, operations research and management science may be seen as the development and extension of the scientific management (SM) movement usually credited to Taylor, Gantt, the Gilbreths, and others. The contributions of these pioneers provided the foundation for the present body of concepts, methods of analysis, and decision models available to decision makers in both the public and private sectors. Their contributions also led to the establishment of industrial engineering, a branch of engineering that has adopted operations research to advance its effectiveness and stature.

Although the "efficiency expert" stigma of the scientific management movement is now shunned, the objective of the movement is just as valid today as it was at the turn of the century. To "scientifically manage" operations is an objective sought by forward-looking decision makers in business, industry, and government. However, the operations under consideration are now being placed in a broader systems context.

Modern approaches to the scientific management of operations have certain distinguishing characteristics. First is the question of scope. Where operations analysis breaks an activity down into small segments for close study, OR/MS emphasizes interdependence and interaction among all parts of the functioning whole. Second is the increasing use of mathematical models in OR/MS to perform indirect instead of direct experimentation on the system. Third is the ultilization of expertise from several disciplines to address the many factors involved through an integrated approach, instead of reliance on the skill of a single "efficiency expert." Fourth, the advent of high-speed digital computers makes possible the assimilation and manipulation of information way beyond that which was possible at the beginning of the scientific management movement.

OR/MS/SM Relationships. In the previous sections, operations research, management science, and scientific management have been discussed separately with little consideration given to their linkages. This section will focus on the place of OR, MS, and SM in a process directed to the improvement of operational systems. The process is illustrated in Figure 1.1.

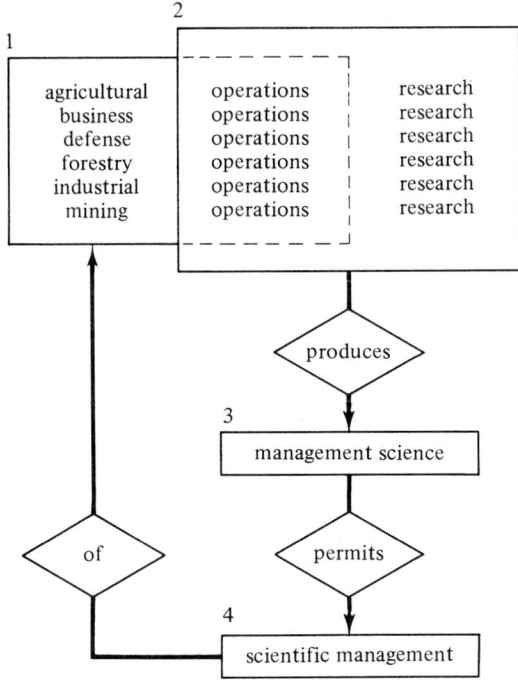

Figure 1.1 OR/MS/SM relationships.

Block 1 lists some of the common operations in existence in the world today. Each of these operational sectors has its own unique characteristics, yet they share much in common. A uniform need of all operations is the requirement for scientific management approaches.

Research is depicted in block 2 as applying to operations in general (operations research), and with consideration of block 1, to specific operations (agricultural operations research, business operations research, etc.). It is research into operations that provides the knowledge base for operational system improvement.

Management science (block 3) is depicted as a body of systematic knowledge about operations produced by successful operations research. Although the body of systematic knowledge called management science is meager when compared to its counterpart in the physical sciences, it is growing rapidly.

Block 4 and the feedback loop depict the utilization of management science in the practice of scientific management: specifically, the scientific management of the operations researched. It is this final phase of Figure 1.1 that is highlighted as the end objective of most OR/MS activities.

Successful operations research adds to the body of systematic knowledge about operations. This body of systematic knowledge, called management sciences, when appropriately utilized, permits the practice of scientific management. Operations analysts, management analysts, systems analysts, industrial engineers, and other staff individuals may utilize this systematic knowledge to assist decision makers in the practice of scientific management.

1.2 HUMAN WANT SATISFACTION

People's wants have always exceeded their means for satisfying them. The relative scarcity of goods and services has been and will continue to be an economic dilemma that all must face. Some wants cannot be satisfied at all, others can be partially satisfied, and a few wants can be fully satisfied. As some wants are satisfied, others are revealed. People are insatiable.

Knowledge about physical phenomena, together with the appropriate selection and pursuit of objectives through organized activity, have enabled human beings to satisfy their wants more fully and continually to improve the general standard of living. The huge investment in producer goods, together with the existence of complex business and industrial organizations, indicates that altering physical factors through organizations has been found to be an effective means for satisfying human wants. In those parts of the world where this process is not working well, human wants are poorly met.

The Creation of Utilities. An accepted economic definition of the term *utility* is the power to satisfy human wants. The utility that an object represents is determined by an individual's subjective evaluation. Thus, the utility of an object is not inherent in the object, but depends on the esteem that a person has for it. It follows that the utility of an object is not ordinarily constant, but may be expected to change over time as the wants of the individual change.

Most things that have utility for an individual are physically manifested. This is readily apparent in such physical objects as a house, an automobile, or a pair of shoes. The situation may be true as well with less tangible things. One can enjoy a television program because light waves impinge on the eye and sound waves strike the ear. Even friendship is realized through the senses and therefore has its physical aspects. The creation of utility is achieved through a change in physical environment.

Two kinds of utility may be considered. The first involves the utility of goods and services that are consumed by the individual. The second is the utility that an object may have as a means to an end, as is the case with producer goods and services. This class of goods includes such items as machine tools, construction equipment, factories, and digital computers. Each has utility as an intermediate step in people's effort to satisfy their wants. They are desired not for themselves, but because they may be coupled with organized activity as an effective means for altering physical factors to produce consumer goods and services.

Certain human wants are more predictable than others. The demand for food, clothing, and shelter needed for bare physical existence is more stable and predictable than the demand for those things that satisfy people's emotional needs. The number of calories of energy needed to sustain life may be determined fairly accurately. Clothing and shelter requirements may be predicted within narrow limits from climatic conditions. Once people are assured of physical existence, they seek satisfactions of a less predictable nature resulting from their being members and products of a society rather than only biological organisms.

The Role of Organization. Organizations are a means for creating and exchanging utility. Through cooperative action, people have been able to overcome their individual limitations. It is apparent that many desired ends may be obtained from the environment more easily by joint action than by individual action. For example, the utility of the harmonic sounds in music is greatly increased by the precise coordination of the efforts of a group of musicians. The utility of steel is increased by a complex manufacturing process which ultimately results in an automobile. Even friendship is enhanced by participation in certain forms of organized activity. To a large degree, the high standard of living enjoyed today may be attributed to the ability of organizations to change the physical environment more effectively than is possible through individual action alone. In this respect, organization may be called humankind's most important innovation.

The function of an organization is to change the physical environment through the appropriate utilization of the activities of contributors. For the organization to be successful, each individual contributor's tangible and intangible satisfactions must exceed his or her contributions as subjectively evaluated. Essentially, organizations are entities to which individuals contribute what they desire less to gain what they desire more.

Organizations come into being as a means for creating and exchanging utility. Their success is dependent on the appropriateness of the series of acts contributed to the system. The majority of these acts are purposeful; that is, they are directed to the accomplishment of some objective. These acts are physical in nature and find purposeful employment in the alteration of the physical environment. As a result, utility is created which, through the process of distribution, makes it possible for the cooperative system to endure.

The function of the management process is the delineation of organizational objectives and the coordination of activity toward the accomplishment of these objectives. The system of coordinated activities must be maintained so that each contributor, including the manager, gains more than he or she contributes. To maintain this system in equilibrium, the decision maker must constantly choose from among a changing set of alternatives. Each member of a set of alternatives may contribute differently to the effectiveness with which organizational objectives are achieved and the contributors satisfied. It is evident from this that mangerial talent is a valuable resource.

1.3 OBJECTIVES AND ALTERNATIVES

Objectives pursued by organizations through alternative courses of action should be directed to the satisfaction of demands resulting from the wants of humankind. Therefore, the determination of appropriate objectives must be preceded by an effort to determine precisely what these wants are. Industrial organizations conduct market studies to learn what consumer goods should be produced. City commissions make surveys to ascertain what civic projects will be of most benefit. Transportation commissions conduct traffic counts to learn what construction programs should be undertaken.

Major and Subordinate Objectives. Any organized effort will involve major and subordinate objectives. For example, an objective to produce and market automobiles is an aim realized only through the accomplishment of subordinate objectives. Design, procurement, and manufacturing objectives must be defined and undertaken. These subordinate objectives will then have objectives subordinate to them that also must be appropriately executed. Specialization in an organization is a direct result of the necessity for executing subordinate objectives.

After the kinds and amounts of required consumer goods have been predicted, the kinds and amounts of producer goods and organized activities needed may be objectively ascertained. If it has been determined that the demand for transportation may be met by producing and marketing 400,000 automobiles of a certain model during a certain period, then the organization of personnel, materials, equipment, and capital becomes a matter of objective determination. The number of assembly workers needed may be determined from production standards. The quantity of steel needed may be calculated from design requirements and a predicted scrap loss. The number of supervisory personnel required may be estimated from past experience. From such data, the objectives that must be achieved by each member of the organization may be specified.

Before the Industrial Revolution, most productive activity was accomplished in small owner-manager enterprises, usually with a single decision maker and simple organizational objectives. Increased technology and the growth of industrial organizations made necessary the establishment of a hierarchy of objectives. This, in turn, required a division of the management function until today a hierarchy of decision makers exists in most organizations. Each decision maker is charged with the responsibility of meeting the objectives of an organizational division. Therefore, he or she may be expected to pursue these objectives in a manner consistent with his or her view of what is good for the organization as a whole. For example, the manager of production strives to meet production requirements and minimize production cost. The marketing manager seeks to maximize sales and minimize selling expense. The personnel manager strives to level out the fluctuations in the work force and to retain competent people. These objectives, and those that are subordinate, are not always consistent with each other.

The Conflict of Objectives. Although high productivity is due in part to the functional division of objectives in organizations, these objectives are often pursued in ways that conflict with each other. Consider the clashing viewpoints of various departments with respect to the inventory policy of a corporation. The production department strives for long uninterrupted production runs which will minimize setup and teardown costs and, hence, total production cost. The end result will be a large inventory of a relatively few product lines. Marketing desires a large inventory, but also requires the availability of diverse product lines so as to maximize sales. Finance strives to minimize inventory levels to reduce capital investment. A stabilized labor force desired by the personnel director can be achieved only by building inventory during periods of slack demand. Conflicting objectives such as these may occur at any level in the organization.

Whenever a hierarchy of objectives is required for the accomplishment of an objective, conflicts are likely to occur. Limited perception at subordinate levels, together with the desire to pursue assigned objectives effectively, may result in action that is appropriate for the subordinate objective but less than best for the organization as a whole. Choice of operating policies for maximum overall benefit requires consideration of how all segments of the whole are related. An attempt is then made to select that course of action which results in the best outcome evaluated with regard to the entire system.

Alternative Courses of Action. Courses of action, among which one expects to choose, are called alternatives. The term *alternative* implies both a means and an end. For example, purchasing from vendor A is a course of action that results in the accumulation of an inventory. But accumulating an inventory may be considered a course of action that will result in the support of manufacturing operations. All proposed alternatives are not equally desirable, since each will involve the consumption of different amounts of scarce resources. The accumulation of an inventory required for the support of manufacturing operations may be accomplished by means other than purchasing from vendor A. Quantitative methods of analysis for evaluating alternatives relative to objectives are finding increased use as an aid in decision making. That course of action most appropriate in the light of the overall objective sought, and the resources consumed, will be judged to be best.

Alternatives not considered cannot be adopted no matter how desirable they might prove to be. Rarely are all possible courses of action known and defined, for the conception of alternatives is a creative process requiring the consumption of time. A fully defined course of action rarely emerges in its final form; it usually begins as an interesting but poorly defined idea requiring further effort for full development. Ordinarily, too few alternatives are considered, but there is a limit beyond which consideration of new possibilities cannot be economically justified.

The Effect of Counteractions. A *counteraction* is a course of action chosen by an opponent which may change the expected outcome of a course of action recently initiated. Evaluating the effects of possible counteractions is important, since an anticipated gain can be converted into a loss by the action of a competitor.

Anticipating and allowing for the results of counteractions is a creative process. It requires considerable experience in situations involving interaction between competing forces. Sometimes a study of the history of competitive counteraction will be helpful. In other cases a rational evaluation of the given situation will help the decision maker. In either case extrapolation to future situations cannot be made with certainty. However, since counteractions will modify expected outcomes, one should try to evaluate their probable effect.

1.4 EFFECTIVENESS AND EFFICIENCY

The objectives of organized activity are not ends in themselves; they are chosen and pursued as a means for satisfying human wants. However, the ultimate success of the organization in satisfying human wants will first depend on its ability to achieve its immediate purpose, stated or otherwise. An automobile company must manufacture and sell automobiles. A garbage collection agency must be able to collect and dispose of garbage. These goals must be accomplished, and they must be accomplished in an economic fashion if the organization is to be successful. The term *effectiveness* will be defined and used as a measure of the economic outcome of a course of action relative to an objective. *Efficiency*, on the other hand, will be applied as a measure of the want-satisfying power of cooperative action for the contributors as subjectively evaluated by them.

Effectiveness. In general, *effectiveness*, as used here, means the degree to which an action leads to the result it was planned to achieve expressed in economic terms. The following examples illustrate this concept. In procurement and inventory operations, the objective is to meet demand. This may be achieved by maintaining a large stock on hand so that a shortage rarely occurs. As a result, the inventory holding cost will be high and the shortage cost will be low. On the other hand, the procurement level and the procurement quantity may be chosen so that the stock on hand is low and shortages occur frequently. In this case the holding cost will be low and the shortage cost will be high. In order to optimize the effectiveness with which the demand is met, the decision maker should choose the procurement level and the procurement quantity so that the sum of the inventory holding cost and the shortage cost is minimized.

In production operations, one objective is to manipulate the process so that the resulting product will conform to specifications. An indication of when the process needs attention may be obtained by sampling from the stream of product and plotting the sample data on a control chart. If the control limits are set close, the chart will frequently indicate an out-of-control condition, often when the process is actually in control. If the control limits are set far apart, the chart will not be as sensitive to an out-of-control condition. In the first case, a cost will be incurred due to production lost while an attempt is made to find the out-of-control condition that may not exist. In the second case, defective products will be produced while the process is out of control, resulting in an associated cost. In order to optimize the effectiveness with which the objective is achieved, the decision maker must set the control limits so as to minimize the sum of the costs arising from lost production on the one hand and from defective product on the other. Thus, the objective of having the product conform to specifications is achieved to the degree that results in optimum effectiveness.

In waiting-line operations, the objective is to service units that arrive. This may be achieved by providing a large service capability so that the units requiring service will rarely need to wait. On the other hand, the service capability may be chosen at some low level that requires considerable waiting. In the first case, the cost of the service facility will be high and the cost of waiting will be low. In the second case, the cost of the facility will be low but the cost of waiting will be high. In this operation the decision maker should choose that service capability which minimizes the cost of the facility and the cost of waiting. By doing so, the objective will be met to the degree that results in optimum effectiveness.

Examples such as these emphasize that the decision maker should meet assigned objectives to the degree that results in optimum effectiveness. To do so, the decision maker must understand the relationships embraced by the operations under his or her control and trade off the relevant economic values. By so doing, the person will be contributing to the overall efficiency of the organization of which he or she is a part.

Efficiency. Efficiency is defined as a mesaure of the result of cooperative action for the contributors as subjectively evaluated by them. The effective pursuit of appropriate organizational objectives contributes directly to organizational efficiency. As used here, efficiency is a measure of the want-satisfying power of the cooperative system as a whole. Thus, efficiency is the aggregate of utilities received from the organization divided by the aggregate of utilities given to the organization, as subjectively evaluated by each contributor.

Consider the following illustration: Assume that the organizational objective to produce 400,000 automobiles is being pursued with optimum effectiveness. That is, assume that each objective subordinate to the overall objective is being met in a manner similar to the examples discussed previously. If this is true, the organization will be able to distribute a greater amount of tangible benefits to its contributors. Assembly-line workers will evaluate the time and effort given to the organization against the wages and intangible benefits they receive. The workers are more likely to make a favorable evaluation if they contribute to a cooperative system with a relatively large amount of tangible benefits to distribute. Similarly, an effective organization can produce more automobiles per unit of labor input and thereby contribute to the maximum satisfaction of its customers. In addition, the owners will enjoy a larger return on their investment, and the material suppliers will find a market for large quantities of their product at an acceptable price.

People are continually seeking to satisfy their wants. In so doing, they join with others in cooperative action and give up certain utilities to the joint effort in order to gain others which they value more. The efficiency of the organization must be greater than unity if the organization is to survive. In fact, efficiency is a conceptual measure of the want-satisfying power of the cooperative system. The relationship of effectiveness and efficiency, as it pertains to the satisfaction of human wants, leads to understanding the function of the decision maker and the management process. Included within this concept is the idea that the effective pursuit of appropriate objectives usually enhances organizational efficiency and the satisfaction of human wants.

1.5 A PLAN FOR APPLYING OR/MS

Operations research and management science has been described as the application of science and the scientific method to operational problems faced by managers. The purpose of OR/MS is to provide the decision maker with an objective basis for evaluating the operations under his or her control. This aim may be achieved with greater success if it is pursued in accordance with a systematic plan. Such a plan is a conceptual construct useful in placing the area of analysis in proper perspective; such a plan seeks to provide a procedure that will result in sound conclusions. The remainder of this chapter presents a systematic plan for the application of OR/MS.

Define the Problem. The problem to which OR/MS may be profitably directed is made up of four major components: the environment, the decision maker, the objectives, and the alternatives. These components must be studied and related to each other before the problem is fully defined.

Of these four components, the environment is the most comprehensive since it embraces and provides a setting for the other three. In general, the environment may be described as the framework within which a system of organized activity is purposefully directed to accomplishing an organizational objective. It involves physical, social, and economic factors which may bear on the problem at hand. For example, such diverse influences as the social acceptance of the product or the legal requirement to acknowledge and deal with a labor union may be important. Defining the problem involves a search for, and a study of, those variables that are significantly related to the effectiveness with which the desired objective is achieved.

The decision maker is the second component of the problem. Implied here is the desire of an individual or group of individuals to achieve an organizational objective, or set of organizational objectives, by the conscious choice from among several possible alternatives. Facts on which to base the decision are sought as part of the task of defining the problem. But before this search can be successful, one must study the decision maker and his or her relationship to the problem in order to determine precisely what the objectives are.

Objectives are the third component of the problem to which analysis must be directed. Questioning by the decision maker is rarely sufficient to formulate all pertinent organizational objectives. Sometimes these objectives may be detected by noting organizational activity. A company may move a plant from one location to another in order to escape from an area of strong union influence. Often it will be necessary to study a situation such as this to uncover objectives not specified by the decision maker. Such study is creative in nature and is an important facet of OR/MS.

Alternatives are the final component of the problem requiring definition. This involves the task of identifying those variables which significantly affect the effectiveness with which the objective may be achieved. When this phase is completed, it is necessary to separate the variables subject to direct control by the decision maker from those not subject to his or her direct control.

Formulate the Model. The first step in formulating an appropriate model is usually taken when the problem is being defined. Models are useful in choosing from among a set of alternatives, since they enable one to determine how various aspects of the modeled entity may respond to a given decision. Thus, the decision maker can evaluate the probable outcome of a given decision without changing the modeled entity itself. The advantage of being able to do this is obvious. Because of the importance of models in OR/MS, this topic is treated in detail in the next chapter.

Operations researchers have identified and modeled many recurrent processes. An increasing number of common problem areas will be explained by the use of models as this research effort continues. These models, in their aggregate, provide a body of quantitative relationships that may be applied, with modification, to the operational problem at hand. In other cases it may be necessary to formulate a model unlike any that exist.

One should not overlook a very useful by-product of model formulation: The individual constructing the model will almost always gain a better understanding of the problem. Since the model must express the relationship of the variables involved, these relationships must be understood initially.

Optimize the Model. In optimizing a model, we seek to determine, for the variables under direct control of the decision maker, values that will yield optimum effectiveness. This may be accomplished analytically or numerically. Each of these has advantages and disadvantages in regard to a given model. Where the model is complex, or where a wide range of operating policies are to be evaluated, a digital or analog computer may be needed. In some cases a large-scale system model applied to a recurrent process will require the permanent use of a computer for that model alone.

A model is never a perfect representation of reality, but if it is properly formulated and correctly optimized, the model will be useful in predicting the effects of changes in controllable variables on the overall system effectiveness. The usefulness of a model may be judged on how well it does predict the effect of these changes. This may be tested in two ways: First, apply the model to historical data and evaluate the difference in system effectiveness that would have resulted had the model been used; and second, apply the model in a parallel fashion to the current decision-making process. One may then judge the worth of the model on the basis of the difference between the current procedure and the procedure that results with the use of the model. If the model proves itself by such a testing procedure, it is ready to implement as an aid in decision making.

Make the Decision. Models of operations are essentially means for taking the decision maker part way to the point of decision. They supply a quantitative basis for evaluating the operations under the decision maker's control. If the model were a complete and accurate representation of reality, the results that it yields could be accepted and applied without judgment. Since, unfortunately, this is not true, it is necessary to give the decision maker both the results derived by use of the model and a formal list of important elements not included in the model. Then, before making the decision, the person may consider the quantitative result together with the irreducible elements. This dual presentation usually improves the decision-making process.

Models, together with automatic data-processing equipment, can be very useful in making routine or repetitive decisions. This process will never completely replace the decision maker because many decisions are based on factors that cannot be included in a model. The general economic situation, world politics, actions of competitors, and technological advances are examples of these. In addition, the judgment of decision makers will always be needed to identify appropriate objectives in a changing decision environment.

In cases where model optimization is to be assigned to the decision maker, it is advisable to take extra time to be sure that the computational procedure is an understandable as possible. This may require the development of a nomograph, a set of tables, or graphs. The importance of making the results of OR/MS acceptable to those who will benefit from their use cannot be overemphasized.

Evaluate the Outcome. Feedback for the purpose of improving future outcomes is essentially in the management process. It is unlikely that future decisions can be improved without knowledge about the results of decisions just reached. Implementing a solution recommended by an OR/MS study is not complete until an evaluation is made of the operational system after the decision is made which affects that system.

Solutions to operational problems developed from decision models may or may not lead to improvements when implemented. Therefore, one should encourage close coordination between those responsible for the decision model and those who will use it for decision making. Between these two parties there will generally be sufficient insight to permit an appropriate evaluation of the outcome.

QUESTIONS

1.1. Develop a definition of operations research.
1.2. Contrast operations research with management science.
1.3. How does OR/MS differ from classical scientific management?
1.4. How may OR/MS contribute to the scientific management of operations?
1.5. Explain how advances in the physical sciences enable people to satisfy their wants more fully.
1.6. Define utilities and explain how they are created.
1.7. Constrast the utility of consumer goods and the utility of producer goods.
1.8. Explain why desired ends may be obtained more easily by joint action than by individual action.
1.9. What is the function of a manager?
1.10. Explain why the objectives of organized activity should be directed to the wants or needs of humankind.

1.11. State an overall objective and list the necessary subordinate objectives for its attainment.

1.12. Describe the conditions under which conflicts of objectives are likely to occur.

1.13. Give an example to show that the term *alternative* implies both a means and an end.

1.14. State an objective and list alternative courses of action that will achieve the objective.

1.15. What is a counteraction?

1.16. Contrast the meaning of effectiveness and efficiency.

1.17. How is the degree of effectiveness related to efficiency?

1.18. Explain why it is possible for organizational efficiency to exceed 100 percent.

1.19. Outline the steps that should be in a systematic OR/MS plan.

2

Models and Simulation in OR/MS

Models and their manipulation are essential in OR/MS. Decision makers must understand the operations for which they are responsible in order to select courses of action appropriate for attaining organizational objectives. The process of simulation employing decision models may be used to gain this understanding. Simulation is the process of manipulating a model of reality rather than reality itself.

A model may be used as a representation of an operational system. It is employed to explain and describe some aspect of the system under study. Models provide the basis for experimental investigation which yields information in less time and at less cost than direct manipulation of the system itself. Although a model is only an abstraction of reality, its value lies in the ease with which it may be manipulated. To manipulate reality is often impossible, as with the solar system, or very costly, as with complex industrial systems. Much of this text has the purpose of providing an understanding of models and model manipulation as key ingredients in OR/MS.

2.1 A CLASSIFICATION OF MODELS

When used as a noun, the word *model* implies representation. A design engineer may construct a clay model as a possible configuration for a new automobile fender or an architect might represent a building she proposes with a scale model. The word may also be used as an adjective. This use of the word carries with it an implication of ideal. Thus, a man may be referred to as a model husband or a child praised as a model student. Finally, the word may be used as a verb, as in the case of a woman employed to model clothes. Here the verb to demonstrate could have been substituted. "Model," as used in OR/MS, retains each of these meanings. Models are designed to represent the operations under study, by an idealized example of reality, in order to explain the essential relationships involved.

Models can be classified by distinguishing physical, schematic, and mathematical types. Physical models are the most easily understood since they look like the object under consideration. Schematic models are traditionally used to study organizational and procedural problems. Mathematical models are an abstraction where symbols rather than physical substitutions are made. Because mathematical models lend themselves well to explaining operational systems, they will be given primary emphasis in OR/MS.

Physical Models. Globes are used in the classroom to demonstrate the shape and orientation of continents, water bodies, and other geographical features of the earth. A model of the solar system is used to demonstrate the orientation of the sun and planets in space. A model of an atomic structure would be similar in appearance but at the other extreme in dimensional reproduction. Each of these models represents reality and is used for demonstration. None of these are customarily manipulated in the experimental sense.

Some physical models are used in the simulation process. An aeronautical engineer may test a specific tail assembly design with a model airplane in a wind tunnel. A pilot plant might be built to test a new process for the purpose of locating operational difficulties before full production. An environmental chamber is used to create conditions anticipated for the component under test.

The use of templates in plant layout is an example of experimentation with a physical model. Templates are either two- or three-dimensional replicas of machinery and equipment which are moved about on a scale model area. The relationship of distance is important and the templates are manipulated until a desirable layout is obtained. Such factors as noise generation, vibration, and lighting are also important, but are not a part of the experimentation and must be considered separately.

Schematic Models. A schematic model is obtained by taking a state or an event and reducing it to a chart or diagram. The schematic model may or may not look like the real-world situation it represents. It is usually possible to achieve a much better understanding of the real-world system described by the model through use of an explicit coding process employed in the construction of the model. The execution of a football play may be diagramed on a blackboard with a simple code. It is the idealized aspect of the model that permits this insight into the football play.

The *organizational chart* is a common schematic model. It is a representation of the state of formal relationships existing between various members of the organization. A *human–machine chart* is another example of a schematic model. It is a model of an event, that is, the time-varying interaction of one or more persons and one or more machines over a complete work cycle. A *flow-process chart* is a schematic model which describes the order of occurrence of a number of events which constitute an objective, such as the assembly of an automobile from many component parts.

In each case, the value of the schematic model lies in its ability to describe the essential aspects of the existing situation. It does not include all extraneous actions and relationships but rather concentrates on a single facet. Thus, the schematic model is not in itself a solution but only facilitates a solution. After the model has been carefully analyzed, a proposed solution can be defined, tested, and implemented.

Mathematical Models. A mathematical model employs the language of mathematics and, like other models, may be a description and then an explanation of the system it represents. Although its symbols may be more difficult to comprehend than verbal symbols, they do provide a much higher degree of abstraction and precision in their application. Because of the logic it incorporates, a mathematical model may be manipulated in accordance with established mathematical procedures.

Almost all mathematical models are used either to predict or to control. The outcome of an alternative course of action may be predicted in terms of a selected measure of effectiveness. For example, a linear programming model may predict the profit associated with various production quantities of a multiproduct process. Mathematical models may be used to control an inventory. In quality control, a mathematical model may be employed to monitor the proportion of defects that will be accepted from a supplier. Such models maintain control over a state of reality.

Mathematical models directed to the study of operations differ from those traditionally used in the physical sciences in two important ways: First, since the system being studied usually involves social and economic factors, these models often must incorporate probabilistic elements to explain their random behavior. Thus, it is appropriate to distinguish *probabilistic models* from *deterministic models*. Second, mathematical models formulated to explain operational systems incorporate two classes of variables: those that are directly under the control of a decision maker and those that are not. The objective is to select values for the variables under the decision maker's control so that some measure of effectiveness is optimized. Thus, these models are directed to decision situations instead of to physical phenomena.

2.2 EXPERIMENTATION THROUGH SIMULATION

The operations with which the decision maker is concerned may be manipulated for experimental purposes over a number of alternative states. This process is costly, and in the case of a corporate organizational structure or its operational procedures, it may be destructive. For example, a plant manager might lose most of the work force by experimenting with different lengths of work week. Models and the process of simulation provide a convenient means whereby the decision maker may be provided with factual information regarding the operations under his or her control without disturbing the operations themselves. Thus, the simulation process is essentially one of indirect experimentation involving the testing of alternative courses of action before they are adopted.

Direct and Indirect Experimentation. In direct experimentation, the object, state, event, and/or the environment is subject to manipulation and the results are observed. For example, the housewife might rearrange the furniture in her living room by this method. Essentially, she, or her husband under her direction, moves the furniture and observes the results. This process may then be repeated with a second move and perhaps a third, until all logical alternatives have been exhausted. Eventually, one such move is subjectively judged best; the furniture is returned to this position, and the experiment is completed. Direct experimentation such as this may be applied to the rearrangement of machinery in a factory. Such a procedure is time consuming, disruptive, and costly. Hence, simulation or indirect experimentation is employed with templates representing the machinery to be moved.

Direct experimentation in aircraft design would involve constructing a full-scale prototype which would be flight-tested under real conditions. Although this is an essential step in the evolution of a new design, it would be very costly as the first step. The usual procedure is evaluating several proposed configurations by building a model of each and then testing in a wind tunnel. This is the process of indirect experimentation, or simulation. It is extensively used in situations where direct experimentation is not economically feasible.

In OR/MS, indirect experimentation is effected through the formulation and manipulation of decision models. This makes it possible to determine how changes in those aspects of the system under control of the decision maker affect the modeled system. Indirect experimentation enables the decision maker to evaluate the probable outcome of a given decision without changing the operational system itself. In effect, indirect experimentation in the study of operations provides a means for making quantitative information available to the decision maker without disturbing the operations under his or her control.

Simulation in OR/MS. In business and industry, the objective sought is the optimization of some measure of effectiveness. Rarely, if ever, can this be done by direct experimentation with the operations under study. For example, a sales price that maximizes profit cannot be determined by changing price over a range of values until the optimum price level is located. Such a method is expensive, time consuming, and in addition may eventually destroy the price structure itself. Hence, operational policies are usually established by intuition, judgment, and simulation rather than by direct experimentation. Mathematical models and other quantitative procedures for doing this are currently being developed at an increasing rate.

As of now, there is no available theory to guide formulation or selection of the best model for a given operational system. The challenge facing operations researchers is to discover fundamental relationships common to classes of operational systems and then to formulate models that capture these relationships with a high degree of fidelity. Management scientists have the continuing challenge of selecting and adapting models to solve management problems. Here the task is to work with the best model for the situation under study.

The remainder of this chapter, and those that follow, will be directed to developing and explaining mathematical decision models as a means for effecting indirect experimentation or simulation. In so doing, it must be remembered that the result sought is the effectiveness with which organizational objectives are achieved.

2.3 MODEL FORMULATION AND OPTIMIZATION

Verbal statements usually precede the formulation of a mathematical decision model. These statements provide a word picture or image of reality from which the mathematical model may evolve. The verbal description and the mathematical model should be closely related, with the model being an extension and quantification of verbal statements. Once a decision model is formulated, it may then be optimized as a means for evaluating alternative operating policies.

Formulating the Model. Formulation of the mathematical decision model requires that an effectiveness function embracing two classes of variables be constructed. These variables have been identified as a dichotomous classification of those factors of importance in the system under consideration.

An effectiveness function is a mathematical statement formally linking a measure of effectiveness with variables under the direct control of the decision maker and variables not under direct control. It provides a means whereby a set of controllable variables, designated X, can be tested in the light of a set of uncontrollable variables, Y. The test is an experimental process performed mathematically. The experimental result is an outcome value for effectiveness,

E. This functional relationship, in its unconstrained form, is expressed as

$$E = f(X, Y),$$

and in its constrained form is subject to a set of constraints expressed as functions of the controllable and uncontrollable variables and a set of constraint constants, B, as

$$g(X, Y) = B,$$

where the equality may also be $\leq$ or $\geq$.

As an example of the effectiveness function structure for an unconstrained decision situation, consider the determination of an optimal procurement quantity for inventory operations. Here the measure of effectiveness is cost, and the objective is to choose a procurement quantity in the face of demand, procurement cost, and holding cost, so that total cost is minimized. The procurement quantity is the variable directly under the control of the decision maker. Demand, procurement cost, and holding cost are not directly under his or her control. The use of a decision model such as this allows the decision maker to arrive at a value for the variable under his or her control that trades off conflicting cost elements.

The effectiveness function structure for a constrained decision situation can be illustrated by the determination of an optimal production mix for a number of products. Here the measure of effectiveness is profit, and the objective is to choose the number of units of each product which should be produced per day to maximize profit. The variables directly under control of the decision maker are the production quantities to be specified. Not directly under his or her control are the profits per unit contributed by each unit produced, the amount of scarce machine time consumed by each unit of product in each processing area, and the amount of machine time available in each processing area each day. A decision model such as this is known as linear programming. It allows the decision maker to optimize a linear effectiveness function in the face of linear constraints, these constraints arising because the activities compete for scarce resources.

In formulating a mathematical decision model, one attempts to consider all components of the system which are relevant to the system's effectiveness. Because of the impossibility of including all parameters in constructing the effectiveness function, it is common practice to consider only those upon which the outcome effectiveness is believed to depend significantly. This necessary viewpoint sometimes leads to the erroneous conclusion that certain segments of the environment are actually isolated from each other. Although it may be feasible to consider only those relationships that are significantly pertinent, one should remember that all elements of operational systems are interdependent.

Even though a diligent search for relevant parameters is made, it is almost certain that some will be unknowingly omitted. Others may be deliberately omitted if their impact on the performance of the model is thought to be small and their contribution to the mathematical complexity is large. To the extent that omitted parameters are significant, the model will provide misleading results until they are detected and included.

Model formulation is often simplified by constructing the model as though it were to be used in a static decision environment. This assumption makes it unnecessary to incorporate dynamic elements into the model. But the model must be updated as the environment changes over time. Finally, some additional simplifications may be made: A variable may be replaced by a constant, a discrete probability distribution may be replaced by a continuous distribution, or a nonlinear relationship may be replaced by one that is linear. If the effect of these simplifications is known to be insignificant, they may be made with confidence. The model should be simplified to the point where the gain in ease of formulation and manipulation ceases to be greater than the loss resulting from an abridged model.

Optimizing the Model. The decision model is not a solution in itself, but is a means for deriving a solution to an operational problem. Once a model has been formulated, it must be manipulated in an experimental sense to test alternative policies. Since models may take on a variety of forms, they may require one of several mathematical or numerical procedures in the manipulation process of optimization.

The form and mathematical characteristics of the effectiveness function and its constraints determine the optimization procedures that can be applied for model manipulation. If the function is well behaved and unconstrained, or subject only to simple constraints, classical optimization techniques from the differential calculus can be utilized with ease. These classical optimization techniques are summarized for review in Appendix B.

If the effectiveness function is linear and subject to linear constraints, a linear programming problem exists. The optimization technique most often utilized is known as the simplex method presented in Chapter 3. Special cases of the general linear programming model have efficient optimization procedures which are presented in Chapter 4.

Effectiveness functions which are not well behaved due to local optima, discreteness, nonlinearities, or discontinuities often require numerical enumeration or search techniques utilizing a digital computer. Sometimes the method of dynamic programming can be used most effectively, as presented in Chapter 6.

Often, an operational system cannot be modeled in closed form and optimized by one of the former approaches. When a decision situation is probabilistic, the probability methods of Appendix C should be utilized to derive an effectiveness function. In these cases it may be necessary to model the operation schematically using a logic diagram. Once the logic of the operation is captured and the probabilistic relationships are determined, it may then be necessary to manipulate the schematic model by simulated sampling techniques as described in Appendix C.

2.4 CONTROL OF THE MODEL SOLUTION

Even though the model may adequately represent the system under study when it is constructed, it may become useless in decision making. This usually occurs as a result of the changing nature of most operational systems. Avoiding obsolescence of the model requires that it incorporate dynamic relationships, or that it be modified over time. Since very few models are designed to cope with a dynamic environment, it will be necessary to review the environment periodically for the purpose of modifying the model under consideration.

The appropriate frequency of review depends on the nature of the changing environment. Two cost elements are pertinent: First, as the frequency of review increases, the cost of review will increase; and second, the cost of incorrect output decisions from the model will decrease with a frequently updated model. The review process should be designed so as to minimize the sum of these two cost components. In effect, a secondary model may be formulated and employed to specify the optimum review period for operational models.

Control of Input Parameters. The input parameters to a decision model are those uncontrolled system elements which may significantly affect the model output or effectiveness. These parameters may include various cost elements as well as such factors as procurement lead time, waiting time, form of arrival distribution, and so forth. Each of these may change over time at a rate depending on a multitude of environmental factors.

Determination of specific values for input parameters involves a process of estimation. Costs may be determined by collecting and analyzing cost accounting data and by projecting anticipated labor, material, and overhead estimates. Distribution parameters may be estimated and distribution forms may be determined. The frequency with which this procedure is followed should be based on the costs involved.

If, upon review of the relevant inputs to the model, the values obtained are significantly different from those currently being used in the model, modification is required. In this way the model is like a road map. All roads shown on the map may still exist, but if new roads have been built, proper information as to the best route to travel is not provided. By frequent revision, the value of the map in decision making is improved. Similarly, revision of input parameters gives assurance that the results obtained from the model can be used with confidence that they are based on the environmental conditions as they currently exist.

Control of Functional Relationships. An effectiveness function is the basic form of the mathematical model used in decision making. It exhibits functional relationships between effectiveness and the two classes of parameters. Any or all of these functional relationships are subject to change over time. If they do change, the model will yield erroneous results.

For example, suppose that an inventory model includes the cost of holding stock based on the average amount on hand during the year. Although this assumption may have been correct when the model was formulated, it may no longer be true. Warehousing practices may now exclude stock consolidation, thus making space vacated by a given product unavailable for other products. If this is so, the cost of holding inventory must now be based on the maximum amount on hand for the year. The decision model must be modified to express holding cost per year as a function of maximum inventory on hand if it is to represent accurately the decision situation as it currently exists.

2.5 THE APPLICATION OF MODELS

One must be cautious in applying a model, since one can come to believe that the model is reality in itself and forget that a model is only an approximation of the situation under study. When the solution derived by the use of a model is not plausible, or when it seems to disagree with what can be expected reasonably, the model should be reevaluated. This is particularly difficult to do when the model is computerized and used to make recurrent decisions.

A decision model cannot be classified as accurate or inaccurate in any absolute sense. It may be considered to be accurate if it is an idealized substitute of the actual system under study. If manipulation of the model would yield the identical result that manipulation of reality would have yielded, the model would be true. If, however, one knew what the manipulation of reality would have yielded, the process of simulation would be unnecessary. Hence, it is difficult to test a model except by an intuitive check for reasonableness.

The Value of Models in Decision Making. Models are valuable primarily because they permit indirect experimentation or simulation; this advantage is particularly worthwhile where direct experimentation is not possible. Indirect experimentation with a model makes it possible to consider a greater range of operating policies at less cost and in less time.

A *decision model* is essentially a device that relates two classes of variables to overall system effectiveness. Without such a device, the decision maker is forced to estimate values for the policy variables directly. When a model of the situation is formulated, however, the relationship of the controllable variables, uncontrollable or system variables, and effectiveness is explicitly stated. One can choose values for the controllable variables with much more certainty by making estimates for the system variables. The values for the policy variables resulting in optimum effectiveness will then depend upon a composite of many estimates. It is generally recognized that the accuracy of estimation can be improved considerably by estimating elements upon which an outcome depends; for example, one can probably estimate the volume of a room more accurately by estimating the length, width, and height of the room, than by estimating volume directly. The effectiveness function allows this principle to be applied to operational systems.

Rarely, however, is it necessary to determine all input parameters to a model by estimation. Usually, a certain amount of data exists that can be used to specify the values that should be assigned to uncontrolled variables. In fact, one advantage of the model is that it specifies which uncontrollable variables are important in the decision situation. One may then begin collecting data directed to the assignment of values to these parameters.

Often, a model is of value in the decision-making process even though it gives biased results. Here the model is valuable because it is consistent; that is, a decison model gives results that do not vary from decision to decision. It is often easier to correct for a biased decision than to compensate for a policy that changes for no apparent reason.

Automation of the Management Process. The delay in developing models to explain complex operational systems may be attributed to an early preoccupation with the physical and biological aspects of the environment. This can be justified, however, since during much of history, the limiting factors in the satisfaction of human wants were predominantly physical and biological. But with the accumulation of knowledge in these sciences, human beings have been able to employ complex systems of productive factors to satisfy their wants. Decision makers are becoming increasingly aware that experience, intuition, and judgment are insufficient for the effective pursuit of operational objectives.

Automation of production has resulted in reducing the number of direct labor hours per unit produced. This reduction may be expected to continue as the move toward more complete automation continues. Decision models are finding increased use as a means to automate the management and decision-making process. Routine decisions embracing recurrent operations may be conveniently handled by properly formulated decision models. These decision models, coupled with the ever-increasing availability and power of computational resources, may be expected to improve the overall effectiveness with which organizational objectives are achieved.

Although, admittedly, mathematical models can be only a partial representation of reality, they do provide a quantitative basis for decision making. This is useful because a model takes the decision maker part way to the point of decision. He or she may then add intuition and judgment to cover that portion of the situation not explained by the model. Thus, this augmented approach to decision making may be expected to improve the decision-making process and the efficiency of operational systems.

QUESTIONS

2.1. Discuss the various meanings of the word *model*.
2.2. Describe briefly physical models, schematic models, and mathematical models.
2.3. How do mathematical models directed to decision situations differ from those traditionally used in the physical sciences?

Chap. 2 Models and Simulation in OR/MS

2.4. Contrast direct and indirect experimentation.
2.5. Describe the role of simulation in OR/MS.
2.6. Write the general form of the effectiveness function and define its symbols.
2.7. Identify a decision situation and indicate the variables under the control of the decision maker and those not directly under his or her control.
2.8. Why is it impossible to formulate a model that accurately represents reality?
2.9. What means may be employed to simplify model construction?
2.10. Outline the means that may be employed to manipulate a decision model.
2.11. Under what conditions may a properly formulated model become useless as an aid in decision making?
2.12. Explain the nature of the cost components that should be considered in deciding how frequently to review a dynamic environment.
2.13. In OR/MS, models are used for prediction and control. Why is it necessary to be concerned with the control of the model itself?
2.14. What caution must be exercised in the use of models?
2.15. Discuss several specific reasons why models are of value in decision making.
2.16. What should be done with those facets of a decision situation that cannot be explained by the model?
2.17. Discuss mathematical models with regard to the automation of the decision-making process.
2.18. Should decision making be classified as an art or as a science?

II

Mathematical Programming Models

3

General Linear Programming Models

Linear programming is a mathematical modeling "system" which has found widespread use in providing decision makers with an efficient means for resolving complex operational alternatives. It is applicable to the general category of problems that require the optimization of a linear effectiveness function subject to linear constraints. These constraints exist because the activities under consideration usually compete for scarce resources. Linearity is assumed in both the effectiveness function and the constraints. Optimization may require minimization of cost, time, or distance, or it may require the maximization of profit, yield, or some other desirable output measure, depending on the situation under consideration.

The initial mathematical formulation of the general linear programming model is credited to George Dantzig and his associates. This formulation grew out of the search for mathematical techniques applicable to military logistics problems. Of primary significance was Dantzig's development of the simplex optimization method in 1947.

3.1 MATHEMATICAL MODEL FORMULATION

The general linear programming model may be formulated mathematically as requiring the optimization of the linear effectiveness function

$$E = \sum_{j=1}^{n} e_j x_j$$

subject to the linear constraints

$$\sum_{j=1}^{n} a_{ij} x_j = b_i \qquad i = 1, 2, \ldots, m$$

$$x_j \geq 0 \qquad j = 1, 2, \ldots, n.$$

The decision maker has direct control of the vector of variables, x_j. Not directly under control is the vector of effectiveness coefficients e_j, the matrix of constants, a_{ij}, and the vector of constants, b_i. This model structure follows the form of the general effectiveness function with constraints, as was presented in Section 2.3.

This mathematical statement of the general linear programming model may be explained in geometric terms. There exist n variables that define an n-dimensional space. Each constraint corresponds to a hyperplane in this space. These constraints surround the region of feasible solutions by hypersurfaces, so that the region is the interior of a convex polyhedron. Since the effectiveness function is linear in the n variables, the requirement that this function have some constant value gives a hyperplane that may or may not cut through the polyhedron. If it does, one or more feasible solutions exist. By changing the value of this constant, a family of hyperplanes parallel to each other is generated. The orthogonal distance from the origin to a member of this family is proportional to the value of the effectiveness function.

Two limiting hyperplanes may be identified: One corresponds to the largest value of the effectiveness function for which the hyperplane just touches the polyhedron; the other corresponds to the smallest value. In most cases, the limiting hyperplanes just touch a single vertex of the limiting polyhedron. This outermost limiting point identifies values for the n variables that optimize the effectiveness function.

Although it is possible to describe verbally the geometric structure of the linear programming model, graphical optimization methods do not exist beyond three dimensions. In the next section graphical optimization is applied to problems of two and three dimensions.

3.2 GRAPHICAL OPTIMIZATION METHODS

A good introduction to the structure and nature of linear programming problems can be obtained by utilizing graphical optimization methods. Although a graphical approach is not feasible for operations with more than three activities competing for scarce resources, these simple cases provide very good insight. The paragraphs that follow present linear programming examples involving two and three variables in which maximization or minimization is required.

Graphical Maximization for Two Activities. When two activities compete for scarce resources, a two-dimenisonal space is defined. Each restriction corresponds to a line on this surface. These restrictions identify a region of feasible solutions. The effectiveness function is also a line, its orthogonal distance from the origin being proportional to its value. The optimum value for the effectiveness function occurs when it is located so that it just touches an extreme point of the region.

Consider the following production example. Two products are to be produced. A single unit of product A requires 2.4 minutes of molding time and 5.0 minutes of assembly time. The profit for product A is $0.60 per unit. A single unit of product B requires 3.0 minutes of molding time and 2.5 minutes of finishing time. The profit for product B is $0.70 per unit. The molding department has time available to allocate to these products of 1,200 minutes per week. The finishing department has idle capacity of 600 minutes per week and the assembly department can supply 1,500 minutes of capacity per week. The production and marketing data for this production situation are summarized in Table 3.1.

Table 3.1. PRODUCTION AND MARKETING DATA FOR TWO PRODUCTS

	Product A	Product B	Capacity
Molding			
Finishing	2.4	3.0	1,200
Welding	0.0	2.5	600
Assembly	5.0	0.0	1,500
Profit	$0.60	$0.70	

In this example, two products compete for the available production time. The objective is to determine the quantity of product A and the quantity of product B to produce per week so that total profit will be maximized. This will require maximizing

$$TP = \$0.60A + \$0.70B \tag{3.1}$$

subject to

$$2.4A + 3.0B \le 1,200 \tag{3.2}$$
$$0.0A + 2.5B \le 600 \tag{3.3}$$
$$5.0A + 0.0B \le 1,500 \tag{3.4}$$
$$A \ge 0 \quad \text{and} \quad B \ge 0.$$

The graphical equivalent of the algebraic statement of this two-product problem is shown in Figure 3.1. The set of linear constraints define a region of

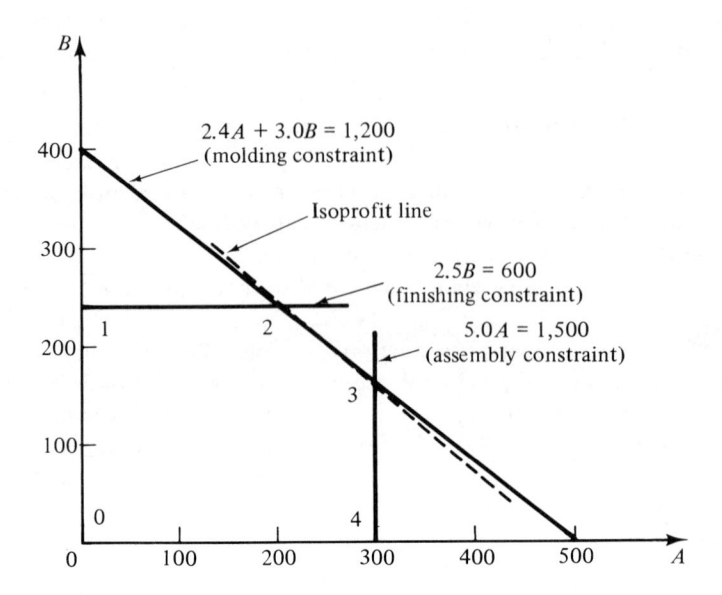

Figure 3.1 Maximizing profit for two-product production.

feasible solutions. This region lies below $2.4A + 3.0B = 1{,}200$ and is constrained further by the requirements that $B \leq 240$, $A \leq 300$, and that both A and B be nonnegative. Thus, the scarce resources determine which combinations of the activities are feasible and which are not feasible.

Feasible production quantity combinations of products A and B may be found at the extreme points by working with the constraints as equalities using linear algebra.[1] First, it is evident that a feasible combination exists at point 0 in Figure 3.1 when $A = 0$ and $B = 0$. From Equation (3.3) it is evident that point 1 in Figure 3.1 exhibits a feasible combination of $A = 0$ and $B = 240$. From Equation (3.4) it is also evident that point 4 exhibits a feasible combination of $A = 300$ and $B = 0$. Next, by utilizing Equation (3.2), the feasible combination at point 2 in Figure 3.1 is found to be

$$
\begin{aligned}
2.4A + 3.0B &= 1{,}200 \\
2.4A + 3.0(240) &= 1{,}200 \\
2.4A &= 1{,}200 - 720 \\
A &= 200
\end{aligned}
$$

since $B = 240$ from Equation (3.3). Finally, by utilizing Equation (3.2), the feasible combination at point 3 in Figure 3.1 is found to be

$$
\begin{aligned}
2.4A + 3.0B &= 1{,}200 \\
2.4(300) + 3.0B &= 1{,}200
\end{aligned}
$$

[1] Linear algebra may be reviewed by reference to Appendix A, Section A.1.

$$3.0B = 1,200 - 720$$
$$B = 160$$

since $A = 300$ from Equation (3.4).

Each of these production quantity combinations may now be evaluated for total profit, TP, by the use of Equation (3.1). For example, when $A = 300$ and $B = 160$ (point 3), total profit is $0.60(300) + $0.70(160) = $292. The results are exhibited in Table 3.2. Inspection of the total profit indicates that profit is maximized at point 3, which has the coordinates 300 and 160. No other production quantity combination of products A and B will result in a higher profit than the $292.00 shown.

Table 3.2. TOTAL PROFIT COMBINATIONS AT EXTREME POINTS OF FIGURE 3.1

Point	Coordinate A	Coordinate B	Total Profit
0	0	0	0
1	0	240	$168.00
2	200	240	288.00
3	300	160	292.00
4	300	0	180.00

A more formal approach to finding the maximum profit combination of products A and B may be utilized by noting that the relationship between A and B is $A = 1.167B$, based on the relative profit contribution of each product. The total profit realized will depend on the production quantity combination chosen. Thus, there is a family of isoprofit lines, one of which will have at least one point in the region of feasible production quantity combinations and be a maximum orthogonal distance from the origin. The member that satisfies this condition intersects the region of feasible solutions at the extreme point $A = 300$, $B = 160$. This is shown as a dashed line in Figure 3.1 and represents a total profit of $292, as was shown algebraically.

Alternative production programs with the same profit might exist in some cases. This occurs when the isoprofit line lies parallel to one of the limiting constraints. For example, if the relative profits of product A and product B were $A = 1.25B$, the isoprofit line in Figure 3.1 would coincide with the constraint $2.4A + 3.0B = 1,200$. In this case, the isoprofit line would touch the region of feasible solutions along a line instead of at a point. All production quantity combinations along the line would maximize profit.

Graphical Maximization for Three Activities. When three activities compete for scarce resources, a three-dimensional space is involved. Each constraint is a plane in this space, and all constraints taken together identify a volume of feasible solutions. The effectiveness function is also a plane, its orthogonal distance from the origin being proportional to its value. The optimum value for the effectiveness function occurs when this plane is located so that it is at the extreme point of the volume of feasible solutions.

As an example, suppose that the production operations in the previous example are to be expanded to include a third product, designated C. A single unit of product C will require 2.0 minutes of molding time. The profit associated with product C is $0.50 per unit. Production and marketing data for this revised situation are summarized in Table 3.3.

Table 3.3. PRODUCTION AND MARKETING DATA FOR THREE PRODUCTS

Molding	Product A	Product B	Product C	Capacity
Finishing	2.4	3.0	2.0	1,200
Welding	0.0	2.5	1.5	600
Assembly	5.0	0.0	2.5	1,500
Profit	$0.60	$0.70	$0.50	

In this example, three products compete for the available production time. The objective is to determine the quantity of product A, the quantity of product B, and the quantity of product C to produce so that total profit will be maximized. This will require maximizing

$$TP = \$0.60A + \$0.70B + \$0.50C \tag{3.5}$$

subject to

$$2.4A + 3.0B + 2.0C \leq 1{,}200 \tag{3.6}$$

$$0.0A + 2.5B + 1.5C \leq 600 \tag{3.7}$$

$$5.0A + 0.0B + 2.5C \leq 1{,}500 \tag{3.8}$$

$$A \geq 0, \quad B \geq 0, \quad \text{and} \quad C \geq 0.$$

The graphical equivalent of the algebraic statement of this three-product production situation is shown in Figure 3.2. The set of constraining planes defines a volume of feasible solutions. This region lies below $2.4A + 3.0B + 2.0C = 1{,}200$ and is restricted further by the requirement that $2.5B + 1.5C \leq 600$, $5.0A + 2.5C \leq 1{,}500$, and that A, B, and C be nonnegative. Thus, the scarce resources determine which combinations of the activities are feasible and which are not feasible.

The production quantity combinations of products A, B, and C that fall within the volume of feasible solutions constitute feasible production programs. That combination or combinations of products A, B, and C which maximizes total profit is sought. The expression $0.60A + 0.70B + 0.50C$ gives the relationship among products A, B, and C based on the relative profit of each. The total profit realized will depend on the production quantity combination chosen. Thus, there exists a family of isoprofit planes, one for each value of total profit.

Chap. 3   General Linear Programming Models   39

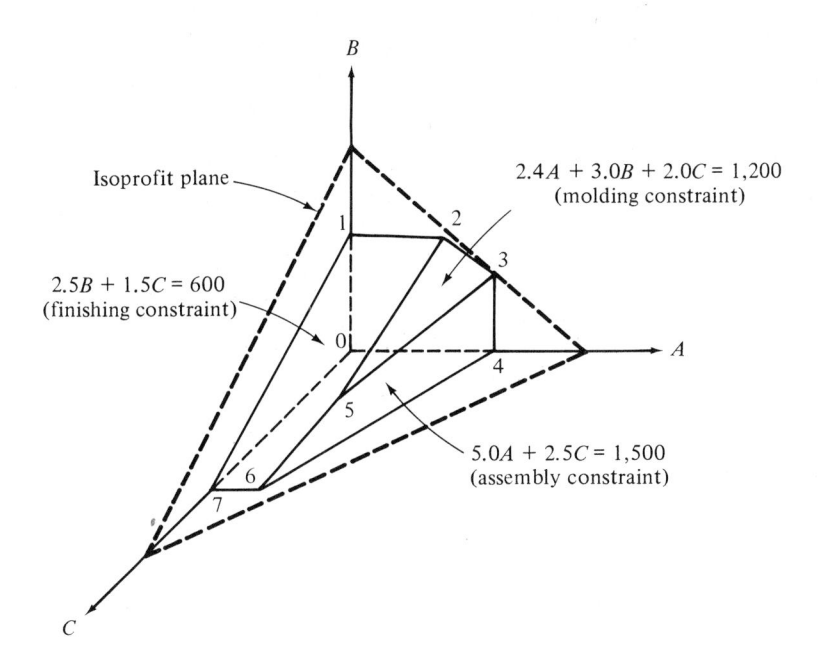

Figure 3.2   Maximizing profit for three-product production.

One of these planes will have at least one point in the volume of feasible solutions and will be a maximum orthogonal distance from the origin. The plane that maximizes profit will intersect the volume at an extreme point.

Feasible production quantity combinations may be found at the extreme points by the use of the elimination substitution technique of linear algebra, as presented in Appendix A. For example, the values of products A, B, and C at extreme point 5 in Figure 3.2 may be found as follows:

1. From Equation (3.7), $B = 240 - 0.6C$.
2. Substitute $B = 240 - 0.6C$ into Equation (3.6), giving $2.4A + 0.2C = 480$.
3. Multiply $2.4A + 0.2C = 480$ by 12.50, giving $30.0A + 2.5C = 6,000$.
4. Subtract $30.0A + 2.5C = 6,000$ from Equation (3.8) and solve for A, giving $A = 180$.
5. Substitute $A = 180$ into Equation (3.8) and solve for C, giving $C = 240$.
6. Substitute $C = 240$ into Equation (3.7) and solve for B, giving $B = 96$.

The total profit resulting from $A = 180$, $B = 96$, and $C = 240$ (point 5) is found from Equation (3.5) as $0.60(180) + \$0.70(96) + \$0.50(240) = \$295.20$. This is recorded in Table 3.4 together with the total profit at all other extreme points in Figure 3.2.

Table 3.4. TOTAL PROFIT VALUES AT EXTREME POINTS OF FIGURE 3.2

Point	Coordinate A	Coordinate B	Coordinate C	Total
0	0	0	0	$ 0
1	0	240	0	$168.00
2	200	240	0	$288.00
3	300	160	0	$292.00
4	300	0	0	$180.00
5	180	96	240	$295.20
6	100	0	400	$260.00
7	0	0	400	$200.00

Inspection of the total profit values in Table 3.4 indicates that profit is maximized at point 5, which has the coordinates 180, 96, and 240. No other production quantity combination of products A, B, and C will result in a higher profit. Also, no alternative optimum solutions exist, since the total profit plane intersects the volume of feasible solutions at only a single point.

Addition of a third product to the two-product production operation increased total profit from $292.00 per week to $295.20 per week. This increase in profit results from reallocation of the available production time and from greater utilization of the idle capacity in the finishing department. The number of units of product A was reduced from 200 to 180 and the number of units of B was reduced from 240 to 96. This made it possible to add 240 units of product C to the production program with the resulting increase in profit.

Graphical Minimization for Two Activities. As an example of optimization by minimization in linear programming, consider a feed-mixing operation that can be described in terms of two activities. The required mixture must contain four kinds of nutrient ingredients, designated w, x, y, and z. Two basic feeds, designated A and B, which contain the required ingredients are available on the market. One pound of feed A contains 0.1 pound of w, 0.1 pound of y, and 0.2 pound of z. One pound of feed B contains 0.1 pound of x, 0.2 pound of y, and 0.1 pound of z.

The feed mixture is to be used to fatten steers which have a daily per head requirement of at least 0.4 pound of ingredient w, 0.6 pound of ingredient x, 2 pounds of ingredient y, and 1.8 pounds of ingredient z. Feed A costs $0.07 per pound and feed B costs $0.05 per pound. The availabilities, requirements, and costs are summarized in Table 3.5.

The objective is to determine the quantity of feed A and the quantity of feed B to include in the mixture so that the total cost will be a minimum. This will require minimizing

Chap. 3   General Linear Programming Models   41

Table 3.5. AVAILABILITIES, REQUIREMENTS, AND COSTS FOR FEED MIXING

Nutrient	Feed A	Feed B	Requirement
w	0.1	0.0	0.4
x	0.0	0.1	0.6
y	0.1	0.2	2.0
z	0.2	0.1	1.8
Cost	$0.07	$0.05	

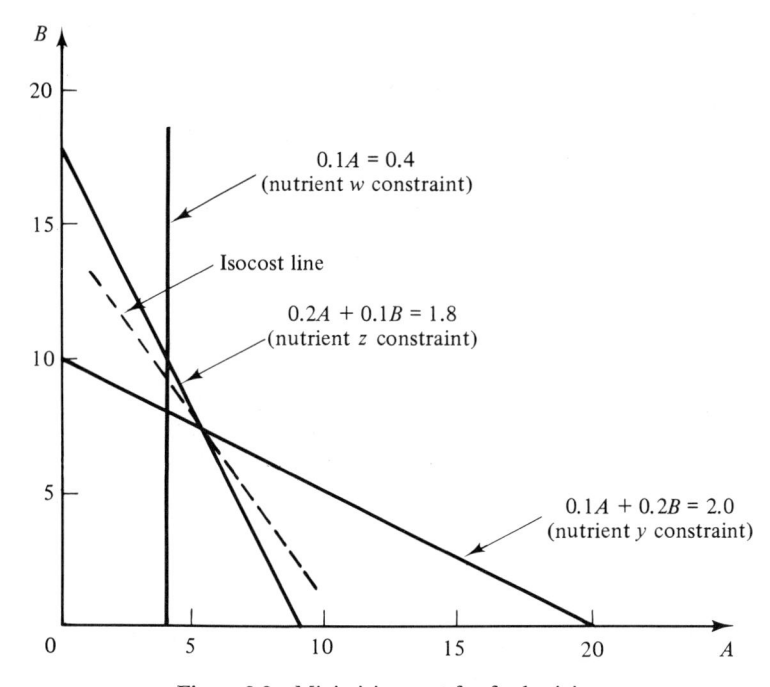

Figure 3.3   Minimizing cost for feed mixing.

$$TC = \$0.07A + \$0.05B$$

subject to

$$0.1A + 0.0B \geq 0.4$$
$$0.0A + 0.1B \geq 0.6$$
$$0.1A + 0.2B \geq 2.0$$
$$0.2A + 0.1B \geq 1.8$$
$$A \geq 0 \quad \text{and} \quad B \geq 0.$$

The graphical equivalent of the algebraic statement of this problem is shown in Figure 3.3. The set of linear constraints define a region of feasible solutions. This region is of a greater than or equal to type, because the problem requires minimization. The region lies above $0.1A + 0.2B = 2.0$ and $0.2A + 0.1B = 1.8$, and is further constrained by $A \geq 4$, $B \geq 6$, and the requirements that A and B be nonnegative. Thus, the minimum nutrient requirements specify which combinations of feeds A and B are feasible and which are not feasible.

The quantity combinations of feeds A and B that fall within the region of feasible solutions constitute feasible feed mixes. That combination or combinations of A and B which minimize total cost is sought. There is a family of isocost lines one of which will have at least one point in the region of feasible solutions and will be a minimum distance from the origin. The member that satisfies this condition intersects the region of feasible solutions at the extreme point $A = 5.33$, $B = 7.34$. This is shown as a dashed line in Figure 3.3 and represents a total cost of $\$0.07(5.33) + \$0.05(7.34) = \$0.74$. No other feed mixture will yield a lower total cost. Also, no alternative optimum solutions exist.

3.3 MAXIMIZING BY THE SIMPLEX METHOD

The simplex method is an algorithm that makes possible the numerical solution of the general linear programming problem. It is not restricted to problems with three activities or fewer, as is the graphical optimization method. The simplex method is an iterative process that begins with a feasible solution, tests for optimality, and proceeds toward an improved solution. It can be shown that the algorithm will finally lead to an optimal solution, if such a solution exists. In this section, the simplex method will be applied to the three-product maximization problem presented graphically. Reference to the graphical solution will help explain certain facets of the computational procedure.

Initial Matrix for Maximization. The three-product production problem under consideration requires the maximization of a total profit equation, subject to certain constraints. These constraints must be converted to equalities of the form specified by the general linear programming model. This requires the addition of three "slack" variables to remove the inequalities. Thus, the constraints become

$$2.4A + 3.0B + 2.0C + S_1 = 1{,}200$$
$$0.0A + 2.5B + 1.5C + S_2 = 600$$
$$5.0A + 0.0B + 2.5C + S_3 = 1{,}500.$$

The amount of departmental time not used in the production program is represented by a slack variable. Thus, each slack variable takes on whatever value is necessary for the equality to exist. If nothing is produced, the slack variables assume values equal to the total production time available in each department. This gives an initial feasible solution expressed as $S_1 = 1{,}200$, $S_2 = 600$, and $S_3 = 1{,}500$. Each slack variable is one of the x_j variables in the model. Since, however, no profit can be derived from idle capacity, total profit may be expressed as

$$TP = \$0.60A + \$0.70B + \$0.50C + \$0S_1 + \$0S_2 + \$0S_3.$$

The initial matrix required by the simplex algorithm may now be set up as shown in Table 3.6. The first column is designated e_i and gives the profit coefficients applicable to the initial feasible solution. These are all zero, since the initial solution involves the allocation of all production time to the slack variables. The second column is designated *Sol* and gives the variables in the initial solution. These are the slack variables that were introduced. The third column is designated b_i and gives the number of minutes of production time associated with the solution variables of the previous column. These reflect the total production capacity in the initial solution. Each of the next three columns is headed by the slack variables, with elements of zero or one depending upon which equation is served by which slack variable. The e_j heading for these columns carries an entry of zero, corresponding to a zero profit. The last three columns are headed by the activity variables with elements entered from the restricting equations. The e_j heading for these columns is the profit associated with each activity variable. The column designated θ, as well as the lower portion of the table, is utilized during the computational process.

Table 3.6. INITIAL MATRIX FOR A THREE-PRODUCT PRODUCTION PROBLEM

	e_j		0	0	0	0.60	0.70	0.50	
e_i	Sol	b_i	S_1	S_2	S_3	A	B	C	θ
0	S_1	1,200	1	0	0	2.4	3.0	2.0	400
0	S_2	600	0	1	0	0	2.5	1.5	240	r
0	S_3	1,500	0	0	1	5.0	0	2.5	∞
	E_j	0	0	0	0	0	0	0	
	$E_j - e_j$		0	0	0	−0.60	−0.70	−0.50	

k

Testing for Optimality. After an initial feasible solution has been obtained, it must be tested to see if a solution with a higher profit can be found. The optimality test is accomplished with the aid of the last two rows in Table 3.6. The required steps are:

1. Enter values in the row designated E_j from the expression $E_j = \sum e_i a_{ij}$, where a_{ij} are the matrix elements in the ith row and the jth column.
2. Calculate $E_j - e_j$, for all positions in the row designated $E_j - e_j$.
3. If $E_j - e_j$ is negative for at least one j, a better solution is possible.

Application of the optimality test to the initial feasible solution is shown in the last two rows of Table 3.6. The first element in the E_j row is calculated as

0(1,200) + 0(600) + 0(1,500) = 0. The second is 0(1) + 0(0) + 0(0) = 0. All values in this row will be zero, since all e_i values are zero in the initial feasible solution. The first element in the $E_j - e_j$ row is $0 - 0 = 0$, the second is $0 - 0 = 0$, the third is $0 - 0 = 0$, the fourth is $0 - 0.60 = -0.60$, and so forth. Since $E_j - e_j$ is negative for at least one j, this initial solution is not optimal.

Iteration Toward an Optimal Solution. If the optimality test indicates that an optimal solution has not been found, the following iterative procedure may be employed:

1. Find the minimum value of $E_j - e_j$ and designate this column k. The variable at the head of this column will be the incoming variable.
2. Calculate entries for the column designated θ from $\theta_i = b_i/a_{ik}$.
3. Find the minimum positive value of θ_i and designate this row r. The variable to the left of this row will be the outgoing variable.
4. Set up a new matrix with the incoming variable substituted for the outgoing variable. Calculate new elements, a'_{ij}, as $a'_{rj} = a_{rj}/a_{rk}$ for $i = r$ and $a'_{ij} = a_{ij} - a_{ik}a'_{rj}$ for $i \neq r$.
5. Perform the optimality test.

Steps (1), (2), and (3) of the iterative procedure are applied to the initial or old matrix. In Table 3.6, step (1) designates B as the incoming variable. Values for θ_i are calculated from step (2). Step (3) designates S_2 as the outgoing variable. The affected column and row are marked with a k and an r, respectively, in Table 3.6.

Steps (4) and (5) require a new matrix, as shown in Table 3.7. The incoming variable B, together with its associated profit, replaces the outgoing variable S_2 with its profit. All other elements in this row are calculated from the first formula of step (4). Elements in the remaining two rows are calculated from the second formula of step (4). Note that after this iteration, the profit at point 1 of Figure 3.2 appears. Comparison of the results in Tables 3.6 and 3.7 with

Table 3.7. FIRST ITERATION FOR A THREE-PRODUCT PRODUCTION PROBLEM

	e_j		0	0	0	0.60	0.70	0.50	
e_i	Sol	b_i	S_1	S_2	S_3	A	B	C	θ
0	S_1	480	1	−1.20	0	2.40	0	0.20	200 r
0.70	B	240	0	0.40	0	0	1	0.60	∞
0	S_3	1,500	0	0	1	5.00	0	2.50	300
	E_j	168	0	0.28	0	0	0.70	0.42	
	$E_j - e_j$		0	0.28	0	−0.60	0	−0.08	

k

the total profit computations in Table 3.4 indicates that the isoprofit plane which began at the origin has now moved away from this initial position to point 1. The gain from this iteration was $168 − $0 = $168. Application of the optimality test indicates that an optimal solution has not yet been reached.

Since the first iteration did not yield an optimal solution, it is necessary to repeat steps (1) through (5). Steps (1), (2), and (3) are applied to Table 3.7 designating A as the incoming variable and S_1 as the outgoing variable. The incoming variable, together with its associated profit, replaces the outgoing variable as shown in Table 3.8. All other elements in this new matrix are calculated from the formulas of step (4). Application of the optimality test indicates that the solution indicated is still not optimal. Table 3.4 and Figure 3.2 show that the isoprofit plane is now at point 2. The gain from this iteration was $288 − $168 = $120.

Table 3.8. SECOND ITERATION FOR A THREE-PRODUCT PRODUCTION PROBLEM

	e_j		0	0	0	0.60	0.70	0.50	
e_i	Sol	b_i	S_1	S_2	S_3	A	B	C	θ
0.60	A	200	0.416	−0.50	0	1	0	0.084	2,381
0.70	B	240	0	0.40	0	0	1	0.60	400
0	S_3	500	−2.08	2.50	1	0	0	2.08	240 r
	E_j	288	0.25	−0.02	0	0.60	0.70	0.47	
	$E_j − e_j$		0.25	−0.02	0	0	0	−0.03	

k

Table 3.8 did not yield an optimal solution, requiring the application of steps (1) through (5) again. Steps (1), (2), and (3) designate C as the incoming variable and S_3 as the outgoing variable. This incoming variable as shown in Table 3.9. All other elements in the matrix are calculated from the formulas of step (4). Application of the optimality test indicates that the solution exhibited by Table 3.9 is optimal. Table 3.4 and Figure 3.2 indicate that the isoprofit

Table 3.9. THIRD ITERATION FOR A THREE-PRODUCT PRODUCTION PROBLEM

	e_j		0	0	0	0.60	0.70	0.50	
e_i	Sol	b_i	S_1	S_2	S_3	A	B	C	θ
0.60	A	180	0.50	−0.60	−0.04	1	0	0	
0.70	B	96	0.60	−0.32	−0.29	0	1	0	
0.50	C	240	−1	1.20	0.48	0	0	1	
	E_j	295.20	0.22	0.016	0.016	0.60	0.70	0.50	
	$E_j − e_j$		0.22	0.016	0.016	0	0	0	

plane is now at point 5. The gain from this iteration was $295.20 − $288 = $7.20.

3.4 MINIMIZING BY THE SIMPLEX METHOD

The computational scheme of Section 3.3 may be used without modification for problems requiring minimization if the signs of the cost coefficients are changed from positive to negative. The principle that maximizing the negative of a function is the same as minimizing the function then applies. If these coefficients are entered in the simplex matrix with their negative signs, the value of the solution will decrease as the computations proceed. In this section, the feed-mixing problem presented graphically in Section 3.2 will be solved by the simplex method.

Initial Matrix for Minimization. The problem under consideration requires the minimization of a total cost equation subject to certain constraints. Changing the sign of each cost coefficient in the total cost equation gives

$$TC = -\$0.07A - \$0.05B.$$

As before, the constraints must be converted to equalities so that the problem will conform to the general linear programming model. This is accomplished by subtracting a slack variable from the left-hand side of each. The constraints then become

$$0.1A + 0.0B - S_1 = 0.4$$
$$0.0A + 0.1B - S_2 = 0.6$$
$$0.1A + 0.2B - S_3 = 2.0$$
$$0.2A + 0.1B - S_4 = 1.8.$$

Although the constraints are now equalities, a feasible solution does not exist. If A and B are set equal to zero, $S_1 = -0.4$, $S_2 = -0.6$, $S_3 = -2.0$, and $S_4 = -1.8$. An initial feasible solution of the correct algebraic form can be forced by adding "artificial" variables, resulting in

$$0.1A + 0.0B - S_1 + A_1 = 0.4$$
$$0.0A + 0.1B - S_2 + A_2 = 0.6$$
$$0.1A + 0.2B - S_3 + A_3 = 2.0$$
$$0.2A + 0.1B - S_4 + A_4 = 1.8.$$

Artificial variables with a value greater than zero destroy the equality required by the general linear programming model. Therefore, they must not appear in the final solution. To assure that they are forced out of the solution, a large penalty will be associated with each. This penalty will be larger than any other effectiveness coefficient and is designated $-M$. With these changes, the total cost equation becomes

$$TC = -\$0.07A - \$0.05B - \$0S_1 - \$0S_2 - \$0S_3$$
$$- \$0S_4 - \$MA_1 - \$MA_2 - \$MA_3 - \$MA_4.$$

The initial matrix required by the simplex algorithm may now be set up as shown in Table 3.10. The intial solution variables are the artificial variables. Effectiveness coefficients for each artificial variable, slack variable, and activity variable are entered in the second row. All other matrix elements are entered from the constraints. The simplex method may be applied to this matrix in the manner outlined for maximization.

Performing the Calculations for Minimization. The last two rows of Table 3.10 are used in the optimality test. Since at least one $E_j - e_j$ is positive, the initial feasible solution is not optimal. Therefore, B becomes the incoming variable. Computation of θ_i identifies A_2 as the outgoing variable. The incoming variable and the outgoing variable are designated k and r, respectively, in Table 3.10. They provide the basis for the first iteration.

The incoming variable B is entered in place of the outgoing variable A_2 in Table 3.11, together with its associated effectiveness coefficient. Each element in this new matrix is calculated from step (4) of the iterative procedure outlined in the preceding section. Application of the optimality test indicates that the solution is still not optimal. This makes the second iteration given in Table 3.12 necessary. Proceeding in this manner results in the third iteration given in Table 3.13, the fourth iteration given in Table 3.14, and the fifth iteration given in Table 3.15. The program indicated by the fifth iteration is optimal. This final table indicates that 5.33 pounds of feed A and 7.34 pounds of feed B should be used in the mixture. The total cost of the mixture will be $0.74, neglecting the negative sign. These results agree with the solution found graphically.

3.5 MATRIX FORMULATION OF LINEAR PROGRAMMING[2]

The general linear programming model may be formulated in matrix notation as requiring the optimization of

$$E = ex$$

subject to

$$Ax = b \quad \text{and} \quad x \geq 0.$$

For the three-product production problem of Section 3.3, x is the vector of real and slack variables A, B, C, S_1, S_2, and S_3, and e is the vector of effec-

---

[2]This section requires familiarity with Appendix A, which presents linear algebra and matrices.

Table 3.10. INITIAL MATRIX FOR A MINIMIZATION PROBLEM

e_j			0	$-M$	0	$-M$	0	$-M$	0	$-M$	-0.07	-0.05	
e_i	Sol	b_i	S_1	A_1	S_2	A_2	S_3	A_3	S_4	A_4	A	B	θ
$-M$	A_1	0.4	-1	1	0	0	0	0	0	0	0.1	0	∞
$-M$	A_2	0.6	0	0	-1	1	0	0	0	0	0	0.1	6
$-M$	A_3	2.0	0	0	0	0	-1	1	0	0	0.1	0.2	10
$-M$	A_4	1.8	0	0	0	0	0	0	-1	1	0.2	0.1	18
	E_j	$-4.8M$	M	$-M$	M	$-M$	M	$-M$	M	$-M$	$-0.4M$	$-0.4M$	
	$E_j - e_j$		M	0	M	0	M	0	M	0	$0.07 - 0.4M$	$0.05 - 0.4M$	

k

Table 3.11. FIRST ITERATION FOR A MINIMIZATION PROBLEM

e_j			0	$-M$	0	$-M$	0	$-M$	0	$-M$	-0.07	-0.05	
e_i	Sol	b_i	S_1	A_1	S_2	A_2	S_3	A_3	S_4	A_4	A	B	θ
$-M$	A_1	0.4	-1	1	0	0	0	0	0	0	0.1	0	∞
-0.05	B	6	0	0	-10	10	0	0	0	0	0	1	-0.6
$-M$	A_3	0.8	0	0	2	-2	-1	1	0	0	0.1	0	0.4
$-M$	A_4	1.2	0	0	1	-1	0	0	-1	1	0.2	0	1.2
	E_j	$-0.3 - 2.4M$	M	$-M$	$0.5 - 3M$	$-0.5 + 3M$	M	$-M$	M	$-M$	$-0.4M$	-0.05	
	$E_j - e_j$		M	0	$0.5 - 3M$	$-0.5 + 4M$	M	0	M	0	$0.07 - 0.4M$	0	

k

48

Table 3.12. SECOND ITERATION FOR A MINIMIZATION PROBLEM

e_j		0	$-M$	0	$-M$	0	$-M$	0	$-M$	-0.07	-0.05	
e_i	Sol	b_i	S_1	A_1	S_2	A_2	S_3	A_3	S_4	A_4	A	B	θ
$-M$	A_1	0.4	-1	1	0	0	0	0	0	0	0.1	0	∞
-0.05	B	10	0	0	0	0	-5	5	0	0	0.5	1	-2
0	S_2	0.4	0	0	1	-1	-0.5	0.5	0	0	0.05	0	-0.8
$-M$	A_4	0.8	0	0	0	0	0.5	-0.5	-1	1	0.15	0	1.6
E_j		$-0.5 - 1.2M$	M	$-M$	0	0	$0.25 - 0.5M$	$-0.25 + 0.5M$	M	$-M$	$-0.025 - 0.25M$	-0.05	
$E_j - e_j$			M	0	0	M	$0.25 - 0.5M$	$-0.25 + 1.5M$	M	0	$0.045 - 0.25M$	0	

k

Table 3.13. THIRD ITERATION FOR A MINIMIZATION PROBLEM

e_j		0	$-M$	0	$-M$	0	$-M$	0	$-M$	-0.07	-0.05	
e_i	Sol	b_i	S_1	A_1	S_2	A_2	S_3	A_3	S_4	A_4	A	B	θ
$-M$	A_1	0.4	-1	1	0	0	0	0	0	0	0.1	0	4
-0.05	B	18	0	0	0	0	0	0	-10	10	2.0	1	9
0	S_2	1.2	0	0	1	-1	0	0	-1	1	0.2	0	6
0	S_3	1.6	0	0	0	0	1	-1	-2	2	0.3	0	5.33
E_j		$-0.9 - 0.4M$	M	$-M$	0	0	0	0	0.5	-0.5	$-0.1M - 0.1$	-0.05	
$E_j - e_j$			M	0	0	M	0	M	0.5	$M - 0.5$	$-0.03 - 0.1M$	0	

k

Table 3.14. FOURTH ITERATION FOR A MINIMIZATION PROBLEM

e_j			0	$-M$	0	$-M$	0	$-M$	0	$-M$	-0.07	-0.05	
e_i	Sol	b_i	S_1	A_1	S_2	A_2	S_3	A_3	S_4	A_4	A	B	θ
-0.07	A	4	-10	10	0	0	0	0	0	0	1	0	-0.4
-0.05	B	10	20	-20	0	0	0	0	-10	10	0	1	0.5
0	S_2	0.4	2	-2	1	-1	0	0	-1	10	0	0	0.2
0	S_3	0.4	3	-3	0	0	1	-1	-2	2	0	0	0.133
	E_j	-0.78	-0.3	0.3	0	0	0	0	0.5	-0.5	-0.07	-0.05	
	$E_j - e_j$		-0.3	$0.3 + M$	0	M	0	M	0.5	$-0.5 + M$	0	0	r

k

Table 3.15. FIFTH ITERATION FOR A MINIMIZATION PROBLEM

e_j			0	$-M$	0	$-M$	0	$-M$	0	$-M$	-0.07	-0.05	
e_i	Sol	b_i	S_1	A_1	S_2	A_2	S_3	A_3	S_4	A_4	A	B	θ
-0.07	A	5.33	0	0	0	0	3.30	-3.30	-6.70	6.70	1	0	
-0.05	B	7.34	0	0	0	0	-6.60	6.60	3.40	-3.40	0	1	
0	S_2	0.134	0	0	1	-1	-0.66	0.66	0.34	-0.34	0	0	
0	S_1	0.133	1	-1	0	0	0.33	-0.33	-0.67	0.67	0	0	
	E_j	-0.74	0	0	0	0	0.099	-0.099	0.299	-0.299	-0.07	-0.05	
	$E_j - e_j$		0	M	0	M	0.099	$-0.099 + M$	0.299	$-0.299 + M$	0	0	

50

Chap. 3   General Linear Programming Models   51

tiveness coefficients $0.60, $0.70, $0.50, and $0. The matrix A is

$$\begin{bmatrix} 2.4 & 3.0 & 2.0 & 1 & 0 & 0 \\ 0 & 2.5 & 1.5 & 0 & 1 & 0 \\ 5.0 & 0 & 2.5 & 0 & 0 & 1 \end{bmatrix}$$

and the vector b is

$$\begin{bmatrix} 1{,}200 \\ 600 \\ 1{,}500 \end{bmatrix}.$$

The vector x can be partitioned into parts. Let x_P include all variables currently included in the program and x_R include all the remaining variables. Then, the constraints $Ax = b$ become

$$[A_P,\ A_R]\begin{bmatrix} x_P \\ x_R \end{bmatrix} = b$$

$$A_P x_P + A_R x_R = b.$$

Multiply both sides by A_P^{-1}:

$$A_P^{-1} A_P x_P + A_P^{-1} A_R x_R = A_P^{-1} b$$

since

$$A_P^{-1} A_P = I$$

$$I x_P + A_P^{-1} A_R x_R = A_P^{-1} b$$

$$I x_P = A_P^{-1}(b - A_R x_R)$$

$$= A_P^{-1} b - A_P^{-1} A_R x_R. \tag{3.9}$$

The identity matrix corresponding to the solution variables can be identified for any iteration of the simplex process. For example, in Table 3.6 columns 3, 4, and 5 of the simplex tableau correspond to the program variables x_1, x_2, and x_3, and these do form an identity matrix.

The current value of the effectiveness function can be stated as

$$E = ex$$

$$= e_P x_P + e_R x_R.$$

Substituting for x_P from Equation (3.9) gives

$$E = e_P[A_P^{-1} b - A_P^{-1} A_R x_R] + e_R x_R$$

$$= e_P A_P^{-1} b - [e_P A_P^{-1} A_R - e_R] x_R.$$

Further, since the variables x_R are not currently in the solution and their numerical value is zero, the current value of effectiveness is $e_P A_P^{-1} b$. The jth component of the vector $[e_P A_P^{-1} A_R - e_R]$ is equivalent to the quantity $E_j - e_j$ computed during the test for optimality. If one unit of any nonprogram variable x_j is added to the program, the effectiveness will be decreased by an amount equal to the jth component of $[e_P A_P^{-1} A_R - e_R]$ or $E_j - e_j$. In this sense the quantity $-(E_j - e_j)$ is the rate of change of the effectiveness function per unit change of a nonprogram variable. This rate of change is also called the marginal profit or shadow price. Obviously, if this rate of change (or the jth component of $[e_P A_P^{-1} A_R - e_R]$) is negative for any nonprogram variable x_j, it implies that the current effectiveness function can be increased by the introduction of x_j into the program, and the current program is not optimal. On the other hand, if none of the components are negative, the current effectiveness cannot be improved.

3.6 THE REVISED SIMPLEX METHOD

The simplex method is very useful for hand computation of small linear programming problems involving few constraints and few variables. However, many applications give rise to linear programming problems of immense size. Problems involving hundreds of constraints and thousands of decision variables are fairly common. It is imperative that these large problems be solved on a digital computer. The revised simplex method was developed as a compact and efficient algorithm for digital computer solution of linear programming problems. Exactly the same computations are carried out in both the simplex and the revised simplex methods. The differences are only in the arrangement of computations and the storage of computed intermediate values, two factors that are of importance when digital computers are used.

Matrix Statement of the Revised Simplex Method. Like the simplex method, the revised simplex method is an iterative procedure that begins from a known feasible solution, tests for optimality, and proceeds toward an improved solution. Let the linear programming problem be stated as:

$$\text{maximize } ex \text{ subject to } Ax = b.$$

Further, let $[x_P, x_R]$ be an intermediate solution such that the variables x_P are currently in the program and the variables x_R are out of the program, and $[A_P, A_R]$ is the partition of A, corresponding to the partition $[x_P, x_R]$. Then, from Section 3.5,

$$I x_P + A_P^{-1} A_R x_R = A_P^{-1} b$$

and

$$E = e_P A_P^{-1} b - [e_P A_P^{-1} A_R - e_R] x_R.$$

The expanded form of these two matrix equations will be identical to the intermediate tableau of the simplex method. Note that the quantities $A_P^{-1} b$, $A_P^{-1} A_R$, $e_P A_P^{-1} b$, and $[e_P A_P^{-1} A_R - e_R]$ can be calculated from the original data if the inverse matrix A_P^{-1} is known. In the revised simplex method, only this inverse matrix is stored instead of the entire simplex tableau. Also, since the variables x_R are currently out of the program and their value is zero, the matrix equations

Chap. 3   General Linear Programming Models

can be written as

$$x_P = A_P^{-1}b$$

and

$$E - e_P A_P^{-1} b = 0$$

or

$$\begin{bmatrix} E \\ x_P \end{bmatrix} = \begin{bmatrix} 1 & e_P A_P^{-1} \\ 0 & A_P^{-1} \end{bmatrix} \begin{bmatrix} 0 \\ b \end{bmatrix}.$$

For any variable x_j, the jth column in the simplex tableau is given by

$$\begin{bmatrix} E_j - e_j \\ A_P^{-1} a_j \end{bmatrix} = \begin{bmatrix} 1 & e_P A_P^{-1} \\ 0 & A_P^{-1} \end{bmatrix} \begin{bmatrix} -e_j \\ a_j \end{bmatrix}.$$

In the equation above, a_j is the column corresponding to x_j in the coefficient matrix A.

Computational Scheme for the Revised Simplex Method. To illustrate the computational scheme, the example problem solved in Section 3.3 by the regular simplex method will be solved by the revised simplex method. This will further demonstrate that computations in both methods are identical, although the form of the computation is different:

STEP 1. Introduce slack and artificial variables to convert all constraint inequations into equations as required by the general linear programming model. Maximize

$$E = ex$$

subject to

$$Ax = b \quad \text{and} \quad x \geq 0.$$

The matrix A and the vectors e' and b are as shown in Section 3.5.

STEP 2. Identify the initial feasible solution as in the case of regular simplex method. In the example problem, the initial feasible solution is easily identified as

$$x_P = \begin{bmatrix} x_4 \\ x_5 \\ x_6 \end{bmatrix} = \begin{bmatrix} 1{,}200 \\ 600 \\ 1{,}500 \end{bmatrix}$$

and

$$x_R = \begin{bmatrix} x_1 \\ x_2 \\ x_3 \end{bmatrix} = \begin{bmatrix} 0 \\ 0 \\ 0 \end{bmatrix}.$$

Also, matrix A_P corresponding to x_P is a 3×3 identity matrix. Obviously, A_P^{-1} is also an identity matrix. In a properly formulated revised simplex format, the matrices A_P and A_P^{-1} will always be identity matrices for the first iterative step.

STEP 3. Formulate the operational matrix D

$$D = \begin{bmatrix} e_p A_P^{-1} & E \\ A_P^{-1} & A_P^{-1}b \end{bmatrix}.$$

Since matrix A_P^{-1} is an identity matrix for the first iteration, the operational matrix becomes

$$\begin{bmatrix} e_p & 0 \\ I & b \end{bmatrix}.$$

This is shown in Table 3.16 for the example. The current solution and effectiveness can be obtained from the operational matrix as $x_4 = 1,200$, $x_5 = 600$, $x_6 = 1,500$, and $E = 0$.

Table 3.16. OPERATIONAL MATRIX D FOR THE FIRST ITERATION

Row Number		Column 1	2	3	4
0	E	0	0	0	0
1	x_4	1	0	0	1,200
2	x_5	0	1	0	600
3	x_6	0	0	1	1,500

STEP 4. Test the current solution for optimality by computing the quantities $E_j - e_j$ or $(e_p A_P^{-1} A_r - e_r)$ for every variable x_j not currently in the solution. E_j is obtained by taking the scalar product of the top row of the first m columns of the operational matrix, $e_p A_P^{-1}$, and the coefficient vector corresponding to the variable x_j, a_j. If none of the quantities $E_j - e_j$ is negative, the solution is optimal. However, if $E_k - e_k$ is negative for any variable x_k, the solution is not optimal, and x_k qualifies as an entering variable. When there are several qualified entering variables, the variable yielding the largest negative value of $E_j - e_j$ is chosen for entry.

For the operational matrix in Table 3.16, x_1, x_2, and x_3 are not currently in the solution, and the quantities $E_1 - e_1$, $E_2 - e_2$, and $E_3 - e_3$ can be calculated using the first three elements of the top row of the operational matrix $[0 \ 0 \ 0]$.

$$E_1 - e_1 = [0 \ 0 \ 0] \begin{bmatrix} 2.4 \\ 0 \\ 5.0 \end{bmatrix} - 0.60 = -0.60.$$

Similarly, $E_2 - e_2 = -0.70$ and $E_3 - e_3 = -0.50$. Since all three evaluations are negative, x_1, x_2, and x_3 qualify as entering variables. However, x_2 is chosen as the entering variable, since the improvement in E per unit of x_2 is greater that which would result if either x_1 or x_3 were chosen.

Chap. 3   General Linear Programming Models   55

Step 5.   Formulate the vector

$$y_k = \begin{bmatrix} E_k - e_k \\ A_P^{-1} a_k \end{bmatrix}$$

and determine the departing variable as the one yielding the smallest positive ratio $d_{2,m+1}/y_{rk}$. Since x_2 is chosen as the entering variable, $k = 2$ giving

$$y_2 = \begin{bmatrix} E_2 - e_2 \\ A_P^{-1} a_2 \end{bmatrix}.$$

However,

$$A_P^{-1} a_2 = \begin{bmatrix} 1 & 0 & 0 \\ 0 & 1 & 0 \\ 0 & 0 & 1 \end{bmatrix} \begin{bmatrix} 3.0 \\ 2.5 \\ 0 \end{bmatrix} = \begin{bmatrix} 3.0 \\ 2.5 \\ 0 \end{bmatrix}.$$

Therefore,

$$y_2 = \begin{bmatrix} -0.70 \\ 3.0 \\ 2.5 \\ 0 \end{bmatrix}.$$

The quantities $d_{r,m+1}$ are the three lower elements of the last column of the operational matrix in Table 3.16. Hence, the ratios are

$$\frac{d_{1,m+1}}{y_{1,k}} = \frac{1,200}{3.0} = 400$$

$$\frac{d_{2,m+1}}{y_{2,k}} = \frac{600}{2.5} = 240$$

$$\frac{d_{3,m+1}}{y_{3,k}} = \frac{1,500}{0} = \infty.$$

It will be noted that these are the same ratios obtained in Table 3.6. Also, they lead to x_5 as the departing variable. The corresponding row number is 2.

Step 6.   Formulate new operational matrix D using the equation $d_{rj} = d_{rj}/y_{rk}$ if $i = r$, and $d_{ij} = d_{ij} - y_{ik} \cdot d_{rj}/y_{rk}$ if $i \neq r$. The new operational matrix is shown in Table 3.17.

Table 3.17. OPERATIONAL MATRIX D FOR THE SECOND ITERATION

E	0	0.28	0	168
x_4	1	−1.20	0	480
x_2	0	0.40	0	240
x_6	0	0	1	1,500

STEP 7. Return to step 4 and apply steps 4, 5, and 6 repeatedly until an optimal solution is found. From Table 3.17 the current solution is $x_2 = 240$, $x_4 = 480$, $x_6 = 1,500$, and the effectiveness $E = 168$.

Since x_1, x_3, and x_5 are not currently in the solution, the quantities $E_1 - e_1$, $E_3 - e_3$, and $E_5 - e_5$ are computed for the optimality test as

$$E_1 - e_1 = -0.60$$
$$E_3 - e_3 = -0.08$$

and

$$E_5 - e_5 = 0.28.$$

Since two of the evaluations are negative, the solution is not optimal and x_1 and x_3 are qualified as entering variables. Selecting x_1 as the entering variable, vector y_1 is formulated as

$$A_P^{-1} a_1 = \begin{bmatrix} 1 & 1.20 & 0 \\ 0 & 0.40 & 0 \\ 0 & 0 & 1 \end{bmatrix} \begin{bmatrix} 2.4 \\ 0 \\ 5.0 \end{bmatrix} = \begin{bmatrix} 2.4 \\ 0 \\ 5.0 \end{bmatrix}$$

and

$$y_1 = \begin{bmatrix} -0.60 \\ 2.4 \\ 0 \\ 5.0 \end{bmatrix}.$$

Selection of the departing variable requires the following ratios:

$$\frac{d_{1,m+1}}{y_{1,k}} = \frac{480}{2.4} = 200$$

$$\frac{d_{2,m+1}}{y_{2,k}} = \frac{240}{0} = \infty$$

$$\frac{d_{3,m+1}}{y_{3,k}} = \frac{1,500}{5.0} = 300.$$

Hence, x_4 is the departing variable.

At this stage the similarity between the regular simplex and revised simplex can be noticed again. The matrix A_P^{-1} in Table 3.17 is the same as the first three columns of the simplex tableau in Table 3.7, the vector y_1 is the same as the vector corresponding to x_1 in Table 3.7, and the ratios $d_{i,m+1}/y_{ik}$ are the same as ratios in the column θ. The new operational matrix is shown in Table 3.18. The evaluations are

$$E_3 - e_3 = -0.03$$
$$E_4 - e_4 = 0.25$$
$$E_5 - e_5 = -0.02.$$

Chap. 3   General Linear Programming Models

Table 3.18. OPERATIONAL MATRIX D FOR THE THIRD ITERATION

E	0.25	−0.02	0	288
x_1	0.416	−0.50	0	200
x_2	0	0.40	0	240
x_6	−2.08	2.50	1	500

From this, x_3 is selected as the entering variable, resulting in

$$A_P^{-1}a_3 = \begin{bmatrix} 0.416 & -0.50 & 0 \\ 0 & 0.40 & 0 \\ -2.08 & 2.50 & 1 \end{bmatrix} \begin{bmatrix} 2.0 \\ 1.5 \\ 2.5 \end{bmatrix} = \begin{bmatrix} 0.084 \\ 0.60 \\ 2.08 \end{bmatrix}$$

$$y_3 = \begin{bmatrix} -0.03 \\ 0.084 \\ 0.60 \\ 2.08 \end{bmatrix}.$$

The ratios are

$$\frac{200}{0.084} = 2{,}381$$

$$\frac{240}{0.60} = 400$$

$$\frac{500}{2.08} = 240.$$

Hence, x_6 is the departing variable. The new operational matrix is shown in Table 3.19. Final evaluations yield

$$E_4 - e_4 = 0.22$$
$$E_5 - e_5 = 0.016$$
$$E_6 - e_6 = 0.016.$$

Since none of the evaluations is negative, the solution is optimal and no further iteration is needed. The optimal solution is $x_1 = 180$, $x_2 = 96$, $x_3 = 240$. The optimal effectiveness is $295.20, as was obtained in Section 3.2.

Table 3.19. OPERATIONAL MATRIX D FOR THE FOURTH ITERATION

E	0.22	0.016	0.016	295.20
x_1	0.50	−0.60	−0.04	180
x_2	0.60	−0.32	−0.29	96
x_3	−1	1.20	0.68	240

3.7 DUALITY IN LINEAR PROGRAMMING

Consider two linear programming problems, expressed in matrix notation, without slack and artificial variables:

PROBLEM 1. Maximize $e'x$ subject to $Ax < b$.

PROBLEM 2. Minimize $b'y$ subject to $A'y > e$.

If A, b, and e are the same in both problems, the problems are called the "duals" of each other. If Problem 1 is the primal, then Problem 2 is its dual, and vice versa.

The feasible solutions for the primal and dual problems are related. Let x^0 and y^0 be feasible solutions for Problems 1 and 2, respectively. The restrictions in Problem 2 can be written in their transposed form as

$$y'A \geq e'.$$

Since x^0 is a feasible solution,

$$Ax^0 \leq b. \tag{3.10}$$

Since y^0 is a feasible solution,

$$y^{0'}A \geq e'. \tag{3.11}$$

Premultiplying Equation (3.10) by $y^{0'}$ and postmultiplying Equation (3.11) by x^0 gives

$$y^{0'}Ax^0 \leq y^{0'}b$$

and

$$y^{0'}Ax^0 \geq e'x^0.$$

Therefore,

$$y^{0'}b \geq e'x^0. \tag{3.12}$$

Equation (3.12) is called the *fundamental relationship of duality*. This relationship leads to significant conclusions.

1. Since the relation holds for any feasible solution y^0, it also holds for the optimal solution y^*. In other words, the minimal effectiveness for Problem 2 is greater than or equal to the effectiveness of any feasible solution for Problem 1. In the same manner the maximal effectiveness for Problem 1, $e'x^*$ is less than or equal to the effectiveness of any feasible solution y^0 for Problem 2.
2. If Problem 1 has a feasible solution, then Problem 2 has an optimal solution, and vice versa.
3. If $x^* = (x_P^*. x_R^*)$ is an optimal solution for Problem 1, then $y^* = e'_P A_P^{-1}$ is an optimal solution for Problem 2, and vice versa.

Chap. 3   General Linear Programming Models   59

4. If x^* and y^* are optimal solutions for Problems 1 and 2, then $y^{*\prime}b = e'_p A_p^{-1} b = e'x^*$. In other words, the optimal values of the effectiveness function for the two problems are equal.

As an example of the application of the dual, consider the feed-mixing problem presented previously. The original algebraic statement of this problem can be transformed to the dual. Maximize

$$0.4y_1 + 0.6y_2 + 2.0y_3 + 1.8y_4$$

subject to the constraints

$$0.1y_1 + 0.0y_2 + 0.1y_3 + 0.2y_4 \leq 0.07$$
$$0.0y_1 + 0.1y_2 + 0.2y_3 + 0.1y_4 \leq 0.05.$$

Adding slack variables results in the initial matrix of Table 3.20. The simplex method may now be applied as was outlined previously. This results in Tables 3.21 and 3.22.

Values for the activity variables of the primal appear in the columns of slack variables in the dual with negative signs. These are indicated in Table 3.22. Finally, the value for the effectiveness function is in the same location in both the primal and dual, but with opposite sign. Table 3.22 should be compared with Table 3.15.

Table 3.20. DUAL MATRIX FOR PRIMAL OF TABLE 3.10

e_i	Sol	b_i	S_1	S_2	y_1	y_2	y_3	y_4	θ	
	e_j		0	0	0.4	0.6	2.0	1.8		
0	S_1	0.07	1	0	0.1	0.0	0.1	0.2	0.70	
0	S_2	0.05	0	1	0.0	0.1	0.2	0.1	0.25	r
	E_j	0	0	0	0	0	0	0		
	$E_j - e_j$		0	0	−0.4	−0.6	−2.0	−1.8		

$$k$$

Table 3.21. FIRST ITERATION FOR DUAL PROBLEM

e_i	Sol	b_i	S_1	S_2	y_1	y_2	y_3	y_4	θ	
	e_j		0	0	0.4	0.6	2.0	1.8		
0	S_1	0.045	1	−0.5	0.1	−0.05	0	0.15	0.30	r
2.0	$\underline{y}_3$	0.250	0	5	0	0.5	1	0.50	0.50	
	E_j	0.50	0	10	0	1	2.0	1.0		
	$E_j - e_j$		0	10	−0.4	0.4	0	−0.81		

$$k$$

Table 3.22. FINAL MATRIX FOR DUAL PROBLEM

e_j			0	0	0.4	0.6	2.0	1.8	
e_i	Sol	b_i	S_1	S_2	y_1	y_2	y_3	y_4	θ
1.8	y_4	0.3	6.6667	−3.3334	0.6667	−0.3334	0	1	
2.0	y_3	0.1	−3.3350	6.6667	−0.3334	0.6667	1	0	
E_j		0.74	5.333	7.333	5.3333	0.7333	2.0	1.8	
$E_j - e_j$			5.333	7.333	1.3333	0.1333	0	0	

3.8 RELATED LINEAR PROGRAMMING TOPICS

This section presents topics that illustrate the versatility of the general linear programming model. *Degeneracy* is a condition that may occur during the computational process of some problems, but it can be overcome. *Equality constraints* may be employed when no slack is allowed in the utilization of certain resources. Finally, *extensions* in a number of areas are mentioned.

Degeneracy in the Simplex Method. Degeneracy becomes evident in the simplex method at the time that the outgoing variable is being selected. In step (3) of the iterative process, the minimum positive value of θ_i determines the outgoing variable. If two or more values of θ_i are minimal, the problem is degenerate. An arbitrary choice of one of the tied variables may result in more iterations than some other choice. More serious, however, is the condition of cycling which might occur because of a poor choice from among the tied variables.

Although cycling seldom occurs in practical problems, it can be prevented by applying the following procedure:

1. Divide each element in the tied rows by the positive coefficients of the kth column progressing from left to right.
2. Compare the resulting ratios from left to right.
3. The row which first contains the smallest algebraic ratio is designated r.

As an example of the preceding procedure, consider the degenerate problem of Table 3.23. A dilemma exists regarding the choice of row 1 or row 2 as the outgoing variable. The first ratio for row 1 is 1/4. Similarly, the first ratio for row 2 is 0/6. Since the second row yields the smallest ratio, it is designated r and the simplex procedure is continued.

Treating Equality Constraints. Some problems solvable by the simplex method of linear programming require that a given resource be fully utilized. For example, a production manager might specify that the entire capacity of the assembly department be utilized in the interest of stabilizing personnel levels.

Chap. 3   General Linear Programming Models   61

Table 3.23. DEGENERATE SIMPLEX PROBLEM

e_i	Sol	b_i	0 S_1	0 S_2	0 S_3	40 A	60 B	80 C	θ
0	S_1	0	1	0	0	−2	0	4	0
0	S_2	0	0	1	0	3	0	6	0
60	B	60	0	0	1	2	1	1	60
E_j		360	0	0	0	120	60	60	
$E_j - e_j$			0	0	0	80	0	−20	

$$k$$

In such cases, the algebraic statement of the problem will contain an equality constraint. This is unlike the foregoing problems, which utilized only inequalities.

The initial simplex matrix for this problem is exhibited in Table 3.24. Note that an artificial variable is employed to yield an initial feasible solution. Although this is a maximization problem, the effectiveness coefficient associated with the artificial variable is $-M$. This is required, since artificial variables are used only to obtain an initial feasible solution and must be forced out of solution as the computations proceed.

Table 3.24. INITIAL SIMPLEX MATRIX FOR EQUALITY CONSTRAINT

e_i	Sol	b_i	$-M$ A_1	0 S_1	12 A	8 B	10 C	θ
$-M$	A_1	240	1	0	3	5	6	
0	S_1	180	0	1	4	4	2	
E_j								
$E_j - e_j$								

The simplex method may be applied to Table 3.24 to find a maximum profit solution. Total profit, however, will be less with the equality constraint than it would be without such a constraint. The production manager will incur a penalty for the desire to utilize available labor hours fully.

As an example of a situation in which an equality constraint is needed, consider the case of a manufacturer who has two manufacturing resources, machine hours and labor hours. In each working day, the manager has 180 machine hours and 240 labor hours to spend on three products, A, B, and C. Product A requires 4 machine hours and 3 labor hours per unit, product B requires 4 machine hours and 5 labor hours per unit, and product C requires 2 machine hours and 6 labor hours per unit. The profit per unit of product A is $12, per unit of product B is $8, and per unit of product C is $10.

The production manager wishes to maximize profit subject to the limitation on machine time and labor hours. She requires, however, that all labor hours be fully utilized so that the level of personnel will remain constant. Therefore, the algebraic statement of this problem requires the maximization of

$$TP = \$12A + \$8B + \$10C$$

subject to

$$3A + 5B + 6C = 240$$
$$4A + 4B + 2C \leq 180$$
$$A \geq 0, \quad B \geq 0, \quad \text{and} \quad C \geq 0.$$

Extensions of the LP Model. This chapter has concentrated on the development of the general linear programming model. Extensions and other applications of the model are presented in subsequent chapters.

In Chapter 4, two special cases of linear programming are considered: the transportation model and the assignment model. Then, in Chapter 5, a formulation of the general linear programming model encompassing multiple goals is presented. Finally, in Chapter 15, a multisource procurement problem is formulated and optimized by the use of the general linear programming model.

PROBLEMS

3.1. Solve graphically for the values of x and y that maximize the function

$$Z = 2.2x + 3.8y$$

subject to the constraints

$$2.4x + 3.2y \leq 140$$
$$0.0x + 2.6y \leq 80$$
$$4.1x + 0.0y \leq 120$$
$$x \geq 0 \quad \text{and} \quad y \geq 0.$$

3.2. Solve graphically for the values of A and B that maximize total profit

$$TP = \$0.37A + \$0.45B$$

subject to the constraints

$$A \leq 51$$
$$B \leq 28$$
$$A + B \leq 74$$
$$A \geq 0 \quad \text{and} \quad B \geq 0.$$

3.3. A small machine shop has capability in turning, milling, drilling, and welding. The machine capacity is 16 hours per day in turning, 8 hours per day in milling, 16 hours per day in drilling, and 8 hours per day in welding. Two products, designated A and B, are under consideration. Each will yield a net profit of $0.35 per unit and will require the following amount of machine time:

	Product A	Product B
Turning	0.046	0.124
Milling	0.112	0.048
Drilling	0.040	0.000
Welding	0.000	0.120

Solve graphically for the number of units of each product that should be scheduled to maximize profit.

3.4. Solve graphically for the values of x, y, and z that maximize the function

$$P = 7.8x + 9.4y + 2.6z$$

subject to the constraints

$$4.2x + 11.7y + 3.5z \leq 1{,}800$$
$$0.8x + 4.3y + 1.9z \leq 2{,}700$$
$$12.7x + 3.8y + 2.5z \leq 950$$
$$x \geq 0, \quad y \geq 0, \quad \text{and} \quad z \geq 0.$$

3.5. Solve graphically for the values of A and B that minimize the function

$$C = 7A + 9B$$

subject to the constraints

$$18A + 7B \geq 250$$
$$9A + 2B \geq 60$$
$$3A + 5B \geq 84$$
$$A \geq 0 \quad \text{and} \quad B \geq 0.$$

3.6. Use the simplex method to find the values of A and B that maximize the function in Problem 3.2.

3.7. Use the simplex method to find the maximum profit production program for the situation given in Problem 3.3.

3.8. Use the simplex method to find the values of x, y, and z that maximize the function given in Problem 3.4.

3.9. Use the simplex method to find the values of A and B that minimize the function given in Problem 3.5.

3.10. Minimize the function given in Problem 3.5 by formulating the dual problem.

3.11. Use the simplex method to find the values for a, b, c, d, and e that maximize total profit expressed as

$$TP = 0.80a + 0.50b + 0.70c + 0.30d + 0.20e$$

subject to the constraints

$$0.50a + 0.40b + 0.20c + 0.20d + 0.10e = 0.8$$
$$0.60a + 0.10b + 0.30c + 0.20d + 0.30e = 1.7$$
$$0.20a + 0.00b + 0.60c + 0.20d + 0.10e \geq 1.0$$
$$a \geq 0, \quad b \geq 0, \quad c \geq 0, \quad d \geq 0, \quad \text{and} \quad e \geq 0.$$

3.12. A soap manufacturing company produces three grades of detergent: soft, medium, and super. Each grade requires additives A, B, and C which are available in the amount of 3,200, 2,800, and 1,200 pounds per day, respectively. One pound of soft detergent requires 0.15 pound of additive A, 0.55 pound of additive B, and 0.30 pound of additive C. One pound of medium detergent requires 0.25 pound of additive A, 0.65 pound of additive B, and 0.10 pound of additive C. One pound of super detergent requires 0.30 pound of additive A, 0.66 pound of additive B, and 0.04 pound of additive C. A profit of $0.015, $0.027, and $0.038 per pound can be realized for soft, medium, and super, respectively. How many pounds of each grade of detergent should be produced each week to maximize profit?

3.13. Sir Francis Drake, operating under a privateer's commission by Queen Elizabeth of England, captured and destroyed the town of Porto Bello on the Isthmus of Panama in 1572. As a result of this victory, he assumed control of 62,000 pounds of silver ornaments, pottery, and other filigree; 44,000 pounds of gold pottery, trinkets, and other ornaments; and 21,000 pounds of precious jewelry, gems, and pearls. His only cargo ship has three holds, forward, center, and aft, with the following capacity limits:

	Pounds	Cubic Feet
Forward	19,800	1,100
Center	30,000	1,340
Aft	15,200	480

The silver filigree, with its necessary packing, will require 0.6 cubic foot of cargo space per pound. The gold pottery will require 0.52 cubic foot per pound and the precious jewelry will require 0.24 cubic foot of cargo space per pound. The weight in each hold must be proportional to the capacity in pounds so that the trim of the ship is preserved. The value of the silver filigree is 24 shillings per ounce, the value of the gold pottery is 32 shillings per ounce, and the value of the precious jewelry is 19 shillings per ounce. How much of each product should be loaded, and how should it be distributed among the holds of the ship so as to maximize the value of the haul to the English Crown?

3.14. A manufacturer has three engine lathes and two profile mills available for machining four products. The unit machining times in hours per unit, the capacities of each machine in hours per week, and the profit per week are summarized below.

Machine	Product A	Product B	Product C	Product D	Capacity
Lathe 1	0.6	0.2	0.5	0.4	30
Lathe 2	0.5	—	—	0.6	50
Lathe 3	0.4	0.3	—	—	24
Mill 1	—	0.5	0.8	0.7	36
Mill 2	0.2	0.6	—	—	40
Profit	$0.15	$0.25	$0.40	$0.30	

Chap. 3 General Linear Programming Models 65

Each product needs processing on only one lathe and/or one mill. The unit times given apply if the designated choice is made. Determine the maximum profit production program.

3.15. Solve Problem 3.2 by the revised simplex method.

3.16. Using the revised simplex method, solve Problem 3.11.

3.17. Solve the following linear programming problem by the revised simplex method.
Minimize
$$z = x_1 + x_2$$
subject to the constraints
$$x_1 + 2x_2 \geq 9$$
$$4x_1 + x_2 \geq 8$$
$$x_1 \geq 0 \quad \text{and} \quad x_2 \geq 0.$$

3.18. Consider the primal requiring the minimization of
$$2A + 1B$$
subject to the constraints
$$4A + 1B \geq 10$$
$$5A + 12B \geq 32$$
$$A \geq 0 \quad \text{and} \quad B \geq 0.$$

Solve the primal and the dual graphically, and verify that optimum effectiveness for the primal is equal to optimum effectiveness for the dual.

3.19. Apply the simplex algorithm to the initial matrix for equality constraint of Table 3.24. What is the maximum profit?

3.20. Change the equality constraint in the problem given by Table 3.24 to a constraint of the less than or equal type. Solve by the simplex method and compare the maximum profit with that of Problem 3.19.

Distribution Models of Linear Programming

This chapter presents two distribution or network models which lend themselves to formulation and manipulation as linear programs. The first is applicable when several origins possess units needed by several destinations. The number of units from each origin to be allocated or distributed to each destination is to be determined optimally. This special case of the general linear programming model is known as the transportation model. The second special case is known as the assignment model. It is applicable to those situations in which it is desired to assign or allocate optimally each of a number of means to an equal number of requirements on a one-for-one basis. An interesting special application of the assignment model is the routing of a traveling salesman.

From the descriptions above, it is observed that distribution problems deal with place utility. They may be solved by the simplex method if properly formulated. However, this approach is not very efficient for these cases. Special algorithms have been developed which are presented in this chapter.

4.1 THE TRANSPORTATION MODEL

The transportation model of linear programming may be described as follows. There exist m origins, with the ith origin possessing a_i units, and n destinations, with the jth destination requiring b_j units. It is not required that m be equal to n, but the sum of the units available at the origins must equal the sum of the requirements at the destinations. Associated with the allocation of 1 unit from the ith origin to the jth destination is a certain effectiveness coefficient, e_{ij}. If x_{ij} is the number of units allocated from the ith origin to the jth destination, the transportation problem may be stated mathematically as that of optimizing the effectiveness function

$$E = \sum_{i=1}^{m} \sum_{j=1}^{n} e_{ij} x_{ij}$$

subject to

$$\sum_{i=1}^{m} x_{ij} = b_j \quad j = 1, 2, \ldots, n$$

$$\sum_{j=1}^{n} x_{ij} = a_i \quad i = 1, 2, \ldots, m,$$

where

$$\sum_{i=1}^{m} a_i = \sum_{j=1}^{n} b_j.$$

Optimization will require either minimization or maximization, depending on the measure of effectiveness involved. The decision maker has under his or her control the allocation matrix, x_{ij}. Not directly under control is the matrix of effectiveness coefficients, e_{ij}. This model structure follows the form of the general effectiveness function with constraints, as was presented in Section 2.3.

The Transportation Matrix. The transportation matrix will contain $m \times n$ nonnegative allocations. Selection of the set of allocations that optimizes the effectiveness function is sought. The paragraphs that follow present a solution improvement algorithm. It starts with any initial allocation and terminates with an optimal allocation.

Consider the following application of the transportation model. Four dealers place orders for new automobiles that are to be shipped from three plants. Dealer A requires 6 automobiles, dealer B requires 5, dealer C requires 4, and dealer D requires 4. Plant 1 has 7 automobiles in stock, plant 2 has 13, and plant 3 has 3. The cost of shipping one automobile from the ith plant to the jth dealer is shown in Table 4.1. For this situation to be classified as a linear programming problem, the linearly assumption is made that the cost of shipping more than one automobile is proportional to the number shipped.

The number of automobiles available at the three plants is 23, whereas the number required by the four dealers is only 19. Therefore, to make this problem conform to the transportation model, it is necessary to add a dummy

Table 4.1. COSTS FOR SHIPPING AUTOMOBILES (dollars)

		Dealer			
		A	B	C	D
Plant	1	50	80	60	70
	2	80	50	60	60
	3	70	60	80	60

destination. This means that some of the available automobiles will not be shipped. The costs associated with the dummy destination are zero.

A transportation matrix exhibiting all information relevant to the situation described is shown as Table 4.2. The number of automobiles available at the respective plants are given in the last column, and the number required at each dealer are given in the last row. The dummy destination is indicated by the next to last column and receives 4 units. As a result, the number of automobiles available is made equal to the number required. The cost per unit shipped for each possible route is entered in the small squares from Table 4.1. The objective is to find the allocation of automobiles to dealers that will satisfy the requirements with a minimum total cost.

Table 4.2. TRANSPORTATION MATRIX FOR SHIPPING AUTOMOBILES

Dealer / Plant	A	B	C	D	Dummy	Available
1	50	80	60	70	0	7
2	80	50	60	60	0	13
3	70	60	80	60	0	3
Required	6	5	4	4	4	23

Finding an Initial Allocation. One formal means for finding an initial allocation is to employ the northwest corner rule. This requires allocating units to the northwest cell in the transportation matrix in such a magnitude that either the origin capacity is exhausted or the destination requirement is satisfied, or both. If the origin capacity is exhausted first, an allocation is made to column 1 from the second origin. This will either exhaust the origin capacity of row 2 or satisfy the remaining requirement of column 1. If the first allocation satisfies the requirement of column 1, an allocation is made in column 2. This will either exhaust the capacity of row 1 or satisfy the requirement of column 2, or both. Continuing in this manner, satisfying the destination requirements and exhausting the origin capacities, one at a time, results in a movement toward the southeast corner with all row and column requirements being satisfied in the process.

Application of the northwest corner rule to the transportation matrix of Table 4.2 results in the allocations shown in Table 4.3. Since 7 automobiles are available at plant 1, dealer A has his requirements completely satisfied from this source. The remaining unit at plant 1 is allocated to dealer B. Four automobiles from plant 2 are used to finish satisfying the requirement of dealer B. Of the remaining 9 units at plant 2, 4 are allocated to dealer C, 4 to dealer D, and 1 to the dummy destination. The 3 automobiles available at plant 3 are allocated to the dummy destination. The resulting solution contains seven allocations. The total cost of this solution may be found from Table 4.3 as 6($50) + 1($80) + 4($50) + 4($60) + 4($60) + 1($0) + 3($0) = $1,060.

Table 4.3. INITIAL ALLOCATION BY THE NORTHWEST CORNER RULE

Dealer Plant	A	B	C	D	Dummy	Available
1	50 6	80 1	60	70	0	7
2	80	50 4	60 4	60 4	0 1	13
3	70	60	80	60	0 3	3
Required	6	5	4	4	4	23

The northwest corner rule does not take into consideration the cost of each allocation. Therefore, it is likely that a scheme considering these costs will result in a lower total cost. One method is to make an allocation to the cell with the lowest cost, up to the maximum allowed by the origin and destination involved. Then, an allocation is made to the next lowest cost cell in view of the remaining capacities and requirements. This process is continued until all origins are emptied and all destinations are filled. If a tie occurs between lowest cost cells, judgment may be used in making the allocation. For small problems, this procedure may result in an optimum solution.

Applying this procedure to the transportation matrix of Table 4.2 results in the allocations shown in Table 4.4. Six units were allocated to dealer A and 5 units were allocated to dealer B, since each involves a minimum shipping cost. The requirement of dealer D is then satisfied from plant 3 at a cost of $60 per unit. Four units from plant 2 are allocated to the dummy destination at no cost. Finally, the remaining requirements are satisfied by allocating 1 unit from plant 1 and 3 units from plant 2 to dealer C, and 1 unit from plant 2

Table 4.4. INITIAL ALLOCATION BY INSPECTION

Plant \ Dealer	A	B	C	D	Dummy	Available
1	50 / 6	80	60 / 1	70	0	7
2	80	50 / 5	60 / 3	60 / 1	0 / 4	13
3	70	60	80	60 / 3	0	3
Required	6	5	4	4	4	23

to dealer D. The total cost of this allocation by inspection is 6($50) + 1($60) + 5($50) + 3($60) + 1($60) + 4($0) + 3($60) = $1,030. This scheme resulted in a $30 improvement over the northwest corner rule.

Testing for Optimality. A basic feasible solution to the transportation problem is one that contains $m + n - 1$ positive allocations. When a basic feasible solution has been obtained, it may be tested to see whether a lower cost allocation can be made. This can be accomplished as follows:

1. Set up a matrix containing the costs associated with the cells for which allocations have been made.
2. Enter a set of numbers, v_j, across the top of the matrix and a set of numbers, u_i, down the left side so that their sums equal the costs entered in step (1).
3. Fill the vacant cells in step (1) with the sums of the u_i and v_j.
4. Subtract the u_i plus v_j values from the original unit cost matrix.
5. If any of the cell evaluations are negative, the basic feasible solution is not optimal.

Table 4.5 illustrates the application of this optimality test to the initial solution of the automobile shipment problem in Table 4.4. The u_i plus v_j matrix was constructed by entering costs in those cells for which allocations were made. These are the boxed values shown. Next, v_1 was arbitrarily set equal to zero to begin the determination of u_i and v_j numbers. This action forces u_1 to be 50 which, in turn, forces v_3 to be 10, u_2 to be 50, v_2 to be 0, v_4 to be 10, v_5 to be -50, and u_3 to be 50. The vacant cells were then filled with the sum of the u_i and v_j giving the u_i plus v_j matrix shown. By subtracting the elements of the u_i plus v_j matrix from those in the unit cost matrix of Table 4.1, the cell evaluation matrix results. Since no elements in the cell evaluation matrix are negative, the initial solution by inspection is optimal.

If the solution by inspection is optimal, the solution by the northwest corner rule cannot be, since it has a higher total cost. This fact is demonstrated by

Table 4.5. TESTING TABLE 4.4 FOR OPTIMALITY

u_i \ v_j	0	0	10	10	−50
50	50	50	60	60	0
50	50	50	60	60	0
50	50	50	60	60	0

u_i plus v_j matrix.

·	30	·	10	0
30	·	·	·	·
20	10	20	·	0

Cell evaluation matrix.

Table 4.6. TESTING TABLE 4.3 FOR OPTIMALITY

u_i \ v_j	0	30	40	40	−20
50	50	80	90	90	30
20	20	50	60	60	0
20	20	50	60	60	0

u_i plus v_j matrix

·	·	−30	−20	−30
60	·	·	·	·
50	10	20	0	·

Cell evaluation matrix.

the optimality test illustrated in Table 4.6. Here three cells in the cell evaluation matrix are negative. When this is the case, an iterative scheme can be used to find an optimal allocation.

Iteration Toward an Optimal Allocation. Since the northwest corner rule did not yield an optimal allocation, the following iterative scheme can be employed:

1. From the cell evaluation matrix, identify the cell with the most negative entry. Make a choice when a tie is involved.

2. Trace a path in the transportation matrix consisting of a series of segments which are alternately horizontal and vertical. The path begins and terminates in the cell identified in step (1). All corners of the path occur in cells for which allocations have been made.
3. Mark the cell identified in step (1) plus and each cell at a corner of the path alternatively minus, plus, minus, and so forth.
4. Make a new allocation in the cell identified in step (1) by entering the smallest allocation on the path which has been given a minus sign.
5. Add and subtract the quantity of the new allocation in step (4) to all cells at the corners of the path maintaining all row and column requirements.

Table 4.7 illustrates the application of steps (1) and (2) to the initial solution of Table 4.3. The "plus–minus" path begins and terminates with the cell that was evaluated to be minus 30. Table 4.8 shows the allocation of 1 unit into this cell. This is the maximum amount that can be reallocated among the members of the loop and still maintain the row and column requirements. The new solution has a total cost of 6($50) + 1($0) + 5($50) + 4($60) + 4($60) + 3($0) = $1,030. This is equal to the optimal cost found by the inspection allocation and is also optimal. Whenever the cell evaluation matrix contains zero elements, alternative optimal solutions exist.

Table 4.7. TRACING THE PLUS–MINUS PATH

Plant \ Dealer	A	B	C	D	Dummy	Available
1	50 / 6	80 / −1	60	70	0 / +	7
2	80 / +4	50 / −4	60 / −4	60 / −4	0 / −1	13
3	70	60	80	60	0 / 3	3
Required	6	5	4	4	4	23

Table 4.8. REALLOCATION BY ADDING AND SUBTRACTING

Plant \ Dealer	A	B	C	D	Dummy	Available
1	50 / 6	80	60	70	0 / 1	7
2	80	50 / 5	60 / 4	60 / 4	0	13
3	70	60	80	60	0 / 3	3
Required	6	5	4	4	4	23

Treating Degeneracy. The allocation given in Table 4.8 is a degenerate basic feasible solution, since it contains less than $m + n - 1$ allocations. When degeneracy exists, a plus–minus path cannot begin in all cells for which allocations have not been made. If further iteration had been necessary, this degeneracy would have had to be resolved before applying the optimality test.

Consider the degenerate solution of Table 4.9 obtained by the northwest corner rule. It is possible to trace a plus–minus path only for cells 1-B and 4-C. In Table 4.8 degeneracy occurred because the reallocation of 1 unit caused two previous allocations to become zero.

Table 4.9. DEGENERATE BASIC FEASIBLE SOLUTION

From \ To	A	B	C	D	Available
1	5				5
2	3	6			9
2			5	1	6
4				6	6
Required	8	6	5	7	26

Degeneracy can be resolved at any stage in the solution by placing an infinitesimally small allocation, ϵ, in an appropriate cell. This small allocation is made by inspection and assumed not to affect the row and column totals. In Table 4.9, plus–minus paths can be traced for all open cells if ϵ is placed in any cell other than 1-B or 4-C. The ϵ allocation is then manipulated in accordance with the rules established previously. It is treated no differently than any other allocation. When an optimal solution is found, ϵ is set equal to zero, thus regaining the original problem.

It can be shown that degeneracy can occur only if the sum of some subset of the row requirements equals the sum of some subset of the column requirements. Since degeneracy can exist only when this condition exists, any adjustment that makes this equality impossible also makes degeneracy impossible. This can be accomplished by making a small perturbation of the row requirements and one of the column requirements before any calculations are made. Applying the perturbation technique to the problem given by Table 4.9 results in the nondegenerate basic feasible solution of Table 4.10. The optimality test and the iterative process can now be applied. Again, the ϵ and the multiples of ϵ are treated no differently than other allocations. When an optimal solution is reached, ϵ is set equal to zero.

Finding a Maximum Profit Allocation. Consider the following maximization problem. A carpet manufacturer has two plants and produces three styles of carpet. For the coming week, plant A has a capacity of 8,400 yards and plant

Table 4.10. PERTURBATION TO ELIMINATE DEGENERACY

From \ To	A	B	C	D	Available
1	$5 + \epsilon$				$5 + \epsilon$
2	$3 - \epsilon$	$6 + 2\epsilon$			$9 + \epsilon$
3		-2ϵ	5	$1 + 3\epsilon$	$6 + \epsilon$
4				$6 + \epsilon$	$6 + \epsilon$
Required	8	6	5	$7 + 4\epsilon$	$26 + 4\epsilon$

B has a capacity of 5,800 yards. This total capacity is to be used to produce 4,200 yards of style 1, 6,100 yards of style 2, and 3,900 yards of style 3 for the week. The estimated profit per yard for each style at each plant is given in Table 4.11. The profit per yard depends on the style and on the plant at which it is manufactured.

Table 4.11. PROFITS FOR CARPET MANUFACTURING (dollars)

		Plant A	Plant B
	1	0.82	0.76
Style	2	0.34	0.41
	3	0.66	0.60

Minimizing the negative of a function is equivalent to maximizing the function. Therefore, the first step in finding a maximum profit allocation of styles to plants is making all elements in the profit matrix of Table 4.11 negative. The transportation method may then be applied as for minimization.

Table 4.12 exhibits the transportation matrix applicable to the carpet manufacturing problem. Since the required total production equals the total

Table 4.12. TRANSPORTATION MATRIX FOR CARPET MANUFACTURING

Style \ Plant	A	B	Production
1	−0.82 / 4,200	−0.76	4,200
2	−0.34 / 300	−0.41 / 5,800	6,100
3	−0.66 / 3,900	−0.60	3,900
Capacity	8,400	5,800	14,200

capacity available, no dummy origins or destinations are needed. Each profit element carries a negative sign, since profit is to be maximized. The basic feasible solution shown was determined by judgment. It represents a total profit of 4,200($0.82) + 300($0.34) + 5,800($0.41) + 3,900($0.66) = $8,498. Application of the optimality test is shown in Table 4.13. Since all cells in the cell evaluation matrix are positive, this solution is optimal. No other allocation will result in a higher profit for the coming week.

Table 4.13. TESTING TABLE 4.12 FOR OPTIMALITY

u_i \ v_j	0	−0.07
−0.82	−0.82	−0.89
−0.34	−0.34	−0.41
−0.66	−0.66	−0.73

u_i plus v_j matrix.

	•	0.13
	•	•
	•	0.13

4.2 VOGEL'S APPROXIMATION METHOD

Vogel's approximation method is offered as an alternative to the method presented previously. The procedure is simple and fast by comparison. Its advocates claim that it will give an optimal allocation for a majority of problems and that the approximation is very good for the remainder. In some applications, the final result of this approximation method may be accepted as is. In others it might be desirable to apply the optimality test and then iterate toward an optimal solution if needed. Normally, use of this scheme to find an initial solution will reduce the number of iterations required by the conventional method.

An Example Application. Suppose that there are three machine centers in a job shop that can process any one of four orders. The capacities of each machine center, as well as the time needed by each order, are expressed in standard machine hours. The capacity for machine center A is 95 standard hours; for machine center B, 115 standard hours; and for machine center C, 50 standard hours. Order 1 needs 66 standard machine hours; order 2, 45 standard hours; order 3, 82 standard hours; and order 4, 44 standard hours. The cost per standard machine hour for each order at each machine center is given in Table 4.14. Costs are a function of the order and the nature of the machine center relative to the order.

Table 4.14. COSTS PER STANDARD MACHINE HOUR (dollars)

	Machine Center		
Order	A	B	C
1	8	7	7
2	9	6	8
3	6	7	9
4	7	8	6

Table 4.15. TRANSPORTATION MATRIX FOR VOGEL'S APPROXIMATION METHOD

Order \ Machine	A	B	C	Needed					
1	X [84]	66 [79]	X [76]	66	3	3	3	3	3
2	X [92]	45 [61]	X [87]	45	26	26	—	—	—
3	82 [60]	X [75]	X [91]	82	15	15	15	—	—
4	13 [78]	4 [80]	27 [69]	44	9	9	9	9	—
Dummy	X [0]	X [0]	23 [0]	23	0	—	—	—	—
Available	95	115	50	260					

	60	61	69
	18	14	7
	18	4	7
	6	1	7
	—	—	—

Table 4.15 exhibits the transportation matrix for this production problem. Since there are 260 standard machine hours available and only 237 required by the four orders, it is necessary to add a dummy order. This dummy order will absorb the extra capacity, thus making the problem conform to the transportation model. Elements in the dummy row are set equal to zero, since no cost is associated with a dummy order that will not be processed.

The Solution Procedure. The solution procedure for Vogel's approximation method may be pursued with the aid of the original transportation matrix. It is not necessary to develop a new matrix for each cycle. Each cycle involves a series of steps repeated in exactly the same manner until the final allocation is made.

Since a minimum cost allocation is required, the first step in the cycle is to inspect the costs in each row and take the difference between the two smallest of these. (If the problem is one of maximization, the difference between the two largest is taken.) These differences form the first column of values to the right of the matrix in Table 4.15. This difference process is now applied to each column in the matrix, and the results form the first row of values across the bottom.

The second step involves identification of the largest difference in the column and row just developed. This occurs in column 3 for the problem under consideration. Thus, column 3 is the first candidate for an allocation.

The third step involves the allocation of needed standard machine hours to the column with the largest difference, up to the maximum allowed by the row and column totals. This allocation is made in the row with the lowest cost or highest profit. Since this row is the dummy with zero cost, 23 hours are allocated. Since all needed machine hours have been allocated, all cells in the row are marked out. If the largest difference had occurred in a row instead of a column, the assignment would have been made to the cell in that row with the lowest cost or highest profit. The procedure is the same in either case. This completes the first cycle.

Each cycle follows the steps just outlined and is applied to the reduced matrix; that is, the matrix remaining after some rows or columns or both are marked out. The difference column and difference row from the previous cycle are disregarded. A new difference column and row are developed for the reduced matrix at the beginning of each cycle. This is shown for each cycle in Table 4.15.

Allocations are made in accordance with the largest differences until all allocations are completed. The total cost for this solution is 66($79) + 45($61) + 82($60) + 13($78) + 4($80) + 27($69) + 23($0) = $16,076. The solution may now be tested for optimality if desired.

4.3 THE ASSIGNMENT MODEL

The assignment model of linear programming is a special case of the transportation model. It may be described as follows. There exist n requirements together with n means for satisfying them. Associated with the assignment of the ith means to the jth requirement, x_{ij}, is a certain effectiveness coefficient, e_{ij}. It is required that $x_{ij} = 1$ if the ith means is used to satisfy the jth requirement, and that $x_{ij} = 0$ if the ith means is not used to satisfy the jth requirement. Since one means can be associated with only one requirement, the assignment problem can be stated mathematically as that of optimizing the effectiveness function

$$E = \sum_{i=1}^{n} \sum_{j=1}^{n} e_{ij} x_{ij}$$

subject to

$$\sum_{i=1}^{n} x_{ij} = 1 \qquad j = 1, 2, \ldots, n$$

$$\sum_{j=1}^{n} x_{ij} = 1 \qquad i = 1, 2, \ldots, n.$$

Optimization will require either minimization or maximization, depending upon the measure of effectiveness involved. The decision maker has control of a matrix of assignments, x_{ij}. Not directly under control is the matrix of effectiveness coefficients, e_{ij}. This model structure follows the form of the general effectiveness function with constraints, as was presented in Section 2.3.

The Assignment Matrix. The assignment matrix will contain $n \times n$ elements with $n!$ possible arrangements. Solution by direct enumeration is ordinarily not possible. For example, if eight requirements are to be satisfied by eight means, there will be 40,320 possible arrangements. The following paragraphs present the Hungarian method for finding the optimal assignment.

Consider the following application of the assignment model. Four different assemblies are to be produced by four contractors. Each contractor is to receive only one assembly to produce. The cost of each assembly is determined by bids submitted by each contractor. This information, when arranged in tabular form, gives an effectiveness matrix shown in Table 4.16. The differences in the bid prices are due to differences in the work to be done and preferences for certain assemblies. The objective is to determine the assignment of assemblies to contractors that will result in a minimum cost.

Table 4.16. COSTS FOR PROCURING ASSEMBLIES (thousands of dollars)

		\multicolumn{4}{c}{Contractor}			
		A	B	C	D
Assembly	1	16	14	15	18
	2	12	13	16	14
	3	14	13	11	12
	4	16	18	15	17

The first step in the Hungarian method is to alter the effectiveness matrix to obtain a reduced matrix. This is accomplished by subtracting the minimum element in each row from all elements in the row, and then by subtracting the minimum element in each column from all elements in the column. The first reduced matrix for the procurement problem of Table 4.16 is shown in Table 4.17. An assignment that minimizes the total for a matrix reduced in this manner also minimizes the total for the original effectiveness matrix.

Chap. 4   Distribution Models of Linear Programming

Table 4.17. FIRST REDUCED COST MATRIX FOR PROCUREMENT

	Contractor			
Assembly	A	B	C	D
1	2	0	1	3
2	0	1	4	1
3	3	2	0	0
4	1	3	0	1

The elements of the first reduced matrix will always be zero or positive. As a result, the total cannot be negative for any assignment. Therefore, all assignments that might be made will have a total that is zero or positive. If an assignment can be made that has a zero total, there cannot be an assignment with a lower total.

Reference to Table 4.17 indicates that an assignment with a zero total can be made. This requires assigning assembly 1 to contractor B, assembly 2 to contractor A, assembly 3 to contractor D, and assembly 4 to contractor C. The resulting assignment matrix is shown in Table 4.18. Its total cost may be found from Tables 4.16 and 4.18 as $14,000 + $12,000 + $12,000 + $15,000 = $53,000. No other assignment will result in a lower total cost.

Table 4.18. ASSIGNMENT MATRIX FOR PROCUREMENT

	Contractor			
Assembly	A	B	C	D
1	0	1	0	0
2	1	0	0	0
3	0	0	0	1
4	0	0	1	0

The problem just described conforms exactly to the assignment model. Sometimes, however, a problem can be made to conform to the assignment model by adding dummy rows or dummy columns. Consider the following example. At the end of a cycle of schedules, a trucking firm has a surplus of one vehicle in cities 1, 2, 3, 4, and 5, and a deficit of one vehicle in cities A, B, C, D, E, and F. The distances between cities with a surplus and the cities with a deficit are shown in Table 4.19. The objective is to find the assignment of surplus vehicles to deficit cities that will result in a minimum total distance.

Inspection of Table 4.19 indicates that there exist more requirements than means. When this is the case, an $n \times n$ effectiveness matrix will result by adding a dummy row, or dummy rows, if required. Elements in the dummy row are zeros, since no cost is associated with not moving a vehicle. The adjusted effectiveness matrix is shown in Table 4.20. If there had been more means than

Table 4.19. DISTANCES FOR MOVING VEHICLES (miles)

		To City					
		A	B	C	D	E	F
	1	13	11	16	23	19	9
	2	11	19	26	16	17	13
From City	3	12	11	4	9	6	10
	4	7	15	9	14	14	13
	5	9	13	12	8	14	11

Table 4.20. ADJUSTED COST MATRIX FOR MOVING VEHICLES

		To City					
		A	B	C	D	E	F
	1	13	11	16	23	19	9
	2	11	19	26	16	17	13
From City	3	12	11	4	9	6	10
	4	7	15	9	14	14	13
	5	9	13	12	8	14	11
	Dummy	0	0	0	0	0	0

requirements, dummy columns would have been added with zeros as elements. Dummy rows mean that some requirements are not met, and dummy columns mean that some means are not used. Adjustment of the effectiveness matrix in this manner makes the problem conform to the assignment model.

The first reduced matrix for this problem is shown in Table 4.21. Inspection indicates that an assignment with a zero total cannot be made. When this is the case, additional computations are necessary to produce more zeros.

Table 4.21. FIRST REDUCED COST MATRIX FOR MOVING VEHICLES

		To City					
		A	B	C	D	E	F
	1	4	2	7	14	10	0
	2	0	8	15	5	6	2
From City	3	8	7	0	5	2	6
	4	0	8	2	7	7	6
	5	1	5	4	0	6	3
	Dummy	0	0	0	0	0	0

Iteration Toward an Optimal Assignment. The following iterative scheme may be employed when the first reduced matrix does not yield an assignment with a zero total:

1. Draw the minimum number of lines that will pass through all zeros in the reduced matrix. There may be several minimum sets. A set is known to be

Chap. 4 Distribution Models of Linear Programming   81

minimum when the number equals the number of independent zeros used in constructing an assignment. Any minimum set may be chosen.

2. Select the smallest element in the reduced matrix that does not have a line through it. Add this element to all elements that occur at the intersection of two lines and subtract it from all elements that do not have a line through them. The other elements of the matrix remain unchanged.

Application of step (1) to the first reduced matrix of the vehicle assignment example results in Table 4.22. The minimum number of lines that can be drawn is five. An assignment with a zero total cannot be made when the minimum number of lines is less than the matrix size. Application of step (2) gives the matrix shown in Table 4.23. It may be called a *modified reduced matrix*. An assignment with a zero total still cannot be made as is indicated by the application of step (1) shown in Table 4.24. Step (2) now yields the final reduced matrix shown in Table 4.25.

Table 4.22. STEP (1), MINIMUM SET OF LINES

To City

		A	B	C	D	E	F
From City	1	4	2	7	14	10	0
	2	0	8	15	5	6	2
	3	8	7	0	5	2	6
	4	0	8	2	7	7	6
	5	1	5	4	0	6	3
	Dummy	0	0	0	0	0	0

Table 4.23. STEP (2), MODIFIED REDUCED MATRIX

To City

		A	B	C	D	E	F
From City	1	4	0	7	14	8	0
	2	0	6	15	5	4	2
	3	8	5	0	5	0	6
	4	0	6	2	7	5	6
	5	1	3	4	0	4	3
	Dummy	2	0	2	2	0	2

Table 4.24. STEP (1), MINIMUM SET OF LINES

To City

		A	B	C	D	E	F
From City	1	4	0	7	14	8	0
	2	0	6	15	5	4	2
	3	8	5	0	5	0	6
	4	0	6	2	7	5	6
	5	1	3	4	0	4	3
	Dummy	2	0	2	2	0	2

Table 4.25. STEP (2), FINAL MODIFIED REDUCED MATRIX

		\multicolumn{6}{c}{To City}
		A	B	C	D	E	F
From City	1	6	0	7	14	8	0
	2	0	4	13	3	2	0
	3	10	5	0	5	0	6
	4	0	4	0	5	3	4
	5	3	3	4	0	4	3
	Dummy	4	0	2	2	0	2

Table 4.26. ASSIGNMENT MATRIX FOR MOVING VEHICLES

		\multicolumn{6}{c}{To City}
		A	B	C	D	E	F
From City	1	0	1	0	0	0	0
	2	0	0	0	0	0	1
	3	0	0	1	0	0	0
	4	1	0	0	0	0	0
	5	0	0	0	1	0	0
	Dummy	0	0	0	0	1	0

An optimal assignment can now be made as is shown in Table 4.26. This will require assigning vehicle 1 to city B, vehicle 2 to city F, vehicle 3 to city C, vehicle 4 to city A, vehicle 5 to city D, and no vehicle to city E. The total distance for this assignment may be found from Tables 4.19 and 4.26 as $11 + 13 + 4 + 7 + 8 + 0 = 43$ miles. No other assignment will result in less total distance for moving the surplus vehicles. An alternative assignment with the same total distance, however, is revealed by Table 4.25. It involves assigning vehicle 1 to city F, vehicle 2 to city A, vehicle 3 to city E, vehicle 4 to city C, vehicle 5 to city D, and no vehicle to city B. There may be some reason why this alternative optimal solution is preferred.

It can be shown that iteration, as demonstrated with this example, will always lead to an optimal assignment in a finite number of cycles. The optimum assignment will occur when the minimum number of lines that can be drawn is equal to the matrix size. This optimum assignment is guaranteed by the existence of one or more assignments with a zero total in the reduced effectiveness matrix.

Finding a Maximum Profit Assignment. Effectiveness is often expressed in terms of profit instead of cost. This requires maximizing the effectiveness function. Maximization may be accomplished by replacing each element of the effectiveness matrix by its negative and proceeding as for minimization. This procedure is valid, since minimizing the negative of a function is equivalent to maximizing the function.

Consider the following maximization problem. A sales manager has four salesmen and four sales districts. After considering the capabilities of the salesmen and the nature of the districts, he estimates that the profit per day for each

Table 4.27. PROFITS FOR SALESMAN ASSIGNMENT (dollars)

		District			
		A	B	C	D
Salesman	1	14	8	12	9
	2	12	9	13	13
	3	13	13	11	10
	4	11	10	12	13

salesman in each district would be as shown in Table 4.27. The objective is to find the assignment of salesmen to districts that will result in a maximum profit.

The first step is to replace each element in Table 4.27 by its negative. Next, the most negative element in each row is subtracted from all elements in the row, and then the most negative element in each column is subtracted from all elements in the column. The resulting first reduced matrix is shown in Table 4.28.

Table 4.28. FIRST REDUCED MATRIX FOR SALESMAN ASSIGNMENT

		District			
		A	B	C	D
Salesman	1	0	6	2	5
	2	1	4	0	0
	3	0	0	2	3
	4	2	3	1	0

Inspection indicates that an assignment with a zero total can be made, as is shown in Table 4.29. This requires assigning salesman 1 to district A, salesman 2 to district C, salesman 3 to district B, and salesman 4 to district D. The total profit from this assignment may be found from Tables 4.27 and 4.29 as $14 + $13 + $13 + $13 = $53. No other assignment will result in a greater profit. If an assignment with a zero total were not produced at this point, it would have been necessary to use the iterative scheme described previously.

When the effectiveness matrix is not square, dummy rows or dummy columns can be added as before. Elements in the dummy rows or dummy col-

Table 4.29. ASSIGNMENT MATRIX FOR SALESMAN ASSIGNMENT

		District			
		A	B	C	D
Salesman	1	1	0	0	0
	2	0	0	1	0
	3	0	1	0	0
	4	0	0	0	1

umns are zeros, since no profit is associated with them. The maximization process then proceeds as previously outlined.

4.4 THE TRAVELING SALESMAN PROBLEM

The traveling salesman problem is closely related to the assignment problem and can be stated as follows. A salesman starts from one city and wishes to visit $n - 1$ other cities once and only once, and then return to the first city. It is assumed that the distance, time, or cost of travel between any pair of cities is known. In what order should he visit the cities so as to minimize the total distance, time, or cost associated with the tour?

A six-city problem corresponds to a 6×6 assignment problem. Since the salesman goes "from" every city once and only once and "to" every city once and only once, the solution to a traveling salesman problem would have a 1 in each row and 1 in each column and there would be exactly six assignments. In this sense the solution to a traveling salesman problem is a feasible solution to the corresponding assignment problem. The converse is not true, however, since a solution to the traveling salesman problem must constiute a complete tour.

Solution by Branch and Bound. Branch and bound is the name given to a solution procedure applicable to a specific class of optimization problems. This class of problems is characterized by the following:

1. The problem involves the selection of the optimal solution out of a large but finite set of possible solutions.
2. Each possible decision would partition the set of all possible solutions into two or more mutually exclusive and exhaustive subsets.
3. For any set of solutions, it is possible to determine a bound or limit such that no solution in the set can possibly be better than the limit.

It is evident that the six-city traveling salesman problem belongs to this class of optimization problems. Specifically, its characteristics are as follows:

1. Each possible solution involves the salesman traveling between six city pairs. Arithmetically, the total distance in the tour equals the sum of six numbers from a distance matrix of 36 numbers. The possible number of ways of selecting 6 out of 36 numbers is large but finite.
2. Each decision about a city pair (i, j) partitions the set of all solutions into two mutually exclusive and exhaustive subsets; i.e., the tours including the city pair, (i, j), and the tours not including the city pair, $\overline{(i, j)}$.
3. Since any tour is a sum of six numbers an obvious bound exists: the sum of the six smallest numbers.

Chap. 4 Distribution Models of Linear Programming   85

Partitioning of the set using decisions is referred to as branching. When several decisions are made sequentially, there is a progressive partitioning of the set of all solutions in a tree-like computational structure. There are two sequential decisions; first A or $\bar{A}$ and then B or $\bar{B}$. The tree structure would appear as in Figure 4.1.

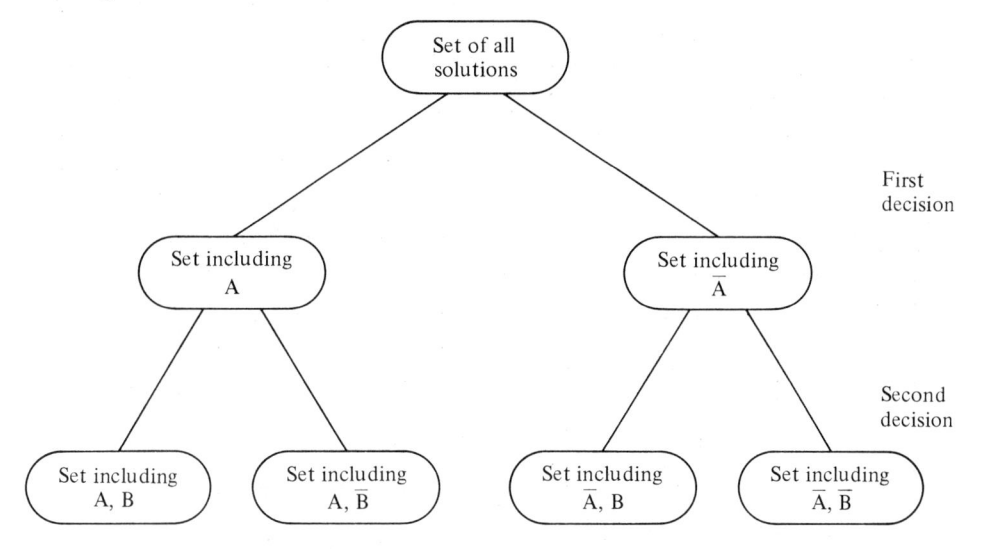

Figure 4.1 Solution tree structure for branch and bound.

The solution to the traveling salesman problem starts with a set containing all tours. Then, a subset (i, j) containing all tours which include the city pair (i, j) and a subset $\overline{(i, j)}$ containing all tours which do not include the city pair (i, j) are formed. Next, a subset (k, l) containing all tours that include both city pairs (i, j) and (k, l) is formed. This branching process is continued until the final subsets each represent a single tour. Figure 4.2 shows the branching method.

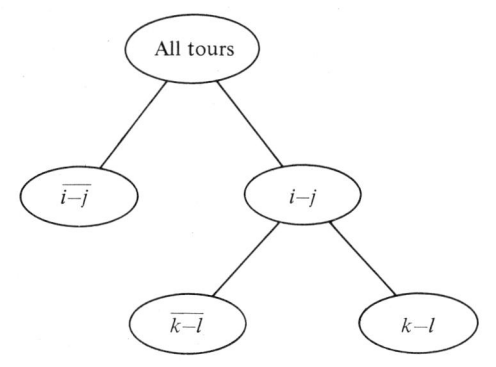

Figure 4.2 Branching method for the traveling salesman problem.

Let $A = [c(i, j)] = $ cost matrix where i and $j = 1, \ldots, n$. The value in the ith row and jth column of this matrix is the cost associated with a tour from city i to city j. The original cost matrix will start with given or assumed costs. A tour, y, can be represented as a set of n ordered city pairs as follows:

$$y = [(1, 2)(2, 3) \cdots (n - 1, n)(n, 1)].$$

The tour is limited to only one visit to each city. The total cost of a tour is the sum of matrix elements representing the ordered pairs in y as follows:

$$TC(y) = \sum c(i, j) | (i, j) \in y.$$

Only one value of the cost in each row and column is included in $TC(y)$.

A reduced cost matrix is obtained by subtracting the smallest element (cost) in each row from all elements in the row and by subtracting the smallest element in each column from all elements in the column. Let $TC(y)$ be the cost of a tour before matrix reduction, $TC^*(y)$ the cost after reduction, and b the sum of constants used in making the reduction. Then,

$$TC(y) = b + TC^*(y).$$

Since the reduced matrix will contain only nonnegative elements, b is a lower bound on the cost of y under the matrix.

If a decision $\overline{(i, j)}$ is made, the city pair (i, j) is not included in any tour in the subset. In the reduced matrix if element (i, j) is zero, the exclusion of (i, j) would involve a certain penalty, as another cell would have to be selected in row i and another cell in column j. Consequently, the best possible choice would be the second smallest numbers in row i and column j, and the lower bound on the cost of tours in subset $\overline{(i, j)}$ would be increased by the sum of the second smallest numbers in row i and column j.

An Example Application. A six-city traveling salesman problem is shown in Table 4.30. Table 4.31 shows the reduced cost matrix. The total reduction by rows and columns is 98. Hence, $TC(y) \geq 98$ for all y. This is shown as the first node of the solution tree in Figure 4.3.

Table 4.30. COST MATRIX FOR TRAVELING SALESMAN PROBLEM

		\multicolumn{6}{c}{To City}
		1	2	3	4	5	6
From City	1	∞	20	23	27	29	34
	2	21	∞	19	26	31	24
	3	26	28	∞	15	36	26
	4	25	16	25	∞	23	18
	5	23	40	23	31	∞	10
	6	27	18	12	35	16	∞

Chap. 4 Distribution Models of Linear Programming

Table 4.31. REDUCED COST MATRIX FOR TRAVELING SALESMAN PROBLEM

From City \ To City

	1	2	3	4	5	6	Row reducing numbers
1	∞	0	3	7	5	14	20
2	0	∞	0	7	8	5	19
3	9	13	∞	0	17	11	15
4	7	0	9	∞	3	2	16
5	11	30	13	21	∞	0	10
6	13	6	0	23	0	∞	12
Column reducing numbers	2	0	0	0	4	0	

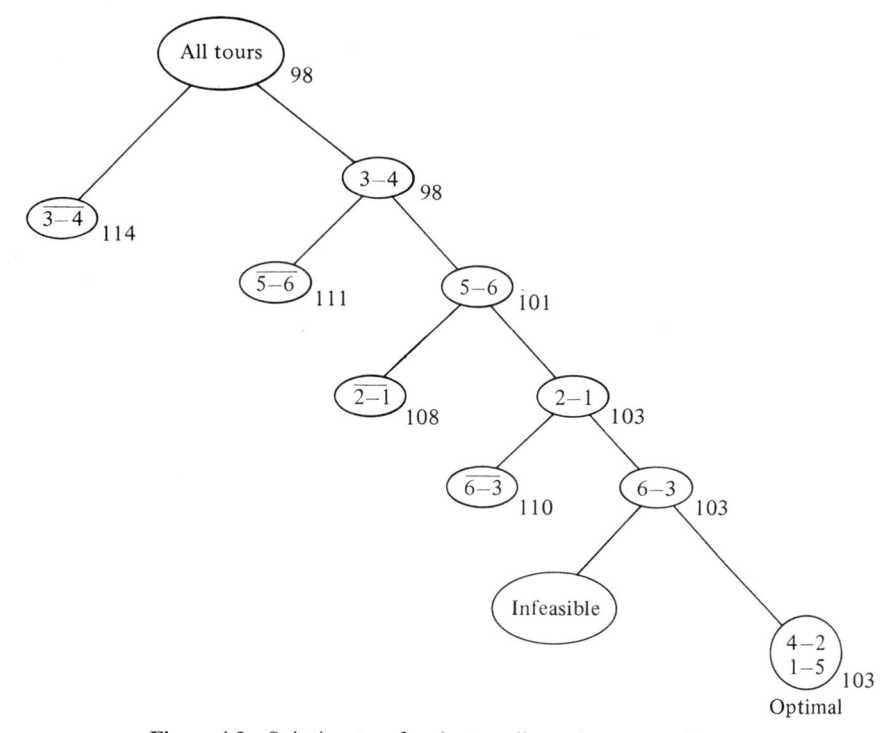

Solution tree:
- All tours: 98
  - $\overline{3-4}$: 114
  - 3-4: 98
    - $\overline{5-6}$: 111
    - 5-6: 101
      - $\overline{2-1}$: 108
      - 2-1: 103
        - $\overline{6-3}$: 110 → Infeasible
        - 6-3: 103
          - 4-2, 1-5: 103 Optimal

Figure 4.3 Solution tree for the traveling salesman problem.

Next, Table 4.32 is developed by adding the second smallest number in each column to the second smallest number in each row and placing the result at the locations where there was a zero in Table 4.31. The city pair which has the maximum value (bracketed number) is chosen for branching in Table 4.32; therefore, the city pair (3, 4) is chosen, since it has a maximum bracketed value of 16. From this the lower bound on $(\overline{3, 4})$ is found to be $98 + 16 = 114$. These nodes are shown on the solution tree.

Table 4.32. CHOOSING A CITY PAIR FOR BRANCHING

		To City						Second smallest row numbers
		1	2	3	4	5	6	
	1	∞	0[3]	3	7	5	14	3
	2	0[7]	∞	0[0]	7	8	5	0
	3	9	13	∞	0[16]	17	11	9
From City	4	7	0[2]	9	∞	3	2	2
	5	11	30	13	21	∞	0[13]	11
	6	13	6	0[0]	23	0[3]	∞	0
Second smallest column numbers		7	0	0	7	3	2	

Table 4.33. COST MATRIX FOR SUBSET (3, 4)

		To City					Second smallest row numbers
		1	2	4 3	5	6	
	1	∞	0[3]	3	5	14	3
	2	0[7]	∞	0[0]	8	5	0
	3 4	7	0[2]	∞	3	2	2
From City	5	11	30	13	∞	0[13]	11
	6	13	6	0[0]	0[3]	∞	0
Second smallest column numbers		7	0	0	3	2	

Next, a cost matrix including subset (3, 4) is developed as in Table 4.33. This is the cost matrix of Table 4.32, with column 4 and row 3 eliminated. This matrix is in reduced form. If this were not the case, it would have to be reduced as was Table 4.31, and the sum of the reducing numbers would have to be added to subset (3, 4).

When column j and row i are deleted as in Table 4.33, care must be taken to avoid the formation of subtours smaller than the complete tour. This is achieved by retaining all ∞ entries in deleted row i in the corresponding position in the row j, and all ∞ entries from the deleted column j in the corresponding position in column i. In this subset, i and j are considered to be a single city with entry possible into i only and departure possible from j only.

Since subset (3, 4) has a lower bound than $\overline{(3, 4)}$, it will contain the optimal tour and may be explored further. This is done by obtaining bracketed numbers, adding the second smallest number in each column to the second smallest number in each row and placing the result at the zero location as shown in Table 4.33. The city pair (5, 6) is chosen for branching as it has the maximum bracketed value of 13. The lower bound on $\overline{(5, 6)}$ is $98 + 13 = 111$. The matrix for (5, 6) is shown in Table 4.34 in reduced form. The lower bound is now $98 + 3 = 101$, since the sum of the reducing numbers is 3. This is shown in Figure 4.3.

Table 4.34. REDUCED COST MATRIX FOR SUBSET (5, 6)

		To City				
				4	6	Row reducing
		1	2	3	5	numbers
From City	1	∞	0	3	5	0
	2	0	∞	0	8	0
	3 4	7	0	∞	3	0
	5 6	13	6	0	∞	0
	Column reducing numbers	0	0	0	3	

The next step is to select a city pair for branching as before. Table 4.35 indicates that city pair (2, 1) is the next basis for branching. The lower bound on subset (2, 1) is 101 plus the sum of reducing numbers in Table 4.36, which is 2, giving 103. The lower bound on $\overline{(2, 1)}$ is obtained by adding the bracketed value of 7 to 101, giving 108. This is shown in Figure 4.3.

Table 4.35. COST MATRIX FOR SUBSET (5, 6)

		To City				
				4	6	Second smallest
		1	2	3	5	row numbers
From City	1	∞	0[2]	3	2	2
	2	0[7]	∞	0[0]	5	0
	3 4	7	0	∞	0[2]	0
	5 6	13	6	0[6]	∞	6
	Second smallest column numbers	7	0	0	2	

Table 4.36. COST MATRIX FOR SUBSET (2, 1)

		To City			
		1	4	6	Row reducing
		2	3	5	numbers
From City	2 1	∞	3	2	2
	3 4	0	∞	0	0
	5 6	6	0	∞	0
	Column reducing numbers	0	0	0	

The next choice for branching is the city pair (5–6, 3–4) called (6, 3) with a lower bound of 103 due to the fact that the cost matrix in Table 4.36 is in reduced form. The lower bound on $\overline{(6, 3)}$ is 103 plus the bracketed value in Table 4.37 of 7, giving 110.

By exploring subset (6, 3) in Table 4.38, it is seen that the inclusion of city pairs (1, 5) and (4, 2) is mandatory, otherwise the tour would be unfeasible.

Table 4.37. COST MATRIX FOR SUBSET (2, 1)

		To City 1 2	4 3	6 5	Second smallest row numbers
From City	2 1	∞	1	0[1]	1
	3 4	0[6]	∞	0[0]	0
	5 6	6	0[7]	∞	6
	Second smallest column numbers	6	1	0	

Table 4.38. COST MATRIX FOR SUBSET (6, 3)

		To City 1 2	4 3 6 5
From City	2 1	∞	0
	5 6 3 4	0	∞

Inclusion of these tours gives the complete tour 3, 4, 2, 1, 5, 6, 3 with a cost of 103. Since this is less than the lower bounds on all subsets not fully explored, the tour is optimal. If this had not been the case, it would have been necessary to start exploration in the subset with the smallest lower bound.

PROBLEMS

4.1. Three plants, 1, 2, and 3, produce 850, 730, and 820 refrigerators per week, respectively. These are to be distributed equally to six warehouses. The cost of shipping in dollars per unit is as follows:

		Warehouse A	B	C	D	E	F
Plant	1	13	14	12	10	17	27
	2	12	20	17	14	33	13
	3	18	24	21	18	12	22

Determine the allocation that will result in a minimum shipping cost. What is the shipping cost per week?

4.2. A company has three warehouses, 1, 2, and 3, containing 10,000, 14,000, and 8,000 units of a certain product. In the next week, 4,500, 6,000, 6,700, 6,900, and 5,000 units must be shipped to retail centers A, B, C, D, and E, respectively. The cost in dollars of shipping one unit from each warehouse to each retail center is as follows:

Chap. 4   Distribution Models of Linear Programming

<table>
<tr><td></td><td></td><td colspan="5">Retail Center</td></tr>
<tr><td></td><td></td><td>A</td><td>B</td><td>C</td><td>D</td><td>E</td></tr>
<tr><td rowspan="3">Warehouse</td><td>1</td><td>0.75</td><td>0.62</td><td>0.87</td><td>1.10</td><td>0.93</td></tr>
<tr><td>2</td><td>0.90</td><td>1.00</td><td>0.78</td><td>1.30</td><td>0.84</td></tr>
<tr><td>3</td><td>0.84</td><td>0.83</td><td>0.62</td><td>0.94</td><td>0.75</td></tr>
</table>

Find the shipping schedule that will result in a minimum shipping cost.

4.3. A company has factories in cities 1, 2, 3, and 4 and supplies warehouses in cities A, B, C, D, and E. Monthly factory capacities are 35, 25, 40, and 32 units, respectively. Monthly warehouse requirements are 15, 12, 22, 30, and 20 units, respectively. Unit shipping costs in dollars are as follows:

<table>
<tr><td></td><td></td><td colspan="5">Warehouse</td></tr>
<tr><td></td><td></td><td>A</td><td>B</td><td>C</td><td>D</td><td>E</td></tr>
<tr><td rowspan="4">Factory</td><td>1</td><td>8</td><td>9</td><td>12</td><td>7</td><td>18</td></tr>
<tr><td>2</td><td>6</td><td>8</td><td>13</td><td>9</td><td>21</td></tr>
<tr><td>3</td><td>20</td><td>7</td><td>10</td><td>11</td><td>8</td></tr>
<tr><td>4</td><td>12</td><td>7</td><td>14</td><td>15</td><td>22</td></tr>
</table>

Determine the initial solution by using the northwest corner rule. What is the optimum distribution for the company?

4.4. There will be a surplus of 8, 7, 9, and 10 trailers in cities 1, 2, 3, and 4, respectively, by the beginning of next week. Cities A, B, C, and D will have a deficit of 6, 7, 9, and 8 trailers, respectively. The cost of moving trailers from each surplus city to each deficit city is given in dollars as follows:

<table>
<tr><td></td><td></td><td colspan="4">Deficit</td></tr>
<tr><td></td><td></td><td>A</td><td>B</td><td>C</td><td>D</td></tr>
<tr><td rowspan="4">Surplus</td><td>1</td><td>26</td><td>32</td><td>27</td><td>33</td></tr>
<tr><td>2</td><td>17</td><td>28</td><td>16</td><td>16</td></tr>
<tr><td>3</td><td>38</td><td>21</td><td>14</td><td>17</td></tr>
<tr><td>4</td><td>22</td><td>25</td><td>24</td><td>27</td></tr>
</table>

Using the perturbation technique to eliminate degeneracy, determine the optimum allocation.

4.5. Six different products are manufactured by three plants A, B, and C, with capacities 14,000, 13,500, and 12,000 units, respectively. The demand for the six products is forecasted as 5,000, 4,800, 3,700, 6,400, 5,200, and 6,800 units. The profit in dollars at each plant for each product is given in the following matrix:

<table>
<tr><td></td><td></td><td colspan="3">Plant</td></tr>
<tr><td></td><td></td><td>A</td><td>B</td><td>C</td></tr>
<tr><td rowspan="6">Product</td><td>1</td><td>2.40</td><td>1.90</td><td>2.30</td></tr>
<tr><td>2</td><td>1.60</td><td>2.20</td><td>1.75</td></tr>
<tr><td>3</td><td>2.60</td><td>2.40</td><td>2.70</td></tr>
<tr><td>4</td><td>2.50</td><td>1.50</td><td>1.90</td></tr>
<tr><td>5</td><td>1.75</td><td>1.75</td><td>2.00</td></tr>
<tr><td>6</td><td>2.00</td><td>2.70</td><td>2.50</td></tr>
</table>

Determine the production allocation that will maximize profit.

4.6. During the Second Punic War, one of the most terrible in antiquity, Hannibal crossed the Alps into Liguria in what is now Italy. In planning this campaign Hannibal decided to procure 250 elephants to carry supplies and for use in battle against the Romans. Hannibal required 100 of these for his own phalanx. Hasdrubal, the brother of Hannibal (not to be confused with Hannibal's brother-in-law of the same name) also required 100. The remaining 50 were to be put at the disposal of Mago, a younger brother of Hannibal, who was given 200,000 gold florins and told to procure the elephants. Mago realized that if he economized on elephants, he could pocket the difference to spend on anticipated pleasures when they reached Rome. He contacted Mutafaet-Al, a sheik and elephant dealer in Alexandria, and received a firm quotation of 900, 875, and 910 florins for the delivered cost per elephant to Hannibal, Hasdrubal, and Mago, respectively. Snuff-en-Stuff, the elephant trader in Bengasi, quoted Mago prices of 750, 790, and 820 florins, respectively, but told Mago that he would be unable to deliver any elephants to Hasdrubal for some time because of an earlier commitment of the available transportation to the slave market in Carthage. The dealers in Cairo and Damascus quoted Mago prices of 800, 900, and 740 florins, and 740, 525, and 600 florins, respectively. Each dealer can supply no more than 100 elephants. If Mago bought his elephants optimally, how much money did he have available to spend in Rome?

4.7. Work centers A through F have capacities of 600, 440, 650, 830, 770, and 550 units of a certain product per day. Work centers 1 through 6 will produce exactly 640 units per day each. The distance in feet from centers 1 through 6 to centers A through F is as follows:

From Center → *To Center*

	A	B	C	D	E	F
1	92	66	84	77	56	64
2	68	92	63	57	60	81
3	84	76	80	82	92	99
4	64	78	97	48	82	64
5	53	66	67	74	92	82
6	88	76	98	86	82	79

How should the production of work centers 1 through 6 be allocated so as to minimize material handling cost? Use Vogel's approximation method.

4.8. Three customers in a certain sales territory have requested technical assistance. Three technicians are available for assignment with the distance in miles from each technician to each customer being as follows:

Technician → *Customer*

	A	B	C
1	470	580	410
2	385	920	740
3	880	550	430

If it costs $0.22 per mile for travel, find the assignment of technicians to customers that will result in a minimum travel cost. Compare this cost with the cost of the next best assignment.

4.9. A lead draftsman has five drafting tasks to accomplish and five idle draftsmen. Each draftsman is estimated to require the following number of hours for each task.

		\multicolumn{5}{c}{Task}
		A	B	C	D	E
	1	60	50	100	85	95
	2	65	45	100	75	90
Draftsman	3	70	60	110	97	85
	4	70	55	105	90	93
	5	60	40	120	85	97

If each draftsman costs the company $15.80 per hour including overhead, find the assignment of draftsmen to tasks that will result in a minimum total cost. What is the total cost?

4.10. Five jobs are to be processed and five machines are available. Any machine can process any job, with the resulting profits in dollars.

		\multicolumn{5}{c}{Machines}
		A	B	C	D	E
	1	40	37	36	21	40
	2	35	24	28	28	37
Jobs	3	27	25	33	30	36
	4	34	33	40	36	40
	5	43	38	42	37	38

What is the maximum profit that may be expected if an optimum assignment is made?

4.11. The owner of a small machine shop has four machinists available to assign to jobs for the day. Five jobs are offered with the expected profit in dollars for each machinist on each job being as follows:

		\multicolumn{5}{c}{Job}
		A	B	C	D	E
	1	7.20	6.50	5.00	10.20	8.40
Machinist	2	6.50	7.30	6.20	7.40	5.70
	3	8.60	9.50	11.00	7.10	8.00
	4	4.80	7.30	8.80	8.30	8.40

Determine the assignment of machinists to jobs that will result in a maximum profit. Which jobs should be declined?

4.12. A toy manufacturer plans on adding four regional warehouses to meet increased demand. The following bid figures in millions of dollars are received for constructing the warehouses:

		\multicolumn{4}{c}{Warehouse}
		A	B	C	D
	1	0.30	0.27	0.31	0.39
	2	0.28	0.18	0.28	0.37
Contractor	3	0.33	0.17	0.29	0.41
	4	0.27	0.18	0.30	0.43
	5	0.40	0.20	0.27	0.36

Determine the assignment of warehouses to contractors that will result in a minimum total cost for the building program.

4.13. Three new automatic feed devices have been made available for existing punch presses. Six presses in the plant can be fitted with this equipment. The plant superintendent estimates that the increased output, together with the labor saved, will result in the following dollar increase in profits per day.

		\multicolumn{6}{c}{Press}
		A	B	C	D	E	F
	1	22	17	22	19	17	18
Device	2	21	19	20	23	20	14
	3	20	21	20	22	23	17

Determine which presses should receive the feed devices so that the benefit to the plant is maximized.

4.14. A salesman estimates that the following would be the additional profits obtained on his route by visiting the five cities as shown in the following table:

		\multicolumn{5}{c}{To City}
		1	2	3	4	5
	1	0	12	22	21	18
	2	13	0	14	17	19
From City	3	17	13	0	22	24
	4	20	19	23	0	24
	5	12	22	15	16	0

The salesman can visit each of the cities once and only once. Determine the optimum sequence the salesman should follow to maximize his additional profit. What is the maximum additional profit?

4.15. Solve Problem 4.9 using the branch-and-bound technique.

4.16. A saleswoman starts from city 1, wishes to visit six other cities once and only once, and then return to city 1. The distance between any pair of cities is given in the following matrix:

		\multicolumn{7}{c}{To City}
		1	2	3	4	5	6	7
	1	∞	16	18	13	22	21	17
	2	21	∞	40	14	23	22	23
	3	18	17	∞	17	18	40	24
From City	4	17	26	29	∞	31	37	26
	5	25	19	33	22	∞	41	18
	6	23	18	22	32	29	∞	12
	7	24	27	17	40	30	36	∞

Determine the sequence of cities the saleswoman should visit so as to minimize the total distance traveled. Use the branch-and-bound technique. What is the total distance traveled?

4.17. Use the transportation method to find the minimum cost assignment for the situation presented in Problem 4.8.

4.18. Solve Problem 4.10 using the branch-and-bound technique.

5

Goal Linear Programming Models

In Chapters 3 and 4, linear programming models were formulated and optimized with effectiveness functions embracing a single measure of effectiveness: profit, cost, distance, time, and so on. Although single measures are easiest to incorporate into a model, they are often not representative of reality. Certain noneconomic goals may be desired together with a "satisfactory" level of profit. These may be concerns for market share, labor stability, environmental impact, or other business or social factors. Also, public sector organizations do not have a profit goal, but a host of social goals. In these cases, the objective may be to attain a satisfactory level of achievement across several measures.

    Goal programming situations are modeled in a manner similar to that for the general linear programming model. The formulation accommodates multiple goals, often with ranking and weighting. Manipulation permits certain more important goals to be achieved at the expense of less important goals. This chapter presents models for deriving the best possible outcome from satisfactory levels of goal attainment.

5.1 GOAL PROGRAMMING MODEL FORMULATION

A goal is a desired result. It may be underachieved, fully achieved, or overachieved. Relative emphasis applied through managerial action contributes to the degree of goal achievement. Symbolically, 1 unit of effort applied to activity x_j might contribute an amount a_{ij} toward the ith goal.

The target level for the ith goal, b_i, is fully achieved if

$$\sum_{j=1}^{n} a_{ij}x_j = b_i.$$

To allow for underachievement or overachievement, let

d_i^- = negative deviation from the ith goal (underachievement)

d_i^+ = positive deviation from the ith goal (overachievement)

From this, the ith goal can be stated in general terms as

$$\sum_{j=1}^{n} a_{ij}x_j + d_i^- - d_i^+ = b_i \quad i = 1, 2, \ldots, m.$$

It is required that one or both of the deviational variables (d_i^- or d_i^+) be zero in the solution, since it is not possible for both underachievement and overachievement to occur at the same time.

The goal programming model must be able to incorporate goal statements, with both ranking and weighting as appropriate. Let

P_k = ranking coefficient for all deviations having the kth priority of being avoided

$W_{i,k}^-$ = relative weight of the d_i^- in the kth rank

$W_{i,k}^+$ = relative weight of the d_i^+ in the kth rank

With m goals, the goal linear programming model may be formulated mathematically as requiring the minimization of the linear weighted ranking function

$$\sum_i \sum_k P_k(W_{i,k}^- d_i^- + W_{i,k}^+ d_i^+)$$

subject to the linear constraints

$$\sum_j a_{ij}x_j + d_i^- - d_i^+ = b_i \quad i = 1, 2, \ldots, m$$

$$x_j, d_i^-, d_i^+ \geq 0.$$

The decision maker has direct control of the vector of variables x_j. Not directly under control is the vector of ranking coefficients, P_k, the vectors of weights, $W_{i,k}^-$ and $W_{i,k}^+$, the matrix of constants, a_{ij}, and the vector of constants, b_i. This model structure follows the form of the general effectiveness function with constraints, as was presented in Section 2.3.

5.2 FORMULATIONS FOR MULTIPLE GOALS

Goal programming seeks satisfactory levels of goal attainment that represents the best possible overall outcome. This aim can be realized if the several goals are stated and formulated mathematically in a manner that will permit their appropriate consideration within the goal programming model. Recognition must be given to the fact that the achievement of each goal may or may not be equally important to the decision maker. Further, within a given goal, there may be subgoals of unequal importance which must be weighted. The two-activity linear programming example of Section 3.2 will be recast in this section to illustrate goal formulations incorporating these possibilities.

In the example cited, two products are to be produced with a single unit of product A requiring 2.4 minutes of molding time and 5.0 minutes of assembly time. The profit for product A is \$0.60 per unit. A single unit of product B requires 3.0 minutes of molding time and 2.5 minutes of finishing time. The profit for product B is \$0.70 per unit.

The single goal of profit maximization led to the formulation of Section 3.2, which is restated below. Maximize

$$TP = \$0.60A + \$0.70B \tag{5.1}$$

subject to

$$2.4A + 3.0B \leq 1{,}200 \tag{5.2}$$

$$0A + 2.5B \leq 600 \tag{5.3}$$

$$5.0A + 0B \leq 1{,}500 \tag{5.4}$$

$$A \text{ and } B \geq 0.$$

Equally Ranked Goals and Deviations. Suppose that the two-product production problem is presented for optimization in the face of several equally ranked goals. Specifically, assume that the production manager wishes to determine the number of units of each product that should be produced per week in consideration of the following set of goals:

1. A profit target of \$350 per week should be met.
2. Overtime should not exceed 20 percent of the available production time in the molding department and should be avoided if possible.
3. Available production time in the finishing and assembly departments should be fully utilized but not exceeded.

The first goal pertains to profit attainment, with a target established at \$350 per week. Equation (5.1) can be restated to allow for underachievement or overachievement as

$$\$0.60A + \$0.70B + d_1^- - d_1^+ = \$350.$$

If this goal is not achieved, d_1^- would take on a positive value and d_1^+ would be zero.

The second goal pertains to overtime in the molding department having the production time constraint given by Equation (5.2). In deviational form, this constraint can be expressed as

$$2.4A + 3.0B + d_2^- - d_2^+ = 1{,}200$$

with overtime represented by d_2^+. By including d_2^+ in this constraint, the goal of avoiding overtime in molding is reflected. However, in addition to deviations below or above the available production time, an overtime goal allowing for deviations below and above the desired maximum of 20 percent must be given as

$$d_2^+ + d_3^- - d_3^+ = 0.2(1{,}200) = 240.$$

This overtime goal statement incorporates d_2^+ to represent overtime beyond 1,200 minutes, d_3^- to represent overtime less than the 20 percent goal constraint, and d_3^+ to represent overtime greater than 20 percent.

The third goal pertains to full capacity utilization in the finishing and assembly departments which have production time constraints given by Equations (5.3) and (5.4). In deviational form, these constraints can be expressed as

$$2.5B + d_4^- = 600$$
$$5.0A + d_5^- = 1{,}500.$$

Deviational variables d_4^- and d_5^- and allow for underutilization, with overutilization ruled out by the omission of deviational variables d_4^+ and d_5^+.

With these goal statements completed, the two-product production problem can be summarized in goal programming model form. Minimize

$$d_1^- + d_2^+ + d_3^+ + d_4^- + d_5^-$$

subject to

$$\$0.60A + \$0.70B + d_1^- - d_1^+ = \$\ 350$$
$$2.4A + 3.0B + d_2^- - d_2^+ = 1{,}200$$
$$d_2^+ + d_3^- - d_3^+ = 240$$
$$2.5B + d_4^- = 600$$
$$5.0A + d_5^- = 1{,}500.$$

The goal programming formulation above can be subjected to an optimization scheme of graphical or mathematical form. Specific values for the policy variables A and B are sought which would minimize the sum of profit underachievement, underachievement in full utilization of production time in finishing and assembly, and overachievement of overtime in molding. However, the result would not be too meaningful due to the assumption of equally ranked goals and deviations. For example, a deviation of $1.00 from the profit goal is equal to 1 minute of overtime in this example. Also, this example gives double weight to overtime in excess of 20 percent in that two deviational variables come into play.

Unequal Goals and Deviations. Stated goals are rarely of equal rank. Therefore, deviations from these goals are not additive. Goal programming can accommodate this if the decision maker will assign a rank to each goal. Then, the goal with first priority is assigned a value of P_1. The goal considered second in priority is asigned a value of P_2, and so on. These priority coefficients are used to rank the goal deviations in the formulation of the effectiveness function to be minimized. They do not assume numerical values in application.

If the decision maker considers two or more goals to be equal in importance, further consideration should be given to goal deviations. When the unit of measurement for the equally important goals is different it will be necessary to derive an equivalent common measure, or to use a conversion factor. For example, if profit and overtime have the same rank, then the decision maker would have to decide if a $1.00 deviation from the profit goal is equivalent to 1 minute of overtime. Since it is probably not, the decision maker could weight the ranking coefficient for overtime minutes by 4, 5, 6 or more to reflect overtime as being worth $15, $12, $10, or less per hour.

With these techniques in mind, the two-product production problem can now be presented with unequal goals and goal deviations. Suppose that the production manager restates the three goals, adds a fourth, and places them in the following priority order:

P_1: Available production time in the finishing and assembly departments should be fully utilized but not exceeded. It is three times as important that this be done in finishing as in assembly.

P_2: Overtime should not exceed 20 percent of the available production time in the molding department.

P_3: A profit target of $350 per week should be met.

P_4: Overtime should be avoided in the molding department.

Each deviational variable in the two-product production problem can now be associated with a priority coefficient from the ranking above. The first is d_1^-, which represents underachievement of the profit goal. Its priority coefficient is P_3, since profit is ranked third in priority. Overtime in molding is represented by d_2^+. It has a priority coefficient of P_4 as given in the priority ranking. But, in addition, overtime in excess of 20 percent is represented by d_3^+ and given a priority ranking of P_2. Finally, deviational variables d_4^- and d_5^- represent the underutilization of production time in finishing and assembly. Priority rank one, P_1, applies to both. Since this is the case, weighting is used within P_1 to reflect the relative importance of fully utilizing time in finishing and assembly. Specifically, $W_{i,k}^-$ is 3 for the finishing department ($W_{4,1}^- = 3$) and 1 for the assembly department ($W_{5,1}^- = 1$).

With all goals stated in terms of deviational variables associated with priority rankings and weighting as appropriate, the next step is to summarize

the goal programming formulation for this two-product production example. It is to minimize
$$P_3 d_1^- + P_4 d_2^+ + P_2 d_3^+ + 3P_1 d_4^- + P_1 d_5^- \tag{5.5}$$
subject to
$$\$0.60A + \$0.70B + d_1^- - d_1^+ = \$\ 350 \tag{5.6}$$
$$2.4A + 3.0B + d_2^- - d_2^+ = 1{,}200 \tag{5.7}$$
$$d_2^+ + d_3^- - d_3^+ = 240 \tag{5.8}$$
$$2.5B + d_4^- = 600 \tag{5.9}$$
$$5.0A + d_5^- = 1{,}500. \tag{5.10}$$

The goal programming formulation above can be subjected to an optimization scheme of graphical or mathematical form. Specific values for the policy variables A and B are sought which would minimize the sum of profit underachievement, overachievement of overtime in molding, and underutilization of available production time in finishing and assembly, with greater weight given to minimizing underutilization in finishing. These goals and weights bring more realism to the example than the preceding formulation, which had equally ranked goals and deviations.

5.3 GRAPHICAL OPTIMIZATION METHOD

The graphical method of optimization for goal programming problems parallels the approach illustrated for general linear programming in Section 3.2, with the exception that the region of feasible solutions is partioned by goal priorities. To illustrate this approach, the two-product production example with unequal goals and deviations will be used as formulated by Equations (5.5) through (5.10).

As a first step, the 20 percent overtime constraint for molding given by Equation (5.8) must be transformed to contain a decision variable. Let
$$d_2^+ = 240 - d_3^- + d_3^+$$
and substitute into Equation (5.7), giving
$$2.4A + 3.0B + d_2^- - (240 - d_3^- + d_3^+) = 1{,}200$$
$$2.4A + 3.0B + d_2^- + d_3^- - d_3^+ = 1{,}440.$$
But since 1,440 exceeds 1,200, the deviational variable d_2^- is zero and can be dropped giving
$$2.4A + 3.0B + d_3^- - d_3^+ = 1{,}440. \tag{5.11}$$

A graphical equivalent of the goal constraints is exhibited in Figure 5.1 together with the direction of positive and negative deviation for each. The first priority goal of fully utilizing available production time in finishing (minimizing

Chap. 5   Goal Linear Programming Models   101

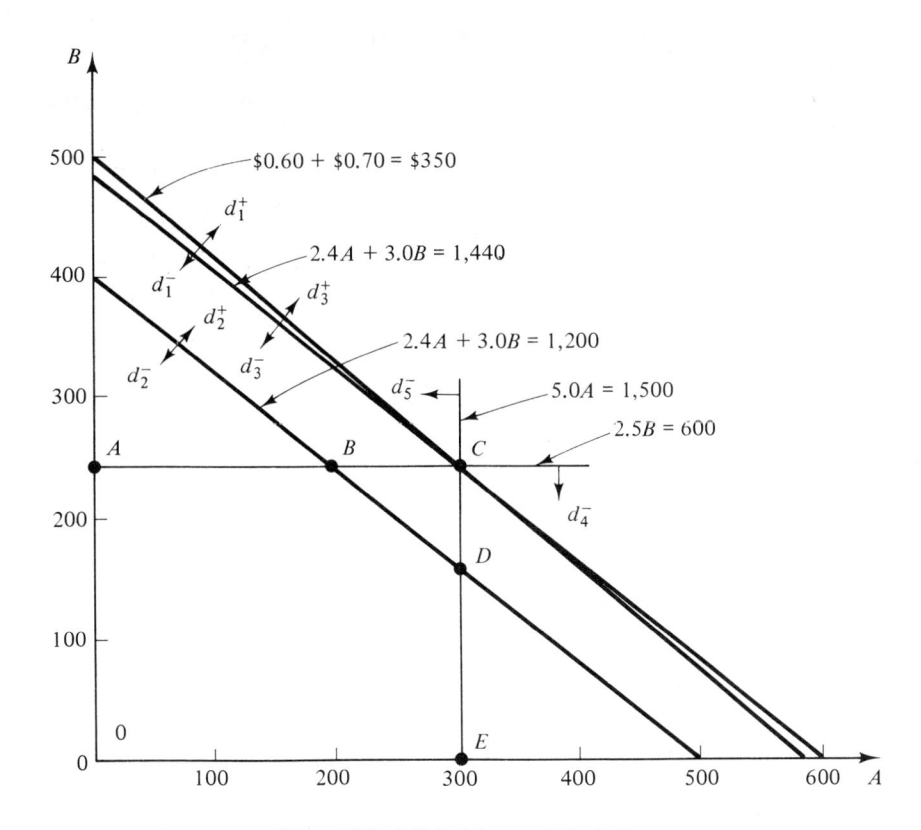

Figure 5.1 Minimizing goal deviations.

d_4^-) and in assembly (minimizing d_5^-) defines the feasible solution space. The second priority goal of not exceeding 20 percent of the available overtime in molding (maximizing d_3^+) leaves only point C as the feasible solution. The third priority goal of meeting the profit target (minimizing d_1^-) retains the feasible solution space of *OACE* together with point C. The fourth priority goal of avoiding overtime in all departments (minimizing d_2^+) also retains *OACE* with point C as the feasible solution space.

The final solution is obviously point C. It is attained by progressing from the origin (point O) to point A to recognize the weight given to finishing over assembly in priority one, and to point C for full utilization of assembly time while simultaneously satisfying priority two on excessive overtime in molding and maximizing profit as priority three. Overtime avoidance as priority four is subordinated to profit maximization.

At point C the degree of goal attainment is very good. P_1 and P_2 are completely attained. P_3 is almost completely attained; the profit amount being $348 instead of $350. Only P_4 is not attained.

5.4 MODIFIED SIMPLEX OPTIMIZATION METHOD

The simplex optimization algorithm, if modified, can be used to optimize the goal linear programming model. It is not restricted to problems with three or fewer activities, as is the graphical optimization method. In this section, a modified version of the simplex algorithm will be presented and applied to the two-product production problem with unequal goals and goal deviations.

The Initial Matrix. Goal programming requires the minimization of a linear weighted ranking function, subject to certain linear constraints. Because these constraints are expressed in goal form by the use of deviational variables, they are equalities of the form specified by the general linear programming model. Thus, the deviational variables in goal programming model formulation take the place of "slack" or "artifical" variables. They assume values as required for the equality to exist. The initial feasible solution will embrace deviational variables instead of slack or artifical variables.

The initial matrix required by the modified simplex algorithm for goal programming can be set up as shown in the upper part of Table 5.1, using the problem given by Equations (5.5) through (5.10) as an example. The first column is designated e_i and gives the weighted ranking coefficients applicable to the initial feasible solution. Some entries are zero because certain deviational variables are not represented in the weighted ranking function of Equation (5.5). The second column is designated *Sol* and gives the deviational variables in the initial solution. These are the d_i^- variables representing underachievement of all goals to which profit and production capacity are initially allocated. The third column is designated b_i and gives the initial deviations in profit and production capacities represented by the deviational variables. The next eight columns give representation to the deviational variables which are part of the initial solution and the others. The e_j heading for these columns carries entries for the weighted ranking coefficients and zeros as applicable to each deviational variable. Matrix elements are entered from the set of goal constraints given by Equations (5.6) through (5.10). The last two columns are headed by the activity variables with matrix elements also entered from the set of goal constraints. The column designated θ, as well as the lower portion of the table, are utilized during the computational process.

Testing for Optimality. After an initial feasible solution has been obtained, it must be tested for optimality. This is accomplished with the aid of the lower portion of Table 5.1 which is an expansion of the $E_j - e_j$ row in the regular simplex method. Preemption priority factors (ranking coefficients) are listed in reverse order in the *Sol* column of this $E_j - e_j$ matrix. All other entries are calculated as part of the optimality test, involving the following steps:

1. Make E_j entries into the column designated b_i by computing $\sum e_i b_i$ from values given in the upper portion of the matrix.

2. Make $E_j - e_j$ entries into all other columns by computing $\sum e_i a_{ij} - e_j$ from values given in the upper portion of the matrix.
3. All $E_j - e_j$ coefficients in the row should be examined to see if there are negative entries at higher priority levels in the same column. Such negative entries signify that an optimal solution has been obtained. A positive $E_j - e_j$ value at a certain priority level, without negative entries at higher unattained priority levels in the same column, signifies that an optimal solution has not been obtained.[1]
4. If the attainment level for each goal in the b_i column is zero, the solution is certainly optimal. But if a positive value exists for one or more unattained priority levels, a better solution may be possible.

Application of the optimality test to the initial feasible solution is shown in the $E_j - e_j$ matrix of Table 5.1. Entries for the column designated b_i are computed from step (1) as $350P_3 + 600 \times 3P_1 + 1{,}500P_1 = 350P_3 + 3{,}300P_1$. Entries for all other columns are computed from step (2) as $1P_3 - P_3 = 0$ for column one, $-1P_3 - 0 = -1P_3$ for column two, ..., $(0.7P_3 + 2.5 \times 3P_1) - 0 = 0.7P_3 + 7.5P_1$ for the last column. Application of step (3) reveals that the attainment level for each goal in the b_i column is not zero, indicating that a better solution may be possible. Positive $E_j - e_j$ values in the P_1 row, without negative entries at higher priority levels in the same columns, signify that this initial feasible solution is not optimal.

Iteration Toward an Optimal Solution. If the optimality test indicates that an optimal solution has not been found, the following iterative procedure may be employed:

1. Find the highest priority level that has not been completely attained by examining the b_i column in the $E_j - e_j$ matrix. Next, identify the column in the $E_j - e_j$ matrix that has the largest positive value without a negative value at a higher priority and designate this column k.[2] The variable at the head of this column will be the incoming variable.
2. Calculate entries for the column designated θ from $\theta_i = b_i/a_{ik}$.
3. Find the minimum positive value of θ_i and designate this row r. The variable to the left of this now will be the outgoing variable.
4. Set up a new matrix with the incoming variable substituted for the outgoing variable. Calculate new elements, a'_{ij}, as $a'_{ij} = a_{rj}/a_{rk}$ for $i = r$ and $a'_{ij} = a_{ij} - a_{ik}a'_{rj}$ for $i \neq r$.
5. Perform the optimality test.

[1] A positive value of $E_j - e_j$ is used since the objective here is to minimize.
[2] A positive value is sought since the modified simplex algorithm for goal programming is used to minimize goal deviations.

Table 5.1. INITIAL MATRIX FOR GOAL PROGRAMMING PROBLEM

e_i	e_j		P_3	0	0	P_4	0	P_2	$3P_1$	P_1	0	0	
	Sol	b_i	d_1^-	d_1^+	d_2^-	$d_2^\pm$	d_3^-	$d_3^\pm$	d_4^-	d_5^-	A	B	θ
P_3	d_1^-	350	1	-1	0	0	0	0	0	0	0.6	0.7	500
0	d_2^-	1,200	0	0	1	-1	0	0	0	0	2.4	3.0	400
0	d_3^-	240	0	0	0	0	1	-1	0	0	0	0	∞
$3P_1$	d_4^-	600	0	0	0	0	0	0	1	0	0	2.5	240
P_1	d_5^-	1,500	0	0	0	0	0	0	0	1	5.0	0	∞
	P_4	0	0	0	0	-1	0	0	0	0	0	0	
$E_j - e_j$	P_3	350	0	-1	0	0	0	0	0	0	0.6	0.7	
	P_2	0	0	0	0	0	0	-1	0	0	0	0	
	P_1	3,300	0	0	0	0	0	0	0	0	5.0	7.5	

k

Table 5.2. FIRST ITERATION FOR GOAL PROGRAMMING PROBLEM

e_i	e_j		P_3	0	0	P_4	0	P_2	$3P_1$	P_1	0	0	
	Sol	b_i	d_1^-	d_1^+	d_2^-	$d_2^\pm$	d_3^-	$d_3^\pm$	d_4^-	d_5^-	A	B	θ
P_3	d_1^-	182	1	-1	0	0	0	0	-0.28	0	0.6	0	303.3
0	d_2^-	480	0	0	1	-1	0	0	-1.20	0	2.4	0	200
0	d_3^-	240	0	0	0	0	1	-1	0	0	0	0	∞
0	B	240	0	0	0	0	0	0	0.4	0	0	1	∞
P_1	d_5^-	1,500	0	0	0	0	0	0	0	1	5.0	0	300
	P_4	0	0	0	0	-1	0	0	0	0	0	0	
$E_j - e_j$	P_3	182	0	-1	0	0	0	0	-0.28	0	0.6	0	
	P_2	0	0	0	0	0	0	-1	0	0	0	0	
	P_1	1,500	0	0	0	0	0	0	-3	0	5.0	0	

k

104

Table 5.3. SECOND ITERATION FOR GOAL PROGRAMMING PROBLEM

e_j			P_3	0	0	P_4	0	0	P_2	$3P_1$	P_1	0	0	
e_i	Sol	b_i	d_1^-	d_1^+	d_2^-	$d_2^\pm$	d_3^-	$d_3^\pm$	d_4^-	d_5^-	A	B	θ
P_3	d_1^-	62	1	-1	-0.25	0.25	0	0	0.02	0	0	0	248
0	A	200	0	0	0.417	-0.417	0	0	-0.5	0	1	0	-480
0	d_3^-	240	0	0	0	1	1	-1	0	0	0	0	240
0	B	240	0	0	0	0	0	0	0.4	0	0	1	0
P_1	d_5^-	500	0	0	-2.08	2.08	0	0	2.5	1	0	0	240
	P_4	0	0	0	0	-1	0	0	0	0	0	0	
$E_j - e_j$	P_3	62	0	-1	-0.25	0.25	0	0	0.02	0	0	0	
	P_2	0	0	0	0	0	0	-1	0	0	0	0	
	P_1	500	0	0	-2.08	2.08	0	0	-0.5	0	0	0	

k

r

Table 5.4. THIRD ITERATION FOR GOAL PROGRAMMING PROBLEM

e_j			P_3	0	0	P_4	0	0	P_2	$3P_1$	P_1	0	0	
e_i	Sol	b_i	d_1^-	d_1^+	d_2^-	$d_2^\pm$	d_3^-	$d_3^\pm$	d_4^-	d_5^-	A	B	θ
P_3	d_1^-	2	1	-1	0	0	0	0	-0.28	-0.12	0	0	
0	A	300	0	0	0	0	0	0	0	2	1	0	
0	d_3^-	0	0	0	1	0	1	-1	-1.2	-0.48	0	0	
0	B	240	0	0	0	0	0	0	0.4	0	0	1	
P_4	$d_2^\pm$	240	0	0	-1	1	0	0	1.2	0.48	0	0	
	P_4	240	0	0	-1	0	0	0	1.2	0.48	0	0	
$E_j - e_j$	P_3	2	0	-1	0	0	0	0	-0.28	-0.12	0	0	
	P_2	0	0	0	0	0	0	-1	0	0	0	0	
	P_1	0	0	0	0	0	0	0	-3	-1	0	0	

105

Steps (1), (2), and (3) of the iterative procedure are applied to the initial or old matrix. In Table 5.1, step (1) designates B as the incoming variable. Values for θ_i are calculated from step (2). Step (3) designates d_4^- as the outgoing variable. The affected column and row are marked with a k and r, respectively, in Table 5.1.

Steps (4) and (5) require a new matrix as is shown in Table 5.2. The incoming variable B, together with its e_j coefficient of zero, replaces the outgoing variable d_4^- with its coefficient of $3P_1$. All other elements in this row are calculated from the first formula of step (4). Elements in the remaining four rows are calculated from the second formula of step (4). Application of the optimality test indicates that an optimal solution has not yet been reached.

Since the first iteration did not yield an optimal solution, it is necessary to repeat steps (1) through (5). Steps (1), (2), and (3) are applied to Table 5.2 designating A as the incoming variable and d_2^- as the outgoing variable. The incoming variable, together with its associated e_j coefficient, replaces the outgoing variable as shown in Table 5.3. All other elements in this new matrix are calculated from the formulas of step (4). Application of the optimality test indicates that the solution is still not optimal.

Table 5.3 did not yield an optimal solution, requiring the application of steps (1) through (5) again. Steps (1), (2), and (3) designated d_2^+ as the incoming variable and d_5^- as the outgoing variable. The incoming variable, together with its e_j coefficient P_4, replaces the outgoing variable as shown in Table 5.4. All other elements in the new matrix are calculated from the formulas of step (4).

Application of the optimality test indicates that the solution exhibited by Table 5.4 is now optimal. It agrees with the solution found graphically in Section 5.3.

PROBLEMS

5.1. Solve the two-product production problem given by Equations (5.1) through (5.4) graphically if the single goal is profit maximization. A target profit of $350 per week is sought.

5.2. Use the modified simplex optimization method to solve the two-product production problem with a single goal as stated in Problem 5.1.

5.3. Present a graphical solution for the two-product production problem with equally ranked goals and deviations as described and formulated in Section 5.2.

5.4. Use the modified simplex optimization method to solve the two-product production problem with equally ranked goals and deviations as described and formulated in Section 5.2. Relate the solution process to the graphical method used in Problem 5.3.

5.5. Two products, A and B, are to be manufactured utilizing time in a manufacturing department and an assembly department. The normal production time available in these departments is 40 hours per week. One hour is required in the manufacturing department to produce one unit of product A, whereas 2 hours are required to produce one unit of product B. Products A and B require 1.5 hours in the assembly department. The profit per unit of product A is $80 and the profit per unit of product B is $100. Find the number of units of A and B to be produced each week so that the following goals ranked in priority order are satisfied:

1. Overtime is not to be allowed.
2. Meet a production quota of 100 units of each product per week.
3. Maximize profit.

5.6. A chemical processing firm has two plants which can meet the demand for an identical pharmacutical support ingredient. The production rate is 20 barrels per hour at plant A and 18 barrels per hour at plant B with the regular production week being 40 hours for each plant. Anticipated profit per barrel is $100. The production manager wants to determine the number of hours to run each plant during the coming week in the face of the following goals which are ranked in priority order.

1. Meet a production goal of 1,800 barrels for the week.
2. Limit overtime at plant A to 5 hours during the week.
3. Fully utilize the available production hours at each plant. It is twice as important that this be accomplished at plant A compared to plant B.
4. Limit total overtime for both plants. This limit should be proportional to the production rate at each plant.

Formulate the problem per the goal linear programming model.

5.7. Present a graphical solution for the two-plant production problem formulated in Problem 5.6.

5.8. Solve the two-plant production problem formulated in Problem 5.6 by the modified simplex optimization method.

Dynamic Programming Models

Nonlinearities, discontinuities, local maxima or minima, and other complications often arise in the mathematical modeling of operations. In these situations, linear programming approaches cannot be successfully applied. Numerical enumeration can be used, but only when the amount of computation required is manageable.

Dynamic programming is a relatively efficient enumeration technique which owes much of its development to the pioneering work of Richard Bellman and his associates at the RAND Corporation. The computational scheme is based on the principle of optimality (developed by Bellman in 1956) which states the following: An optimal policy has the property that, whatever the initial state and initial decisions are, the remaining decisions must constitute an optimal policy with regard to the state resulting from the first decision. *This principle implies a sequential decision process in which a problem involving several variables is broken down in a sequence of simpler problems each involving a single variable, with prior decisions not affected by subsequent decisions. Each component problem can then be solved by the best available procedure, usually enumeration.*

6.1 DYNAMIC PROGRAMMING MODEL FORMULATION

A general dynamic programming model may be formulated quite easily for single-dimensional processes from the principle of optimality. The programming situation involves a certain quantity of an economic resource, such as space, money, people, or equipment which can be allocated to a number of different activities. A conflict arises from the numerous ways in which the allocation can be made. A certain return is derived from the allocation of all or part of the resource to a given activity. The magnitude of the return depends jointly on the specific activity and the quantity of the resource allocated. The objective is to allocate the available resource among the various activities so as to maximize the total return.

Let the number of activities be designated by n, enumerated in fixed order, $1, 2, \ldots, n$. Associated with each activity is a return function which gives the dependence of the return from the activity on the quantity of the resource allocated. The quantity of the resource allocated to the jth activity may be designated x_j, and $r_j(x_j)$ denotes the return function. Since it was assumed that the activities are independent and that the returns from all activities are additive, the total return may be expressed as

$$R(x_1, x_2, \ldots, x_n) = r_1(x_1) + r_2(x_2) + \cdots + r_n(x)_n. \qquad (6.1)$$

The limited quantity of the resource, Q, leads to the constraint

$$Q = x_1 + x_2 + \cdots + x_n \qquad x_j \geq 0.$$

The objective is to maximize the total return over all x_j, subject to the constraint above.

The problem of maximizing the total return from the allocation process is viewed as one member of a sequence of allocation processes. The quantity of the resource, Q, and the number of activities, n, will not be assumed to be fixed, but may take on any value subject to the restriction that n be an integer. It is artificially required that the allocations be made one at a time; that is, a quantity of the resource is allocated to the nth activity, then to the $(n-1)$th activity, and so on.

Since the maximization of R depends on Q and n, the dependence must be explicitly stated by a sequence of functions

$$f_n(Q) = \max_{x_j} \{R(x_1, x_2, \ldots, x_n)\}. \qquad (6.2)$$

The function $f_n(Q)$ represents the maximum return from the allocation of the resource Q to the n activities. If it is assumed that $r_j(0) = 0$ for each activity, it is evident that

$$f_n(0) = 0 \qquad n = 1, 2, \ldots$$

and that

$$f_1(Q) = r_1(Q). \qquad (6.3)$$

These two statements express the return to be expected from the nth activity if no resources are allocated and the return to be expected from the first activity if all the resources are allocated to it.

A functional relation connecting $f_n(Q)$ and $f_{n-1}(Q)$ for arbitrary values of n and Q may be developed by the following procedure. If x_n, $0 \leq x_n \leq Q$, is the allocation of the resource to the nth activity, then, regardless of the value of x_n, a quantity of resource $Q - x_n$ will remain. The return from the $n - 1$ activities may be expressed as $f_{n-1}(Q - x_n)$. Therefore, the total return from the n activity process may be expressed as

$$r_n(x_n) + f_{n-1}(Q - x_n). \tag{6.4}$$

An optimal choice of x_n would be that choice which maximizes the foregoing function. Thus, the general dynamic programming model may be written as

$$f_n(Q) = \max_{0 \leq x_n \leq Q} \{r_n(x_n) + f_{n-1}(Q - x_n)\} \qquad n = 2, 3, \ldots$$

where $f_1(Q)$ is determined from Equation (6.3).

The dynamic programming model gives the best results when the effectiveness functions are additive; that is, when it can be assumed that the returns from different activities can be measured in a common unit. In addition, the return from any activity must be independent of the level of other activities and the total return must be the sum of returns from individual activities. The model developed in this section and examples in subsequent sections are based on the assumption of separable effectiveness functions, the sequential decision process, and the application of the principle of optimality.

6.2 SOME COMPUTATIONAL PROCEDURES

Equation (6.4) is based on the principle of optimality. It offers a computational procedure for obtaining the sequence $f_n(Q)$ once $f_1(Q)$ is known. Since $f_1(Q)$ determines $f_2(Q)$, it also follows that $f_2(Q)$ leads to an evaluation of $f_3(Q)$. The recursive relationship progresses in this manner until $f_{n-1}(Q)$ determines $f_n(Q)$, at which time the computational procedure stops.

In dynamic programming, a sequence of univariate enumerations is substituted for multivariate enumeration. This almost always results in a significant increase in computational efficiency. Consider a problem with three decision variables, each capable of assuming 10 different integer values. Multivariate enumeration would require 10^3, or 1,000, evaluations, whereas a sequence of three univariate enumerations would require only $10 + 10 + 10 = 30$ evaluations.

Network Flow Procedures. Consider the network illustrated in Figure 6.1 with three possible origins, A, B, and C, and three possible destinations, a, b, and c. The effectiveness coefficients (distance, time, profit, etc.) for traversing

Chap. 6   Dynamic Programming Models   111

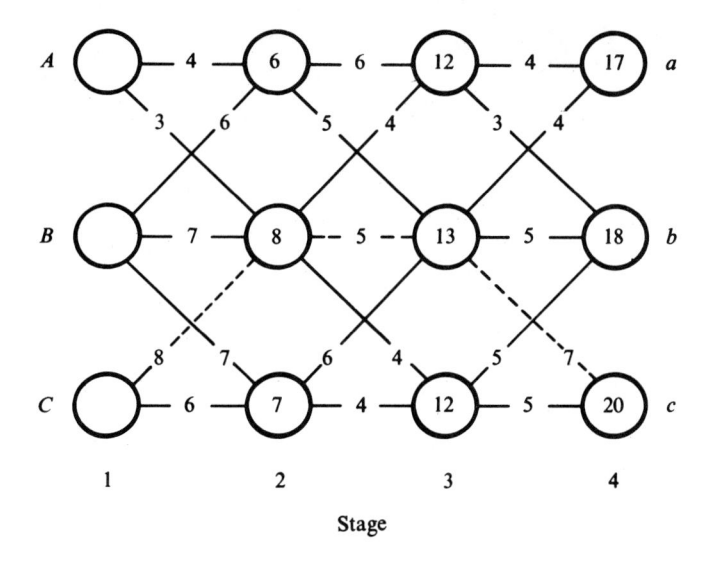

Figure 6.1 Network flow diagram.

from stage to stage are entered on each of the possible paths. Depending on the measure of effectiveness involved, the objective would be to maximize or minimize across all stages and to identify the optimal path. This might be accomplished by identifying all possible paths and calculating the value of each. However, this approach requires much calculation and suffers from the possibility that a path could be overlooked.

By utilizing the dynamic programming approach, optimization is viewed as a stagewise process. If the measure of effectiveness is revenue generated, or profit, the maximum path is sought. This is determined by first finding the maximum path from stage 1 to stage 2 by entering the value of the maximum path from stage 1 to stage 2 for each terminal point of stage 2, as shown in Figure 6.2. This occurs because whatever the starting point chosen, the path to the terminal point must be a maximum for an optimal two-stage policy to exist. Thus, the optimal two-stage policy is easily identified with little calculation. The optimal three-stage policy is found by again calculating the maximum of each terminal point from a knowledge of the results of the optimal two-stage policies. Continuing to the fourth stage with the same philosophy results in an optimal four-stage policy. This maximum path will have a value of 20. The maximum path may now be identified by searching backward, as indicated by the dashed line in Figure 6.2.

Alternatively, a minimum path through the network may be desired if the measure of effectiveness is distance, time, or cost. If the minimum path through the network of Figure 6.1 is sought, the minimum path from stage 1

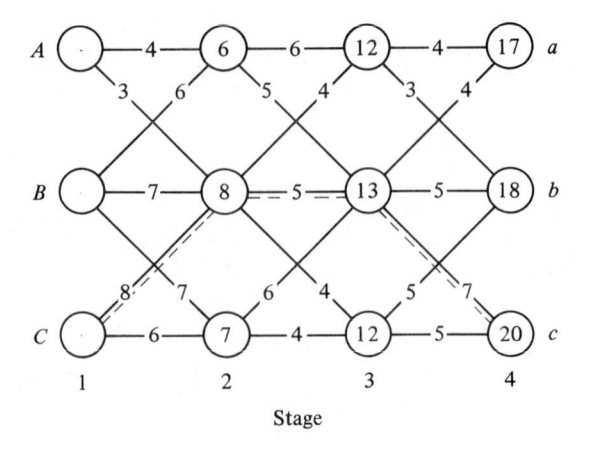

Figure 6.2 Network flow maximization.

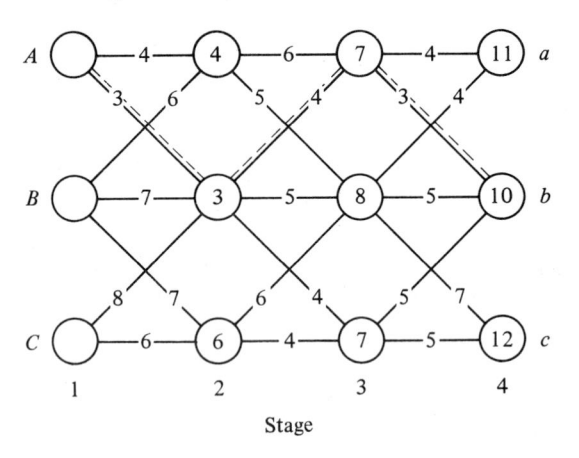

Figure 6.3 Network flow minimization.

to stage 2 is entered for each terminal point of stage 2, as shown in Figure 6.3. In like manner, the optimal three-stage policies are found and entered from knowledge of the results of the optimal two-stage policies. By repeating for the fourth stage, an optimal four-stage policy is found. This minimum path will have a value of 10. This minimum path may now be identified by searching backward, as indicated by the dashed line in Figure 6.3.

Resource Allocation Procedure. The computational procedure for resource allocation optimization differs from that for network optimization. It is based on the general dynamic model of Equation (6.4). In this model, the entire set of values $f_n(Q)$ in the range 0 to Q may be found by assuming a finite grid of points. Each element of the sequence $f_n(Q)$ may be evaluated and tabulated at each of these grid points. Maximization of Equation (6.4) may be performed when $n = 1$, since $f_1(Q) = r_1(Q)$. A set of values $f_1(Q)$ may be computed and tabulated. Equation (6.4) may then be used to compute $f_2(Q)$ for $n = 2$; that is,

$$f_2(Q) = \max_{0 \leq x_2 \leq Q} \{r_2(x_2) + f_1(Q - x_2)\}.$$

The maximization process begins by evaluating $r_2(0) + f_1(Q)$ and $r_2(\Delta) + f_1(Q - \Delta)$. The larger of these values is retained and compared with the values $r_2(2\Delta) + f_1(Q - 2\Delta)$. As before, the larger of these values is retained and compared with $r_2(3\Delta) + f_1(Q - 3\Delta)$. This process is continued until all values of Δ are considered. The result is a table of values for $f_2(Q)$ at the Q values of $0, \Delta, 2\Delta, \ldots$, as given by Table 6.1. For any given value of Q, subject to the

Table 6.1. TABULAR REPRESENTATION OF COMPUTATIONAL SCHEME

Q	x_1	$f_1(Q)$	x_2	$f_2(Q)$	$\ldots$
0					
Δ					
2Δ					
.					
.					

grid established, the table gives the corresponding allocation, x_2, for the second activity, $n = 2$, since only a two-stage process was considered. Once the allocation of x_2 to the second activity is determined, the allocation of the remaining resources, $Q - x_2$, to the first activity may be determined. The computational procedure can be extended for n stages, giving an expanded table and a means for determining all allocations through a backward search.

6.3 CAPITAL ALLOCATION PROBLEM

As a simple application of the dynamic programming model, consider the following situation. A conflict rises from the numerous ways in which a fixed amount of capital can be allocated to a number of activities. A certain return is derived as a result of allocating all or part of the captial to a given activity. The total return depends on the manner in which the allocation is made. Therefore, the objective is to find that allocation which maximizes

$$R = \sum_{j=1}^{n} r_j x_j$$

subject to

$$\sum_{j=1}^{n} x_j = Q \quad j = 1, 2, \ldots, n$$

$$x_j \geq 0.$$

This is a restatement of the model developed in Section 6.1. The decision maker has control over the vector of variables x_j. Not directly under control is the vector of return coefficients, r_j, and the fixed amount of capital, Q.

Problem Description. Suppose that 8 units of capital are available and that three different activities are under consideration. The return functions for each venture are given in Table 6.2, with each return being measured in a common unit. The return from each activity is independent of the allocations to the other activities. In addition, the total return is the sum of the individual returns. Each activity exhibits a return function that increases for a portion of its range and then levels off. This is attributable to the law of diminishing returns and is typical of many activities.

Table 6.2. RETURN FUNCTIONS FOR CAPITAL INVESTMENT

Q	$r_1(Q)$	$r_2(Q)$	$r_3(Q)$
0	0	0	0
1	5	5	4
2	15	15	26
3	40	40	40
4	80	60	45
5	90	70	50
6	95	73	51
7	98	74	52
8	100	75	53

A finite grid of points is established for this problem by the discrete nature of the return functions. Direct enumeration of all ways in which the 8 units of capital can be allocated to the three activities would be possible. However, the dynamic programming model may be used with a saving in computational effort.

The Computational Procedure. The return expected from the first activity if all the available capital is allocated to it is determined from Equation (6.3) as

$$f_1(0) = r_1(0) = 0$$
$$f_1(1) = r_1(1) = 5$$
$$f_1(2) = r_1(2) = 15$$
$$f_1(3) = r_1(3) = 40$$
$$f_1(4) = r_1(4) = 80$$
$$f_1(5) = r_1(5) = 90$$
$$f_1(6) = r_1(6) = 95$$
$$f_1(7) = r_1(7) = 98$$
$$f_1(8) = r_1(8) = 100.$$

This completes the computation of $f_1(Q)$. Each value is entered in the first stage of Table 6.3.

Table 6.3. TABULAR SOLUTION FOR A CAPITAL INVESTMENT PROBLEM

Q	x_1	$f_1(Q)$	x_2	$f_2(Q)$	x_3	$f_3(Q)$
0	0	0	0	0	0	0
1	1	5	1	5	0	5
2	2	15	2	15	2	26
3	3	40	3	40	3	40
4	4*	80	0	80	0	80
5	5	90	0	90	0	90
6	6	95	2	95	2	106
7	7	98	3	120	3	120
8	8	100	4*	140	0*	140

From the results of $f_1(Q)$, $f_2(Q)$ may be computed by use of Equation (6.4). It is evident that when $Q = 0$, $f_2(Q) = 0$. When $Q = 1$,

$$f_2(1) = \max_{0 \leq x_2 \leq 1} \{r_2(x_2) + f_1(1 - x_2)\}.$$

For values of x_2 ranging from 0 to 1, this gives

$$f_2(1) = \max \begin{cases} r_2(0) + f_1(1) = 5 \\ r_2(1) + f_1(0) = 5 \end{cases}.$$

When $Q = 2$,

$$f_2(2) = \max_{0 \leq x_2 \leq 2} \{r_2(x_2) + f_1(2 - x_2)\}.$$

For values of x_2 ranging from 0 to 2, this gives

$$f_2(2) = \max \begin{cases} r_2(0) + f_1(2) = 15 \\ r_2(1) + f_1(1) = 10 \\ r_2(2) + f_1(0) = 15 \end{cases}.$$

When $Q = 3$,

$$f_2(3) = \max_{0 \leq x_2 \leq 3} \{r_2(x_2) + f_1(3 - x_2)\}.$$

For values of x_2 ranging from 0 to 3, this gives

$$f_2(3) = \max \begin{cases} r_2(0) + f_1(3) = 40 \\ r_2(1) + f_1(2) = 20 \\ r_2(2) + f_1(1) = 20 \\ r_2(3) + f_1(0) = 40 \end{cases}.$$

This process is continued until $f_2(8)$ is evaluated. The maximum value of $f_2(Q)$ is identified for each value of Q and entered in the second stage of Table 6.3 together with its associated value of x_2. An arbitrary choice may be made when a tie is involved.

The third stage is considered next. Using the results of $f_2(Q)$, $f_3(Q)$ may be computed by use of Equation (6.4). As before, when $Q = 0$, $f_3(Q) = 0$. When $Q = 1$,

$$f_3(1) = \max_{0 \le x_3 \le 1} \{r_3(x_3) + f_2(1 - x_3)\}.$$

For values of x_3 ranging from 0 to 1, this gives

$$f_3(1) = \max \begin{Bmatrix} r_3(0) + f_2(1) = 5 \\ r_3(1) + f_2(0) = 4 \end{Bmatrix}.$$

When $Q = 2$,

$$f_3(2) = \max_{0 \le x_3 \le 2} \{r_3(x_3) + f_2(2 - x_3)\}.$$

For values of x_3 ranging from 0 to 2, this gives

$$f_3(2) = \max \begin{Bmatrix} r_3(0) + f_2(2) = 15 \\ r_3(1) + f_2(1) = 9 \\ r_3(2) + f_2(0) = 26 \end{Bmatrix}.$$

When $Q = 3$,

$$f_3(3) = \max_{0 \le x_3 \le 3} \{r_3(x_3) + f_2(3 - x_3)\}.$$

For values of x_3 ranging from 0 to 3, this gives

$$f_3(3) = \max \begin{Bmatrix} r_3(0) + f_2(3) = 40 \\ r_3(1) + f_2(2) = 19 \\ r_3(2) + f_2(1) = 31 \\ r_3(3) + f_2(0) = 40 \end{Bmatrix}.$$

Again, this process is continued until $f_3(8)$ is evaluated. The maximum value of $f_3(Q)$ is identified for each value of Q and entered in the third stage of Table 6.3 together with its associated value of x_3.

Table 6.3 may now be used to find the maximum return allocation of capital. This maximum is found in the third stage of the table to be 140 units. The allocation of capital associated with this return may be found by noting that $x_3 = 0$ at $f_3(Q) = 140$. Therefore, 8 units of capital remain for the two-stage process giving a value for x_2 of 4 units. This leaves 4 units for the first stage; $x_1 = 4$. Each allocation is indicated with an asterisk in Table 6.3.

Note that Table 6.3 can be used to find the maximum return investment policy for investments ranging from 1 to 8 units of capital. It may also be used to find the optimal policy for a reduced number of activities. For example, if 6 units of capital are to be invested in activities 1 and 2, the solution will be found by noting that $x_2 = 2$ at $f_2(Q) = 95$. This means that 4 units will remain for the first activity; $x_1 = 4$. Thus, the maximization of R depends on Q and n, as expressed in Equation (6.2).

Chap. 6   Dynamic Programming Models

6.4 SHIPPING OR "KNAPSACK" PROBLEM

A given number of items, each with a different weight and value, are to make up a shipment or fill a "knapsack." The total weight of the shipment must not exceed a certain maximum. The objective is to select the number of each item to include in the shipment so that its value will be a maximum.

Problems such as this arise in shipping operations where the value of the shipment may be measured in terms of its worth to the receiver, or where its value is a function of the shipping revenue. The latter case will be considered in the example of this section, which requires the maximization of

$$V = \sum_{n=1}^{N} v_n x_n$$

subject to

$$\sum_{n=1}^{N} w_n x_n \leq W \quad n = 1, 2, \ldots, N$$

$$x_n \geq 0,$$

where N = number of different items
v_n = unit value of item n
x_n = number of item n to ship
w_n = unit weight of item n
W = total weight limit.

The decision maker has control over the vector of variables x_n. Not directly under control is the number of different items to be considered, N, the unit value of each item, v_n, the unit weight of each item, w_n, and the total weight limit, W.

Problem Description. Suppose that four items with different weights and values are to form a shipment with a total weight of not more than 9 tons. Table 6.4 gives the weight and net profit to be derived from shipping each item.

Table 6.4. WEIGHTS AND VALUES OF ITEMS

Item	Weight (tons)	Net Profit (dollars)
1	2	50
2	4	120
3	5	170
4	3	80

In this problem, the weight of the shipment is a restriction and constitutes a resource to be distributed or allocated to the four items. Thus, the dynamic programming model may be used if the problem is properly structured.

The first step in the solution is to determine the return functions for each individual item. This is accomplished by considering different weights to be allocated to each item and by identifying the whole number of items that can be accommodated within these weights. By reference to Table 6.4, the return functions of Table 6.5 are developed. Each function gives the return to be expected from allocating designated amounts of the scarce resource (shipping weight) to each activity (item).

Table 6.5. RETURN FUNCTIONS FOR SHIPPING PROBLEMS

W	$r_1(W)$	$r_2(W)$	$r_3(W)$	$r_4(W)$
0	0	0	0	0
1	0	0	0	0
2	50	0	0	0
3	50	0	0	80
4	100	120	0	80
5	100	120	170	80
6	150	120	170	160
7	150	120	170	160
8	200	240	170	160
9	200	240	170	240

Performing the Calculations. First, the return to be expected from the first item if all the available weight is allocated to it must be determined from Equation (6.3) as

$$f_1(0) = r_1(0) = 0$$
$$f_1(1) = r_1(1) = 0$$
$$f_1(2) = r_1(2) = 50$$
$$f_1(3) = r_1(3) = 50$$
$$f_1(4) = r_1(4) = 100$$
$$f_1(5) = r_1(5) = 100$$
$$f_1(6) = r_1(6) = 150$$
$$f_1(7) = r_1(7) = 150$$
$$f_1(8) = r_1(8) = 200$$
$$f_1(9) = r_1(9) = 200.$$

This completes the computation of $f_1(W)$. Each value is entered in the first stage of Table 6.6.

From the results of $f_1(W)$, $f_2(W)$ may be computed by use of Equation (6.4). When $W = 0$, $f_2(0) = 0$. When $W = 1$,

$$f_2(1) = \max_{0 \leq x_2 \leq 1} \{r_2(x_2) + f_1(1 - x_2)\}.$$

For values of x_2 ranging from 0 to 1, this gives

$$f_2(1) = \max \begin{Bmatrix} r_2(0) + f_1(1) = 0 \\ r_2(1) + f_1(0) = 0 \end{Bmatrix}.$$

Chap. 6   Dynamic Programming Models   119

Table 6.6. TABULAR SOLUTION FOR A SHIPPING PROBLEM

W	k_1	$f_1(W)$	k_2	$f_2(W)$	x_3	$f_3(W)$	k_4	$f_4(W)$
0	0*	0	0	0	0	0	0	0
1	1	0	0	0	0	0	0	0
2	2	50	0	50	0	50	0	50
3	3	50	1	50	1	50	3	80
4	4	100	4*	120	0	120	0	120
5	5	100	5	120	5	170	0	170
6	6	150	4	170	6	170	1	170
7	7	150	5	170	5	220	0	220
8	8	200	8	240	0	240	3	250
9	9	200	9	240	5*	290	0*	290

When $W = 2$,
$$f_2(2) = \max_{0 \leq x_2 \leq 2} \{r_2(x_2) + f_1(2 - x_2)\}.$$
For values of x_2 ranging from 0 to 2, this gives
$$f_2(2) = \max \begin{cases} r_2(0) + f_1(2) = 50 \\ r_2(1) + f_1(1) = 0 \\ r_2(2) + f_1(0) = 0 \end{cases}.$$
When $W = 3$,
$$f_2(3) = \max_{0 \leq x_2 \leq 3} \{r_2(x_2) + f_1(3 - x_1)\}.$$
For values of x_2 ranging from 0 to 3, this gives
$$f_2(3) = \max \begin{cases} r_2(0) + f_1(3) = 50 \\ r_2(1) + f_1(2) = 50 \\ r_2(2) + f_1(1) = 0 \\ r_2(3) + f_1(0) = 0 \end{cases}.$$

This process is continued until $f_2(9)$ is evaluated. The maximum values of $f_2(W)$ are identified for each value of W and entered in the second stage of Table 6.6 together with their associated values of x_2.

The third stage is considered next. Using the results of $f_2(W)$, $f_3(W)$ may be computed by use of Equation (6.4). As before, when $Q = 0$, $f_3(W) = 0$.
When $W = 1$,
$$f_3(1) = \max_{0 \leq x_3 \leq 1} \{r_3(x_3) + f_2(1 - x_3)\}.$$
For values of x_3 ranging from 0 to 1, this gives
$$f_3(1) = \max \begin{cases} r_3(0) + f_2(1) = 0 \\ r_3(1) + f_2(0) = 0 \end{cases}.$$
When $W = 2$,
$$f_3(2) = \max_{0 \leq x_3 \leq 2} \{r_3(x_3) + f_2(2 - x_3)\}.$$

For values of x_3 ranging from 0 to 2, this gives

$$f_3(2) = \max \begin{Bmatrix} r_3(0) + f_2(2) = 50 \\ r_3(1) + f_2(1) = 0 \\ r_3(2) + f_2(0) = 0 \end{Bmatrix}.$$

When $W = 3$,

$$f_3(3) = \max_{0 \leq x_3 \leq 3} \{r_3(x_3) + f_2(3 - x_3)\}.$$

For values of x_3 ranging from 0 to 2, this gives

$$f_3(3) = \max \begin{Bmatrix} r_3(0) + f_2(3) = 50 \\ r_3(1) + f_2(2) = 50 \\ r_3(2) + f_2(1) = 0 \\ r_3(3) + f_2(0) = 0 \end{Bmatrix}.$$

Again, this process is continued until $f_3(9)$ is evaluated. The maximum values of $f_3(Q)$ are identified for each value of W and entered in the third stage of Table 6.6 together with their associated values of x_3.

By continuing this pattern for the fourth stage, Table 6.6 is completed. The maximum profit is found in stage 4 to be $290. The number of tons to be allocated to item 4 is found by noting that $x_4 = 0$ at $f_4(Q) = \$290$. Since 9 tons are still available, x_3 will be 5. This leaves 4 tons for item 2 and none for item 1. Thus, the shipment resulting in a maximum profit will contain one each of items 2 and 3.

PROBLEMS

6.1. Consider the network flow diagram of Figure 6.1. Use the concept of dynamic programming to find the maximum path if the origin is B and the destination is b.

6.2. If the origin is either A or B and the destination is either b or c in Figure 6.1, find the minimum path from stage 1 to stage 4 using the concept of dynamic programming.

6.3. Use dynamic programming to find the shortest path from node 1 to node 8 in the network below. What is the longest path?

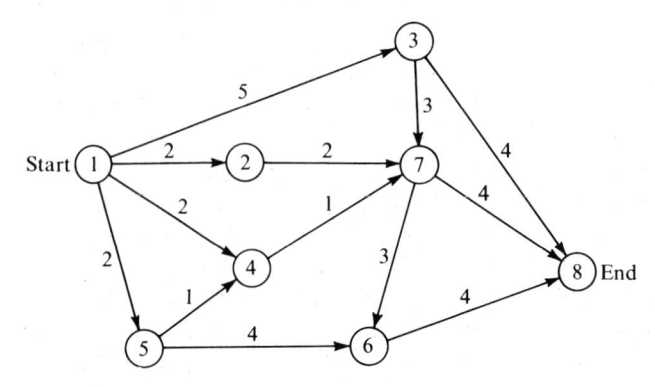

Chap. 6 Dynamic Programming Models

6.4. Eight units of capital can be invested in three activities with the return from each activity given in the accompanying table. Determine the capital allocation to each activity that will maximize the total return. What will be the total return if the available capital is reduced by 2 units?

Q	$g_1(Q)$	$g_2(Q)$	$g_3(Q)$
0	0	0	0
1	2	2	2
2	3	4	4
3	4	5	6
4	6	7	6
5	8	7	8
6	9	8	9
7	10	9	9
8	10	11	12

6.5. The profit associated with each of the four activities as a function of the labor hours allocated to each is given in the following table. If 8 labor hours are available each day, how should the allocation of time be made so that the profit per day is maximized?

H	$g_1(H)$	$g_2(H)$	$g_3(H)$	$g_4(H)$
0	0	0	0	0
1	2	1	2	3
2	4	2	3	4
3	6	3	4	6
4	9	5	7	7
5	13	8	11	9
6	14	10	13	10
7	15	12	13	13
8	16	15	13	16

6.6. The athletic director of Fun State University has 16 athletic scholarships available to allocate to the minor sports of tennis, golf, and volley ball. During the coming season, Fun State will play 10 games of tennis, 10 of golf, and 10 of volley ball. Being quite concerned with the reputation of his institution as an academic power house, the athletic director wishes to be sure that the total number of games won in these minor sports is maximized. He estimates that the number of games won as a function of the allocation of scholarships will be as given in the accompanying table. How should the available scholarships be allocated so as to maximize the esteem of Fun State in minor sports?

Q	Tennis $g_1(Q)$	Golf $g_2(Q)$	Volley Ball $g_3(Q)$
0	2	3	1
1	2	3	2
2	3	3	3
3	3	4	3
4	3	4	4
5	4	4	4
6	4	5	4
7	4	5	4
8	4	5	4
9	5	5	4
10	5	6	5
11	5	6	5
12	6	6	6
13	7	7	6
14	8	7	6
15	8	8	6
16	9	8	7

6.7. Determine the number of each of the four items to include in a package so that the value of the package will be a maximum. The total weight of the package must not exceed 15 pounds.

Item	Weight (pounds)	Value (dollars)
1	2	5
2	4	7
3	3	7
4	5	9

6.8. Determine the number of each of five items to include in a package so that the cost of the package will be a minimum. The weight of the package has to be at least 13 ounces.

Item	Weight (ounces)	Cost (dollars)
1	4	1.25
2	2	0.50
3	3	1.50
4	5	0.75
5	4	2.00

6.9. A trucking company plans to load a certain group of trucks with a selection of certain heavy items which will result in maximizing the revenue per truck. The capacity of a truck is 1,500 cubic feet, and the following table shows the items to be shipped. Determine the number of each of the four items to be included in each load.

Item	Volume (cubic feet)	Revenue (dollars)
1	200	15
2	100	6
3	300	17
4	400	25

III

Models for Decision Alternatives

7

Decision and Game Models

One organizing concept for scientifically approaching decisions is that of formulating and optimizing an effectiveness function having the structure introduced in Section 2.3. Another focuses on alternatives as discrete entities from among which the decision maker is obliged to choose in the face of several possible futures. Decision and game models fit this latter case and are of considerable importance in OR/MS.

In this chapter, four categories of decision situations are developed and presented. The first postulates the state of certainty in which it is assumed that only a single known future will occur. The second is the state of risk in which the several factors that exist can be assigned probabilities of occurrence. The third is the state of uncertainity in which it is inappropriate or impossible to assign probabilities to the futures. The fourth category stands apart from the other three in that the decision maker is in competition with a goal-seeking opponent, instead of with a passive opponent often called "nature." This category is approached through game models for analyzing competitive situations.

7.1 THE PAYOFF MATRIX MODEL

A *payoff matrix model* is a formal way of exhibiting the interaction of a finite set of alternatives and a finite set of possible futures (or states of nature). In this usage, alternatives have the meaning presented in Section 1.3; that is, they are courses of action among which a decision maker expects to choose. The states of nature are normally not natural events such as rain, sleet, or snow, but are a wide variety of future outcomes over which the decision maker has no direct control.

The general payoff matrix is a model depicting the positive or negative results that will occur for each alternative under each possible future. In abstract form, this model is structured as shown in Figure 7.1. Its symbols are defined as follows:[1]

A_i = an alternative available for selection by the decision maker, where $i = 1, 2, \ldots, m$

F_j = a future not under control of the decision maker, where $j = 1, 2, \ldots, n$

P_j = the probability that the jth future will occur, where $j = 1, 2, \ldots, n$

θ_{ij} = the payoff outcome (positive or negative) associated with the ith alternative and the jth future

A_i \ F_j \ P_j	P_1 F_1	P_2 F_2	$\cdots$	P_n F_n
A_1	θ_{11}	θ_{12}	$\cdots$	θ_{1n}
A_2	θ_{21}	θ_{22}	$\cdots$	θ_{2n}
$\vdots$	$\vdots$	$\vdots$		$\vdots$
A_m	θ_{m1}	θ_{m2}	$\cdots$	θ_{mn}

Figure 7.1 Payoff matrix model.

Several assumptions underlie the application of this payoff matrix model to decision making under assumed certainty, risk, and uncertainty. Foremost among these is the presumption that all viable alternatives have been considered and all possible futures have been identified. Alternatives not considered cannot be adopted, no matter how desirable they may prove to be. Possible futures not identified can significantly affect the actual outcome relative to the planned outcome.

---

[1] It is interesting to note that A_i and F_j have a meaning analogous to X and Y in $E = F(X, Y)$, in the sense of alternatives (policy variables) and futures (system parameters).

Payoff values in the matrix model are associated with outcomes which may be either objective or subjective. The most common case is one in which the outcome values are objective and therefore subject to quantitative expression in cardinal form. For example, the payoffs may be profits expressed in dollars, yield expressed in pounds, costs (negative payoffs) expressed in dollars, or other desirable or undesirable measures. Subjective outcomes, on the other hand, are those which are valued on an ordinal or ranking scale. Examples are expressions of preference, such as a good corporate image being preferred to a poor image, higher-quality outputs being preferred to those of lower quality, and so forth.

Other assumptions of importance in the payoff matrix representation of decisions are:

1. The occurrence of one future precludes the occurrence of any other future (futures are mutually exclusive).
2. The occurrence of a specific future is not influenced by the alternative selected.
3. The occurrence of a specific future is not known with certainty, even though certainty may be assumed for analysis purposes.

The payoff matrix for game situations has many characteristics in common with those of Figure 7.1. However, there are enough differences to justify its deferral until Section 7.5, where game models will be presented.

7.2 DECISIONS UNDER ASSUMED CERTAINTY

In dealing with physical aspects of the environment, physical scientists and engineers have a body of systematic knowledge and physical laws upon which to base their reasoning. Such laws as Boyle's law, Ohm's law, and Newton's laws of motion were developed primarily by collecting and comparing many comparable instances and by the use of an inductive process. These laws may then be applied with a high degree of certainty to specific instances. They are supplemented by many models for physical phenomena which enable conclusions to be reached about the physical environment that match the facts within narrow limits. Much is known with certainty about the physical environment.

Much less, particularly of a quantitative nature, is known about the environment within which managerial decisions are made. Nonetheless, the primary aim of operations research and management science is to bring the scientific approach to bear to a maximum feasible extent. This is done with the aid of conceptual simplifications and models of reality, the most common being the assumption of a single known future. It is not claimed that knowledge about the future is in hand. Rather, the supression of risk and uncertainty is one of the ways in which the scientific approach simplifies reality in order to gain insight. Such insight can assist greatly in decision making, provided that its shortcomings are recognized and accommodated.

The payoff matrix for decision making under assumed certainty is not a matrix at all. It is a vector with as many elements (payoffs) as there are alternatives, with these payoffs constituting a single column. This decision vector is a special case of the decision matrix of Figure 7.1. It appears as in Figure 7.2, with the payoffs represented by θ_i, where $i = 1, 2, \ldots, m$. The single future, which is assumed to occur with certainty, actually carries a probability of unity ($P = 1.0$) in the payoff matrix. All other futures are suppressed by carrying probabilities of zero ($P = 0.0$).

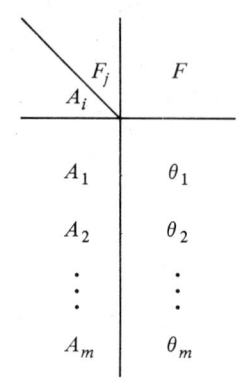

Figure 7.2 Payoff vector model.

When the outcome payoffs, θ_i, are stated in monetary terms (cost or profit), the decision rule or principle of choice is quite simple. If the alternatives are equal in all other respects, one would choose the alternative that minimizes cost or maximizes profit. In the case of cost, one would choose

$$\min_i \{\theta_i\} \quad \text{for } i = 1, 2, \ldots, m.$$

For profit, one would choose

$$\max_i \{\theta_i\} \quad \text{for } i = 1, 2, \ldots, m.$$

It is often not possible to accept the premise that only the cost or the profit differences are important, with intangibles and irreducibles having little or no effect. Unquantifiable nonmonetary factors may be significant enough to outweigh calculated costs or profit differences among alternatives. In other cases, the outcome is not easily expressed in monetary terms, or even in quantitative terms of some other effectiveness measure, such as time, percent of market, and so forth. Valid qualitative comparisons may be made when the quantitative outcomes cannot stand alone and/or when the outcomes are nonquantitative.

The use of outcome scales often makes possible a somewhat rational choice from among a number of nonquantifiable alternatives, each with an outcome rating determined by expert opinion, estimation, history, or other means.

Foremost among these are ordinal comparisons. Where intangibles and irreducibles are significant, ranking each outcome above or below every other outcome leads to a preferred choice. To do this, each outcome can be compared to a common standard, or the outcome can be paired and compared. As an example of the paired approach, suppose that four alternatives are assumed to lead (with certainty) to four outcomes $\theta_1, \theta_2, \theta_3$, and θ_4. Suppose further that the six possible pairs are arranged according to preference as follows:[2]

$$\theta_1 > \theta_3 \quad \theta_2 > \theta_3 \quad \theta_2 > \theta_1$$
$$\theta_2 > \theta_4 \quad \theta_3 > \theta_4 \quad \theta_1 > \theta_4.$$

In these comparisons, θ_2 is preferred three times; θ_1 twice; θ_3 once; and θ_4 not at all. Accordingly, the preference ranking is

$$\theta_2 > \theta_1 > \theta_3 > \theta_4.$$

Thus far in this book, only certainty has been assumed. The mathematical programming models of Part II were formulated and optimized as though only a single known future exists. In the next two sections, some models are presented for decision alternatives under risk and uncertainty. Then, at selected points in subsequent chapters, models incorporating probabilistic and other approaches for handling risk and uncertainty will be developed.

7.3 DECISIONS UNDER RISK

The lack of certainty about future outcomes makes decision making one of the most difficult tasks faced by individuals, by business and industry, and by governmental agencies. Decision making under risk occurs when the decision maker does not suppress acknowledged ignorance about the future, but makes it explicit through the assignment of probabilities. Such probabilities may be based on experimental evidence, expert opinion, subjective judgment, or a combination of these.

It is the incorporation of probabilities that classifies a decision situation as occurring under risk. Consider the following example. A computer systems firm has the opportunity to bid on two related contracts being advertised by a municipality. The first pertains to the selection and installation of hardware for a central computing facility together with required software. The second involves the development of a distributed computing network involving the selection and installation of hardware and software. The firm may be awarded either contract C_1 or contract C_2, or both contract C_1 and C_2. Thus, there are three possible outcomes.

Careful consideration of the possible approaches leads to the identification of five alternatives. The first is for the firm to subcontract the hardware selection

---

[2]The symbol $>$ is used to indicate that the outcome identified first is preferred to its counterpart.

and installation, but to develop the software itself. The second is for the firm to subcontract the software development, but to select and install the hardware itself. The third is for the firm to handle both the hardware and software tasks itself. The fourth is for the firm to bid jointly with a partner firm on both the hardware and software projects. The fifth alternative is for the firm to serve only as project manager, subcontracting all hardware and software tasks.

With the possible outcomes and various alternatives identified, the next step is to determine payoff values. Also to be determined are the probabilities for each of the three futures, where the sum of these probabilities must be unity. Suppose that these determinations lead to the payoff profits and probabilities given in Table 7.1.

Table 7.1. DECISION ALTERNATIVE MATRIX (Payoffs in Thousands of Dollars)

Probability: Future:	(0.3) C_1	(0.2) C_2	(0.5) $C_1 + C_2$
Alternative A_1	100	100	400
A_2	−200	150	600
A_3	0	200	500
A_4	100	300	200
A_5	−400	100	200

Table 7.1 is structured in accordance with the format of the payoff matrix model exhibited in Figure 7.1. It is observed that the firm anticipates a profit of $100,000 if alternative A_1 is chosen and contract C_1 is secured. If contract C_2 is secured, the profit would also be $100,000. However, if both contract C_1 and C_2 are secured, the profit anticipated is $400,000. Similar information is exhibited for the other alternatives, with each row of the payoff matrix representing the outcome expected for each state of nature (column) for a particular alternative.

Elimination of Dominance. Before proceeding to the application of criteria for the choice from among alternatives, the payoff matrix should be examined for dominance. Any alternatives that are clearly not preferred, regardless of the state of nature which occurs, may be dropped from consideration. If the payoffs for alternative x are better than the payoffs for alternative y for all possible futures, alternative x is said to *dominate* alternative y, and y can be eliminated as a possible choice.

The computer systems firm, facing the payoff matrix of Table 7.1, may eliminate A_5 from consideration since it is dominated by all other alternatives. This means that the possible choice of serving only as project manager is inferior to each and every one of the other alternatives, regardless of the way in which the projects are awarded. Therefore, the payoff matrix can be reduced to that given in Table 7.2. The decision criteria in the sections that follow may be used to assist in the selection from among alternatives A_1 through A_4.

Table 7.2. REDUCED PAYOFF MATRIX (Thousands of Dollars)

Probability: Future:	(0.3) C_1	(0.2) C_2	(0.5) $C_1 + C_2$
Alternative A_1	100	100	400
A_2	−200	150	600
A_3	0	200	500
A_4	100	300	200

The Aspiration Level Criterion. Some form of aspiration level exists in most personal and business decision making. An aspiration level is some desired level of achievement such as profit, or some undesirable result level to be avoided, such as loss. In decision making under risk, the aspiration level criterion involves selecting some level of achievement that is to be met, followed by a selection of that alternative which maximizes the probability of achieving the stated aspiration level.

The computer systems firm is now at the point of selecting from among alternatives A_1 through A_4, as presented in the reduced payoff matrix of Table 7.2. Under the aspiration level criterion, management must set a minimum aspiration level for profit and possibly a maximum aspiration level for loss. Suppose that the profit level is set to be at least $400,000 and the loss level is set to be no more than $100,000. Under these aspiration level choices, alternatives A_1, A_2, and A_3 qualify as to profit potential, but alternative A_2 fails the loss test and must be eliminated. The choice could now be made between A_1 and A_3 by some other criterion, even though both satisfy the aspiration level criterion.

The Most Probable Future Criterion. A basic human tendency is to focus on the most probable outcome from among several that could occur. This approach to decision making suggests that all except the most probable future be disregarded. Although somewhat equivalent to decision making under certainty this criterion works well when the most probable future has a significantly high probability so as to partially "dominate."

Under the most probable future criterion, the computer systems firm would focus its selection process from among the four alternatives on the profits associated with the future designated $C_1 + C_2$ (both contracts awarded). This is because the probability of this future occurring is 0.5, the most probable possibility. Alternative A_2 is preferred by this approach.

The most probable future criterion could be applied to select between A_1 and A_3, as identified under the aspiration level criterion. If this is done, the firm would choose alternative A_3.

The Expected Value Criterion. Many decision makers strive to make choices that will maximize expected profit or minimize expected loss. This is ordinarily justified in repetitive situations where the choice is to be made over and over again with increasing confidence that the calculated expected outcome will be achieved. This criterion is viewed with caution only when the payoff consequences of possible outcomes are disproportionately large, making a result that deviates from the expected outcome a distinct possibility.

The calculation of the expected value requires weighting all payoffs by their probabilities of occurrence. These weighted payoffs are then summed across all futures for each alternative. For the computer systems firm, alternatives A_1 through A_4 yield the following expected values (in thousands):

A_1: $\$100(0.3) + \$100(0.2) + \$400(0.5) = \$250$

A_2: $\$-200(0.3) + \$150(0.2) + \$600(0.5) = \$270$

A_3: $\$0(0.3) + \$200(0.2) + \$500(0.5) = \$290$

A_4: $\$100(0.3) + \$300(0.2) + \$200(0.5) = \$190$.

From this analysis it is clear that alternative A_3 would be selected. Further, if this criterion were to be used to resolve the choice of either A_1 or A_3 under the aspiration level approach, the choice would be alternative A_3.

Summary of Alternative Selections. It is evident that there is no one best selection when these criteria are utilized for decision making under risk. The decision made is dependent on the decision criterion adopted by the decision maker. For the example of this section, the alternatives selected under each criterion were:

Aspiration level criterion: A_1 or A_3

Most probable future criterion: A_2

Expected value criterion: A_3

If the application of the latter two criteria to the resolution of A_1 or A_3 chosen under the aspiration level criterion is accepted as valid, then A_3 is preferred twice and A_2 once. From this it might be appropriate to suggest that A_3 is the best alternative arising from the use of these three criteria.

7.4 DECISIONS UNDER UNCERTAINTY

It may be inappropriate or impossible to assign probabilities to the several futures identified for a given decision situation. Often no meaningful data are available from which probabilities may be developed. In other instances the decision maker may be unwilling to assign a subjective probability, as is the case when the future could prove to be unpleasant. When probabilities are not available for assignment to future events, the situation is classified as decision making under uncertainty.

As compared with decision making under certainty and under risk, decisions under uncertainty are made in a more abstract environment. In this section several decision criteria will be applied to the example of Section 7.3 to illustrate the formal approaches that are available.

The Laplace Criterion. Suppose that the computer systems firm is unwilling to assess the states of nature in terms of probabilities. Specifically, the firm is unwilling to differentiate between the likelihood at acquiring contract 1, contract 2, and contract 1 and contract 2. In the absence of these probabilities one might reason that each possible state of nature is as likely to occur as any other. The rationale of this assumption is that there is no stated basis for one state of nature to be more likely than any other. This is called the *Laplace principle* or the *principle of insufficient reason* based on the philosophy that nature is assumed to be indifferent.

Under the Laplace principle, the probability of the occurrence of each future state of nature is assumed to be $1/n$, where n is the number of possible future states. To select the best alternative one would compute the arithmetic average for each. For the payoff matrix of Table 7.2 this is accomplished as shown in Table 7.3. Alternative A_3 results in a maximum profit of $233,000 and would be selected.

Table 7.3. COMPUTATION OF AVERAGE PAYOFF (Thousands of Dollars)

Alternative	Average Payoff
A_1	($100 + $100 + $400) ÷ 3 = $200
A_2	($−200 + $150 + $600) ÷ 3 = $183
A_3	($0 + $200 + $500) ÷ 3 = $233
A_4	($100 + $300 + $200) ÷ 3 = $200

The Maximin and Maximax Rules. Two simple decision rules are available for dealing with decision under uncertainty. The first is the *maximin* rule, based on an extremely pessimistic view of the outcome of nature. The use of this rule would be justified if it is judged that nature will do its worst. The second is the *maximax* rule, based on an extremely optimistic view of the outcome of nature. Use of this rule is justified if it is judged that nature will do its best.

Because of the pessimism enbraced by the maximin rule, its application will lead to the alternative that assures the best of the worst possible outcomes. If θ_{ij} is used to represent the payoff for the ith alternative and the jth state of nature, the required computation is

$$\max_i \{\min_j \theta_{ij}\}.$$

Consider the decision situation described by the payoff matrix of Table 7.2. The application of the maximin rule requires that the minimum value in each row be selected. Then the maximum value is identified from these and associated with the alternative that would produce it. This procedure is illustrated in Table 7.4. Selection of either alternative A_1 or A_4 assures the firm of a payoff of at least $100,000 regardless of the outcome of nature.

Table 7.4. PAYOFF BY THE MAXIMIN RULE
(Thousands of Dollars)

Alternative	$\text{Min}_j \theta_{ij}$
A_1	$ 100
A_2	−200
A_3	0
A_4	100

The optimism of the maximax rule is in sharp contrast to the pessimism of the maximin rule. Its application will choose the alternative that assures the best of the best possible outcomes. As before, if θ_{ij} represents the payoff for the ith alternative and the jth state of nature, the required computation is

$$\max_i \{\max_j \theta_{ij}\}.$$

Consider the decision situation of Table 7.2 again. The application of the maximax rule requires that the maximum value in each row be selected. Then the maximum value is identified from these and associated with the alternative that would produce it. This procedure is illustrated in Table 7.5. Selection of alternative A_2 is indicated. Thus, the decision maker may receive a payoff of $600,000 if nature is benevolent.

Table 7.5. PAYOFF BY THE MAXIMAX RULE
(Thousands of Dollars)

Alternative	$\text{Max}_j \theta_{ij}$
A_1	$400
A_2	600
A_3	500
A_4	300

A decision maker who chooses the maximin rule considers only the worst possible occurrence for each alternative and selects that alternative which promises the best of the worst possible outcomes. In the example where A_1 was chosen, the firm would be assured of a payoff of at least $100,000, but it could not receive a payoff any greater than $400,000. Or, if A_4 were chosen, the firm could not receive a payoff any greater than $300,000. Conversely, the firm that chooses the maximax rule is optimistic and decides solely on the basis of the highest payoff offered for each alternative. Accordingly, in the example in which A_2 was chosen, the firm faces the possibility of a loss of $200,000 while seeking a payoff of $600,000.

The Hurwicz Criterion. Because the decision rules presented above are extreme, they are shunned by many decision makers. Most people have a degree of optimism or pessimism somewhere between the extremes. A third approach to decision making under uncertainty involves an index of relative optimism and pessimism. It is called the *Hurwicz rule*.

A compromise between optimism and pessimism is embraced in the Hurwicz rule by allowing the decision maker to select an index of optimism, α, such that $0 \leq \alpha \leq 1$. When $\alpha = 0$ the decision maker is pessimistic about the outcome of nature, while an $\alpha = 1$ indicates optimism about nature. Once α is selected, the Hurwicz rule requires the computation of

$$\max_i \{\alpha[\max_j \theta_{ij}] + (1-\alpha)[\min_j \theta_{ij}]\}, \quad (7.1)$$

where θ_{ij} is the payoff for the ith alternative and the jth state of nature.

As an example of the Hurwicz rule, consider the payoff matrix of Table 7.2 with $\alpha = 0.2$. The required computations are shown in Table 7.6 and alternative A_1 would be chosen by the firm.

Table 7.6. PAYOFF BY THE HURWICZ RULE WITH $\alpha = 0.2$
(Thousands of Dollars)

Alternative	$\alpha[\max_j \theta_{ij}] + (1-\alpha)[\min_j \theta_{ij}]$
A_1	0.2($400) + 0.8($100) = $160
A_2	0.2($600) + 0.8($-200) = $-40
A_3	0.2($500) + 0.8(0) = $100
A_4	0.2($300) + 0.8($100) = $140

Additional insight into the Hurwicz rule can be obtained by graphing each alternative for all values of α between zero and one. This makes it possible to identify the value of α for which each alternative would be favored. Such a graph is shown in Figure 7.3. It may be observed that alternative A_1 yields a maximum expected payoff for all values of $\alpha \leq \frac{1}{2}$. Alternative A_3 exhibits a maximum for $\frac{1}{2} \leq \alpha \leq \frac{2}{3}$ and alternative A_2 gives a maximum for $\frac{2}{3} \leq \alpha \leq 1$. There is no value of α for which alternative A_4 would be best except at $\alpha = 0$, where it is as good an alternative as A_1.

When $\alpha = 0$, the Hurwicz rule gives the same result as the maximin rule, and when $\alpha = 1$, it is the same as the maximax rule. This may be shown for the case where $\alpha = 0$ as

$$\max_i \{0[\max_j \theta_{ij}] + (1-0)[\min_j \theta_{ij}]\} = \max_i [\min_j \theta_{ij}].$$

For the case where $\alpha = 1$,

$$\max_i \{1[\max_j \theta_{ij}] + (1-1)[\min_j \theta_{ij}]\} = \max_i [\max_j \theta_{ij}].$$

Thus, the maximin rule and the maximax rule are special cases of the Hurwicz rule.

The philosophy behind the Hurwicz rule is that focus on the most extreme outcomes or consequences bounds or brackets the decision. By use of this rule, the decision maker may weight the extremes in such a manner as to reflect their relative importance.

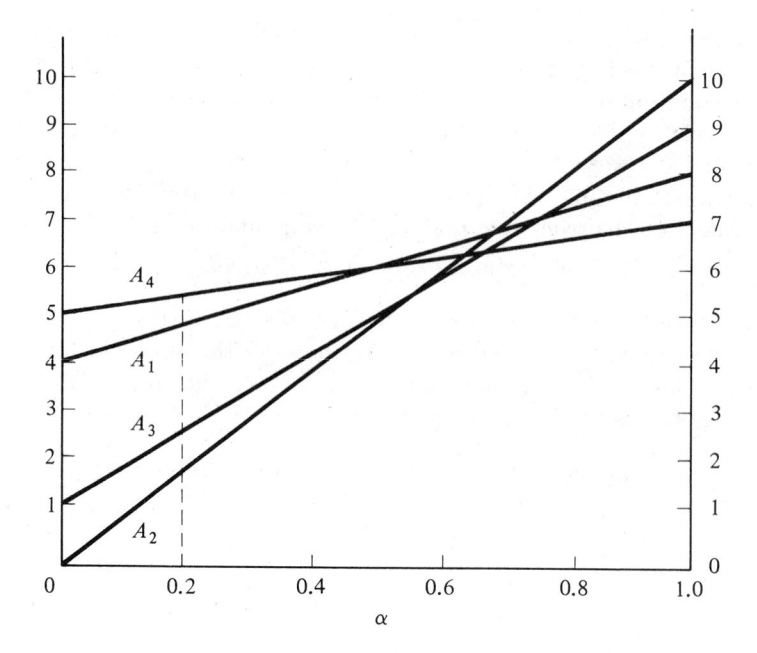

Figure 7.3 Values for the Hurwicz rule representing four alternatives.

The Minimax Regret Criterion. A decision maker will "regret" the selection of an alternative if a state of nature occurs such that he or she could have done better by having selected another alternative. This regret is the difference between the payoff that could have been achieved with perfect knowledge of the future and the payoff that was actually received from the alternative chosen. The *minimax regret rule* is based on the premise that a decision maker wishes to avoid any regret, or at least to minimize the maximum regret resulting from a decision.

Application of the minimax regret rule requires the formulation of a regret matrix. This is accomplished by identifying the maximum payoff for each state (column). Next, each payoff in the column is subtracted from the maximum payoff identified. This is repeated for each column. For the payoff matrix of Table 7.2 the maximum payoffs are $100, $300, and $600 for C_1, C_2, and C_1 and C_2, respectively. Thus, the regrets for C_1, applicable to alternatives A_1 through A_4, are $100 − $100 = 0; $100 − ($−200) = $300; $100 − $0 = $100; $100 − $100 = $0. Repeating this computation for each state results in the regret matrix shown in Table 7.7.

If the regret values are designated R_{ij} for the ith alternative and the jth state, the minimax regret rule requires the computation of

$$\min_i \{\max_j R_{ij}\}.$$

Table 7.7. REGRET MATRIX (Thousands of Dollars)

Alternative	State of Nature		
	C_1	C_2	C_1 and C_2
A_1	0	200	200
A_2	300	150	0
A_3	100	100	100
A_4	0	0	400

Table 7.8. PAYOFF BY THE MINIMAX REGRET RULE
(Thousands of Dollars)

Alternative	$\underset{j}{Max}\ R_{ij}$
A_1	$200
A_2	300
A_3	100
A_4	400

This computation is shown in Table 7.8. Selection of alternative A_3 assures the firm of a maximum regret of $100,000.

A decision maker who uses the minimax regret rule as a decision criterion will make that decision which will result in the least possible opportunity loss. Individuals who have a strong aversion to criticism would be tempted to apply this rule since it puts them in a relatively safe position with respect to the future states of nature which might occur. Thus, this criterion has a conservative underlying philosophy.

Summary of Alternative Selections. As was the case for the decision criteria applied for decision making under risk, it is evident that there is no one best criterion for decision making under uncertainty. The decision made is dependent on the decision criterion adopted by the decision maker. For the examples of this section, the alternatives selected were:

Laplace criterion: A_3
Maximin criterion: A_1 or A_4
Maximax criterion: A_2
Hurwicz criterion ($\alpha = 0.2$): A_1
Minimax regret criterion: A_3

Examination of the selections recommended by the five decision rules indicates that each has its own merit. Several factors may influence a decision maker's choice of a rule in a given decision situation. The decision maker's attitude toward uncertainty (pessimistic or optimistic) and his or her personal utility function are important influences. Thus, the choice of a particular decision rule for a given decision situation must be based on subjective judgment.

7.5 GAME DECISION MODELS

This section presents decision models which are generally similar to those of the preceding sections. The main difference is that the payoffs result from the actions of a rational goal-seeking opponent, rather than a passive opponent referred to as "nature." Contract negotiations between labor and management, decisions made by military commanders in combat, price–volume negotiations in procurement, and market-share interactions between competing firms are examples of conditions under which conflict occurs. Competitive situations such as these can be partially understood by the application of game models.

Game models may be classified into two general types which depend on how payoffs occur for the players. If each game or positive payoff for one player comes at the expense or negative payoff for the other player, the net payoff resulting from any action is zero. This situation is called a *zero-sum game* in that one player's gains are equal to the losses of the other player. If one player's gain is not necessarily another player's loss, a *non-zero-sum game* is defined. It is quite easy to classify a game situation as zero-sum or non-zero-sum when the payoffs are expressed in monetary terms, but difficult when payoffs require utility comparisons between individuals. Only zero-sum games are presented in this section with payoffs expressed as costs or profits.

The Payoff Matrix. A general payoff matrix for a two-person zero-sum game is shown in Figure 7.4. Player A has m available actions and player B has n. The matrix entries $p_{11}, p_{12}, \ldots, p_{mn}$ represent payoffs to player A. These same entries are payoff outcomes to player B, but of opposite magnitude. That is, if action a_2 is taken by player A and action b_1 is taken by player B, the payoff amount p_{21} gained (lost) by player A is lost (gained) by player B. This condition must exist for the game to meet the zero-sum definition.

		Player B			
a_i \ b_j		b_1	b_2	$\cdots$	b_n
Player A	a_1	p_{11}	p_{12}	$\cdots$	p_{1n}
	a_2	p_{21}	p_{22}	$\cdots$	p_{2n}
	$\vdots$	$\vdots$	$\vdots$		$\vdots$
	a_m	p_{m1}	p_{m2}	$\cdots$	p_{mn}

Figure 7.4 Payoff matrix model.

The payoff matrix model for a two-person zero-sum game is based on some assumptions beyond that of zero-sum for payoffs. It is assumed that each player has a finite number of alternative actions. Each player knows in advance all available alternatives on both sides. All gains or losses are quantitative and expressible as a single number. Finally, both players are assumed to know in advance all outcomes that can occur from each possible action taken by the other player.

Game models allow for repeated decisions to reflect competitive interaction. This is in contrast to the single decision approach, where the decision maker is dealing with states of nature. An objective of a game model is to prescribe a strategy for choosing from among alternative actions that are the same each time the game is played. Such a strategy is classified as a *pure strategy* which, if optimal for both players, identified the game as having a *saddle point*. Games that do not have a saddle point require each player to choose actions according to a specified probability distribution in order to implement optimal strategies. This is classified as a *mixed strategy* situation.

Games with Saddle Points. Consider a zero-sum game in which each player has four possible courses of action as given in Table 7.9. The payoffs exhibited are assumed to be monetary amounts equally desired by player A and player B. If player A selects alternative a_2 and player B selects alternative b_3, the outcome is a gain of $4,000 for A and a loss of $4,000 for B. Positive entries in Table 7.9 are gains for A and negative entries are gains for B. But in

Table 7.9. GAME WITH SADDLE POINT

		Player B			
		b_1	b_2	b_3	b_4
Player A	a_1	$ 5,000	$ 4,500	$−2,500	$−1,000
	a_2	−2,000	−3,000	4,000	−1,000
	a_3	2,500	1,000	3,000	500
	a_4	1,000	3,000	−3,000	−2,000

either case, the sum of the payoffs for any choice of alternatives is zero. The amount lost by one player is the amount gained by the other making this game zero-sum.

As with other decision models, the first step in the analysis is to look for *dominance*. In game matrices the rows and the columns represent alternatives making it necessary to check both. If one dominant relationship is found, another may be revealed. This is the case with the example of Table 7.9. An examination of the alternatives available to player B reveals that b_2 is preferred to b_1 for all outcomes except for the entry in the last row. But from the alternatives available to player A it is evident that the last row, a_4, would never be selected since a_1 is always preferred. Therefore, both b_2 and a_4 can be eliminated from the matrix giving the reduced game matrix of Table 7.10. This reduction,

Table 7.10. REDUCED GAME MATRIX WITH SADDLE POINT IDENTIFIED

		Player B			
		b_1	b_3	b_4	Row Min
	a_1	$ 5,000	$−2,500	$−1,000	$−2,500
Player A	a_2	−2,000	4,000	−1,000	−2,000
	a_3	2,500	3,000	500	500 Maximin
	Col. Max	$ 5,000	$ 4,000	$500 Minimax	

due to dominance, is justified on the grounds that both players are intelligent. Player B would feel certain that player A would never use alternative a_4, making it unnecessary for him or her to use alternative b_2.

The next step is to search for a saddle point. A saddle point will be present if it is advantageous for both players to use pure strategies. It is identified by an outcome that is both the smallest number in its row and the largest number in its column. These smallest row numbers and largest column numbers are given with the matrix in Table 7.10. The outcome $500 at a_3, b_4 satisfies the saddle point requirement.

It is the players' motives that attach significance to the saddle point. Alternative a_1 is attractive to A because of the potential gain of $5,000. Likewise, alternative a_2 is attractive to A due to a potential gain of $4,000. However, B can assure A a loss of $1,000 by choosing b_4 whenever A chooses to use a_1 or a_2. A would be interested in a_3 because it cannot result in a negative outcome. B can minimize A's gain by again utilizing b_4. A recognizes the advantage b_4 affords B, and would select the alternative that minimizes B's gain. This alternative for A is a_3.

In this example, both players would use pure strategies. Player A would always employ alternative a_3 and player B would always employ alternative b_4. The result is a gain of $500 for A and a corresponding loss of $500 for B (zero sum). Thus, the *value of the game* is $500 as identified by the saddle point amount. The principle of choice is maximin-minimax in that A seeks the least of her minimum gains and B seeks the least of her maximum losses. This choice strategy is consistent with the conservative rational approach of maximizing gains or minimizing losses.

Games Without Saddle Points. When no saddle point exists, the players will utilize a *mixed strategy* approach. A mixed strategy involves the utilization of different alternatives for a fixed proportion of the plays, with each play being a random choice from among all available choices. The value of the game will be the average return that results from each player following an optimal mixed strategy.

As an example of a game without a saddle point, consider the two-player zero-sum game illustrated in Table 7.11 representing expected payoffs from market competition between two firms. The lack of a saddle point is confirmed

Table 7.11. GAME WITHOUT SADDLE POINT

		Firm B		Row Min	
		b_1	b_2		
Firm A	a_1	8%	−6%	−6%	
	a_2	4%	10%	4%	Maximin
Col. Max		8%	10%		
		Minimax			

by the maximin-minimax computation shown in the table. By choosing the maximin alternative (a_2), firm A will receive a payoff percentage increase in market share of at least 4%. If firm B chooses the minimax alternative (b_1), it is guaranteed a loss of market share no greater than 8%. From this it is evident that the value of this game, v, is between 4% and 8%, where maximin $\leq v \leq$ minimax.

Firm A, in considering the situation, would want to pursue a marketing strategy with a potential payoff greater than the maximin value of 4%. If the pure strategy a_2 is chosen, firm B will certainly choose b_1 to hold its market share loss to 4%. Alternatively, if firm A chooses the pure strategy a_1, firm B will counter by choosing b_2 and enjoy a market share gain of 6%. Accordingly, the best strategy for firm A is to keep firm B off balance by randomly selecting from a_1 and a_2 in accordance with some probability distribution.

By employing a mixed strategy, firm A can be assured of an expected payoff regardless of the actions of firm B. The possibility of firm A being outguessed by firm B can be eliminated by deriving an optimal mixed strategy. Let

$E(b_1)$ = expected payoff to firm A when firm B chooses strategy b_1

$E(b_2)$ = expected payoff to firm A when firm B chooses strategy b_2

$P(a_1)$ = probability that firm A chooses strategy a_1

$P(a_2)$ = probability that firm A chooses strategy a_2

The mixed strategy for firm A is $P(a_1)$ and $P(a_2)$, a probability distribution with $P(a_1) + P(a_2) = 1.00$. Further, $E(b_1)$ must be equal to $E(b_2)$ for firm A's payoff expectation to be independent of firm B's strategy.

Specific values for $E(b_1)$ and $E(b_2)$ can now be calculated from

$$E(b_1) = P(a_1)(p_{11}) + [1 - P(a_1)](p_{21}) \tag{7.2}$$

$$E(b_2) = P(a_1)(p_{12}) + [1 - P(a_1)](p_{22}) \tag{7.3}$$

where $p_{11}, \ldots, p_{22}$ are payoffs as illustrated in Figure 7.4. By utilizing the actual values for firm A and firm B given in Table 7.11, Equations (7.2) and (7.3) become

$$E(b_1) = P(a_1)(0.08) + [1 - P(a_1)](0.04)$$

$$E(b_2) = P(a_1)(-0.06) + [1 - P(a_1)](0.10).$$

Setting $E(b_1) = E(b_2)$ gives

$$P(a_1)(0.08) + [1 - P(a_1)](0.04) = P(a_1)(-0.06) + [1 - P(a_1)](0.10).$$

Solving for $P(a_1)$ yields

$$P(a_1)(0.08) + 0.04 - P(a_1)(0.04) = P(a_1)(-0.06) + 0.10 - P(a_1)(0.10)$$

$$P(a_1)(0.20) = 0.06$$

$$P(a_1) = 0.30$$

and

$$P(a_2) = 1 - P(a_1) = 1 - 0.30 = 0.7.$$

From the analysis above, firm A can proceed to implement strategy a_1, with probability 0.3 and strategy a_2 with probability 0.7. This is the optimal mixed strategy for firm A. It will yield an expected payoff greater than the maximin value of 4%. This expected payoff is

$$E(b_1) = 0.3(0.08) + 0.7(0.04) = 0.052$$

$$E(b_2) = 0.3(-0.06) + 0.7(0.10) = 0.052,$$

or 5.2%. Regardless of the strategy utilized by firm B, firm A will experience an average payoff of a 5.2% increase in market share by playing its optimal mixed strategy. Of course, firm A can gain as much as 8% or as little as 4% on any one play of the game.

The value of the game in this example is 5.2% to firm A and, since zero-sum was assumed, the value to firm B is -5.2%. There is an optimal strategy for firm B that guarantees a loss no greater than 5.2% on the average. This can be found by calculating

$$E(a_1) = P(b_1)(p_{11}) + [1 - P(b_1)](p_{12}) \tag{7.4}$$

$$E(a_2) = P(b_1)(p_{21}) + [1 - P(b_1)](p_{22}), \tag{7.5}$$

where $p_{11}, \ldots, p_{22}$ are payoffs as illustrated in Figure 7.4. By utilizing the actual values for firm B and firm A as given in Table 7.11, Equations (7.4) and (7.5) become

$$E(a_1) = P(b_1)(0.08) + [1 - P(b_1)](-0.06)$$

$$E(a_2) = P(b_1)(0.04) + [1 - P(b_1)](0.10).$$

Setting $E(a_1) = E(a_2)$ gives

$$P(b_1)(0.08) + [1 - P(b_1)](-0.06) = P(b_1)(0.04) + [1 - P(b_1)](0.10).$$

Solving for $P(b_1)$ yields

$$P(b_1)(0.08) - 0.06 + P(b_1)(0.06) = P(b_1)(0.04) + 0.10 - P(b_1)(0.10)$$

$$P(b_1)0.20 = 0.16$$

$$P(b_1) = 0.80$$

and

$$P(b_2) = 1 - P(b_1) = 1 - 0.80 = 0.2.$$

The optimal mixed strategy for firm B is to implement strategy b_1 with probability 0.8 and strategy b_2 with probability 0.2. This will yield an expected payoff loss for firm B less than the minimax value of 8%. This expected payoff is

$$E(a_1) = 0.8(0.08) + 0.2(-0.06) = 0.052$$
$$E(a_2) = 0.8(0.04) + 0.2(0.10) = 0.052,$$

or 5.2%, which is equal to the average payoff value for firm A. It is also positive since the payoff matrix was structured in terms of gains to firm A. Actually, the expected market gain by firm A of 5.2% is an expected market loss of 5.2% by firm B. Firm B can be guaranteed to lose no more than this average amount by implementing its optimal mixed strategy as derived above.

Optimal mixed strategies can be determined graphically for two-person 2 × 2 games like the example just presented. This is illustrated in Figure 7.5 from the perspective of firm A, although the perspective of firm B could have been used. The horizontal scale represents the probabilities $P(a_1)$ and $P(a_2)$ and the vertical scale represents transfers from firm A to firm B. Firm A's pure strategy of selecting a_1 is shown on the left and firm A's pure strategy of selecting a_2 is shown on the right. Lines b_1 and b_2 represent the two strategies available

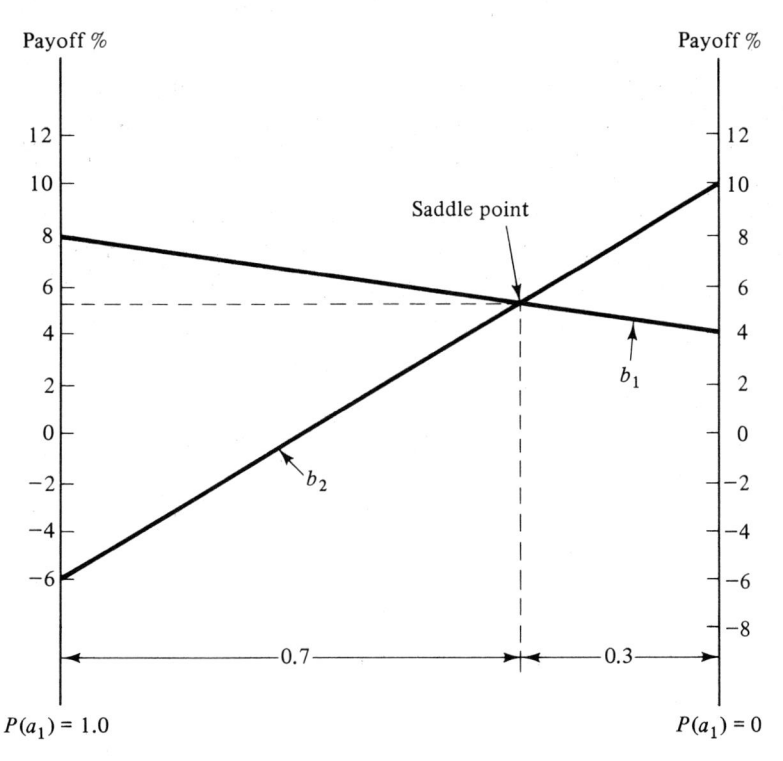

Figure 7.5 Graphical game solution.

to firm B. Points between the vertical lines which lie on b_1 and b_2 represent all possible mixed strategies for firm A. The optimal mixed strategy for firm A occurs where $E(b_1) = E(b_2)$, which is at the intersection of b_1 and b_2. This intersection identifies $P(a_1)$, $P(a_2)$, and the value of the game.

QUESTIONS

7.1. Formulate the payoff matrix for a hypothetical decision situation of your choice.

7.2. Formulate the payoff vector for a hypothetical decision situation under assumed certainty.

7.3. Discuss general linear programming as a decision under assumed certainty by formulating a payoff vector.

7.4. Develop an example to illustrate the application of paired outcomes in decision making among a number of nonquantifiable alternatives.

7.5. What approaches may be used to assign probabilities to future outcomes?

7.6. What is the role of dominance in decision making among alternatives?

7.7. Give an example of an aspiration level in decision making.

7.8. When would one follow the most probable future criterion in decision making?

7.9. What drawback exists in using the most probable future criterion?

7.10. How does the Laplace criterion for decision making under uncertainty actually convert the situation to decision making under risk?

7.11. Discuss the maximin and the minimax rules as special cases of the Hurwicz rule.

7.12. Under what condition would a decision maker want to minimize her maximum regret?

7.13. In what ways do game models differ from models for decision making under risk and uncertainty?

PROBLEMS

7.1. The cost of developing an internal training program for office automation is unknown but described by the following probability distribution:

Cost	Probability of Occurrence
$ 80,000	0.20
95,000	0.30
105,000	0.25
115,000	0.20
130,000	0.05

What is the expected cost of the course? What is the most probable cost? What is the maximum cost that will occur with a 95 percent assurance?

7.2. Net profit has been calculated for five investment opportunities under three possible futures. Which alternative should be selected under the most probable future criterion; the expected value criterion?

	(0.3) F_1	(0.2) F_2	(0.5) F_3
A_1	$ 100,000	$100,000	$380,000
A_2	−200,000	160,000	590,000
A_3	0	180,000	500,000
A_4	110,000	280,000	200,000
A_5	400,000	90,000	180,000

7.3. Daily positive and negative payoffs are given for five alternatives and five futures in the matrix below. Which alternative should be chosen to maximize the probability of receiving a payoff of at least 9? What choice would be made by using the most probable future criterion?

	(0.15) F_1	(0.20) F_2	(0.30) F_3	(0.20) F_4	(0.15) F_5
A_1	12	8	−4	0	9
A_2	10	0	5	10	16
A_3	6	5	10	15	−4
A_4	4	14	20	6	12
A_5	−8	22	12	4	9

7.4. The following matrix gives the payoffs in utiles (a measure of utility) for three alternatives and three possible states of nature.

		State of Nature		
		S_1	S_2	S_3
Alternative	A_1	50	80	80
	A_2	60	70	20
	A_3	90	30	60

Which alternative would be chosen under the Laplace principle? The maximin rule? The maximax rule? The Hurwicz rule with $\alpha = 0.75$? The minimax regret rule?

7.5. The following payoff matrix indicates the costs associated with three decision options and four states of nature.

		State of Nature			
		S_1	S_2	S_3	S_4
Option	T_1	20	25	30	35
	T_2	40	30	40	20
	T_3	10	60	30	25

Select the decision option that should be selected for the maximin rule; the maximax rule; the Laplace rule; the minimax regret rule; and the Hurwicz rule with $\alpha = 0.2$. How do the rules applied to the cost matrix differ from those that are applied to a payoff matrix of profits?

7.6. The following matrix gives the expected profit in thousands of dollars for five marketing strategies and five potential levels of sales.

		\multicolumn{5}{c}{Level of Sales}
		L_1	L_2	L_3	L_4	L_5
Strategy	M_1	10	20	30	40	50
	M_2	20	25	25	30	35
	M_3	50	40	5	15	20
	M_4	40	35	30	25	25
	M_5	10	20	25	30	20

Which marketing strategy would be chosen under the maximin rule? The maximax rule? The Hurwicz rule with $\alpha = 0.4$? The minimax regret rule?

7.7. Graph the Hurwicz rule for all values of α using the payoff matrix of Problem 7.6.

7.8. A firm has a sum of money to invest and has narrowed the possibilities to the following:

A_1: Invest in its own stock

A_2: Invest in blue chip stocks

A_3: Invest in government bonds

Three future states are being considered by the firm:

S_1: Economic progress

S_2: Economic stability

S_3: Economic recession

Analysis leads to the following rates of return in prospect:

	S_1	S_2	S_3
A_1	20	1	-6
A_2	9	8	0
A_3	4	4	4

(a) What course of action do the following decision criteria indicate: Laplace, maximin, maximax, and Hurwicz with $\alpha = 0.5$?
(b) Which investment is preferred? Why?

7.9. Determine the optimal strategy and the value of the following two-person zero-sum game:

4	6
-1	3

7.10. Determine the optimal strategy and the value of the following two-person zero-sum game:

-1	6
7	2

7.11. Two firms now share equally in the market for their two competing products. If no changes are made in the current advertising, the status quo will continue. However, both firms are planning advertising campaign modifications and the firm with the strongest campaign will capture a majority percentage of the market. Each firm will strive to select appropriate advertising media and knows that 50 percent of the potential customers can be reached by radio, 30 percent through television, and 20 percent through newspapers. Formulate this competitive situation as a two-person zero-sum game. Does the game have a saddle point?

8

Models for Production Operations

Business and industrial organizations come into being as a means for creating and exchanging utility, often through the establishment and coordination of production operations. This coordination alters physical inputs to create products and services intended to satisfy human wants. Because of the utility that may be ascribed to the goods and services produced, the organization receives an income from their exchange. But there are costs associated with the acquisition and employment of inputs to the production process. To the extent that the income received exceeds cost, the economic efficiency of the process will exceed 100 percent.

This chapter presents some economic decision models for production operations. Each model illustrates some aspect of the need for economic efficiency to exceed 100 percent as a necessary but not sufficient condition for business success. As explained in Chapter 1, an organization will endure only as long as its organizational efficiency exceeds unity. Although economic models can increase economic efficiency, the real test must be the degree to which organizational efficiency is enhanced thereby.

8.1 THE PRODUCTION SYSTEM

The *production system* may be described as a process for converting some combination of inputs to one or more forms of output. This conversion process may be quite simple, but is usually very complex. An essential feature of the process is the conversion of inputs through altering physical factors, thus creating an output of increased utility. This section describes the inputs and outputs associated with a production system and presents the concept of economic efficiency.

Inputs. Many distinct classes of elements serve as inputs to a production system. It is not feasible to enumerate all of these, but a broad classification will be useful.

An organization consists of the coordinated activities of people. The labor input must be remunerated for its contributions. Human contributions to the production process can be divided into the subclasses of direct labor, indirect labor, and supervision. There may also be an investigation and research group concerned with the development of new products and processes. Expenditures may also be made for promotional effort in an attempt to increase consumer demand for the goods and services. Finally, there will be a management group responsible for coordination of the production process itself.

Many different forms of materials may be required to meet the objectives of the organization. These are usually classified into the two categories of direct material and indirect material. In the first category are the raw materials physically altered and directly converted into finished goods and services. In the second category are materials that may be employed and consumed in support of the production process.

Producer goods are a third major input to the production system. These may include land and buildings as well as the equipment directly employed in physically altering the input materials. Most producer goods are consumed in the production process. This consumption, and the eventual necessity for replacement, must be treated as an input element requiring the outlay of capital. The life of equipment may vary from only a short time to a period of many years. Depreciation during this life must be estimated and included as a cost of production.

Besides the input elements of labor, material, and producer goods, it is necessary to consider capital as an input and then to consider interest charges on this capital as a cost. Most firms require the use of capital to meet operating expenses, and interest charges represent a rental for the use of this money. In addition to interest charges as an outlay, most firms pay taxes to compensate for government services. Although interest and taxes may not have the same physical aspects as labor, material, and equipment, they are costs of production.

Outputs. The outputs of business organizations are as diverse as the products and services that possess utility. Usually, the specification of an output is the first step in the formation of an industrial organization. An existing organization may, however, search for and find an additional product or service that it may produce and market.

Goods and services are sold in a marketplace that is dynamic. New opportunities continually develop while existing products and services may lose their utility for people. A new material or a new process may suggest an output that was previously uneconomical or technologically unfeasible. Shifting demand may end the market for an existing product and require the development of a replacement product. The utility of an existing product or service, or the potential utility of a proposed product, will be of vital concern to the business organization.

Once a product or service has been specified, the total income resulting from sales will depend on the price of each unit and the total number of units sold. These two factors are not independent. A decision in regard to each must be based on estimates that may require market surveys and forecasting techniques.

Economic Efficiency. The production system may be viewed as an input–output process, as illustrated in Figure 8.1. Although this illustration does not include intangible inputs and outputs, which are subjectively evaluated by the contributors, it provides a useful simplification of a complex system. Figure 8.1 is actually only one part of the illustration that would be required to describe the organized activity associated with production.

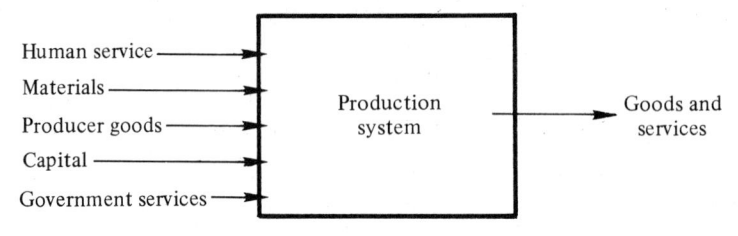

Figure 8.1 Schematic illustration of the production system.

If the income received for the goods and services produced exceeds the cost of the required input elements, a profit will result. This is a fundamental measure of success. Another measure is that of economic efficiency expressed as

$$\text{economic efficiency} = \frac{\text{income}}{\text{cost}}.$$

It is well known that physical efficiencies cannot exceed 100 percent. However, economic efficiencies can exceed 100 percent and must do so for economic undertakings to be successful.

Economic efficiency is related to physical efficiency. A plant to produce electricity from natural gas may be profitable in economic terms even though its physical efficiency in converting units of energy in natural gas to electrical energy may be relatively low. In a certain plant, assume that the physical efficiency is only 40 percent. If the output Btu (British thermal units, a measure of heat consumption) in the form of electrical energy have an economic value of $14.50 per million and the input Btu in the form of natural gas have an economic value of $2.40, then

$$\text{economic efficiency} = \frac{\text{Btu output} \times \text{value of electricity}}{\text{Btu input} \times \text{value of natural gas}}$$

$$= 0.40\left(\frac{\$14.50}{\$2.40}\right) = 242 \text{ percent.}$$

Business activities are feasible only if they attain economic efficiencies greater than 100 percent. In production, the economic worth per unit of physical output must always be greater than the economic cost per unit of physical input. Consequently, economic efficiency must depend more on the income and cost per unit of physical outputs and inputs than on physical efficiency. Physical efficiency is significant, but only to the extent that it contributes to economic efficiency. Further, economic efficiency is significant through its contribution to organizational efficiency.

8.2 CLASSIFICATION OF PRODUCTION COST

A production process is an intermediate step in an input–output system and acts as the converter. It is responsible for the increased utility attached to the output of the system. The outlay of money in return for input elements is considered the cost of this operation. Costs can be attributed to human service, materials, and producer goods. Also, costs arise from the use of capital and government services. Each of these costs must be the subject of careful study.

Production costs may be classified across another pertinent dimension: that of their independence or dependence upon the level of production. In the first class are fixed costs, and in the second class are variable costs. In addition, costs can be viewed in the framework of cost extensions for added levels of production. The latter view of costs leads to the concept of incremental cost analysis. Fixed, variable, and incremental costs are considered in this section.

Fixed Costs. A cost thought to remain fairly constant over a complete range of operational activity is considered to be fixed. Cost items in this class are more or less fixed in amount over a time period, such as a year, regardless of the number of units produced. In general, managerial expenses as well as sales, promotional, and research inputs are independent of production levels. The cost of some indirect materials, together with depreciation and rental expenses, may be regarded as fixed. In addition, interest charges on capital will be constant if the capital requirements do not change with the level of production activity.

Fixed costs usually arise because of preparation for the future. A machine is bought now so that labor costs may be reduced. Materials are purchased in large quantities and stored in order to avoid idleness of production facilities and people. Research is carried out with no immediate benefit in view in hope that it will pay in the long run. Investments that give rise to fixed costs are made in the present with the anticipation that they will be recovered with a profit in the future.

Variable Costs. A second classification of costs assumes that the consumption of some input elements will increase in a linear relationship with increases in production. Thus, the cost per unit of output will be a constant. Direct labor and direct material are typically considered as input elements which can be linearly related to output. Their cost will therefore vary with the production quantity. To some extent, indirect labor and supervision can be classified in this category.

Classifying costs as either fixed or variable permits a rather definitive cost-output projection. In practice many costs are not so easily defined. Some costs are a mixture of fixed and variable expenses, with the latter not linearly related to output. A production increase may require overtime labor input at premium rates. Depreciation may be partially dependent on time and partially dependent on wear and tear. Obsolescence is particularly difficult to categorize. Some expenses may be expected to follow one pattern over a range of output and then change as a second range is entered. As an example, utility expenses may decrease as a lower rate is attained at a higher level of power consumption. Material costs may increase with output if less efficient production facilities are put into operation.

Most costs should properly be considered as neither fixed nor variable. Nevertheless, they may be placed in one class or the other if the approximation does not result in a great sacrifice in accuracy. Alternatively, a cost may be prorated with a portion assigned to one class and the remainder to the other. The advantage to be gained in simple projections of cost-output relationships may warrant this dichotomous classification system.

A schematic representation of fixed and variable costs is given in Figure 8.2. Note that the fixed costs are assumed constant over the appropriate range of output, whereas the variable costs are linearly increasing over this range. In some cases, the fixed costs will be quite significant in comparison to the unit variable cost. In other cases the fixed costs may be negligible. Where these two cases produce the same product or service output, analyses can be made and the selection of an alternative will rest on the anticipated total cost. This will be treated in the next section.

Incremental Costs. The use of incremental analysis requires that the outcome of alternative courses of action be estimated in terms of changes in revenue in comparison to changes in cost. With this reasoning, a decision is

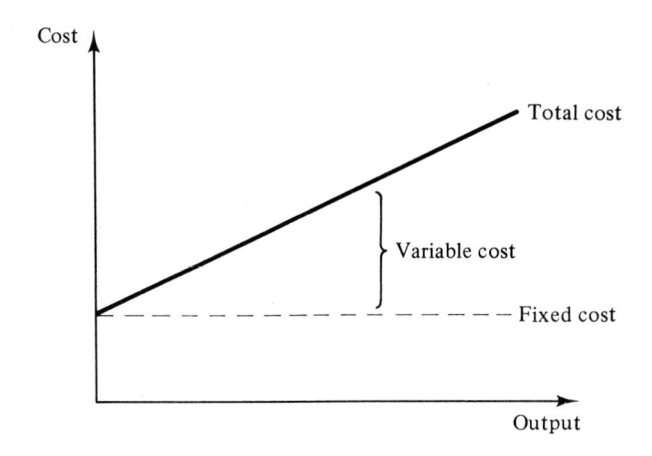

Figure 8.2 Fixed and variable portions of a total cost function.

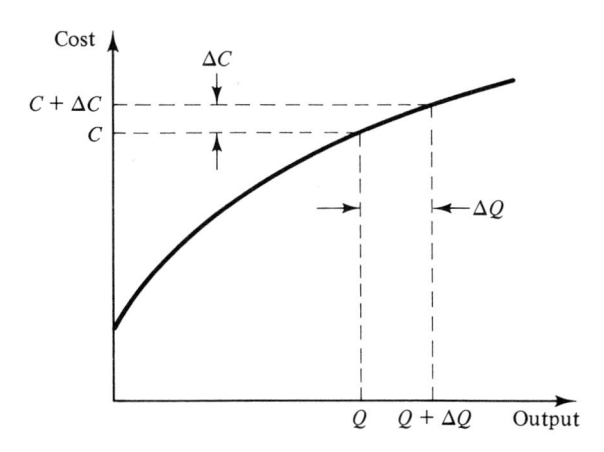

Figure 8.3 Incremental cost ΔC, resulting from the incremental output ΔQ.

profitable if it increases revenue more than it increases cost. The measurement of incremental cost is illustrated in Figure 8.3.

Incremental cost analysis can be useful, provided that some discretion is used in its application. Consider the following example. The total cost of producing 300 units per year is $3,600. This gives an average cost of $12 per unit. The opportunity of selling an additional 10 units for a total of $100 has presented itself. At $10 per unit this would appear to result in a loss of $2 per unit. The total cost of producing 310 units has, however, been estimated to be $3,650. Then, using the incremental cost concept, $\Delta C = \$3{,}650 - \$3{,}600$ or $50 and $\Delta Q = 110 - 100$, or 10, units. The incremental cost would be $\Delta C/\Delta Q = \$50/10$, or $5 per unit. Thus, the sale of an additional 10 units would result in a profit of $5 per unit rather than a loss of $2 per unit. This profit would not have been realized unless the incremental cost of production had been recognized and considered.

Caution must be exercised in the use of the incremental cost concept. Although a decision is sound if it increases revenue more than cost, or reduces cost more than revenue, the total effect of the decision must be evaluated. In the preceding example, customers may learn of the dual price structure and resent paying the higher price in subsequent transactions. A second lot of 10 units may be immediately requested at the same price of $10 per unit. This added output may require additional fixed costs to add to production capacity. Alternatively, a subsequent order may have been placed at the original price, and now this order cannot be met because this last sale exhausted available capacity.

Incremental analysis is actually a method of reasoning whereby receipts and expenditures that have already occurred are considered to be beyond control of the decision maker. Subsequent receipts and expenditures are evaluated only in terms of their added amounts, and action is taken in accordance with their relative magnitudes.

8.3 PRODUCTION QUANTITY DECISIONS

The profit or loss that results from production operations depends on the income received from the sale of product and the cost of production. In many cases, profit can be maximized by selecting a production quantity that yields the greatest economic efficiency. In this section, graphical models are used to illustrate the relationship between costs, income, and production quantity.

Profit Related to Production Quantity. Assume that production quantities ranging from 1 through 10 units of output may be produced and sold each period of time, such as a day, month, quarter, or year. The cost and income associated with these production levels are given in Table 8.1. In this example,

Table 8.1. INCOME AND COST DATA FOR VARYING PRODUCTION QUANTITIES

Production Output, Q (A)	Fixed Cost (B)	Variable Cost (C)	Total Cost (B + C) (D)	Income (E)	Profit (E − D) (F)
1	$300	$100	$400	$125	$−275
2	300	180	480	250	−230
3	300	240	540	375	−165
4	300	290	590	500	−90
5	300	345	645	625	−20
6	300	415	715	745	+30
7	300	505	805	860	+55
8	300	620	920	970	+50
9	300	765	1,065	1,065	0
10	300	945	1,245	1,135	−110

the variable cost, given in column C, is increasing at a nonlinear rate. The income, given in column E, becomes nonlinear in the higher ranges of output. The difference between income and total cost represents the profit of the operation within the time period, at the production level indicated. This is shown in column F. Profit is maximized for an output of 7 units, where income less total cost is $55. At this point, the economic efficiency is $860 $\div$ $805 = 107 percent.

The data of Table 8.1 are illustrated in Figure 8.4. This graph illustrates the relationships among fixed cost, variable cost, total cost, and production quantity, as well as income and production quantity. The range of profitable operation occurs at that output where income exceeds total cost. In this example,

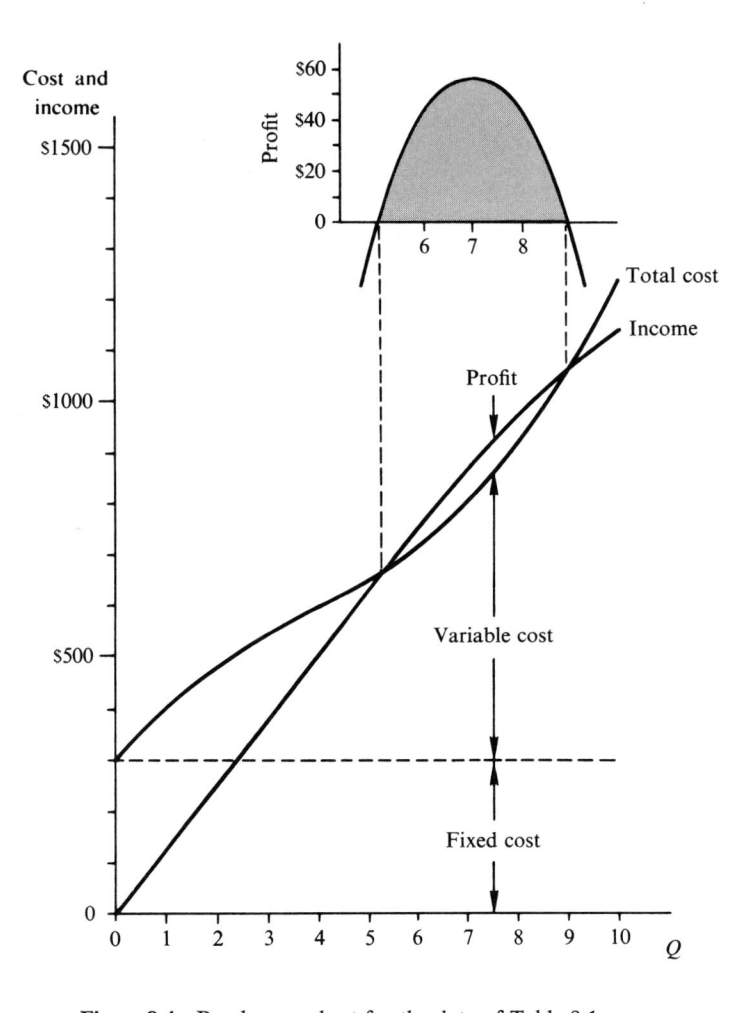

Figure 8.4 Break-even chart for the data of Table 8.1.

profitable operation occurs for the range of output from 6 through 8 units, with the maximum return and economic efficiency at 7 units.

This analysis identifies two break-even points. A *break-even point* occurs at the production quantities where total cost and income are equal: in this case, at about 5 and at 9 units. Break-even points are very useful in decision making for they identify the production quantities at which the economic efficiencies go from negative to positive or, possibly, from positive to negative as in this example.

The data of Table 8.1 can be analyzed on an incremental basis. Table 8.2 gives a continuation of Table 8.1 with columns G and H listing the average cost and income per unit. The incremental cost and incremental income are given in columns I and J. Each of these is sketched in Figure 8.5, permitting another insight to the original example.

Table 8.2. AVERAGE AND INCREMENTAL VALUES FOR THE DATA OF TABLE 8.1

Production Output, Q (A)	Average Cost $(D \div A)$ (G)	Average Income $(E \div A)$ (H)	Incremental Cost $(D_Q - D_{Q-1})$ (I)	Incremental Income $(E_Q - E_{Q-1})$ (J)
1	$400	$125	—	—
2	240	125	$80	$125
3	180	125	60	125
4	148	125	50	125
5	129	125	55	125
6	119	124	70	120
7	115	123	90	115
8	115	121	115	110
9	118	118	145	95
10	125	114	180	70

Note that the average cost is initially quite high. As more units are produced, the fixed cost is distributed over a wider base and it becomes a less significant portion of the total cost. Eventually, the unit variable cost may begin to increase as the production system becomes overburdened and less efficient. Then the sum of the diminishing average fixed cost and average variable cost begins to increase. In this example, the average income is assumed constant through a range of 5 units. As the demand is assumed to drop off, the unit income diminishes and the average income drops off to a lesser extent. At any level of production output, total profit will be the average income less average cost times the number of units of output.

Figure 8.5 permits incremental analysis of the production situation. Through 7 units of output, the incremental income exceeds the incremental cost. The cost of producing the eighth unit, however, is more than the revenue that

Chap. 8   Models for Production Operations   157

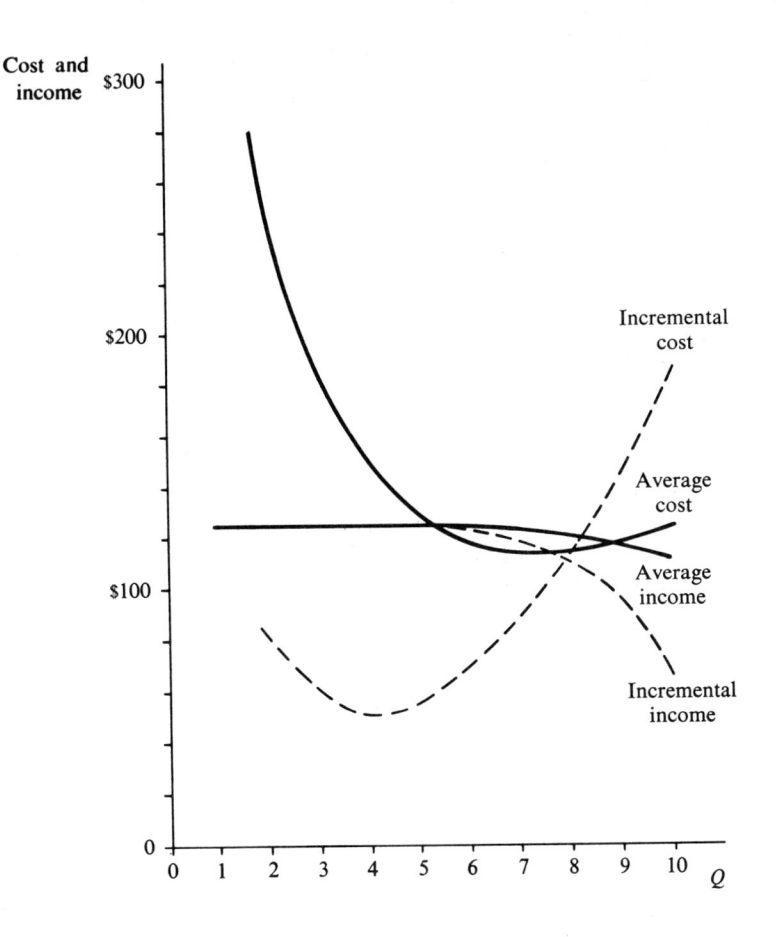

Figure 8.5   Graph for the data of Table 8.2.

will be received from its sale. Seven units is the optimum production quantity. It is at this production quantity that the economic efficiency of the system is maximized.

Profit Related to Production Quantity and Price.   Profit may often depend on the combined result of efforts to produce and distribute at a given price. Price and the costs of production and distribution must be considered in relation to their joint effect. Either one is meaningless when considered independently of the other. One aspect of this joint relationship will be illustrated by an example.

A firm had been marketing a specialized product for a number of years. On the basis of experience, sales, research, and estimates, curves were drawn

Table 8.3. RELATIONSHIP OF SELLING PRICE, SALES, SALES EFFORT, AND INCOME

Q, units produced and sold	\multicolumn{9}{c}{SELLING PRICE PER UNIT}
	\multicolumn{3}{c}{$p_1 = \$90$}	\multicolumn{3}{c}{$p_2 = \$100$}	\multicolumn{3}{c}{$p_3 = \$110$}
	I, income $= Q \times p_1$	S, sales effort cost	N, net income from sales, $N = I - S$	I, income $= Q \times p_2$	S, sales effort cost	N, net income from sales, $N = I - S$	I, income $= Q \times p_3$	S, sales effort cost	N, net income from sales, $N = I - S$
10	$ 900	$ 40	$ 860	$ 1,000	$ 70	$ 930	$ 1,100	$ 90	$1,010
20	1,800	130	1,670	2,000	200	1,800	2,200	220	1,950
30	2,700	240	2,460	3,000	380	2,620	3,300	420	2,880
40	3,600	400	3,200	4,000	640	3,360	4,400	730	3,670
50	4,500	630	3,870	5,000	1,000	4,000	5,500	1,260	4,240
60	5,400	970	4,430	6,000	1,500	4,500	6,600	2,090	4,510
70	6,300	1,530	4,770	7,000	2,130	4,870	7,700	3,070	4,630
80	7,200	2,170	5,030	8,000	2,800	5,110	8,800	4,140	4,660
90	8,100	2,940	5,160	9,000	3,770	5,230	9,900	5,320	4,580
100	9,000	3,770	5,230	10,000	4,770	5,230	11,000	6,550	4,450
110	9,900	4,650	5,250	11,000	5,900	5,100	12,100	7,900	4,200
120	10,800	5,600	5,200	12,000	7,150	4,850	13,200	9,300	3,900

showing the relationship between price, cost of sales effort, and the number of units produced and sold. Data taken and values calculated from these curves are given in Table 8.3. From this table curves representing the relationship of net income from sales, $I - S$, and the number of units sold, Q, were plotted as shown in Figure 8.6. The cost of production is composed of a fixed cost of $3,000 and a variable cost of $20 per unit. For the conditions given, the maximum profit will be approximately $5,230 for the sale of approximately 90 to 100 units at a price of $100. Corresponding values for selling prices of $90 and $110 are $5,250 and $4,660 for the sale of 110 and 60 units, respectively. These results illustrate the fact that sales effort, price, and cost of production must be considered jointly.

8.4 LINEAR BREAK-EVEN MODELS

Production quantity decision models are often formulated with an emphasis on break-even analysis. This emphasis is very useful for the planning of production systems not yet in operation. The lack of data from operating

Chap. 8   Models for Production Operations

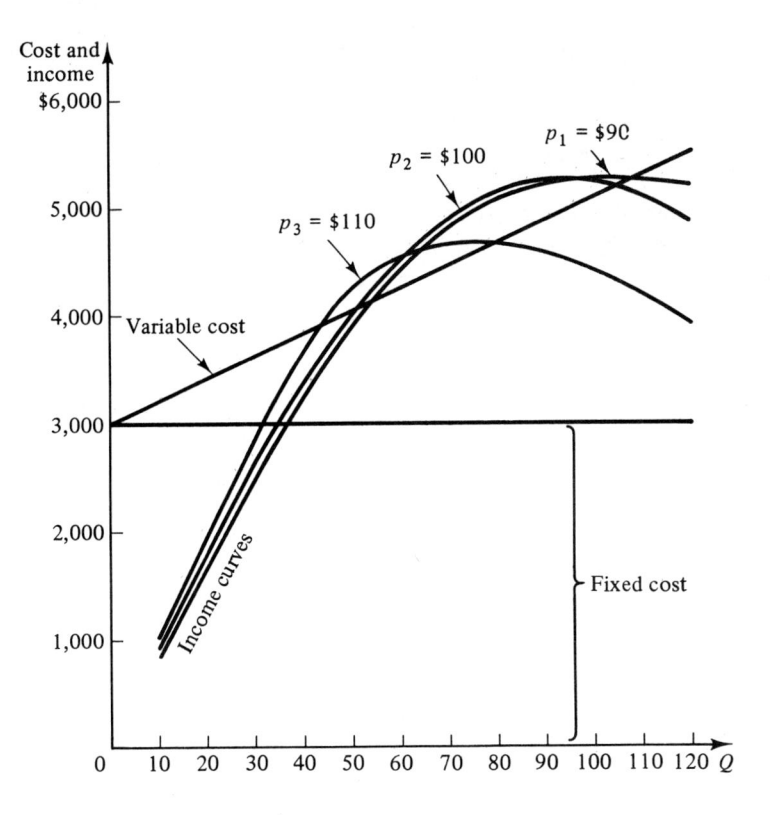

Figure 8.6 Graph of income from sales for different sale prices.

experience justifies the assumption of linearity when the objective is to identify the broad regions of potential profit or loss.

Finding the Break-Even Point. Under the assumption of linear cost and income functions, finding the break-even point is quite easy. Let

Q = number of units produced and sold during each time period
p = price received per unit of product sold
$I = Qp$, the income from Q units of product
F = fixed cost per period
V = variable cost per unit of product

$C = F + QV$, the sum of the fixed and variable costs for Q units of product

$TP = I - C$, the total profit per time period from Q units of product; a negative value of TP represents a loss

A number of algebraic relationships can now be developed by using the graph of Figure 8.7. In this case, the fixed cost, F, is $10; the variable cost, V, is $2.50 per unit; the price, p, is $5 per unit; and the production capacity, N, is 8 units.

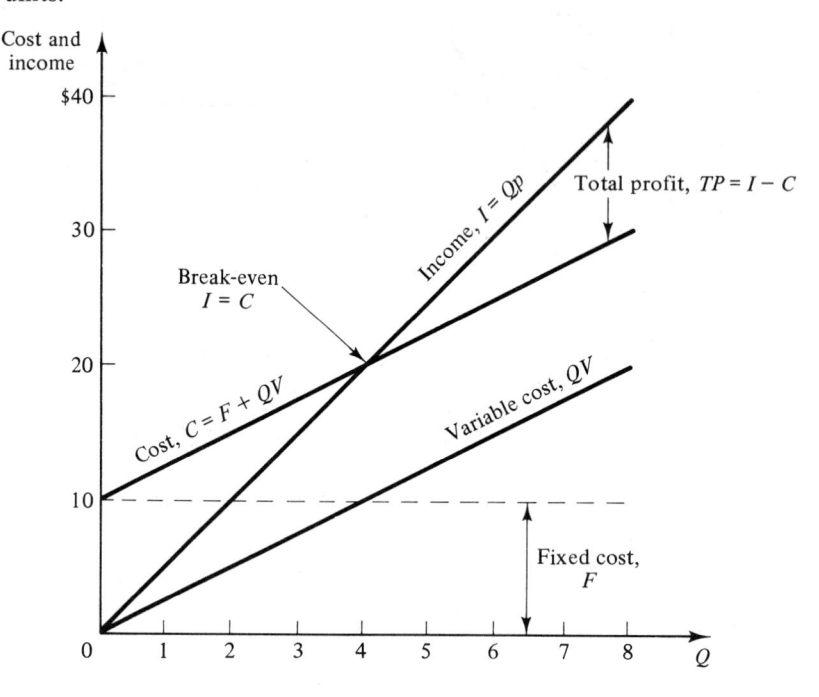

Figure 8.7 Break-even chart with linear cost and income.

The break-even point may be defined as that value of Q where income equals cost, or $Qp = F + QV$. Solving for Q gives

$$Q = \frac{F}{p - V}. \tag{8.1}$$

In this example

$$Q = \frac{\$10}{\$5 - \$2.50} = 4 \text{ units.}$$

The ordinate of the break-even point may be found by substituting $F/(p - V)$ for Q in $I = Qp$ or $C = F + QV$. The value of the ordinate in dollars will be

$$I = p\left(\frac{F}{p-V}\right) \quad \text{or} \quad C = F + V\left(\frac{F}{p-V}\right). \tag{8.2}$$

In this example

$$I = \$5\left(\frac{\$10}{\$5 - \$2.50}\right) = \$20 \quad \text{or} \quad C = \$10 + \$2.50\left(\frac{\$10}{\$5 - \$2.50}\right) = \$20.$$

Since *TP* is the total profit per time period, it is often desirable to express *TP* as a function of Q, the number of units produced and sold. This relationship may be derived as

$$\begin{aligned} TP &= I - C \\ &= Qp - (F + QV) \\ &= Q(p - V) - F. \end{aligned} \tag{8.3}$$

In this example, the total profit, at an output of 6 units, would be $TP = 6(\$5 - \$2.50) - \$10 = \$5$. And, at an output of 3 units, $TP = 3(\$5 - \$2.50) - \$10 = -\$2.50$. The negative sign indicates a loss in the amount of $2.50.

Production Above Normal Capacity. Suppose now that a production output of 10 units per time period is desired and possible, but at a variable cost of $4 per unit for the 2 units of output exceeding the normal capacity of 8 units. This can be described by letting Q' and V' represent the respective units and variable cost of output exceeding normal capacity. The graph of this extended example is given in Figure 8.8. The cost of production now becomes

$$C = F + QV + Q'V' \tag{8.4}$$

with Q limited to the range of the maximum normal production, $Q = 8$. The cost of producing 10 units would be $C = \$10 + 8(\$2.50) + 2(\$4) = \$38$. Equation (8.3) can be modified and profit defined as

$$\begin{aligned} TP &= I - C \\ &= Qp + Q'p - F - QV - Q'V' \\ &= p(Q + Q') - F - QV - Q'V'. \end{aligned} \tag{8.5}$$

The profits realized by producing at the rate of 10 units per period would be $TP = \$5(8 + 2) - \$10 - 8(\$2.50) - 2(\$4) = \$12$. As long as the slope of the income function exceeds the slope of the cost function, production at extended capacity can be pursued with profit.

The Effect of Dumping. In some instances, a constant unit price can be realized for the sale of a product only over a specific range of production. At a level exceeding this value, the added units must be sold at a reduced price. This is sometimes referred to as *dumping*. Returning to the original example, assume that the price, p, can be obtained for the first 6 units. The next 2 units,

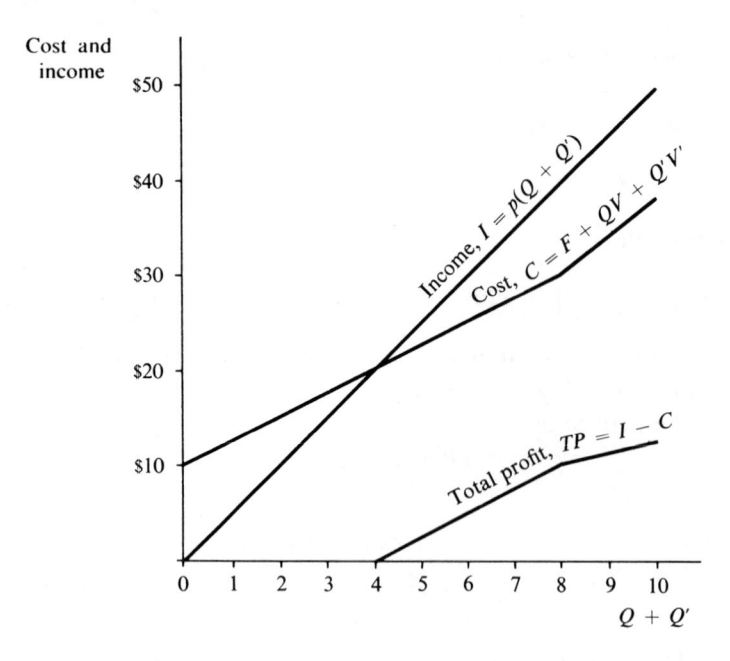

Figure 8.8 Break-even chart indicating the effect of extended production operations.

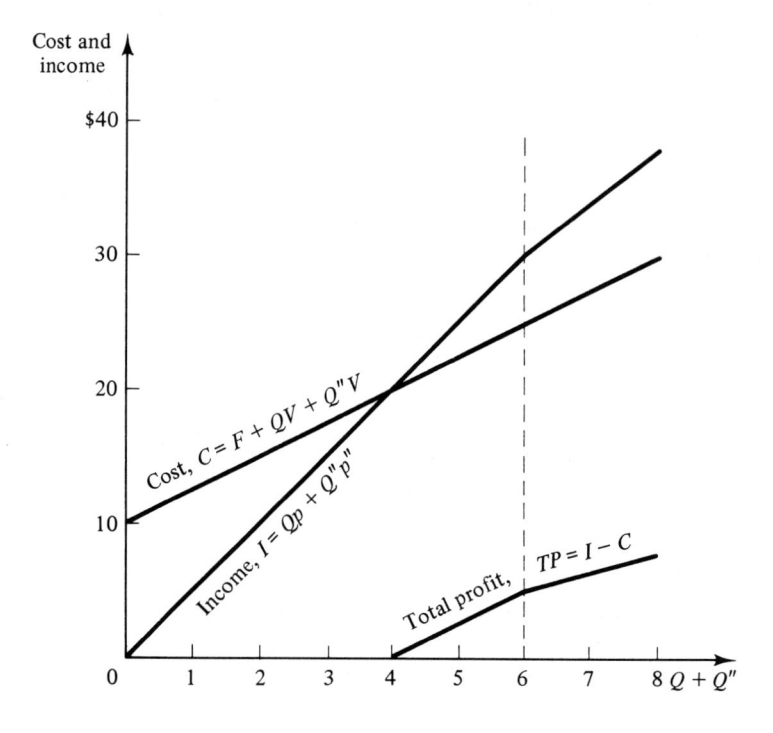

Figure 8.9 Break-even chart indicating the effect of dumping.

162

Chap. 8 Models for Production Operations   163

Q'', must be sold at the reduced price of $p'' = \$4$. The effect of dumping can be seen in Figure 8.9. The income realized is now

$$I = Qp + Q''p'' \tag{8.6}$$

with Q limited to a value of 6 units. The total profit may be expressed as

$$\begin{aligned} TP &= Qp + Q''p'' - F - QV - Q''V \\ &= Q(p - V) + Q''(p'' - V) - F. \end{aligned} \tag{8.7}$$

The total profit realized from the sale of 8 units is $TP = 6(\$5 - \$2.50) + 2(\$4 - \$2.50) - \$10 = \$8$.

The practice of dumping is profitable if the reduced price exceeds the variable cost of production. This is governed by the law of diminishing returns. As soon as the price drops below the variable cost of production, the optimum profit level has been passed and total profit will diminish.

8.5 THE PRODUCTION FUNCTION

The production process is essentially a means for converting some combination of inputs into an output of increased utility. Often, a production system can utilize varying levels of inputs to produce an identical output. When total cost or total profit can be expressed as a function of the input quantity combination, it may be possible to select that quantity combination of input elements that leads to an optimum result. Such an expression is called a *production function*, since it gives the relationship between rates and combinations of inputs and the rate of output. This section deals with the determination of the quantity combination of input elements, under direct control of a decision maker, that minimizes cost or maximizes profit.

The Input–Output Function. A production function defines the relationship between the input and output of a production process. If Q represents the rate of output, this function can be expressed in general terms as

$$Q = f(a_1, a_2, \ldots, a_n) \tag{8.8}$$

where $a_1, a_2, \ldots, a_n$ represent continuously divisible production factors. The relationship given by Equation (8.8) is one of rates rather than simple quantities. Output may be units per hour, week, or year. The inputs are not simply labor, machines, and land but rather their services measured in units per time period, such as labor hours per hour, machine hours per day, or acre-years per year.

Production is a time-dependent process, and a production function must incorporate this time dimension. The production function does not incorporate cost, although inputs and the output can eventually be converted to a common cost base. Also, the relationship applies to only one production process. Other processes are assumed to require separate functions. Finally, input factors not directly included in the production function are regarded as fixed over the range of output being considered.

The relationship between a single input variable and output, Q, may be described with a curve. The relationship between two input variables and output may be described with a surface oriented in three dimensions. As more input variables are included in the functional relationship, the input–output surface assumes added dimensions. In order to permit graphical analysis, production factors are often grouped into the two input classes of labor, L, and capital, C. Under this assumption, Equation (8.8) becomes

$$Q = f(L, C). \qquad (8.9)$$

There is some justification for this grouping of inputs. Labor is the coordinated human effort required in production. Capital can then be taken to include the cost of material, equipment, land, and all other physical inputs. A trade-off is then possible when equipment is utilized to replace human effort.

As various combinations of L and C are substituted into the production function, Q assumes different values. The surface thus traced is called a *production surface*. It is oriented in three-dimensional space, with any point on its surface representing a specific output for a specific combination of labor and capital input. Such a production surface might assume the form illustrated by Figure 8.10. Usually, Q is zero along both the L and C axes, indicating that no output is possible unless both inputs are present. As both labor and capital inputs increase, the surface usually rises. The surface may reach a peak, indicating that a level has been achieved beyond which additions will result in a decrease in output. Up to this point, the surface normally increases at a decreasing rate due to the law of diminishing returns. The form of the surface will depend on the functional relationship given by Equation (8.9).

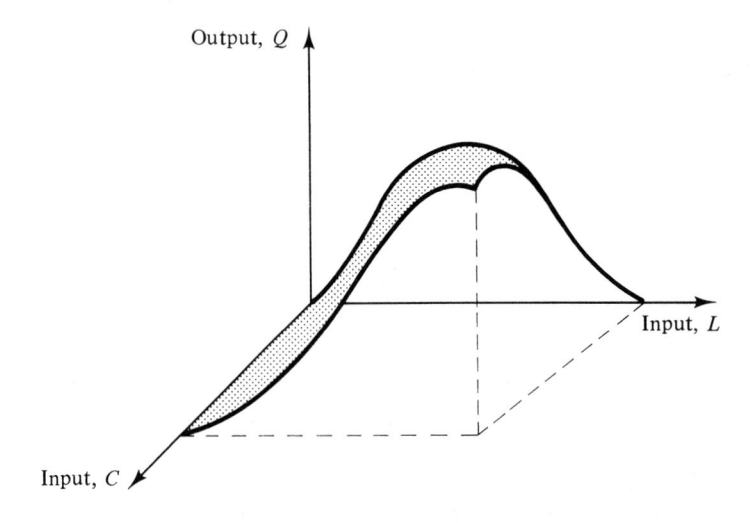

Figure 8.10 Production surface with labor and capital inputs.

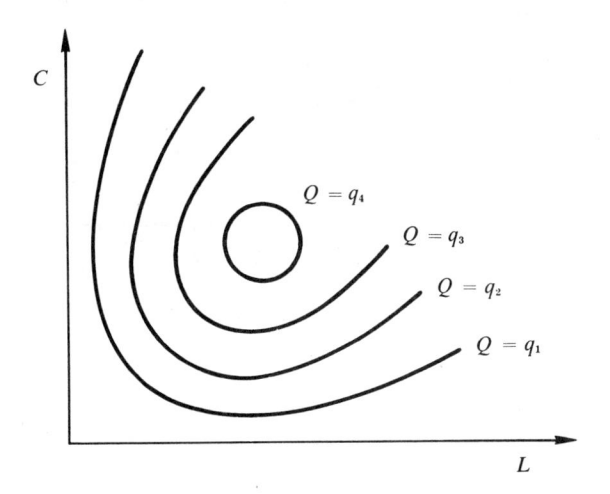

Figure 8.11 Family of constant output curves.

By holding one variable constant, the surface can be described with curves on a two-dimensional plane. By holding Q constant, curves of constant product output (isoquants) may be traced as illustrated by Figure 8.11. By holding either L or C constant, the relationship between the remaining variable and Q can be illustrated. For example, if C is held constant, the effect of L on Q is as shown in Figure 8.12.

A simple graphical analysis of output can be undertaken in two dimensions by holding one input variable constant. As an example, if the output curve $C = c_2$ from Figure 8.12 were to be studied on an average and an incremental

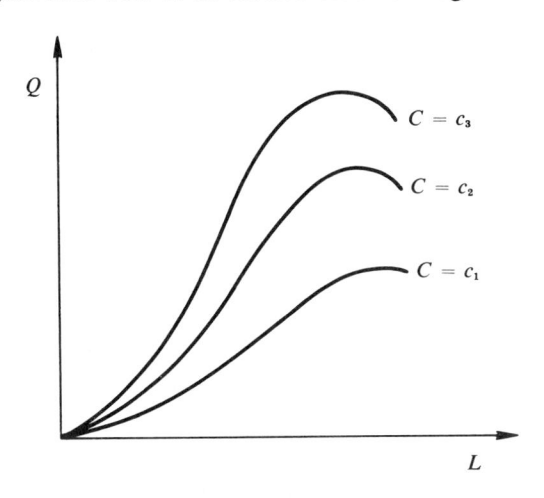

Figure 8.12 Family of output curves of constant capital inputs.

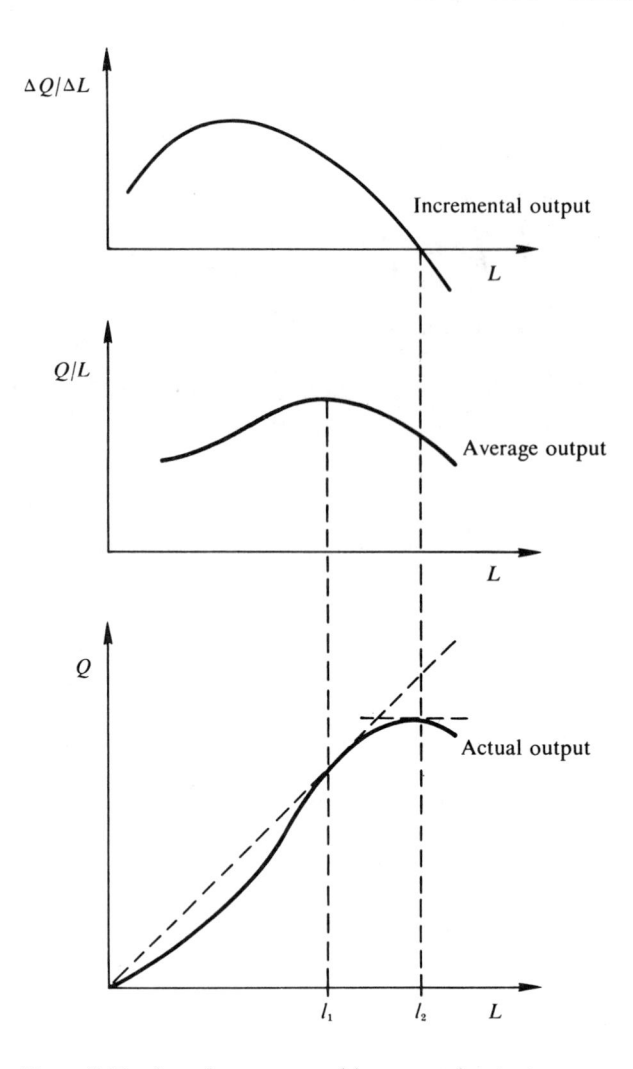

Figure 8.13 Actual, average, and incremental output curves.

basis, the results would be as indicated in Figure 8.13. The maximum output would be achieved at an input of l_2. Beyond this point the incremental output is negative. The maximum average output per unit of input would be achieved at l_1. This occurs at the point at which a line tangent to the actual output function just touches that function. An output increase beyond l_1 occurs, but at a reduction in the ratio Q/L.

The Minimum Cost–Input Rate Combination. Use of the production function as a decision model requires that inputs and outputs be related by a common economic measure. The dollar is the measure most frequently used. It is usually assumed that costs in dollars are known with certainty at varying rates of input, and that an optimum combination of inputs is one that either minimizes costs to achieve a desired output or maximizes output at a specified total dollar input.

Under the assumption of two inputs, L and C, minimum cost will be achieved when the ratio of the incremental outputs of labor and capital is equal to the ratio of the price of each. Symbolically, the minimum cost occurs when

$$\frac{\Delta Q/\Delta L}{\Delta Q/\Delta C} = \frac{p_L}{p_C} \qquad (8.10)$$

where p_L and p_C are the prices of a unit of labor input and a unit of capital input, respectively. Equation (8.10) may be expressed in equivalent derivative notation as

$$\frac{\partial Q/\partial L}{\partial Q/\partial C} = \frac{p_L}{p_C}. \qquad (8.11)$$

Equation (8.10) or (8.11) indicates that the cost of production is minimum when the input factors have been combined in such a fashion that the marginal or incremental cost of the marginal input of every factor is identical. Thus, factors will be added to the production process until their incremental cost per incremental unit of output exceeds other available factors. The optimum mix will be achieved when these costs are equal.

As an example of the application of Equation (8.11), consider the simple production function

$$Q = L^{1/2}C^{1/2}.$$

The surface described by this production function is a hyperbolic paraboloid, illustrated by Figure 8.14. If the cost of labor is $10 per unit and the required return per unit of capital is also $10, the minimum cost combination of labor and capital may be found from Equation (8.11) as

$$\frac{C^{1/2}\tfrac{1}{2}L^{-1/2}}{L^{1/2}\tfrac{1}{2}C^{-1/2}} = \frac{\$10}{\$10}$$

$$\$10(C^{1/2}\tfrac{1}{2}L^{-1/2}) = \$10(L^{1/2}\tfrac{1}{2}C^{-1/2})$$

$$L = C.$$

As a further illustration, assume that a total of $1,000 is available to spend for labor and capital. Since the price of labor equals the price of capital, each of which is $10 per unit, this will provide 100 units of these inputs. A minimum cost output is achieved when $L = C$, thus making the optimum mix of labor and capital equal to 50 units of each. This will result in an output of

$$Q = 50^{1/2}50^{1/2} = 50 \text{ units}.$$

The Maximum Profit–Input Rate Combination. Consider an extension of the preceding example. Assume that the price received for each unit of output, P_Q, is a function of the total output expressed as

$$p_Q = \$30 - \frac{Q}{1,000}.$$

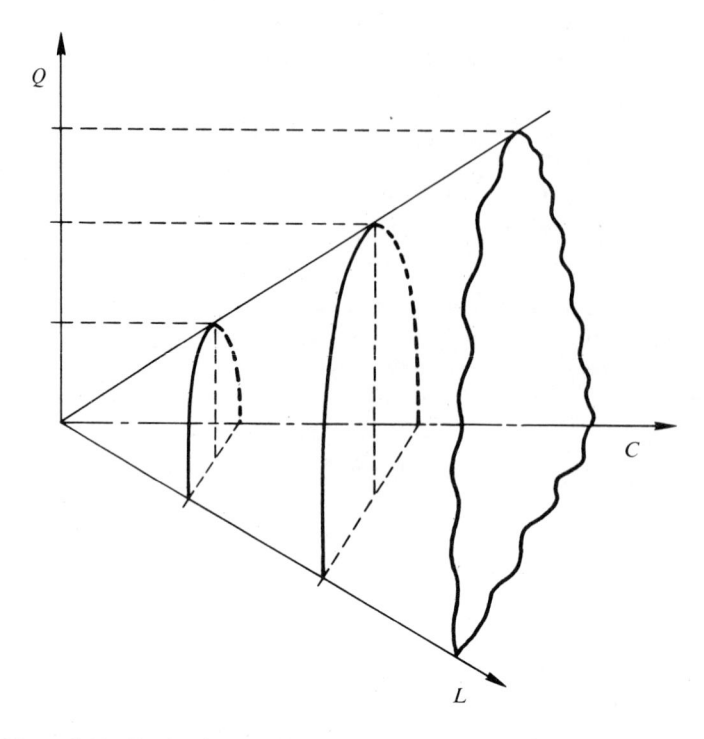

Figure 8.14 Production surface described by the function $Q = L^{1/2}C^{1/2}$.

The input rate combination of labor and capital that results in a maximum profit is sought. This requires the formulation of a total profit expression in terms of L and C. Total profit will be total revenue minus total cost, which may be expressed as

$$TP = p_Q(Q) - [p_L(L) + p_C(C)]$$
$$= \left(\$30Q - \frac{Q^2}{1,000}\right) - (\$10L + \$10C).$$

But since

$$Q = L^{1/2}C^{1/2},$$

$$TP = \left[\$30(L^{1/2}C^{1/2}) - \frac{L(C)}{1,000}\right] - (\$10L + \$10C). \tag{8.12}$$

The maximum profit combination of L and C may be found by taking the partial derivative of total profit with respect to L, and then with respect to C, and setting the results equal to zero. This results in

$$\frac{\partial TP}{\partial L} = C^{1/2}15L^{-1/2} - \frac{C}{1,000} - 10 = 0 \tag{8.13}$$

$$\frac{\partial TP}{\partial C} = L^{1/2}15C^{-1/2} - \frac{L}{1,000} - 10 = 0. \tag{8.14}$$

From Equation (8.14),
$$C^{1/2} = \frac{15{,}000 L^{1/2}}{L + 10{,}000}. \tag{8.15}$$

Substituting Equation (8.15) into Equation (8.13) gives
$$\frac{15{,}000 L^{1/2} 15 L^{-1/2}}{L + 10{,}000} - \frac{1}{1{,}000}\left(\frac{15{,}000 L^{1/2}}{L + 10{,}000}\right)^2 - 10 = 0.$$

Solving for L gives $L = 5{,}000$. Substituting into Equation (8.15) gives $C = 5{,}000$. This input rate combination will result in a maximum profit, and it satisfies the condition $L = C$ required for optimality.

The total profit resulting from this input combination may be found by substituting into Equation (8.12) as follows:

$$TP = \$30(5{,}000)^{1/2}(5{,}000)^{1/2} - \frac{5{,}000(5{,}000)}{1{,}000} - \$10(5{,}000) - \$10(5{,}000)$$
$$= \$150{,}000 - \$25{,}000 - \$100{,}000 = \$25{,}000.$$

This profit occurs at an output of
$$Q = (5{,}000)^{1/2}(5{,}000)^{1/2} = 5{,}000 \text{ units}.$$

Suppose that the price of capital changes from $10 per unit to $12 per unit. The optimum mix of labor and capital would be
$$\frac{C^{1/2}\tfrac{1}{2}L^{-1/2}}{L^{1/2}\tfrac{1}{2}C^{-1/2}} = \frac{\$10}{\$12}$$
$$\$12(C^{1/2}\tfrac{1}{2}L^{-1/2}) = \$10(L^{1/2}\tfrac{1}{2}C^{-1/2})$$
$$L = \tfrac{6}{5}C.$$

The total profit would be
$$TP = \left[\$30(L^{1/2}C^{1/2}) - \frac{L(C)}{1{,}000}\right] - (\$10L + \$12C). \tag{8.16}$$

Taking the partial derivatives with respect to L and C and setting these equal to zero gives
$$\frac{\partial TP}{\partial L} = C^{1/2} 15 L^{-1/2} - \frac{C}{1{,}000} - 10 = 0 \tag{8.17}$$
$$\frac{\partial TP}{\partial C} = L^{1/2} 15 C^{-1/2} - \frac{L}{1{,}000} - 12 = 0. \tag{8.18}$$

From Equation (8.18),
$$C^{1/2} = \frac{15{,}000 L^{1/2}}{L + 12{,}000}. \tag{8.19}$$

Substituting Equation (8.19) into Equation (8.17) gives
$$\frac{15{,}000 L^{1/2} 15 L^{-1/2}}{L + 12{,}000} - \frac{1}{1{,}000}\left(\frac{15{,}000 L^{1/2}}{L + 12{,}000}\right)^2 - 10 = 0.$$

Solving for L gives $L = 4{,}432$. Substituting into Equation (8.19) gives $C = 3{,}693$. This input rate combination results in a maximum profit and satisfies the condition $L = \frac{8}{3}C$ required for optimality.

The total profit resulting from this input combination may be found by substituting into Equation (8.16) as follows:

$$TP = \$30(4{,}432)^{1/2}(3{,}693)^{1/2} - \frac{(4{,}432)(3{,}693)}{1{,}000} - \$10(4{,}432) - \$12(3{,}693)$$

$$= \$121{,}370 - \$16{,}367 - \$44{,}320 - \$44{,}316 = \$16{,}367.$$

This profit occurs at an output of

$$Q = (4{,}432)^{1/2}(3{,}693)^{1/2} = 4{,}046 \text{ units.}$$

Thus, an increase in the price of capital caused a shift in the utilization of each input from $L = C$ to $L = \frac{8}{3}C$. The result was a reduction in total profit from \$25,000 to \$16,367.

The effect of varying labor and capital inputs from the optimum mix can be demonstrated numerically. Table 8.4 gives the total profit and the output which results from changes of 100 units in each input element. The profit which results in each case is less than that achieved with the optimum mix.

Table 8.4 suggests a means for finding the maximum profit numerically. By a systematic series of trials it is possible to find the combination of labor and capital that will maximize profit. This procedure must be used when the total profit equation cannot be differentiated.

Table 8.4. LABOR AND CAPITAL INPUTS AND THEIR RESULT ON PROFIT AND OUTPUT

Labor Input L	Capital Input C	Total Profit $TP(s)$	Output Q
4,432	3,693	\$16,367	4,046
4,332(−100)	3,593(−100)	16,349	3,945
4,532(+100)	3,793(+100)	16,354	4,146
4,332(−100)	3,793(+100)	16,353	4,054
4,532(+100)	3,593(−100)	16,331	4,035

QUESTIONS

8.1. Describe the production system as an input–output process.

8.2. What are the three categories of physical inputs to the production system?

8.3. What are the two nonphysical inputs to the production system?

8.4. Why must the output of the production system be geared to a dynamic marketplace?
8.5. How is economic efficiency related to physical efficiency?
8.6. Why is it essential that economic efficiency exceed 100 percent?
8.7. Give some examples of fixed cost.
8.8. Give some examples of variable costs.
8.9. What is an incremental cost?
8.10. What is a break-even point?
8.11. Discuss the break-even chart in terms of $E = f(X, Y)$.
8.12. Discuss the production function in terms of $E = f(X, Y)$.
8.13. What condition must be satisfied if the optimum mix of input factors to a production function has been found?

PROBLEMS

8.1. A certain power plant for generating electricity consumes 1 Btu in the form of coal for each 0.32 Btu equivalent produced in the form of electrical energy. The cost of coal is $1.80 per 1,000,000 Btu and the value of electrical energy produced per 1,000,000 Btu equivalent is $14.10. What is the economic efficiency of this power plant?

8.2. Plot economic efficiency as a function of physical efficiency for the range 0.28 to 0.36 utilizing the data from Problem 8.1.

8.3. A manufacturing firm estimates that its expenses per year for different levels of operation would be as follows:

	Output (units of product)					
	0	10	20	30	40	50
Administrative and sales cost	$4,900	$ 5,700	$ 6,200	$ 6,700	$ 7,100	$ 7,500
Direct labor and material cost	0	2,500	4,600	6,400	8,100	9,800
Overhead expense	4,120	4,190	4,270	4,350	4,400	4,550
Total cost	$9,020	$12,390	$15,070	$17,450	$19,600	$21,850

(a) What is the incremental cost of maintaining the plant ready to operate (the incremental cost of making zero units of product)?
(b) What is the average incremental cost per unit of manufacturing the first increment of 10 units of product per year?
(c) What is the average incremental cost per unit of manufacturing the increment of 31 to 40 units per year?
(d) What is the average total cost per unit when manufacturing at the rate of 30 units per year?
(e) At a time when the rate of manufacture is 20 units per year, a salesman reports that he can sell 10 additional units at $310 per unit without disturbing

the market in which the company sells. Would it be profitable for the company to undertake the production of the 10 additional units?

8.4. The product of an enterprise has a fixed selling price of $76. An analysis of production and sales costs and the market in which the product is sold has produced the following results:

Level of Operation	Total Production and Selling Cost (Units of Product)	Level of Operation	Total Production and Selling Cost (Units of Product)
0	$13,200	600	$35,000
100	17,900	700	38,600
200	21,400	800	47,100
300	24,600	900	55,600
400	27,200	1,000	65,400
500	31,500	1,100	74,000

(a) Determine the profit for each level of operation.
(b) Plot production and selling cost, income from sales, profit, average incremental production and selling cost per unit, and average incremental income per unit for each level of operation.

8.5. Sketch the break-even chart described by $F = \$6,000$, $V = \$15$ per unit, and $p = \$20$ per unit. Indicate the break-even point.

8.6. Solve for the break-even point in Problem 8.5 by algebraic analysis. What is the profit at an output of 2,500 units?

8.7. If the maximum production capacity of 2,500 units in Problem 8.6 can be exceeded by 600 units at a variable cost of $17 per unit, solve graphically and algebraically for the additional profit.

8.8. If the last 400 of 600 units in Problem 8.7 must be dumped at a price of $10 per unit, solve graphically and algebraically for the incremental effect of these added 600 units.

8.9. A market survey of cities A, B, and C reveals that it will be possible to sell 1,200, 900, and 750 tires per week in each city, respectively. At the present time two alternatives are being considered to meet this demand. In the first, one plant could be located equidistant between the three cities which would produce 3,350 tires at a fixed cost of $10,000 per week. The variable cost would be $9 per tire. Alternatively, plants of capacity 1,500, 1,000, and 850 tires, respectively, could be located in each of the cities. The fixed cost in each case would be $6,000, $4,000, and $3,200 per week. The variable cost would be only $8 per tire, owing to the elimination of transportation costs. If the market survey proves correct, which alternative would be most desirable? If sales were to increase to production capacity, which alternative would be best?

8.10. In Problem 8.9, consider a third alternative—to locate two plants, one in city A and the other equidistant between cities B and C. Plant 2 has a capacity of 1,850 tires, with a fixed cost of $6,500 per week and a variable cost of $8.50 per tire. Which of the three alternatives should be chosen if the market survey proves correct? Which should be chosen if the sales increase to production capacity?

8.11. A firm has the capacity to produce 750,000 units per year. At present, it is operating at 80 percent of capacity. The annual income is $0.09 per unit, regardless of output. Annual fixed costs are $21,000 and the variable cost is $0.049 per unit.
(a) What is the annual profit or loss at this capacity?
(b) At what percentage of capacity does the firm break even?
(c) What will be the profit or loss at 50 percent and 75 percent of capacity?

8.12. A plant is operating at its normal capacity of 50,000 units per year. The annual fixed costs are $19,000 and the variable cost is $0.12 per unit.
(a) What must be the minimum unit selling price if a loss situation is to be prevented?
(b) If the demand increases to 70,000 units per year, the plant can operate on an overtime basis at an additional variable cost of $0.03 per unit. Assuming the selling price calculated in part (a), what would be the annual profit?

8.13. A firm has priced its product at $1.00 per unit and is operating at a loss. Sales at this price total 860,000 units per year. The fixed costs of manufacturing and selling total $480,000 per year, and the variable cost is $0.48 per unit. A market survey indicates that price reductions of $0.10, $0.15, and $0.20 per unit from the present price will result in total annual sales of 1,200,000, 1,380,000, and 1,500,000 units, respectively. Calculate the annual profit that will result from each selling price given, assuming that the variable cost per unit will be the same for all volumes.

8.14. Sketch the production function $Q = 13X - 3X^2$ between $X = 0$ and $X = 5$, where X is hundreds of unit of input and Q is tens of units of output. Sketch the average output and marginal output curves.

8.15. If the price received per unit in Problem 8.14 is $100 and the input units cost $3 each, what is the maximum profit that can be realized? At what level of input and output does this maximum occur? At what level does profit occur?

8.16. A plant producing two products, A and B, has a capacity of 1,500 and 2,000 units per hour, respectively, and the total production time available is 4,000 hours. The fixed costs are $50,000 per year. The variable costs are $0.12 and $(4n \times 10^{-8} + 0.15)$ per unit, respectively, where n is the annual production. Product A is sold at $0.40 per unit, while product B is sold at $0.55 per unit. What is the distribution of production that will maximize profit?

8.17. Find the optimum mix of labor and capital for the production function $Q = L^{1/2}C^{1/2}$ with $p_Q = \$30 - Q/1,000$, $p_L = \$15$, and $p_C = \$5$. What profit is realized with this mix?

8.18. In the mid-1700s a number of significant breakthroughs occurred in England in the technology of the textile industry. Everyone today is familiar with these inventions, but in the late 1700s, the water frame, the mule spinner, the power loom, the spinning jenny, and the flying shuttle represented a novel means of transferring skill to machines. Under these conditions, capital expenditures for equipment could be considered as a partial substitute for labor. Immediately following the War of 1812, an enterprising English aeronautical engineer, after being laid off by a defense contractor, took up employment in a textile concern. He single-handedly developed a production function for the entire industry. By employing women and children to work 14 hours per day, the age of the machine could be implemented and output, Q, in square rods of cloth, could be represented as $Q = L^{1/2}C^{1/2}$. With $p_Q = £50 - Q/500$ and $p_L = £5$, and $p_C = £10$, what profit could be realized with the optimum quantity and mix of labor and capital? ($£ = 1$ pound sterling.)

9

Models for Economic Equivalence

Organizational objectives are often achieved by selecting and implementing one alternative from an available set. Each member of the set may contribute differently to the effectiveness with which these objectives are achieved. The selection of a specific alternative is usually straightforward if the available alternatives are reduced to a common economic base for comparison. When this is done, the decision models of Chapter 7 may be used in the selection process.

Many operational alternatives may be described in terms of their receipts and disbursements over time. When this is the case, reducing these economic values to an equivalent basis is essential in decision making. This chapter deals with the specific models for economic equivalence. The time value of money is incorporated through the development of interest formulas. Several methods for the calculation of equivalence are illustrated. Finally, the common methods for evaluating a single alternative and for comparing multiple alternatives on an equivalent economic basis are presented.

9.1 THE TIME VALUE OF MONEY

Fundamentally, the rent paid for the use of a building is essentially the same as interest paid for the use of capital. The ethics and economics of charging a rent for the use of money have been discussed by philosophers, economists, and others throughout the ages. Regardless of the ethics of the practice, its economic aspect must be considered in deciding between alternatives that involve receipts and disbursements over time. This section deals with the time value of money, expressed as an interest rate, together with its impact on decision making.

Interest Rate and Interest. The interest rate is the ratio of the rent either paid or received for the use of money to the amount of money itself, over a period of time, usually 1 year. This ratio is generally expressed as a percentage. For example, if $18 is paid for the use of $100 for 1 year, the interest rate is 18 percent. The lender may consider interest received as a result of investing funds as a gain or profit. The borrower may consider interest as a charge or cost.

A person who owns a sum of money has a number of choices regarding its use. One of these involves lending this money on condition that the borrower repay the initial sum plus interest at some future date. If this is the choice, a number of factors should be considered in specifying an interest rate: First, the probability that the borrower will not repay the loan; this will depend on the borrower's integrity as well as on the security granted to the lender. If the chances are 3 in 100 that the loan will not be repaid, the lender is justified in charging 3 percent of the sum to compensate for the risk of loss. This reasoning is most appropriate in the case of a lender who is lending many such sums of money. Then, in the long run, with a constant 3 percent risk of loss, a 3 percent charge on each loan will compensate for those loans that are not repaid. A second consideration in lending money is the cost of investigating the borrower, together with the administrative costs of monitoring the actual disbursement and receipt of money. If this cost is $2 per $100 per year, a 2 percent administrative charge might be included. Finally, the net amount that will compensate the lender for being deprived of the use of the money for the time period is important, especially in times of high inflation. This charge might be considered as pure gain and might amount to $13 for a $100 loan. On the basis of the preceding analysis, a total interest rate of 18 percent might be charged.

To the borrower, the interest charge represents an expense for the use of money. One will evaluate the magnitude of the interest charge by considering the use to which the money will be put. If it is borrowed to finance an operation that will result in some expected gain, this gain must exceed the interest cost.

Most production operations are partially financed with borrowed money. Thus, the charge for the use of money should be considered together with the charges for materials, labor, and producer goods. The sum of these charges should be less than the receipts for the products or services. The net difference represents the profit of the operation. The use of borrowed money to finance the cost of production with the expectation of making a profit is sometimes referred to as the *earning power of money.*

Simple Interest. The rent for a sum of money is usually expressed as the rate for the use of the money for a period of 1 year. The amount of interest charged on repayment of a loan is proportional to the duration of the loan expressed in years.

In simple interest, money is earned only on the principal sum. With P as the principal sum, n as the number of years, and i as the interest rate, simple interest can be expressed as

$$I = Pni. \tag{9.1}$$

As an example, consider a sum of $1,000 borrowed for 4 years at an interest rate of 15 percent per annum. The interest earned may be calculated from Equation (9.1) as

$$I = \$1,000(4)(0.15) = \$600.$$

The amount of simple interest earned or charged is $600. At the end of the 4-year period, the principal sum of $1,000 is returned together with this $600.

Compound Interest. Under compound interest, the money earned at the end of each interest period either becomes due at that time or earns interest upon itself. In the example just given, the total interest of $600 could be paid in four equal payments of $150, one at the end of each year of the loan. This would satisfy the requirement of compound interest.

Alternatively, the interest earned during the life of the loan would earn interest on itself and would be paid at the end of the 4-year period. The total amount of money paid at the end of the loan of the preceding example, with compound interest, is shown in Table 9.1 to be $1,749. When the interest earned each year is added to the amount of the loan for the purpose of calculating interest charges, interest is said to be compounded annually. Annual compounding for this example resulted in $749 of interest instead of $600 under the simple interest case.

Table 9.1. CALCULATION OF COMPOUND INTEREST AND PRINCIPAL WHEN INTEREST IS PERMITTED TO COMPOUND

Year	Amount Owed at Beginning of Year (A)	Interest Added at End of Year (B)	Amount Owed at End of Year (A + B)	Amount Paid at End of Year
1	$1,000.00	$1,000.00 × 0.15 = $150.00	$1,000(1.15) = $1,150.00	0
2	1,150.00	$1,150.00 × 0.15 = $172.50	$1,000(1.15)² = $1,322.50	0
3	1,322.50	$1,322.50 × 0.15 = $198.38	$1,000(1.15)³ = $1,520.88	0
4	1,520.88	$1,520.88 × 0.15 = $228.13	$1,000(1.15)⁴ = $1,749.00	$1,749.00

Effective Interest Rates. An interest rate quoted for an interest period of 1 year is called a *nominal annual rate*. The compound-interest example given above was based on the assumption of annual compounding interest. Sometimes, however, interest may be compounded more frequently. The result of this more frequent compounding will be an effective interest rate that will be higher than the nominal annual rate.

As an example, consider a nominal annual interest rate of 8 percent which is to be compounded every 6 months. This is equivalent to an actual rate of 4 percent compounded each half year. The compound amount can be found as $(1.04)^2 = 1.0816$. Thus, the effective interest rate is 8.16 percent. The effective interest rate may be expressed as

$$\left(1 + \frac{i}{c}\right)^c - 1,$$

where c is the number of interest periods per year and i is the nominal annual interest rate.

9.2 INTEREST AND INTEREST FORMULAS

Under compound interest, the interest earned at the end of an interest period is either paid at that time or it earns interest upon itself. Formulas for the case where interest earns interest on itself are presented in this section. Let

i = nominal annual rate of interest

n = number of interest periods, usually annual

P = principal sum, at a time regarded to be the present

A = single payment in a series of n equal payments, made at the end of each interest period

F = sum, n interest periods hence, equal to the compound amount of a principal sum, P, or the sum of the compound amounts of the payments, A, at the interest rate i

Single-Payment Compound-Amount Factor. When interest is permitted to compound as in Table 9.1, the interest earned during each interest period is added to the principal sum at the beginning of the next interest period. By substituting general terms in Table 9.1, the relationship between F, P, n, and i can be developed as shown in Table 9.2. The resulting factor, $(1 + i)^n$, is known as the *single-payment compound-amount factor*.

The single-payment compound-amount factor may be used to express the equivalence between a present sum, P, and a future sum, F at an interest rate i for n years. The relationship is

$$F = P(1 + i)^n. \qquad (9.2)$$

Table 9.2. THE SINGLE-PAYMENT COMPOUND-AMOUNT FACTOR

Year	Amount at Beginning of Year	Interest Earned During Year	Compound Amount at End of Year
1	P	Pi	$P + Pi = P(1 + i)$
2	$P(1 + i)$	$P(1 + i)i$	$P(1 + i) + P(1 + i)i = P(1 + i)^2$
3	$P(1 + i)^2$	$P(1 + i)^2 i$	$P(1 + i)^2 + P(1 + i)^2 i = P(1 + i)^3$
n	$P(1 + i)^{n-1}$	$P(1 + i)^{n-1} i$	$P(1 + i)^{n-1} + P(1 + i)^{n-1} i = P(1 + i)^n = F$

In convenient functional designation form, Equation (9.2) may be expressed as[1]

$$F = P(\overset{F/P,i,n}{\quad}).$$

Values for the ($\overset{F/P,i,n}{\quad}$) factor and those that follow are tabulated in Appendix E, Tables E.1 through E.13.

The compound amount of $1,000 in 6 years at 12 percent interest compounded annually may be found from Equation (9.2) as

$$F = \$1,000(1 + 0.12)^6$$
$$= \$1,000(1.974) = \$1,974.$$

Or, by use of the factor designation and the tabular value in Table E.7,

$$F = \$1,000(1.974\overset{F/P,12,6}{\quad}) = \$1,974.$$

Single-Payment Present-Worth Factor. The single-payment compound-amount relationship given in Equation (9.2) may be solved for P and expressed as

$$P = F\left[\frac{1}{(1 + i)^n}\right]. \tag{9.3}$$

The resulting factor, $1/(1 + i)^n$, is known as the *single-payment present-worth factor* and is designated ($\overset{P/F,i,n}{\quad}$). This factor may be used to express the equivalence between a future sum, F, and a present sum, P, at an interest rate i for n years. This relationship may be expressed in functional form as

$$P = F(\overset{P/F,i,n}{\quad}).$$

As an example, assume that it is desired to accumulate $10,000 in 4 years. If the interest rate is 14 percent, the amount of money that must be deposited is formed from Equation (9.3) as

---

[1] The functional factor designation system is summarized in Table 9.3. It will be used throughout this text.

$$P = \$10,000 \left[\frac{1}{(1.14)^4} \right]$$

$$= \$10,000 \left(\frac{1}{1.689} \right)$$

$$= \$10,000(0.5921) = \$5,921.$$

Or, by use of the factor designation and the tabular value in Table E.9,

$$P = \$10,000(\overset{P/F,14,4}{0.5921}) = \$5,921.$$

Equal-Payment Series Compound-Amount Factor. In some situations, a series of receipts or disbursements occurring uniformly at the end of each year may be encountered. The sum of the compound amounts of this series may be derived by reference to Figure 9.1.

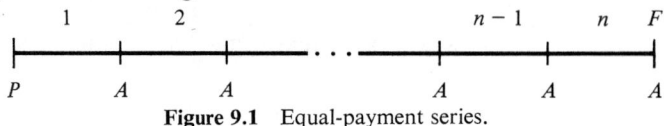

Figure 9.1 Equal-payment series.

The A dollars deposited at the end of the nth year will earn no interest and will contribute only A dollars to F. The A dollars deposited at the end of period $n-1$ will earn interest in the amount of Ai, and $A(1+i)$ will be contributed to the sum. The payment made at the end of $n-2$ will contribute $A(1+i)^2$. The sum of this series will be

$$F = A(1) + A(1+i) + A(1+i)^2 + \cdots + A(1+i)^{n-2} + A(1+i)^{n-1}.$$

Multiplying this series by $(1+i)$ gives

$$F(1+i) = A[(1+i) + (1+i)^2 + (1+i)^3 + \cdots + (1+i)^{n-1} + (1+i)^n].$$

Then, subtracting the first equation from the second gives

$$F(1+i) - F = A[(1+i)^n - 1]$$

$$iF = A[(1+i)^n - 1]$$

$$F = A \left[\frac{(1+i)^n - 1}{i} \right]. \tag{9.4}$$

The resulting factor, $[(1+i)^n - 1]/i$, is known as the *equal-payment series compound-amount factor* and is designated ($\overset{F/A,i,n}{\quad}$). This factor may be used to express the equivalence between an equal-payment series, A, and a future sum, F, at an interest rate i for n years. This relationship may be expressed in functional form as

$$F = A(\overset{F/A,i,n}{\quad}).$$

As an example, suppose that $500 is to be invested at the end of each year for 10 years at 10 percent interest. The amount accumulated can be found from

Chap. 9   Models for Economic Equivalence   181

Equation (9.4) as

$$F = \$500\left[\frac{(1+0.10)^{10}-1}{0.10}\right]$$

$$= \$500\left[\frac{(2.5937)-1}{0.10}\right]$$

$$= \$500(15.937) = \$7,969.$$

Or, by use of the factor designation and the tabular value in Table E.5,

$$F = \$500(\overset{F/A,10,10}{15.937}) = \$7,969.$$

Equal-Payment Series Sinking-Fund Factor. The equal-payment series compound-amount relationship in Equation (9.4) may be solved for A and expressed as

$$A = F\left[\frac{i}{(1+i)^n - 1}\right]. \qquad (9.5)$$

The resulting factor, $i/[(1+i)^n - 1]$, is known as the *equal-payment series sinking-fund factor* and is designated ($\overset{A/F,i,n}{}$). This factor may be used to express the equivalence between a future sum, F, and an equal-payment series, A, at an interest rate i for n years. This relationship may be expressed in functional form as

$$A = F(\overset{A/F,i,n}{}).$$

As an example, suppose that it is desired to deposit a series of uniform, year-end payments over 10 years in order to provide a total of \$5,000 at the end of that period. The amount that should be deposited each year at an interest rate of 14 percent is found from Equation (9.5) as

$$A = \$5,000\left[\frac{0.14}{(1+0.14)^{10}-1}\right]$$

$$= \$5,000\left[\frac{0.14}{(3.7072)-1}\right]$$

$$= \$5,000(0.0517) = \$259.$$

Or, by use of the factor designation and the tabular value in Table E.9,

$$A = \$5,000(0.0517) = \$259.$$

Equal-Payment Series Capital-Recovery Factor. The substitution of $P(1+i)^n$ for F in the equal-payment series sinking-fund relationship given in Equation (9.5) gives

$$A = P(1+i)^n\left[\frac{i}{(1+i)^n - 1}\right]$$

$$= P\left[\frac{i(1+i)^n}{(1+i)^n - 1}\right]. \qquad (9.6)$$

The resulting factor, $i(1+i)^n/[(1+i)^n - 1]$, is known as the *equal-payment series capital-recovery factor* and is designated ($\overset{A/P,i,n}{}$). This factor may be used to express the equivalence between a present amount, P, and an equal-payment series, A, in the future at an interest rate i for n years. This relationship may be expressed in functional form as

$$A = P(\overset{A/P,i,n}{}).$$

As an example, assume that a firm borrowed $100,000 at 9 percent interest which it must repay in equal end-of-year amounts over the next 8 years. The amount that must be repaid at the end of each year may be found from Equation (9.6) as

$$A = \$100{,}000\left[\frac{0.09(1+0.09)^8}{(1+0.09)^8 - 1}\right]$$

$$= \$100{,}000\left[\frac{0.09(1.9926)}{(1.9926) - 1}\right]$$

$$= \$100{,}000(0.1807) = \$18{,}070.$$

Or, by use of the factor designation and the tabular value in Table E.4,

$$A = \$100{,}000(\overset{A/P,9,8}{0.1807}) = \$18{,}070.$$

Equal-Payment Series Present-Worth Factor. The equal-payment series capital-recovery relationship in Equation (9.6) can be solved for P and expressed as

$$P = A\left[\frac{(1+i)^n - 1}{i(1+i)^n}\right]. \tag{9.7}$$

The resulting factor, $[(1+i)^n - 1]/i(1+i)^n$, is known as the *equal-payment series present-worth factor* and is designated ($\overset{P/A,i,n}{}$). This factor may be used to express the equivalence between future equal-payment series, A, and a present amount, P, at an interest rate i for n years. This relationship may be expressed in functional form as

$$P = A(\overset{P/A,i,n}{}).$$

As an example of this formula, assume that a machine will save $4,000 per year in operating costs over the next 10 years. If an interest rate of 10 percent is used, the present worth of these savings may be found from Equation (9.7) as

$$P = \$4{,}000\left[\frac{(1+0.10)^{10} - 1}{0.10(1+0.10)^{10}}\right]$$

$$= \$4{,}000\left[\frac{(2.5937) - 1}{0.10(2.5937)}\right]$$

$$= \$4{,}000(6.1446) = \$24{,}578.$$

Or, by use of the factor designation and the tabular value in Table E.5,

$$P = \$4,000(6.1446 \overset{P/A,10,10}{)} = \$24,578.$$

Summary of Interest Formulas. The interest formulas derived in the previous paragraphs express relationships among P, A, F, i, and n. In any given application an equivalence between F and P, P and F, F and A, A and F, P and A, or A and P is required for an interest rate and a number of years n. Table 9.3 may be used to select the interest factor needed in a given situation. The factor designation scheme summarized in the last column makes it possible to set up a problem symbolically before determining the value of the factor.

Table 9.3. SUMMARY OF INTEREST FORMULAS

Single-payment compound-amount	Given P, find F	$F = P(1+i)^n$	$F = P(^{F/P,i,n})$
Single-payment present-worth	Given F, find P	$P = F\dfrac{1}{(1+i)^n}$	$P = F(^{P/F,i,n})$
Equal-payment series compound-amount	Given A, find F	$F = A\left[\dfrac{(1+i)^n - 1}{i}\right]$	$F = A(^{F/A,i,n})$
Equal-payment series sinking-fund	Given F, find A	$A = F\left[\dfrac{i}{(1+i)^n - 1}\right]$	$A = F(^{A/F,i,n})$
Equal-payment series present-worth	Given A, find P	$P = A\left[\dfrac{(1+i)^n - 1}{i(1+i)^n}\right]$	$P = A(^{P/A,i,n})$
Equal-payment series capital-recovery	Given P, find A	$A = P\left[\dfrac{i(1+i)^n}{(1+i)^n - 1}\right]$	$A = P(^{A/P,i,n})$

Numerical values corresponding to each of the factor designations for the most frequently used ranges of i and n are given in Appendix E, Tables E.1 through E.13. Individual tabular values are given to a number of decimal places sufficient for most applications. Linear interpolation may be used for either i or n with fairly accurate results. If results with a degree of accuracy beyond that which may be obtained by the use of tabular values are required, it will be necessary to use the formulas directly, together with logarithmic operations, a financial calculator, or a digital computer.

9.3 THE CALCULATION OF EQUIVALENCE

Two monetary amounts are equivalent when they have the same value in exchange. Three factors are involved in the equivalence of sums of money. They are (1) the amount of the sums, (2) the time occurrence of the sums, and (3) the interest rate. Some example calculations of monetary equivalence are presented in this section.

Interest Formula Equivalence Calculations. At an interest rate of 14 percent, with $n = 5$ years, a P of \$1 is equivalent to an F of \$1.925. This is found from the single-payment compound-amount factor as

$$F = \$1(\overset{F/P,14,5}{1.925}) = \$1.925.$$

An application of this equivalence statement is that \$1 spent today must result in a revenue receipt (or avoid a cost) of \$1.925 five years hence if the interest rate is 14 percent.

A reciprocal situation is where $i = 14$ percent, $n = 5$ years, and $F = \$1$. The P that is equivalent to F is found from the single-payment present-worth factor as

$$P = \$1(\overset{P/F,14,5}{0.5194}) = \$0.519.$$

An application of this statement of equivalence is that no more than \$0.519 can be spent today to secure a revenue receipt of \$1 (or avoid a like cost) 5 years hence if the interest rate is 14 percent.

If $i = 12$ percent and $n = 8$ years, the F that is equivalent to an A of \$1 is found from the equal-payment series compound-amount factor as

$$F = \$1(\overset{F/A,12,8}{12.300}) = \$12.30.$$

An application of this equivalence statement is that \$1 spent each year for 8 years must result in a revenue receipt (or avoid a cost) of \$12.30 eight years hence if the interest rate is 12 percent.

A reciprocal situation is where $i = 12$ percent, $n = 8$ years, and $F = \$1$. The A that is equivalent to F is found from the equal-payment series present-worth factor as

$$A = \$1(\overset{A/F,12,8}{0.0813}) = \$0.081.$$

An application of this statement of equivalence is that \$0.081 must be received each year for 8 years to be equivalent to a receipt of \$1 eight years hence.

If $i = 15$ percent, $n = 4$ years, and A is \$1, the P that is equivalent to A is found from the equal-payment series present-worth factor as

$$P = \$1(\overset{P/A,15,4}{2.8550}) = \$2.855.$$

An application of this equivalence statement is that an investment of \$2.855 today must yield an annual income (or avoid an annual cost) of \$1 each year for 4 years if the interest rate is 15 percent.

A reciprocal situation is where $i = 15$ percent, $n = 4$ years, and $P = \$1$. The A that is equivalent to P is

$$A = \$1(\overset{A/P,15,4}{0.3503}) = \$0.35.$$

Chap. 9   Models for Economic Equivalence   **185**

An application of this statement of equivalence is that $1 can be invested today to yield an annual income (or avoid an annual cost) of $0.35 each year for 4 years if the interest rate is 15 percent.

Equivalence Function Diagrams.   A useful analysis technique for exhibiting the equivalence of monetary amounts is to plot present value as a function of the interest rate. For example, the value of i that will make a P of $600 equivalent to an F of $1,000 if $n = 5$ years is stated as

$$\$600 = \$1,000(\overset{P/F,i,5}{}).$$

The solution is illustrated graphically in Figure 9.2 to be 10.75 percent.

Present value may also be plotted as a function of n as a useful technique for exhibiting equivalence of monetary amounts. For example, the value of n that will make a P of $900 equivalent to an F of $1,800 if $i = 12$ percent is

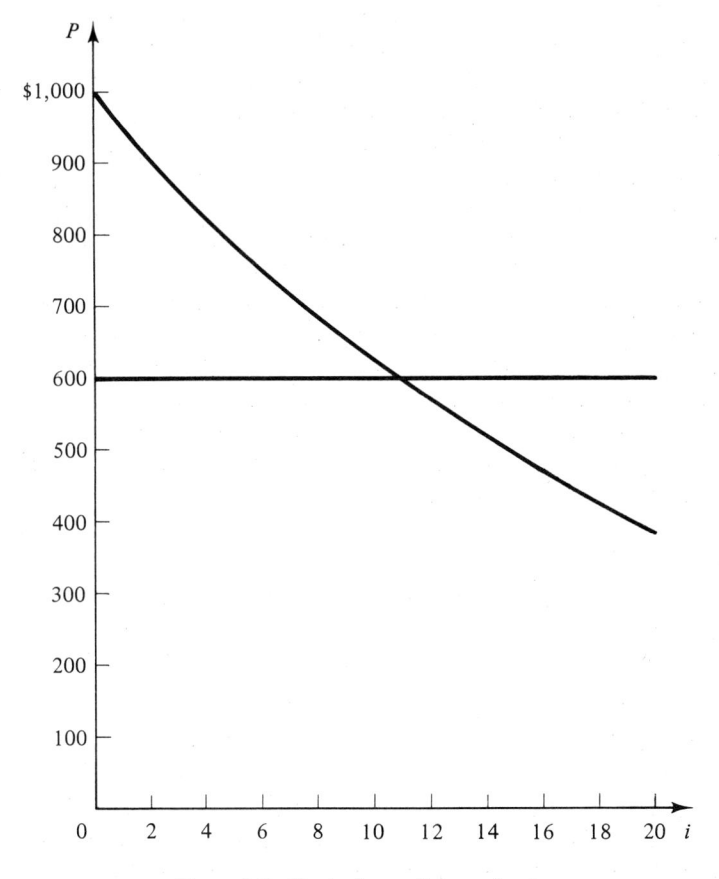

Figure 9.2   Equivalence diagram for i.

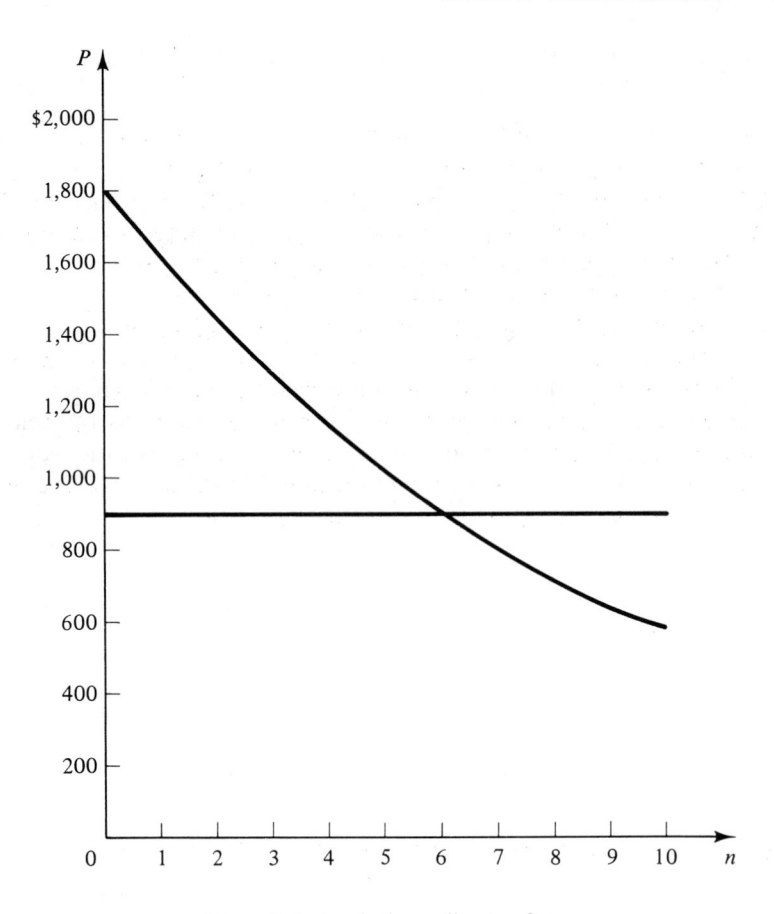

Figure 9.3 Equivalence diagram for n.

stated as

$$\$900 = \$1,800(\overset{P/F,12,n}{\quad\quad}).$$

The solution is illustrated graphically in Figure 9.3 to be 6 years.

Equivalent Annual Cost of an Asset. Regardless of the depreciation function that describes the reduction in value of an asset over time, its annual equivalent cost may be expressed as the annual equivalent first cost less the annual equivalent salvage value. This annual equivalent cost is the amount an asset must earn each year if the invested capital is to be recovered together with interest on the investment. It is derived as follows:

$$A = P(\overset{A/P,i,n}{\quad\quad}) - F(\overset{A/F,i,n}{\quad\quad})$$
$$= P\left[\frac{i(1+i)^n}{(1+i)^n - 1}\right] - F\left[\frac{i}{(1+i)^n - 1}\right]$$

$$= P\left[\frac{i(1+i)^n}{(1+i)^n - 1}\right] - F\left[\frac{i(1+i)^n}{(1+i)^n - 1} - i\right]$$

$$= (P - F)\left[\frac{i(1+i)^n}{(1+i)^n - 1}\right] + F(i)$$

$$= (P - F)(\overset{A/P,i,n}{}) + F(i). \qquad (9.8)$$

As an example of the application of Equation (9.8), consider the following situation. A small business computer is purchased for $12,800 with an anticipated salvage value of $4,000 in 5 years. At an interest rate of 15 percent, the annual equivalent cost of the computer is

$$(\$12,800 - \$4,000)(\overset{A/P,15,5}{0.2983}) + \$4,000(0.15) = \$3,225.$$

9.4 EVALUATING A SINGLE ALTERNATIVE

The economic evaluation of alternatives involving receipts and disbursements over time may be accomplished by reducing these alternatives to an equivalent economic base. It is necessary to reduce alternatives to an equivalent base in order that apparent differences become real differences, with the time value of money considered. When expressed in terms of an equivalent base, real differences become directly comparable and may be used in decision making. The most common bases for comparison are the present-worth amount, the equivalent annual amount, the rate of return, and the payout period.

In most cases, a decision must be reached by selecting one alternative from among two or more feasible alternatives. Sometimes, however, the decision is limited to acceptance or rejection of a single alternative. In such a case the decision will be based on the relative merit of the alternative and other opportunities believed to exist, even though none of the latter have been crystallized into definite proposals. When only one specified alternative exists, it should be evaluated within a framework that will permit its desirability to be compared to other opportunities that may exist, but which are unspecified. The following example illustrates the several bases of evaluation when the decision to accept or reject a proposal must be made and there is no specific alternative proposed for comparison.

The purchase of an air-driven drill is being considered by an equipment rental business for rental to construction contractors who need and use such equipment on a temporary basis. The anticipated receipts and disbursements of this alternative are given in Table 9.4. With the exception of the initial cost, these transactions and dates are only estimates of what will occur in the future. For convenience, the disbursements and receipts that may occur during the year are assumed due and payable at the end of that year or the start of the next year, considered to be the same point in time. There is some small error in the

Table 9.4. DISBURSEMENTS AND RECEIPTS FOR A SINGLE ALTERNATIVE

Item	Date	Disbursements	Net Receipts
Cost	1-1-19×0	$18,500	—
Rental, first year	1-1-19×1	—	$7,500
Rental, second year	1-1-19×2	—	7,500
Overhaul	1-1-19×2	2,500	—
Rental, third year	1-1-19×3	—	7,500
Rental, fourth year	1-1-19×4	—	7,500
Salvage value	1-1-19×4	—	6,000

practice of considering receipts and disbursements as year-end payments. This error is insignificant, however, in comparison to the usual errors in estimates, except under extremely high interest rates. In the foregoing example, consider an interest rate of 12 percent as the cost of money and consider January 1, 19x0, to be the present.

Present-Worth Evaluation. The present worth of future receipts and disbursements is easily computed and understood. In this example, the present worth of receipts as of January 1, 19x0, is

$$\$7,500(\overset{P/A,12,4}{3.0374}) + \$6,000(\overset{P/F,12,4}{0.6355}) = \$26,594.$$

The present worth of disbursements as of January 1, 19x0, is $18,500. The present worth of receipts less disbursements is $26,594 less $18,500, or $8,094.

If these estimates prove to be correct, the significance of this analysis is that if the $18,500 is invested, a return of 12 percent will be received in addition to an equivalent receipt of $8,093 at the present time. To decide whether to purchase the drill, this anticipated gain must be compared with or against a feeling or opinion regarding nonspecified opportunities that may present themselves.

Equivalent Annual Evaluation. This method of analysis is similar to the present-worth method except that the difference between receipts and disbursements is now expressed as an equivalent annual amount. Using the same interest rate, the equivalent annual amount of receipts is

$$\$7,500(1) + \$6,000(\overset{A/F,12,4}{0.2092}) = \$8,755.$$

The equivalent annual amount of disbursements is

$$\$18,500(\overset{A/P,12,4}{0.3292}) = \$6,090.$$

The equivalent annual amount of receipts less disbursements is $8,755 less $6,090, or $2,665. As a verification, the equivalent annual amount of the present-worth difference between receipts and disbursements is

$$\$8,094(\overset{A/P,12,4}{0.3292}) = \$2,665.$$

This result means that if $18,500 is invested on January 1, 19x0, a 12 percent return will be received plus the equivalent of receipts of $2,665 on January 1, 19x1, 19x2, 19x3, and 19x4.

Rate-of-Return Evaluation. This is probably the best method for comparing a specific proposal with other opportunities believed to exist but not delineated. The rate of return is a universal measure of economic success. Rates of return from different classes of opportunities are usually well established and generally known. This permits comparison of an alternative against accepted norms. Thus, this characteristic makes the rate-of-return comparison well adapted to the situation where the choice is to accept or reject a single alternative.

The equipment rental proposal can be evaluated on the basis of the rate of return that would be secured from the invested funds. In effect, a rate of interest will be specified that makes the receipts and disbursements equivalent. This can be done either in terms of present worth or equivalent annual amount. In this case a present-worth evaluation will be utilized.

To find the value of i, it is necessary to make the present worth of receipts less the present worth of disbursements equal to zero. Thus, solution for i in

$$\$7{,}500(\overset{P/A,i,4}{}) + \$6{,}000(\overset{P/F,i,4}{}) - \$18{,}500 = 0$$

will give the rate of return sought. Try $i = 25$ percent:

$$\$7{,}500(\overset{P/A,25,4}{2.3616}) + \$6{,}000(\overset{P/F,25,4}{0.4096}) - \$18{,}500 = \$1{,}670.$$

Try $i = 30$ percent:

$$\$7{,}500(\overset{P/A,30,4}{2.1663}) + \$6{,}000(\overset{P/F,30,4}{0.3501}) - \$18{,}500 = -\$152.$$

By linear interpolation

$$i = 25 + (5)\frac{\$1{,}670 - 0}{\$1{,}670 - (\$-152)} = 29.6 \text{ percent.}$$

This result means that the investment of $18,500 in the air-driven drill should yield an approximate 29.6 percent return over the 4-year rental period. Since the cost of money was assumed to be 12 percent, this venture promises a substantial contribution to profit for the equipment rental firm.

Payout Evaluation. Often, a proposed asset is evaluated in terms of how long it will take the asset to pay for itself. Assets that tend to pay for themselves quickly are desirable, in that there is less uncertainty associated with estimates of short duration. This comparison also directs attention to the life embraced by an alternative.

Consider the rental example of the previous paragraphs in which the cost of money was 12 percent. With the receipts in Table 9.4, the present amount that will have accumulated in 3 years is

$$\$7{,}500(\overset{P/A,12,3}{2.4018}) = \$18{,}014.$$

The present amount that will have accumulated in 4 years is

$$\$7{,}500(\overset{P/A,12,4}{3.0374}) = \$22{,}781.$$

By linear interpolation

$$n = 3 + (1)\frac{\$18{,}500 - \$18{,}014}{\$22{,}781 - \$18{,}014} = 3.1 \text{ years}.$$

This result means that the investment of $18,500 in the air-driven drill will be returned with 12 percent interest in 3.1 years. Remaining rental income will make a contribution to profit for the equipment rental firm.

9.5 COMPARING MULTIPLE ALTERNATIVES

Where a number of feasible alternatives provide service of equal value, it is desirable to compare them directly against each other. Where service of unequal value is provided by multiple alternatives, each alternative must be evaluated as a single alternative and is accepted or rejected on the basis of one or more of the comparisons suggested in the preceding section. In many cases, however, the available alternatives do provide outputs which are identical or equal in value. Under this condition, the objective is to select the alternative that provides the desired service at least cost.

Assume that a company is considering the purchase of a new computer controller. A semiautomatic controller will cost $10,000 and can be expected to last 6 years with a salvage value of $1,000. Operating cost will be $6,000 per year. A fully automatic controller will cost $16,000, should also last 6 years, and will have a salvage value of $4,000. Operating cost will be $4,000 per year. The service provided by each device will be identical. With a desired interest rate of 15 percent, the alternative that meets the criterion of least cost should be selected.

Present-Worth Comparison. Under this method, the two alternatives may be compared in equivalent costs at a time taken to be the present. The present-worth cost of the semiautomatic controller is

$$\$10{,}000 + \$6{,}000(\overset{P/A,15,6}{3.7845}) - \$1{,}000(\overset{P/F,15,6}{0.4323}) = \$32{,}275.$$

The present-worth cost of the fully automatic controller is

$$\$16{,}000 + \$4{,}000(\overset{P/A,15,6}{3.7845}) - \$4{,}000(\overset{P/F,15,6}{0.4323}) = \$29{,}409.$$

This comparison shows the present-worth cost of the fully automatic controller to be less than the present-worth cost of the semiautomatic controller by $32,275 less $29,409, or $2,866.

Equivalent Annual Cost Comparison. The equivalent annual costs are taken as an equal-cost series over the life of the assets. The equivalent annual cost of the semiautomatic controller is

$$\$10,000(\underset{A/P,15,6}{0.2642}) + \$6,000 - \$1,000(\underset{A/F,15,6}{0.1142}) = \$8,528.$$

The equivalent annual cost of the fully automatic controller is

$$\$16,000(\underset{A/P,15,6}{0.2642}) + \$4,000 - \$4,000(\underset{A/F,15,6}{0.1142}) = \$7,770.$$

The equivalent annual difference of $8,528 less $7,770, or $758, is the equivalent annual cost superiority of the fully automatic controller. As a verification, the equivalent annual amount of the present-worth difference is

$$\$2,866(\underset{A/P,15,6}{0.2642}) = \$757.$$

Rate-of-Return Comparison. The previous cost comparisons have indicated that the fully automatic controller was more desirable at an interest rate of 15 percent. At some higher interest rate, however, the semiautomatic controller will be less expensive because of its lower initial cost.

The interest rate at which the costs of the two alternatives are identical can be determined by setting them equal to each other and solving for the interest rate, i. Thus,

$$\$10,000 + \$6,000(\underset{P/A,i,6}{\quad}) - \$1,000(\underset{P/F,i,6}{\quad})$$

$$= \$16,000 + \$4,000(\underset{P/A,i,6}{\quad}) - \$4,000(\underset{P/F,i,6}{\quad})$$

$$\$2,000(\underset{P/A,i,6}{\quad}) + \$3,000(\underset{P/F,i,6}{\quad}) = \$6,000.$$

For $i = 25$ percent,

$$\$2,000(\underset{P/A,25,6}{2.9514}) + \$3,000(\underset{P/F,25,6}{0.2622}) = \$6,689.$$

For $i = 30$ percent,

$$\$2,000(\underset{P/A,30,6}{2.6428}) + \$3,000(\underset{P/A,30,6}{0.2072}) = \$5,907.$$

By linear interpolation

$$i = 25 + (5)\frac{\$6,689 - \$6,000}{\$6,689 - \$5,907} = 29.4 \text{ percent.}$$

When funds are considered to earn less than 29.4 percent, the fully automatic controller will be the most desirable. When funds earn more than 29.4 percent, the semiautomatic controller will be preferred.

Service Life Comparison. The service life of 6 years for each of the two controllers is the result of estimates and may be in error. If the services are needed for shorter or longer periods of time and if the assets are capable of providing the service for a longer period of time, the advantage may pass from one alternative to the other. Just as there is an interest rate at which two alternatives may be equal, there may be a service life at which the equivalent cost may be identical. This service life may be obtained by setting the alternatives equal to each other and solving for the life, n. Thus, for an interest rate of 15 percent,

$$\$10,000 + \$6,000(\overset{P/A,15,n}{\quad}) - \$1,000(\overset{P/F,15,n}{\quad})$$
$$= \$16,000 + \$4,000(\overset{P/A,15,n}{\quad}) - \$4,000(\overset{P/F,15,n}{\quad})$$
$$\$2,000(\overset{P/A,15,n}{\quad}) + \$3,000(\overset{P/F,15,n}{\quad}) = \$6,000.$$

For $n = 2$ years,

$$\$2,000(\overset{P/A,15,2}{1.6257}) + \$3,000(\overset{P/F,15,2}{0.7562}) = \$5,520.$$

For $n = 3$ years,

$$\$2,000(\overset{P/A,15,3}{2.2832}) + \$3,000(\overset{P/F,15,3}{0.6575}) = \$6,539.$$

By linear interpolation

$$n = 2 + (1)\frac{\$6,000 - \$5,520}{\$6,539 - \$5,520} = 2.47 \text{ years.}$$

If the controller were to be used less than 2.47 years, the semiautomatic model would be the most economical.

QUESTIONS

9.1. Define interest and interest rate.
9.2. From the viewpoint of the lender, what three factors might be considered in specifying an interest rate?
9.3. Define simple interest and compound interest.
9.4. What are a nominal interest rate and an effective interest rate?
9.5. What is meant by capital recovery plus return?
9.6. List the four bases for evaluating alternatives.
9.7. Under what condition would the evaluation of multiple alternatives be conducted as if each were a single alternative?

PROBLEMS

9.1. If an investment of $1,000 earns $100 in 9 months, what is the annual rate of interest?
9.2. How long must $1,000 be invested to amount to $2,000 if 18 percent simple interest per annum is earned?
9.3. What effective interest rate corresponds to the following?

(a) Nominal interest rate of 12 percent compounded semiannually.
(b) Nominal interest rate of 10 percent compounded quarterly.

9.4. What amount will be accumulated by each of the following investments?
(a) $3,500 at 13 percent compounded annually over 10 years.
(b) $52,500 at 8 percent compounded annually over 5 years.
(c) $800 at 12 percent compounded semiannually over 2 years.

9.5. What is the present worth of the following?
(a) A year-end series of payments of $600 compounded annually at 14 percent for 5 years.
(b) A sum of $600 to be received in 2 years at 12 percent compounded annually.

9.6. How much money must be invested now to accumulate the following future amounts?
(a) $1,000 in 10 years at 8 percent compounded annually.
(b) $1,000 in 7 years at 9 percent compounded semiannually.

9.7. What interest rate compounded annually is involved if $5,000 results in $8,000 in 4 years?

9.8. How many years will it take $4,000 to reach a sum of $8,000 at an interest rate of 10 percent compounded annually?

9.9. What interest rate is necessary for a sum of money to double itself in 6 years?

9.10. Plot P as a function of i to find the value for i which will make $10,000 to be received 8 years hence equivalent to $4,000 now.

9.11. Plot P as a function of n to find the value for n which will make $8,000 in the future equivalent to $5,000 now, if the interest rate is 10 percent.

9.12. An asset was purchased for $20,000 with the anticipation that it would last for 8 years and be worth $2,000 as scrap. After 5 years of operation the asset was sold for $2,000. The interest rate is 13 percent.
(a) What was the anticipated equivalent annual cost?
(b) What was the actual annual equivalent cost?

9.13. How much can be paid for an asset with a salvage value anticipated to be 20 percent of its first cost if its service life is estimated to be 6 years, if the interest rate is 12 percent, and if it will result in an annual saving of $22,500?

9.14. A cement mixer purchased for $24,000 has an estimated salvage value of $6,000 and an expected life of 3 years. Approximately 250 cubic yards of concrete per month will be produced by the mixer.
(a) Calculate the equivalent annual cost of the mixer at an interest rate of 12 percent.
(b) Calculate the equivalent annual cost of capital recovery plus return per cubic yard of concrete produced.

9.15. The table below shows the receipts and disbursements for a given venture.

End of the Year	Receipts	Disbursements
0	$ 0	$500
1	600	0
2	500	400
3	500	0
4	1,200	100

Determine the desirability of the venture for a 10 percent interest rate based on the present-worth evaluation and the equivalent annual evaluation.

9.16. A man wishes to invest $8,000 in an automobile to be used as a taxi. He anticipates a net profit before overhaul expense $2,800, $2,600, $2,400, and $2,200 at the end of the first through the fourth years of operation. The overhaul will cost $1,400 at the end of the second year. At the end of 4 years, a salvage value of $1,000 is expected. Use an interest rate of 12 percent, and evaluate the desirability of the investment on the basis of present-worth and equivalent annual methods.

9.17. A new automatic machine can be purchased for $30,000 and will have a $3,000 salvage value at any age. This machine will increase net profits by $5,000 per year.
   (a) What rate of return is expected if the machine is used for 8 years?
   (b) For what life will the automatic machine give a return of 15 percent?

9.18. An automobile can be purchased for $6,000. A down payment of $1,500 is required, and the balance may be paid in 16 quarterly installments plus 12 percent on the unpaid balance. As an alternative, the automobile can be purchased for $5,500 cash. At what interest rate are the plans equivalent?

9.19. An investor plans on purchasing a bus for $35,000 that will have a capacity of 80 passengers. As an alternative he can purchase another bus for $45,000 which will have a capacity of 100 passengers. The salvage value of both buses is estimated at $2,000 after a 10-year life. If an annual net profit of $100 can be realized per passenger, which alternative would you recommend, using an interest rate of 15 percent?

9.20. A manufacturing plant and its equipment are insured for $710,000. The present annual insurance premium is $0.85 per $100 of coverage. A sprinkler system with an estimated life of 20 years and no salvage value can be installed for $18,000. Annual maintenance and operating cost is estimated to be $360. The premium will be reduced to $0.40 per $100 coverage if the sprinkler system is installed.
   (a) Write an expression that may be used to find the rate of return if the sprinkler is installed.
   (b) With interest at 14 percent, find the payout period for the sprinkler system.

10

Depreciation and Replacement Models

Mass production has been found to be an effective means for satisfying human wants. This process requires a complex industrial organization, together with a large investment in producer goods. Producer goods are employed to alter physical factors to create consumer goods. In the process, they depreciate in value, become obsolete, inadequate, or otherwise become candidates for replacement.

This chapter begins by presenting the concept and several models for depreciation. Then, two categories of replacement models are considered. The first deals with the case where equipment deteriorates with time. The choice between an existing asset and its potential replacement is based on the difference in cost expressed on an equivalent basis for comparison. The second deals with replacement models used to establish a renewal policy for items that do not deteriorate appreciably with time, but fail instantaneously and completely. Replacement models for items that fail require the use of probabilistic concepts and the statistics of failure data.

10.1 THE CONCEPT OF DEPRECIATION

The production of goods and services is directly dependent on the employment of large quantities of producer goods which require considerable investment. Although this investment results in high worker productivity, this economy must be sufficient to absorb the reduction in value of these facilities as they are consumed in the production process. Alternative operational proposals may involve different programs of capital investment; hence, it is essential that the cost of capital consumed be considered in evaluating these alternatives.

Classifications of Depreciation. With the possible exception of land, physical assets are likely to lessen in value with the passage of time. This reduction in value may be due to physical depreciation, functional depreciation, or accident.

Physical depreciation results from the physical impairment of an asset. Commonly referred to as *wear and tear* or *deterioration*, physical impairment may manifest itself as corrosion, abrasion, or cracking. This type of depreciation lowers the ability of the physical asset to perform its intended service.

Functional depreciation rests not on a reduction in the ability of the asset to perform its intended service, but rather on a change in the demand for the service rendered by the asset. This reduction in demand for the product or service produced by the asset may be due to obsolescence resulting from the discovery of a second asset that makes it uneconomical to continue to use the first asset. Another form of functional depreciation occurs when the asset can no longer meet the demands placed upon it. The service has not changed. Rather, the demand for the service has changed, making it no longer feasible for this particular asset to satisfy demand. Finally, an asset that is no longer needed becomes obsolete with a resulting reduction in value.

Accidents may cause a sudden reduction in the value of an asset. Although insurable losses are usually not classified as depreciation, minor uninsured losses reduce the value of the asset and may be treated as depreciation.

The Value-Time Function. The capital that should be recovered over the life of a depreciable asset is equal to the first cost less its salvage value at the time of retirement. In addition to this recovery of investment, interest should be earned on the unrecovered balance during the life of the asset. Understanding the concept of depreciation is complicated because two aspects must be considered. First is the actual lessening in value of the asset with use and the passage of time. Thus, the bearings on a machine may wear and structural elements may deteriorate. A building may become functionally obsolete. This is actual depreciation. The second aspect is accounting for this lessening in value. These two aspects are usually identical when the asset is first obtained. There are some advantages to these being identical when the asset is finally removed, either at the end of its estimated life or some time earlier or later than this estimated date. This is not always possible, however, since accounting for the lessening in value of a physical asset requires an estimate of the future.

In considering depreciation as a cost of production, it is necessary to predict the pattern of future value of an asset. It is customary to assume that the value of an asset decreases yearly in accordance with one of several mathematical functions. The choice of a particular depreciation model is not an easy task. This choice involves an estimate of the effective life of the asset, its salvage value at the end of this life, and the form of the mathematical function. Once a value-time function has been selected, it is chosen to represent the value of the asset at any point in time. A general value-time function is illustrated in Figure 10.1.

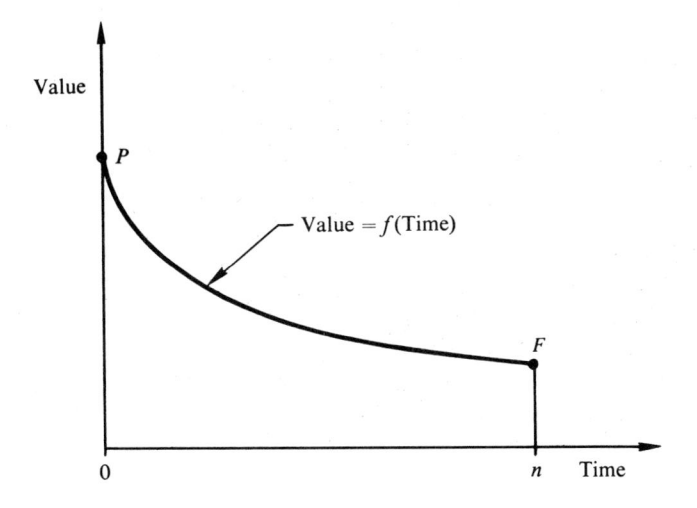

Figure 10.1 General value-time function.

Depreciation is a cost of production. If the cost of capital consumption is neglected, profits will appear higher by the amount equal to the capital consumed. Then, at the end of the life of the asset, there may have been no financial provision made for its replacement.

The calculated amount of decrease in value from one point in time to the next depends on the initial cost of the asset, the method of depreciation selected, and the estimated salvage value. Once these estimates have been made, they are acted upon as if they represent actual facts until another decision is made. When a new decision is made, it is based on the facts as they exist at that time.

Capital Recovery Plus Return. Capital assets are purchased with the belief that they will earn more than they cost. One part of the anticipated earnings is considered to be *capital recovered*. The capital invested in an asset is recovered in the form of earnings resulting from the sale of products or services produced by the asset. Additional capital may be recovered in the form of the final sale of the asset at the end of its useful life. If a machine provided services in the amount of $1,800 during its useful life, and if it was finally sold at a salvage value of $200, a total of $2,000 is considered to be recovered capital. If the asset initially cost $2,000, the capital invested in it will have been fully recovered.

A second part of the prospective earnings of an asset will be considered to be *return*. Since capital invested in an asset is recovered in small increments over time, it is necessary to consider the interest on the undepreciated balance as a cost of ownership. An investment in an asset is expected to return not only the capital invested in the asset, but also to provide for interest earnings on the diminishing investment remaining. These two forms of earnings are collectively referred to as *capital recovery plus return*.

10.2 SOME DEPRECIATION MODELS

One aim in accounting for the depreciation of an asset is to have a monetary measure of the capital worth of the enterprise. A more immediate aim is to arrive at the physical expenditure of physical capital, in monetary terms, that has been occasioned by each unit of product produced. This aim permits an accounting for the cost of the goods or service. The accounting objective is difficult because the physical depreciation per unit of product depends upon the total depreciation and the number of units produced, neither of which can be known until after the asset has been consumed. Nevertheless, an estimate of these must be made in advance. This section is concerned with depreciation models which may be used in accounting for the consumption of capital assets.

The Straight-Line Model. The straight-line depreciation model assumes that the value of an asset decreases at a constant rate. Expressions for capital recovered, capital unrecovered, return, and capital recovered plus return may be developed for each year of the asset's life. Let

$P = $ first cost of the asset

$F = $ estimated salvage value

$n = $ estimated life

$i = $ interest rate

The capital recovered each year by the straight-line model may be expressed as $(P - F)/n$.

As an example of the application of the straight-line model, assume that an asset has a first cost of $7,000, an estimated life of 6 years, and an estimated salvage value of $1,000. The total depreciation will be $7,000 - $1,000 = $6,000 over a period of 6 years. The depreciation each year will be $1,000.

For the conditions assumed, the investment in the asset during the first year is $7,000, during the second year $6,000, during the third year $5,000, and so forth. If the desired rate of return on the investment is 8 percent, the return for the first year will be $7,000 \times 0.08 = \$560$, for the second year $6,000 \times 0.08 = \$480$, for the third year $5,000 \times 0.08 = \$400$, and so forth. The capital recovered, capital unrecovered, return, and capital recovered plus return for each year of the asset's life are given in Table 10.1. General expressions for these terms may be developed from the numerical example and are given in Table 10.2.

Table 10.1. EXAMPLE OF THE STRAIGHT-LINE DEPRECIATION MODEL

Year	Capital Recovered	Capital Unrecovered Beginning of Year	Return on the Capital Unrecovered	Capital Recovered Plus Return
1	$1,000	$7,000	$560	$1,560
2	1,000	6,000	480	1,480
3	1,000	5,000	400	1,400
4	1,000	4,000	320	1,320
5	1,000	3,000	240	1,240
6	1,000	2,000	160	1,160

Table 10.2. GENERAL EXPRESSIONS FOR THE STRAIGHT-LINE DEPRECIATION MODEL

Year	Capital Recovered	Capital Unrecovered Beginning of Year	Return on Capital Unrecovered	Capital Recovered plus Return
1	$\frac{P-F}{n}$	P	Pi	$\frac{P-F}{n} + Pi$
2	$\frac{P-F}{n}$	$P - \left(\frac{P-F}{n}\right)$	$\left[P - \left(\frac{P-F}{n}\right)\right]i$	$\frac{P-F}{n} + \left[P - \left(\frac{P-F}{n}\right)\right]i$
3	$\frac{P-F}{n}$	$P - 2\left(\frac{P-F}{n}\right)$	$\left[P - 2\left(\frac{P-F}{n}\right)\right]i$	$\frac{P-F}{n} + \left[P - 2\left(\frac{P-F}{n}\right)\right]i$
r	$\frac{P-F}{n}$	$P - (r-1)\left(\frac{P-F}{n}\right)$	$\left[P - (r-1)\left(\frac{P-F}{n}\right)\right]i$	$\frac{P-F}{n} + \left[P - (r-1)\left(\frac{P-F}{n}\right)\right]i$
n	$\frac{P-F}{n}$	$P - (n-1)\left(\frac{P-F}{n}\right)$	$\left[P - (n-1)\left(\frac{P-F}{n}\right)\right]i$	$\frac{P-F}{n} + \left[P - (n-1)\left(\frac{P-F}{n}\right)\right]i$

The equivalent end-of-service value of capital recovered plus return may be found by multiplying the capital recovered plus return for the rth year by the compound-amount factor for the rth year, and summing over all r years. Let F equal the equivalent end-of-service-life value of capital recovered plus return. Then

$$F = \sum_{r=1}^{n} \left\{\frac{P-F}{n} + \left[P - (r-1)\left(\frac{P-F}{n}\right)\right]i\right\}(1+i)^{n-r}$$

$$= \sum_{r=1}^{n} \left[\frac{P-F}{n} + Pi + \frac{P-F}{n}i\right](1+i)^{n-r} - \sum_{r=1}^{n} i\left(\frac{P-F}{n}\right)r(1+i)^{n-r}$$

$$= \left[\frac{P-F}{n}(1+i) + Pi\right]\sum_{r=1}^{n}(1+i)^{n-r} - i\left[\frac{P-F}{n}\right]\sum_{r=1}^{n} r(1+i)^{n-r}.$$

But

$$\sum_{r=1}^{n}(1+i)^{n-r} = (1+i)^{n-1} + (1+i)^{n-2} + \cdots + (1+i) + 1$$
$$= \frac{(1+i)^n - 1}{i}.$$

Let

$$\rho = \sum_{r=1}^{n} r(1+i)^{n-r}$$
$$= (1+i)^{n-1} + 2(1+i)^{n-2} + \cdots + (n-1)(1+i) + n.$$
$$(1+i)\rho = (1+i)^n + 2(1+i)^{n-1} + \cdots + n(1+i) + 1 - 1.$$

Subtracting ρ from $(1+i)\rho$, term by term yields

$$i\rho = (1+i)^n + \sum_{r=1}^{n}(1+i)^{n-r} - (n+1)$$
$$= (1+i)^n + \frac{(i+i)^n - 1}{i} - (n+1).$$

Substituting these evaluations into the expression for F gives

$$F = \left[\frac{P-F}{n}(1+i) + Pi\right]\frac{(1+i)^n - 1}{i} - i\left(\frac{P-F}{n}\right)\left[\frac{(1+i)^n}{i}\right.$$
$$\left. + \frac{(1+i)^n - 1}{i^2} - \frac{n+1}{i}\right]$$
$$= Pi\frac{(1+i)^n - 1}{i} + \frac{P-F}{n}\left[\frac{(1+i)^n - 1}{i} + (1+i)^n - 1 - (1+i)^n\right.$$
$$\left. - \frac{(1+i)^n - 1}{i} + n + 1\right]$$
$$= P(1+i)^n - P + \frac{P-F}{n}(n) = P(1+i)^n - F.$$

An expression for the equivalent annual cost of capital recovered plus return may be derived by multiplying the equivalent end-of-service-life value of capital recovered plus return by the sinking-fund factor as follows:

$$[P(1+i)^n - F]\left[\frac{i}{(1+i)^n - 1}\right] = P\left[\frac{i(1+i)^n}{(1+i)^n - 1}\right] - F\left[\frac{i}{(1+i)^n - 1}\right]$$
$$= P\left[\frac{i(1+i)^n}{(1+i)^n - 1}\right] - F\left[\frac{i(1+i)^n}{(1+i)^n - 1} - i\right]$$
$$= (P-F)\left[\frac{i(1+i)^n}{(1+i)^n - 1}\right] + F(i)$$
$$= (P-F)(\overset{A/P,i,n}{}) + F(i). \qquad (10.1)$$

This is the same result as that obtained in Equation (9.8). Regardless of the depreciation model chosen to represent the value of an asset over time, the equivalent annual cost of capital recovered plus return is given by Equation (9.8) or (10.1).

The Sinking-Fund Model. The sinking-fund depreciation model assumes that the value of an asset decreases at an increasing rate. One of a series of equal amounts is assumed to be deposited into a sinking fund at the end of each year of the asset's life. The sinking fund is ordinarily compounded annually, and at the end of the estimated life of the asset, the amount accumulated equals the total depreciation of the asset. Thus, if an asset has a first cost of $7,000, an estimated life of 6 years, an estimated salvage value of $1,000, and if an interest rate of 8 percent is used, the amount deposited into the sinking fund at the end of each year will be

$$(\$7,000 - \$1,000)(\overset{A/F,8,6}{0.13632}) = \$817.92.$$

The capital recovered during any year is the sum of the amount deposited into the sinking fund at the end of the year and the amount of interest earned on the sinking fund during the year. For the foregoing example, the capital recovered during the first year will be $817.92, during the second year $817.92 + $817.92 × 0.08 = $883.35, during the third year $817.92 + $1,701.27 × 0.08 = $954.02, and so forth. These values are given in the first section of Table 10.3.

Table 10.3. EXAMPLE OF THE SINKING-FUND DEPRECIATION MODEL

Year	Capital Recovered	Capital Unrecovered Beginning of Year	Return on the Capital Unrecovered	Capital Recovered plus Return
1	$817.92	$7,000.00	$560.00	$1,377.92
2	883.35	6,182.08	494.57	1,377.92
3	954.02	5,298.73	423.90	1,377.92
4	1,030.35	4,344.61	347.57	1,377.92
5	1,112.78	3,314.26	265.14	1,377.92
6	1,201.80	2,201.48	176.12	1,377.92

The investment in the asset during the first year is $7,000, during the second year $6,182.08, during the third year $5,298.73, and so forth. The return for the first year would be $7,000 × 0.08 = $560, for the second year $6,182.08 × 0.08 = $494.57, for the third year $5,298.73 × 0.08 = $423.90, and so forth. The capital recovery plus return will be a constant $1,377.92 each year, as indicated in Table 10.3. General expressions for the sinking-fund model are given in Table 10.4.

The Fixed-Percentage Model. The fixed-percentage depreciation model assumes that the reduction in the value of an asset decreases at a decreasing rate. In effect, the depreciation during any year is equal to the undepreciated amount at the beginning of that year times D, where $D \times 100$ is the fixed percentage rate of depreciation. The undepreciated balance remaining at the end

Table 10.4. GENERAL EXPRESSIONS FOR THE SINKING-FUND DEPRECIATION MODEL.

Year	Capital Recovered	Capital Unrecovered Beginning of Year	Return on the Capital Unrecovered	Capital Recovered plus Return
1	$\dfrac{(P-F)i}{(1+i)^n - 1}$	P	Pi	$Pi + \dfrac{(P-F)i}{(1+i)^n - 1}$
2	$\dfrac{(P-F)i(1+i)}{(1+i)^n - 1}$	$P - \dfrac{(P-F)i}{(1+i)^n - 1}$	$Pi - \dfrac{(P-F)i^2}{(1+i)^n - 1}$	$Pi + \dfrac{(P-F)i}{(1+i)^n - 1}$
3	$\dfrac{(P-F)i(1+i)^2}{(1+i)^n - 1}$	$P - \dfrac{(P-F)[(1+i)^2 - 1]}{(1+i)^n - 1}$	$Pi - \dfrac{(P-F)i[(1+i)^2 - 1]}{(1+i)^n - 1}$	$Pi + \dfrac{(P-F)i}{(1+i)^n - 1}$
r	$\dfrac{(P-F)i(1+i)^{r-1}}{(1+i)^n - 1}$	$P - \dfrac{(P-F)[(1+i)^{r-1} - 1]}{(1+i)^n - 1}$	$Pi - \dfrac{(P-F)i[(1+i)^{r-1} - 1]}{(1+i)^n - 1}$	$Pi + \dfrac{(P-F)i}{(1+i)^n - 1}$
n	$\dfrac{(P-F)i(1+i)^{n-1}}{(1+i)^n - 1}$	$P - \dfrac{(P-F)[(1+i)^{n-1} - 1]}{(1+i)^n - 1}$	$Pi - \dfrac{(P-F)i[(1+i)^{n-1} - 1]}{(1+i)^n - 1}$	$Pi + \dfrac{(P-F)i}{(1+i)^n - 1}$

of any year equals the unrecovered balance at the beginning of that year times $(1 - D)$. The unrecovered capital at the end of the first, second, and nth year is then $P(1 - D)$, $P(1 - D)^2$, and $P(1 - D)^n$, respectively, with $P(1 - D)^n = F$. The general expression for determining D, given P, F, and n is then

$$D = 1 - \left(\frac{F}{P}\right)^{1/n}, \qquad F > 0. \tag{10.2}$$

In the preceding example, where $P = \$7,000$, $F = \$1,000$, and $n = 6$ years,

$$D = 1 - \left(\frac{1,000}{7,000}\right)^{1/6} = 1 - 0.723 = 0.277.$$

The capital recovered during the first year will be $\$7,000.00 \times 0.277 = \$1,939.00$, during the second year ($\$7,000.00 - \$1,939.00) \times 0.277 = \$1,401.90$, during the third year ($\$7,000.00 - \$1,939.00 - \$1,401.90) \times 0.277 = \$1,013.57$, and so forth. These values are given in the first section of Table 10.5.

Table 10.5. EXAMPLE OF THE FIXED-PERCENTAGE DEPRECIATION MODEL

Year	Capital Recovered	Capital Unrecovered Beginning of Year	Return on the Capital Unrecovered	Capital Recovered plus Return
1	$1,939.00	$7,000.00	$560.00	$2,499.00
2	1,401.90	5,061.00	404.88	1,806.78
3	1,013.57	3,659.10	292.73	1,306.30
4	732.81	2,645.53	211.64	944.45
5	529.82	1,912.72	153.02	682.84
6	382.84	1,382.10	110.57	493.41

The investment in the asset during the first year will be $\$7,000.00$, for the second year $\$5,061.00$, for the third year $\$3,659.10$, and so forth. With an interest rate of 8 percent, the return for the first year will be $\$7,000.00 \times 0.08 = \$560.00$, for the second year $\$5,061.00 \times 0.08 = \$404.88$, for the third year $\$3,659.10 \times 0.08 = \$292.73$, and so forth. The capital unrecovered, return, and capital recovery plus return are given in Table 10.5 for each year of the asset's life. General expressions for the fixed-percentage model are given in Table 10.6.

The Sum-of-the-Years Model. The sum-of-the-years model of depreciation also assumes that the value of an asset decreases at a decreasing rate. The sum of the numbers from 1 to n is used as the denominator for a series of fractions, n in number, used to calculate annual depreciation. The numerator of the fraction for any specific year is the life expectancy as of that year. The depreciation allocation for any year is found by multiplying the specific fraction by the depreciable amount.

Returning to the example of $P = \$7,000$, $n = 6$, and $F = \$1,000$, then $1 + 2 + 3 + 4 + 5 + 6 = 21$, and the depreciation during the first year will be

Table 10.6. GENERAL EXPRESSIONS FOR THE FIXED-PERCENTAGE DEPRECIATION MODEL

Year	Capital Recovered	Capital Unrecovered Beginning of Year	Return on the Capital Unrecovered	Capital Recovered plus Return
1	$P\left[1 - \sqrt[n]{\dfrac{F}{P}}\right]$	P	Pi	$P\left(1 - \sqrt[n]{\dfrac{F}{P}}\right) + Pi$
2	$P\left[1 - \sqrt[n]{\dfrac{F}{P}}\right]\left(\dfrac{F}{P}\right)^{1/n}$	$P\left(\dfrac{F}{P}\right)^{1/n}$	$Pi\left(\dfrac{F}{P}\right)^{1/n}$	$\left[P\left(1 - \sqrt[n]{\dfrac{F}{P}}\right) + Pi\right]\left(\dfrac{F}{P}\right)^{1/n}$
3	$P\left[1 - \sqrt[n]{\dfrac{F}{P}}\right]\left(\dfrac{F}{P}\right)^{2/n}$	$P\left(\dfrac{F}{P}\right)^{2/n}$	$Pi\left(\dfrac{F}{P}\right)^{2/n}$	$\left[P\left(1 - \sqrt[n]{\dfrac{F}{P}}\right) + Pi\right]\left(\dfrac{F}{P}\right)^{2/n}$
r	$P\left[1 - \sqrt[n]{\dfrac{F}{P}}\right]\left(\dfrac{F}{P}\right)^{(r-1)/n}$	$P\left(\dfrac{F}{P}\right)^{(r-1)/n}$	$Pi\left(\dfrac{F}{P}\right)^{(r-1)/n}$	$\left[P\left(1 - \sqrt[n]{\dfrac{F}{P}}\right) + Pi\right]\left(\dfrac{F}{P}\right)^{(r-1)/n}$
n	$P\left[1 - \sqrt[n]{\dfrac{F}{P}}\right]\left(\dfrac{F}{P}\right)^{(n-1)/n}$	$P\left(\dfrac{F}{P}\right)^{(n-1)/n}$	$Pi\left(\dfrac{F}{P}\right)^{(n-1)/n}$	$\left[P\left(1 - \sqrt[n]{\dfrac{F}{P}}\right) + Pi\right]\left(\dfrac{F}{P}\right)^{(n-1)/n}$

$$(P - F)\frac{n}{\sum n} = (\$7{,}000 - 1{,}000)\left(\frac{6}{21}\right) = \$1{,}714.29. \qquad (10.3)$$

During the second year, the depreciation will be ($7,000 − $1,000)(5/21) = $1,428.57, during the third year ($7,000 − $1,000)(4/21) = $1,142.86, and so forth. These values are given in the first section of Table 10.7.

Table 10.7. EXAMPLE OF THE SUM-OF-THE-YEARS DEPRECIATION MODEL

Year	Capital Recovered	Capital Unrecovered Beginning of Year	Return on the Capital Unrecovered	Capital Recovered Plus Return
1	$1,714.29	$7,000.00	$560.00	$2,274.29
2	1,428.57	5,285.71	422.86	1,851.43
3	1,142.86	3,857.14	308.57	1,451.43
4	857.14	2,714.28	217.14	1,074.28
5	571.43	1,857.14	148.57	720.00
6	285.72	1,285.71	102.86	388.58

The unrecovered capital will be $7,000 during the first year, $7,000 − $1,714.29 = $5,285.71 during the second year, $5,285.71 − $1,428.57 = $3,857.14 during the third year, and so forth. With an 8 percent interest rate, the return for the first year will be $7,000 × 0.08 = $560.00, for the second year $5,285.71 × 0.08 = $422.86, for the third year $3,857.13 × 0.08 = $308.57, and so forth. The capital unrecovered plus return for each year of the asset's life is given in Table 10.7. General expressions for the sum-of-the-years model are given in Table 10.8.

Equivalence of Depreciation Models. In economic analysis it is often necessary to compute the equivalent annual cost of capital recovered plus return so that alternatives involving competitive assets may be compared on an equivalent basis. As a numerical example of the equivalence of depreciation methods, consider the example used in this section. The present worth of capital recovered plus return for each year from the straight-line model of Table 10.1 is given in Table 10.9. The total present worth is $6,369.69. Similarly, the present worth of capital recovered plus return for each year from the sinking-fund model of Table 10.3 is given in Table 10.10. The total present worth is $6,369.85. The slight difference is due to the use of tabular values with too few decimal places.

There are actually only two real transactions in an asset's life: the first cost, P, and the receipt from salvage after n years, F. From these, the equivalent annual cost of capital recovery and return can be calculated. The annual equivalent for an expenditure P at present and receipt F after n years is given by

$$(P - F)(\overset{A/P,i,n}{\qquad}) + F(i)$$

as was shown previously.

Table 10.8. GENERAL EXPRESSIONS FOR THE SUM-OF-THE-YEARS DEPRECIATION MODEL

Year	Capital Recovered	Capital Unrecovered Beginning of Year	Return on the Capital Unrecovered	Capital Recovered plus Return
1	$\dfrac{n}{\sum n}(P-F)$	P	Pi	$\dfrac{n}{\sum n}(P-F)+Pi$
2	$\dfrac{n-1}{\sum n}(P-F)$	$\dfrac{\sum(n-1)}{\sum n}(P-F)+F$	$\left[\dfrac{\sum(n-1)}{\sum n}(P-F)+F\right]i$	$\dfrac{n-1}{\sum n}(P-F)+\left[\dfrac{\sum(n-1)}{\sum n}(P-F)+F\right]i$
3	$\dfrac{n-2}{\sum n}(P-F)$	$\dfrac{\sum(n-2)}{\sum n}(P-F)+F$	$\left[\dfrac{\sum(n-2)}{\sum n}(P-F)+F\right]i$	$\dfrac{n-2}{\sum n}(P-F)+\left[\dfrac{\sum(n-2)}{\sum n}(P-F)+F\right]i$
r	$\dfrac{n-r+1}{\sum n}(P-F)$	$\dfrac{\sum(n-r+1)}{\sum n}(P-F)+F$	$\left[\dfrac{\sum(n-r+1)}{\sum n}(P-F)+F\right]i$	$\dfrac{n-r+1}{\sum n}(P-F)+\left[\dfrac{\sum(n-r+1)}{\sum n}(P-F)+F\right]i$
n	$\dfrac{1}{\sum n}(P-F)$	$\dfrac{1}{\sum n}(P-F)+F$	$\left[\dfrac{1}{\sum n}(P-F)+F\right]i$	$\dfrac{1}{\sum n}(P-F)+\left[\dfrac{1}{\sum n}(P-F)+F\right]i$

Table 10.9. PRESENT WORTH OF CAPITAL RECOVERY PLUS RETURN FOR STRAIGHT-LINE DEPRECIATION MODEL

Year	Capital Recovered plus Return	Single-Payment Present-Worth Factor	Present Worth
1	$1,560	$P/F, 8, 1$ (0.9259)	$1,444.40
2	1,480	$P/F, 8, 2$ (0.8573)	1,268.80
3	1,400	$P/F, 8, 3$ (0.7938)	1,111.32
4	1,320	$P/F, 8, 4$ (0.7350)	970.20
5	1,240	$P/F, 8, 5$ (0.6806)	843.94
6	1,160	$P/F, 8, 6$ (0.6302)	731.03

Table 10.10. PRESENT WORTH OF CAPITAL RECOVERY PLUS RETURN FOR SINKING-FUND DEPRECIATION MODEL

Year	Capital Recovered plus Return	Present-Worth Factor	Present Worth
1	$1,377.92	$P/F, 8, 1$ (0.9259)	$1,275.82
2	1,377.92	$P/F, 8, 2$ (0.8573)	1,181.29
3	1,377.92	$P/F, 8, 3$ (0.7938)	1,093.79
4	1,377.92	$P/F, 8, 4$ (0.7350)	1,012.77
5	1,377.92	$P/F, 8, 5$ (0.6806)	937.81
6	1,377.92	$P/F, 8, 6$ (0.6302)	868.37

10.3 THE BASIC REPLACEMENT MODEL

The basic replacement model is a simple economic comparison of the desirability of retaining an asset against that of replacing it with a proposed asset. These alternatives are usually delineated as present and future receipts and disbursements and compared on an equivalent cost basis. This comparison is sometimes difficult, however, because aspects of the asset's use or life may not be directly comparable. These differences may not be easily reduced to economic terms. Also, the future of a present asset is less cause for concern because of its shorter remaining life and lower value. In addition, a decision not to replace the existing asset can be reviewed and reversed at any time in the future.

Considerations Leading to Replacement. When replacement is being considered, two assets must be evaluated: the present asset and its potential replacement. Since the success of an industrial organization depends on profit, replacement should generally occur if an economic advantage will result.

Replacing an asset before it is completely worn out contradicts the concept of thrift held by many decision makers. Part of the reluctance to replace physically satisfactory but economically inferior equipment arises because a decision to replace is much more binding than a decision to continue with the present asset. Continuing production with the existing asset is a course of action that may be reviewed at any time, whereas a decision to replace is a commitment for a longer period into the future. Caution in this respect is justified.

A machine or other asset may be incapable of meeting the changing demand required of it. This is often manifested by equipment of fixed capacity and a requirement that sometimes exceeds this capacity. A machine tool may not be capable of handling larger workpieces. A motor may not be able to meet an increased load. In each case the usable piece of equipment may be in excellent condition, with consideration of its replacement being forced by the need for greater capacity.

New equipment is continually being developed that will perform the same operations as existing equipment but at substantial savings. When this occurs, the existing asset may be replaced because of this technological obsolescence. The existing asset may still be capable of meeting the production demands placed on it, without excessive maintenance cost and at a satisfactory level of operating efficiency. If, however, an economic advantage can be gained by replacement, the existing asset should be retired.

Machines and other complex items of equipment rarely incur uniform wear. Some elements or components are likely to deteriorate faster and fail before others. Under these conditions it is often economical to repair the component to extend the useful life of the asset. Some repairs are minor; others are quite extensive. Some may follow an unpredictable pattern; others are periodic and can be planned. A piece of equipment may become a candidate for replacement when it needs repair. Equipment is more likely to be replaced when the needed repairs are extensive and when it appears that additional and excessive repairs will soon be needed.

Equipment sometimes operates at an initial peak efficiency which declines with time and use. The reduction in efficiency may require increased power consumption and longer use to accomplish the same operation. This, in turn, may result in increased costs of operation which will make the equipment a candidate for replacement. As with the case of increasing maintenance costs, increasing costs of operation can be analyzed with a tabular review of equivalent average annual cost of service. This leads to the identification of the minimum equivalent average annual cost.

In most situations, an asset is replaced for more than one cause. An asset may begin to require more maintenance, and/or it may begin to operate at a reduced level of efficiency. It may not always be capable of meeting the demands placed on it. The availability of a potential replacement, which may have a higher initial cost but which is more economical to operate, may result in an analysis of the economic feasibility of replacing the existing asset.

Whatever the reasons leading to the consideration of replacement, the analysis and decision must be based on estimates of what will occur in the future. The past is irrelevant in replacement analysis and must not be allowed to influence the replacement decision.

The Treatment of Sunk Costs. When an asset is purchased and placed into operation, a depreciation model is usually selected to reflect the changing value of the asset. This is done for a number of reasons, one of which is to reflect the cost of the consumption of that asset. When the asset is eventually replaced either before, at, or after its estimated life, there may be some discrepancy existing between the value of the asset as reflected in the depreciation schedule and the actual price received for it. If more money is received for the asset than the worth established by the depreciation schedule, a capital gain is realized because of this difference. If the reverse is true and the asset is sold for less than its depreciated value, a sunk cost has occurred. In evaluating replacements, especially where an asset is being considered for replacement sooner than its intended life, it is likely that a sunk cost will be encountered.

Consider the following example as an illustration of the correct and incorrect treatment of sunk costs. Machine A was purchased 6 years ago for $22,000. It was intended to have a life of 10 years and a salvage value after 10 years of $2,000. The depreciation schedule, using the straight-line model of depreciation, indicates that the asset is presently worth $22,000 − 6($2,000) = $10,000. The operating expenses of the machine average $8,000 per year. Machine B, presently being considered as a replacement, is being offered for $30,000. It will have an estimated life of 10 years with no salvage value and an annual operating cost of $3,000. If the proposed asset is purchased, machine A can be sold for $4,000. This sale price is taken to reflect the true market value of used machines of this type in comparison with new machines like that being considered. With an interest rate of 10 percent, should machine A be replaced?

The proper decision in this example rests on the treatment of the sunk cost. The following analysis is based on the "outsider" viewpoint which assumes that a party exists who owns neither machine A nor machine B and needs the service that can be provided by one of these two assets. The equivalent annual cost of machine A to this "outsider" will be

$$(\$4{,}000 - \$2{,}000)(0.3155 \overset{A/P,10,4}{}) + \$2{,}000(0.10) + \$8{,}000 = \$8{,}831.$$

Machine B will be obtained and operated for

$$(\$30{,}000)(0.1628 \overset{A/P,10,10}{}) + \$3{,}000 = \$7{,}884.$$

Under these conditions, the "outsider" would select machine B with an equivalent annual saving of $8,831 − $7,884 = $949 over the next 4 years. The savings or loss over the 6 years following these 4 cannot be ascertained because no information is available concerning a replacement for machine A, had it been kept for the next 4 years.

Even though a sunk cost cannot be recovered, it is natural to attempt to charge the sunk cost to the contemplated replacement. This practice is fallacious because it reduces the possibility of selecting this alternative and of realizing the potential savings. Even if the replacement is selected, the actual savings will be incorrectly reported. A sunk cost must be recognized as such and removed from consideration in the analysis of machine replacements. This requires accepting the fact that a sunk cost is revealed and not caused by replacement.

The Treatment of Unequal Service Life. An existing and a proposed asset should be compared, as far as possible, on an equivalent cost basis. If the remaining life of an existing asset and the expected life of a proposed asset are identical, a direct comparison can be made if other aspects of their service are similar. Normally, however, the life of the proposed asset will extend beyond the remaining years of the present asset, as was the case in the previous example. The following paragraphs present a general method for placing alternatives on a comparative basis by the selection of a study period. Under this procedure, comparison is made on the basis of receipts and disbursements occurring during the selected period. The effect of receipts or disbursements occurring after the study period is either ignored or included in the analysis, depending on the situation.

Consider the following example utilizing an interest rate of 12 percent: At the present time, machine A is being used to perform a certain operation. This machine has a present market value of $500 and an estimated remaining life of 2 years, with no anticipated salvage value. Operating costs are $1,000 per year. It is presently planned to replace machine A in 2 years with machine B. This replacement will have an acquisition cost, an estimated service life, salvage value, and yearly operating expense of $20,000, 8 years, none, and $600, respectively.

The opportunity of replacing machine A immediately with machine C has presented itself. Machine C will have an acquisition cost, an estimated service life, salvage value, and yearly operating expense of $11,000, 6 years, none, and $800, respectively. The two alternatives are exhibited in Table 10.11. Because these alternatives have unequal service lives, an arbitrary time period will be selected for their comparison. Since it is difficult to make forecasts, an arbitrary study period will be specified as 6 years, the life of machine C.

If machine A is retained for 2 years and replaced by machine B, this asset will have a life of 4 years within the study period and 4 years extending beyond the study period. Under an equitable allocation of costs, the equivalent annual cost for machine B during its life is

$$\$20{,}000(0.2013 \overset{A/P,12,8}{}) + \$600 = \$4{,}626.$$

Chap. 10   Depreciation and Replacement Models   211

Table 10.11. MACHINE REPLACEMENT ANALYSIS OVER A SELECTED STUDY PERIOD

	Retain Existing Asset		Replace Existing Asset	
Year End	Investment Cost	Operating Costs	Investment Cost	Operating Costs
0	$ 500 (A)		$11,000 (C)	
1		$1,000		$800
2	20,000 (B)	1,000		800
3		6,600		800
4		600		800
5		600		800
6		600		800
7		600		
8		600		
9		600		
10		600		

(Study Period is years 0 through 6.)

The present-worth cost of the 6 years of service in the study period is

$$\$500 + \$1{,}000(\underset{P/A,12,2}{1.6901}) + \$4{,}626(\underset{P/A,12,4}{3.0374})(\underset{P/F,12,2}{0.7972}) = \$13{,}392.$$

If the existing asset is replaced with machine C, the present-worth cost of the 6 years of service is

$$\$11{,}000 + \$800(\underset{P/A,12,6}{4.1114}) = \$14{,}289.$$

On the basis of this comparison, the existing asset and plan for its replacement would be retained.

Had the value of machine B at the end of the selected study period been disregarded, the other alternative might have been selected. This assumes that the asset will be retired at the end of the study period for analysis. The equivalent annual cost of machine B is calculated as

$$\$20{,}000(\underset{A/P,12,4}{0.3292}) + \$600 = \$7{,}184.$$

The present-worth cost of 6 years of service in the study period is

$$\$500 + \$1{,}000(\underset{P/A,12,2}{1.6901}) + \$7{,}184(\underset{P/A,12,4}{3.0374})(\underset{P/F,12,2}{0.7972}) = \$19{,}586.$$

Thus, retaining machine A and purchasing machine B in 2 years exceeds the cost of replacing machine A immediately with machine C. As a result, the latter alternative would probably be selected.

The practice of disregarding value remaining in an asset introduces error equivalent to that value actually remaining. The practice of ignoring the remaining value in an asset is difficult to defend because it does not greatly reduce the burden of calculations nor does it lean toward a policy of conservation in machine replacement.

10.4 THE OPTIMUM REPLACEMENT INTERVAL

Although it is mathematically attractive to forecast the optimum life of an asset when it is installed, this is more of an ideal than a reality. The decision to replace an asset is almost always made just before the actual replacement and is the result of the analysis of factors that exist at that time. There are a number of reasons for this. Rarely are the future cost data of an asset, particularly the maintenance cost, available when the asset is purchased. In addition, the decision to replace an asset depends on the economic advantage of the proposed replacement. It is equally unlikely that the characteristics and cost of an asset's replacement are available in a meaningful form when the original asset is purchased. Nevertheless, treatment of the optimum replacement interval of an asset is proposed in this section.

It will be assumed that the future costs of an asset can be predicted with some reasonable degree of accuracy at the time the asset is purchased. To simplify the development, only maintenance costs are treated. It is also assumed that the replacement is identical in cost and characteristics to the original asset.

Patterns of Maintenance Costs. The decision to replace an asset is dependent on the pattern of costs which must be incurred to maintain that asset properly through its service life. For classification, these costs may be considered to be sporadic, relatively constant, or increasing over the life of the asset. It will be demonstrated that only increasing costs are grounds for equipment replacement.

Consider the example of a machine purchased for $600 with no anticipated salvage value. An interest rate of zero is assumed for simplicity. The pattern of maintenance costs is shown in Table 10.12. Averaging these costs as shown in

Table 10.12. ECONOMIC HISTORY OF A MACHINE UNDER SPORADIC MAINTENANCE COSTS

End of Year (A)	Maintenance Cost at End of Year (B)	Summation of Maintenance Costs (Σ B) (C)	Average Cost of Maintenance (C ÷ A) (D)	Average Capital Cost ($600 ÷ A) (E)	Average Total Cost (D + E) (F)
1	$100	$100	$100	$600	$700
2	400	500	250	300	550
3	100	600	200	200	400
4	100	700	175	150	325
5	400	1,100	220	120	340
6	100	1,200	200	100	300
7	400	1,600	229	86	315
8	100	1,700	213	75	288

column D tends to smooth their sporadic occurrence. The average yearly capital costs decrease as the number of years increases. Replacement with a minimum average yearly cost is more likely just before a large maintenance expenditure, since there is no clearly defined minimum cost point.

Under constant maintenance costs, there will never be justification for replacement. Extending the life of the asset will reduce the average capital cost and the average yearly cost. Only under increasing maintenance costs will there be justification for replacement. This will hold true with or without interest charges.

Consider a modification of the preceding example involving maintenance costs which begin at zero and increase $100 each year. The pattern of average total costs is given in Table 10.13. With the rising average maintenance costs counterbalanced by the diminishing average capital costs, a year will be reached where the sum of these costs is a minimum. In this example, the minimum cost of $300 is achieved after either 3 or 4 years. Retaining the asset longer than 4 years or disposing of it before 3 years will result in a cost penalty.

Table 10.13. ECONOMIC HISTORY OF A MACHINE UNDER INCREASING MAINTENANCE COSTS

End of Year (A)	Maintenance Cost at End of Year (B)	Summation of Maintenance Costs (Σ B) (C)	Average Cost of Maintenance (C $\div$ A) (D)	Average Capital Cost ($600 $\div$ A) (E)	Average Total Cost (D + E) (F)
1	$ 0	$ 0	0	$600	$600
2	100	100	$ 50	300	350
3	200	300	100	200	300
4	300	600	150	150	300
5	400	1,000	200	120	320
6	500	1,500	250	100	350

Finding the Optimum Replacement Interval. When there exists a predictable and rising trend in maintenance cost, it is possible to formulate a model that may be used to find the optimum replacement interval. If interest is neglected, the average annual total cost of an asset under increasing maintenance costs can be expressed as

$$TC = \frac{P}{n} + O + (n-1)\frac{m}{2}, \qquad (10.4)$$

where P = initial cost of the asset
O = annual operating costs plus constant portion of maintenance costs
m = the amount by which maintenance costs increase each year
n = life of the asset in years.

If Equation (10.4) is differentiated with respect to n, set equal to zero, and solved for n, the optimum replacement interval will result. This gives

$$\frac{dTC}{dn} = -\frac{P}{n^2} + \frac{m}{2} = 0$$

$$n = \sqrt{\frac{2P}{m}}. \qquad (10.5)$$

Using Equation (10.5), the optimum life of the example given by Table 10.13 is

$$n = \sqrt{\frac{2(\$600)}{\$100}} = 3.46 \text{ years.}$$

The average annual total cost may be found from Equation (10.4) as

$$TC = \frac{\$600}{3.46} + 2.46\left(\frac{\$100}{2}\right) = \$296.$$

As an illustration of the effect of interest, consider a modification of the example above. Table 10.14 exhibits the same information as Table 10.13 except

Table 10.14. ECONOMIC HISTORY OF A MACHINE UNDER INCREASING MAINTENANCE COSTS WITH INTEREST

(A) End of Year	(B) Maintenance Cost at End of Year	(C) Present-Worth Factor $P/F, 10, n$	(D) Present Worth of Maintenance (B × C)	(E) Summation of Present Worths (Σ D)	(F) Capital Recovery Factor $A/P, 10, n$	(G) Equivalent Annual Cost of Maintenance (E × F)	(H) Equivalent Annual Cost of Capital Recovery (F × $600)	(I) Total Equivalent Annual Cost (G + H)
1	0	0.9091	0	0	1.1000	0	$660	$660
2	$100	0.8265	$ 83	$ 83	0.5762	$ 48	346	394
3	200	0.7513	150	233	0.4021	94	241	335
4	300	0.6830	205	438	0.3155	138	189	327
5	400	0.6209	248	686	0.2638	181	158	339
6	500	0.5645	282	968	0.2296	222	138	360

for the consideration of an interest rate of 10 percent. The optimum replacement interval is close to that found without interest. This is illustrated graphically in Figure 10.2 together with the effect of interest on the cost components. Since the total cost function is flat in the region of its minimum, Equation (10.5) may be used as an approximation for the optimum replacement interval for cases involving interest. The tabular approach can always be used when an exact solution is required.

Chap. 10 Depreciation and Replacement Models

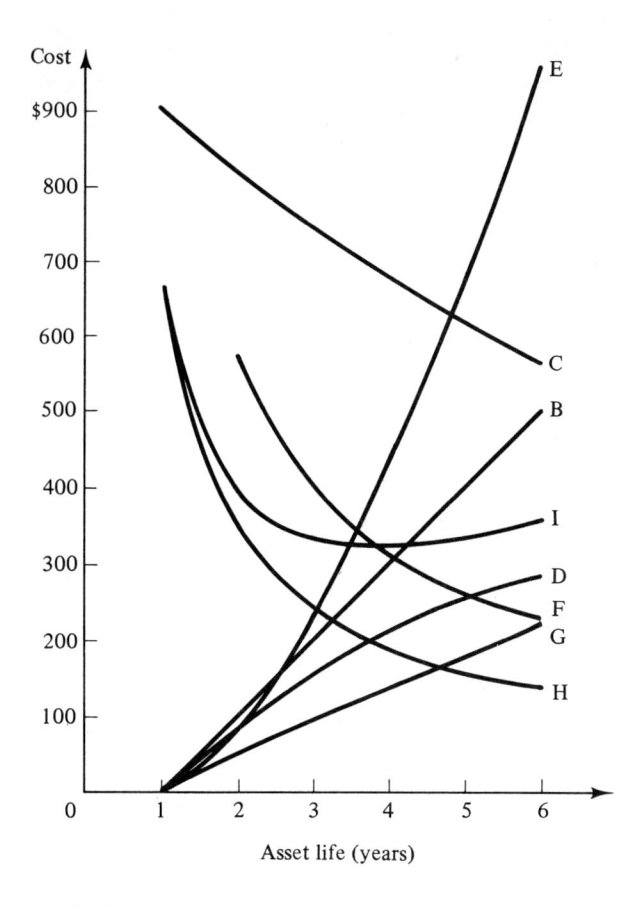

Figure 10.2 Optimum replacement intervals for the data of Tables 10.13 and 10.14.

10.5 A DYNAMIC REPLACEMENT MODEL

Because of deterioration and the passage of time, the net revenue earned by an asset may become less and less. A series of decisions of whether to keep an existing asset or purchase a replacement must be made. From a set of future revenue and cost predictions for the existing asset and subsequent replacements, a sequence of replacement decisions that maximize profit may be derived using dynamic programming.

Definitions and Problem Formulation. The following terminology will be used in formulating the machine replacement problem.

$R(t, n)$ = revenue during year n resulting from operating a machine built in year t

$C(t, n)$ = cost of replacing a machine built in year t by a machine built at the beginning of year n

$f(t, n)$ = total return in years $n, n+1, \ldots, N$ from the best operating policy if the existing machine was built in year t

In addition, it is assumed that the decisions are made only at the beginning of each year, replacement is instantaneous, and an existing machine can only be replaced by a new machine. Thus, only two alternatives are considered: Keep the existing machine, designated K, or purchase a new machine, designated P.

If the planning horizon consists of N years, it can be assumed that

$$f(t, N + 1) = 0 \quad \text{for all } t. \tag{10.6}$$

This assumption considers all transactions after the year N to be irrelevant. If the existing machine at the beginning of year n was built in year t, the best return from a decision to keep the machine one more year will be

$$g_k(t, n) = R(t, n) + f(t, n + 1).$$

Similarly, the best return from a decision to purchase a new machine will be

$$g_P(t, n) = R(n, n) - C(t, n) + f(n, n + 1).$$

Application of the principle of optimality yields the following functional equation:

$$\begin{aligned} f(t, n) &= \max \begin{Bmatrix} g_k(t, n) \\ g_P(t, n) \end{Bmatrix} \\ &= \max \begin{Bmatrix} R(t, n) + f(t, n + 1) \\ R(n, n) - C(t, n) + f(n, n + 1) \end{Bmatrix}. \end{aligned} \tag{10.7}$$

Equation (10.7) takes the form of the maximum of the expected revenue from the present stage plus the decisions from the subsequent stage and a reverse sequence of decisions from the year N, to year $N - 1$, and so forth, until the beginning is obtained. The starting conditions for this computational procedure are obtained from Equation (10.6).

As an example of the application of Equation (10.7) assume that the net revenues to be derived from a machine are a function of the year of replacement and the year of manufacture as given in Table 10.15. Also assume that the

Table 10.15. NET REVENUES FOR MACHINE REPLACEMENT

Year of Decision	Year of Manufacture of Machine				
	1	2	3	4	5
1	10				
2	9	14			
3	8	12	15		
4	7	11	13	14	
5	6	9	12	13	17
Totals	40	46	40	27	17

replacement cost is a function of the year of decision and the year of manufacture as given in Table 10.16. The objective is to determine a series of decisions, one for each year, that specifies whether the existing machine should be kept or the replacement should be purchased.

Table 10.16. REPLACEMENT COST FOR MACHINE REPLACEMENT

Year of Replacement	Existing Machine Manufactured in Year				
	1	2	3	4	5
1	0				
2	5	0			
3	8	4	0		
4	12	5	3	0	
5	14	8	5	4	0

Table 10.17. TOTAL RETURN AND OPTIMAL POLICY

Year of Decision	Existing Machine Manufactured in Year					Optimal Policy
	1	2	3	4	5	
1	55					P
2	45	50				P
3	32	36	40			P
4	15	22	25	27		K
5	6	9	12	13	17	P or K

The Solution Procedure. The solution procedure utilizes Equation (10.7). For each year of decision the quantity $f(t, n)$ is computed for all values of t less than or equal to n. The quantities $f(t, n)$ are shown in Table 10.17. For ease of computation Equation (10.7) is modified to the following form:

$$f(n, n) = R(n, n) + f(n, n + 1) \qquad (10.8)$$

and

$$f(t, n) = \max \begin{Bmatrix} R(t, n) + f(t, n + 1) \\ -C(t, n) + f(n, n) \end{Bmatrix} \quad t < n. \qquad (10.9)$$

Starting from $n = N = 5$, the computations proceed in a reverse sequence to $n = 1$. For $n = 5$:

$$f(5, 5) = R(5, 5) + 0 = 17$$

$$f(4, 5) = \max \begin{Bmatrix} R(4, 5) + f(4, 6) \\ -C(4, 5) + f(5, 5) \end{Bmatrix}$$

$$= \max \begin{Bmatrix} 13 + 0 \\ -4 + 17 \end{Bmatrix} = 13(P, K)$$

$$f(3, 5) = \max \begin{Bmatrix} R(3, 5) + f(3, 6) \\ -C(3, 5) + f(5, 5) \end{Bmatrix}$$

$$= \max \begin{Bmatrix} 12 + 0 \\ -5 + 17 \end{Bmatrix} = 12(P, K)$$

$$f(2, 5) = \max \begin{Bmatrix} R(2, 5) + f(2, 6) \\ -C(2, 5) + f(5, 5) \end{Bmatrix}$$

$$= \max \begin{Bmatrix} 9 + 0 \\ -8 + 17 \end{Bmatrix} = 9(P, K)$$

$$f(1, 5) = \max \begin{Bmatrix} R(1, 5) + f(1, 6) \\ -C(1, 5) + f(5, 5) \end{Bmatrix}$$

$$= \max \begin{Bmatrix} 6 + 0 \\ -14 + 17 \end{Bmatrix} = 6(K).$$

The designation within the parentheses indicates that the return is obtained for the purchase action, P, or the keep action, K. The remainder of the calculations are as follows:

For $n = 4$:

$$f(4, 4) = R(4, 4) + f(4, 5)$$
$$= 14 + 13 = 27$$

$$f(3, 4) = \max \begin{Bmatrix} R(3, 4) + f(3, 5) \\ -C(3, 4) + f(4, 4) \end{Bmatrix}$$

$$= \max \begin{Bmatrix} 13 + 12 \\ -3 + 27 \end{Bmatrix} = 25(K)$$

$$f(2, 4) = \max \begin{Bmatrix} R(2, 4) + f(2, 5) \\ -C(2, 4) + f(4, 4) \end{Bmatrix}$$

$$= \max \begin{Bmatrix} 11 + 9 \\ -5 + 27 \end{Bmatrix} = 22(P)$$

$$f(1, 4) = \max \begin{Bmatrix} R(1, 4) + f(1, 5) \\ -C(1, 4) + f(4, 4) \end{Bmatrix}$$

$$= \max \begin{Bmatrix} 7 + 6 \\ -12 + 27 \end{Bmatrix} = 15(P).$$

For $n = 3$:

$$f(3, 3) = R(3, 3) + f(3, 4)$$
$$= 15 + 25 = 40$$

$$f(2, 3) = \max \begin{Bmatrix} R(2, 3) + f(2, 4) \\ -C(2, 3) + f(3, 3) \end{Bmatrix}$$

$$= \max \begin{Bmatrix} 12 + 22 \\ -4 + 40 \end{Bmatrix} = 36(P)$$

$$f(1, 3) = \max \begin{Bmatrix} R(1, 3) + f(1, 4) \\ -C(1, 3) + f(3, 3) \end{Bmatrix}$$

$$= \max \begin{Bmatrix} 8 + 15 \\ -8 + 40 \end{Bmatrix} = 32(P).$$

For $n = 2$:

$$f(2, 2) = R(2, 2) + f(2, 3)$$
$$= 14 + 36 = 50$$

$$f(1, 2) = \max \begin{Bmatrix} R(1, 2) + f(1, 3) \\ -C(1, 2) + f(2, 2) \end{Bmatrix}$$

$$= \max \begin{Bmatrix} 9 + 32 \\ -5 + 50 \end{Bmatrix} = 45(P).$$

For $n = 1$:

$$f(1, 1) = R(1, 1) + f(1, 2)$$
$$= 10 + 45 = 55.$$

The optimal policy is obtained by proceeding backward from $n = 1$ to $n = 5$. The obvious optimal policy in year 1 is to purchase. The machine on hand at the beginning of year 2 will be the machine built in year 1. The computation for $f(1, 2)$ indicates a purchase decision. The machine on hand at the beginning of year 3 will then be a machine built in year 2. The optimal policy in year 3 is to purchase as the computations for $f(2, 3)$ indicate. The machine on hand at the beginning of year 4 will be a machine built in year 3. The optimal policy in year 4 is to keep the existing machine as indicated by the computations of $f(3, 4)$. Finally, the machine on hand at the beginning of year 5 will be a machine built in year 3. The optimal policy in year 5 is either to purchase a new machine or to keep the old as is indicated by $f(3, 5)$.

10.6 REPLACEMENTS OF UNITS THAT FAIL

An asset will be replaced when it has failed completely. A unit may be replaced while it is functioning properly if it has achieved a specific probability of failure and if an economic advantage will result. This section is directed to the problem of determining whether to replace on an individual or on a group basis. If the decision is to replace on a group basis, the additional problem of determining the minimum cost replacement interval arises. Since light bulbs exhibit the characteristic of instantaneous and complete failure, they will be used in the examples of this section.

Analysis of Failure Data. The development of replacement policy for units that fail must be preceded by an analysis of failure data. Suppose that a group of 10,000 light bulbs are installed, and at the end of t time periods the number of bulbs surviving is some function of t. If the population of bulbs is homogeneous, each bulb has the same probability of being in operation at time t as any other bulb.

Although failures would be continuous, it is likely that failure data would be collected and recorded within discrete time intervals. Column B of Table 10.18 gives the number of bulbs functioning properly at the end of each time period. Column C gives the number of bulbs which failed within each time period. The probability of a bulb failing within each time period is given in column D. These probabilities are calculated from

$$P(t) = \frac{N_{t-1} - N_t}{N_o}, \qquad (10.10)$$

where $P(t)$ = probability of failure during the time period t
N_o = initial number of units in the group
N_t = number of survivors through time t
N_{t-1} = number of survivors through time $t - 1$.

Table 10.18. ANALYSIS OF LIGHT BULB FAILURE DATA

Period (A)	Survivors (B)	Failures (C)	$P(t)$ (D)	$P_c(t)$ (E)	$P_s(t)$ (F)
0	10,000	—	—	—	1.00
1	9,000	1,000	0.10	0.10	0.90
2	7,000	2,000	0.20	0.22	0.70
3	4,000	3,000	0.30	0.43	0.40
4	2,000	2,000	0.20	0.50	0.20
5	500	1,500	0.15	0.75	0.05
6	0	500	0.05	1.00	0
7	0	0	0	—	—

The probability that a bulb, having survived to an age $t - 1$, will fail during the interval $t - 1$ to t can be defined as the *conditional probability* of failure. These conditional probabilities are given in column E. They are calculated from

$$P_c(t) = \frac{N_{t-1} - N_t}{N_{t-1}}. \qquad (10.11)$$

Column F gives the probability of survival to an age t. These survival probabilities are calculated from

$$P_s(t) = \frac{N_t}{N_o}. \qquad (10.12)$$

The probabilities $P(t)$, $P_c(t)$, and $P_s(t)$ in Table 10.18 are calculated from the basic data in column B. In an actual analysis of failure data, more precision would be obtained by increasing the number of time periods and dividing the survivor data more finely. This example is based on empirical data. If there is good reason to believe that failure data conform to a known theoretical distribution, the entries in column B can be found by calculation. From these, the respective probabilities can be found.

The Number of Replacements per Period. If the policy of replacing units as they fail is followed, the number of replacements needed in each time period may be found. For simplicity assume that failures occur only at the end of a time period. If failures are replaced, the replacements themselves will eventually fail and must be replaced. These replacements will also fail and require replacement, thus giving rise to the replacement of replacements. If x_t denotes the number of replacements made at the end of the tth period, the number of replacements at the end of each period will be

$$x_0 = x_0$$
$$x_1 = x_0[P(1)]$$
$$x_2 = x_0[P(2)] + x_1[P(1)]$$
$$x_3 = x_0[P(3)] + x_1[P(2)] + x_2[P(1)],$$

and so forth. A general expression for x_t is

$$x_t = N_o \left\{ P(t) + \sum_{j=1}^{t-1} P(j)P(t-j) + \sum_{b=1}^{t-1} \left[\sum_{j=1}^{b-1} P(j)P(b-j) \right] P(t-b) + \cdots \right\}.$$
(10.13)

As an example, the number of replacements at the end of the third time period is given by

$$x_3 = 10{,}000 \left\{ P(3) + \sum_{j=1}^{2} P(j)P(3-j) \right.$$

$$\left. + \sum_{b=2}^{2} \left[\sum_{j=1}^{b-1} P(j)P(b-j) \right] P(3-b) + \cdots \right\}$$

$$= 10{,}000[0.30 + 0.10(0.20) + 0.20(0.10) + 0.10(0.10)(0.10)] = 3{,}410.$$

Table 10.19 provides a systematic means for calculating x_t. The calculations can be extended beyond the 13 periods shown. Figure 10.3 illustrates that the number of replacements required per period oscillates until a steady-state condition is achieved. This is called the *maintenance rate*, and it reaches a finite limit as the number of periods increases. The maintenance rate is in its permanent state when it is essentially constant and equal to the reciprocal of the average life.

The average life of the units under consideration is given by the expression

$$\sum_{t=0}^{n} t[P(t)]$$

For example, the average life of the light bulbs is $1(0.10) + 2(0.20) + 3(0.30) + 4(0.20) + 5(0.15) + 6(0.05) = 3.25$ periods. Hence, the number of replacements required per time period in the steady-state condition is $10{,}000/3.25$, or approximately 3,080. This value agrees with that illustrated in Figure 10.3.

Table 10.19. CALCULATION OF THE NUMBER OF REPLACEMENTS PER TIME PERIOD

$P(t)$ \ x_1	$x_0=$ 10,000	$x_1=$ 1,000	$x_2=$ 2,100	$x_3=$ 3,410	$x_4=$ 3,061	$x_5=$ 3,318	$x_6=$ 3,036	$x_7=$ 2,933	$x_8=$ 3,126	$x_9=$ 3,105	$x_{10}=$ 3,075	$x_{11}=$ 3,074	$x_{12}=$ 3,070	$x_{13}=$ 3,080
$P(6)=0.05$	500	50	105	170	153	166	152	147	156					
$P(5)=0.15$	1,500	150	315	512	459	498	456	441	468	465				
$P(4)=0.20$	2,000	200	420	682	612	664	608	588	624	620	616			
$P(3)=0.30$	3,000	300	630	1,023	918	996	912	882	936	930	924	921		
$P(2)=0.20$	2,000	200	420	682	612	664	608	588	624	620	616	614	616	
$P(1)=0.10$	1,000	100	210	341	306	332	304	294	312	310	308	307	307	308

222

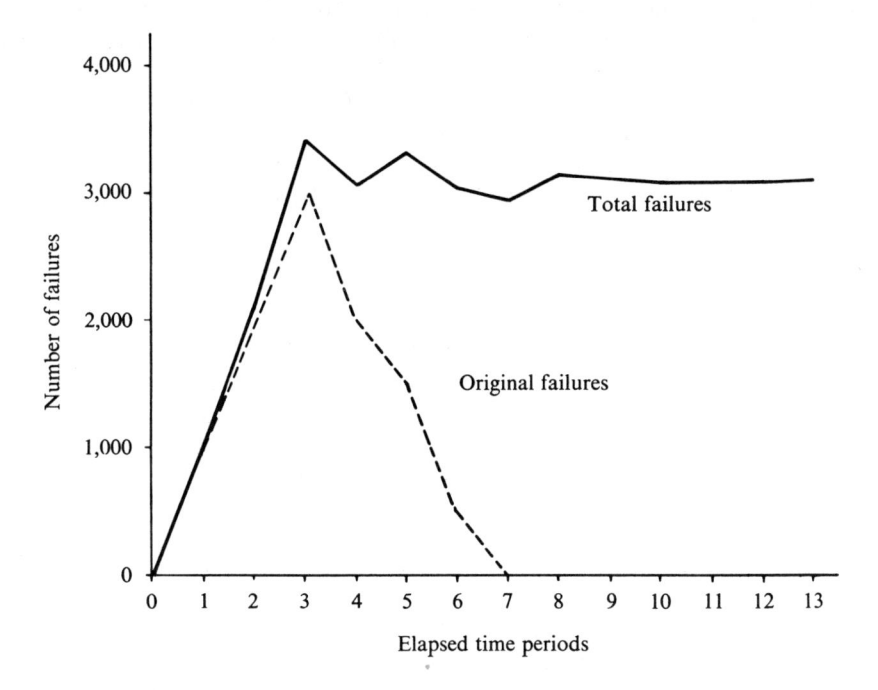

Figure 10.3 Total failures per time period and failures per time period of the original units.

If the cost of replacing 1 unit is $0.10, the cost per period would be $0.10(3,080), or $308. This period cost should be compared with the policy of group replacement. For the comparison to be valid, however, the minimum cost group replacement interval must be found.

The Minimum Cost Group Replacement Interval. Assume that units are replaced as they fail, but in addition, all units will be replaced at a specified interval. Let

TC = total replacement cost per period through t periods
C_u = cost of unit replacement per unit
C_g = cost of group replacement per unit

The total cost per period will be the cost of unit replacement per period plus the cost of group replacement per period, or

$$TC = UC + GC.$$

The cost of unit replacement per period may be expressed as

$$UC = \frac{C_u \sum_{t}^{t-1} x_t}{t},$$

where the summation of x_t is over $t-1$ periods, to allow for the replacement of failures in period t as part of the group. The cost of group replacement per period may be expressed as

$$GC = \frac{C_g N_o}{t}.$$

Therefore, the total cost per period with group replacement may be expressed as

$$TC = \frac{C_u \sum_{t}^{t-1} x_t}{t} + \frac{C_g N_o}{t}. \tag{10.14}$$

As an example, assume that the population of 10,000 bulbs has a group replacement cost of $0.05 per unit. As before, assume that the cost of unit replacement per unit is $0.10. The total cost per period for various group replacement intervals is calculated from Equation (10.14) and is given in Table 10.20.

Table 10.20. TOTAL COST PER PERIOD FOR GROUP REPLACEMENT

Period t	$\sum^{t-1} x_t$	UC	GC	TC
1	0	$ 0	$500	$500
2	1,000	50	250	300
3	3,100	103	167	270
4	6,510	163	125	288

A group replacement interval of three periods will result in a minimum total cost per period. Since this cost is $270, a saving of $308 less $270, or $38 per period, will result if the policy of group replacement is implemented.

QUESTIONS

10.1. Discuss the difference between functional and physical depreciation.
10.2. Why should capital consumption be included as a cost of production?
10.3. Name the essential components of the value-time function.
10.4. Discuss criteria other than economic that might be included in the replacement decision.
10.5. Outline the primary considerations leading to replacement.
10.6. What is a sunk cost, and how should it be treated in replacement analysis?
10.7. Discuss the treatment of unequal service life in replacement analysis.
10.8. Discuss the minimum cost replacement model in terms of $E = f(x_i, y_j)$.
10.9. Under what conditions is the minimum cost replacement model applicable?
10.10. What replacement policies are available for the case of units that fail?

PROBLEMS

10.1. An asset has a first cost of $8,000 and an estimated salvage value of $1,000 at the end of 4 years. The interest rate is 12 percent. Tabulate capital recovery, return, and capital recovery plus return for each year by the straight-line model of depreciation, the sinking-fund model of depreciation, the fixed-percentage model of depreciation, and the sum-of-the-years model of depreciation.

10.2. A drill press was purchased 10 years ago for $2,500. It is being depreciated to no salvage value over a life of 20 years by the straight-line model of depreciation. With an interest rate of 10 percent, what would have been the difference in present book value if the sinking-fund method of depreciation were used?

10.3. An asset is purchased for $1,000; it has an estimated life of 2 years and a salvage value of $100. With an interest rate of 15 percent, what will be the book value after 1 year under the straight-line, sinking-fund, sum-of-the-years, and fixed-percentage models of depreciation?

10.4. Two years ago an aerospace manufacturer purchased a numerically controlled machine tool for $400,000 to use in connection with a 6-year contract. The machine is being depreciated in accordance with the fixed-percentage model to a salvage value of $40,000 at the end of the contract period, and its current book value is an accurate measure of its value. Annual costs of operation and programming are $120,000. A replacement capable of being programmed by a digital computer can be purchased for $500,000 and sold for $150,000 at the end of 4 years. The annual cost of operation and programming will be only $42,000. If the interest rate is 12 percent, find the equivalent annual cost difference between the old and new machines.

10.5. A small community secures its water supply from a system of wells. A 6-inch centrifugal pump in good condition is presently being used. The pump was purchased 4 years ago for $2,200 and has a present book value of $1,200, having been depreciated on the basis of an expected life of 8 years. Design improvements have made the demand for this type of pump small. The present resale value of the pump is only $500; it is expected to be only $200 in 4 years. An improved pump can be purchased for $4,000 which will have an estimated life of 10 years and a $200 trade-in value. The pumping demand is 320 cubic feet per minute against an average head of 200 feet. The present pump has an efficiency of 80 percent when furnishing the foregoing demand. The new pump will have an efficiency of 90 percent. Power costs $0.062 per horsepower-hour, and either pump must operate 2,400 hours per year. Do the improvements in design justify the purchase of a new pump if the interest rate is 10 percent?

10.6. A rancher is considering two bridge designs for a structure to cross a small stream over which he must move livestock. The wooden design will cost $800 and last 10 years. The steel design will cost $1,100 and last 15 years. Each structure has no salvage value and will require the same amount of maintenance. Compare the two alternatives for a life of 30 years at an interest rate of 15 percent.

10.7. The following two alternatives are available for purchasing an automobile: A new automobile can be purchased for $8,000 and has an estimated life of

10 years, with an average annual maintenance cost of $100. As an alternative, a used automobile can be purchased for $4,000, with an estimated life of 6 years and an average annual maintenance cost of $400. Which of the two alternatives would you choose, with an interest rate of 12 percent? Assume that the salvage value is negligible in both alternatives and the automobile is required for a 5-year period.

10.8. A vehicle was purchased 5 years ago at a cost of $9,600. The following table is a record of its annual operating costs, maintenance costs, book value, and salvage value.

Year of Service	Operating Costs for Year	Maintenance Costs for Year	Book Value at End of Year	Salvage Value at End of Year
1	$4,600	$ 150	$8,100	$500
2	4,650	400	6,600	500
3	4,950	700	5,100	500
4	5,350	900	3,600	500
5	5,800	1,900	2,100	500

If interest is neglected, what is the average annual cost of each year of service? At what service was this average annual cost minimized?

10.9. A special-purpose computer is installed at a first cost of $8,000. The table below provides other relevent data.

Year of Service	Maintenance and Operating Costs	Book Value at End of Year	Resale Value at End of Year
1	$5,000	$7,500	$3,500
2	5,250	7,000	3,000
3	5,500	6,500	2,500
4	5,750	6,000	2,000
5	6,000	5,500	1,500
6	6,250	5,000	1,000
7	6,500	4,500	500
8	6,750	4,000	0

Neglect interest and compute the service life for which the annual cost would be a minimum.

10.10. Determine the sequence of decisions regarding replacement that will result in a maximum profit for the 5-year period shown below, if the assumptions of Section 10.5 are applicable.

Chap. 10   Depreciation and Replacement Models   227

Revenue
Year of Manufacture

		1	2	3	4	5
Year of Decision	1	8				
	2	7	10			
	3	6	8	12		
	4	5	6	10	14	
	5	4	3	6	12	15

Replacement Cost
Existing Machine Year

		1	2	3	4	5
Year of Replacement	1	0				
	2	4	0			
	3	7	3	0		
	4	9	4	2	0	
	5	11	5	3	4	0

10.11. Assume that the failure pattern of 12,000 light bulbs will follow a Poisson distribution with a mean failure rate of 6 time units. Assuming that data are recorded in integer time units, tabulate and sketch $P(t)$.

10.12. Calculate and plot the number of replacements needed in Problem 10.11 until the steady-state condition is achieved.

10.13. The failure pattern of 5,000 semiconductors is given to follow a Poisson distribution, with a mean failure rate of 4 time units. The cost of group replacement is $0.15 and that of unit replacement is $0.25. Determine the optimal number of time units between group replacement and the total cost per period under this optimal time interval.

10.14. Plot the *TC* function for the data in the Problem 10.13.

10.15. Solve Problem 10.11 for an exponential distribution with a mean failure rate of 2 time units.

10.16. Plot the number of replacements needed in Problem 10.15 until the steady-state condition is achieved.

10.17. With the same costs of Problem 10.13, calculate the average total cost per period under the optimum replacement interval.

IV

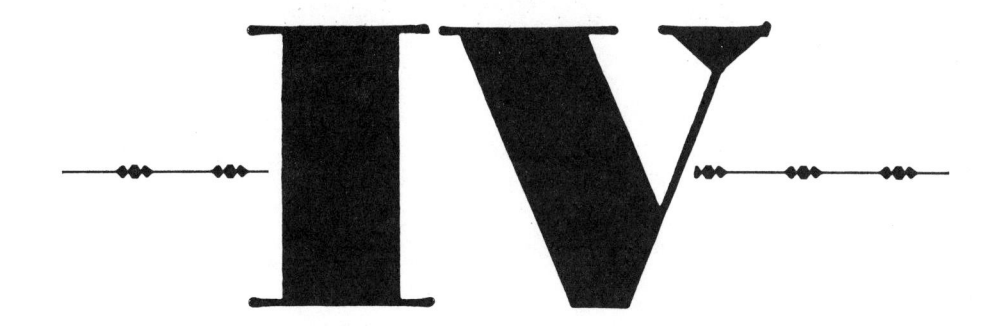

*Models for Production
and Operations Control*

11

Production Progress Models

Production and other operations require a coordinated set of activities that are often repeated over time. This repetition makes possible the reduction in production time per unit as the number of units produced increases. Other operations are characterized by improvements in the rate at which activities are performed. The decision maker needs a means to predict the effect of production progress and/or operations improvement on the system under consideration. The production progress model may be used to make this prediction.

The progress model is a simple graphical or mathematical expression that may be used to predict a reduction in direct labor hours. This forecasting model is known by a number of names. Experience curve, improvement curve, production acceleration curve, manufacturing progress functions, and learning curve have all been used to describe the phenomenon of a predicted reduction in time. Although these different names may add confusion, the mechanics of each is almost identical. This chapter presents models that may be used to explain the phenomenon of production progress.

11.1 PRODUCTION TIME IMPROVEMENTS

The production progress model is an expression of the anticipated time improvement in the production process. It serves as a standard which may be used in calculating production costs and determining production schedules. It is based on the following assumptions: (1) The amount of time required to complete a given task or unit of product will be less each time the task is undertaken; (2) the unit time will decrease at a decreasing rate; and (3) the reduction in unit time will follow a specific predictable pattern.

The empirical evidence that supports these assumptions was first noted in the aircraft industry. The reduction in direct labor hours required to build aircraft was observed and found to be predictable. Since then, the progress function has found applications in other industries, particularly in those with low production volume, such as machine tool manufacturing and shipbuilding.

The Rate of Improvement. The production progress function rests on the assumption that the direct labor hours necessary to complete a unit of product will decrease by a constant percentage each time the production quantity is doubled. For example, a typical rate of improvement in the aircraft industry is 20 percent between doubled quantities. This establishes an 80 percent progress function and means that the direct labor hours necessary to build the second aircraft will be 80 percent of those required to build the first. The fourth aircraft will require 80 percent of the hours that the second required, the eighth will require 80 percent of the fourth, the sixteenth will be 80 percent of the eighth, and so forth. The rate of improvement is constant with regard to doubled production quantities, but diminishes with time.

The situation described can be illustrated with an example. Suppose that the first production aircraft requires 100,000 direct labor hours to complete and that an 80 percent progress function is to be used to predict subsequent improvements. Under the assumptions of the example, the second unit will require $100,000(0.80) = 80,000$ direct labor hours; the fourth unit will require $80,000(0.80) = 64,000$ direct labor hours. If this analysis is continued for doubled production units, it will be found that unit 128 will require 20,972 direct labor hours and unit 256 will require 16,777 direct labor hours. The foregoing shows why "follow-on" contracts in low-volume production are much more economical than the original contract and why low-volume military aircraft and spacecraft production is so expensive.

Consider an example in mass production, that of building automobiles. For simplicity, assume that the necessary direct labor hours are diminishing over time because of technological improvements. Also, assume that the set of coordinated acts necessary to complete an automobile is not changing radically from one year to the next. Assume further that a manufacturer has built a total of 10,000,000 units to date, and that they will build 1,000,000 automobiles each year in the future. At this rate it will take 10 years to double production. A 20 percent reduction in direct labor hours will be realized during these 10 years if an 80 percent manufacturing progress function applies. This amounts to approximately a 2 percent per year improvement—a realistic figure for technological improvements in a mass production industry. This example has been oversimplified, but it does illustrate the relative magnitude of improvement when the production quantities are in the millions. In addition, it illustrates why the rate of improvement in relation to time or from one unit to the next may be so small as to appear negligible.

Production Improvements and Learning   The production progress model is sometimes referred to as a *learning curve*. This is unfortunate, since it implies that all improvements are a result of direct labor learning. Actually, the contribution of the direct labor employee may be only a part of the total reduction in the time required to complete a production unit. Other improvements will come from management and, in large part, from supporting staff organizations. It is difficult to quantify the contributions of each group, since they vary over time and from one industrial environment to another. It is possible, however, to describe these contributions in qualitative terms.

The production employee's performance will improve as he or she becomes familiar with the task. This improvement should be evident in the completion of more units of product per increment of time. The employee's learning may take the form of increased familiarity with the correct method or assembly technique, familiarity with the tooling, or with the inspection requirements and workpiece specifications. The employee may also acquire a better understanding of the proper position of his or her task in relation to the total production process. The learning of the individual worker will have an immediate effect in terms of manufacturing improvement. This learning, however, will probably not result in significant improvements over a long period of time, particularly in repetitive and short-cycle operations.

Improvement resulting from management or direct labor supervision will be felt only through staff functions and production employees, respectively. These improvements will depend on managerial capabilities and, in particular, on the attention given a specific product when more than one product is being produced. A major portion of the improvement will result from the efforts of personnel in supporting staff organizations. These contributions will be as diverse as the staff functions themselves, although all have as an objective, and should contribute to, the reduction in direct labor hours necessary to complete a cycle of work.

The extent to which tooling is established before production and the tooling refinements made during production will influence the magnitude of manufacturing improvement. Modifications in tool design and the correction of tooling errors will reduce the unit production time. Increased or supplementary production requirements may result in more elaborate tooling, which should, in turn, reduce the unit production time.

The degree to which manufacturing methods have been developed and specified prior to production, together with the emphasis placed on improving these methods during production, will affect manufacturing improvements. In a broader sense, this work simplification includes revisions in plant layout and materials handling which should also influence the unit production time.

Production control personnel may facilitate improvement through better planning, routing, scheduling, dispatching, and follow-up. This will result in an increased utilization of machines, tools, and labor and should ultimately produce a reduction in the direct labor hours per unit.

The materials management organization deals with the purchase of raw materials and component parts, as well as with the control and storage of preproduction, in-process, and finished inventory. As this function is improved, material shortages and the resulting disruption of production should be reduced or eliminated.

The engineering department is responsible for product design and testing. The manner in which this function is accomplished before and during production will affect total manufacturing improvement. Contributions, such as the correction of specification errors, the simplification of product design, and the incorporation of requested design changes, will be an important factor in manufacturing improvement after production has begun.

How far a quality assurance program can reduce the number of rejects and thus reduce losses and/or the necessity for rework and repair will influence the total manufacturing improvement. An especially important function of the quality control program is serving as a feedback mechanism in notifying operating personnel of deviations or shifts in the manufacturing process. The extent and rapidity with which this mechanism acts will influence manufacturing improvement.

Many other factors might reduce unit production time. The installation and maintenance of a wage incentive system may affect productivity. An employee suggestion system might produce some improvements. Intangibles that raise morale, such as a program of noise reduction, an employee newsletter, or various fringe benefits, may serve to reduce unit manufacturing time. It may also be desirable to inform production employees of the present and projected production rates. If these are realistic, employees may concertedly attempt to meet them. The degree to which the foregoing factors influence manufacturing improvement largely depends on the amount of available improvement remaining immediately after the first unit has been completed and also on the subsequent attempt to accomplish as much improvement as possible.

The Shape of the Progress Function. The production progress function is assumed to describe a constant percentage improvement as the production quantities double. All progress functions rest on this assumption and differ only in the percentage improvement between doubled production quantities and in the direct labor hours required to complete the first production unit. Therefore, all progress functions will have the same general shape. Any function may be defined if the number of direct labor hours required to complete the first unit is established and if the subsequent rate of improvement is specified.

The number of direct labor hours required to complete the first production unit depends on three major factors. First, previous experience and the relevance of this experience; a firm with extensive, directly applicable experience will require fewer direct labor hours for the first unit than will a firm with little experience. Second, the amount of effort that the organization expends in preparation for production will influence the time to complete the first unit; the firm may expend extensive time and energy in tooling-up for the required manufacturing process. Hence, the first unit will require less manufacturing time. Third the characteristics of the unit itself will affect first-unit time. The complexity and the size of the unit will have a direct bearing on its production time.

The rate of improvement that will be experienced as additional units are produced is also a function of the preceding factors. Two additional, related factors will also influence this rate: (1) the effort that the organization puts forth to improve or reduce manufacturing times should affect the ultimate rate of improvement; and (2) the opportunity for improvement will also determine the improvement rate. If the time required to manufacture the first unit is high, subsequent improvement may come rather easily. If the reverse is true, subsequent improvement will be difficult. The latter case may be the more desirable even though the reduction in production time may be less striking than a higher first unit with more improvement. An important aspect of this is that the hours required for the first unit and the rate of improvement must be considered simultaneously in assessing production performance.

11.2 THE GRAPHICAL PROGRESS FUNCTION

One reason for the initial acceptance and popularity of the production progress model is the relative ease with which it can be applied. The relationship between direct labor hours and units produced can be expressed as a curve on graph paper from only a few plotted points. Thus, the information needed for a specific unit of production can be taken directly from this graph. On log-log paper the progress function will result in a straight line. This is the usual method of expressing the relationship between the unit number and the direct labor hours. Before proceeding to the log-log representation, however, the function will be exhibited on arithmetic graph paper.

The Function on Arithmetic Paper. Consider the previous example of an aircraft model that requires 100,000 direct labor hours to produce the first unit. Assume that in producing subsequent units a reduction of 20 percent in the direct labor hours between doubled production units can be expected. This

Table 11.1. UNIT, CUMULATIVE, AND CUMULATIVE AVERAGE DIRECT LABOR HOURS REQUIRED FOR AN 80 PERCENT PROGRESS FUNCTION WITH UNIT 1 AT 100,000 HOURS

Unit Number	Unit Direct Labor Hours	Cumulative Direct Labor Hours	Cumulative Average Direct Labor Hours
1	100,000	100,000	100,000
2	80,000	180,000	90,000
4	64,000	314,210	78,553
8	51,200	534,591	66,824
16	40,960	892,014	55,751
32	32,768	1,467,862	45,871
64	26,214	2,392,453	37,382
128	20,972	3,874,395	30,269
256	16,777	6,247,318	24,404

establishes an 80 percent progress function expressed in tabular form for movements of doubled production quantities in Table 11.1. The cumulative values shown in the table were computed after first finding the unit times for all units.

The cumulative average direct labor hours shown in Table 11.1 were obtained by dividing the cumulative values by the unit number. Thus, the first eight aircraft will require a total of 534,591 direct labor hours. The average of direct labor hours per aircraft is therefore $534,591/8 = 66,824$. Units and cumulative average values for this example are illustrated in Figure 11.1 for units 1-16 and in Figure 11.2 for units 1 through 2,048.

It is possible to determine any unit values or cumulative average value through unit 16. Thus, aircraft 11 should require 46,000 direct labor hours. The first 11 aircraft should require a total of 11(61,500), or 676,500, hours. Figure 11.2 shows that unit 700 will require approximately 12,000 direct labor hours. The first 800 aircraft will require 800(17,000), or 13,600,000, direct labor hours. Thus, with these two graphs it is possible to plot the given unit and cumulative average values, sketch in a curve to connect these points, and then read off any other required value from the curves. There are some difficulties in this method. First, it is not easy to draw in accurately a smooth curve which connects the given points. Second, it is possible to obtain only an approximate reading from the curve. The first objection can be eliminated and the second partially overcome by using log-log rather than arithmetic graph paper.

The Function on Log-Log Paper. On arithmetic graph paper, equal numerical differences are represented by equal distances. For example, the linear distance between 1 and 3 will be the same as between 8 and 10. On logarithmic graph paper, the linear distance between any two quantities is dependent upon the ratio of those two quantities. Two pairs of quantities having the

Chap. 11 Production Progress Models 237

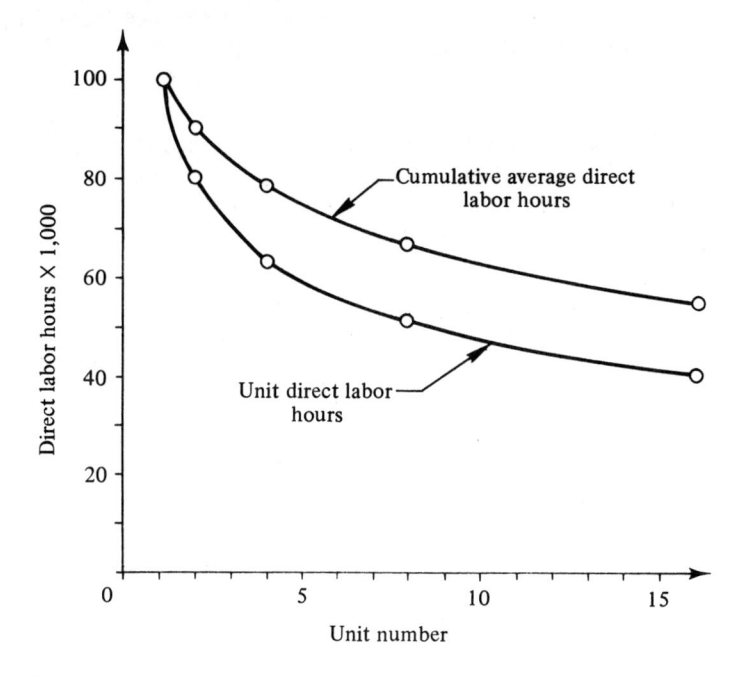

Figure 11.1 Eighty percent progress curve with unit one at 100,000 hours.

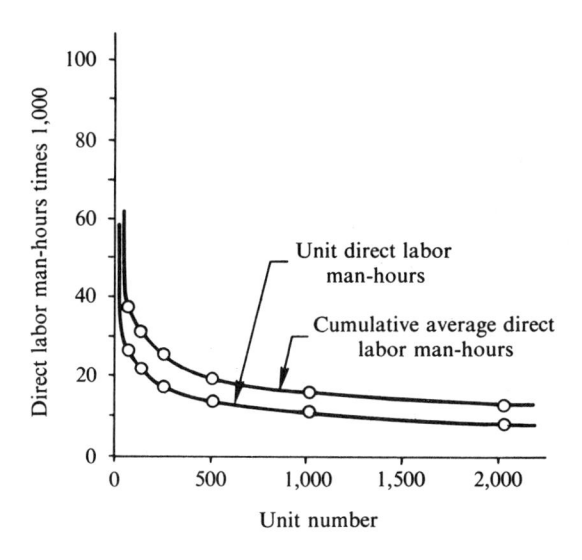

Figure 11.2 Eighty percent progress curve with unit one at 100,000 hours.

same ratio will be equally spaced. For example, the distance from 2 to 4 will be the same as from 30 to 60 or from 1,000 to 2,000.

If the progress function is plotted on double logarithmic paper, both the abscissa and the ordinate are represented logarithmically. This permits the progress function to be plotted as a straight line. A power function may be plotted as a straight line on log-log paper. Hence, the progress function can be plotted either from two points or one point and the slope, such as unit 1 and the percent improvement. Also, by using log-log paper, the values for a large quantity of units can be presented on a single graph. Arithmetic graph paper, on the other hand, generally requires more values to define a curve. Either two separate graphs or one extremely large graph is required to present the curve over a wide range of units. Extrapolation or projection from a few points is difficult.

Figure 11.3 exhibits the same unit and cumulative average values that were used to construct the function on arithmetic paper, except that these are plotted on log-log paper. Reading from Figure 11.3, unit 300 will require 16,000 direct labor hours. A total of 300 units should require 300(23,000), or 6,900,000, hours. Note that the function in Figure 11.3 representing the cumulative average direct labor hours is above, and nearly parallel to, the unit function, after the first few units.

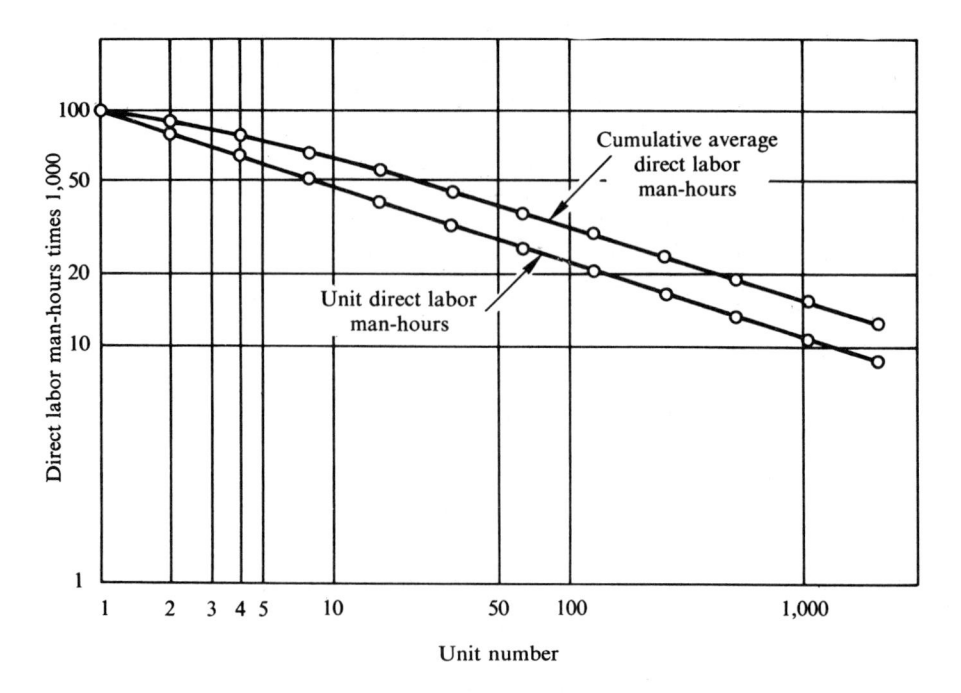

Figure 11.3 Eighty percent progress curve with unit one at 100,000 hours (logarithmic scale).

Chap. 11   Production Progress Models   239

The relative ease of using a double logarithmic graphical representation of the progress function should be evident from the preceding example. In practice, this representation is extensively used. The progress curve, representing a projection or a forecast, is first established. Then, as production units are completed, the actual values are recorded on the graph. This provides a current exhibit of the actual production progress compared to the planned progress. If the actual progress deviates significantly from the planned progress function, the forecast must be revised or corrective action must be applied to the production process.

11.3 THE MATHEMATICAL PROGRESS MODEL

The manufacturing progress model has been described as an empirical concept. It has been suggested that the relationship between direct labor hours and units produced will follow a predictable pattern. If this is true, the relationship can be defined with a mathematical function. This section is concerned with analytical methods of determining the unit, the cumulative, and the cumulative average values of direct labor hours for various production quantities.

Development of the Unit Formula. An analytical expression for the production progress function will be developed from the assumption that the number of direct labor hours required to produce doubled production units is reduced by a constant percentage. Let

$x =$ unit number
$Y_x =$ number of direct labor hours required to produce the xth unit
$K =$ number of direct labor hours required to produce the first unit
$\phi =$ slope parameter of the production progress function

From the assumption of a constant percentage reduction in direct labor hours for doubled production units,

$$Y_x = K\phi^0 \quad \text{where} \quad x = 2^0 = 1$$
$$Y_x = K\phi^1 \quad \text{where} \quad x = 2^1 = 2$$
$$Y_x = K\phi^2 \quad \text{where} \quad x = 2^2 = 4$$
$$Y_x = K\phi^3 \quad \text{where} \quad x = 2^3 = 8.$$

Therefore,
$$Y_x = K\phi^d \quad \text{where} \quad x = 2^d.$$

Taking the common logarithm gives
$$\log Y_x = \log K + d \log \phi \quad \text{where} \quad \log x = d \log 2.$$

Solving for d gives
$$d = \frac{\log Y_x - \log K}{\log \phi} \quad \text{and} \quad d = \frac{\log x}{\log 2},$$

from which
$$\frac{\log Y_x - \log K}{\log \phi} = \frac{\log x}{\log 2}$$
$$\log Y_x - \log K = \frac{\log x (\log \phi)}{\log 2}.$$

Let
$$n = \frac{\log \phi}{\log 2}.$$

Therefore,
$$\log Y_x - \log K = n \log x.$$

Taking the antilog of both sides gives
$$\frac{Y_x}{K} = x^n$$
$$Y_x = Kx^n. \tag{11.1}$$

Application of Equation (11.1) can be illustrated by reference to the example of an 80 percent progress function with unit 1 at 100,000 direct labor hours. Solving for Y_8, the number of direct labor hours required to build the eighth unit gives

$$Y_8 = 100,000(8)^{-(\log 0.8/\log 2)}$$
$$= 100,000(8)^{-0.322}$$
$$= \frac{100,000}{(8)^{0.322}} = 51,192.$$

As an additional example, consider the situation with unit 1 at 120,000 direct labor hours and a 90 percent progress function. The number of direct labor hours required for unit 50 is

$$Y_{50} = 12,000(50)^{(\log 0.9/\log 2)}$$
$$= 120,000(50)^{-0.152}$$
$$= \frac{120,000}{50^{0.152}} = 66,212.$$

The Cumulative and Cumulative Average Formulas. The cumulative number of direct labor hours required to produce N units may be expressed as

$$T_N = Y_1 + Y_2 + \cdots + Y_N = \sum_{x=1}^{N} Y_x. \tag{11.2}$$

A fairly good approximation for Equation (11.2) is possible by integrating from 0.5 to $N + 0.5$ as follows:

$$T_N \simeq \int_{0.5}^{N+0.5} Y_x \, dx = K \int_{0.5}^{N+0.5} x^n \, dx$$
$$\simeq \frac{K}{1+n}[(N + 0.5)^{(1+n)} - (0.5)^{(1+n)}]. \tag{11.3}$$

Chap. 11   Production Progress Models   241

As an example of the use of Equation (11.3) suppose that the approximate cumulative direct labor hours required to build 4 units, T_4, under an 80 percent progress function with unit 1 at 100,000 hours is needed.

$$T_4 \simeq \frac{100{,}000}{1 + (\log 0.8/\log 2)} \times [(4 + 0.5)^{[1 + (\log 0.8/\log 2)]} - (0.5)^{[1 + (\log 0.8/\log 2)]}]$$

$$\simeq \frac{100{,}000}{0.678}[(4.5)^{0.678} - (0.5)^{0.678}]$$

$$\simeq 147{,}493[2.773 - 0.625] = 316{,}815.$$

Application of Equation (11.2) would give a value for T_4 of 314,210 direct labor hours. Thus, the approximation method gives an error of $+0.83$ percent. This error would be even less for larger values of N.

The cumulative average direct labor hours required to produce N units may be expressed as

$$V_N = \frac{Y_1 + Y_2 + \cdots + Y_N}{N} = \frac{\sum_{x=1}^{N} Y_x}{N}. \tag{11.4}$$

By substituting Equation (11.3) a fairly good approximation for Equation (11.4) is obtained. Thus,

$$V_N \simeq \frac{K}{N(1 + n)}[(N + 0.5)^{(1+n)} - (0.5)^{(1+n)}]. \tag{11.5}$$

An example of the application of Equation (11.5) can be illustrated with a 90 percent progress function with unit 1 at 120,000 direct labor hours. The cumulative average direct labor hours required to build a total of 50 units may be calculated as

$$Y_{50} \simeq \frac{120{,}000}{50[1 + (\log 0.9/\log 2)]} \times [(50 + 0.5)^{[1 + (\log 0.9/\log 2)]} - (0.5)^{[1 + (\log 0.9/\log 2)]}]$$

$$\simeq \frac{120{,}000}{42.4}[(50.5)^{0.848} - (0.5)^{0.848}]$$

$$\simeq 2{,}830(27.822 - 0.556) = 77{,}163.$$

Consider another approximation for the cumulative direct labor hours, given by the integral

$$T_N \simeq \int_0^N Y_x \, dx$$

$$\simeq K \int_0^N x^n \, dx$$

$$\simeq K \left(\frac{N^{n+1}}{n+1}\right). \tag{11.6}$$

Dividing Equation (11.6) by N gives an approximation for the cumulative average number of direct labor hours expressed as

$$V_N \simeq \frac{1}{n+1}(KN^n). \tag{11.7}$$

Inspection of Equation (11.7) indicates that the cumulative average number of direct labor hours can be obtained by multiplying the unit value by the factor $1/(n + 1)$. For the example above,

$$V_{50} \simeq \frac{1}{(\log 0.9/\log 2) + 1}(120{,}000)(50)^{(\log 0.9/\log 2)}$$

$$\simeq \frac{1}{0.848}(120{,}000)(50^{-0.152})$$

$$\simeq 78{,}080.$$

The factor $1/(1 + n)$ does not yield a value for the cumulative direct labor hours that is as accurate as the previous approximation. It is simple to use, however, and give fairly good results for large values of x.

The Use of Tabular Values. Application of the manufacturing progress function is facilitated by the use of tabular values. Appendix F gives unit and cumulative values for selected slope parameters with unit 1 at 1 direct labor hour. The unit values in Table F.1 were obtained from $Y_x = Kx^n$. The cumulative values in Table F.2 were obtained by summing the unit values of Table F.1. Cumulative average values can be found from Table F.2 by dividing the cumulative value by the number of units involved.

Solutions to specific values require multiplying the tabular values that apply by K. For example, if $K = 65$ direct labor hours, multiply the tabular value by 65. This is necessary, since the tables are based on a K value of unity.

Interpolation may be employed for either x or ϕ or both if the small loss of accuracy is relatively unimportant. If the loss of accuracy is important, the formulas may be used directly, or a table with the required parameters may be constructed.

11.4 DEFINING THE PROGRESS MODEL

It has been empirically demonstrated that improvements in production operations can often be described by a constant percentage improvement between doubled production quantities. Thus, the progress model is based on empirical evidence. This does not mean that the progress model cannot be a good forecasting device. It does mean that the model must be supported in each case through the collection and analysis of data from this or a similar operation or product to determine whether the progress function is appropriate. Then the member of the family of functions that is applicable can be specified. Once this has been done, the progress function may serve as the basis for forecasting in production operations.

Determining the Progress Function from Production Standards. Direct labor hours for the first production unit and a subsequent rate of improvement must be estimated for each application of the production progress function.

There are two common production standard methods of approach in obtaining these estimates. The first requires development of a work standard from a system of elemental standard data. The second requires use of data from similar, but already completed, jobs. In either case, the rate of improvement is considered to be constant and dependent upon the general production capabilities of the firm. It is assumed not to vary over time or from one job to another. Then, all that needs to be defined is the direct labor hours necessary to complete the first production unit.

In using elemental standard data, a detailed study is made of the operation, and a standard time is set under the assumption that most of the improvement has already been realized. Then, either of two alternatives is followed. (1) A constant may be applied to modify this standard time to obtain an estimate for the first production unit hours. For example, a given production facility may be approximately and repeatedly 35 percent efficient on the first production unit. The standard time is then divided by 0.35 to obtain the time for the first production unit. This constant will be determined by the preproduction effort expended and will rarely vary from one job to another. If it did, it would have to be estimated with each new job. (2) The standard time will be estimated as the time to complete some specific unit of production some time in the future. As before, this information would be obtained from previous experience. For example, the standard direct labor hours can be attained by production unit 1,000. Then the time for the first production unit will be estimated by calculating from this reference point using the estimated slope.

A second method for defining the progress function also rests on the assumption that the rate of improvement is constant for a given production facility. It is only required that the number of direct labor hours needed for the first production unit be estimated. This may be established from comparison with similar jobs. In the aircraft industry it is common practice to estimate the time for the first unit from the basic air-frame weight. The weight of the aircraft less engines, instruments, and auxiliary gear is multiplied by a constant obtained from previous experience in building similar aircraft. This estimate for the number of direct labor hours, together with the assumed rate of improvement, specifies a progress function for any new model under consideration.

Fitting the Progress Function to More Than Two Points. In some applications, a set of data exists for which a specific progress function must be specified. This can be done most simply by plotting the data on log-log graph paper and sketching a straight line that appears to fit these data. When more than two values are plotted, it is unlikely that a straight line exists that will pass through all these values. The method of least squares may be used to specify the line of best fit for such data.

The general progress function, $Y_x = Kx^n$, when expressed in logarithmic form, is the straight-line $\log Y_x = \log K + n \log x$. Log K is the intercept at $\log x = 0$ or $x = 1$, and n is the slope of the line. Thus, the general progress function can be defined by specifying n and log K. The method of least squares will yield

$$n = \frac{\sum [\log Y][\log x - (\sum \log x/M)]}{\sum [\log x - (\sum \log x/M)]^2}. \tag{11.8}$$

$$\log K = \frac{\sum \log Y - n \sum \log x}{M}. \tag{11.9}$$

The number of data points is designated M.

The development of a line of best fit by specification of the parameters n and log K can be illustrated with an example. Assume that data have been collected on production items 10, 20, 30, 40, and 50. It is desired to determine the general progress function that best fit these data in order to make predictions about future production rates. Five unit numbers and the direct labor hours for each of these units are given. These data can be expressed in tabular form as shown in Table 11.2. The parameters can be calculated from the completed table and Equations (11.8) and (11.9) as

$$n = \frac{-0.07239}{0.30474} = -0.2375.$$

Since $\log \phi = n \log 2$,

$$\log \phi = -0.2375(0.3010) = -0.0715$$

Taking the antilog gives $\phi = 0.848$. Thus, an 84.8 percent progress function describes these data. Also,

$$\log K = \frac{8.3480 - (-0.2375)(7.0792)}{5} = 2.0058.$$

Taking the antilog gives $K = 101.3$ hours. Therefore, the manufacturing progress function is defined as

$$Y_x = 101.3 x^{-0.2375}.$$

Table 11.2. CALCULATIONS LEADING TO A LINE OF LEAST SQUARES

Unit Number x	$\log x$	$\log x - \dfrac{\sum \log x}{M}$	Direct Labor Hours Y	$\log Y$	$\log Y \left(\log x - \dfrac{\sum \log x}{M} \right)$
10	1.0000	−0.41584	59.2	1.7723	−0.73699
20	1.3010	−0.11484	48.5	1.6857	−0.19359
30	1.4771	+0.06126	46.1	1.6637	+0.10192
40	1.6021	+0.18626	42.0	1.6232	+0.30234
50	1.6990	+0.28316	40.1	1.6031	+0.45393
	7.0792			8.3480	
		$\sum \left(\log x - \dfrac{\sum \log x}{M} \right)^2$ = +0.30474			$\sum \left[\log Y \left(\log x - \dfrac{\sum \log x}{M} \right) \right]$ = −0.07239

Refinements of the Progress Function. It has been assumed that the progress function is linear when plotted on log-log graph paper. The graphical and analytical solutions, and the examples given in the preceding sections, rest on the assumption that the direct labor hours required to complete a unit of product will decrease according to an exponential function that is linear when expressed on logarithmic grids. It has been suggested that there is no logical or analytical proof of this relationship; only empirical evidence can be developed. The characteristic of linearity on logarithmic grids, however, and the resulting ease with which the curve can be applied seem to account in a large measure for the general acceptance and continued popularity of the concept of the progress function.

Almost since its initial use, suggestions have been made for refinements to the manufacturing progress function. Since the assumption of linearity rests on only empirical evidence, it would be logical to assume that attempts would be made to choose a nonlinear curve. Such a choice would be an improvement if it were to "fit" empirical data better than the classical linear formulation. Most refinements have started with the premise that the linear function on logarithmic grids, $Y_x = Kx^n$, does not describe empirical data as well as could be expected. Examples have been offered to illustrate the magnitude of the error in specific situations. Refinements have been proposed and developed. The Stanford "B" curve and "S" curve, the Rand modified progress curve, and the Boeing modified progress curve are such refinements. Both the Stanford "B" curve and "S" curve deviate from the linear hypothesis in that they have an initial humped or arched segment which is concave downward when plotted on logarithmic grids. The Stanford "B" curve approximates linearity; the "S" curve, as the name implies, calls for a convex segment before becoming linear. The Rand modified progress curve assumes linearity for the initial portion of the curve followed by a convex segment which eventually brings the curve into a flat and constant standard of production. The Boeing modified progress curve is an attempt to account for and predict irregularities in the curve due to major design changes in the product. That curve seeks to decribe a particular situation more precisely rather than to redefine the linear function, as is done in the first three cases.

11.5 APPLICATIONS OF THE PROGRESS MODEL

The production progress function may form the basis for decision making in the procurement, production, and financial aspects of an enterprise. In procurement, the function can be used to determine the item cost for manufacturing and as a basis for the manufacture or purchase decision. In production, the progress function may be used to determine equipment loading and personnel schedules. In finance, decisions related to bidding, pricing, and capital requirements may be based on the progress function. In each of these applications, the function acts as a forecasting device against which actual performance can be measured. This section presents selected applications of the progress function.

Procurement Applications. Once a specific production progress function has been selected, it may be used to determine the average item cost for manufacturing over a given production run. Item cost per unit is expressed in terms of the direct labor cost, the direct material cost, and the factory burden cost. Direct labor cost will require computation of the average number of direct labor hours per unit. Direct material cost will be a constant charge per unit of product. Factory burden cost will be related to direct labor cost by the use of a percentage. Let

lr = direct labor hourly rate
dm = direct material cost per unit
fb = factory burden rate expressed as a decimal fraction of the direct labor hourly rate

Item cost per unit, C_i, can be expressed as

$$C_i = V_N(lr) + dm + V_N(lr)(fb).$$

Substituting Equation (11.7) for V_N gives

$$C_i = \frac{KN^n}{n+1}(lr)(1 + fb) + dm. \tag{11.10}$$

If C_i' is the item cost per unit for a purchased item, the number of units that must be produced for a break-even item cost may be expressed as

$$C_i' = \frac{KN^n}{n+1}(lr)(1 + fb) + dm$$

$$\frac{KN^n}{n+1} = \frac{C_i' - dm}{lr(1 + fb)}$$

$$N = \left[\frac{(C_i' - dm)(n + 1)}{lr(1 + fb)K}\right]^{1/n}. \tag{11.11}$$

As an example, consider a situation in which 50 units are to be manufactured. The direct labor hourly rate is $8 per hour, the direct material cost per unit is $210, and the factory burden rate is 0.70. It is estimated that the first unit will require 100 direct labor hours to produce and that a 90 percent progress function is applicable. Suppose that the item can be purchased for $910 per unit. The number of units that must be produced in order that the manufacturing alternative be as attractive as purchasing can be found from Equation (11.11) as

$$N = \left[\frac{(\$910 - \$210)(0.848)}{\$8.00(1.70)100}\right]^{(-1/0.152)}$$

$$= (0.4365)^{-6.58} = 234.$$

Production Applications. The production progress model can be used as the basis for production scheduling. The function provides information concerning the anticipated time required to perform an operation or a series of operations. Such information is a prerequisite to many production decisions. Information extracted from the function may be used to establish requirements for personnel, floor space, machinery, and tools. If the size of the work force is constant, the reduction in time required to process 1 unit should result in a reduction in flow time and an increase in the rate of delivery. Materials and purchased components must arrive on this schedule. The quality assurance program must be geared to meet the increasing flow of the product. Thus, all manufacturing operations that support production must be geared to production and the production progress function.

As an example of the application of the manufacturing progress function to the determination of personnel requirements, consider the following situation. A supervisor has shown a consistent performance improvement in his or her department. Production to date has involved a total of 150 units. The average number of hours per unit was 7.0. Production is to be increased over the next 4 weeks, and the supervisor wishes to determine the number of people required to produce 40 units in the first week, 60 in the second, 90 in the third, and 140 in the fourth.

Without considering the effect of a reduction in direct labor hours, the supervisor multiplies the number of units required each week by 7.0 and divides by 40. This will give a projected requirement of 7 people in the first week, 11 in the second, 16 in the third, and 25 in the fourth. By scheduling a predicted improvement in performance, however, a more realistic personnel requirement can be established.

Suppose that analysis of the direct labor hours associated with the initial 150 units of production gives an estimated first-unit value of 12.8 hours with a 90 percent progress function. Then, from Table F.1 of Appendix F it can be determined that the first 190 units will require a total of 1,285 hours. The first 150 units require a total of 1,050 hours, giving projected hour requirement for the first week of 235. This should require 6 people for a 40-hour week. Adding the units required in the second week gives a total hour requirement of 1,619 for the production of 250 units. The projected hours for the second week are 1,619 less 1,285, or 334. For a 40-hour week this will require 9 people. Proceeding in this manner gives a projected personnel requirement of 13 people in the third week and 20 people in the fourth week.

The analysis presented is based on two assumptions: (1) that a 90 percent progress function will apply for the future production schedule, and (2) that the new personnel needed each week will be just as productive as those carried over from previous weeks. Note that in the fourth week only 5.6 hours will be required per unit produced.

Financial Applications. With the production progress model as a statement of manufacturing capabilities, one can use the function for preparing bids, setting prices for new products, or extending existing contracts. Alternatively, the function can be used to check the reasonableness of subcontracted bids or purchase prices in some situations. Once a financial decision has been made, the function may be used to maintain financial control. The starting load costs of the product can be calculated, forecasts of capital requirements can be made, budgets can be prepared, and financial control can be implemented. After the product is in production, financial control can be maintained and deviations or cost trends can be analyzed and questioned.

Assume that a plant has produced a total of 790 units and that 2,765 hours have been expended to date at an average rate of $8.40 per hour. The number of units manufactured each month has steadily increased, but so has the number of hours. The plant manager wishes to determine whether the increased number of hours will raise the average unit labor cost above the $18.50 originally estimated for a run of 2,000 units.

Production data for this situation are given in columns A and C of Table 11.3. The plant manager is interested in estimating the cumulative average hours per unit when 2,000 units are completed. More specifically, he or she wishes to project the cumulative average costs to determine whether they will reach $18.50 per unit at 2,000 units. This will be accomplished graphically under the assumption that the cumulative average curve is a straight line on log-log paper after 20 units.

Table 11.3. MONTHLY PRODUCTION DATA AND HOURS EXPENDED PER MONTH

Month	Units per Month (A)	Cumulative Units (B)	Hours per Month (C)	Cumulative Hours (D)	Cumulative Average Hours per Unit (E)
1	—	—	258.0	258.0	—
2	92	92	340.0	598.0	6.50
3	103	195	373.1	971.1	4.98
4	115	310	302.2	1,373.3	4.43
5	133	443	407.6	1,780.9	4.02
6	152	595	450.4	2,231.3	3.75
7	195	790	533.7	2,765.0	3.50

Columns B, D, and E of Table 11.3 are completed as indicated. The monthly units and monthly hours are accumulated to complete the cumulative units and cumulative hours columns. Then, the values in column D are divided by those in column B to obtain the cumulative average hour values of column E. These values are recorded on log-log graph paper as indicated in Figure 11.4. It is noted that the cumulative average trend line shows a constant improvement

Chap. 11   Production Progress Models   249

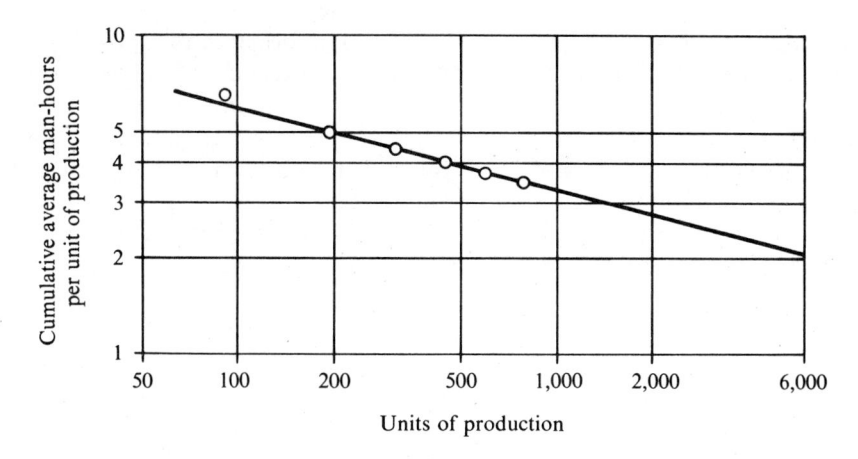

Figure 11.4 Cumulative function for the data of Table 11.3.

after unit 195. When 2,000 units are reached, the average labor hours per unit will have declined to 2.75. At a labor rate of $8.40 per hour, the average labor cost per unit for the run of 2,000 units will be $23.10 rather than the original estimate of $18.50. Thus, the original estimate was in error. It might then be asked how many units must be produced to reduce the average unit cost to $18.50. This amounts to the average unit hour rate of 2.20 units per hour ($18.50 per unit divided by $8.40 per hour). From Figure 11.4 it appears that it would be necessary to produce 6,000 units in order to reduce the average cost to $18.50 per unit.

This problem can be approached analytically. A line of cast squares can be fitted to the given data and the intercept (the hours for the first unit) and the slope (the percentage improvement) calculated. Then the approximation formula can be used to answer the original question. With the data as given in this problem, however, it is not possible to specify the unit hours for any specific unit. Hence, it is necessary to find the line of best fit for the cumulative average curve, realizing that a straight line is appropriate on log-log paper only after about 20 units of production. This approach will be satisfactory in solving for the cumulative average value at unit 2,000.

The Reliability of Data. At least two questions concerning the reliability of progress data should be considered. First, consider the situation where a production progress curve is specified and the resulting production conforms to this curve. It appears that a desirable situation exists, as this is what was originally intended. Once a control or quantitative objective is imposed on an operation, however, strong forces are created to make performance conform to the objective. This would be desirable if the progress curve represented a valid standard, one that could just be attained through diligence on the part of all employees. If this standard is very easily attained, then in all probability, the standard is all that will be attained. Eventual conformance to a progress curve is not evidence that the specified curve was the correct curve. Rather, evidence must be gathered as to the relative effort expended in conforming to the specified curve. Using a certain progress function for all work is not only dangerous but is indefensible on the basis of empirical evidence if, during the same period of time, the function was used as a control device.

The second issue concerning the reliability of production progress data is the definition of the data itself. If direct labor hours are recorded and charged against a product, there will be a strong temptation to classify questionable work as indirect labor. Thus, if direct labor hours are decreasing while indirect labor hours are on the rise, no real progress has been attained. Similarly, it may even be difficult to obtain an accurate production count. Where a simplified design change is introduced, one must use judgment to decide whether this is an improvement contributed from a supporting staff organization or a new model which should be treated with a new progress function. The issues just described are not insurmountable in the use of the progress model, but they should be recognized and considered during its application.

QUESTIONS

11.1. Describe the manufacturing progress function.

11.2. Describe the three classes or types of contributions that may lead to manufacturing improvements.

11.3. How may the shape of a specific progress curve be defined? What factors might contribute to this relative shape?

11.4. What are some of the disadvantages of expressing the progress curve on arithmetic graph paper?

11.5. Give the unit, the cumulative, and the cumulative average formulas for the progress function.

11.6. Describe the two classes of methods that are used to determine a specific progress function.

11.7. Why is it sometimes desirable to fit a progress function to two or more data points?

11.8. What criterion may be used in fitting a line of least squares to data?

11.9. What are the three areas of application of the progress curve?

PROBLEMS

11.1. Sketch the progress curve $k = 12$ hours, $\phi = 0.80$ on arithmetic graph paper through 20 units. How long should units 8 and 16 take to complete?

11.2. Solve Problem 11.1 using the unit formula.

11.3. Solve Problem 11.1 for the cumulative average.

Chap. 11   Production Progress Models   251

11.4. A poor but honest tenant farmer, Dudley Forthumbs, was experiencing some difficulty in keeping flying creatures out of the kitchen of his home. The insects and small birds were not consuming too much food, but some of the larger birds were often able to make off with the best portion of the family meal. At the insistence of his wife, Dud set out to build the 12 screens necessary to cover the 12 windows in the kitchen. After some setup time, he was finally able to complete the first screen in 50 hours. He then became discouraged and was about to go fishing. His wife, however, reminded him that manufacturing improvements could be expected and that the last screen would probably be accomplished in half the time the first one took. If Dud's wife was correct, how much time would be required to build the total of 12 screens?

11.5. If the homeowner in Problem 11.4 were to continue his project and build 10 additional screens, what would be the best estimate of the average time to complete each of the second batch of 10 screens?

11.6. The following data were collected on alternate production units:

Unit Number	Direct Labor Hours
2	100
4	90
6	80
8	75
10	60
12	50

What is the best estimate of the cumulative average time to complete a total of 100 such units? Solve graphically and verify the result analytically.

11.7. The following data are provided for Problem 11.6:

Direct material cost $3.50 per piece
Direct labor rate $7.10 per hour
Factory burden rate   1.10

What is the average unit cost of the 100 units? If the units can be purchased for $37.00 per unit, how many units should be produced so that the cost of manufacturing and purchasing will be equal?

11.8. A product can be manufactured under a direct labor hourly rate of $4.50 per hour, a direct material cost of $21 per unit, and a factory burden rate of 1.20. The first production unit will require 4 hours to complete. Improvements of 25 percent between doubled quantities can be expected. The product can also be purchased for $45. At what total quantity are the two alternatives equal in cost?

11.9. Rework the example of Section 11.5 to find out how much can be saved by manufacturing instead of purchasing at a price of $910 per unit if the number of units required is 300.

11.10. An assembly department assembled 200 microcomputers in the past week and the average number of hours per assembly was 3.6. The demand is expected to be 350, 400, and 500 units in the next 3 weeks. If the slope parameter for the progress function is 0.8 and each worker is expected to provide 7 effective hours per day 5 days per week, calculate the labor requirements for the next 3 weeks.

11.11. Under the assumptions of the linear cumulative average model, if the first production unit took 40 days to complete and $\phi = 0.80$, how long would it take to complete 5 units?

11.12. In Problem 11.11, how long would the fifth unit take to complete?

11.13. The following data were complied from the production of engines. Sketch the curve of direct hours versus engines produced on log-log paper and fit a linear cumulative average model.

(a) If, in the month of November, the number of hours is expected to be 4,500, how many engines will be produced?

(b) How many hours will be required to produce a total of 4,000 engines?

Month	Engines Produced	Hours of Labor
May	72	4,441
June	78	4,260
July	86	4,513
August	95	4,150
September	106	4,450
October	119	4,380

11.14. Solve Problem 11.13 using the model of Section 11.4.

12

Models for Production Sequencing

Production sequencing decisions arise whenever there is a choice as to the order in which a number of jobs can be performed. The democratic and commonly accepted first-come, first-served rule may work well in society when people are waiting for service, but there are better sequencing rules when production orders or jobs are involved. The effectiveness of a specific sequence may be measured in terms of makespan time, average completion time, due date performance, machine utilization, inventory of jobs in process, and so forth. A decision maker will prefer that sequence which optimizes the chosen measure of effectiveness.

Sequencing problems occur in flow-shop production systems and in job-shop production systems. In the former, each production order goes across the same set of machine centers. The jobs may be fixed in number or they may arrive over time. In a job-shop production system, jobs flow across machine centers on many different routes. In this chapter simple flow-shop problems are presented for the case where the job set is fixed in number. Then the job-shop problem is presented for the dynamic case involving the continuous arrival of jobs over time. Both algebraic and computer simulation approaches are presented in this chapter.

12.1 FLOW-SHOP SEQUENCING FOR TWO MACHINES

The two-machine flow-shop operation presented in this section may be described as follows. Similar production equipment and skills are grouped into two machine or production centers. There exists a set of n jobs, all simultaneously available, which are to be processed.

Two constraints exist. First, each machine can process only one job at a time. Second, each job can be in process on only one machine at a time.

Formulating the Sequencing Problem. The objective in determining a production sequence for the set of n jobs is to minimize the maximum flow time. Let

$A(i) =$ processing time (including set up time if any) on the first machine for the ith job

$B(i) =$ processing time (including set up time if any) on the second machine for the ith job

$F(i) =$ time at which the ith job is completed

Each job consists of a pair of times $A(i)$ and $B(i)$, where $A(i)$ is the time on the first machine and $B(i)$ is the time on the second machine. This ordering is the same for each of the n jobs. Some of the $A(i)$'s and $B(i)$'s may be zero if a job requires only a single operation.

The two-machine flow-shop sequencing problem may now be formulated as follows: Given the $2n$ time values, $A(1), A(2), \ldots, A(n)$, and $B(1), B(2), \ldots, B(n)$, find the ordering of jobs on each of the two machines so that neither of the constraints is violated and the maximum of $F(i)$ is minimized.

Consider the two-machine situation illustrated in Figure 12.1. The last job cannot be completed earlier than the time required to process each job on machine A plus the time needed to perform the second operation of the last

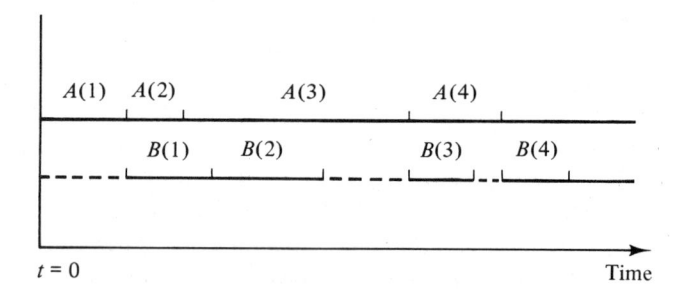

Figure 12.1 Sequence for two-machine flow shop.

job, since $B(n)$ cannot overlap $A(n)$. Therefore,

$$F_{\max} \geq \sum_{i=1}^{n} A(i) + B(n).$$

Similarly, the last job cannot be completed in less time than it takes to process each job on machine B plus the time caused by the delay before machine B can begin, since B(1) cannot overlap A(1). Therefore,

$$F_{max} \geq A(1) + \sum_{i=1}^{n} B(i).$$

It will be noted that the sum of $A(i)$'s and the sum of $B(i)$'s are direct consequences of the given processing times and are entirely unaffected by the ordering of the jobs. Thus, to reduce F_{max} one can only influence $B(n)$ and $A(1)$ by the choice of sequence. Hence, choose the smallest of the set of $2n$ values of $A(i)$'s and $B(i)$'s. If this value happens to be an $A(i)$, put this job first in sequence so as to make $A(1)$ as small as possible. If the smallest processing time happened to be $B(i)$, this job would go last in sequence so as to make $B(n)$ as small as possible. Once the position of one job is determined, the same procedure can be used for the set of $(n - 1)$ remaining jobs.

A Two-Machine Sequencing Example. Assume that six jobs are to be processed on two machines, A and B. Each job is processed first on machine A and then on machine B. The processing times are given in Table 12.1. The objective is to find the job sequence that will minimize the maximum flow time.

The first step in the solution procedure is to select the job with the shortest processing time. Table 12.1 indicates that this is 2 hours for job 1 on machine A.

Table 12.1. PROCESSING TIMES FOR SIX JOBS

Job	Processing Time (hours)	
	Machine A	Machine B
1	2	6
2	7	3
3	9	7
4	11	5
5	7	10
6	4	8

Job 1 is assigned to the first available position in sequence. Next, the processing time for the remaining jobs are studied to find the shortest time. This is 3 hours for job 2 on machine B. Thus, job 2 is assigned to the last sequence position, which is 6. The next smallest processing time is 4 hours for job 6 on machine A. This job is assigned to the first available sequence position. In this case the job is assigned to position 2. Table 12.1 indicates that the next smallest processing time is 5 hours for job 4 on machine B. This job will be assigned to the last available sequence position, which is 5.

Now it is noted that there is a tie for the next shortest processing time. This is 7 hours each for job 3 on machine B and job 5 on machine A. An arbitrary choice of assigning job 5 to position 3 and job 3 to position 4 can be made. Ties among smallest processing times can always be resolved arbitrarily, without a detrimental effect on the optimal sequence.

In the example presented the optimal sequence is 1, 6, 5, 3, 4, 2, as illustrated in Figure 12.2. The value of F_{max} is 43 hours.

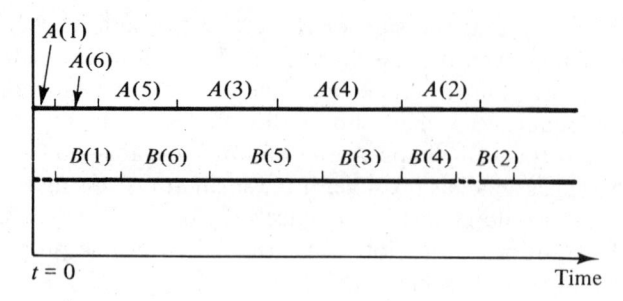

Figure 12.2 Optimal sequence for six-job problem.

12.2 FLOW-SHOP SEQUENCING FOR SEVERAL MACHINES

Flow-shop sequencing problems involving three or more machines require very complex solution procedures. In this section a special three-machine problem is presented which may be converted into an equivalent two-machine problem for solution by the previous procedure. Next, a general three-machine problem is solved using a branch-and-bound technique. Finally, heuristic methods of solution are discussed.

A Special Three-Machine Problem. Assume that there are three machines, A, B, and C, in a flow shop. Each job is processed in the order A, B, C, and the processing time is smallest on machine B for every job—that is, $A(i) \leq B(i)$ and $C(i) \geq B(i)$. Under these conditions the three-machine problem can be converted into an equivalent two-machine problem with processing times

$$G(i) = A(i) + B(i)$$

and

$$H(i) = B(i) + C(i).$$

As an example, consider the following three-machine problem. Five jobs are to be processed on three machines, A, B, and C. The processing times are given in Table 12.2.

Comparing the processing times on machine B with those on machines A and C reveals that the conditions for the special case are satisfied. The equivalent problem can be stated with processing times shown in Table 12.3.

By applying the algorithm of Section 12.1, the optimal sequence is found to be 3, 4, 1, 5, 2. This is also the optimal sequence for the three-machine problem.

Table 12.2. PROCESSING TIMES FOR FIVE JOBS

Job	Processing Times (hours)		
	Machine A	Machine B	Machine C
1	10	6	7
2	8	2	5
3	5	2	10
4	6	6	7
5	8	5	6

Table 12.3. EQUIVALENT TWO-MACHINE PROBLEM

Job	Processing Times (hours)	
	Machine G	Machine H
1	16	13
2	10	7
3	7	12
4	12	13
5	13	11

The General Three-Machine Sequencing Problem.[1] The branch and bound procedure described in Chapter 4 can be used to sequence n jobs through 3 machines. For n jobs there are $n!$ possible sequences. The objective is to find the one with the minimum makespan.

For purposes of branching or partitioning the sets of solutions, a partial sequence (one with less than n jobs sequenced) is used to identify the subset of all possible sequences arising out of the partial sequence. Branching is illustrated in Figure 12.3, where subset 3xx is the subset of all sequences with job 3 in first place.

A lower bound on each subset is determined such that the makespan for any sequence in the subset is greater than or equal to this bound. After every branching the subset with the lowest lower bound is chosen for further exploration. The procedure terminates when a complete sequence is obtained for which the makespan is equal to or less than the lower bounds on all unexplored subsets. The complete sequence is then optimal. Figure 12.3 shows the complete solution tree for the branch and bound procedure.

In the three-machine makespan problem, each node represents a sequence of between 1 and n jobs. Consider a node corresponding to partial sequence y, where y contains a particular subset of the n jobs of size r. Let $TA(y)$, $TB(y)$,

---

[1] Porcedure adapted from E. Ignall and L. E. Schrage, "Application of the Branch-and-Bound Technique to Some Flow-Shop Scheduling Problems," *Operations Research*, XIII, No. 3 (May–June 1965), pp. 400–412.

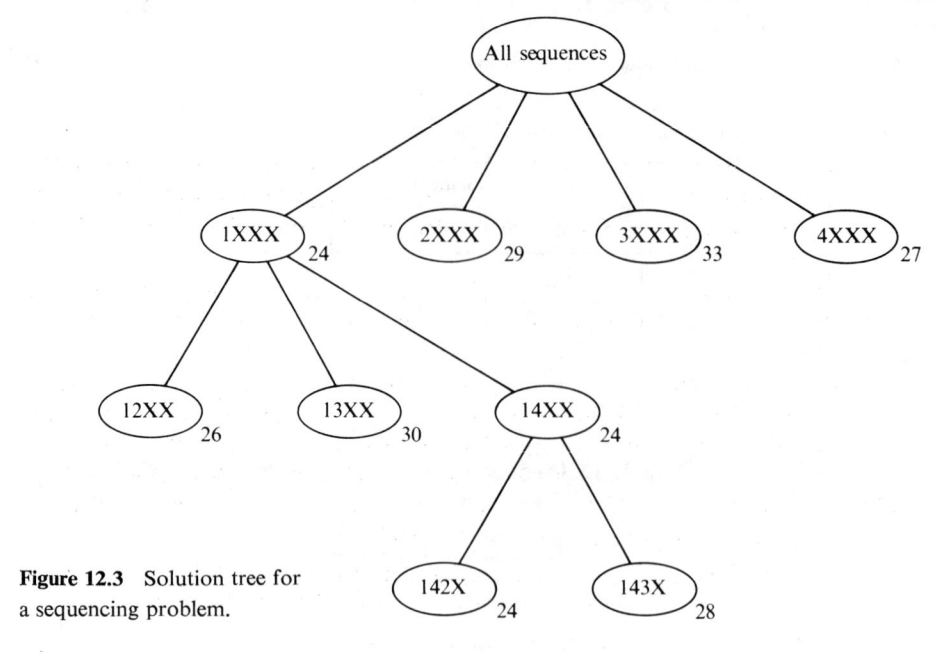

Figure 12.3 Solution tree for a sequencing problem.

and $TC(y)$ be the times at which machines A, B, and C, respectively, complete processing the last of the jobs in the subset.

A lower bound on the makespan of all schedules that begin with sequence y is

$$LB(y) = \max \begin{cases} TA(y) + \sum_{\bar{y}} A(i) + \min_{\bar{y}} [B(i) + C(i)] \\ TB(y) + \sum_{\bar{y}} B(i) + \min_{\bar{y}} [C(i)] \\ TC(y) + \sum_{\bar{y}} C(i). \end{cases}, \qquad (12.1)$$

where $A(i)$, $B(i)$, and $C(i)$ are the processing times of the ith job on machines A, B, and C, respectively, and $\bar{y}$ is the set of $n - r$ jobs that have not been assigned a position in partial sequence y. $LB(y)$ is a lower bound on the makespan for any node that branches from node y, since all such nodes represent sequences of from $r + 1$ to n jobs that begin with sequence y.

The branch-and-bound technique is applied as follows:

1. Develop a list of nodes ranked by lower bounds such that the node with the smallest lower bound is first.
2. Retain a set of attributes (partial sequence y, TA, TB, TC, etc.) for each node.
3. Start by listing only the node that has scheduled none of the jobs.
4. Update the list recursively as described below until an optimum is obtained.
5. Remove the first node from the list.
6. Create a new node for every job that the "just-removed" node has not yet

258

scheduled. This is done by attaching the unscheduled job to the end of the sequence of scheduled jobs.

7. Compute the lower bounds and other attributes for those newly created nodes and insert them ranked on the list.
8. Go back to step (5). The first time that a node which has scheduled all n jobs is first on the list the problem is solved. The node's sequence is an optimal one.

To illustrate the use of this technique, consider a three-machine, four-job problem. The processing times on the machines are given in Table 12.4. From the processing times $\sum A(i) = 16$, $\sum B(i) = 22$, and $\sum C(i) = 17$.

To simplify the calculations in Equation (12.1), $C(i)$ and the sums $B(i) + C(i)$ are arranged in ascending order as shown in Table 12.5.

Table 12.4. THREE-MACHINE, FOUR-JOB PROBLEM

Job	Processing Times (hours)		
	Machine A	Machine B	Machine C
1	1	4	8
2	6	4	5
3	8	5	1
4	1	9	3

Table 12.5. COMPUTATIONS FOR FOUR-JOB PROBLEM

$C(i)$	Job	$C(i) + B(i)$	Job
1	3	6	3
3	4	9	2
5	2	12	4
8	1	12	1

From Tables 12.4 and 12.5 the following lower bounds may be calculated:

$$LB(1) = \max \begin{Bmatrix} 1 + 15 + 6 \\ 5 + 18 + 1 \\ 13 + 9 \end{Bmatrix} \quad LB(2) = \max \begin{Bmatrix} 6 + 10 + 6 \\ 10 + 18 + 1 \\ 15 + 12 \end{Bmatrix}$$

$$= 24 \qquad\qquad\qquad = 29$$

$$LB(3) = \max \begin{Bmatrix} 8 + 8 + 9 \\ 13 + 17 + 3 \\ 14 + 16 \end{Bmatrix} \quad LB(4) = \max \begin{Bmatrix} 1 + 15 + 6 \\ 10 + 13 + 1 \\ 13 + 14 \end{Bmatrix}$$

$$= 33 \qquad\qquad\qquad = 27.$$

Since $LB(1) = 24$ is the smallest of these values, 1 is chosen as the starting job in the sequence. $LB(1, 2)$, $LB(1, 3)$, and $LB(1, 4)$ are computed next:

$$LB(1, 2) = \max \begin{Bmatrix} 7 + 9 + 6 \\ 11 + 14 + 1 \\ 18 + 4 \end{Bmatrix} \quad LB(1, 3) = \max \begin{Bmatrix} 9 + 7 + 9 \\ 14 + 13 + 3 \\ 15 + 8 \end{Bmatrix}$$
$$= 26 \qquad\qquad\qquad\qquad\qquad = 30$$

$$LB(1, 4) = \max \begin{Bmatrix} 2 + 14 + 6 \\ 14 + 9 + 1 \\ 17 + 6 \end{Bmatrix}$$
$$= 24.$$

Since $LB(1, 4)$ gives the minimum, it is chosen as the next starting partial sequence.

Next, $LB(1, 4, 2)$ and $LB(1, 4, 3)$ are computed:

$$LB(1, 4, 2) = \max \begin{Bmatrix} 8 + 8 + 6 \\ 18 + 5 + 1 \\ 23 + 1 \end{Bmatrix} \quad LB(1, 4, 3) = \max \begin{Bmatrix} 10 + 6 + 9 \\ 19 + 4 + 5 \\ 20 + 5 \end{Bmatrix}$$
$$= 24 \qquad\qquad\qquad\qquad\qquad = 28.$$

Since $LB(1, 4, 2)$ is the smaller of these, and since 1, 4, 2, 3 will include every job to be sequenced, the next calculation is that of the total makespan. This is $TC(y) + \sum_{\bar{y}} C(i) = 23 + 1 = 24.$

The makespan of 24 is less than any of the lower bounds of partial sequences not contained in 1, 4, 2, 3. Thus, the calculations are completed. These are shown in Figure 12.3. If the makespan for 1, 4, 2, 3 were greater than one of those lower bounds, it would be necessary to calculate the lower bounds for the sequences not eliminated in a similar manner.

Flow-Shop Sequencing on n Machines. A common characteristic of all algorithms for the solution of sequencing problems is the magnitude of the computations required. Although most heuristic approaches involve much less computation than complete enumeration, the required time increases rapidly as the size of the problem increases. Consequently, practical size-sequencing problems are beyond the reach of total enumeration and must be subjected to heuristic methods of solution. However, heuristic methods do not guarantee an optimal solution.

One heuristic solution procedure will be presented below. Let

Chap. 12   Models for Production Sequencing   261

$$T_{ij} \begin{cases} i = 1, \ldots, n \\ j = 1, \ldots, m \end{cases}$$

represent the processing time for the ith job on the jth machine in an n-job, m-machine, makespan sequencing problem. Then p auxiliary n-job, two-machine problems can be defined. In the kth auxiliary problem, where k is the sequence number equal to or less than p,

$$\theta_{i1}^k = \sum_{j=1}^{k} T_{ij} = \text{processing time for the } i\text{th job on the first machine}$$

$$\theta_{i2}^k = \sum_{j=m+1-k}^{m} T_{ij} = \text{processing time for the } i\text{th job on the second machine.}$$

For each auxiliary problem the two-machine algorithm of Section 12.1 may be used. The result is a set of sequences $S_1, S_2, \ldots, S_p$ for the p auxiliary problems. The best sequence of the set would be chosen.

Consider the four-machine, six-job problem given in Table 12.6. Three auxiliary problems may be formulated as given in Tables 12.7, 12.8, and 12.9. The optimal sequence for each auxiliary problem is given in Table 12.10. The sequence 2, 6, 3, 1, 4, 5 is best, although not necessarily optimal.

Table 12.6. FOUR-MACHINE, SIX-JOB PROBLEM

	Processing Time (hours)			
Job	Machine A	Machine B	Machine C	Machine D
1	10	6	8	7
2	3	8	7	9
3	6	8	10	6
4	7	9	9	5
5	15	6	8	5
6	8	6	10	13

Table 12.7. AUXILIARY PROBLEM 1

	Processing Time (hours)	
Job	Machine A	Machine B
1	10	21
2	3	24
3	6	24
4	7	23
5	15	19
6	8	29

Table 12.8. AUXILIARY PROBLEM 2

Job	Processing Time (hours) Machine A	Machine B
1	16	15
2	11	16
3	14	16
4	16	14
5	21	13
6	14	23

Table 12.9. AUXILIARY PROBLEM 3

Job	Processing Time (hours) Machine A	Machine B
1	24	7
2	18	9
3	24	6
4	25	5
5	29	5
6	24	13

Table 12.10. BEST SEQUENCES FOR AUXILIARY PROBLEMS

Auxiliary Problem	Optimal Sequence	Makespan (hours)
1	2, 3, 4, 6, 1, 5	73
2	2, 6, 3, 1, 4, 5	68
3	6, 2, 1, 3, 4, 5	71

12.3 THE JOB-SHOP SEQUENCING PROBLEM[2]

In this section a relatively more complex production system known as the job shop is presented. The job-shop system may be described as follows. Similar production facilities and skills are grouped and constitute a finite number of machine centers. Each committed production order or job is either awaiting release to the first machine center on its route or it is in process. The route for each job involves n downstream machine centers and is specified by a routing sheet. The routes for all jobs are determined by technological processing considerations and constitute a network of interwoven paths. Completion of a

[2] Adapted from W. J. Fabrycky and J. E. Shamblin, "A Probability-Based Sequencing Algorithm," *Journal of Industrial Engineering*, XVIII, No. 6 (June 1966).

given job is a composite task requiring the completion of a finite number of subtasks, each consuming scarce machine time. A schematic illustration of the job shop is shown in Figure 12.4.

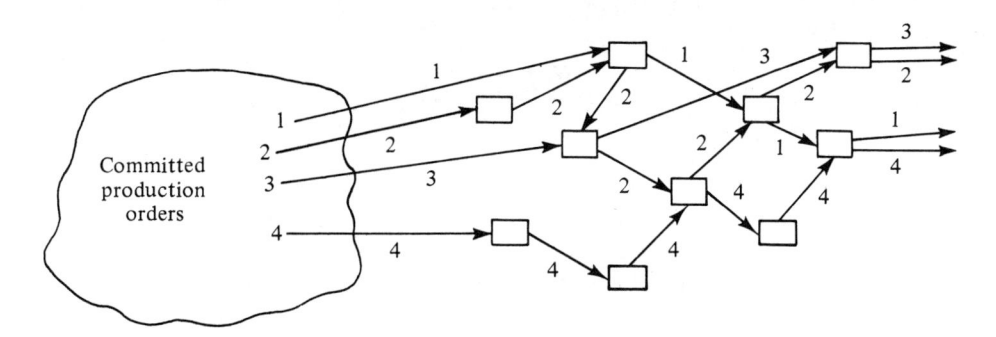

Figure 12.4 Job-shop production system.

An important part of the production management task is the sequencing of jobs at machine centers to achieve some desired performance objective. This section assumes that management is primarily concerned with the due date performance of completed production orders. Because of this, time is the primary variable of interest. Thus, we will use a daily production calendar for time which consists of the positive set of integers increasing with time and without bound.

An Urgency Factor Model. Order flow time through the jth machine center is uncertain and may be viewed as a random variable. A gross classification of its elements would be move time, queue time, setup time, and processing time.

If t_j is used to designate flow time across the jth machine center, then total flow time for the ith order may be expressed as $T_i = \sum t_j$ for $j = 1, 2, \ldots, n$. Since t_j is a random variable, it follows that T_i will also be a random variable.

Assuming that the flow times across machine centers are independently distributed random variables with means μ_j and variances σ_j^2, the distribution of T_i will have parameters

$$\mu_i = \sum_j \mu_j$$
$$\sigma_i^2 = \sum_j \sigma_j^2 \qquad \text{for } j = 1, 2, \ldots, n.$$

Further, it can be assumed that T_i is distributed approximately normal due to a version of the central limit theorem.

Regardless of the position of the order in the production system, there is a certain upstream history and a certain downstream future that has a bearing on the probability of completing the order by its due date. If the current date is designated C, the time in days remaining before the due date for the ith order is $D_i - C$. For an order at machine center $k(k = 1, 2, \ldots, n)$ the expected flow time before completion will be $\sum_{j=k}^{n} \mu_j$. The flow-time variance will be $\sum_{j=k}^{n} \sigma_j^2$. The factor

$$z_i = \frac{(D_i - C) - \sum_{j=k}^{n} \mu_j}{\sqrt{\sum_{j=k}^{n} \sigma_j^2}}$$

is a percentage point on the distribution of remaining flow time. If the distributions of remaining flow times are identical for all orders at a certain machine center, the order with the smallest algebraic factor is the most urgent.

The relative urgency of orders in each queue is based solely upon the time remaining before due date and the statistical properties of downstream flow time. Although the distribution of flow time will deviate from normality as $k \to n$, this is important only to the extent that the flow-time distributions differ for orders being sequenced. Of course, if t_j is normal, total flow time will be normal regardless of the number of remaining downstream machine centers.

The Urgency Factor Algorithm. The urgency factor model may be programmed for a digital computer. Required as inputs are current estimates of μ_j and σ_j^2 for each machine center, the due dates for each order, the routing for each order, and the current date. A computer run is made each day to determine an urgency factor for all orders awaiting release to the manufacturing system and for all orders in process. The passage of one day, the availability of updated estimates of μ_j and σ_j^2, and the fact that k will increase by one when the order flows through a machine center will alter the previously computed value of z_i.

Each order awaiting release, or at machine center k, has an assigned urgency factor from the computer run. Each z_i implicitly reflects the probability of completing the order by its due date. Thus, z_i states which order should be worked first, which should be worked second, and so forth. Actually, the urgency factors rank the downstream routes for orders in queue in accordance with their relative urgencies. The algorithm gives precedence to those orders which have the smallest implied probability of being completed by due date. Thus, probability sequencing is an expediting process that shifts scarce production time from those orders that probably will be completed before due date to those that have less probability of being completed before the due date. The probabilities, although not explicitly specified, are implicitly reflected in the urgency factors.

Probability sequencing is compatible with the random nature of job-shop flow time. It provides a dynamic queue discipline that is a function of the total time remaining before the due date for the order and the statistical properties of downstream flow time. As flow time conditions change in the system, the sequencing algorithm will adapt itself by allocating scarce production time to those orders with the lowest probability of completion by their due dates. The scheme will not generate production capacity. Probability sequencing simply distributes the available capacity among the orders competing for the capacity in such a way that each has an approximately equal probability of being completed by its due date.

Probability sequencing is a dynamic queue discipline based on the criterion of completion by the due date. Effectiveness is expressed in terms of due date performance of completed orders. In operation, three important characteristics are noted:

1. Orders with high relative probability of completion by due date wait in the queue, relinquishing machine time to those that have a low relative probability of completion by the due date.
2. After clearing a congested machine center, the probability of completion by the due date improves and the order becomes less urgent.
3. As the due date for an order approaches, the effect of the passage of one day becomes increasingly significant.

The operational characteristics listed above are a direct result of the sequencing algorithm. To verify these characteristics, a job-shop simulation utilizing probability sequencing was programmed on a digital computer. Some features of the digital simulator are:

1. The shop consists of 10 independent machine centers which receive orders from a random generation process.
2. The number of machining operations, the machine times, and the routing are randomly selected. An order can be scheduled through any combination of the 10 machine centers, including return trips.
3. The due date for an order is selected at random, but it is a function of the number of machine centers in the routing.
4. The individual μ_j and σ_j are updated each day utilizing a weighted combination of past history and flow-time data for orders waiting in queue.

An Example of Completion Performance. When the actual completion date, A_i, is compared with the due date, D_i, the due date performance of the ith order may be expressed as $E_i = A_i - D_i$. If a histogram of E is plotted for an interval of time, it may be used as a measure of effectiveness. Its mean and standard deviation may be designated μ_E and σ_E, respectively. Ideally, $\mu_E = 0$ and $\sigma_E = 0$. This cannot be achieved in practice. A desirable situation would be to have $\mu_E < 0$ with σ_E small. Thus, the distribution of E is of primary interest in discussing completion performance during the interval of time under study.

To illustrate a due date performance histogram for job-shop operations, a 100-day simulation was run on a digital computer. The service rate of the shop as a whole was set at 1.5 times the arrival rate to avoid an explosive condition. At the end of the simulation, the histogram of completed orders appeared as shown in Figure 12.5. Its mean was 2.5 days early and its standard deviation was 3.4 days.

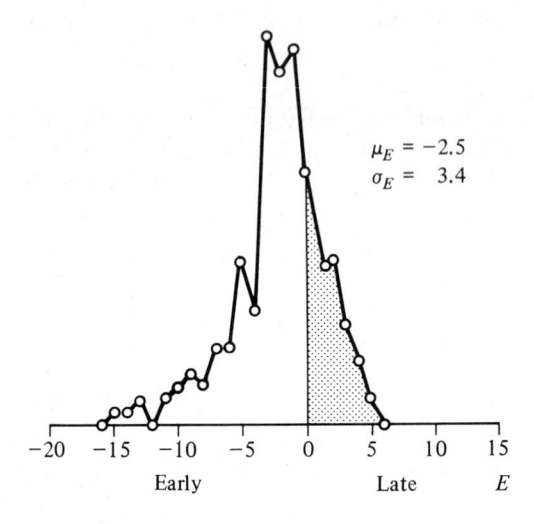

Figure 12.5 Histogram of due date performance.

12.4 COMPARISON OF JOB-SHOP SEQUENCING RULES[3]

In addition to the probability sequencing rule developed in the preceding section there are many others used in practice. Observation indicates that these rules can be divided into three classes. Rules in the first class are completely independent of any characteristics of the job or the shop. Rules in the second class depend on a characteristic of the job. Sequencing rules that depend on both job and shop characteristics fall in the third class.

The simplest example of a rule that does not depend on any characteristic of the job or the shop is the first-come, first-served (FCFS) rule. This sequencing

---

[3] Adapted from W. J. Fabrycky, V. Chachra, and D. C. Montgomery, "A Simulation Study of Three Classes of Job-Shop Sequencing Rules," Proceedings, 13th Annual International Meeting, *American Production and Inventory Control Society*, Cincinnati, Ohio, October 1970.

rule assigns priority to jobs in the order in which they join the queue at a machine center. Symbolically, if p_{ij} is the priority of the ith job behind the jth machine center and s_j is the set of integers denoting the jobs in queue behind machine center j, in arrival order, then for this rule

$$\max \{p_{ij}\} = \{s_j^1\}$$

where s_j^1 is the first element of the set s_j. Obviously, the assignment of priority by this rule in no way depends on either job or shop characteristics.

A very useful rule known as the shortest processing time (SPT) rule is an example of a sequencing policy which depends on a job characteristic but does not depend on any characteristic of the shop. This sequencing rule assigns the highest priority to that job in the queue having the shortest processing time at the machine center in question. If t_{ij} is the processing time of the ith job at the jth machine center, then for this rule

$$\max \{p_{ij}\} = \min \{t_{ij}\}.$$

The assignment of priority by this rule depends on the job characteristic of processing time but does not depend on any shop characteristic.

Probability sequencing (PS) as developed in the preceding section is an example of a sequencing rule that depends on both job and shop characteristics. Priority is assigned to jobs at each machine center in accordance with

$$\max \{p_{ij}\} = \min \{z_{ij}\},$$

where z_{ij} is the urgency factor for the ith job at the jth machine center. This sequencing rule assigns priorities that depend on both job and shop characteristics as was indicated in the previous section.

Job-Shop Simulation. Comparison of job-shop sequencing rules can be accomplished only by use of digital simulation. Such simulation permits indirect experimentation in a situation where direct experimentation is virtually impossible. The rules discussed above were compared on a digital computer programmed to behave like a job shop.

The simulator models a production system with 12 machine centers from which routes for jobs are selected. A job entering the system joins the queue behind the first machine center on its routing. When the machine is free, a job is selected in accordance with a sequencing rule and is allowed to occupy the machine for a time equal to its predetermined processing time. When the job is completed, it moves into the queue behind the next machine center on its routing. A machine center is idle if no job is in process at that center. A job is complete when it has been processed through all centers on its route.

Performance statistics for the job shop are generated with each event that occurs in the simulator. Data are collected continuously through the entire period of simulation as follows:

1. Cumulative time that each queue is of a given length behind each machine center. This is used in calculating queue probabilities.
2. Cumulative time that each machine center is busy. This is used in calculating machine utilizations.
3. Due date performance of each job processed.
4. Total number of jobs processed.
5. Waiting time history at each machine center for the last 15 jobs processed. This is used to compute μ_j and σ_j^2 for the probability sequencing rule.

The simulator is general in that it can handle variable shop sizes, different simulation durations, and several operating conditions. The operating conditions may be chosen by suitably modifying the four subroutines briefly described as follows:

1. Subroutine RAND: This subroutine generates interarrival times for jobs. The negative exponential distribution with a mean of 2.04 hours was chosen for this study.
2. Subroutine SUBJOB: This subroutine determines the routing for each order, the processing time at each machine center, and the due date. The average route was chosen to be 11 machine centers, the processing time is distributed uniformly with a mean of 2.0 hours and a variance of 0.33 hour, and the due date is established by summing the processing times and multiplying by a factor.
3. Subroutine DECIDE: This subroutine determines which order is to be worked next at each machine center. It operates in one of three modes depending on the sequencing rule chosen.
4. Subroutine PROB: New urgency factors are computed by this subroutine at the end of each day for use in sequencing by subroutine DECIDE when the probability sequencing rule is being used.

In this study the simulated interval used and the number of jobs generated are kept constant with the number of jobs completed allowed to vary. In other investigations, comparisons were made for the same number of jobs processed. It is recognized that, in the approach of this investigation, steady state is a necessary condition for valid comparisons.

The values of machine utilizations were used as indicators of steady state. A test run was made with a shop size of 12 machine centers operating under the FCFS sequencing rule. Machine utilization values were printed at intervals of 6 days starting at day 8. Utilization figures for six machine centers picked at random are plotted in Figure 12.6.

Inspection of the curves in Figure 12.6 shows that 50 days is a sufficient interval for initializing the shop. In order to be consistent between runs, the shop was initialized for a period of 50 days under the FCFS sequencing rule for

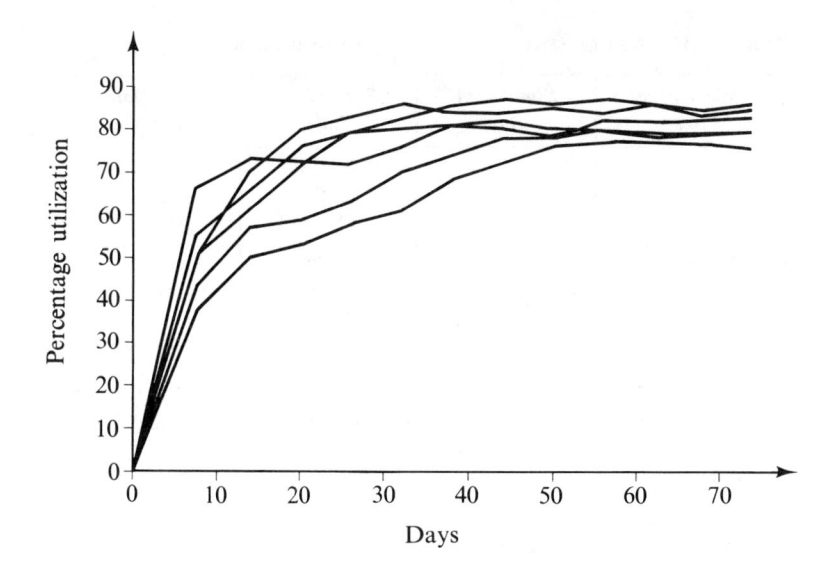

Figure 12.6 Convergence of machine utilization.

all experimental runs. If the sequencing rule being tested was not FCFS, a switchover took place after 50 days from FCFS to the sequencing rule being studied.

The total interval of simulation was 300 days, of which 50 days constituted the initialization period. Performance data were gathered for the last 250 days only. Computer time restrictions and sample size considerations entered into the choice of the simulation interval. Since Figure 12.6 indicates that this simulator was operating near steady state, it was decided to keep the simulation interval constant. The number of jobs processed in this interval was used as a performance measure.

In this experiment the means of the arrival time and service time distributions were chosen so that a traffic density of approximately 0.9 would result. A low traffic density situation leads to short queues and little opportunity for sequencing rules to have an effect; thus it was avoided.

Six experimental runs were made under two sets of operating conditions. In set I the allowable flow time was small and represents a tight due date condition. Set II had a larger allowable flow time representing a normal due date condition. The actual values selected for the two sets of test conditions are presented in Table 12.11.

Simulated Outputs. The actual outputs from the simulation runs were machine utilizations, queue probabilities, and histograms of due date performance. The due date performance histograms for the test conditions are presented in Figures 12.7 through 12.12. In these histograms the abscissa is

Table 12.11. TEST CONDITIONS FOR JOB-SHOP SIMULATION

Experimental Set	Simulation Run	Sequencing Rule	Due Date Multiplier
I	1 2 3	FCFS SPT PS	2.5
II	4 5 6	FCFS SPT PS	5.0

given as days with negative values representing days early and positive values representing days late. The dashed portion of the histogram indicates that values beyond that point have been grouped.

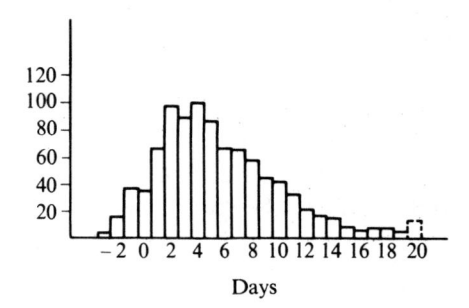

Figure 12.7 Due date performance—set I, run 1.

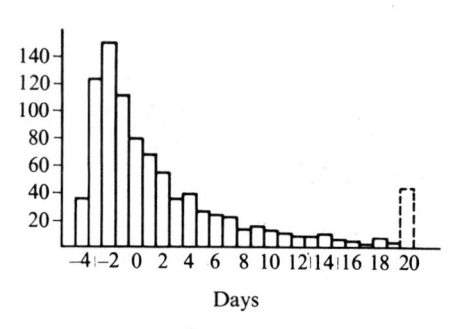

Figure 12.8 Due date performance—set I, run 2.

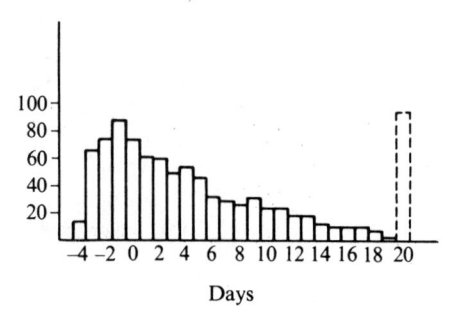

Figure 12.9 Due date performance—set I, run 3.

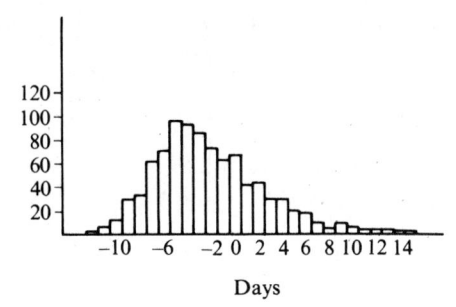

Figure 12.10 Due date performance—set II, run 4.

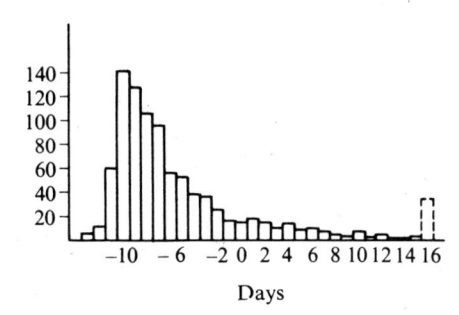

Figure 12.11 Due date performance—set II, run 5.

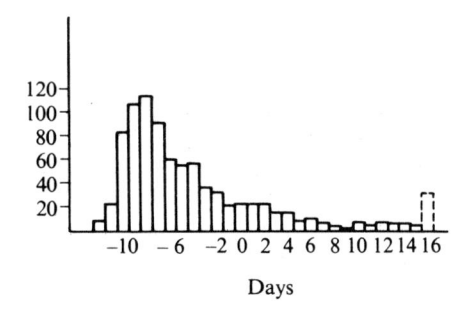

Figure 12.12 Due date performance—set II, run 6.

Further calculations were made utilizing these results to obtain measures of the number of jobs late, mean lateness, and in-process inventory. These are summarized in Table 12.12 for all test conditions.

Observations and Discussion. There are five observations that may be made from the simulation results summarized in this section. Each is presented separately followed by an explanatory discussion.

OBSERVATION 1.

Operation of the job shop under SPT leads to the lowest in-process inventory level.

Table 12.12 shows that the in-process inventory level for SPT is 38.18 and that this value is well below that for FCFS or PS under each experimental set. The in-process inventory level depends upon queue lengths and the durations

Table 12.12. SUMMARY OF RESULTS FOR JOB-SHOP SIMULATION

Test Condition	Set I FCFS	Set I SPT	Set I PS	Set II FCFS	Set II SPT	Set II PS
Total jobs processed	924	932	921	924	932	931
Total jobs late	844	453	627	254	142	208
Mean lateness	6.02	6.99	8.25	3.81	9.32	8.99
In-process inventory	48.70	38.18	50.13	48.70	38.18	46.50
Per cent utilization	86.30	86.90	85.40	86.30	86.90	85.90

for which the queue is of different lengths. The SPT sequencing rule assigns the highest priority to the job that has the smallest processing time at the machine center, whereas FCFS and PS do not. Since jobs with small processing times are processed first, SPT would process the largest number of jobs in any given interval of time. This keeps the queue behind each machine center at a minimum. As a result, the in-process inventory level for the job shop is a minimum.

OBSERVATION 2.

The mean lateness in the case of SPT sequencing is greater than that for FCFS sequencing, even though the number of jobs late is greater in FCFS than in SPT.

The SPT sequencing rule has the inherent tendency of reducing queues to a minimum. Hence, the number of jobs in the shop is relatively small and so are the number of jobs late. However, the jobs that tend to be late in SPT are the jobs with large processing times, as these jobs stay in queue while jobs with shorter processing times move ahead. Thus, the jobs that are late under SPT sequencing are very late. This explains the fact that, even though the number of jobs late for SPT is small, the mean lateness is larger than in FCFS.

No simple explanation can be given for the PS rule, as the results depend both on the extra allowable flow time available between set I and set II and the resulting change in priority assignment. Under FCFS and SPT sequencing, the change between set I and set II results only from the change in allowable flow time, with the assignment of priorities remaining unaltered. The change in allowable flow time has the simple effect of measuring jobs that are late from a new reference point.

OBSERVATION 3.

The difference in mean lateness between SPT and FCFS is less under tight due date commitments than under normal due date commitments.

Chap. 12   Models for Production Sequencing   273

The difference in mean lateness is 0.97 day for the tight case and 5.51 days for the normal case. This can be explained by comparing the number of jobs late. In the case of tight commitments, the effect of jobs that are very late for SPT is distributed over a larger number of jobs giving a smaller difference between SPT and FCFS. In the normal case since fewer jobs are late, the effect of very late jobs in SPT is more predominant, causing the larger difference between FCFS and SPT.

OBSERVATION 4.

The in-process inventory level for the PS rule increases with decreasing allowable flow time, whereas the inventory level for FCFS and SPT does not change with changes in allowable flow time.

Table 12.12 shows that the in-process inventory level for both the FCFS and the SPT sequencing rules remain unchanged between the test conditions of set I and set II, whereas this is not the case under the PS rule. As stated earlier, the in-process inventory level is a function of queue lengths and queue durations. When the allowable flow time is changed, the priority assignment for the FCFS and SPT sequencing rules is in no way affected, since these rules are independent of due dates. Thus, the queue lengths and queue durations are unchanged leading to the same in-process inventory level.

In the case of PS, the priority assignment depends upon the due date, and hence the inventory level may be expected to change with changes in allowable flow time. The reason for the increase in inventory level with decreasing allowable flow time becomes clear on studying the probability sequencing formula presented earlier.

If N is the number of remaining machine centers on the route for an order and if t, μ, and σ^2 are average values such that $\sum t = Nt$, $\sum \mu = N\mu$, and $\sum \sigma^2 = N\sigma^2$, then

$$z_i = \frac{[(D_i - C) - Nt] - N\mu}{\sqrt{N\sigma^2}}$$

or

$$z_i = \frac{N}{\sqrt{N\sigma^2}} \left[\frac{(D_i - C)}{N} - (t + \mu) \right].$$

Thus, z_i is proportional to N times the average allowable flow time per machine center, $(D_i - C)/N$, less the average anticipated flow time per machine center, $t + \mu$.

When the expression in the brackets is positive, a large value of N gives a large positive z value and a low priority. On the other hand, if the expression in the brackets is negative, a large value of N gives a large negative z value and a high priority. Thus, when the average allowable flow time is less than the average anticipated flow time, the jobs with longer routings will be processed first. Since attention is directed to those jobs which will be in process longest, a high in-process inventory level is to be expected as compared with the case where allowable flow time is normal.

OBSERVATION 5.

The number of jobs processed under PS is a function of the allowable flow time and decreases with decreasing allowable flow time, whereas this is not the case for FCFS and SPT.

Table 12.12 indicates that the total number of jobs processed is identical in sets I and II for the FCFS and SPT sequencing rules. This is to be expected, since these rules assign priority independent of allowable flow time.

The reasoning given in connection with Observation 4 indicates that jobs with larger routings are given attention under a tight flow-time condition. Thus, in any given interval of time a smaller number of jobs will be processed as compared with the case where allowable flow time is normal.

Direct experimentation with job-shop type production systems is often not possible or leads to erroneous conclusions. This is because the job-shop system is extremely complex and difficult to understand. Thus, digital computer simulation is being used more frequently to support indirect experimentation for the purpose of gaining a simplifying insight.

Simulation stuides such as those reported here give the investigator a basis for conclusions concerning the comparative effect of sequencing rules and methods of establishing due dates. Often, these conclusions cannot be reached by intuition alone. Simulation can point out the reasons for overserved differences in job-shop behavior and identify the cause-and-effect relationships involved. This understanding is often valid and applicable for real-world job-shop systems and can lead to the improvement of production operations.

PROBLEMS

12.1. A flow shop receives seven jobs which are to be processed on two machines, A and B. Each of the seven jobs are processed first on machine A and then on machine B. The processing times are given below.

Job	Processing Time (hours)	
	Machine A	Machine B
1	4	3
2	5	12
3	7	10
4	12	3
5	9	7
6	13	15
7	6	8

Determine the job sequence that will minimize the makespan.

12.2. The following table gives the processing times on a lathe and a milling machine for 10 jobs. Each job has to be processed first on the lathe and then on the milling machine.

| | Processing Time (minutes) ||
Job	Lathe	Milling Machine
1	32	58
2	43	25
3	68	37
4	53	75
5	27	53
6	18	29
7	55	18
8	36	63
9	29	36
10	75	45

Determine the optimal job sequence for minimizing the makespan.

12.3. A flow shop has three machines, A, B, and C, to process eight jobs. Each job is processed in the order A, B, C. The processing times are given below.

| | Processing Time (hours) |||
Job	Machine A	Machine B	Machine C
1	12	12	14
2	14	9	10
3	5	5	12
4	7	3	4
5	15	6	8
6	8	7	11
7	9	9	13
8	10	5	6

Determine the optimal job sequence for minimizing the makespan.

12.4. Solve the three-machine, five-job problem given below to determine the optimal sequence for the five jobs. Use the branch-and-bound technique.

| | Processing Time (hours) |||
Job	Machine A	Machine B	Machine C
1	2	3	5
2	7	4	6
3	3	9	7
4	5	10	12
5	1	4	6

12.5. The foreman of a flow shop wishes to minimize the makespan for the six jobs he has just received. From past experience, he estimates the processing times of each of the six jobs on each of the three machines to be as given below.

	Processing Time (minutes)		
Job	Machine A	Machine B	Machine C
1	30	50	45
2	25	60	20
3	55	40	45
4	40	55	35
5	60	30	70
6	15	55	30

(a) Which technique would you recommend to solve the problem?
(b) Solve the problem to determine the optimal job sequence.

12.6. The following table gives the estimated time for processing five jobs in a flow shop with machines x, y, and z. Using the branch-and-bound solution procedure, determine the optimal job sequence to minimize total time.

	Processing Time		
Job	Machine x	Machine y	Machine z
1	25	35	50
2	15	75	10
3	40	30	60
4	20	15	40
5	45	25	35

12.7. Determine the optimal job sequence of Problem 12.6, using the heuristic solution procedure discussed in Section 12.2. Is the sequence determined optimal?

12.8. A flow shop must process six jobs through five machines, A, B, C, D, and E. The processing times are given in the following table.

	Processing Time (hours)				
	Machine				
Job	A	B	C	D	E
1	8	7	5	9	12
2	4	6	6	10	9
3	5	13	11	7	7
4	12	9	10	4	10
5	7	5	8	11	13
6	6	4	14	9	8

Determine heuristic sequence(s) for the six jobs.

12.9. The table below shows the relevant data for a job shop. All five jobs are waiting in queue at machine center A. If the current date is 3 and the routing for each of the orders is to be A, B, C, determine the urgency factor, z_1, for each of the five jobs. What sequence would you recommend at machine center A?

	\multicolumn{6}{c	}{Machine Centers}	
	\multicolumn{2}{c	}{A}	\multicolumn{2}{c	}{B}	\multicolumn{2}{c	}{C}	
Job	μ_A	σ_A^2	μ_B	σ_B^2	μ_C	σ_C^2	Due Date
1	6	2	7	3	8	4	6
2	7	3	12	7	9	6	9
3	9	5	10	5	11	7	8
4	8	4	6	3	9	5	12
5	9	6	11	6	6	2	13

12.10. Determine the urgency factor, z_i, for the six jobs, if all jobs are in the source queue awaiting to be processed on machine centers A, B, and C, in that order. Give the sequence of jobs based on the urgency factors.

	\multicolumn{8}{c	}{Machine Centers}	
	\multicolumn{2}{c	}{A}	\multicolumn{2}{c	}{B}	\multicolumn{2}{c	}{C}	\multicolumn{2}{c	}{D}	
Job	μ_A	σ_A^2	μ_B	σ_B^2	μ_C	σ_C^2	μ_D	σ_D^2	Due Date
1	8	3	6	2	7	3	9	4	10
2	8	4	11	5	9	4	14	7	13
3	6	2	7	3	11	6	8	3	12
4	10	5	10	6	13	7	13	8	19
5	7	2	8	4	10	5	8	4	17
6	12	7	4	1	6	2	10	5	23

12.11. The table below shows the processing time for six jobs to be processed at four machines of a job shop.

	\multicolumn{4}{c	}{Processing Time (hours)}
	\multicolumn{4}{c	}{Machine}
Job	A	B	C	D
1	4	7	3	8
2	4	9	2	6
3	3	4	7	4
4	6	8	3	7
5	9	7	6	3
6	8	3	7	6

Determine the sequence of the jobs you would recommend, using (a) the first-come, first-served rule, and (b) the shortest processing time rule. What is the total processing time by each method?

12.12. A job shop is to process five jobs through four machines. The processing times are estimated to be as follows:

	\multicolumn{4}{c}{Processing Time (minutes)}
	\multicolumn{4}{c}{Machine}
Job	A	B	C	D
1	40	30	70	65
2	35	65	40	90
3	65	75	25	55
4	85	35	65	40
5	75	45	60	80

What sequence would the foreman follow if he uses (a) the first-come, first-served rule, and (b) the shortest processing time rule? Compare the total processing time using the rules above. Which rule would you recommend?

13

Project Planning and Control Models

A project is composed of a series of activities directed to the accomplishment of a desired objective. Projects differ from production processes in that they are normally nonrepetitive. They usually confront the decision maker with a unique situation in which prior experience and information for control is nonexistent. Therefore, models for project control should meet two conditions: (1) *during the planning phase of a project they should make possible the determination of a logical, preferably optimal, project plan, and* (2) *during the execution phase of a project they should make possible the evaluation of project progress against the plan.*

The planning and control of a large-scale project may be accomplished by utilizing an activity network as the modeling technique. Such techniques may be classified into deterministic procedures designated CPM (critical path method) or probabilistic procedures designated PERT (program evaluation and review technique). Acceptance of these procedures has been widespread by project management for the following reasons: (1) *the concepts are easy to understand and apply,* (2) *they introduce objectivity in planning and control, and* (3) *they reduce the complexity of the planning process by breaking the project down into its individual components.*

13.1 DETERMINISTIC PROJECT CONTROL—CPM

The critical path method is based on certain definitions derived from network or graph theory. These definitions are:

Element or arc: An arc is a specified line segment.

Oriented arc: An oriented arc is a line segment for which the direction or orientation is specified.

Vertex: A vertex is an end point of an arc.

Network or graph: A network or graph is a group of arcs, no two of which meet at a point other than a vertex.

Path: A path is a string of arcs connecting two vertices such that every arc is connected to not more than one arc at each of its vertices or end points.

Connected graph: A connected graph is a graph in which there is at least one path connecting any pair of vertices.

Circuit: A circuit is an unoriented path connecting a vertex to itself.

Cycle: A cycle is an oriented path connecting a vertex to itself.

For the purpose of developing a graphical model, each activity in the project is assumed to be defined by two events: the start of activity and the completion of the activity. In a graphical representation there are two alternatives available. In one, the activities are represented by the vertices of the graph. Although this leads to a feasible representation, it is not very commonly used. In the other, the activities are represented by an oriented arc, with the start and completion events represented by vertices. The orientation of the arc is in the direction from start to completion.

The physical nature of the project constrains the execution of activities to some specified order. This specified order gives rise to precedence and succession relationships between the events and the activities. The principal relationships are:

1. The start event of an activity precedes the end event for the same activity by a time duration called the activity time.
2. The start event of an activity succeeds end events for all activities preceding it.
3. The event *project start* precedes all activities and events in the project.
4. The event *project end* succeeds all activities and events in the project.

The relationships described above can be expressed graphically in the form of a network. The nodes of the network represent events, and the arcs represent activities. The direction of time flow is shown on each arc from the start toward the end. Thus, all arrows point away from the event *project start* and toward the event *project end*. Each event on this network is labeled by a nonnegative integer. It is usually more convenient to have $i < j$, whenever event i precedes event j directly or indirectly. However, this is not mathematically necessary. An activity that has its start labeled i and its end labeled j is represented by the double subscript (i, j).

Associated with each activity is an estimate of the expected time required for its completion. This is represented by the lengths of the arcs in the network. The basic difference in CPM and PERT occurs from the different methods of arriving at the time estimate. In CPM only one time estimate is made, and this value, Y_{ij}, is treated as a known value. Similarly, there are two chronological times TE_i and TL_i associated with each event or node of the graph:

$TE_i =$ earliest possible time of the occurrence of event, i, for a given project start, TE_0

$TL_i =$ latest possible time of occurrence of event, i, which would not be incompatible with a given project end, TL_s

From the network relationships between events and activities, it is possible to develop the following recursive relationships for computing TE_i and TL_i:

$$TE_i = \begin{cases} TE_0 & i = 0 \\ \max{(TE_k + Y_{ki})} & \text{for all } (k, i) \in P \end{cases} \quad (13.1)$$

and

$$TL_i = \begin{cases} TL_s & i = s \\ \min{(TL_k - Y_{ik})} & \text{for all } (i, k) \in P \end{cases} \quad (13.2)$$

From these equations, it is possible to compute the following information about each activity (i, j) included in the project P:

$$\begin{aligned}&\text{(1) Earliest starting time, } TE_i \\ &\text{(2) Latest starting time, } TL_j - Y_{ij} \\ &\text{(3) Earliest completion time, } TE_i + Y_{ij} \\ &\text{(4) Latest completion time, } TL_j \\ &\text{(5) Maximum available time, } TL_j - TE_i \\ &\text{(6) Slack, } TL_j - TE_i - Y_{ij}\end{aligned} \quad (13.3)$$

The information above becomes the basic foundation on which management decisions about a particular activity are based. Slack represents the amount of latitude available to the decision maker in the scheduling of that activity. If the slack is zero, the activity is critical because the sequencing decision is no longer controlled by the decision maker. In CPM it can be shown that there is always a connected chain of critical activities from project start to project end. This is called the *critical path*.

13.2 AN EXAMPLE OF PROJECT CONTROL WITH CPM

Figure 13.1 shows the graphical representation of a project as an activity network. The project represented consists of 22 activities shown by arrows. For each activity an estimate is made for the time required to complete the activity. These estimates are given in Table 13.1.

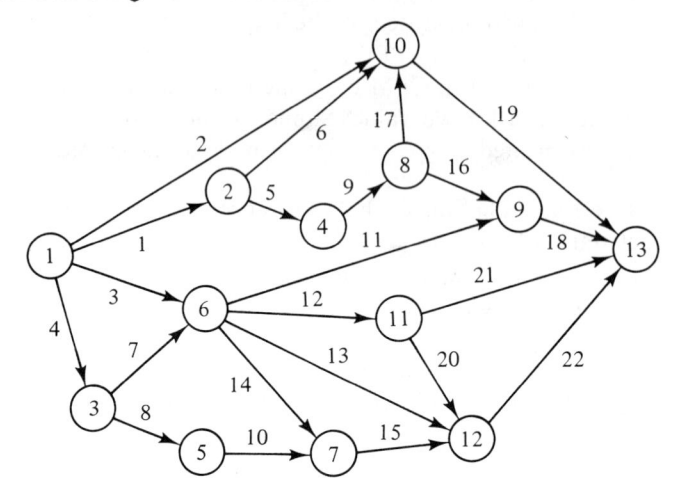

Figure 13.1 Activity network for a project.

The interrelationships of activities determined by technological considerations may be shown as a precedence matrix as in Table 13.2. In the precedence matrix, element m_{ij} is one if activity i cannot be started until activity j is completed. Figure 13.1 is a compact method for representing precedence relationships.

Computing the Earliest Occurrence of Events. The first analysis step in the critical path method is to compute the earliest occurrence of events, TE_i. The earliest occurrence time for event 1, project start, is set to be zero. Then the earliest occurrence times for other events may be computed by using the recursive relationship of Equation (13.1).

As an example of the computations required, consider event 3. The earliest occurrence of event 3 is

$$TE_3 = \max_k \{TE_k + Y_{ki}\} \quad \text{for all } (k, i) \in P.$$

The only activity preceding event 3 is activity 4. Therefore,

$$TE_3 = 0 + 20 = 20.$$

Next, consider event 6 which is preceded by activities 3 and 7. The earliest occurrence of event 6 is

Table 13.1. ESTIMATES OF ACTIVITY TIMES

Activity	Start	End	Time
1	1	2	20
2	1	10	75
3	1	6	35
4	1	3	20
5	2	4	20
6	2	10	55
7	3	6	20
8	3	5	20
9	4	8	20
10	5	7	20
11	6	9	45
12	6	11	30
13	6	12	50
14	6	7	20
15	7	12	20
16	8	9	20
17	8	10	25
18	9	13	20
19	10	13	35
20	11	12	5
21	11	13	20
22	12	13	20

Table 13.2. PRECEDENCE MATRIX FOR ACTIVITIES

	1	2	3	4	5	6	7	8	9	10	11	12	13	14	15	16	17	18	19	20	21	22
1	0	0	0	0	0	0	0	0	0	0	0	0	0	0	0	0	0	0	0	0	0	0
2	0	0	0	0	0	0	0	0	0	0	0	0	0	0	0	0	0	0	0	0	0	0
3	0	0	0	0	0	0	0	0	0	0	0	0	0	0	0	0	0	0	0	0	0	0
4	0	0	0	0	0	0	0	0	0	0	0	0	0	0	0	0	0	0	0	0	0	0
5	1	0	0	0	0	0	0	0	0	0	0	0	0	0	0	0	0	0	0	0	0	0
6	1	0	0	0	0	0	0	0	0	0	0	0	0	0	0	0	0	0	0	0	0	0
7	0	0	0	1	0	0	0	0	0	0	0	0	0	0	0	0	0	0	0	0	0	0
8	0	0	0	1	0	0	0	0	0	0	0	0	0	0	0	0	0	0	0	0	0	0
9	0	0	0	0	1	0	0	0	0	0	0	0	0	0	0	0	0	0	0	0	0	0
10	0	0	0	0	0	0	0	1	0	0	0	0	0	0	0	0	0	0	0	0	0	0
11	0	0	1	0	0	0	1	0	0	0	0	0	0	0	0	0	0	0	0	0	0	0
12	0	0	1	0	0	0	1	0	0	0	0	0	0	0	0	0	0	0	0	0	0	0
13	0	0	1	0	0	0	1	0	0	0	0	0	0	0	0	0	0	0	0	0	0	0
14	0	0	0	1	0	0	0	1	0	0	0	0	0	0	0	0	0	0	0	0	0	0
15	0	0	0	0	0	0	0	0	0	1	0	0	0	1	0	0	0	0	0	0	0	0
16	0	0	0	0	0	0	0	0	1	0	0	0	0	0	0	0	0	0	0	0	0	0
17	0	0	0	0	0	0	0	0	1	0	0	0	0	0	0	0	0	0	0	0	0	0
18	0	0	0	0	0	0	0	0	0	1	0	0	0	1	0	0	0	0	0	0	0	0
19	0	1	0	0	0	1	0	0	0	0	0	0	0	0	1	0	0	0	0	0	0	0
20	0	0	0	0	0	0	0	0	0	0	1	0	0	0	0	0	0	0	0	0	0	0
21	0	0	0	0	0	0	0	0	0	0	1	0	0	0	0	0	0	0	0	0	0	0
22	0	0	0	0	0	0	0	0	0	0	0	1	0	1	0	0	0	0	1	0	0	0

$$TE_6 = \max \begin{Bmatrix} TE_1 + Y_{1,6} \\ TE_3 + Y_{3,6} \end{Bmatrix}$$

$$= \max \begin{Bmatrix} 0 + 35 \\ 20 + 20 \end{Bmatrix} = 40.$$

Similar computations will lead to the earliest occurrence for all events. These are given in the second column of Table 13.3.

Table 13.3. EARLIEST AND LATEST EVENT TIMES

Event	Earliest Time	Latest Time
1	0	0 *
2	20	20 *
3	20	30
4	40	40 *
5	40	60
6	40	50
7	60	80
8	60	60 *
9	85	100
10	85	85
11	70	95
12	90	100
13	120	120 *

Computing the Latest Occurrence of Events. The computations for the latest occurrence of events, TL_i, begins by working with the event *project end*. The time for the latest occurrence of *project end*, event 13 in the example, is set equal to the time for the earliest occurrence of the event, TE_{13} (Alternatively, TL_{13} can be set at some predetermined scheduled date for the completion of the project.) Then, the latest occurrence times for other events can be computed by using the recursive relationships of Equation (13.2).

As an example of the procedure above, consider event 9. The latest occurrence of event 9 is

$$TL_9 = \min_k \{TL_k - Y_{ik}\} \quad \text{for all } (i, k) \in P.$$

The only activity succeeding event 9 is activity 18. Hence,

$$TL_9 = 120 - 20 = 100.$$

Similar computations can be performed to obtain the latest occurrences for all events. These are given in the third column of Table 13.3. The asterisks indicate the events for which the time for the latest occurrence coincides with the earliest occurrence.

Determination of Critical Activities and Critical Path. After the earliest and the latest occurrences of the events are computed, information about each activity in the project can be computed using Equations (13.3). For example, consider activity 6 (starting event 2, end event 10) with $i = 2$ and $j = 10$.

Earliest starting time $= TE_i = 20$
Latest starting time $= TL_j - Y_{ij} = 85 - 55 = 30$
Earliest completion time $= TE_i + Y_{ij} = 20 + 55 = 75$
Latest completion time $= TL_j = 85$
Maximum available time $= TL_j - TE_i = 85 - 20 = 65$
Slack $= TL_j - TE_i - Y_{ij} = 85 - 20 - 55 = 10$

The information for all activities is given in Table 13.4.

Table 13.4. ACTIVITY INFORMATION TABLE

Activity	Earliest Starting Time	Latest Starting Time	Earliest Completion Time	Latest Completion Time	Maximum Available Time	Activity Slack Time
1	0	0	20	20	20	0
2	0	10	75	85	85	10
3	0	15	35	50	50	15
4	0	10	20	30	30	10
5	20	20	40	40	20	0
6	20	30	75	85	65	10
7	20	30	40	50	30	10
8	20	40	20	60	40	20
9	40	40	60	60	20	0
10	40	60	60	80	40	20
11	40	55	85	100	60	15
12	40	65	70	95	55	25
13	40	50	90	100	60	10
14	40	60	60	80	40	20
15	60	80	80	100	60	40
16	60	80	80	100	40	20
17	60	80	85	85	25	0
18	85	100	105	120	35	15
19	85	85	120	120	35	0
20	70	95	75	100	30	25
21	70	100	90	120	50	30
22	90	100	110	120	30	10

An activity is considered critical if there is no slack time available. Further, it has been shown that if there is at least one critical activity, then there exists a continuous chain of critical activities from project start to project end. This chain is called a critical path. From Table 13.4 it can be seen that activities 1, 5, 9, 17, and 19 are critical and that the critical path is 1, 2, 4, 8, 10, 13. The critical path is shown by boldface lines in Figure 13.2.

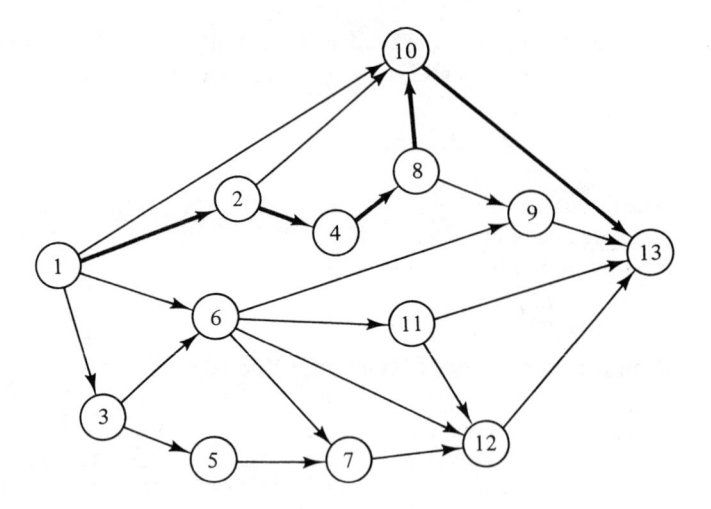

Figure 13.2 Critical path.

13.3 PROBABILISTIC PROJECT CONTROL—PERT

Both CPM and PERT are similar in their logical structure. Projects are represented by sets of required activities, with the principal difference being the treatment of estimated time for the completion of each activity. In PERT, activity time is considered to be a random variable with an assumed probability distribution.

In CPM only one time estimate was made, and the value Y_{ij} was treated as a known value. In PERT, three time estimates are made:

1. The probable earliest completion time, a
2. The probable latest completion time, b
3. The most probable completion time, m

Value Y_{ij} is defined as a random variable with a beta distribution and with range from a to b and mode m. The expected value of this distribution is used as the length of the corresponding arc.

The advantage of the PERT approach is that it offers a method of dealing with random variation, making it possible to allow for chance in the scheduling calculations. Also, it may be used as a basis for computing the probability that the project will be completed on or before its scheduled date.

The term *critical path* was explained in the preceding section, as a connected chain of critical activities from project start to project end. In PERT networks, there is no single critical path, but each activity has a certain probability of being critical. The activities that may become critical with a high probability are considered more critical than those having a smaller probability of becoming critical.

Probabilistic project control with PERT utilizes the expected values of the hypothetical distribution of actual performance times as shown in Figure 13.3.

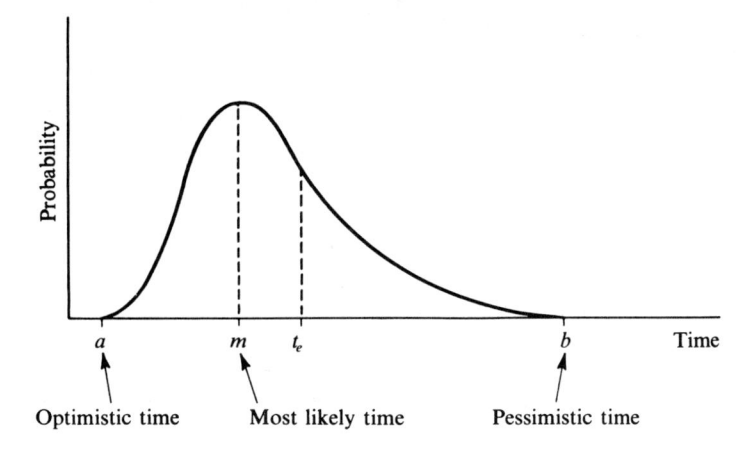

Figure 13.3 Beta distribution of activity times.

All computations are made prior to performance of the activity. Hence, the basis for PERT computations does not involve any statistical sampling, but rather depends on the judgment of the person knowledgeable about the activity. The person involved estimates the three times based on his or her general experience, knowledge of the requirements of the activity, and the personnel and facilities available. These times are:

a = optimistic time, the probable earliest completion time if all goes well

b = pessimistic time, the probable longest completion time if everything goes wrong

m = most likely time, the most probable completion time

From the three time estimates given above, an assumed beta distribution for the activity time is obtained with mean $t_e = (a + 4m + b)/6$ and variance $\sigma^2 = [(b - a)/6]^2$ for each activity.

13.4 AN EXAMPLE OF PROJECT CONTROL WITH PERT

Suppose that a project with 13 activities may be represented graphically as shown in Figure 13.4. For each activity three time estimates are made. Table 13.5 shows the time estimates assumed for this example together with other calculated values.

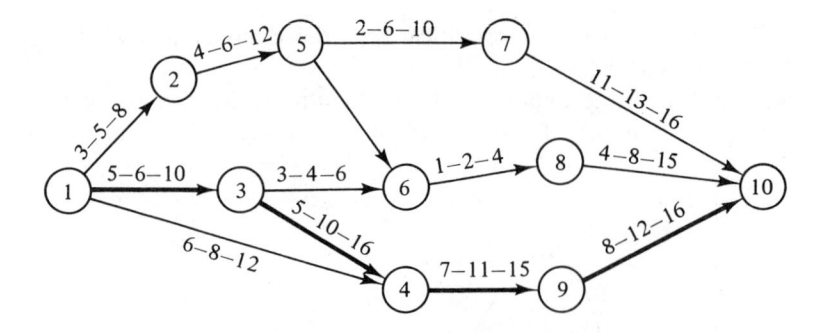

Models for Production and Operations Control Part IV

Figure 13.4 Network for a probabilistic project.

Table 13.5. TIME ESTIMATES AND CALCULATIONS

Event	Previous Event	a	m	b	$t_e = \dfrac{a+4m+b}{6}$	$\sigma^2 = \left(\dfrac{b-a}{6}\right)^2$	TE	TL	TL− TE	TS	P
10	7	11	13	16	13.2	0.69				38.0	0.27
	8	4	8	15	8.5	3.36					
	9	8	12	16	12.0	1.78	39.7	39.7	0.0		
9	4	7	11	15	11.0	1.78	27.7	27.7	0.0		
8	6	1	2	4	2.2	0.25	26.8	31.2	4.4		
7	5	2	6	10	6	1.78	17.9	26.5	8.6		
4	3	5	10	16	10.2	3.36	16.7	16.7	0.0		
	1	6	8	12	8.3	1.00					
6	3	3	4	6	4.2	0.25	24.6	29.0	4.4		
	5	9	13	15	12.7	1.00					
5	2	4	6	12	6.7	1.78	11.9	16.3	4.4		
3	1	5	6	10	6.5	0.69	6.5	6.5	0.0		
2	1	3	5	8	5.2	0.69	5.2	9.6	4.4		
1	—	—	—	—	—	—	—	—	—		

Performing the PERT Network Analysis. The PERT network analysis is performed as follows:

1. Each event is listed beginning with the last event and proceeding to the start event.
2. The preceding events are listed beside each event, thus having a succeeding and preceding event for each activity.
3. The optimistic, most likely, and pessimistic times, a, m, and b, respectively, are listed.
4. The expected value, t_e, is calculated for each activity, using the relationship $t_e = (a + 4m + b)/6$.
5. The variance, σ^2, is calculated for each activity using the relationship $\sigma^2 = [(b - a)/6]^2$.

6. The earliest expected time, TE, of the completion of the event is calculated by adding the expected time (t_e) of each activity to the cumulative total of expected times through the preceding event, staying on the same path from start to finish. When more than one activity leads to an event, that activity whose expected time (t_e) gives the maximum value up to that event is chosen as the expected time for that event. For example, path 1, 2, 5, 7, 10 sums up to 31.1 units, while path 1, 3, 4, 9, 10 sums up to 39.7 units.

7. The latest time, TL, for each event is calculated by fixing the earliest time of the end event as its latest time. Then the latest times for all preceding events are obtained by subtracting the expected activity time (t_e) from the latest time for the succeeding event, staying on the same path and working backward from finish to start. When more than one activity leads from an event, the activity which gives the minimum value through that event is selected. For example, activity 3, 6 has a latest time (TL) of 29.0 units. This value is obtained by subtracting the expected times for the activities 6, 8 and 8, 10 from the earliest expected time (TE) as $39.7 - (2.2 + 8.5) = 29.0$ units.

8. The slack time for each event is obtained by subtracting the earliest expected time from the latest time $(TL - TE)$. The critical path in the PERT network is obtained from the activities having zero slack. The critical path in this example is 1, 3, 4, 9, 10, as can be obtained from the $TL - TE$ values. The second critical path can be obtained as 1, 3, 6, 8, 10, and so on.

Probability of Meeting the Scheduled Time. Assuming the scheduled time (TS) to be 38.0 units, the probability of meeting a scheduled time is calculated as follows:

$$\frac{\text{scheduled time} - \text{earliest expected time}}{\text{standard deviation of sum of activity times}} = \text{area under normal curve}$$

$$\frac{TS - TE}{\sqrt{\text{sum of variance}}} = \frac{38.0 - 39.7}{\sqrt{0.69 + 3.36 + 1.78 + 1.78}}$$

$$= -\frac{1.7}{\sqrt{7.61}} = -0.616.$$

The probability from the normal curve tables given in Appendix D for the calculated value of -0.616 is 0.2689. Thus, the probability of meeting the scheduled time of 38 units is approximately 27 percent.

Probability values between 25 and 60 percent indicate an acceptable range to proceed with a program as depicted in the network. Probability values less than 25 percent assume that the scheduled time cannot be met reasonably with the given resources. Probability values higher than 60 percent may indicate that excess resources are committed to the project, which should be considered for other projects. When the scheduled time and the earliest expected time are equal

($TS = TE$), the probability of completing the project on schedule is approximately 50 percent.

13.5 ECONOMIC ASPECTS OF PROJECT CONTROL

Deterministic and probabilistic project planning and control techniques were explained in detail with illustrative examples in the previous sections. These techniques provide a feasible approach during the planning phase of the project and a basis for evaluation and management during the execution phase of the project.

The estimated time for the completion of an activity was considered to be deterministic in CPM and to be a random variable with an assumed probability distribution in PERT. In either of these techniques, the project manager estimates the activity times based on his or her experience, knowledge of the requirements of the activity, and the resources available.

All required computations are made prior to activity performance. If the calculated probability of meeting the scheduled time ranges between the values of 25 and 60 percent, the project can be started. Otherwise, the critical path is reviewed again with the relevant personnel involved, and reassessments are made where required. This process can be repeated until the decision maker is convinced of the feasibility of the project schedule. Thus, these techniques provide a means of simulating project control during the planning phase.

The slack time ($TL - TE$) provides data to determine the best critical path and the next best critical path. Different critical paths enable the decision maker to determine which path to use based on the probability of meeting the scheduled time. While the project is in progress, the actual times required by the various activities can be compared to the expected value (t_e) and thus determine whether or not the project is in control. If a particular activity is utilizing more than the expected time, necessary measures can be taken to keep the actual activity time within or closer to the expected value. The equipment or personnel can be changed depending on the requirements. Thus, the techniques of CPM and PERT provide a means for exercising control during the execution phase of the project.

Cost can be the parameter of interest in PERT. In the example given previously, only time was considered as a variable. Other variables such as resources and cost can be taken into consideration in the analysis. This technique can be utilized for maximizing profits or minimizing the total costs. The various critical paths can be computed, and the total cost involved in each of these alternatives will enable management to choose the best one.

In the planning of a project, it is generally accepted that there is an inverse relationship between the amount of resources allocated to an activity and the time needed for its completion. This means that an activity can be expedited by allocating additional resources. Conversely, the completion time of an activity can be delayed by curtailing the resources allocated.

Referring to the PERT example given earlier, consider the resource allocations for critical path 1, 3, 4, 9, 10 and another path 1, 2, 5, 7, 10 as given in Table 13.6.

Table 13.6. COSTS FOR PERT NETWORK

\multicolumn{4}{c}{Path 1, 3, 4, 9, 10}	\multicolumn{4}{c}{Path 1, 2, 5, 7, 10}
Event	Previous Event	t_e	Estimated Activity Cost	Event	Previous Event	t_e	Estimated Activity Cost
10	9	12.0	$1,200	10	7	13.2	$1,320
9	4	11.0	1,100	7	5	6.0	600
4	3	10.2	1,020	5	2	6.7	670
3	1	6.5	650	2	1	5.2	520
Total		39.7	$3,970	Total		31.1	$3,110

Although path 1, 3, 4, 9, 10 is critical, the alternative path 1, 2, 5, 7, 10 has a slack of $(39.7 - 31.1) = 8.6$ units. Since the time for the completion of the project is governed by the critical path, the decision maker is concerned with resource allocation to the activities along the critical path. In this situation there is a possibility of reallocating some of the resources from an activity along the alternative path to an activity along the critical path. The effect of the reallocation would be to decrease the total time along the critical path and the completion of the project. The slack in the alternative path will also be decreased. For example, assume that $100 is reallocated from activity 7, 10 to activity 9, 10. As a consequence, activity 7, 10 requires 14.0 time units and activity 9, 10 requires 11.3 time units. The total time along the critical path is reduced, and the project is completed in 39.0 time units. The time along the alternative path is increased to 31.9 units, and the slack is reduced to $(39.0 - 31.9) = 7.1$ units. Now the problem must be reworked to determine the critical path after the changes have been made. Thus, resource allocation plays an important role in determining the critical path and hence the estimated project completion time.

There are other costs involved in the performance of an activity, which may not be linear with reference to time. Further, in some cases additional resource allocations may not necessarily influence (reduce) the expected activity time. Thus, choosing the best critical path requires careful consideration of the various costs involved.

The job-costing structures generally found in industry need a great deal of interpretation to relate actual costs to actual progress. They are rarely related to the scheduling plans. Resource and labor restrictions have considerable effect on the success of a project. The CPM and PERT project control techniques are simple both to understand and apply. These techniques are the most economical ones to apply to any type of project. They reduce the complexity of the project by network analysis of the individual activities. Finally, they provide for efficient project control during both the planning and execution phases.

PROBLEMS

13.1. Determine the critical path of the network shown below.

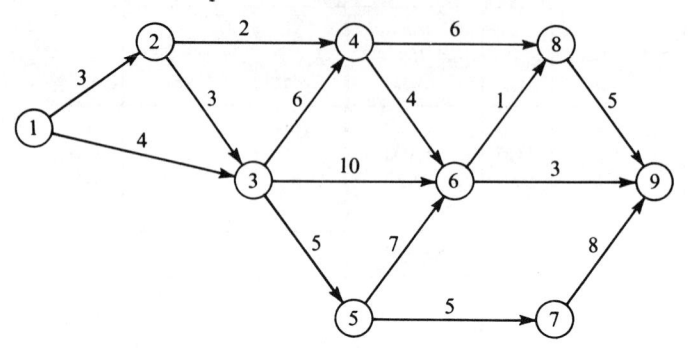

13.2. Find the critical path of the network shown below.

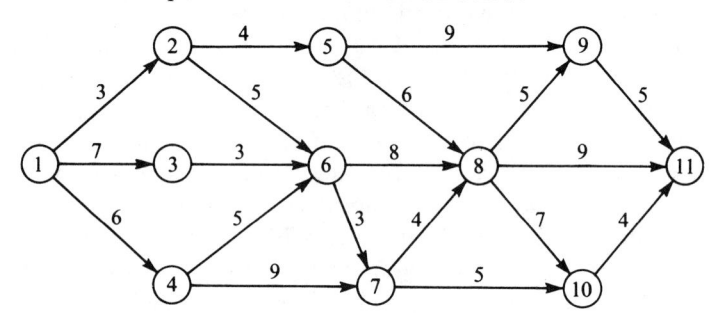

13.3. Write the precedence matrix for the activity network in Problem 13.2.

13.4. Determine the critical path and the second most critical path of the network shown below.

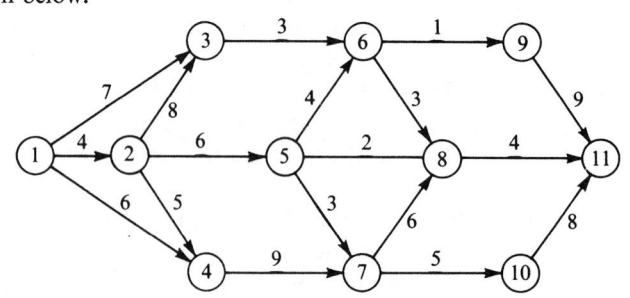

Chap. 13   Project Planning and Control Models   293

13.5. The estimated activity cost for the network given in Problem 13.2 is given in the following table.

Event	Previous Event	Estimated Activity Cost	Event	Previous Event	Estimated Activity Cost
11	10	$200	7	6	$150
	9	250		4	450
	8	450	6	4	250
10	8	350		3	150
	7	250		2	250
9	8	250	5	2	200
	5	450	4	1	300
8	7	200	3	1	350
	6	400	2	1	150
	5	300			

Calculate the estimated costs for the critical path and the second most critical path. If $100 can be reallocated from activity 2, 5 to activity 10, 11, activity 2, 5 will require 7 units of time, and activity 10, 11 will require 2 units of time. Determine the new critical path after the reallocation and the estimated project cost.

13.6. Determine the critical path for the network given below. The estimated costs for the activities are given in the following table.

Event	Previous Event	Estimated Activity Cost	Event	Previous Event	Estimated Activity Cost
13	12	$800	7	6	$600
	11	800		4	200
	10	900		3	600
12	8	300	6	5	200
	7	700		3	400
11	9	400		2	500
10	9	700	5	2	400
	7	500		1	700
	6	400	4	3	400
9	5	500		1	600
8	7	100	3	2	300
	4	300		1	500
			2	1	200

Determine the estimated cost for the completion of the project. By reallocating $100 from activity 11, 13, the time for activity 12, 13 can be reduced to 6 units, while the activity 11, 13 will require 11 units of time. Would the critical path be different after this reallocation? Find the new estimated project cost.

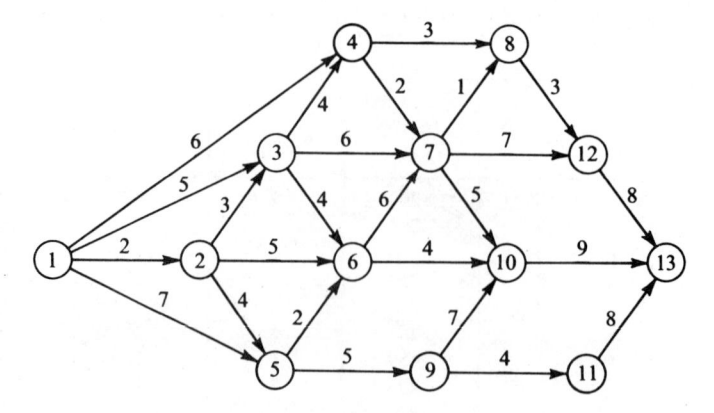

13.7. Determine the critical path of the PERT network below. What is the second most critical path?

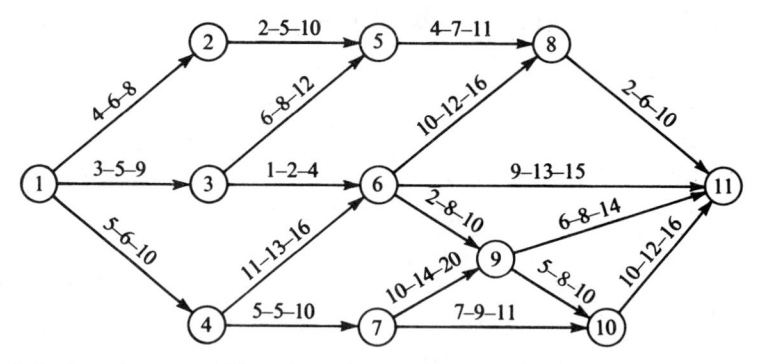

13.8. Calculate the probability of meeting a scheduled time of 50 units for the PERT network given below.

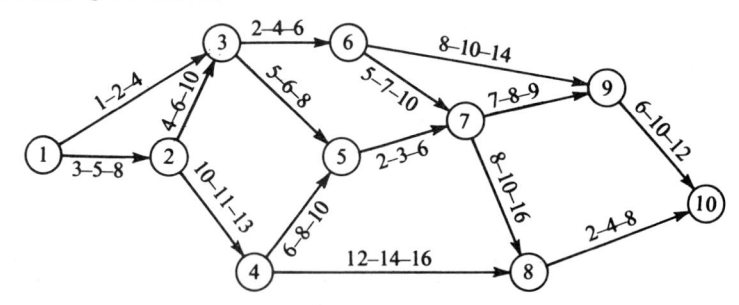

13.9. Determine the critical path and the second most critical path of the PERT network given below.

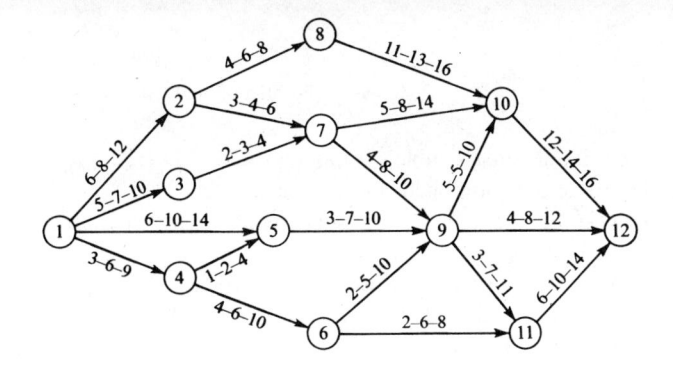

13.10. The following table shows the estimated activity cost for the PERT network given in Problem 13.8.

Event	Previous Event	Estimated Activity Cost	Event	Previous Event	Estimated Activity Cost
10	9	$580	6	3	$240
	8	260	5	4	800
9	7	480		3	370
	6	620	4	2	670
8	7	640	3	2	380
	4	840		1	130
7	6	430	2	1	310
	5	200			

Calculate the estimated costs for the critical path and the second most critical path. If $120 is reallocated from activity 8, 10 to activity 9, 10, activity 8, 10 will require 5.5 units of time and activity 9, 10 will require 9.2 units of time. What is the project completion time? Determine the new critical path after the changes above have been made.

13.11. An electronic industry receives a contract for the manufacture of certain prototype. The manager decides to utilize the PERT network technique to determine the best critical path and to reallocate $400 from the second most critical path to the best critical path so that the total project completion time will be minimized. The three estimates (optimistic, most likely, and pessimistic) are given in parentheses for each of the following activities to be performed for completion of the project.

  1. Process the contract (1, 2, 2).
  2. Request for and receive quotations from vendors for subassembled items (2, 2, 4).
  3. Place purchase orders and receive the subassembled items (10, 16, 18).
  4. Place purchase orders and receive the raw materials for in-plant manufacture (4, 6, 8).
  5. Manufacture component A (5, 6, 8).
  6. Manufacture component B (3, 5, 8).
  7. Inspect and subassemble components A and B (2, 3, 3).
  8. Manufacture component C (6, 7, 10).
  9. Manufacture component D (4, 6, 9).

10. Inspect and subassemble components C and D (1, 2, 4).
11. Manufacture component E (2, 4, 5).
12. Inspect component E and subassemble with components C and D (2, 2, 3).
13. Subassemble all manufactured components (1, 2, 3).
14. Inspect the purchased (subassembled) items (1, 2, 2).
15. Assemble and inspect all manufactured and purchased items (3, 4, 6).

Determine the best and second best critical path before and after the reallocation of the $400 if the reallocation reduces the expected value (t_e) of activity 2, 4 by 1.5 units and increases the expected value (t_e) of activity 2, 3 by 3.0 units.

13.12. Determine the estimated project cost given the PERT network below.

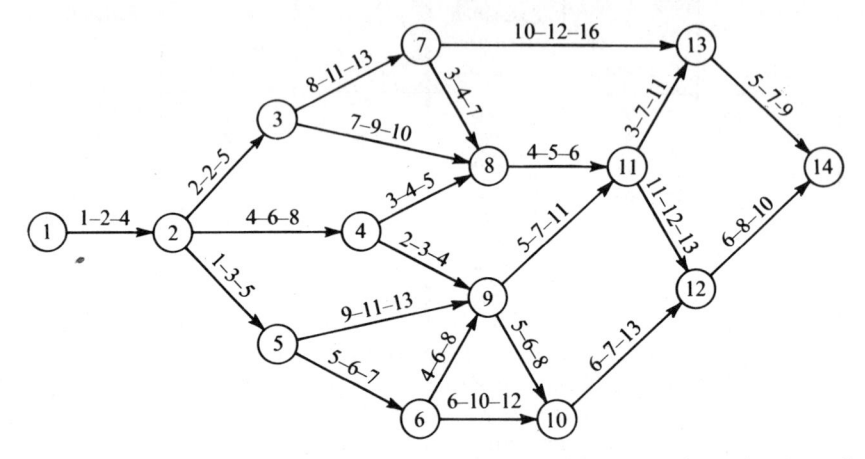

If $200 can be reallocated to an activity on the critical path from the event that has the maximum slack, the expected time of the critical activity will be reduced by 2 units and that of the noncritical activity will be increased by 3 units. Calculate the new project completion time and the estimated cost.

Event	Previous Event	Estimated Activity Cost	Event	Previous Event	Estimated Activity Cost
14	13	$ 700	9	6	$ 600
	12	800		5	1,100
13	11	700		4	300
	7	1,250	8	7	450
12	11	1,200		4	400
	10	800		3	900
11	9	730	7	3	1,100
	8	500	6	5	600
10	9	620	5	2	300
	6	1,000	4	2	600
			3	2	250
			2	1	200

14

Statistical Control Models for Operations

Most operations occur within an environment composed of a multitude of random events, many of which can be treated statistically to facilitate decision making. Others may be analyzed to ascertain their stability over time. The decision maker cannot eliminate variation, but can measure and control variation through the use of statistical control models. Such models help decision makers draw conclusions about the stability of random variable processes. The control models presented in this chapter deal with continuous measurements through $\bar{X}$ and R charts, or with attributes through p or c charts.

When concern occurs beyond the point of process control, acceptance sampling models may be employed. These models determine whether a discrete quantity of the output of a process is acceptable against some criterion. Acceptance sampling models presented in this chapter are used most often in quality determination. But they can also be applied to the verification of accounting and cost records, to determine the accuracy of clerical work, and to numerous other situations in business and industry.

14.1 THE CONCEPT OF STATISTICAL CONTROL[1]

Variation is inherent in most aspects of the decision environment. A multitude of chance causes, few of which can be predicted with certainty, may produce a pattern of variation for such diverse characteristics as the dimension of a finished part, the number of defectives per unit quantity of a part, the procurement lead time of an item, and the number of arrivals per time period. Essential in the concept of statistical control is the employment of control limits within which sample values must fall in order that the operation under study be considered "in control." When a sample value falls outside these limits, the decision maker may infer that a stable system of chance causes no longer exists. Action may then be taken to find the cause of the apparent change. If such a cause exists, the operation may be brought back into control, or compensation made for the change in the pattern of variation. This is the concept on which statistical control models are based.

Patterns of Statistical Variation. A stable or probabilistic steady-state pattern of variation exists when the parameters of the statistical distribution describing the system of chance causes remain constant over time. Steady-state variation of this type is normally an exception rather than the rule. Many operations will produce a probabilistic non-steady-state pattern of variation over time. When this is the case, the mean and/or the variance of the distribution describing the pattern change with time. Sometimes, the form of the distribution will also undergo change.

A probabilistic non-steady-state pattern of variation is exhibited in Figure 14.1. Assume that each point shown represents the measured diameter of a small part. A part was produced and measured each minute giving the 4-hour pattern of variation shown. The nature of the variation exhibited may be generally described as follows. The mean and the variance of the process remained constant during the first hour. During the second hour, the mean exhibited an increase while the variance remained constant. The variance increased moderately for the third hour while the mean stabilized. During the last hour, the variance maintained its previous value as the mean decreased.

A more specific description of the pattern of variation is possible by developing a histogram of the data for each hour. This requires collecting all data for the hour and treating them as though the process was in a steady-state condition during the hour. Although this leads to an erroneous conclusion about the pattern of variation during the hour, there is no satisfactory alternative. Reducing the time interval from which the data are taken will improve the situation to a degree but will result in less data from which to construct the histogram. Therefore, the gain from choosing a small interval is partially lost in the description provided by a histogram. The histogram given at the end of

---

[1] Probability and statistical concepts may be reviewed by a study of Appendix C.

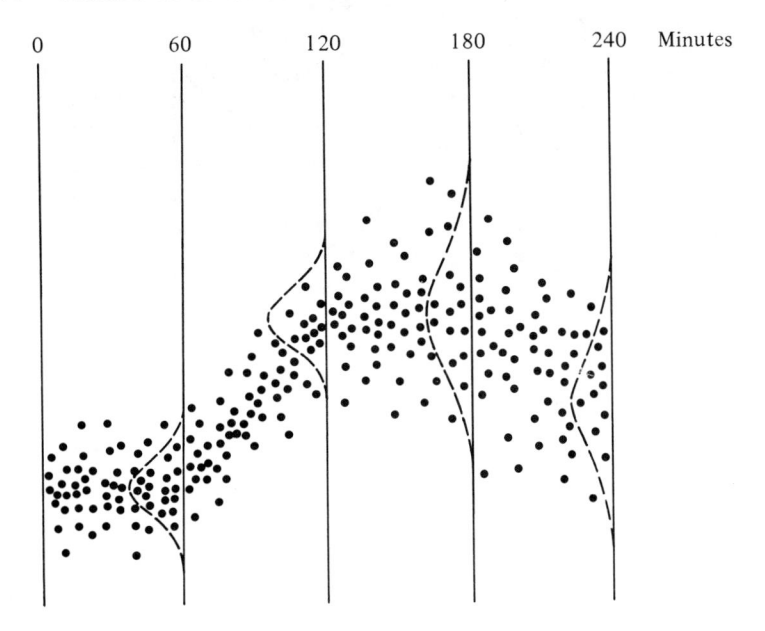

Figure 14.1 Probabilitistic non-steady-state pattern of variation.

each hour in Figure 14.1 is an approximate representation of the distribution of values at the end of that hour, although it cannot be developed from the single point at the end of the hour.

Control limits may be placed about the initial stable pattern of variation to detect subsequent changes from that pattern. In effect, a statistical inference is made when a sample value is considered. If the sample falls within the control limits, the process under study is said to be *in control*. If the sample falls outside the limits, the process is deemed to have changed and is said to be *out of control*.

Figure 14.2 is a representation of control limits placed at a distance $k\sigma$ from the mean of the initial stable pattern of variation of Figure 14.1. If a sample value falls outside the control limits, and the process has not changed, a Type I error of probability α has been made. On the other hand, if a sample value falls within these limits and the process has changed, a Type II error of probability β has been made. In the first case, the null hypothesis has been rejected in error. In the second, the null hypothesis has not been rejected, with a resulting error. Control limits placed about the histogram of the first hour's data in Figure 14.1 are almost certain to detect a changed pattern of variation for the second hour.

Control by Control Chart. A control chart is a graphical representation of a mathematical model used to monitor a random variable process in order to detect changes in a parameter of that process. Charting statistical data is a test of the null hypothesis that the process from which the sample came has

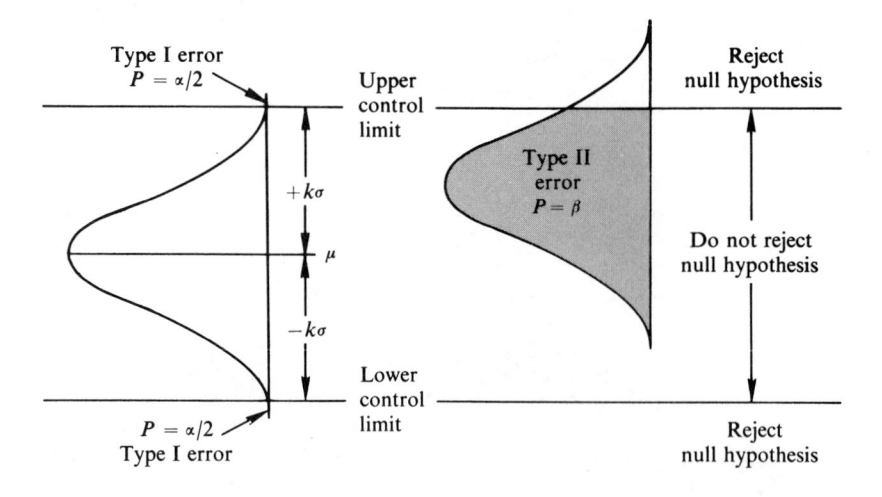

Figure 14.2 Stable and charged pattern of variation.

not changed. A control chart is directed to distinguishing between the existence of a stable pattern of variation and the occurrence of an unstable pattern. If an unstable pattern of variation is detected, action may be initiated to discover the cause of the instability. Removal of the assignable cause should permit the process to return to the stable pattern of variation. The control chart finds its most frequent application in this role.

If the limits on a control chart are set relatively far apart, it is unlikely that a Type I error will be made. The control, however, is then not likely to detect small shifts in the parameter. In effect, the probability, β, of a Type II error is large. If the other approach is taken and the limits are placed relatively close to the initial stable pattern of variation, the value of α will increase. The advantage gained is greater sensitivity of the chart for the shifts that may occur. The ultimate criterion will be the costs associated with the making of Type I and Type II errors. The limits should be established to minimize the sum of these two costs.

The control chart may also be used for monitoring the solution obtained from a decision model. Most decision models are static in that they do not adapt themselves to the instability of the decision environment. These models are constructed at a point in time for a specific set of values for input parameters. A solution derived from a decision model will be optimal only as long as the input parameters to the model retain the values initially established. An optimum procurement policy will be less than optimum if the actual procurement lead time is out of control with respect to the value initially determined and used in the decision model. An optimum level of service capability in a waiting-line system will cease to be optimum if the statistically described arrival pattern is out of control with respect to the derived model. Models of statistical control provide a means for warning the decision maker that inputs to the model need revision. In this role, control charts provide a means for converting static to dynamic decision models so that they may be applied in a non-steady-state environment.

14.2 CONTROL MODELS FOR VARIABLES

When a continuous operation exists, control models for variables can be applied. Specifically, two models are available for operations of this type. The $\bar{X}$ chart is a plot over time of sample means taken from a process. It is primarily employed to detect changes in the mean of the process from which the samples came. The R chart is a plot over time of the ranges of these same samples. It is employed to detect changes in the dispersion of the process. These charts are often employed together in control operations.

Constructing the $\bar{X}$ Chart. The $\bar{X}$ chart receives its input as the mean of a sample taken from the process under study. Usually, the sample will contain four or five observations, a number sufficient to make the central limit theorem applicable. Accepting an approximately normal distribution of the sample means allows one to establish control limits with a predetermined knowledge of the probability of making a Type I error. It is not necessary to know the form of the distribution of the process.

The first step in constructing an $\bar{X}$ chart is to estimate the process mean, μ, and the process variance, σ^2. This requires taking m samples each of size n and calculating the mean, $\bar{X}$, and the range, R, for each sample. Table 14.1

Table 14.1. COMPUTATIONAL FORMAT FOR DETERMINING $\bar{X}$ AND R

Sample Number	Sample Values	Mean $\bar{X}$	Range R
1	$x_{11}, x_{12}, \ldots, x_{1n}$	$\bar{X}_1$	R_1
2	$x_{21}, x_{22}, \ldots, x_{2n}$	$\bar{X}_2$	R_2
.	. . .	.	.
.	. . .	.	.
.	. . .	.	.
m	$x_{m1}, x_{m2}, \ldots, x_{mn}$	$\bar{X}_m$	R_m

illustrates the format that may be used in the calculations. The mean of the sample means, $\bar{\bar{X}}$, is used as an estimate of μ and is calculated as

$$\bar{\bar{X}} = \frac{\sum_{i=1}^{m} \bar{X}_i}{m}. \tag{14.1}$$

The mean of the sample ranges, $\bar{R}$, is calculated as

$$\bar{R} = \frac{\sum_{i=1}^{m} R_i}{m}. \tag{14.2}$$

The expected ratio between the average range, $\bar{R}$, and the standard deviation of the process has been computed for various sample sizes, n. This ratio is designated d_2 and is expressed as

$$d_2 = \frac{\bar{R}}{\sigma}.$$

Therefore, σ can be estimated from the sample statistic, $\bar{R}$, as

$$\sigma = \frac{\bar{R}}{d_2}. \qquad (14.3)$$

Values of d_2 as a function of the sample size are given in Table 14.2.

Table 14.2. FACTORS FOR THE CONSTRUCTION OF $\bar{X}$ AND R CHARTS*

Sample Size, n	$\bar{X}$ Chart d_2	$\bar{X}$ Chart A_2	R Chart D_3	R Chart D_4
2	1.128	1.880	0	3.267
3	1.693	1.023	0	2.575
4	2.059	0.729	0	2.282
5	2.326	0.577	0	2.115
6	2.534	0.482	0	2.004
7	2.704	0.419	0.076	1.924
8	2.847	0.373	0.136	1.864
9	2.970	0.337	0.184	1.816
10	3.078	0.308	0.223	1.777
11	3.173	0.285	0.256	1.744
12	3.258	0.266	0.284	1.716
13	3.336	0.249	0.308	1.692
14	3.407	0.235	0.329	1.671
15	3.472	0.223	0.348	1.652
16	3.532	0.212	0.364	1.636
17	3.588	0.203	0.379	1.621
18	3.640	0.194	0.392	1.608
19	3.687	0.187	0.404	1.596
20	3.735	0.180	0.414	1.586

The mean of the $\bar{X}$ chart is set at $\bar{\bar{X}}$. The control limits are normally set at $\pm 3\sigma_{\bar{x}}$, which results in the probability of making a Type I error of 0.0027. Since

$$\sigma_{\bar{x}} = \frac{\sigma}{\sqrt{n}},$$

substitution into Equation (14.3) gives

$$\sigma_{\bar{x}} = \frac{\bar{R}}{d_2\sqrt{n}}$$

and

$$3\sigma_{\bar{X}} = \frac{3\bar{R}}{d_2\sqrt{n}}. \tag{14.4}$$

The factor $3/d_2\sqrt{n}$ has been tabulated as A_2 in Table 14.2. Therefore, the upper and lower control limits for the $\bar{X}$ chart may be specified as

$$\text{UCL}_{\bar{X}} = \bar{\bar{X}} + A_2\bar{R}. \tag{14.5}$$

$$\text{LCL}_{\bar{X}} = \bar{\bar{X}} - A_2\bar{R}. \tag{14.6}$$

Constructing the R Chart. The R chart is constructed in a manner similar to the $\bar{X}$ chart. If the $\bar{X}$ chart has already been completed, R has been calculated from Equation (14.2). Tabular values of three sigma control limits for the range have been compiled for varying sample sizes and are included in Table 14.2. The upper and lower control limits for the R chart are then specified as

$$\text{UCL}_R = D_4\bar{R} \tag{14.7}$$

$$\text{LCL}_R = D_3\bar{R}. \tag{14.8}$$

Since $D_3 = 0$ for sample sizes of $n \leq 6$ in Table 14.2, the $\text{LCL}_R = 0$. Actually, three sigma limits yield a negative lower control limit which is recorded as zero. This means that, with samples of six or fewer, it will be impossible for a value on the R chart to fall outside the lower limit. In effect, the R chart will not be capable of detecting reductions in the dispersion of the process output.

Application of the $\bar{X}$ and R Charts. Once the control limits have been specified for each chart, the data used in constructing the limits are plotted on these same charts. Should all values fall within both sets of limits, the charts are ready for use. Should one or more values fall outside one set of limits, however, further inquiry is needed. A value outside the limits on the $\bar{X}$ chart indicates that the process may have undergone some change in regard to its central tendency. A value outside the limits on the R chart is evidence that the process variability may have been out of control. In either case, one should search for the source of the change in process behavior. If one or two values fall outside the limits and an assignable cause can be found, then these one or two values may be discarded and revised control limits calculated. If the revised limits contain all the remaining values, the control chart is ready for implementation. If they do not, the procedure may be repeated before using the control chart.

There is an advantage to constructing and testing the R chart first. Since an estimate of the variance of the sample means is obtained from $\bar{R}$, the construction of the $\bar{X}$ chart will depend on the control of process variability. If the $\bar{X}$ chart is first constructed and all $\bar{X}$ values fall within the limits, the chart may have to be revised if process variability is not in control after constructing the R chart. In effect, a revised estimate of process variation will have to be included in new limits on both the R and $\bar{X}$ charts.

Assume that control charts are to be established to monitor the weight in ounces of the contents of containers being filled on an assembly line. The containers should hold at least 10 ounces. To guarantee this weight, the process must be set to deliver slightly more than this amount. Samples of five have been taken every 30 minutes. The sample data, together with the sample means and sample ranges, are given in Table 14.3.

Table 14.3. WEIGHT OF THE CONTENTS OF CONTAINERS (ounces)

Sample Number	Sample Values					Mean $\bar{X}$	Range R
1	11.3	10.5	12.4	12.2	12.0	11.7	1.9
2	9.6	11.7	13.0	11.4	12.8	11.7	3.4
3	11.4	12.4	11.7	11.4	12.4	11.9	1.0
4	12.0	11.9	13.2	11.9	12.2	12.2	1.3
5	12.4	11.9	11.7	11.6	10.5	11.6	1.9
6	13.8	12.5	13.9	11.9	11.4	12.7	2.5
7	13.3	11.6	13.2	10.7	11.4	12.0	2.6
8	11.1	11.3	13.2	12.8	12.0	12.1	2.1
9	12.5	11.9	13.8	11.6	13.0	12.6	2.2
10	12.1	11.7	12.0	11.7	12.9	12.1	1.2
11	11.7	12.6	12.3	11.2	10.8	11.7	1.8
12	13.8	12.3	12.4	14.1	11.3	12.8	2.8
13	10.6	11.8	13.1	12.8	11.7	12.0	2.5
14	12.0	11.2	12.1	11.7	12.1	11.8	0.9
15	11.5	13.1	13.9	11.9	10.7	12.2	3.2
16	13.4	12.6	12.4	11.9	11.8	12.4	1.6
17	12.1	13.1	14.1	11.4	12.3	12.6	2.7
18	11.5	13.2	12.4	12.6	12.2	12.4	1.7
19	13.8	14.2	13.5	13.2	12.8	13.5	1.4
20	11.5	11.4	13.1	11.6	10.8	11.7	2.3

An R chart is first constructed from these data. Using Equation (14.2), $\bar{R}$ is calculated as 2.05. The control limits are then determined from Equations (14.7) and (14.8) as

$$\text{UCL}_R = 2.115(2.05) = 4.34$$

$$\text{LCL}_R = 0(2.05) = 0.$$

These limits are used to construct the R chart of Figure 14.3. Since all values fall within the control limits, the R chart is accepted as a means of assessing subsequent process variation. Had a point fallen outside the calculated limits, that point would have had to be discarded and limits recalculated. Attention should next be directed to the $\bar{X}$ chart. The mean of the sample means, $\bar{\bar{X}}$, is found from Equation (14.1) to be 12.19. The mean of the sample ranges, $\bar{R}$, has already been calculated as 2.05. Preliminary control limits for the $\bar{X}$ chart can

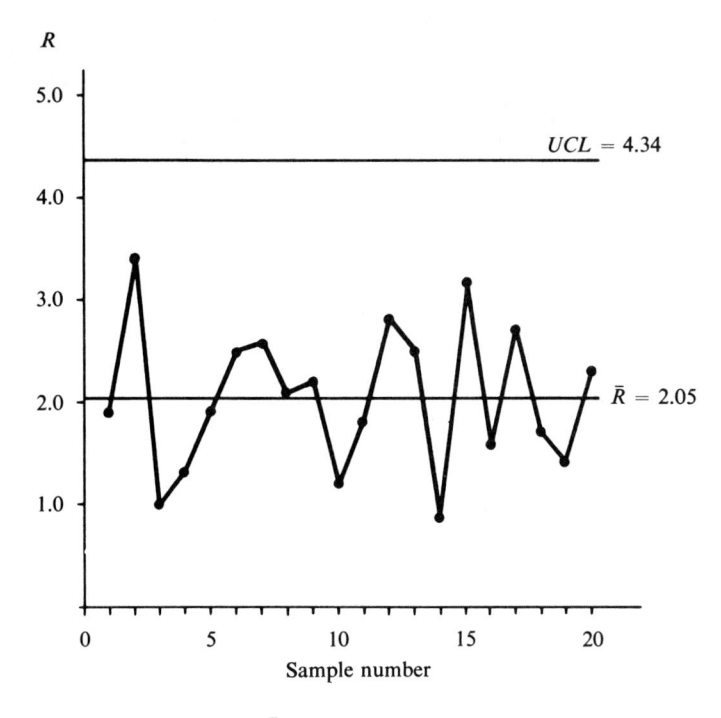

Chap. 14   Statistical Control Models for Operations   305

Figure 14.3 $\bar{R}$ chart for the data of Table 14.3.

now be calculated from Equations (14.5) and (14.6) as

$$\text{UCL}_{\bar{x}} = 12.19 + 0.577(2.05) = 13.37$$
$$\text{LCL}_{\bar{x}} = 12.19 - 0.577(2.05) = 11.01.$$

These limits are used to construct the $\bar{X}$ chart shown in Figure 14.4.

The 20 sample means may now be plotted. It is noted that the mean of sample 19 exceeds the upper control limit. This would indicate that at this point in time, the universe from which this sample was selected was not exhibiting a stable pattern of variation. Some change occurred between the time of selecting sample 18 and sample 19. It is further noted that after sample 19, the process returned to its original state. One may base action on the assumption that these statements are true, particularly if one thinks that some recognized assignable cause effected the change. Actually, the mean of sample 19 might have exceeded the control limit by chance, and a Type I error might have been made. Alternatively, the pattern of variation might have shifted some time before sample 18 and/or not returned after this time. Then a Type II error would have been made at these other points in time.

The data of sample 19 should now be discarded and the control limits recalculated for the remaining pattern of variation. The mean of the remaining

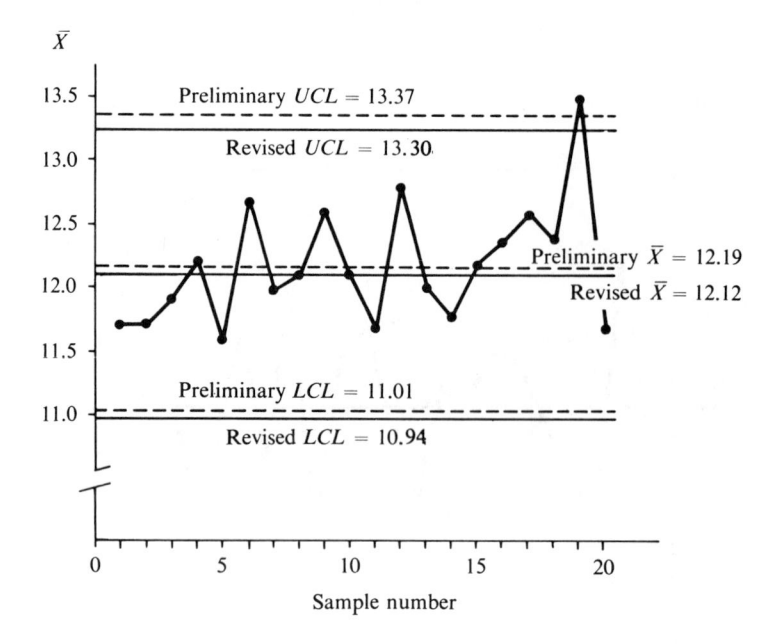

Figure 14.4 $\bar{X}$ chart for the data of Table 14.3.

sample means is 12.12. The range is not recalculated because it is assumed that the process variation did not change when sample 19 was selected. The control limits are now revised to

$$\text{UCL}_{\bar{x}} = 12.12 + 0.577(2.05) = 13.30$$
$$\text{LCL}_{\bar{x}} = 12.12 - 0.577(2.05) = 10.94$$

These are indicated on the control chart of Figure 14.4 and again checked to determine that no sample means exceed these limits. It is noted that no further changes are necessary, and the control chart of Figure 14.4, with the revised limits, and the chart of Figure 14.3 may now be employed to monitor the process. This control model may be implemented to test future process variation to see that it does not change from that used to construct the chart.

14.3 OPERATING CHARACTERISTICS OF $\bar{X}$ CHARTS

The decision to implement a control model should be based upon its anticipated operating effectiveness. This requires consideration of the objective sought and the actual design, implementation, and maintenance of the chart. This section discusses two features of the control chart as an operational model. The first deals with the relationship between specification limits and control limits. The second discusses the power of the control chart to detect changes in the pattern of variation and is directly related to the objective sought by the decision maker. Although the illustrations presented are directed to the control of quality by the $\bar{X}$ chart, note that the concepts are applicable to satistical control and statistical control models in general.

Specification Limits and Control Limits. Two limits may be established for the dimension of a workpiece. The *specification limit* is that limit within which the dimension must fall for the workpiece to be classified as acceptable. This limit is sometimes called a *tolerance* limit and is specified when the part is designed. A *control limit*, on the other hand, is a measure of the inherent capability of the process producing the part. It is a measure of process dispersion when the process is operating in a steady-state or "in-control" condition.

As an example of the relationship of the specification limits to the control limits, consider the situation illustrated in Figure 14.5. Note that the process capability of six sigma limits is within the specification limits. If the workpiece dimension can be centered at 5.000, there should be no control problems other than the routine assessment of the stability of the pattern of variation. If

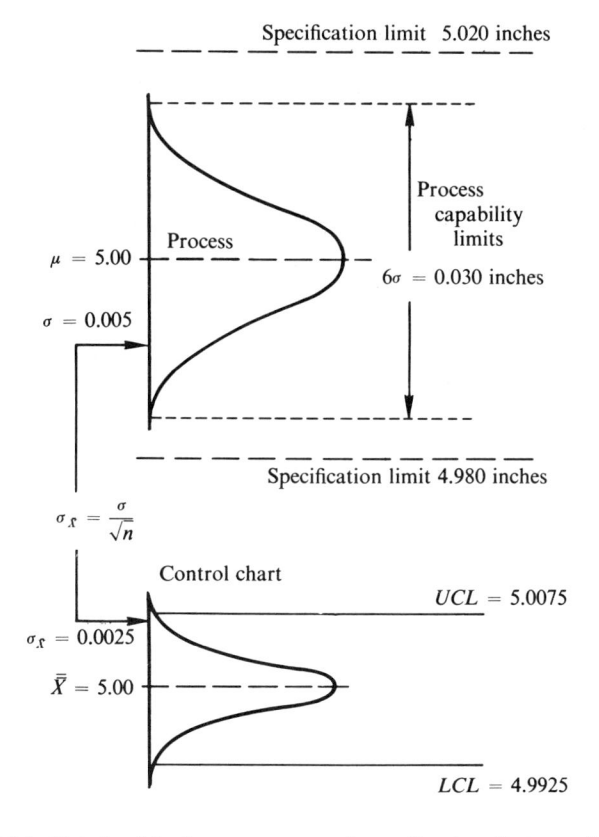

Figure 14.5 Relationship between a set of specification limits and control limits.

samples of $n = 4$ are taken, control limits of $\alpha = 0.0027$ will be established as $\text{UCL}_{\bar{x}} = 5.0075$ and $\text{LCL}_{\bar{x}} = 4.9925$.

Under the conditions of Figure 14.5, it is possible for the mean of the process to shift and for the dimensions of all workpieces still to be within the specification limits. A process being out of control does not mean that defectives are being produced. Should the specification limits be approximately the same as the process capability, a shift detected on the $\bar{X}$ chart is a good indication that a proportion of the produced units are defective. Under these conditions, it is likely that a large sample size will be taken at frequent intervals to detect shifts in the process as quickly as possible. In a few instances, the process capability limits may exceed the specification limits. Then, even though the process is maintained in control, defectives will be produced.

Three alternatives are available in this latter situation: First, one may accept the production of some defectives. These will either be sorted and removed through 100 percent inspection or permitted to remain with the acceptable units. Second, one might redesign the product. In particular, the need for the specification limit might be questioned. This limit might be increased without a sacrifice in the performance of the product. Third, one might change the manufacturing process to permit production with a tighter process capability. This alternative would probably be implemented only after the first two had been attempted and rejected.

The Power of the Control Chart. Control charts are employed to detect changes in a pattern of variation. The probability of the chart indicating that a change has occurred, when in fact it has not, is the probability of making a Type I error. If three sigma limits are used on the $\bar{X}$ chart, this probability is approximately 0.0027, an unlikely event.

Of at least equal concern to the decision maker is the probability of making or not making a Type II error. When changes in the pattern of variation do occur, the decision maker is concerned with the model's ability to detect these changes. The probability of making a Type II error can be demonstrated with an operating characteristic or OC curve. An OC curve for an $\bar{X}$ chart of three sigma limits is illustrated in Figure 14.6. The ordinate is the probability of not detecting a shift in the mean of a pattern of variation, assuming that only the mean and not the dispersion has shifted. The magnitude of the shift in the mean is defined in terms of k as $\mu + k\sigma_{\bar{x}}$. This permits one such OC curve to describe all $\bar{X}$ charts with three sigma limits. Superimposed on the OC curve of Figure 14.6 are a series of distributions of changes of $\mu + 1\sigma_{\bar{x}}$, $\mu + 2\sigma_{\bar{x}}$, and so forth. The shaded area in each case represents the probability of a point falling within the limits after the shift, and hence the probability of making a Type II error. Note that the new mean of the process is defined as μ', and that the dispersion is assumed to remain constant.

Consider the following examples. Using the data given in Figure 14.6, $\text{UCL}_{\bar{x}} = 5.0075$ and $\text{LCL}_{\bar{x}} = 4.9925$, and samples of $n = 4$ are taken. Assume

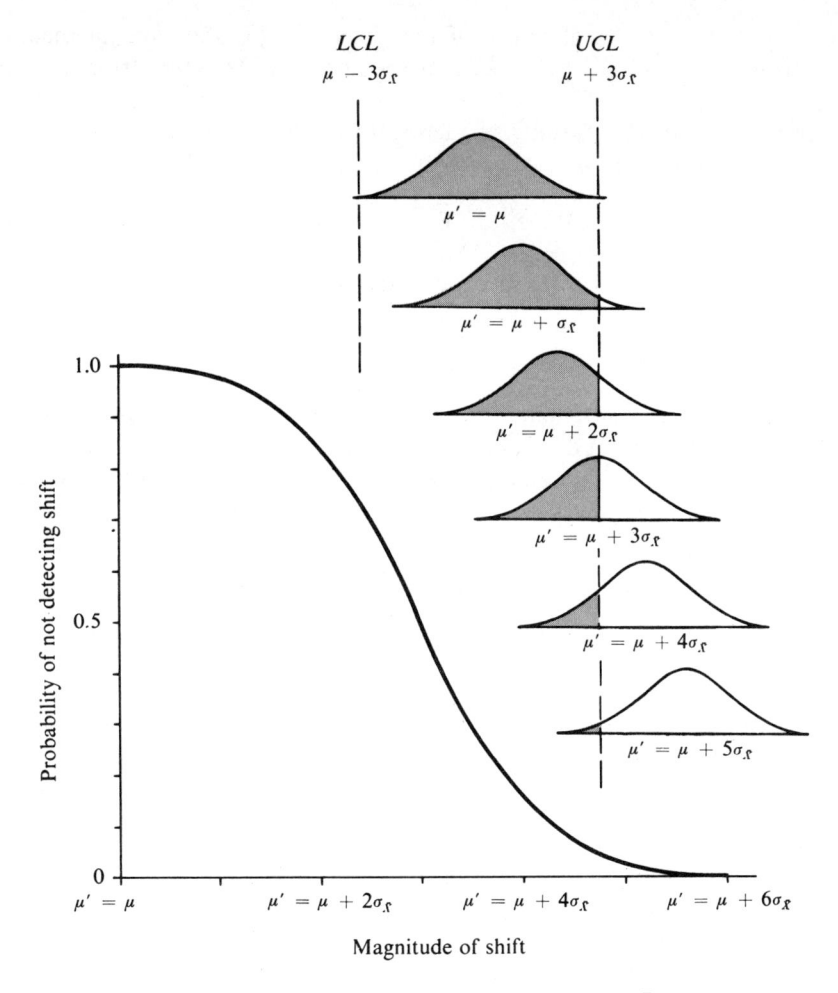

Figure 14.6 Operating characteristic curve for an $\bar{X}$ chart.

that the process variation remains constant at $\sigma = 0.005$ and that the mean of the process has shifted to $\mu' = 5.005$. The question raised concerns the probability of detecting this shift in the first sample. This shift can be expressed as

$$\mu' = 5.005$$
$$= \mu + k\sigma_{\bar{x}}$$

where

$$\mu = 5.000 \quad \text{and} \quad \sigma_{\bar{x}} = \frac{\sigma}{\sqrt{n}} = \frac{0.005}{2} = 0.0025.$$

Thus,

$$\mu' = \mu + 2\sigma_{\bar{x}}.$$

From Figure 14.6, the probability of not detecting this shift and of making a Type II error is 0.84, or the area under the normal distribution from $-\infty$ to $+1\sigma$.

In the second case, assume an identical situation except that a sample of $n = 9$ is being used. The shift can now be expressed as

$$\mu' = \mu + k\sigma_{\bar{x}}$$

with

$$\sigma_{\bar{x}} = \frac{0.005}{\sqrt{9}} = 0.0017.$$

Thus,

$$\mu' = \mu + 3\sigma_{\bar{x}}.$$

From Figure 14.6, the probability of not detecting this shift reduces to 0.50, or the area under the normal distribution from $-\infty$ to 0.0σ.

In the last case, again assume a sample of $n = 4$, this time with a shift in the process mean to $\mu' = 5.010$. This shift is expressed as

$$\mu' = 5.010$$
$$= \mu + k\sigma_{\bar{x}}$$

with

$$\mu = 5.000$$

and

$$\sigma_{\bar{x}} = 0.0025.$$

Thus,

$$\mu' = \mu + 4\sigma_{\bar{x}}.$$

The probability of not detecting this shift is only 0.16, or the area under the normal distribution from $-\infty$ to -1σ.

The $\bar{X}$ chart has been described as the control device used primarily in detecting shifts in the mean of the basic pattern of variation. The R chart is designed to detect shifts in the dispersion. It is possible to construct an OC curve for R charts after a table of the distribution of ranges has been compiled. If OC curves are constructed for both $\bar{X}$ and R charts, it is possible to calculate the probability of detecting a shift in both the mean and dispersion on either the $\bar{X}$ or R chart or both. It is also possible to construct OC curves for control charts by attributes. In each case, the OC curve provides a measure of the relative ability of the control chart to detect changes in the basic pattern of variation.

14.4 CONTROL MODELS FOR ATTRIBUTES

Often an observation yields only a two-valued classification: a simple yes or no, correct or incorrect, acceptable or defective. A milling machine may be either in use or idle. The surface finish of a piece of furniture may be acceptable or not. The dimension of a part may either fall within or outside a set of specification limits. With such a classification system, the proportion of measurements falling in one class during a specified time period or other sample unit may be monitored over time or over many such samples with a *p* chart. In other cases, observation may yield a multivalued, but still discrete, classification system. A clerical operation may have been performed correctly, or it may contain one, two, or more errors. An employee may suffer none, one, or more lost-time accidents during a given time period. The number of arrivals to a service facility during a specified hour of the day will be a discrete number. In general, the number of objects, states, or events occurring during a period of time, or within a sample unit, may be monitored with a *c* chart. This section develops control models that may be used with attribute sampling.

The p Chart. When the item sampled is assessed and then placed into one of two defined classes, the proportion of units falling into one class may be controlled over time or from one sample to another with a *p* chart. The probability distribution describing this situation is the binomial. The mean of this distribution and its standard deviation are given in Appendix C as

$$\mu = np$$
$$\sigma = \sqrt{np(1-p)}.$$

These parameters may be expressed as proportions by dividing by the sample size, n. If $\bar{p}$ is then defined as an estimate of the proportion parameter μ/n, and s_p as an estimate of σ/n, then these statistics can be expressed as

$$\bar{p} = \frac{\text{total number in the class}}{\text{total number of observations}}. \qquad (14.9)$$

$$s_p = \sqrt{\frac{\bar{p}(1-\bar{p})}{n}}. \qquad (14.10)$$

The application of the *p* chart will be illustrated with an example of a work-sampling study. This work measurement technique is used to obtain information about the activities of people or machines, usually in less time and at lower cost than by conventional means. Random and instantaneous observations are taken by classifying the activity at a point in time into one and only one category. In the most simple form, the categories "idle" and "at work" are used. The control chart is useful in work-sampling studies in that the observed proportions can be verified as "in control" and following a stable pattern of variation or "out of control" with an unstable pattern. In the latter case, a search can be undertaken for an assignable cause.

Consider the case of a work-sampling study involving desk calculators in an office. The objective was to determine the proportion of time the calculators were in use as opposed to the time they were idle. One hundred observations were taken each day over all working days in a month. The number of times the calculators were in use, and the proportion for each day are given in Table 14.4.

Table 14.4. NUMBER OF TIMES A DAY THE DESK CALCULATORS ARE IN USE

Working Day	Times in Use	Proportion	Working Day	Times in Use	Proportion
1	22	0.22	12	46	0.46
2	33	0.33	13	31	0.31
3	24	0.24	14	24	0.24
4	20	0.20	15	22	0.22
5	18	0.18	16	22	0.22
6	24	0.24	17	29	0.29
7	24	0.24	18	31	0.31
8	29	0.29	19	21	0.21
9	18	0.18	20	26	0.26
10	27	0.27	21	24	0.24
11	31	0.31	Total	546	

From this table and Equation (14.4), $\bar{p}$ is established as

$$\bar{p} = \frac{546}{(21)(100)} = 0.260.$$

The standard deviation of the data is calculated with Equation (14.10) as

$$s_p = \sqrt{\frac{(0.26)(0.74)}{100}} = 0.044.$$

With $\bar{p} = 0.26$ as the best estimate of the population proportion, a control chart may now be constructed. Control limits in work sampling are usually established at $\bar{p} \pm 2s_p$, and these limits will not vary from one day to another in this example, since a constant sample size has been maintained for each day. With these control limits, the probability of making a Type I error may be defined as $\alpha = 0.0456$ if the normal distribution is used as an approximation. Such an approximation is realistic for this example since the binomial will approximate the normal distribution if $n > 50$ and $0.20 < p < 0.80$. If these requirements were not met or a more accurate estimate were needed, the binomial distribution would have had to be employed. The control limits for the p chart are defined and calculated as

$$\begin{aligned} \text{UCL}_p &= \bar{p} + 2s_p \\ &= 0.260 + 2(0.044) = 0.348 \end{aligned} \quad (14.11)$$

$$\begin{aligned} \text{LCL}_p &= \bar{p} - 2s_p \\ &= 0.260 - 2(0.044) = 0.172. \end{aligned} \quad (14.12)$$

The p chart is constructed as shown in Figure 14.7. A plot of the data indicates that day 12 was not typical of the pattern of use established by the rest of the month. Subsequent investigation reveals that personnel from another department were also using the machines that one day because their equipment

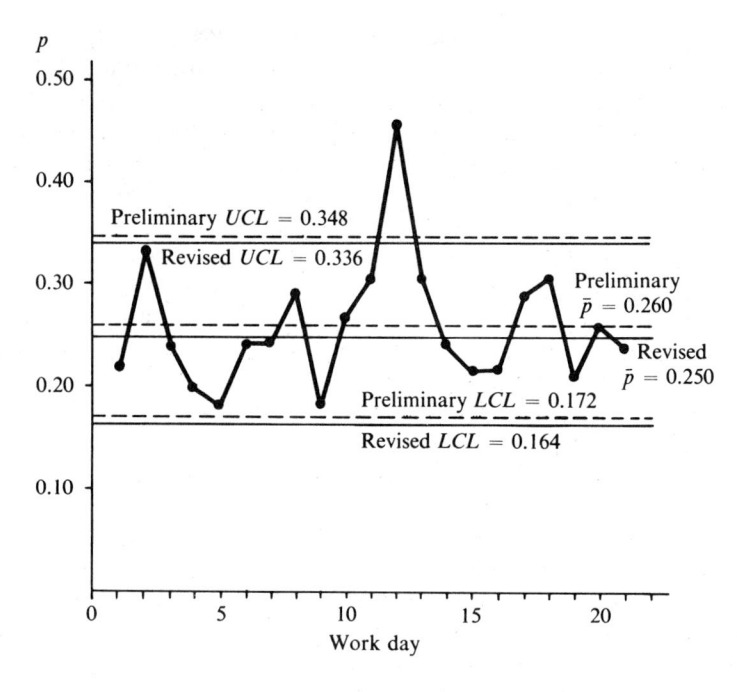

Figure 14.7 *p* chart of daily desk calculator usage.

had preceded them in a move to another building. As this is an atypical situation, the sample is discarded and a revised mean and standard deviation are calculated as

$$\bar{p} = \frac{500}{(20)(100)} = 0.250$$

$$s_p = \sqrt{\frac{(0.25)(0.75)}{100}} = 0.043.$$

Revised control limits are now calculated and placed on the same control chart as

$$\text{UCL}_p = \bar{p} + 2s_p$$
$$= 0.250 + 2(0.043) = 0.336$$
$$\text{LCL}_p = \bar{p} - 2s_p$$
$$= 0.250 - 2(0.043) = 0.164.$$

It is noted that no further days fall outside these limits and that the chart and data, without day 12, can be taken as a stable pattern of variation of calculator usage.

The c Chart. Some random variable processes may provide numerical data that are recorded as a number rather than a proportion. For example, the number of arrivals per hour demanding service at a toll booth is of interest when deciding upon the level of service capability to provide. If the number of arrivals per hour deviates from the stable pattern of variation, it may be necessary to compensate by either opening or closing certain toll booths. Since the arrival process described is not under the control of the decision maker, this is his only possible course of action if he is to maintain a minimum cost service policy.

The Poisson distribution is usually used to describe the number of arrivals per time period. Here, the opportunity for the occurrence of an event, n, is large but the probability of each occurrence, p, is quite small. The mean and the variance of the Poisson distribution are equal and expressed as $\mu = \sigma^2 = np$. These parameters can be estimated from the statistics with $\bar{c}$ and s_c^2 defined as these estimates. In many applications, values for n and p cannot be determined but their product np can be established. Then the mean and variance can be estimated as

$$\bar{c} = s_c^2 = \frac{\sum (np)}{m}. \tag{14.13}$$

Consider the application of a c chart to the arrival process previously described. Data for the past 20 hours have been collected and are presented in Table 14.5. The mean of the arrival population may be estimated from $\bar{c}$ with Equation (14.13) as

$$\bar{c} = \frac{84}{20} = 4.20.$$

The standard deviation may be estimated as

$$s_c = \sqrt{\bar{c}}$$
$$= \sqrt{4.20} = 2.05.$$

Table 14.5. NUMBER OF ARRIVALS PER HOUR DEMANDING SERVICE AT A TOLL BOOTH

Hour Number	np: Number of Arrivals	Hour Number	np: Number of Arrivals
1	6	11	6
2	4	12	4
3	3	13	2
4	5	14	2
5	4	15	4
6	6	16	8
7	5	17	2
8	4	18	3
9	2	19	5
10	5	20	4
		Total	= 84

With these estimates, the control chart may now be constructed. Control limits may be established as $\bar{c} \pm 3s_c$. The probability of making a Type I error can be determined either from the cumulative values of Appendix D, Table D.1, or from the Thorndike chart of Table D.2. For the example under consideration,

$$\begin{aligned} \text{UCL}_c &= \bar{c} + 3s_c \\ &= 4.2 + 3(2.05) = 10.35. \end{aligned} \tag{14.14}$$

$$\begin{aligned} \text{LCL}_c &= \bar{c} - 3s_c \\ &= 4.2 - 3(2.05) < 0. \end{aligned} \tag{14.15}$$

There is no lower control limit. The probability of making a Type I error is the probability of 11 or more arrivals in a given hour from a population with $\bar{c} = 4.2$. This is $1 - P(10 \text{ or less})$ or $1 - 0.996 = 0.004$. Alternatively, the control limit could have been defined as a probability limit. If it were thought desirable to define $\alpha \leq 0.01$, the control limit would have been specified as 9.5. Under this control policy the probability of detecting 10 or more arrivals would satisfy $\alpha \leq 0.01$.

In the c chart of Figure 14.8, all values fell within the control limits and the chart can be installed as originally formulated. Had a value exceeded a limit, this value would have to be discarded and revisions made. This will be the case when, in using the chart, a value appears outside the limit. Action will be initiated to alter the service capability to meet the new demand pattern. At the same time, a new chart based on the recent data will be constructed and implemented. In this way the decision maker is informed of conditions in the system that require modification of operating policy.

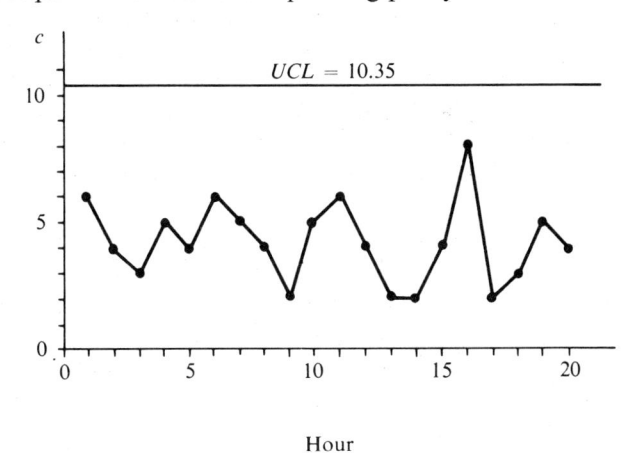

Figure 14.8 c chart of the number of arrivals per hour requiring service at a toll booth.

14.5 ACCEPTANCE SAMPLING MODELS

The control models of the previous sections dealt with the statistical stability of a pattern of variation. These statistical control models were applied as a direct monitor on the process through verifying its output. The acceptance sampling methods presented in this section are concerned with the output of a process beyond the point of immediate process control. Their objective is to determine whether a discrete quantity of the output of a process is acceptable against some criterion of quality. Consequently, a sample from the lot must be assessed and the lot must be either accepted or rejected in accordance with the findings of the sample.

Methods of acceptance sampling lend themselves to inspection requirements, for acceptance purposes, in product quality control. Inspection can be applied to incoming materials, to materials and components in the manufacturing process, or to the finished product. Inspection may also be applied to verify accounting records and to determine the accuracy of clerical work. In each case, the quality of the submitted lot is judged on the basis of a sample taken from the lot.

The Concept of Acceptance Sampling. The quality of a group of items may be verified in one of three ways. Every item in the lot may be inspected, a sample of items may be taken from the lot and inspected, or no inspection may be used. In the third case it is assumed that the quality of the lot certainly exceeds some minimum acceptable standard. In the former cases, the lot may be accepted or rejected, depending on the outcome of the inspection process.

The level of verification chosen should consider the cost of inspection measured against the cost of accepting and perhaps using defective items. In general, acceptance sampling will be more economical than 100 percent inspection when the occurrence of a defective in an accepted lot is not prohibitively expensive or when an inspection process requires the destruction of the item. Acceptance sampling will be more economical than no inspection when some expense is incurred in accepting defectives and the number of defectives differs from one lot to the next.

Acceptance sampling plans call for the random selection of a sample of size n, from a lot containing N items. The entire lot is then accepted if the number of defectives found in the sample is equal to or less than c, the acceptance number. For example, a sampling inspection plan might be defined as $N = 1,000$, $n = 50$, and $c = 1$. This designation means that a sample of 50 items is to be taken from the lot of 1,000. If zero or one defective is found in the sample, the whole lot is accepted. If more than one defective is found, the lot is rejected. A rejected lot can either be returned to the producer or it can be retained and subjected to a 100 percent screening process. The former action is called a *nonrectifying inspection program*, the latter, a *rectifying* inspection program.

The type of inspection sampling described by N, n, and c uses inspection by attributes and a single sample of size n. Other attribute inspection plans

Chap. 14 Statistical Control Models for Operations   317

might use two samples before requiring the acceptance or rejection of a lot. A third procedure might use multiple samples or a sequential sampling process in evaluating a lot. Each of these methods—single, double, and multiple sampling—rests on a system of inspection by attributes of items logically grouped into lots.

The Operating Characteristics Curve. Acceptance sampling plans attempt to discriminate between lots of acceptable and lots of unacceptable items. The relative ability of a sampling plan to meet this objective can be demonstrated with an operating characteristic curve. An OC curve defines the probability of a lot being accepted (or finding c or fewer defectives in a sample) for different levels of proportion defective.

An operating characteristic curve for the sampling plan $N = 1,000$, $n = 50$, $c = 1$ is illustrated in Figure 14.9. The abscissa refers to the proportion defective in the lot. The ordinate refers to the probability of accepting a lot at a specified level of proportion defective. Note that if N contains no defectives and if $p = 0$, the lot is certain to be accepted. If the lot contains 10 defectives and if $p = 0.01$, the probability of accepting the lot is 0.91. The probability distribution appropriate to these calculations is the hypergeometric. For ease of calculation, however, the Poisson distribution is used as an approximation. In Appendix D, Table D.1 (Cumulative Poisson Probabilities), or Table D.2

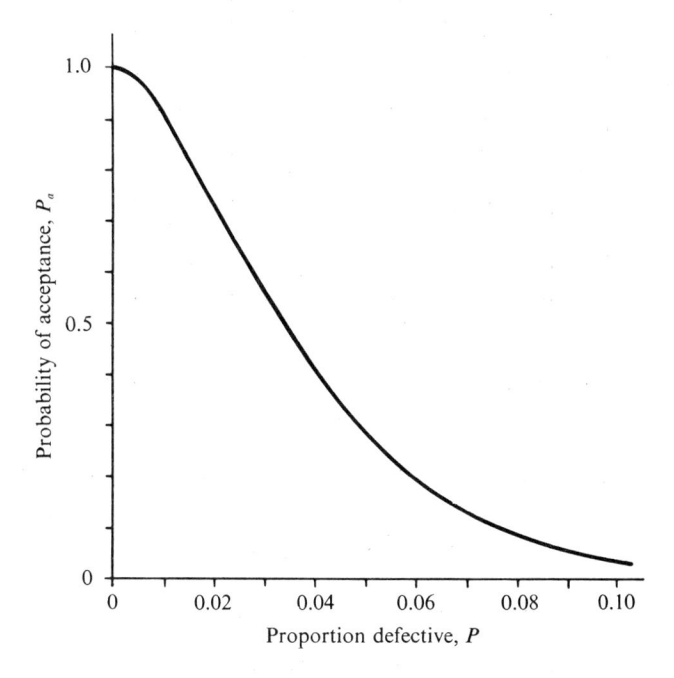

Figure 14.9 Operating characteristic curve for the sampling plan $n = 50$, $c = 1$.

(Cumulative Poisson Probability Curves) may be used to develop an OC curve quickly. As an example, at $p = 0.03$ in Figure 14.9, $np = (50)(0.03) = 1.50$ and the probability of the occurrence of one or fewer defects would be 0.56. Note that because the Poisson distribution is used as an approximation, the OC curve is independent of the lot size.

A good sampling plan will have a high probability of accepting those lots that contain few defectives and a low probability of accepting lots having an excessive number of defectives. The OC curve illustrates how well a given sampling plan discriminates between good and bad lots. *Good* and *bad* are relative terms, and a lot containing 1 percent defective might be considered quite good in one instance and very poor in another.

Two parties are involved in an inspection sampling procedure, the party submitting the lot and the party to whom the lot is consigned if accepted. These two parties are referred to as the *producer* and the *consumer*, respectively. The parties may represent a seller and a buyer of a product, or they may represent two departments within the same organization. As an example, castings from a foundry department may be delivered for acceptance to the machining department. In another situation, the producer may be an accounting department and the consumer may be represented by an auditor who either accepts or rejects a number of accounting records against some criterion of accounting quality. In each case, the producer usually desires that material relatively free from defectives have a high probability of being accepted. The consumer desires that it will be unlikely for the lot to be accepted if it contains a high proportion of defectives.

The concept of producer and consumer risks can be defined in terms of two points on an operating characteristic curve. The producer risk point occurs at a fraction defective, p_1; the consumer risk point occurs at p_2. Four values are used to specify these two points, which, in turn, may be used to construct the OC curve for a specific acceptance sampling plan.

1. Acceptable quality level, AQL: This indicates a good level of quality and low proportion of fraction defective, referred to as p_1, for which it is desired to have a high probability of acceptance.

2. Producer's risk, α: The probability that lots of the quality level given as the AQL will not be accepted where $\alpha = 1 - P_a$. In effect, this is the probability of making a Type I error, that is, of rejecting a lot when it should be accepted.

3. Lot tolerance percent defective, LTPD: This level of quality, given as p_2, is deemed to be quite poor and it is desired to reject lots of this quality or at least have a low probability of acceptance.

4. Consumer's risk β: The probability, P_a, that lots of a quality level at the LTPD will be accepted. A value of $P_a = 0.10$ at p_2 is often used in accep-

Chap. 14   Statistical Control Models for Operations   319

tance sampling. This probability represents the likelihood of making a Type II or β error, that is, of accepting a lot when it should be rejected.

Each of these values is illustrated on the OC curve of Figure 14.10.

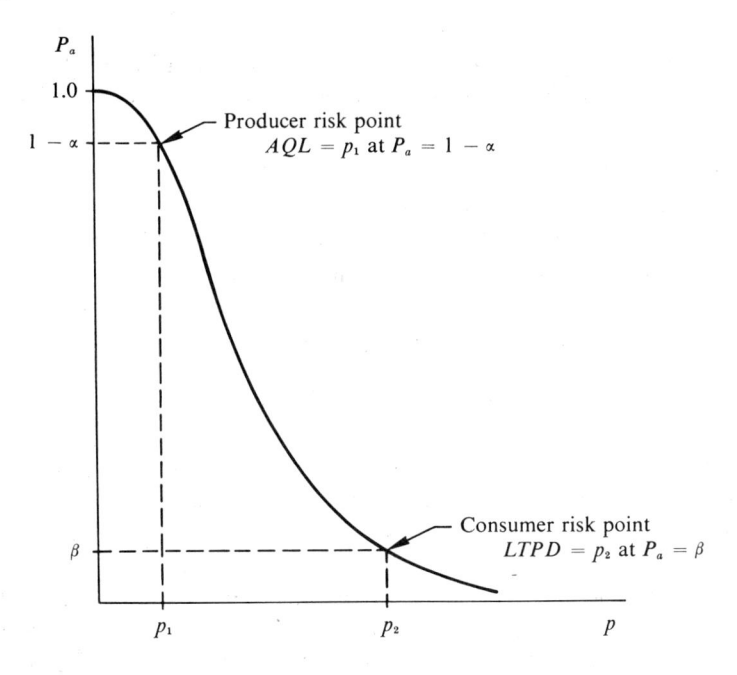

Figure 14.10 OC curve passing through a consumer risk point and a producer risk point and possessing a unique value of n and c.

Deriving an Acceptance Sampling Plan. Most acceptance sampling plans involve inspection by attributes. Often a unit can be assessed only in the two-valued classification of acceptable or defective. In other situations, it may be advantageous to take a continuous dimension and reduce it to a dichotomous assessment of within specifications and acceptable, or defective and outside specification limits. In either case, the function of the acceptance sampling model is to accept those lots containing few defectives and reject those lots containing many defectives. This objective is often defined in terms of a producer and a consumer risk.

When two required points, such as a consumer and a producer risk point, are given as the basis for a sampling plan, the effect is to require the solution to two equations for two unknowns. An iterative, trial-and-error solution, using the Poisson distribution as an approximation, can be easily effected using the cumulative Poisson tables in Appendix D, Table D.1, or from Table D.2.

As an example, assume that a single sampling plan is desired that will yield an OC curve passing through a producer risk of $\alpha = 0.05$ at an AQL of 0.01, and a consumer risk, of $\beta = 0.10$ at an LTPD of 0.04. The solution is facilitated if a table is constructed as illustrated in Table 14.6. This table permits the solution for n and c in the following equations:

$$1 - 0.05 = \sum_0^c \frac{e^{-0.01n}(0.01n)^c}{c!}$$

$$0.10 = \sum_0^c \frac{e^{-0.04n}(0.04n)^c}{c!}.$$

These equations represent the producer and consumer risk points, respectively.

Table 14.6. TABLE USED TO DETERMINE A SINGLE SAMPLING PLAN APPROXIMATING $\alpha = 0.05$ AT AQL = 0.01 AND $\beta = 0.10$ AT LTPD = 0.04

c	$p_1 n$ ($P_a = 0.95$)	$p_2 n$ ($P_a = 0.10$)	$\frac{p_2 n}{p_1 n}$	
0	0.05	2.30	46.00	
1	0.35	3.89	11.10	
2	0.82	5.32	6.49	
3	1.37	6.68	4.88	
4	1.97	8.00	4.06	LTPD
5	2.61	9.28	3.56	AQL
6	3.29	10.53	3.20	
7	3.98	11.77	2.96	
8	4.70	13.00	2.77	

In Table 14.6, if an acceptance number of $c = 0$ is required and if $P_a = 0.95$, then $p_1 n$ must be 0.05. This value was obtained by interpolation in the cumulative Poisson tables in Appendix D. Less precise values may be obtained more quickly from the Thorndike chart in Table D.2, although this specific value lies outside the limits of the chart. The second value, for $c = 1$ at $P_a = 0.95$, yields $p_1 n = 0.35$. If $c = 2$ and $P_a = 0.95$, then $p_1 n = 0.82$, and so forth. This process is repeated for $P_a = 0.10$ to find the values given in the third column. The fourth column in Table 14.6 is completed by recording the ratio p_2/p_1. In this example, the ratio of fraction defective of consumer to producer risk points was given as $0.04/0.01 = 4.0$. Therefore, this process is continued until the desired ratio of $p_2/p_1 = 4.0$ is bracketed.

The desired sampling plan calls for an acceptance number somewhere between $c = 4$ and $c = 5$. Because both the acceptance number and the sample size must be integers, it is not possible to achieve the precise requirement that was given. One of the four plans listed in Table 14.7 must be selected with the associated degree of protection. The data from Table 14.7 are developed directly from Table 14.6 as follows. With $c = 4$ and $P_a = 0.95$, $p_1 n$ was taken to be 1.97,

Chap. 14   Statistical Control Models for Operations

Table 14.7. FOUR SAMPLING PLANS THAT BRACKET
$\alpha = 0.05$ AT AQL $= 0.01$ AND $\beta = 0.10$
AT LTPD $= 0.04$

Plan	α at p_1	β at p_2
$c = 4, n = 197$	0.050	0.107
$c = 4, n = 200$	0.053	0.100
$c = 5, n = 261$	0.050	0.052
$c = 5, n = 232$	0.032	0.100

and if $p = 0.01$ at the producer risk point, then $n = 197$. This sampling plan of $c = 4$, $n = 197$ will yield an $\alpha = 0.05$ as required but will yield a $\beta = 0.107$, which is slightly higher than desired. If $c = 4$ and it is desired that the OC curve go through the consumer risk point, then $n = p_2 n/p_2 = 8.00/0.04 = 200$. With $c = 4$ and $n = 200$, β is established at 0.10 and α will be $1 - P_a$, or $1 - 0.947 = 0.053$. Similarly, α and β can be found for $c = 5$.

The four plans of Table 14.7 were obtained by alternating in holding α as required and solving for β and then maintaining β while solving for α. These four plans are sketched in Figure 14.11 with the risk point bracketing effect magnified so that it will be more evident. Once these four plans have been defined, it is likely that a plan will be selected and used which results in a compromise in regard to α and β. In this example $c = 4$ yields two plans fairly

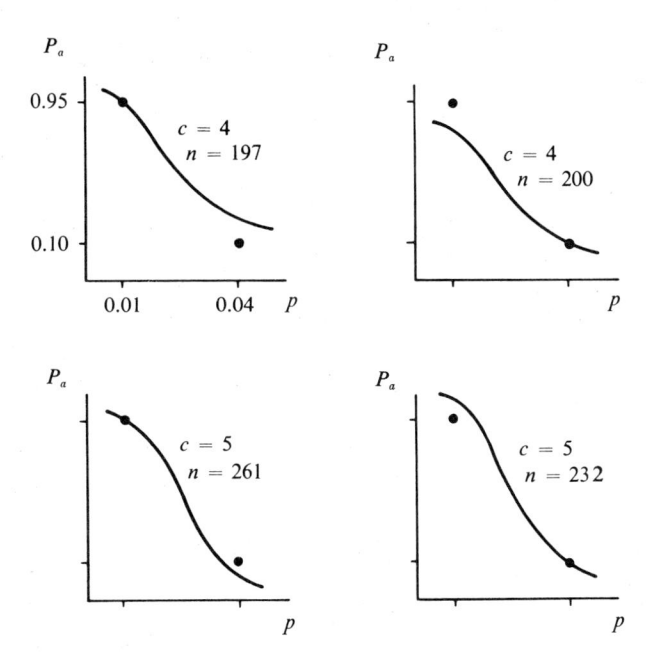

Figure 14.11   Four sampling plans of Table 14.7 (not to scale).

close to the consumer and producer risk points. One or the other might be selected. The plan $c = 4$, $n = 200$ would have the advantage of a convenient sample size which would facilitate subsequent computations. In other cases, the average sample size for one or the other acceptance number could be used.

Average Outgoing Quality. When rejected lots are returned to the supplier, the acceptance sampling plan does not significantly improve the quality level of lots submitted to the plan. A few defectives may be detected and discarded from samples of accepted lots, but no profound improvements can be realized here without resulting in the rejection of the lot. The sampling plan can and should function as a screening process and permit the acceptance of good lots and the rejection and return of poor quality lots. This will result in some improvement if there is a large variation in the level of quality from one lot to another.

When a rectifying inspection program is employed and rejected lots are subjected to 100 percent inspection, significant and predictable quality improvements can be realized. Under a rectifying inspection program, an average outgoing level, AOQ, and an average inspection load, I, can be predicted for varying levels of incoming fraction defective. In addition, an average outgoing quality limit, AOQL, the worst possible average outgoing quality level, can be forecast and related to a specific incoming level of fraction defective. This latter value gives assurance regarding the poorest average quality level that might leave the inspection station.

If it is assumed that all lots arriving at an inspection station contain the same proportion of defectives, p, and if rejected lots are subjected to 100 percent inspection,

$$\text{AOQ} = \frac{P_a(p)(N - n)}{N - pn - (1 - P_a)p(N - n)}. \tag{14.16}$$

The numerator in Equation (14.16) represents the average number of defectives in each lot beyond the point of inspection. Defectives will be found only in the proportion of lots that have been accepted, P_a, and will constitute $p(N - n)$ in number. The denominator represents the average lot size, where N is the original lot size, pn is the reduction in size due to defectives found and discarded in the sample, and $(1 - P_a)p(N - n)$ is the reduction in lot size due to defectives found and discarded during the 100 percent screening process. By similar reasoning, the average inspection can be shown to be

$$I = n + (1 - P_a)(N - n). \tag{14.17}$$

As an example, if a lot size of $N = 10{,}000$ is assumed and each lot contains 200 defectives, then for the sampling plan previously developed of $n = 200$ and $c = 5$, P_a can be found to be 0.785, and from Equation (14.16),

$$\text{AOQ} = \frac{(0.785)(0.02)(9{,}800)}{10{,}000 - (0.02)(200) - (0.215)(0.02)(9{,}800)}$$

$$= \frac{153.86}{10{,}000 - 4 - 42.14} = 0.01546.$$

The average inspection can be found from Equation (14.17) to be

$$I = 200 + (0.215)(9{,}800) = 2{,}307$$

It should be recognized that these values of AOQ and of I are expected or average values that will be approached in the long run over many lots. In regard to the proportion defective, one specific lot will either contain somewhere between 195 to 200 defectives if the lot is accepted and it is assumed to contain no defectives if the lot is rejected. By the same token, either 200 items will be inspected if the lot is accepted or the total of 10,000 units will be verified if it is rejected. In the long run, however, the foregoing results for AOQ and I will represent the average for all lots submitted at a value of $p = 0.02$.

Under some conditions, it might be desired to retain a constant lot size whether a lot is accepted or rejected and regardless of the number of defectives discarded during the sampling and/or screening process. A constant lot size can be maintained if defectives are replaced by units which are assumed to be selected, inspected, and inserted in the place of the defectives if they are acceptable. Under these conditions of replacement,

$$\text{AOQ} = \frac{P_a(p)(N - n)}{N}. \tag{14.18}$$

The average inspection increases slightly to

$$I = \frac{n + (1 - P_a)(N - n)}{1 - p}. \tag{14.19}$$

The average outgoing quality and the average inspection will vary as a function of the level of incoming proportion defective. With the sampling plan $n = 200$, $c = 5$, under the condition of nonreplacement of defectives, AOQ and I are given in Table 14.8. Note that the average outgoing quality increases as the proportion defective in incoming lots increases until it reaches a maximum

Table 14.8. AVERAGE OUTGOING QUALITY AND AVERAGE INSPECTION FOR THE SINGLE SAMPLING PLAN OF $N = 10{,}000$, $n = 200$, $c = 5$ UNDER RECTIFYING INSPECTION WITHOUT REPLACEMENT

Proportion Defective in Submitted Lots, p	Probability of Acceptance, P_a	Average Outgoing Quality (AOQ)	Average Inspection, I
0	1.000	0	200.0
0.005	0.999	0.00490	209.8
0.010	0.983	0.00964	366.6
0.015	0.916	0.01349	1,023.2
0.020	0.785	0.01546	2,307.0
0.025	0.616	0.01524	3,924.0
0.030	0.446	0.01334	5,629.2
0.035	0.301	0.01059	7,050.2
0.040	0.191	0.00774	8,128.2
0.045	0.116	0.00533	8,863.2
0.050	0.067	0.00344	9,343.4

value. This value is referred to as the *average outgoing quality limit*, AOQL. From this point on, a pronounced number of lots are being rejected and screened under 100 percent inspection. The latter effect is resulting in a continuing reduction in the average outgoing quality, as can be seen in Table 14.8. The concept of an average outgoing quality limit is often employed in specifying a sampling plan. Sampling plans have been devised for varying values of AOQL and presented in tabular form. With this limit as the worst average quality level that can be expected to occur, a plan with a known AOQL can be selected along with other desired criteria.

The concept of a level of average outgoing quality and a level of average inspection rests upon the assumption of the detection and removal of all defectives from screened lots. Further, the values obtained for AOQ and I are expected values that will occur in the long run. Over a short time period some variation from these values can be expected. The concept of an average outgoing quality level and average inspection has found wide application in the field of product acceptance. In recent years it has also been found applicable in auditing accounting records and verifying clerical activities.

QUESTIONS

14.1. What is the relationship between a stable pattern of variation, control limits, and a Type I error?

14.2. What is the relationship between an unstable pattern of variation, control limits, and a Type II error?

14.3. What are the primary functions of the $\bar{X}$ chart and the R chart in relation to detecting unstable patterns of variations?

14.4. Under what conditions is it necessary to construct "revised" control limits?

14.5. What are process capability limits? How are they important in product design?

14.6. What is meant by the *power* of a control chart? What factors influence this value?

14.7. What are the two types of control charts for attributes? Give an example of a process that might be controlled by each.

14.8. How does the objective of an inspection sampling plan differ from that of a control model?

14.9. What does an operating characteristic curve illustrate?

14.10. Why is it usually necessary to bracket the two desired points on an OC curve?

14.11. Why is it usually necessary to bracket the two desired points on an OC curve?

14.12. Discuss the relationship between the average outgoing quality limit and the average outgoing quality.

PROBLEMS

14.1. Samples of $n = 10$ were taken from a process for a period of time. The process average was estimated to be $\bar{\bar{X}} = 0.0250$ inch and the process range was estimated as $\bar{R} = 0.0020$ inch. Specify the control limits for an $\bar{X}$ chart and for an R chart.

14.2. Control charts by variables are to be established on the tensile strength in pounds of a yarn. Samples of five have been taken each hour for the past 20 hours. These were recorded as follows:

									Hour											
1	2	3	4	5	6	7	8	9	10	11	12	13	14	15	16	17	18	19	20
50	44	44	48	47	47	44	52	44	43	47	49	47	43	44	45	45	50	46	48
51	46	44	52	46	44	46	46	46	44	44	48	51	46	43	47	45	49	47	44
49	50	44	49	46	43	46	45	46	49	44	41	50	46	40	51	47	45	48	49
42	47	47	49	48	40	48	42	46	47	42	46	48	48	40	48	47	49	46	50
43	48	48	46	50	45	46	55	43	45	50	46	42	46	46	46	46	48	45	46

(a) Construct an $\bar{X}$ chart based on these data.
(b) Construct an R chart based on these data.

14.3. A lower specification limit of 42 pounds is required for the condition of Problem 14.2. Sketch the relationship between the specification limit and the control limits. What proportion, if any, of the yarn will be defective?

14.4. Control limits are established on a process with a mean of 20,000 psi and a standard deviation of 1,000 psi. Samples of four units are taken and tested every 30 minutes. A lower or minimum specification of 15,000 psi has been established. Should the process mean shift to 18,000 psi, what proportion of produced units will be defective?

14.5. In Problem 14.4, should the process mean shift to 18,000 psi and the dispersion double, what proportion of produced units will be defective?

14.6. In Problem 14.4, after how many samples would it be 99 percent certain that a shift on the $\bar{X}$ chart would be detected?

14.7. The total number of accidents during the long weekends and the number of fatalities are given below for a 10-year period.

Weekend	Number of Accidents	Number of Fatalities	Weekend	Number of Accidents	Number of Fatalities
1	2,378	426	16	3,943	523
2	3,375	511	17	3,950	557
3	3,108	498	18	4,358	536
4	3,756	525	19	4,217	533
5	3,947	564	20	3,959	547
6	2,953	475	21	4,108	554
7	3,075	490	22	4,379	579
8	3,173	504	23	4,455	598
9	3,479	528	24	4,753	585
10	3,545	555	25	4,276	543
11	3,865	537	26	3,868	507
12	3,747	529	27	3,947	523
13	4,011	569	28	3,665	575
14	3,108	470	29	4,078	569
15	3,207	510	30	4,025	578

Assuming that the process is in control with regard to the proportion of fatalities, construct a p chart and record the data of the last eight weekends.

14.8. Develop a stabilized p chart for the situation given in Problem 14.7, and plot the data for the last eight weekends.

14.9. Recently, geese have been used to weed cotton fields in southern Texas, sometimes replacing migratory farm workers or chemical weed killers. *Cotton goosing*, the term used to describe this process, can be accomplished with approximately two geese per acre. One farmer is reported to have tested the weeding habits of a sample of 100 geese to determine the proportion of time the geese were idle or not weeding. His work-sampling data represent the idle portion of the 100 geese observed each day for a period of 1 month. Were the work habits of the cotton-goosing geese in control for this month?

Date	Number Idle	Date	Number Idle	Date	Number Idle
1	13	11	6	21	6
2	11	12	5	22	8
3	5	13	11	23	7
4	8	14	7	24	7
5	15	15	9	25	13
6	5	16	8	26	8
7	6	17	13	27	7
8	7	18	5	28	8
9	4	19	8	29	11
10	4	20	4	30	10

14.10. A p chart has indicated that the process average is 0.05. Assuming that this now changes to 0.10, what is the probability of detecting this shift if an inspection unit consists of 100 units? Use the Poisson approximation.

14.11. During a 4-week production period, the following number of defects were found in a sample of 400 electronic components:

Date	Number of Defects	Date	Number of Defects
1	7	11	6
2	8	12	8
3	9	13	16
4	8	14	2
5	3	15	4
6	9	16	2
7	5	17	6
8	6	18	5
9	15	19	3
10	9	20	7

Construct a c chart for these data. Does it appear as though there existed an assignable cause of variation during any of this time?

14.12. A survey during a safety month showed the number of defective cars on a highway as given in the table below.

Date	Defective Cars	Date	Defective Cars	Date	Defective Cars
1	12	11	9	21	9
2	15	12	7	22	8
3	13	13	13	23	17
4	9	14	12	24	16
5	14	15	6	25	13
6	17	16	18	26	18
7	8	17	15	27	12
8	21	18	5	28	9
9	12	19	14	29	11
10	14	20	12	30	19

A sample of 100 cars was taken during each day. Construct a c chart for these data. Is there any assignable cause of variation during this period?

14.13. Sketch the OC curves for the sampling plans $c = 0$, $n = 100$; $c = 1$, $n = 100$; $c = 2$, $n = 100$.

14.14. Sketch the OC curves for the sampling plans $c = 1$, $n = 100$; $c = 2$, $n = 200$; $c = 5$, $n = 500$.

14.15. Develop the four single sampling plans that bracket the producer and consumer risk points of $\alpha = 0.05$ at AQL $= 0.02$ and $\beta = 0.10$ at LTPD $= 0.05$.

14.16. Develop the plans that bracket $\alpha = 0.05$ at AQL $= 0.02$ and $\beta = 0.10$ at LTPD $= 0.10$.

14.17. Sketch I and AOQ, and specify AOQL for the plan $c = 1$, $n = 100$, and $N = 1{,}000$ under rectifying inspection with nonreplacement of defectives. Do the same for $c = 0$, $n = 50$, and $N = 1{,}000$.

V

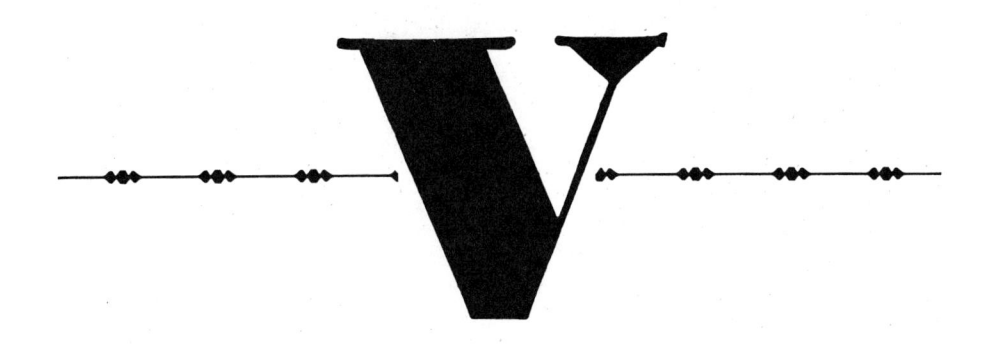

Procurement and Inventory Models

15

Deterministic Procurement and Inventory Models

The procurement and inventory process under consideration in this chapter may be described as follows. A stock of a certain item is maintained to meet a demand. When the number of these items on hand and on order falls to a predetermined level, action is initiated to procure a replenishment quantity from one of several possible sources. The objective is to determine the procurement level, the procurement quantity, and the procurement source in the light of the relevant costs and the properties of demand and procurement lead time so that the sum of all costs associated with the procurement and inventory system will be minimized.

Systems having the foregoing characteristics are found in many operational settings. A procurement and inventory process may exist to meet the demand for raw materials and component parts in manufacturing, to meet the demand for consumer goods at the factory, wholesale, or retail level, to meet the demand for spare parts caused by a wing of military aircraft, and so forth. The first portion of this chapter describes the procurement and inventory system in general terms. The deterministic models that follow are based on the supposition that any item is available from more than one source. By considering the item in this multisource context, these models can be used to make source decisions. This will be illustrated by applying each model to situations requiring determination of the procurement level, the procurement quantity, and the procurement source.

15.1 THE PROCUREMENT AND INVENTORY SYSTEM

A multisource procurement and inventory system is illustrated schematically in Figure 15.1. It exists as a result of the demand stimulus, D. The inventory holding portion of the system (stock) is of primary importance. It serves as a means for making procurement action independent of demand upon the system. Maintaining the stock on hand at an appropriate level contributes to the economy of the procurement and inventory process. Therefore, in satisfying demand, the procurement manager must decide *when* to procure, *how much* to procure, and *from what source* to procure. The following paragraphs describe the source alternatives available to the decision maker and indicate the source-dependent parameters associated with each.

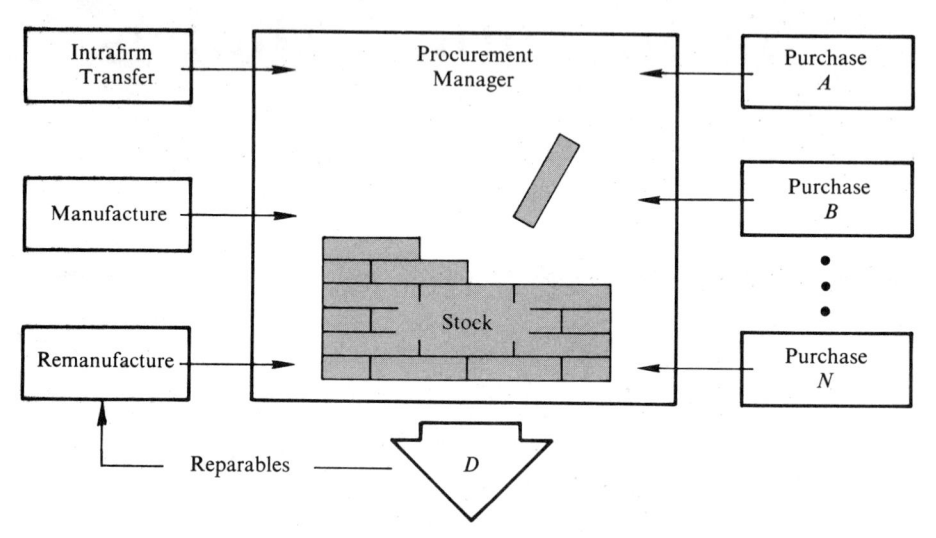

Figure 15.1 Multisource procurement and inventory system.

The Purchase Alternative. Purchasing may be one of the inventory replenishment sources that exist. Actually, several vendors, represented by $A, B, \ldots, N$ in Figure 15.1, may come under consideration.

Associated with each vendor will be a certain procurement lead time capability. The simplest lead time pattern may be described as deterministic. In this special case, the future lead time for a given procurement order can be predicted with certainty. Procurement lead time considered in this restricted sense is only an approximation of reality. In the general case, *lead time* may be described as a random variable that takes on values in accordance with a specific probability distribution. Since lead time is a component of the inventory process and since alternative vendors are unlikely to exhibit identical lead time characteristics, this source-dependent parameter indicates that the inventory process and the procurement process are related.

The replenishment rate for purchasing will be essentially instantaneous, since replenishment stock is usually received in one shipment. Under this condition, the stock on hand will increase by an amount equal to the procurement quantity in an instant of time.

The cost per unit of the item procured will depend on the vendor chosen. Each vendor resides in a unique supply–demand environment and may be expected to price the item accordingly. In addition to differing unit price, it is unlikely that each vendor will quote an identical quantity discount schedule. Therefore, item cost should be considered as an important difference in alternative vendors.

Procurement cost is the summation of the cost elements arising from the series of acts beginning with the initiation of procurement action and ending with the receipt of replenishment stock. Certain of these costs will depend on the vendor chosen as, for instance, the cost of follow-up action required to ensure timely delivery. Since procurement cost is a component of the inventory process as well as a function of the vendor chosen, this is further indication of the relationship between the inventory process and the procurement process.

The Intrafirm Transfer Alternative. An important variation of the purchase alternative is the transfer of stock between procurement managers who are members of the same organization. As an example, assume that a factory distributor in need of replenishment stock places an order with another factory distributor in an adjacent territory. Such action is justified if it results in an economic advantage to the organization as a whole.

Procurement lead time for the intrafirm transfer of stock is usually shorter than that for the purchase alternative. It has the same characteristics, however, and is usually made up of many of the same time elements. A reduced lead time is often the primary incentive for considering the intrafirm transfer alternative.

The replenishment rate for intrafirm transfer would normally be instantaneous. If the requested item is in stock, it will usually be shipped to the requesting organizational unit in one batch and in the amount requested.

Item cost to the receiving organization unit should simply be equal to the cost of the item to the shipping organizational unit plus handling and inventory expenses involved. The addition of a profit for intrafirm transfer is not usually justified, since the interests of the organization as a whole are of prime importance.

Procurement cost for the intrafirm transfer alternative will be made up of cost components similar to those for the purchase alternative. Because of the nature of each source, however, it is not likely that the two will be the same.

The Manufacture Alternative. It may be enocomically advantageous to procure replenishment stock from a manufacturing facility within the organization if such a facility exists. When this is the case, the procurement manager is faced with a manufacture or purchase decision.

Associated with the manufacturing source will be a certain procurement lead time capability. Although manufacturing lead time will be a random variable, its variance may be more easily controlled than the variance in purchase lead time.

The replenishment rate for remanufacturing is normally finite. Items being manufactured accumulate as they are made, whereas purchased items are received at one time. This is an important difference between the manufacture and purchase alternatives.

Item cost for the manufacture alternative involves a summation of the costs of direct labor, direct material, and factory burden. In addition, manufacturing progress or learning will occur, which may result in a significant reduction in the number of direct labor hours per unit as the number of units produced increases. This brings about a corresponding reduction in item cost analogous to the price discount schedule for the purchase alternative.

Procurement cost for manufacturing will be composed of the cost elements incurred in production planning, setup and teardown, scheduling, and other costs arising from the set of acts required in the initiation of manufacturing action. Evidently, this cost will differ significantly from procurement cost for the purchase alternative.

The Remanufacture Alternative. The possibility of remanufacturing should be considered in those cases where a remanufactured item may be used to satisfy demand. This is often the case with automotive and aircraft components.

Remanufacturing lead time may be considerably shorter than the procurement lead time from any other source. This occurs, in part, because the process normally requires only a few manufacturing operations. The replenishment rate for remanufacturing will be finite because remanufactured items accumulate as they are made in the same manner as manufactured items.

As for manufacturing, item cost will involve the cost elements of direct labor, direct material, and factory burden. The direct material item must include the cost of repairables, a necessary input for this source alternative. In addition, manufacturing progress will be experienced during remanufacturing with its resulting effects.

Procurement cost for the remanufacturing alternative will be analogous to that for the manufacturing alternative. It will be composed of those cost elements arising from the set of acts required in preparation for remanufacturing.

15.2 THE DECISION ENVIRONMENT

The procurement and inventory system described in Section 15.1 includes parameters dependent on the source and some which are independent of it. Four of these—procurement lead time, the replenishment rate, item cost, and procurement cost—were discussed in Section 15.1. Each was classified as source dependent, since its specific value depends upon the source chosen. Three others —demand, holding cost, and shortage cost—are source independent. These are discussed in the following paragraphs. Finally, the general structure of decision models for procurement and inventory operations will be presented.

Demand. Demand is the primary stimulus on the procurement and inventory system and is the justification for its existence. Specifically, the system may exist to meet the demand of customers, the spare parts demand of an operational weapons system, the demand of the next step in a manufacturing process, and so forth. The characteristics of demand, although independent of the source chosen to replenish inventories, will depend on the nature of the environment giving rise to demand.

The simplest demand pattern may be classified as deterministic. In this special case, the future demand for an item may be predicted with certainty. Demand considered in this restricted sense is only an approximation of reality. In the general case, demand may be described as a random variable that takes on values in accordance with a specific probability distribution.

Holding Cost. Inventory holding costs are incurred as a function of the quantity on hand and the time duration involved. Included in these costs are the real out-of-pocket costs, such as insurance, taxes, obsolescence, and warehouse rental or other space charges, and operating costs such as light, heat, maintenance, and security. In addition, capital invested in inventories is unavailable for investment elsewhere. The rate of return forgone represents a cost of carrying inventory.

The inventory holding cost per unit of time may be thought of as the sum of several cost components. Some of these may depend on the maximum inventory level incurred. Others may depend on the average inventory level. Still others, like the cost of capital invested, will depend on the value of the inventory during the time period. The determination of holding cost per unit for a specified time period depends on a detailed analysis of each cost component.

Shortage Cost. Shortage cost is the penalty incurred for being unable to meet a demand when it occurs. This cost does not depend on the source chosen to replenish stock but is a function of the number of units short and the time duration involved.

The specific dollar penalty incurred when a shortage exists depends on the nature of the demand. For instance, if the demand is that of customers on a retail establishment, the shortage cost will include the loss of good will. In this case, shortage cost will be small relative to the cost of the item. If, however, the demand is that of the next step in a manufacturing process, the cost of a shortage may be high relative to the cost of the item. Being unable to meet the requirement for raw material or a component part may result in lost production or even closing of the plant. Therefore, in establishing shortage cost, the seriousness of the shortage condition and its time duration must be considered.

The Decision Model. The inventory process resulting from procurement action and demand will exhibit a saw-toothed function which depends on the procurement level, the procurement quantity, the demand rate, the procurement lead time, and the replenishment rate. The total system cost will depend on the exhibited geometry and the item cost, the procurement cost, the holding cost, and the shortage cost. Since procurement lead time, the replenishment rate, item cost, and procurement cost are source dependent, evidently both the geometry of the inventory process and the total system cost will be source dependent. If both demand and procurement lead time are deterministic, as is assumed in this chapter, the resulting inventory process will be deterministic, as shown in Figure 15.2.

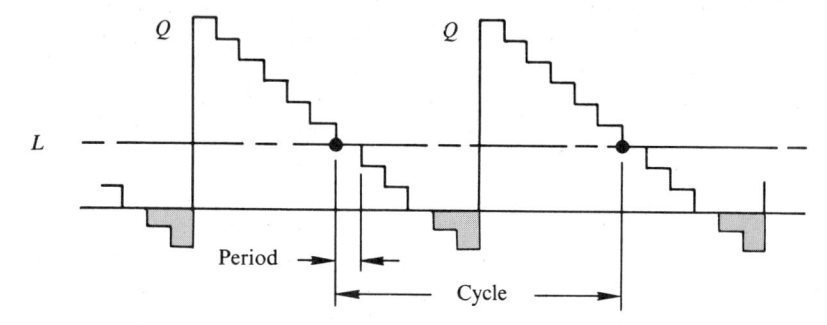

Figure 15.2 Deterministic inventory process with instantaneous replenishment.

The inventory function is illustrated as it would appear to the bookkeeping system. Two basic time elements are involved which may be defined as follows:

1. Period: the element of elapsed time between review of the stock position. This is usually 1 day, but it may be any other time unit.
2. Cycle: the number of periods occurring between successive procurement actions.

Stock level review and adjustment occur at the end of each period resulting in the step function shown. The stock level at the end of one period is equal to the stock level at the beginning of the next. In this context, the inventory level is periodically reviewed as opposed to a theoretical continuous review process.

The primary objective of the procurement and inventory system is to meet demand at minimum cost. This involves the assignment of appropriate values to the decision variables of when to procure, how much to procure, and from what source to procure by constructing and optimizing a mathematical model of the form[1]

$$E = f(x_i, y_j),$$

[1] Some optimization techniques used in this chapter require a familiarity with Appendix B.

where E = measure of effectiveness sought (minimize total system cost)
x_i = policy variables of when to procure and how much to procure
y_j = source-dependent and source-independent parameters of procurement lead time, the replenishment rate, item cost, procurement cost, demand, holding cost, and shortage cost.

The following sections deal with the development of deterministic decision models having these general characteristics. The following symbolism will be adopted:

TC = total system cost per period
L = procurement level
Q = procurement quantity
D = demand rate in units per period
T = lead time in periods
P = number of periods per cycle
R = replenishment rate in units per period
C_i = item cost per unit
C_p = procurement cost per procurement
C_h = holding cost per unit per period
C_s = shortage cost per unit short per period

Additional notation will be adopted and defined as required for the derivation of specific decision models.

15.3 THE PURCHASE ALTERNATIVE

If demand for the item is to be met by purchasing (or intrafirm transfer) once per year, the cost incident to purchasing will occur once per year, but the large quantity received will result in a relatively high inventory holding cost for the year. Conversely, if purchasing action is initiated several times per year, the cost incident to purchasing will be incurred several times per year, but since small quantities will be received, the cost of holding inventory will be relatively small. If the decision is to be based on economy of the total operation, the procurement level and procurement quantity resulting in a minimum cost for each vendor must be determined.

A Purchase Decision Model. If it is assumed that the demand for the item is deterministic, that the procurement lead time is deterministic, that the replenishment rate is infinite, and that shortage cost is infinite, the resulting inventory process may be represented graphically as in Figure 15.3.

The total system cost per period will be the sum of the item cost for the period, the procurement cost for the period, and the holding cost for the period; that is,

$$TC = IC + PC + HC.$$

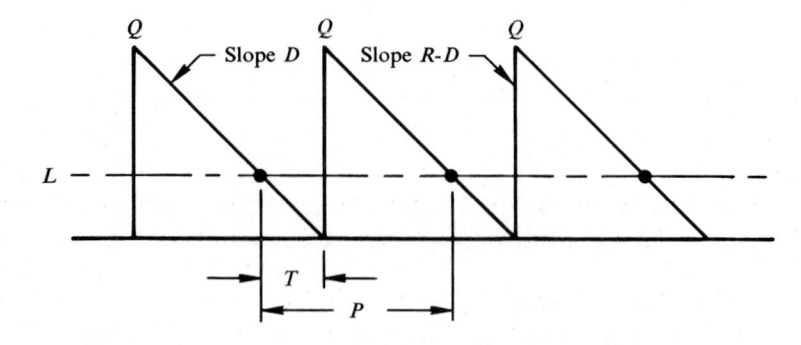

Figure 15.3 Infinite replacement rate with infinite shortage cost.

The item cost for the period will be the item cost per unit times the demand rate in units per period, or

$$IC = C_i D.$$

The procurement cost for the period will be the purchase cost per purchase divided by the number of periods per cycle, or

$$PC = \frac{C_p}{P}.$$

But since P is the procurement quantity divided by the demand rate,

$$PC = \frac{C_p D}{Q}.$$

Since the maximum number of units in stock is Q, the average inventory during the period will be $Q/2$. Therefore, the holding cost for the period will be the holding cost per unit times the average number of units on hand for the period, or

$$HC = \frac{C_h Q}{2}.$$

The total system cost per period will be the sum of the item cost per period, the procurement cost per period, and the holding cost per period, or

$$TC = C_i D + \frac{C_p D}{Q} + \frac{C_h Q}{2}. \tag{15.1}$$

The procurement quantity resulting in a minimum total system cost may be found by differentiating with respect to Q, setting the result equal to zero, and solving for Q as follows:

$$\frac{dTC}{dQ} = -\frac{C_p D}{Q^2} + \frac{C_h}{2} = 0$$

$$Q = \sqrt{\frac{2 C_p D}{C_h}}. \tag{15.2}$$

In this simple model, no shortages were allowed, since shortage cost was assumed to be infinite. Since this is the case, the procurement level will be

$$L = DT. \tag{15.3}$$

The minimum total system cost may be found by substituting the minimum cost procurement quantity into Equation (15.1) as follows:

$$TC_{\min} = C_i D + \frac{C_p D}{\sqrt{2C_p D/C_h}} + \frac{C_h \sqrt{2C_p D/C_h}}{2} \tag{15.4}$$
$$= C_i D + \sqrt{2C_p C_h D}.$$

A Purchase Decision. For simplicity, assume that only one vendor is under consideration as a possible source of replenishment stock. In this case, it is necessary to determine only the procurement level and the procurement quantity resulting in a minimum cost, the source being fixed by restriction. Suppose that the item has a demand of three units per period, the procurement lead time is 16 periods, the item cost is $6.10 per unit, the procurement cost is $8.00 per procurement, and the holding cost per unit per period is $0.004.

Item cost per period, procurement cost per period, holding cost per period, and total cost per period may be tabulated as a function of Q to illustrate the nature of the cost components. The results shown in Table 15.1 were developed from Equation (15.1). It is evident from the table that item cost per period is costant, procurement cost per period decreases, and holding cost per period increases with increasing values of Q. It is not possible to pick the minimum cost procurement quantity from the table because of the number of decimal places exhibited. The curve generated by these points is flat in the region of its minimum.

Table 15.1. COST COMPONENTS FOR PURCHASE DECISION

Q	IC	PC	HC	TC
0	$18.30	$∞	$0.00	$∞
10	18.30	2.40	0.02	20.72
20	18.30	1.20	0.04	19.54
30	18.30	0.80	0.06	19.16
40	18.30	0.60	0.08	18.98
50	18.30	0.48	0.10	18.88
60	18.30	0.40	0.12	18.82
70	18.30	0.34	0.14	18.78
80	18.30	0.30	0.16	18.76
90	18.30	0.27	0.18	18.75
100	18.30	0.24	0.20	18.74
110	18.30	0.22	0.22	18.74
120	18.30	0.20	0.24	18.74
130	18.30	0.18	0.26	18.74
140	18.30	0.17	0.28	18.75

The minimum cost procurement quantity and procurement level may be found directly by substituting into Equation (15.2) and Equation (15.3) as follows:

$$Q = \sqrt{\frac{2(\$8)(3)}{\$0.004}} = 110 \text{ units}$$

$$L = 3(16) = 48 \text{ units}.$$

Under the conditions assumed, the procurement manager would initiate purchasing action when the stock falls to 48 units for a purchase quantity of 110 units from the vendor specified.

15.4 THE MANUFACTURE ALTERNATIVE

If demand for the item is to be met by manufacturing (or remanufacturing) once per year, the cost of initiating manufacturing action will occur only once per year, but the large quantity produced will result in a relatively high inventory holding cost for the year. Conversely, if manufacturing action is initiated several times per year, this cost will be incurred several times per year, but since small quantities will be produced, the cost of holding inventory will be relatively small. If the decision is to be based on economy of the total operation, the procurement level and procurement quantity resulting in a minimum cost must be determined.

A Manufacture Decision Model. Minimum cost manufacturing quantities are determined in a manner similar to that employed in determining minimum cost purchase quantities. The difference in analysis occurs because a purchased lot is received at one time, whereas a production lot accumulates as it is made. If it is assumed that demand for the item is deterministic, that procurement lead time is deterministic, that the replenishment rate is finite ($R > D$), and that shortage cost is infinite, the resulting inventory process may be represented graphically as in Figure 15.4.

The total system cost per period will be the sum of the item cost for the period, the procurement cost for the period, and the holding cost for the period; that is,

$$TC = IC + PC + HC.$$

The item cost for the period will be the item cost per unit times the demand in units per period, or

$$IC = C_i D.$$

The procurement cost for the period will be setup cost per setup divided by the number of periods in the cycle, or

$$PC = \frac{C_p}{P}.$$

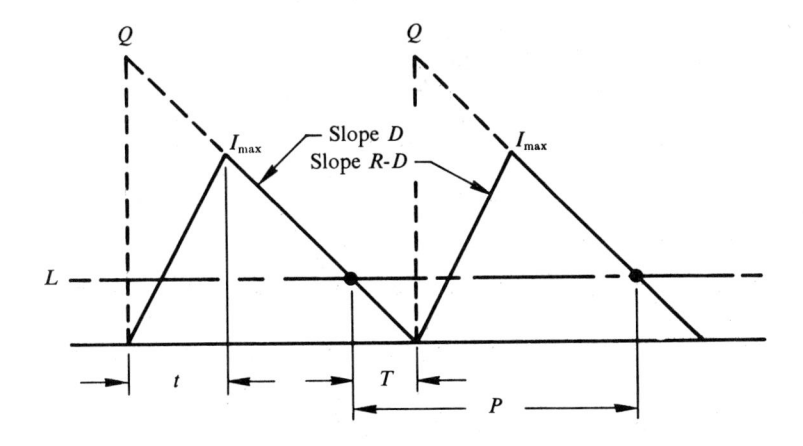

Figure 15.4 Finite replenishment rate with infinite shortage cost.

But since P is the procurement quantity divided by the demand rate,

$$PC = \frac{C_p D}{Q}.$$

The maximum number of units in stock may be expressed as

$$I_{max} = t(R - D) = \frac{Q}{R}(R - D).$$

The average number of units on hand during the period will be the maximum number of units in stock divided by 2, and the holding cost for the period will be the holding cost per unit per period times the average number of units on hand for the period, or

$$HC = \frac{C_h Q}{2R}(R - D).$$

The total system cost per period will be the sum of the item cost per period, the procurement cost per period, and the holding cost per period, or

$$TC = C_i D + \frac{C_p D}{Q} + \frac{C_h Q}{2R}(R - D). \tag{15.5}$$

The procurement quantity resulting in a minimum total system cost may be found by differentiating with respect to Q, setting the result equal to zero, and solving for Q as follows:

$$\frac{dTC}{dQ} = -\frac{C_p D}{Q^2} + \frac{C_h}{2R}(R - D) = 0$$

$$Q^2 = \frac{2C_p D}{C_h[1 - (D/R)]} \tag{15.6}$$

$$Q = \sqrt{\frac{2C_p D}{C_h[1 - (D/R)]}}.$$

As for the purchase decision model, no shortages were allowed since shortage cost was assumed to be infinite. Since this is the case, the procurement level will be

$$L = DT. \tag{15.7}$$

The minimum total system cost may be found by substituting the minimum cost procurement quantity into Equation (15.5) as follows:

$$\begin{aligned} TC_{\min} &= C_i D + \frac{C_p D}{\sqrt{2C_p D/C_h[1-(D/R)]}} \\ &\quad + \frac{C_h\sqrt{2C_p D/C_h[1-(D/R)]}}{2R}(R-D) \\ &= C_i D + \sqrt{2C_p\left(1-\frac{D}{R}\right)C_h D}. \end{aligned} \tag{15.8}$$

Equation (15.6) reduces to Equation (15.2), and Equation (15.8) reduces to Equation (15.4) as $R \rightarrow \infty$. Thus, the purchase decision model is a special case of the manufacture decision model.

A Manufacture Decision. Suppose that the item under consideration is to be manufactured and that the item cost due to manufacturing is $6.00 per unit. Also suppose that the demand is 3 units per perod, the procurement lead time is 12 periods, the procurement (setup) cost is $50, the holding cost per unit per period is $0.004, and the production rate is 18 units per period.

Item cost per period, procurement cost per period, holding cost per period, and total cost per period may be tabulated as a function of Q to illustrate the nature of the cost components. From Equation (15.5) the results of Table 15.2 may be developed. It is evident from the table that item cost per period is constant, procurement cost per period decreases, and holding cost per period

Table 15.2. COST COMPONENTS FOR MANUFACTURE DECISION

Q	IC	PC	HC	TC
0	$18.00	∞	$0.00	∞
30	18.00	$5.00	0.05	$23.05
60	18.00	2.50	0.10	20.60
90	18.00	1.67	0.15	19.82
120	18.00	1.25	0.20	19.45
150	18.00	1.00	0.25	19.25
180	18.00	0.83	0.30	19.13
210	18.00	0.71	0.35	19.06
240	18.00	0.63	0.40	19.03
270	18.00	0.56	0.45	19.01
300	18.00	0.50	0.50	19.00
330	18.00	0.45	0.55	19.00
360	18.00	0.42	0.60	19.02

increases with increasing values of Q. As before, it is not possible to pick the minimum cost procurement quantity because of the number of decimal places given. Again, the curve generated by these points is flat in the region of its minimum.

The minimum cost procurement level and procurement quantity may be found directly by substituting into Equations (15.6) and (15.7) as follows:

$$Q = \sqrt{\frac{2(\$50)(3)}{\$0.004[1 - (3/18)]}} = 300 \text{ units}$$

$$L = 3(12) = 36 \text{ units.}$$

Under the conditions assumed, the procurement manager would initiate manufacturing action when the stock falls to 36 units for a manufacturing quantity of 300 units from the manufacturing source specified.

15.5 MAKING THE SOURCE DECISION

The examples of the previous sections assumed that the source was fixed by restriction. Suppose now that no such restriction exists and that the procurement level, procurement quantity, and procurement source are to be determined. The computational procedure required involves the determination of the minimum total system cost for each source. The source giving rise to the minimum of the minimum costs is the source chosen. The procurement level and procurement quantity at which the absolute minimum occurred is also specified. The end result is the operation of the procurement and inventory system at minimum cost. The following paragraphs are presented in order to illustrate the computational procedure.

Purchase or Manufacture. Suppose that the demand for a given item may be met by either purchasing or manufacturing. Also assume that the item in question is the item used in the examples of the previous sections. The demand rate assumed was 3 units per period and the holding cost per unit per period was $0.004. Source-dependent parameters assumed were as follows:

	Purchase	Manufacture
Procurement lead time	16	12
Item cost	$6.10	$ 6.00
Procurement cost	$8.00	$50.00
Replenishment rate	∞	18

The minimum total system cost for the purchase alternative may be found from Equation (15.4) as

$$TC_{\min} = \$6.10(3) + \sqrt{2(\$8)(\$0.004)(3)} = \$18.74.$$

The minimum total system cost for the manufacture alternative may be computed from Equation (15.8) as

$$TC_{min} = \$6.00(3) + \sqrt{2(\$50)[1 - (3/18)](\$0.004)(3)} = \$19.00.$$

Therefore, the minimum cost procurement source is the purchase alternative, even though the item cost for purchasing is higher than the item cost for manufacturing. Comparison of the values given in Table 15.1 and Table 15.2 verifies this conclusion.

The minimum cost purchase quantity was shown previously to be 110 units, and the minimum cost procurement level was 48 units. Therefore, the minimum cost procurement and inventory policy for this example is that policy requiring procurement action to be initiated when the stock falls to 48 units, for a procurement quantity of 110 units, from the purchase source.

Evaluating Alternate Vendors. Suppose that the demand for an item may be met by purchasing from one of two vendors. Also, assume that the demand rate is 3 units per period and that the holding cost per unit per period is $0.003. The source-dependent parameters are as follows:

	Vendor A	Vendor B
Procurement lead time	14	10
Item cost	$4.20	$4.35
Procurement cost	$9.00	$7.00

The minimum total system cost for vendor A may be found from Equation (15.4) as

$$TC_{min} = \$4.20(3) + \sqrt{2(\$9)(\$0.003)(3)} = \$13.00.$$

For vendor B the same equation may be used, giving

$$TC_{min} = \$4.35(3) + \sqrt{2(\$7)(\$0.003)(3)} = \$13.40.$$

Therefore, the minimum cost procurement source is vendor A. The minimum cost procurement quantity may be computed from Equation (15.2) as

$$Q = \sqrt{\frac{2(\$9)(3)}{\$0.003}} = 134 \text{ units.}$$

The minimum cost procurement level may be found from Equation (15.3) as

$$L = 3(14) = 42 \text{ units.}$$

For the conditions of this example, the minimum cost procurement and inventory policy is that policy requiring procurement action to be initiated when the stock level falls to 42 units, for a procurement quantity of 134 units from vendor A. The situation is illustrated graphically in Figure 15.5. The total cost curves for each vendor were developed from Equation (15.1). As is usually the case, the curves are flat in the region of their minimums.

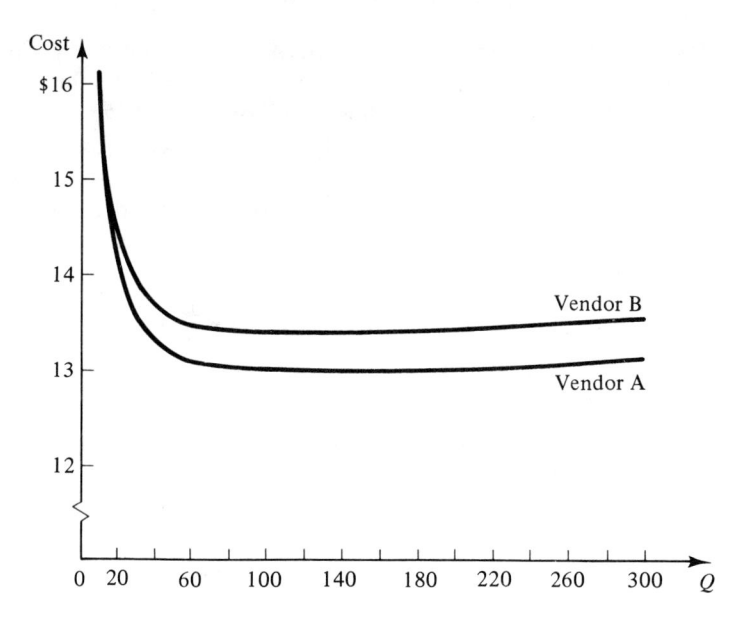

Figure 15.5 Total cost curves for evaluating alternative vendors.

15.6 MODELS FOR VARIABLE ITEM COST

Item cost is a source-dependent parameter in that its value depends on the procurement source chosen. This fact was illustrated in the examples presented in the preceding section. In those examples, however, item cost was not taken to be a function of the procurement quantity. This is an exception rather than the rule. Most vendors will quote a price discount schedule which allows for a reduction in the price per unit as the number of units purchased increases. Similarly, the reduction in the number of direct labor hours per unit as the number of units produced increases will result in a reduction in item cost. In each case, item cost will be a function of the procurement quantity chosen. The following paragraphs present, for the previously developed models, modifications that take variable item cost into consideration.

Purchase Decision with Variable Item Cost. In the purchase alternative, item cost may depend on the procurement quantity, owing to discounts allowed by the vendor for large orders. The price per unit is usually quoted for various purchase quantities as follows:

Purchase Quantity	Price per Unit
$1 \leq Q \leq Q_1$	C_{i_1}
$Q_1 < Q \leq Q_2$	C_{i_2}
$Q_2 < Q \leq Q_3$	C_{i_3}

Total system cost for the purchase alternative was given by Equation (15.1). Since the first term involves C_i, this equation will result in a different total cost function for each price in the schedule. Each price will have an applicable range, as previously indicated. Consequently, each total cost function will be valid for only a segment of its range and is, therefore, discontinuous. Hence, the least cost procurement quantity cannot be found by direct differentiation. It will be necessary to use the following procedure to find the minimum cost procurement quantity:

1. Calculate the minimum cost Q by use of Equation (15.2).
2. Find the total system cost by use of Equation (15.4), using the C_i value applicable to the Q value found in step (1).
3. Calculate the total system cost for the smallest Q in the next higher Q range using Equation (15.1).
4. If the TC value found in step (3) is greater than the TC value found in step (2), the result in step (2) is a minimum total system cost. If the TC value found in step (3) is less than the TC value found in step (2), proceed to step (5).
5. Calculate the total system cost for the smallest Q in the next higher Q range using Equation (15.1).
6. If the TC value found in step (5) is greater than the TC value found in step (3), the Q value of step (3) will result in a minimum total system cost. If the TC value found in step (5) is less than the TC value found in step (3), proceed to the next Q range and repeat steps (5) and (6) until the TC value starts increasing.
7. If the highest Q range is reached without the total cost increasing, then the smallest Q in the highest Q range will give the minimum total system cost.

As an example of the application of the price discount procedure just outlined, consider the following situation: A specified vendor is supplying replenishment stock to meet a demand of 10 units per period. Procurement cost is $16.00 per procurement, holding cost is $0.20 per unit per period, procurement lead time is 12 periods, and item cost is quoted in accordance with the following schedule:

Purchase Quantity	Price per Unit
1–49	$5.20
50–99	4.90
100 and above	4.60

Application of Equation (15.2) gives the minimum cost procurement quantity of

$$Q = \sqrt{\frac{2(\$16)10}{\$0.20}} = 40 \text{ units.}$$

Since this procurement quantity falls in the first price break, $5.20 is used as the item cost in Equation (15.4), resulting in

$$TC = \$5.20(10) + \sqrt{2(\$16)(\$0.20)(10)} = \$60.00.$$

Next, the total system cost resulting from the smallest Q in the next higher price range is found from Equation (15.1) as

$$TC = \$4.90(10) + \frac{\$16(10)}{50} + \frac{\$0.20(50)}{2} = \$57.20.$$

Since this value is less than the total system cost of the preceding step, the total system cost for the smallest Q in the next higher price range is calculated from Equation (15.1) as

$$TC = \$4.60(10) + \frac{\$16(10)}{100} + \frac{\$0.20(100)}{2} = \$57.60.$$

This value is now greater than the total system cost of the previous step. Therefore, the minimum cost procurement quantity is 50 units The minimum cost procurement level is found from Equation (15.3) to be $10(12) = 120$ units.

In this example, the procurement level is greater than the procurement quantity. Therefore, the stock on hand will always be lower than the procurement level. This requires that procurement action be initiated when the stock on hand plus the stock on order falls to the procurement level. The number of periods per cycle will be 50/10 or five. Thus, procurement action would be initiated every five periods for a procurement quantity of 50 units.

Production Decision with Variable Item Cost. It was shown in Chapter 11 that item cost is a function of the number of items produced, the manufacturing progress factor, the number of direct labor hours required for the first unit, the direct labor rate, the factory burden rate, and the direct material cost. Item cost was given by Equation (11.10).

Total system cost for manufacturing or remanufacturing was given by Equation (15.5). Since item cost occurs in only the first term, the minimum cost procurement quantity given by Equation (15.6) and the minimum cost procurement level given by Equation (15.7) will still hold. The effect of manufacturing progress, however, is lowering of the total system cost. This reduction in total system cost will affect the source decision only.

Equation (15.8) expresses the minimum total system cost for the manufacturing alternative when item cost is not modified because of manufacturing progress. If it is assumed that the discontinuous nature of manufacturing operations does not affect the item cost given by Equation (11.10), Equation (15.8) becomes

$$TC_{min} = \left[\frac{KN^n}{n+1}(lr)(1+fb) + dm\right]D + \sqrt{2C_p\left(1 - \frac{D}{R}\right)C_h D}, \quad (15.9)$$

where

$$n = \frac{\log \phi}{\log 2}.$$

This equation may be used to find the minimum total system cost for production where item cost is subject to manufacturing progress.

As an illustration of the analysis required for the manufacturing model with variable item cost, consider the following situation. Suppose that a manufacturing source is being considered as an alternative to the purchase source of the previous example. Data relating to the manufacturing source under consideration are as follows:

$$\phi = 0.80$$
$$K = 2 \text{ hours}$$
$$lr = \$6.00 \text{ per hour}$$
$$dm = \$2.40 \text{ per unit}$$
$$fb = 0.80 \text{ of direct labor cost}$$
$$C_p = \$100 \text{ per procurement}$$
$$R = 20 \text{ units per period}$$
$$N = 3,000 \text{ units}$$
$$T = 8 \text{ periods}$$

The minimum total system cost for this alternative may be found from Equation (15.9) as

$$TC_{\min} = \left[\frac{2(3,000)^{\log 0.8/\log 2}}{(\log 0.80/\log 2) + 1}(\$6.00)(1 + 0.80) + \$2.40\right]10$$

$$+ \sqrt{2(\$100)\left(1 - \frac{10}{20}\right)(\$0.20)(10)}$$

$$= \left[\frac{2(3,000)^{-0.3219}}{0.6781}(\$10.80) + \$2.40\right]10 + \sqrt{\$200}$$

$$= \$48.20 + \$14.14 = \$62.34.$$

Since this value is greater than the minimum total system cost for the purchase alternative, this source of replenishment stock should be rejected.

15.7 MODELS FOR FINITE SHORTAGE COST

All derivations up to this point were based on the assumption that shortage cost was infinite. As a result, the decision models presented involved a trade-off between procurement cost and holding cost. When shortage cost is finite, an economic advantage may be gained by allowing some shortages to occur. One seeks the trade-off between procurement cost, holding cost, and shortage cost that will result in a minimum total system cost. Normally, the increase in total system cost due to the shortage condition is more than compensated by the reduction in holding cost. The following paragraphs develop models for the case where shortage cost is finite.

Chap. 15 Deterministic Procurement and Inventory Models

A Purchase Decision Model. If it is assumed that demand for the item is deterministic, that procurement lead time is deterministic, that the replenishment rate is infinite, that shortage cost is finite, and that unsatisfied demand is not lost, the resulting inventory process may be represented graphically as in Figure 15.6.

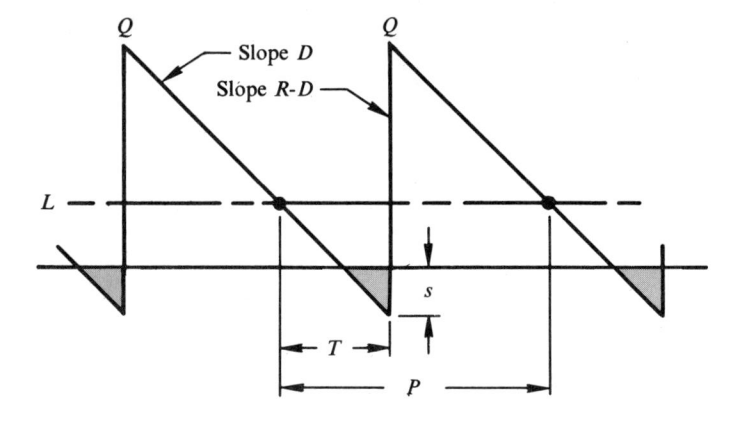

Figure 15.6 Infinite replenishment rate with finite shortage cost.

The number of periods per cycle may be expressed as

$$P = T + \frac{Q - DT}{D} = \frac{Q}{D}.$$

The average number of unit periods of stock on hand during the cycle is

$$I = \frac{Q + L - DT}{2}\left(\frac{Q + L - DT}{D}\right)$$
$$= \frac{(Q + L - DT)^2}{2D}.$$

The average number of unit periods of shortage during the cycle is

$$S = \frac{DT - L}{2}\left(\frac{DT - L}{D}\right)$$
$$= \frac{(DT - L)^2}{2D}.$$

The total system cost per period will be the sum of the item cost for the period, the procurement cost for the period, the holding cost for the period, and the shortage cost for the period; that is,

$$TC = IC + PC + HC + SC.$$

$$TC = C_i D + \frac{C_p D}{Q} + \frac{C_h}{2Q}(Q + L - DT)^2 + \frac{C_s}{2Q}(DT - L)^2. \quad (15.10)$$

Equation (15.10) may be modified as follows:

$$TC = C_i D + \frac{C_p D}{Q} + \frac{C_h Q}{2} - C_h(DT - L) + \frac{C_h(DT - L)^2}{2Q} + \frac{C_s(DT - L)^2}{2Q}.$$

Total system cost is a function of two independent variables, L and Q. Taking the partial derivatives of TC with respect to Q and $DT - L$ and setting these equal to zero gives

$$\frac{\partial TC}{\partial Q} = -\frac{C_p D}{Q^2} + \frac{C_h}{2} - \frac{C_h(DT-L)^2}{2Q^2} - \frac{C_s(DT-L)^2}{2Q^2} = 0 \quad (15.11)$$

$$\frac{\partial TC}{\partial (DT-L)} = -C_h + \frac{C_h(DT-L)}{Q} + \frac{C_s(DT-L)}{Q} = 0. \quad (15.12)$$

From Equation (15.12)

$$\frac{DT - L}{Q} = \frac{C_h}{C_h + C_s}. \quad (15.13)$$

Substituting Equation (15.13) into Equation (15.11) gives

$$-\frac{C_p D}{Q^2} + \frac{C_h}{2} - \frac{C_h + C_s}{2}\left(\frac{C_h}{C_h + C_s}\right)^2 = 0$$

$$\frac{C_p D}{Q^2} = \frac{C_h(C_h + C_s) - C_h^2}{2(C_h + C_s)}$$

$$Q^2 = \frac{2 C_p D (C_h + C_s)}{C_h C_s} \quad (15.14)$$

$$Q = \sqrt{\frac{2 C_p D}{C_h} + \frac{2 C_p D}{C_s}}.$$

Equation (15.14) gives the minimum cost procurement quantity as a function of demand, procurement cost, holding cost, and shortage cost.

The minimum cost procurement level may be derived from Equation (15.13) as

$$L = DT - \frac{C_h}{C_h + C_s}(Q).$$

Substituting Equation (15.14) for Q gives

$$L = DT - \frac{C_h}{C_h + C_s}\sqrt{\frac{2 C_p D}{C_h} + \frac{2 C_p D}{C_s}}$$

$$= DT - \sqrt{\frac{2 C_h C_p D}{C_s(C_h + C_s)}}. \quad (15.15)$$

Equations (15.14) and (15.15) may now be substituted back into the total cost equation to yield an expression for minimum total system cost. Rewriting Equation (15.10) gives

$$TC = C_i D + \frac{C_p D}{Q} + \frac{C_h Q}{2}\left(1 - \frac{DT-L}{Q}\right)^2 + \frac{C_s Q}{2}\left(\frac{DT-L}{Q}\right)^2.$$

Substituting Equations (15.13) and (15.14) gives

$$TC_{\min} = C_i D + \frac{C_p D}{Q} + \frac{C_h Q}{2}\left[\frac{C_s^2}{(C_h + C_s)^2}\right] + \frac{C_s D}{2}\left[\frac{C_h^2}{(C_h + C_s)^2}\right]$$

$$= C_i D + C_p D \sqrt{\frac{C_h C_s}{2(C_h + C_s)C_p D}} + \frac{C_h C_s}{2(C_h + C_s)}\left(\sqrt{\frac{2(C_h + C_s)C_p D}{C_h C_s}}\right)$$

$$= C_i D + \sqrt{\frac{2 C_p C_h C_s D}{C_h + C_s}}. \tag{15.16}$$

Equation (15.14) reduces to Equation (15.2), Equation (15.15) reduces to Equation (15.3), and Equation (15.16) reduces to Equation (15.4) as $C_s \to \infty$. Thus, the purchase model with infinite shortage cost is a special case of the purchase model with finite shortage cost.

A Purchase Decision for Finite Shortage Cost. As an example of the computations required in the application of the purchase model for finite shortage cost, consider the following situation. A specified vendor is supplying replenishment stock to meet a demand of 10 units per period. Purchasing lead time is 16 periods, item cost is $5.00 per unit, procurement cost is $16.00 per procurement, holding cost is $0.20 per unit per period, and shortage cost is $0.10 per unit short per period.

Total system cost per period may be tabulated as a function of L and Q by the use of Equation (15.10). The resulting values in the region of the minimum cost point are given in Table 15.3. The minimum cost Q and L may be found by inspection. As was expected, the surface generated by the values exhibited is seen to be rather flat.

The minimum cost procurement quantity and procurement level may be found directly by substituting into Equations (15.14) and (15.15) as follows:

$$Q = \sqrt{\frac{2(\$16)(10)}{\$0.20} + \frac{2(\$16)(10)}{\$0.10}} = 69 \text{ units}$$

$$L = 10(16) - \sqrt{\frac{2(\$16)(10)}{\$0.10[1 + (\$0.10/\$0.20)]}} = 114 \text{ units}.$$

Table 15.3. TOTAL SYSTEM COST AS A FUNCTION OF L AND Q (DOLLARS)

L \ Q	66	67	68	69	70	71	72
109	54.735	54.711	54.690	54.673	54.659	54.648	54.640
110	54.706	54.685	54.667	54.653	54.642	54.635	54.630
111	54.681	54.663	54.649	54.638	54.630	54.626	54.624
112	54.660	54.646	54.635	54.627	54.622	54.621	54.622
113	54.644	54.633	54.625	54.621	54.619	54.620	54.624
114	54.633	54.625	54.620	54.619	54.619	54.623	54.630
115	54.626	54.621	54.619	54.621	54.624	54.631	54.640
116	54.624	54.622	54.623	54.627	54.634	54.643	54.655
117	54.626	54.627	54.631	54.638	54.647	54.659	54.674
118	54.633	54.637	54.644	54.655	54.665	54.680	54.697
119	54.644	54.651	54.661	54.673	54.687	54.704	54.724

The resulting total system cost at the minimum cost procurement quantity and procurement level may be found from Equation (15.16) as

$$TC_{min} = \$5.00(10) + \sqrt{\frac{2(\$16)(\$0.20)(\$0.10)(10)}{\$0.20 + \$0.10}} = \$54.62.$$

Actually, however, a slightly modified policy must be adopted because the procurement quantity is less than the procurement level and because it is not a multiple of the demand. In this case, the number of periods per cycle is 69/10, or 6.9 periods. Thus, procurement action should be initiated every 7 periods for a procurement quantity of 70 units. This would result in a slightly higher total system cost.

A Manufacture Decision Model. If it is assumed that demand for the item is deterministic, that procurement lead time is deterministic, that the replenishment rate is finite ($R > D$), that shortage cost is finite, and that unsatisfied demand is not lost, the resulting inventory process may be represented graphically as in Figure 15.7. As before, the number of periods per cycle may be expressed as

$$P = \frac{Q}{D}.$$

The net rate of accumulation during time $t_1 + t_2$ is $R - D$. The maximum accumulation is designated I_{max} in Figure 15.7. The following algebraic relationships are evident:

$$(t_1 + t_2)(R - D) = (t_3 + t_4)D. \tag{15.17}$$

$$t_1 + t_2 = \frac{Q}{R}. \tag{15.18}$$

$$t_3 + t_4 = \frac{I_{max} + DT - L}{D}. \tag{15.19}$$

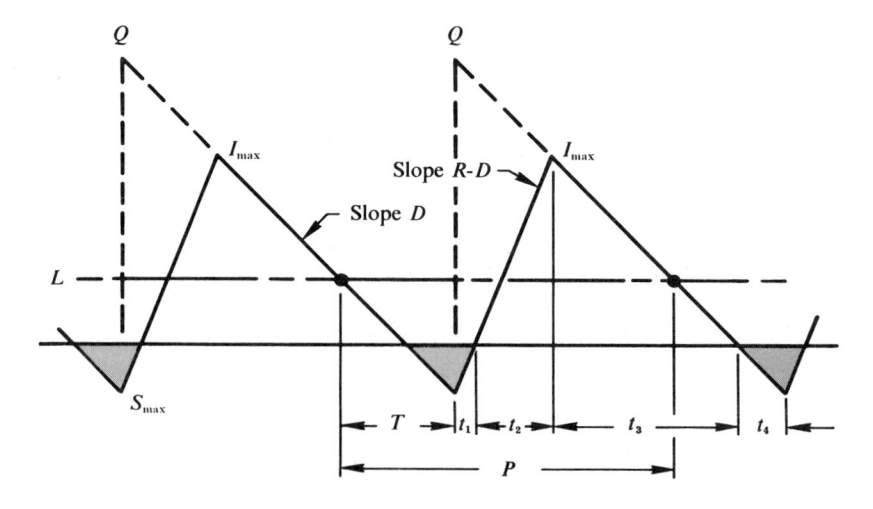

Figure 15.7 Finite replenishment rate with finite shortage cost.

Chap. 15   Deterministic Procurement and Inventory Models   353

From Equations (15.17), (15.18), and (15.19),

$$I_{max} + DT - L = \frac{Q}{R}(R - D)$$

$$I_{max} = \frac{Q}{R}(R - D) + L - DT \qquad (15.20)$$

$$= Q\left(1 - \frac{D}{R}\right) + L - DT.$$

The total number of unit periods of stock on hand during the inventory cycle is

$$I = \frac{I_{max}}{2}(t_2 + t_3)$$

$$= \frac{I^2_{max}}{2(R - D)} + \frac{I^2_{max}}{2D}$$

$$= \frac{I^2_{max}}{2}\left(\frac{1}{R - D} + \frac{1}{D}\right).$$

Substituting Equation (15.20) for I_{max} gives

$$I = \frac{[Q(1 - D/R) + L - DT]^2}{2D(1 - D/R)}. \qquad (15.21)$$

The total number of unit periods of shortage during the cycle is

$$S = \frac{S_{max}}{2}(t_1 + t_4)$$

$$= \frac{S^2_{max}}{2(R - D)} + \frac{S^2_{max}}{2D}.$$

But since $S_{max} = DT - L$,

$$S = \frac{(DT - L)^2}{2D(1 - D/R)}. \qquad (15.22)$$

As for the purchase model, the total system cost per period will be the item cost for the period, the procurement cost for the period, the holding cost for the period, and the shortage cost for the period; that is,

$$TC = IC + PC + HC + SC.$$

$$TC = C_iD + \frac{C_pD}{Q} + \frac{C_h}{2Q(1 - D/R)}\left[Q\left(1 - \frac{D}{R}\right) + L - DT\right]^2 \qquad (15.23)$$

$$+ \frac{C_s(DT - L)^2}{2Q(1 - D/R)}.$$

Equation (15.23) may be modified as follows:

$$TC = C_iD + \frac{C_pD}{Q} + \frac{C_hQ(1 - D/R)}{2} - C_h(DT - L)$$

$$+ \frac{C_h(DT - L)^2}{2Q(1 - D/R)} + \frac{C_s(DT - L)^2}{2Q(1 - D/R)}.$$

As for the purchase model, total system cost is a function of two independent variables, L and Q. Taking the partial derivative of TC with respect to Q and $DT - L$ and setting these equal to zero gives

$$\frac{\partial TC}{\partial Q} = -\frac{C_p D}{Q^2} + \frac{C_h(1 - D/R)}{2} - \frac{C_h(DT - L)^2}{2Q^2(1 - D/R)} - \frac{C_s(DT - L)^2}{2Q^2(1 - D/R)} = 0 \quad (15.24)$$

$$\frac{\partial TC}{\partial (DT - L)} = -C_h + \frac{C_h(DT - L)}{Q(1 - D/R)} + \frac{C_s(DT - L)}{Q(1 - D/R)} = 0. \quad (15.25)$$

From Equation (15.25)

$$\frac{DT - L}{Q} = \frac{C_h(1 - D/R)}{C_h + C_s}. \quad (15.26)$$

Substituting Equation (15.26) into Equation (15.24) gives

$$-\frac{C_p D}{Q^2} + \frac{C_h(1 - D/R)}{2} - \frac{C_h^2(1 - D/R)}{2(C_h + C_s)^2} - \frac{C_s C_h^2(1 - D/R)}{2(C_h + C_s)^2} = 0$$

$$\frac{C_p D}{Q^2} = \frac{C_h C_s(1 - D/R)}{2(C_h + C_s)}$$

$$Q = \sqrt{\frac{2C_p D(C_h + C_s)}{C_h C_s(1 - D/R)}} \quad (15.27)$$

$$Q = \sqrt{\frac{1}{1 - D/R}} \sqrt{\frac{2C_p D}{C_h} + \frac{2C_p D}{C_s}}.$$

Equation (15.27) gives the minimum cost procurement quantity as a function of demand, the replenishment rate, procurement cost, holding cost, and shortage cost.

The minimum cost procurement level may be derived from Equation (15.26) as

$$L = DT - \frac{C_h(1 - D/R)}{C_h + C_s} \sqrt{\frac{1}{1 - D/R}} \sqrt{\frac{2C_p D}{C_h} + \frac{2C_p D}{C_s}}$$

$$= DT - \sqrt{1 - \frac{D}{R}} \sqrt{\frac{2C_p D}{C_s(1 + C_s/C_h)}}. \quad (15.28)$$

Equations (15.27) and (15.28) may now be substituted back into the total cost equation to yield an expression for minimum total system cost. The result is

$$TC_{\min} = C_i D + \sqrt{1 - \frac{D}{R}} \sqrt{\frac{2C_p C_h C_s D}{C_h + C_s}}. \quad (15.29)$$

Equation (15.27) reduces to Equation (15.14), Equation (15.28) reduces to Equation (15.15), and Equation (15.29) reduces to Equation (15.16) as $R \to \infty$. Thus, the purchase model with finite shortage cost is a special case of the manufacture model with finite shortage cost. In fact, it can be shown that all previously derived models are special cases of the manufacture model with finite shortage cost.

Chap. 15   Deterministic Procurement and Inventory Models   355

A Manufacture Decision for Finite Shortage Cost. To illustrate the analysis required for the manufacturing model with finite shortage cost, assume that a manufacturing source is being considered as an alternative to the purchase source of the previous example. For simplicity, item cost will not be a function of the procurement quantity; that is, manufacturing progress does not occur. Data relating to the manufacturing source indicate that item cost is $4.80 per unit, procurement cost is $100, the production rate is 20 units per period, and the lead time is 12 periods.

The minimum total system cost may be calculated from Equation (15.29) as follows:

$$TC_{min} = \$4.80(10) + \sqrt{1 - \frac{10}{20}} \sqrt{\frac{2(\$100)(\$0.20)(\$0.10)(10)}{\$0.20 + \$0.10}} = \$56.16$$

Since this minimum total system cost is higher than the minimum total system cost for the purchase alternative, purchasing is to be preferred. The minimum cost procurement quantity and procurement level may be found from Equations (15.27) and (15.28) as follows:

$$Q = \sqrt{\frac{1}{1 - (10/20)}} \sqrt{\frac{2(\$100)(10)}{\$0.20} + \frac{2(\$100)(10)}{\$0.10}} = 245 \text{ units}$$

$$L = 10(12) - \sqrt{1 - \frac{10}{20}} \sqrt{\frac{2(\$100)(10)}{\$0.10[1 + (\$0.10/\$0.20)]}} = 38 \text{ units.}$$

The demand for the item will be met by purchasing in lots of 69 units when the stock on hand and on order falls to 114 units. It should be noted that the item in question is to be purchased in spite of the fact that the item cost per unit is $5.00 − $4.80 = $0.20 more than for manufacturing.

15.8 PROCUREMENT TO MEET VARIABLE DEMAND

A procurement model for a sequence of decisions over time is presented in this section for the case of variable demand. The amount to procure to meet demand must be determined at the beginning of each time period. The demand over a planning horizon is specified, the cost of procurement is known, and the cost of holding stock is specified. The objective is to minimize total cost over the planning horizon.

Formulation of the Problem. The problem under consideration is based on the following assumptions:

1. Procurement lead time is zero.
2. Procurement action can be initiated only at the beginning of a period.
3. There is no stock on hand at the beginning of the first or at the end of the last period.

4. Demand occurs at the beginning of the period.
5. No shortages are allowed.

Demand for the item is to span a five-period planning horizon with a requirement schedule of 10, 20, 30, 30, and 20 units. Procurement quantities must be in increments of 10 units with a maximum quantity of 60 units. Procurement cost is $20 per procurement. Holding cost for the period is based on the stock level at the end of the period and is $0.10 per unit per period. The maximum stock level is 40 units.

Let I_i be the stock level during period i, let Q_i be the quantity procured at the beginning of the period, and let D_i be the demand at the beginning of the period. Also, let $(PC)_i$ be the procurement cost for the period and $(HC)_i$ be the holding cost for the period. The objective is to minimize total system cost over the N period planning horizon. This may be expressed as

$$TC = \sum_{i=1}^{N} [(PC)_i + (HC)_i]. \tag{15.30}$$

A decision to procure a quantity Q_i at the beginning of the ith period will bring the stock level up to I_i in the period. This requires that

$$I_{i-1} = I_i + D_i - Q_i. \tag{15.31}$$

Since the stock level cannot exceed 40 units or be less than 0 units,

$$0 \leq I_{i-1} \leq 40.$$

Substituting Equation (15.31) for I_{i-1} gives

$$0 \leq I_i + D_i - Q_i \leq 40.$$

Solving for Q_i gives

$$I_i + D_i \geq Q_i \geq I_i + D_i - 40. \tag{15.32}$$

The principle of optimality from Chapter 6 on dynamic programming yields the following functional equation, which may be used to find a vector of procurement quantities that minimize total system cost over the planning horizon:

$$f_N(I_N) = \min_{I_N + D_N \geq Q_N \geq I_N + D_N - 40} \{g_N(Q_N + I_N) + f_{N-1}(I_{N-1})\}.$$

Substituting Equation (15.31) for I_{N-1} gives

$$f_N(I_N) = \min_{I_N + D_N \geq Q_N \geq I_N + D_N - 40} \{g_N(Q_N + I_N) + f_{N-1}(I_N + D_N - Q_N)\}. \tag{15.33}$$

The Computational Procedure. First, the cost of a one-stage process is computed from Equation (15.33) as

$$f_1(I_1) = \min \{g_1(Q_1 + I_1)\}.$$

For values of I_2 ranging from 0 to 40 units and $D_1 = 10$, this gives

$$f_1(\ 0) = g_1(10 + \ 0) = 20 + 0 = 20$$

Chap. 15 Deterministic Procurement and Inventory Models

$$f_1(10) = g_1(20 + 10) = 20 + 1 = 21$$
$$f_1(20) = g_1(30 + 20) = 20 + 2 = 22$$
$$f_1(30) = g_1(40 + 30) = 20 + 3 = 23$$
$$f_1(40) = g_1(50 + 40) = 20 + 4 = 24.$$

This completes the computation of $f_1(I_1)$. Each value is entered in the first stage of Table 15.4 together with its associated value of Q_1.

Table 15.4. TABULAR SOLUTION FOR VARIABLE DEMAND PROCUREMENT

I	Q_1	$f_1(I)$	Q_2	$f_2(I)$	Q_3	$f_3(I)$	Q_4	$f_4(I)$	Q_5	$f_5(I)$
0	10	20	0*	22	30*	42	0	45	0*	64
10	20	21	0	24	40	43	0	49	30	66
20	30*	22	0	26	50	44	50*	64	40	67
30	40	23	50	43	60	45	60	65	50	68
40	50	24	60	44	60	48	60	67	60	69

The second-period values, $f_2(I_2)$, may be computed using the results of $f_1(I_1)$. Thus, for the second period

$$f_2(I_2) = \min_{I_2 + D_2 \geq Q_2 \geq I_2 + D_2 - 40} \{g_2(Q_2 + I_2) + f_1(I_2 + D_2 - Q_2)\}.$$

When $I_2 = 0$,

$$f_2(0) = \min_{0 \leq Q_2 \leq 20} \{g_2(Q_2 + 0) + f_1(0 + 20 - Q_2)\}.$$

For values of Q_2 ranging from 0 to 20, this gives

$$f_2(0) = \min \begin{cases} g_2(\ 0 + 0) + f_1(0 + 20 - \ 0) = 0 + 0 + 22 = 22 \\ g_2(10 + 0) + f_1(0 + 20 - 10) = 20 + 0 + 21 = 41 \\ g_2(20 + 0) + f_1(0 + 20 - 20) = 20 + 0 + 20 = 40 \end{cases}.$$

When $I_2 = 10$,

$$f_2(10) = \min_{0 \leq Q_2 \leq 30} \{g_2(Q_2 + 10) + f_1(10 + 20 - Q_2)\}.$$

For values of Q_2 ranging from 0 to 30, this gives

$$f_2(10) = \min \begin{cases} g_2(\ 0 + 10) + f_1(10 + 20 - \ 0) = 0 + 1 + 23 = 24 \\ g_2(10 + 10) + f_1(10 + 20 - 10) = 20 + 1 + 22 = 43 \\ g_2(20 + 10) + f_1(10 + 20 - 20) = 20 + 1 + 21 = 42 \\ g_2(30 + 10) + f_1(10 + 20 - 30) = 20 + 1 + 20 = 41 \end{cases}.$$

When $I_2 = 20$,

$$f_2(20) = \min_{0 \leq Q_2 \leq 40} \{g_2(Q_2 + 20) + f_1(20 + 20 - Q_2)\}.$$

For values of Q_2 ranging from 0 to 40, this gives

$$f_2(20) = \min \begin{cases} g_2(\ 0 + 20) + f_1(20 + 20 - \ 0) = \ 0 + 2 + 24 = 26 \\ g_2(10 + 20) + f_1(20 + 20 - 10) = 20 + 2 + 23 = 45 \\ g_2(20 + 20) + f_1(20 + 20 - 20) = 20 + 2 + 22 = 44 \\ g_2(30 + 20) + f_1(20 + 20 - 30) = 20 + 2 + 21 = 43 \\ g_2(40 + 20) + f_1(20 + 20 - 40) = 20 + 2 + 20 = 42 \end{cases}.$$

When $I_2 = 30$,

$$f_2(30) \quad \min_{10 \leq Q_2 \leq 50} \{g_2(Q_2 + 30) + f_1(30 + 20 - Q_2)\}.$$

For values of Q_2 ranging from 10 to 50, this gives

$$f_2(30) = \min \begin{cases} g_2(10 + 30) + f_1(30 + 20 - 10) = 20 + 3 + 24 = 47 \\ g_2(20 + 30) + f_1(30 + 20 - 20) = 20 + 3 + 23 = 46 \\ g_2(30 + 30) + f_1(30 + 20 - 30) = 20 + 3 + 22 = 45 \\ g_2(40 + 30) + f_1(30 + 20 - 40) = 20 + 3 + 21 = 44 \\ g_2(50 + 30) + f_1(30 + 20 - 50) = 20 + 3 + 20 = 43 \end{cases}.$$

When $I_2 = 40$,

$$f_2(40) = \min_{20 \leq Q_2 \leq 60} \{g_2(Q_2 + 40) + f_1(40 + 20 - Q_2)\}.$$

For values of Q_2 ranging from 20 to 60, this gives

$$f_2(40) = \min \begin{cases} g_2(20 + 40) + f_1(40 + 20 - 20) = 20 + 4 + 24 = 48 \\ g_2(30 + 40) + f_1(40 + 20 - 30) = 20 + 4 + 23 = 47 \\ g_2(40 + 40) + f_1(40 + 20 - 40) = 20 + 4 + 22 = 46 \\ g_2(50 + 40) + f_1(40 + 20 - 50) = 20 + 4 + 21 = 45 \\ g_2(60 + 40) + f_1(40 + 20 - 60) = 20 + 4 + 20 = 44 \end{cases}.$$

This completes the computation of $f_2(I_2)$. The minimum value of $f_2(I_2)$ is identified for each value of I_2 and entered in the second stage of Table 15.4 together with its associated value of Q_2. The third, fourth, and fifth stages are calculated in the same manner, and the minimum results are used to complete Table 15.4.

The sequence of procurement quantities resulting in a minimum cost can now be found. First, the total system cost for the planning horizon is seen to be $64 from Table 15.4. This has an associated Q_5 of 0 units. From Equation (15.31) the value of I_4 is found to be $0 + 20 - 0 = 20$. Reference to Table 15.4 indicates that Q_4 should be 50 units. Again applying Equation (15.31) gives a value for I_3 of $20 + 30 - 50 = 0$. This gives a value for Q_3 of 30 units in Table 15.4. Continuing the foregoing analysis gives $Q_2 = 0$ and $Q_1 = 30$. The vector of procurement quantities previously identified is designated by asterisks in Table 15.4.

15.9 PROCUREMENT BASED ONLY ON ITEM COST

Procurement and inventory models presented up to this point took into consideration item cost, procurement cost, holding cost, and shortage cost. In this section it is assumed that the decision maker wishes to focus only on item cost as the basis for making the procurement source decision. Other costs known to exist are assumed to be equal for each source considered, or they are purposely ignored.

As a trivial example of item cost procurement, consider a situation in which an item is experiencing a demand of 8 units per period. Two vendors are under consideration as potential sources for the item. Vendor A quotes a per unit price of $28 and vendor B quotes a per unit price of $31. The total cost per period for purchasing from vendor A is $224 and the total cost per period for purchasing from vendor B is $248. Thus, vendor A would be chosen as the procurement source.

As an expanded example, suppose that the decision maker may consider manufacturing the item in question. Parameters associated with the manufacturing facility for this item are as follows:

$$\phi = 0.85$$
$$K = 4 \text{ hours}$$
$$N = 400 \text{ units}$$
$$dl = \$7.00 \text{ per hour}$$
$$dm = \$7.90 \text{ per unit}$$
$$fb = 0.80$$

The average item cost per unit may be found from Equation (11.10) as follows:

$$C_i = \frac{4(400)^{(\log 0.85/\log 2)}}{(\log 0.85/\log 2) + 1}(\$7.00)(1 + 0.80) + \$7.90$$

$$= \frac{0.978}{0.765}(\$12.60) + \$7.90 = \$24.$$

Therefore, with a demand of 8 units per period, the total cost per period for manufacturing is $192, which makes it the minimum cost procurement alternative.

Suppose that the decision maker, in the situation above, faces a source capacity constraint on the manufacturing facility. Each unit manufactured will consume 1.5 hours of scarce machine time. No more than 9 hours of machine time may be assigned to this product per period. The vendors under consideration may supply the item in unlimited quantity; that is, they can meet any demand schedule presented by the decision maker.

The capacity constraint on the manufacturing facility requires that no more than 6 units per period be procured from the manufacturing facility. The remaining 2 units required each period must be purchased. Therefore, the total number of units to be manufactured is reduced from 400 to 300. The item cost per unit for manufacturing is now

$$C_i = \frac{4(300)^{(\log 0.85/\log 2)}}{(\log 0.85/\log 2) + 1}(\$7.00)(1 + 0.80) + \$7.90$$

$$= \frac{1.05}{0.765}(\$12.60) + \$7.90 = \$25.20.$$

Parameters pertaining to this procurement situation are given in Table 15.5.

Table 15.5. PARAMETERS FOR ITEM COST PROCUREMENT

Parameter	Vendor A	Vendor B	Manufacture
C_i	$28.00	$31.00	$25.20
h	—	—	1.5
H	—	—	9

The total system cost is minimized by procuring 6 units per period from the manufacturing facility and 2 units per period from vendor A. The total system cost is $25.20(6) + $28.00(2) = $207.20 per period. Thus, the system manager suffers a penalty of $207.20 − $192.00 = $15.20 per period due to the existence of a capacity constraint.

The general solution method for problems of this type is to allocate the required quantity to the least cost source up to the maximum allowed by the constraint. Remaining requirements are allocated to the source exhibiting the next lowest cost up to the maximum allowed by its constraint. The procedure is continued until all requirements are met or all source capacities are exhausted.

In general, if there are n sources, with each source requiring h_j hours of scarce capacity for each unit and having H_j hours of total capacity, the problem requires the minimization of

$$TC = C_{i1}d_1 + C_{i2}d_2 + \cdots + C_{in}d_n$$

subject to

$$d_1 + d_2 + \cdots + d_n = D$$

and

$$h_1 d_1 \leq H_1$$
$$h_2 d_2 \leq H_2$$
$$\vdots$$
$$h_n d_n \leq H_n,$$

where $d_1, d_2, \ldots, d_n$ are the portions of demand to be satisfied from each source.

This general statement of the multisource procurement problem with source capacity constraints conforms to the general linear programming model. Therefore, graphical procedures or the simplex procedure may be used for its solution. As an example of the graphical approach, consider the procurement situation given earlier. Minimize

$$TC = \$28.00d_A + \$25.20d_M$$

subject to

$$d_A + d_M = 8$$

and

$$1.5d_M \leq 9,$$

where d_A and d_M are the portions of demand to be met by vendor A and from the manufacturing facility, respectively.

Figure 15.8 exhibits the graphical approach to minimizing the total cost function. The region of feasible solution is bounded by the demand restriction and the source capacity restriction. The minimum cost procurement program occurs when the isocost line is a minimum orthognal distance from the origin with at least one point in the region of feasible solution. This occurs at $d_A = 2$ and $d_M = 6$, as was indicated previously.

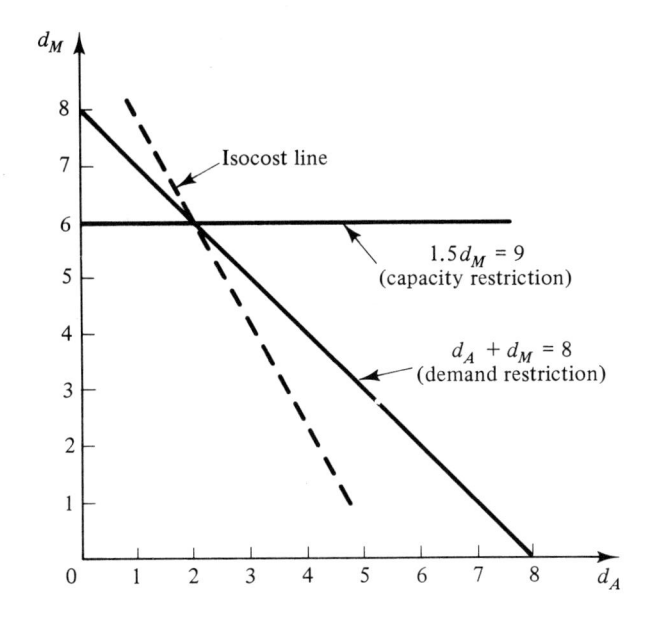

Figure 15.8 Graphical solution for constrained procurement problem.

QUESTIONS

15.1. What is the justification for procuring and holding inventory?

15.2. Describe the source alternatives available to the inventory manager.

15.3. Give several reasons why procurement lead time will depend on the source chosen.

15.4. Give several reasons why item cost will depend on the source chosen.

15.5. Give several reasons why procurement cost will depend on the source chosen.

15.6. What factors should be considered in arriving at a specific value for holding cost?

15.7. What factors should be considered in arriving at a specific value for shortage cost?

15.8. Classify all parameters of the procurement and inventory system in terms of $E = f(x_i, y_j)$.

15.9. Describe the trade-off relationships in the models for infinite shortage cost and finite shortage cost.

15.10. Item cost may be a function of both the source and the procurement quantity. Explain.

PROBLEMS

15.1. A contractor has a requirement for cement that amounts to 300 bags per day. No shortages are to be allowed. Cement costs $3.80 per bag, holding cost is $0.01 per bag per day, and it costs $60 to process a purchase order.
  (a) Find the minimum cost purchase quantity.
  (b) Find the minimum cost procurement level if the purchase lead time is 2 days.
  (c) Calculate the total system cost per day.

15.2. An engine manufacturer requires 82 pistons per day in his assembly operations. No shortages are to be allowed. The machine shop can produce 500 pistons per day. The cost associated with initiating manufacturing action is $400, and the holding cost is $0.45 per piston per day. The manufacturing cost is $105 per piston.
  (a) Find the minimum cost production quantity.
  (b) Find the minimum cost procurement level if production lead time is 8 days.
  (c) Calculate the total system cost per day.

15.3. Show that Q becomes infinite and TC approaches $C_i D$ as D approaches R for the production model with infinite shortage cost.

15.4. The demand for a certain item is 12 units per period. No shortages are to be allowed. Holding cost is $0.02 per unit per period. Demand can be met either by purchasing or manufacturing, with each source described by the following data:

	Purchase	*Manufacture*
Procurement lead time	18 periods	13 periods
Item cost	$11.00	$9.60
Procurement cost	$20.00	$90.00
Replenishment rate	∞	25 units per period

  (a) Find the minimum cost procurement source and calculate its economic advantage over its alternative source.

(b) Find the minimum cost procurement quantity.
(c) Find the minimum cost procurement level.

15.5. The army mess sergeant at Camp Swampy is responsible for meeting a demand of 6 bushels of potatoes per day. No shortages are permitted under technical order CS-174. Holding cost for potatoes is $0.04 per bushel per day. The demand can be met from one of three government-certified farmers in the immediate area. Farmer Brown requires a lead time of 6 days and attempts to gouge the army to the extent of $8.40 per bushel. Farmer Smith requires 8 days lead time but only charges $8.30 per bushel. The procurement cost from either of these two farmers is $12.00. Farmer Jones sells his wormy potatoes for only $8.10 per bushel. The procurement cost of dealing with Jones is $14.00 with a lead time of 10 days.
(a) Find the minimum cost procurement source.
(b) Find the minimum cost procurement quantity.
(c) Find the minimum cost procurement level.

15.6. Suppose that the price per bag of cement required by the contractor of Problem 15.1 is quoted in accordance with the following schedule:

Purchase Quantity (bags)	Price per Bag
0–1,999	$3.80
2,000–3,999	3.60
4,000–5,999	3.40
6,000 or more	3.20

(a) Find the minimum cost procurement quantity and procurement level.
(b) Calculate the total system cost per day for meeting the demand and compare with the result of Problem 15.1.

15.7. Suppose that the learning factor associated with the manufacture of pistons described in Problem 15.2 is found to be 0.90. The following data describe the manufacturing facility:

$$K = 20 \text{ hours}$$
$$lr = \$5.50 \text{ per hour}$$
$$dm = \$65.00 \text{ per piston}$$
$$fb = 0.75 \text{ of direct labor cost}$$
$$R = 500 \text{ units per period}$$

(a) What is the minimum total system cost per day with and without learning, if the total number of units required is 5,000?
(b) Find the minimum cost procurement quantity and procurement level.

15.8. A subcontractor has been found who can supply pistons to the manufacturer described in Problem 15.2. Procurement cost will be $90 per purchase order. The cost per unit is a function of the purchase quantity as follows:

Purchase Quantity	Price per Piston
1–199	$115
200–499	110
500 or more	100

(a) Calculate the minimum total system cost per day for purchasing from the subcontractor.

(b) What is the economic advantage of adopting the minimum cost source?

15.9. The demand for a certain item is 16 units per period. Unsatisfied demand causes a shortage cost of $0.75 per unit short per period. The cost of initiating purchasing action is $15 per purchase and the holding cost is $0.05 per unit per period. The item cost is $8.00 per unit.

(a) Find the minimum cost purchase quantity.

(b) Find the minimum cost procurement level if lead time is 8 periods.

(c) Calculate the total system cost per period.

15.10. A television set manufacturing firm has a demand of 250 units per period. It costs $400 to initiate manufacturing action to produce at the rate of 600 units per period. The unit production cost is $90. The holding cost is $0.15 per unit per period and the shortage cost is $3.25 per unit short per period for unsatisfied demand. Determine (a) the minimum cost manufacturing quantity, (b) the minimum cost procurement level if production lead time is 12 periods, and (c) the total system cost per period.

15.11. An electronics firm requires 25 pounds (1 pound = 5,000 feet) of 30 AWG stranded wire per day. The shortage cost is $0.005 per 1,000 feet per day, and the holding cost is $0.01 per 1,000 feet per day. The following data apply to the purchase and the manufacture alternatives:

	Purchase	Manufacture
Item cost per pound	$20.00	$17.50
Procurement cost	$15.00	$225.00
Replenishment rate	∞	80 pounds per day

Determine whether it is more economical to purchase or produce the wire.

15.12. In Problem 15.10, the learning factor associated with the manufacture of television sets is found to be 0.85. The following data apply to the facility:

$K = 24$ hours
$lr = \$6.00$ per hour
$dm = \$40.00$ per television set
$fb = 1.10$ of direct labor cost
$R = 600$ units per period

Determine (a) the minimum cost procurement quantity and procurement level, and (b) the minimum total system cost per period with and without learning, if the total number of units required is 6,000.

15.13. Show that Q becomes infinite and TC approaches $C_i D$ as D approaches R for the production model with finite shortage cost.

15.14. Show that Equations (15.27) and (15.28) reduce to Equations (15.14) and (15.15), respectively, when R approaches infinity.

15.15. Show that Equations (15.27) and (15.28) reduce to Equations (15.2) and (15.3), respectively, when both R and C_s approach infinity.

Chap. 15 Deterministic Procurement and Inventory Models

15.16. Derive expressions for the minimum cost procurement quantity and minimum cost procurement level when C_h is assumed to be infinite. Name a real-world situation where such a model would apply.

15.17. The demand for electric heaters during the next six periods is expected to be 200, 300, 400, 300, 300, and 200 units. The procurement cost is $15 per procurement, and the storage cost is $0.03 per unit per period. Procurements can only be made in lot sizes of 100 units, with a maximum of 700 units. The maximum stock level is 500 units. Determine the maximum profit procurement schedule based on the assumptions in Section 15.8.

15.18. Two needed items may be procured from either of two sources of supply. Data pertaining to each item and each source are given below. Find the procurement source for each item that will result in a minimum total system cost per period. Compare this procurement policy with the next best policy and find the per period cost difference.

	Source A	Source B	
Item 1	$C_i = \$4$	$C_i = \$5$	$D = 6$
Item 2	$C_i = \$6$	$C_i = \$8$	$D = 9$

15.19. Suppose that the procurement situation in Problem 15.18 is subject to the constraints given in the table below. Find the number of each unit to procure from each source so that the total cost per period is minimized.

	Source A	Source B	
Item 1	$C_i = \$4$, $h = 5$	$C_i = \$5$, $h = 6$	$D = 6$
Item 2	$C_i = \$6$, $h = 7$	$C_i = \$8$, $h = 8$	$D = 9$
	$H = 25$	$H = 80$	

16

Probabilistic Inventory Models

A probabilistic procurement and inventory process will result if either demand or procurement lead time, or both, are random variables. Under these conditions, it is not possible to keep both the procurement quantity and the number of periods per cycle fixed, as is the case with the deterministic assumption of Chapter 15. The most common inventory system is that in which the procurement quantity is fixed and the procurement interval is allowed to vary. Models for the probabilistic inventory process will be developed from expressions for expected values under the assumption that the probability distribution function of future demand is known.

The derivation of optimal policy is simplified in this chapter by the consideration of expected outcomes. Also, this chapter avoids the complication of multiple replenishment sources. The additional simplification of an infinite replenishment rate is adopted. The resulting inventory models may be used to derive the minimum cost procurement level and procurement quantity for a single source. Numerical methods must be used for finding this minimum in most cases. Mathematical minimization is illustrated by formulating a simplified system. The probabilistic models of this chapter can be used to make source decisions if source parameters are considered in the manner of Chapter 15.

16.1 SIMULATION OF INVENTORY FLOW[1]

The probabilistic inventory process may be most easily described by performing simulated sampling or Monte Carlo analysis of inventory flow over time. This does not mean that the simulated flow exactly parallels the real-world process that it patterns. The simulation never deviates from the policies established, whereas in the real world such compliance will not occur. Nevertheless, the results provide a useful standard against which expressions for expected values for the probabilistic inventory system can be checked. Thus, simulated sampling analysis provides the basis for deriving probabilistic inventory models.

Demand and Lead Time Distributions. The probabilistic inventory process usually involves both a demand distribution and a procurement lead time distribution. The form and parameters of these distributions must be specified. The cumulative distributions may then be developed and used as a source of demand and lead time data needed in the simulated sampling analysis.

For the example under consideration, assume that demand has a Poisson distribution with a mean of 0.6 unit per period. Lead time will be assumed to have an empirical distribution with a mean of 4.3 periods. Figure 16.1 is an illustration of these distributions giving specific values for the random variables, together with their associated probabilities. Note that D_x and T_x are used to designate demand and lead time random variables, respectively, and that D_m and T_m are mean or expected values of the distributions.

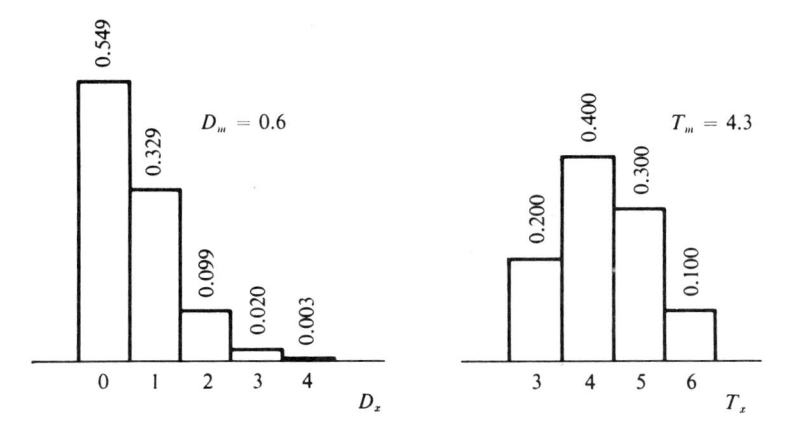

Figure 16.1 Demand and lead time distributions.

By summing the probabilities from left to right, and plotting the results, cumulative distributions may be developed. Figure 16.2 illustrates the cumulative distributions that result from the demand and lead time distributions of Figure

---

[1] It is suggested that Appendix C, Section C.5, be reviewed as a prerequisite to this section.

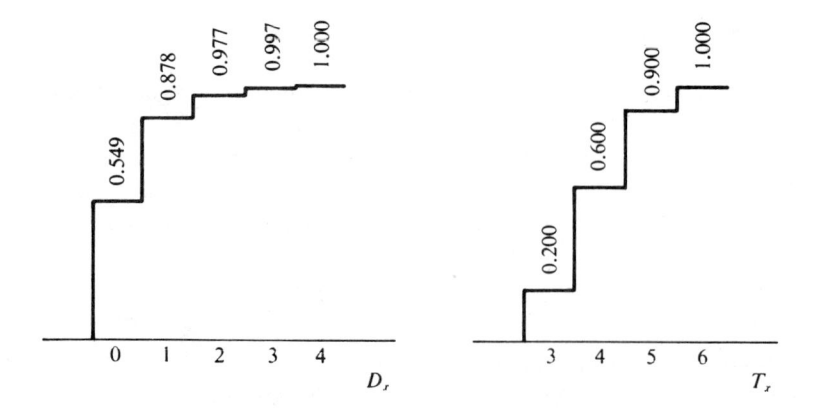

Figure 16.2 Cumulative demand and lead time distributions.

16.1. These are used with random rectangular variables to generate demand and lead time data for the simulated inventory flow process.

The Simulated Sampling Analysis. The inventory flow process operates in accordance with certain policies established by the decision maker. These must be obeyed in the analysis. For this example, assume that the procurement level is 3 units and that the procurement quantity is 12 units. It will be shown later that these policies lead to a minimum total system cost for the example under consideration.

The simulation process of this example begins with the stock on hand equal to the procurement level. At the beginning of each period, stock on hand plus stock on order is checked against the procurement level. If the procurement level has been reached or exceeded, an order is placed for an amount equal to the procurement quantity. A value is then drawn at random from the lead time distribution and retained.

If the procurement level has not been reached, a value is drawn at random from the demand distribution. This value is subtracted from the stock on hand, resulting in a new stock level at the end of the period. Since one period has passed, 1 is subtracted from all outstanding lead time values. If a lead time value is reduced to zero, an amount equal to the procurement quantity is added to the stock on hand. The statistics for the period are calculated and the next period is considered. If a lead time value is not reduced to zero, period statistics are calculated and the next period is considered. Refer to Table 16.1 and Figure 16.3 in order to get a more complete understanding of the simulation scheme.

Column C of Table 16.1 indicates that the stock on hand at the beginning of the first cycle is 3 units. Since the procurement level has been reached, a procurement order for 12 units is placed. This is shown by the dashed line in Figure 16.3. Next, a value is drawn at random from the cumulative lead time distribution of Figure 16.2 and entered in column D. A value is then drawn at random from the cumulative demand distribution of Figure 16.3 and entered

Table 16.1. SIMULATED SAMPLING ANALYSIS OF INVENTORY FLOW

(A) Cycle	(B) Period	(C) Initial Stock	(D) Lead Time, T_x	(E) Demand, D_x	(F) Final Stock	(G) Units on Hand	(H) Units Short
1	1	3	4	0	3	3	0
	2	3		1	2	3	0
	3	2		0	2	2	0
	4	2		0	14	2	0
	5	14		1	13	14	0
	6	13		0	13	13	0
	7	13		1	12	13	0
	8	12		1	11	12	0
	9	11		2	9	11	0
	10	9		0	9	9	0
	11	9		0	9	9	0
	12	9		0	9	9	0
	13	9		0	9	9	0
	14	9		1	8	9	0
	15	8		3	5	8	0
	16	5		1	4	5	0
	17	4		1	3	4	0
2	1	3	5	3	3	3	0
	2	3		0	3	3	0
	3	3		1	2	3	0
	4	2		0	2	2	0
	5	2		0	14	2	0
	6	14		1	13	14	0
	7	13		1	12	13	0
	8	12		0	12	12	0
	9	12		0	12	12	0
	10	12		0	12	12	0
	11	12		1	11	12	0
	12	11		0	11	11	0
	13	11		1	10	11	0
	14	10		0	10	10	0
	15	10		0	10	10	0
	16	10		3	7	10	0
	17	7		1	6	7	0
	18	6		0	6	6	0
	19	6		2	4	6	0
	20	4		2	2	4	0
3	1	2	4	0	2	2	0
	⋮	⋮	⋮	⋮	⋮	⋮	⋮

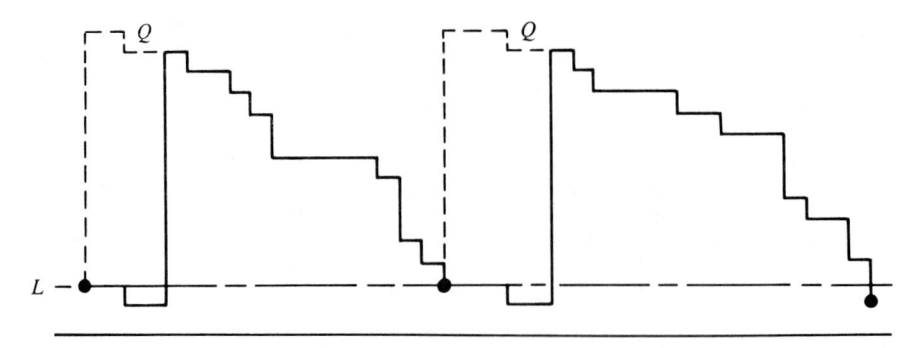

Figure 16.3 Monte Carlo analysis of inventory flow.

in column E. Since this value was 0 units, the final stock position of column F remains at 3 units.

Since one period is completed, it is now possible to compute three important statistics. First, it is noted that one period is added to the total number of periods for the cycle. This total number will appear in column B just before the beginning of the next cycle. The number of units on hand or short, as the case may be, is recorded in column G or H as required. These data will provide values for the total number of unit periods of stock on hand for the cycle and the total number of unit periods of shortage for the cycle.

The second period of this example begins with 3 units on hand, since the first period ended with 3 units. A random draw from the demand distribution gives a value of 1, which reduces the final stock for the period to 2 units. Since it is assumed that the demand occurs at the end of the period, the number of units on hand for the period is recorded in column G as 3. The third period begins with 2 units on hand, experienced no demand, and, therefore, had 2 units on hand. No demand was experienced for the fourth period, thus maintaining the stock on hand at 2 units. As a result of 4 lead time periods having elapsed, 12 units are added to the final stock position in column G. This is shown in Figure 16.3 at the point where the stock on hand rises sharply and the dashed line representing stock on order vanishes. Period 5 begins with 14 units on hand, experiences 1 demand, and ends with 13 units. Thus units on hand during the period are recorded as 14. Two complete cycles of inventory flow are developed and exhibited in Table 16.1. The entries for each period were developed as just outlined.

Output Statistics for Computer Simulation. As the simulated sampling analysis continues and cycle summary data are developed, a composite picture of the probabilistic inventory process begins to develop. Table 16.2 is an abridged cycle-by-cycle summary of the simulated inventory flow performed on a digital computer for 1,000 cycles. Column A gives the cycle number. Column B gives the number of periods in the cycle, designated P_x, since it is a random variable. Column C gives the running average, P_m, of the individual values in

Table 16.2. OUTPUT STATISTICS FOR COMPUTER SIMULATION

(A) Cycle	(B) P_x	(C) P_m	(D) I_x	(E) I_m	(F) S_x	(G) S_m
1	17	17.000	135	135.000	0	0.000
2	20	18.500	163	149.000	0	0.000
3	25	20.667	176	158.000	0	0.000
4	27	22.250	233	176.750	0	0.000
5	17	21.200	115	164.400	0	0.000
6	30	22.667	214	172.667	0	0.000
7	16	21.714	129	166.429	0	0.000
8	17	21.125	108	159.125	0	0.000
9	22	21.222	170	160.333	0	0.000
10	18	20.900	101	154.400	0	0.000
11	12	20.091	44	144.364	7	0.636
12	14	19.583	78	138.833	0	0.583
13	25	20.000	200	143.538	0	0.538
14	18	19.875	112	141.286	0	0.500
15	22	20.000	154	142.133	1	0.533
986	14	20.185	85	140.990	0	0.577
987	35	20.200	325	141.176	0	0.576
988	12	20.191	49	141.083	6	0.582
989	10	20.181	70	141.011	0	0.581
990	47	20.208	410	141.283	0	0.581
991	13	20.201	65	141.206	2	0.582
992	26	20.207	217	141.282	0	0.582
993	25	20.211	162	141.303	0	0.581
994	24	20.215	119	141.281	5	0.586
995	26	20.221	199	141.339	0	0.585
996	20	20.221	137	141.334	0	0.584
997	20	20.221	142	141.335	0	0.584
998	21	20.221	119	141.313	3	0.586
999	21	20.222	140	141.311	0	0.586
1000	19	20.221	135	141.305	0	0.585

column B. Column D gives the total number of unit periods of stock on hand for the cycle. This is designated I_x, since it is also a random variable. Its running average, I_m, is given in column E. Column F gives the total number of unit periods of shortage for the cycle. This is a random variable and is designated S_x. Its running mean, S_m, is given in column G. Table 16.1 and Figure 16.3 may be used to verify the values for P_x, I_x, and S_x given for cycles 1 and 2 in Table 16.2.

Each of these random variables may be histogrammed to describe further the nature of the probabilistic inventory process. These histograms are exhibited in Figures 16.4, 16.5, and 16.6. Although 1,000 cycles are not sufficient to give perfectly smooth histograms, a good idea of the distribution of each random variable is given.

The values for P_m, I_m, and S_m given at cycle 1,000 represent estimates of

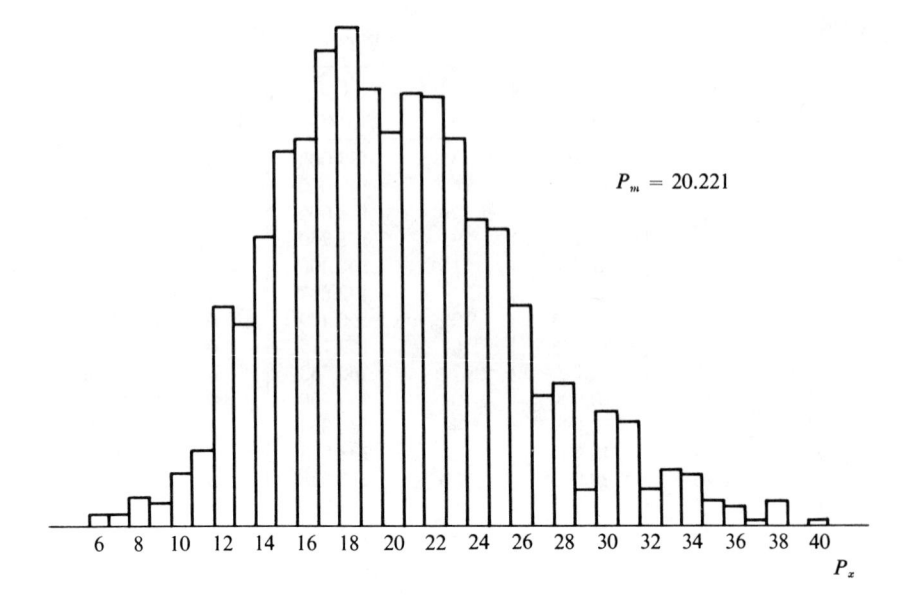

Figure 16.4 Distribution of number of periods per cycle.

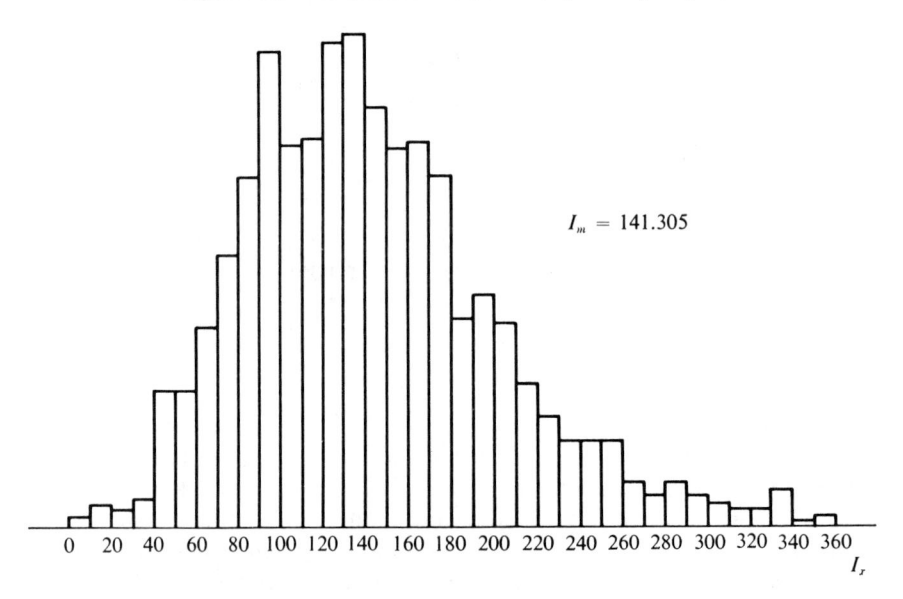

Figure 16.5 Distribution of total number of unit periods of stock per cycle.

the expected values for P_x, I_x, and S_x, respectively. The relative stability of the mean values may be noted by comparing the terminal cycles with the initial cycles in Table 16.2. Continuing the simulation beyond 1,000 cycles would contribute further to their stability.

Chap. 16   Probabilistic Inventory Models   373

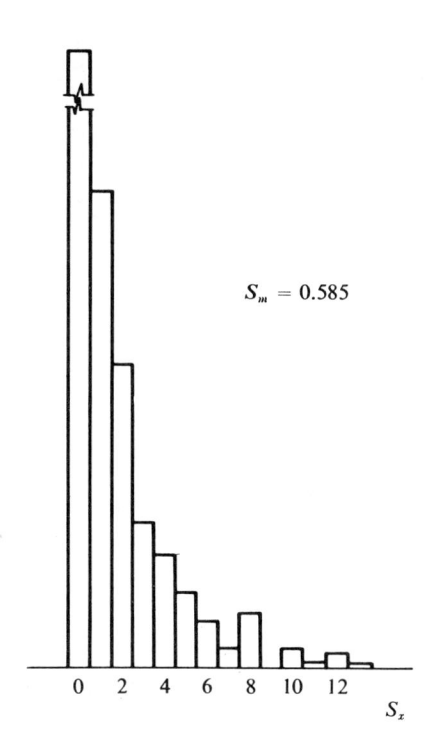

$S_m = 0.585$

Figure 16.6 Distribution of total number of unit periods of shortage per cycle.

0   2   4   6   8   10   12

S_x

16.2 EXPRESSIONS FOR EXPECTED VALUES

The simulation process of the preceding section provides expected values for three important random variables associated with the probabilistic inventory system. These values are needed in developing decision models for the process. Use of the simulation method to derive expected values for even a limited number of procurement level and procurement quantity combinations is obviously extremely time consuming. Hence, this section will derive expressions that approximate P_m and I_m. A direct development for S_m is presented in the following sections.

The Expected Inventory Geometry. Figure 16.3 illustrates the inventory process as it occurs under the influence of random elements. If variance were not present, the process would operate in accordance with its expected values. Inventory flow over time would appear as in Figure 16.7.

The geometry of the inventory process shown in Figure 16.7 does not differ from that for the deterministic system with instantaneous replenishment. Its orientation, however, is different. Provision is made for safety stock to absorb fluctuations in stock level from cycle to cycle. The need for this extra stock may be attributed to the presence of random elements.

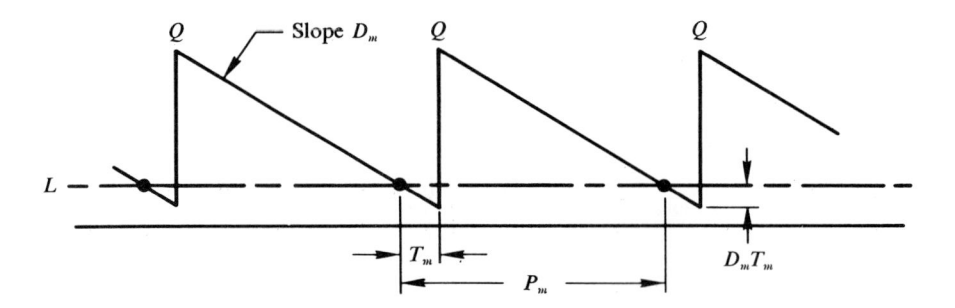

Figure 16.7 Expected inventory flow process.

The Expected Number of Periods per Cycle. Reference to Figure 16.7 indicates that the expected number of periods per cycle may be expressed as

$$P_m = T_m + \frac{Q - D_m T_m}{D_m} = \frac{Q}{D_m}. \tag{16.1}$$

The validity of this expression as a measure of the expected number of periods per cycle may be checked by reference to the simulated process. Substituting the values for Q and D_m used in the simulation results in

$$P_m = \frac{12}{0.6} = 20.000 \text{ periods}.$$

Since the value found by simulation was 20.221, it may be concluded that Equation (16.1) gives a good means for approximating the expected number of periods per cycle for the probabilistic inventory process. Intuitive reasoning indicates that this expression yields an exact value, the discrepancy being due to the lack of complete convergence at 1,000 cycles.

The Expected Total Number of Unit Periods of Stock. Figure 16.7 indicates that the expected total number of unit periods of stock on hand during the cycle is the sum of two components which may be approximated as

$$I_m = P_m\left(\frac{Q}{2}\right) + P_m(L - D_m T_m)$$

$$= \frac{Q}{D_m}\left[\frac{Q}{2} + (L - D_m T_m)\right]. \tag{16.2}$$

The validity of Equation (16.2) as an approximation for the total number of unit periods of stock on hand for the cycle may be checked by substituting the values of Q, L, D_m, and T_m used in the simulation. This results in

$$I_m = \frac{12}{0.6}\left[\frac{12}{2} + 3 - 0.6(4.3)\right] = 128.40 \text{ unit periods}.$$

The value found by simulation was 141.305 unit periods. This can be reduced by $\frac{1}{2}P_m D_m = \frac{1}{2}(20)(0.6) = 6$ unit periods to compensate because the simulation charged the entire period for the stock level at the beginning of the period. The simulated result is, therefore, 135.305 unit periods, which is comparable with the value found from Equation (16.2).

It may be concluded that Equation (16.2) yields only an approximation for the total number of unit periods of stock on hand for the cycle. This conclusion is supported by intuitive considerations and by the unlikelihood of a discrepancy of seven unit periods being entirely due to the lack of complete convergence at 1,000 cycles. Using expected values to derive an expression for expected area yields a biased result.

16.3 THE DISTRIBUTION OF LEAD TIME DEMAND

Expressions for the expected number of periods per inventory cycle, P_m, and for the expected number of unit periods of stock on hand for the cycle, I_m, were developed in the previous section. The derivation of an expression for the expected number of unit periods of shortage for the cycle, S_m, will deviate from the procedure used there. It requires the development of the distribution of lead time demand as an important intermediate step. The following paragraphs present an exact numerical method for developing this distribution.

Lead Time Demand. Lead time demand is demand summed over the lead time. When both demand and lead time are random variables, lead time demand may be expressed symbolically as

$$V_x = \sum^{T_x} D_x. \tag{16.3}$$

This expression indicates that lead time demand is the sum of all demand over the lead time. With the distribution of D_x and T_x given, it is possible to develop the distribution of V_x by Monte Carlo analysis. The method, however, requires considerable computational effort to give a good approximation of the actual distribution. For complete generality, it is necessary to have an exact method for developing the lead time demand distribution.

Figure 16.8 illustrates conditional distributions of lead time demand for several specific values of lead time. When viewed as a single distribution, Figure 16.8 may be called a *joint distribution of demand and lead time* if the total probability is adjusted to unity. The probability associated with any specific value of lead time demand may then be found by summing for that value across all lead time values.

The previous qualitative description may be quantified by adopting the following notation:

$V_x | T =$ lead time demand random variable, given that lead time is T periods

$f(V_x | T) =$ conditional lead time demand distribution, given that lead time is T periods

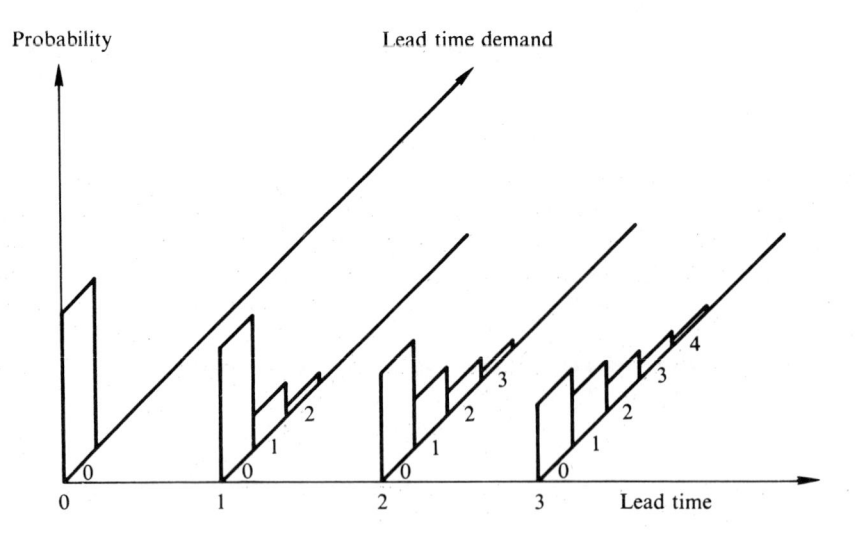

Figure 16.8 Joint distribution of demand and lead time.

The probability of $V_x \geq V$ for a specific lead time (conditional probability) is

$$P(V_x \geq V \mid T) = \sum_{V_x=V}^{V_{max}} f(V_x \mid T).$$

Multiplying by $f(T_x)$ and summing over all values of T gives

$$P(V_x \geq V) = \sum_{T=0}^{T_{max}} \left[f(T_x) \sum_{V_x=V}^{V_{max}} f(V_x \mid T) \right]. \tag{16.4}$$

The probability associated with each integral value of V_x may be found from Equation (16.4). This procedure is now illustrated with an example based on the distributions of Figure 16.1.

Numerical Development of Lead Time Demand. The computational procedure required in developing the distribution of lead time demand may best be explained by reference to Table 16.3. The first section is analogous to Figure 16.8 in that it gives the conditional distribution of lead time demand associated with each lead time value. For the case under consideration, conditional distributions are required for lead time values of 3, 4, 5, and 6. These conditional distributions are selected in accordance with the following rules:

1. If lead time is one period, the basic demand distribution is the lead time demand distribution. The probabilities of each value of D_x would be associated with the respective values of V_x under $T_x = 1$, if $T_x = 1$ were called for.
2. Enter V_x probabilities under $T_x = 2$, $T_x = 3, \ldots,$ associated with a demand distribution of the same form as the basic demand distribution,

Table 16.3. NUMERICAL DEVELOPMENT OF LEAD TIME DEMAND DISTRIBUTION

V_x	$P[V_x \mid T_x]$				$P(T_x, V_x) = P(T_x) \cdot P(V_x \mid T_x)$				$P(V_x)$
	$T_x=3$	$T_x=4$	$T_x=5$	$T_x=6$	$P(T_x=3)$ $=0.2$	$P(T_x=4)$ $=0.4$	$P(T_x=5)$ $=0.3$	$P(T_x=6)$ $=0.1$	
0	0.1653	0.0907	0.0498	0.0273	0.03306	0.03628	0.01494	0.00273	0.08701
1	0.2975	0.2177	0.1494	0.0984	0.05950	0.08708	0.04482	0.00984	0.20124
2	0.2678	0.2613	0.2240	0.1771	0.05356	0.10542	0.06720	0.01771	0.24299
3	0.1607	0.2090	0.2240	0.2125	0.03214	0.08360	0.06720	0.02125	0.20419
4	0.0723	0.1254	0.1680	0.1912	0.01446	0.05016	0.05040	0.01912	0.13414
5	0.0260	0.0602	0.1008	0.1377	0.00520	0.02408	0.03024	0.01377	0.07329
6	0.0078	0.0241	0.0504	0.0826	0.00156	0.00964	0.01512	0.00826	0.03458
7	0.0020	0.0083	0.0216	0.0425	0.00040	0.00332	0.00648	0.00425	0.01445
8	0.0005	0.0025	0.0081	0.0191	0.00010	0.00100	0.00243	0.00191	0.00544
9	0.0001	0.0007	0.0027	0.0076	0.00002	0.00028	0.00081	0.00076	0.00187
10		0.0002	0.0008	0.0028		0.00008	0.00024	0.00028	0.00060
11			0.0002	0.0009			0.00006	0.00009	0.00016
12			0.0001	0.0003			0.00003	0.00003	0.00004*
13				0.0001				0.00001	0.00001

but with parameters multiplied by 2, 3, ... In Table 16.3, this calls for Poisson probabilities for distributions with mean values of 1.8, 2.4, 3.0, and 3.6.

The second section of Table 16.3 involves adjustment of the total probability so it will sum to unity. The procedure is described by Equation (16.4) and is accomplished by multiplying each value of each conditional distribution by the probability of T_x taking its associated value. The result is a joint probability density function from which the lead time demand distribution may be developed.

The probability of lead time demand assuming the specific values specified as V_x in Table 16.3 may be found by summing across all values of $P(T_x, V_x)$ in the second section. The results are entered under $P(V_x)$ in the last column and make up a demand marginal distribution. This demand marginal distribution is the required lead time demand distribution for the demand and lead time distribution of Figure 16.1. It is histogrammed in Figure 16.9.

The numerical procedure presented in this section is applicable in those cases where demand has a Poisson, normal, or certain other distributions. In selecting the conditional distributions, it is necessary only to increase the parameters of the basic demand distribution by multiplying by the specific conditional lead time value. If demand obeys some other distribution form, this method for selecting the conditional distributions does not hold. The distribution of lead time need not conform to any specific form. Any theoretical or empirical distribution may be used.

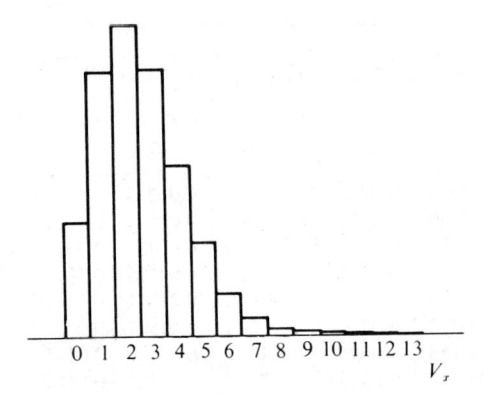

Figure 16.9 Distribution of lead time demand.

16.4 EXPRESSIONS FOR SHORTAGE CONDITION

Lead time demand is independent of the procurement level. A lead time demand distribution simply exhibits the number of demands that may occur during the lead time. The shortage condition at the end of the inventory cycle depends jointly upon the distribution of lead time demand and choice of procurement level. In this section, approximations for the probability of an empty warehouse, the probability of one or more shortages, the expected number of shortages, and the expected number of unit periods of shortage are developed. Completion of this phase will provide the third expected value needed in the derivation of effectiveness functions for the probabilistic inventory process.

The Probability of an Empty Warehouse. An empty warehouse will result if lead time demand is equal to or greater than the procurement level. If the lead time demand distribution is continuous, the probability of an empty warehouse at the end of the inventory cycle may be expressed as

$$P\{\text{empty warehouse}\} = \int_L^\infty f(V_x)\, dV_x.$$

For the discrete lead time demand distribution of Figure 16.9, the probability of an empty warehouse is

$$P\{\text{empty warehouse}\} = \sum_L^{V_{\max}} f(V_x).$$

The second column of Table 16.4 gives the probability of an empty warehouse as a function of the procurement level.

The probability of an empty warehouse, as an expression for shortage condition, fails to give a measure of the magnitude of the shortage condition (if any) or the time duration involved. As such, it is very difficult to establish a value for shortage cost. In fact, an empty warehouse is desirable if during the period no demand occurs.

Table 16.4. SHORTAGE PROBABILITIES AS A FUNCTION OF L

L	P {empty warehouse}	P {1 or more short}
0	1.00000	0.91299
1	0.91299	0.71175
2	0.71175	0.46876
3	0.46876	0.26457
4	0.26457	0.13043
5	0.13043	0.05714
6	0.05714	0.02256
7	0.02256	0.00811
8	0.00811	0.00267
9	0.00267	0.00080
10	0.00080	0.00020
11	0.00020	0.00005
12	0.00005	0.00001
13	0.00001	0.00000

The Probability of One or More Shortages. One or more shortages will result if lead time demand is greater than the procurement level. If the lead time demand distribution is continuous, the probability of one or more shortages at the end of the inventory cycle may be expressed as

$$P\{1 \text{ or more short}\} = \int_{L+1}^{\infty} f(V_x)\, dV_x.$$

For the discrete lead time demand distribution of Figure 16.9 the probability of one or more shortages is

$$P\{1 \text{ or more short}\} = \sum_{L+1}^{V_{max}} f(V_x).$$

The third column of Table 16.4 gives the probability of one or more shortages as a function of the procurement level.

The probability of one or more shortages establishes with certainty the existence of a shortage condition. Like the probability of an empty warehouse, however, it does not give a measure of the magnitude of the shortage condition or its time duration. It is, therefore, difficult to establish a value of shortage when using this measure.

The Expected Number of Shortages. If the lead time demand distribution is continuous, the expected number of shortages per inventory cycle may be expressed as

$$E\{\text{number of shortages}\} = \int_{L+1}^{\infty} (V_x - L)f(V_x)\, dV_x.$$

For the discrete lead time demand distribution of Figure 16.9, the expected number of shortages is

$$E\{\text{number of shortages}\} = \sum_{L+1}^{V_{max}} (V_x - L)f(V_x). \qquad (16.5)$$

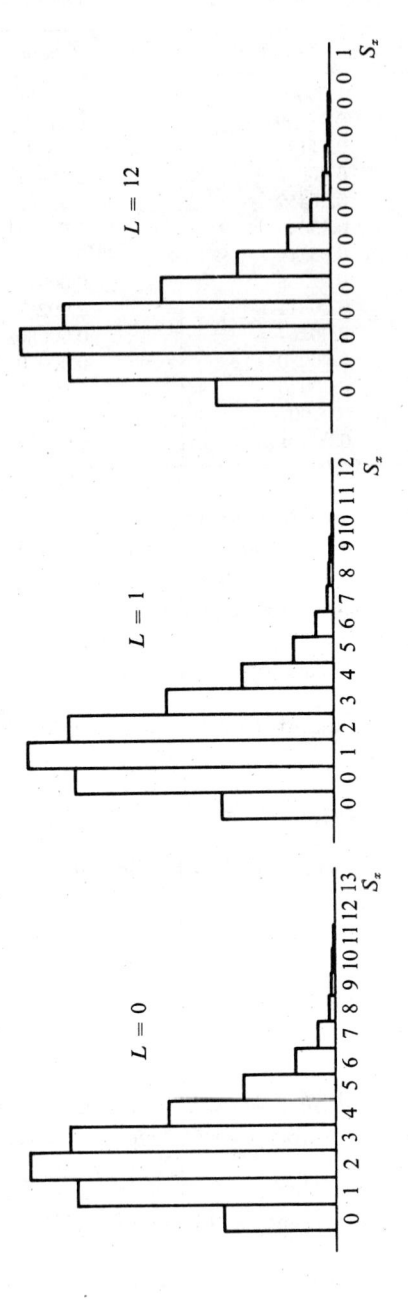

Figure 16.10 Development of shortage distributions.

The application of Equation (16.5) is illustrated in Figure 16.10 and requires the development of one shortage distribution for each procurement level choice. When $L = 0$, the lead time demand distribution is the shortage distribution. This is verified by reasoning as follows: If no demands occur during the lead time, no shortages will result; if one demand occurs, one shortage will result; if two demands occur, two shortages will result; and so forth. The probability of each of these events is given by the lead time demand distribution. Therefore, the expected number of shortages for $L = 0$ is the mean of the shortage distribution for that L choice. This is shown as the first phase of Figure 16.10.

The second phase of Figure 16.10 gives the shortage distribution for the case where $L = 1$. It is developed by reasoning thus: If no demands occur during the lead time, no shortages will result; if one demand occurs, no shortages will result; if two demands occur, one shortage will result; if three demands occur, two shortages will result; and so forth. Again, the probability of each of these events is given by the lead time demand distribution. The mean for the resulting shortage distribution is calculated in Figure 16.10.

The process just outlined is continued for all values of L up to $L = V_{max}$. For $L = 12$, it is evident that no shortages will occur for all values of lead time demand except 13. If lead time demand is 13, one shortage will occur. This is shown in the last phase of Figure 16.10. The expected value for the resulting shortage distribution is calculated as before and is found to be 0.00001. If $L = 13$, it is evident that no shortages will occur for any allowable value of lead time demand up to and including V_{max}. Therefore the expected number of shortages for this last case will be zero. The second column of Table 16.5

Table 16.5. SHORTAGE EXPECTATION AS A FUNCTION OF L

L	$E\{shortages\}$	S_m
0	2.58004	5.5472
1	1.66705	2.3159
2	0.95530	0.7605
3	0.48654	0.1973
4	0.22197	0.0411
5	0.09154	0.0070
6	0.03440	0.0010
7	0.01184	0.0001
8	0.00373	0.0000
9	0.00106	0.0000
10	0.00026	0.0000
11	0.00006	0.0000
12	0.00001	0.0000
13	0.00000	0.0000

gives the expected number of shortages per inventory cycle as a function of the procurement level.

A measure of the magnitude of the shortage condition is provided by an expression for the expected number of shortages. Although the time duration involved is not specified, it is possible to establish a fairly good value of shortage cost when using this expression.

The Expected Number of Unit Periods of Shortage. By utilizing the values for the expected number of shortages per inventory cycle, it is possible to derive an approximate expression for the expected number of unit periods of shortage. This is the value previously developed by simulation. It is an area which may be approximated by

$$S_m = \frac{[E\{S_x\}]^2}{2D_m}. \tag{16.6}$$

The third column of Table 16.5 gives specific values for S_m as a function of L. Since these values are based on the same inputs as were used in the simulation, a comparison can be made. The simulated value for S_m given in Table 16.2 is 0.585 unit periods. Since the procurement level was set at three units, this is to be compared to 0.197 given in Table 16.5. The discrepancy may be explained first because using expected values to find an area is bias, as was the case with the expected total number of unit periods of stock. Second, the simulation charges the period for the number of shortages at the beginning of the period, whereas Equation (16.6) is based on the average number short for the period. This should almost double the value found by simulation. Finally, procurement action is initiated after the stock level falls below L for some cycles. This occurred on the second cycle of Figure 16.3 and will also contribute to an increase in the simulated value. Its effect is to force a more severe shortage condition than the assumption that procurement action is initiated exactly on the procurement level.

The expected number of unit periods of shortage per cycle gives a measure of the magnitude and time duration of the shortage condition. As a result, assigning a value for shortage cost is not as difficult as for the previous expressions for shortage condition. Although the derived value for S_m does not agree with the simulated value, it deviates to the small side, as does the value of I_m. As such, the errors introduced will tend to cancel, since effectiveness functions utilizing these expected values trade off costs based on their magnitudes. This compensation may be noted in the analysis of the next section.

16.5 THE MINIMUM COST INVENTORY POLICIES

In inventory models involving demand and/or lead time as a random variable, the effectiveness measure will also be a random variable. In general, the effectiveness function $E = f(x_i, y_j)$ will be a random variable whenever one or more system parameters are a random variable. Consequently, it is difficult to determine optimal policy variables which optimize E. Under these circumstances, the decision maker would attempt to determine values for the x_i's which optimize this expectation of the effectiveness E.

By utilizing the previously derived approximations for P_m, I_m, and S_m, it is possible to develop effectiveness functions that may be used to find the minimum cost inventory policies. This section will present two specific cases: The first deals with an expected total variable cost model trading off holding cost per period and shortage cost per period with the procurement quantity fixed. The second deals with an expected total variable cost model trading off procurement cost per period, holding cost per period, and shortage cost per period. It will provide a means for finding the minimum cost procurement level and procurement quantity simultaneously.

Expected Total Variable Cost as a Function of* L *Given* Q. If the procurement quantity is assumed to be fixed, the expected total variable cost per period will be the sum of the expected holding cost per period and the expected shortage cost per period; that is,

$$TC_m = HC_m + SC_m.$$

The expected holding cost per period will be the holding cost per unit per period multiplied by the expected number of units in stock for the period, or

$$HC_m = \frac{C_h I_m}{P_m}.$$

Substituting Equation (16.1) for P_m and Equation (16.2) for I_m gives

$$HC_m = C_h \left[\frac{Q}{2} + (L - D_m T_m) \right].$$

The expected shortage cost per period will be the shortage cost per unit short per period multiplied by the expected number of unit periods of shortage for the period, or

$$SC_m = \frac{C_s S_m}{P_m}.$$

Substituting Equation (16.1) for P_m gives

$$SC_m = \frac{C_s D_m S_m}{Q}.$$

The expected total variable cost per period will be a summation of the two cost components previously developed and may be expressed as

$$TC_m = C_h \left[\frac{Q}{2} + (L - D_m T_m) \right] + \frac{C_s D_m S_m}{Q}. \qquad (16.7)$$

Minimization of Equation (16.7) by taking a derivative is not possible because S_m cannot be expressed as a mathematical function of L. It can only be numerically related to L, as in Table 16.5.

As an example of the determination of the minimum cost procurement level when the procurement quantity is fixed, consider the following situation:

Demand and lead time are distributed as shown in Figure 16.1. Holding cost per unit per period is $0.09 and shortage cost per unit short per period is $3.50. The procurement quantity is fixed at 10 units. Therefore, the expected total variable cost as a function of the procurement level is

$$TC_m = \$0.09\left[\frac{10}{2} + (L - 2.58)\right] + \$3.50\left(\frac{0.6}{10}\right)S_m.$$

The expected total variable cost as a function of L when Q is fixed at 10 units is given in the second column of Table 16.6. Each value is computed from the foregoing equation by reference to Table 16.5 for values of S_m. Actually, each total cost value shown is an expected value from a total cost distribution. Choosing the L giving a minimum expected cost is equivalent to maximizing the probability of minimizing the sum of holding cost per period and shortage cost per period.

Table 16.6. EXPECTED TOTAL VARIABLE COST AS A FUNCTION OF L GIVEN Q (dollars)

L	TC_m at $Q = 10$	TC_m at $Q = 14$
0	1.383	1.230
1	0.794	0.835
2	0.558	0.692
3	0.529	0.698
4	0.586	0.764
5	0.669	0.849
6	0.758	0.938

The third column of Table 16.6 gives expected total variable cost values for the case where Q is fixed at 14 units. Comparison with the values for $Q = 10$ indicates that the expected minimum total system cost depends on both L and Q. Thus, at this point, it is not certain what value of Q will yield a minimum expected total variable cost.

Expected Total Variable Cost as a Function of L and Q. When the procurement quantity is not restricted to a specific value, the expected total variable cost per period will be the sum of the expected procurement cost per period, the expected holding cost per period, and the expected shortage cost per period; that is,

$$TC_m = PC_m + HC_m + SC_m.$$

The expected procurement cost per period is the procurement cost per procurement divided by the expected number of periods per inventory cycle, or

$$PC_m = \frac{C_p}{P_m}.$$

Substituting Equation (16.1) for P_m gives

$$PC_m = \frac{C_p D_m}{Q}.$$

The expected holding cost per period and the expected shortage cost per period were derived in the previous paragraphs. Therefore, the expected total system cost per period may be expressed as

$$TC_m = \frac{C_p D_m}{Q} + C_h \left[\frac{Q}{2} + (L - D_m T_m) \right] + \frac{C_s D_m S_m}{Q}. \qquad (16.8)$$

Minimization of Equation (16.8) by partial differentiation is not possible. Like Equation (16.7), it contains S_m, which is only numerically related to L. As an example of the determination of the minimum cost procurement level and procurement quantity, consider the following situation: Demand and lead time are distributed as shown in Figure 16.1. Procurement cost per procurement is $10. Holding cost per unit per period is $0.09 and shortage cost per unit per period is $3.50. Therefore, the expected total variable cost as a function of the procurement level and procurement quantity is

$$TC_m = \frac{\$10(0.6)}{Q} + \$0.09 \left[\frac{Q}{2} + (L - 2.58) \right] + \$3.50 \left(\frac{0.6}{Q} \right) S_m.$$

The expected total variable cost as a function of L and Q is given in Table 16.7. Each value is computed from the preceding expression with reference to Table 16.5 for values of S_m. As before, each entry is actually an expected value from a total variable cost distribution. Choosing the L and Q giving a minimum expected cost is equivalent to maximizing the probability of minimizing the sum of procurement cost per period, holding cost per period, and shortage cost per period.

Table 16.7. EXPECTED TOTAL VARIABLE COST AS A FUNCTION OF L AND Q (dollars)

L \ Q	10	11	12	13	14
0	1.983	1.867	1.779	1.711	1.659
1	1.494	1.340	1.303	1.303	1.264
2	1.158	1.133	1.121	1.118	1.121
3	1.129	1.116	1.113	1.117	1.127
4	1.187	1.176	1.175	1.182	1.193
5	1.269	1.259	1.259	1.266	1.278
6	1.358	1.348	1.348	1.355	1.367

The minimum expected cost procurement level and procurement quantity is found by inspection to be 3 and 12, respectively. These are the values that were used in the Monte Carlo analysis. They give an expected total variable cost of $1.113 when used with the expressions for expected values. Any error in these values will be reflected in the expected total variable cost. Making adjustments in the expected values found by Monte Carlo analysis and using them to compute the expected total system cost gives a value of $1.142.

16.6 MINIMUM COST POLICIES FOR A SIMPLIFIED SYSTEM

The effectiveness functions derived in the previous section could not be minimized by direct mathematical means. This occurred primarily because the term S_m was not a mathematical function of L. This section adopts two simplifications in order to demonstrate the method of finding mathematically minimum cost inventory policies for the probabilistic system. Specifically, this will require that shortage cost be based on the expected number of shortages, and that the lead time demand distribution be a simple continuous function. Although other choices may be made, it is assumed in this section that lead time demand is distributed uniformly in the interval 0 to q units, $f(V_x) = 1/q$.

Expected Total Variable Cost as a Function of L Given Q. If the procurement quantity is assumed to be fixed, the expected total variable cost per period will be the sum of the expected holding cost per period and the expected shortage cost per period; that is,

$$TC_m = HC_m + SC_m.$$

The expected holding cost was derived in the previous section and was shown to be

$$HC_m = C_h \left[\frac{Q}{2} + (L - D_m T_m) \right].$$

The expected shortage cost per period will be the shortage cost per unit short, designated C'_s, multiplied by the expected number of shortages per period, or

$$SC_m = \frac{C'_s E\{S_x\}}{P_m}.$$

Substituting a continuous approximation of Equation (16.5) for $E\{S_x\}$ and Equation (16.1) for P_m gives

$$SC_m = \frac{C'_s D_m}{Q} \int_{L+1}^{q} (V_x - L) f(V_x) \, dV_x.$$

Substituting $f(V_x) = 1/q$ and evaluating gives

$$SC_m = \frac{C'_s D_m}{qQ} \left[\int_{L+1}^{q} (V_x) \, dV_x - \int_{L+1}^{q} (L) \, dV_x \right]$$

$$= \frac{C'_s D_m}{qQ} \left[\frac{V_x^2}{2} \Big|_{L+1}^{q} - L(V_x) \Big|_{L+1}^{q} \right]$$

$$= \frac{C'_s D_m}{qQ} \left[\frac{q^2}{2} - \frac{(L+1)^2}{2} - Lq + L(L+1) \right]$$

$$= \frac{C'_s D_m}{Q} \left(\frac{q}{2} - L + \frac{L^2 - 1}{2q} \right).$$

The expected total variable cost per period will be the sum of the expected holding cost for the period and the expected shortage cost for the period and may be expressed as

$$TC_m = C_h\left[\frac{Q}{2} + (L - D_m T_m)\right] + \frac{C'_s D_m}{Q}\left(\frac{q}{2} - L + \frac{L^2 - 1}{2q}\right). \quad (16.9)$$

The minimum cost procurement level for any given procurement quantity may be found by taking the derivative with respect to L, setting the result equal to zero, and solving for L as follows:

$$\frac{dTC_m}{dL} = C_h - \frac{C'_s(D_m)}{Q} + \frac{L(C'_s)(D_m)}{qQ} = 0$$

$$L = -\frac{q(Q)C_h}{C'_s D_m} + q \quad (16.10)$$

$$= q\left[1 - \frac{(Q)C_h}{C'_s D_m}\right].$$

Equation (16.10) gives the minimum cost procurement level for a fixed procurement quantity as a function of the expected demand, the maximum value of lead time demand, the holding cost, and the shortage cost.

As an example of the application of Equation (16.10), consider the following situation. The expected demand for a certain item is 1 unit per period. Lead time demand is distributed uniformly in the interval 1 to 10 units. Holding cost is $0.05 per unit per period and shortage cost is $3 per unit short. The item is procured in lots of 24 units. Under these conditions, the minimum cost procurement level is

$$L = 10\left[1 - \frac{(24)\$0.05}{\$3(1)}\right] = 6 \text{ units}.$$

As before, it is not certain as to what value of L and Q will yield a minimum expected total system cost.

Expected Total Variable Cost as a Function of* L *and* Q. When the procurement quantity is not restricted to a specific value, the expected total system cost per period will be the sum of the expected procurement cost per period, the expected holding cost per period, and the expected shortage cost per period; that is,

$$TC_m = PC_m + HC_m + SC_m.$$

The expected procurement cost per period, the expected holding cost per period, and the expected shortage cost per period were derived previously. Therefore, the expected total variable cost per period may be expressed as

$$TC_m = \frac{C_p D_m}{Q} + C_h\left[\frac{Q}{2} + (L - D_m T_m)\right] + \frac{C'_s D_m}{Q}\left(\frac{q}{2} - L + \frac{L^2 - 1}{2q}\right). \quad (16.11)$$

The procurement level and procurement quantity resulting in a minimum expected total variable cost may be found by taking the partial derivatives of

TC_m with respect to L and Q, setting the results equal to zero, and solving for L and Q as follows:

$$\frac{\partial TC_m}{\partial Q} = -\frac{C_p D_m}{Q^2} + \frac{C_h}{2} - \frac{C'_s D_m}{Q^2}\left(\frac{q}{2} - L + \frac{L^2 - 1}{2q}\right) = 0. \quad (16.12)$$

$$\frac{\partial TC_m}{\delta L} = C_h - \frac{C'_s D_m}{Q} + \frac{L(C'_s)(D_m)}{qQ} = 0. \quad (16.13)$$

From Equation (16.13)

$$L = q - \frac{q(C_h)Q}{C'_s D_m}. \quad (16.14)$$

Substituting Equation (16.14) into Equation (16.12) and simplifying gives

$$Q = D_m \sqrt{\frac{C'_s}{qC_h}\left(\frac{C'_s - 2qC_p}{qC_h - C'_s D_m}\right)}. \quad (16.15)$$

Equation (16.15) gives the minimum cost procurement quantity as a function of the expected demand, the maximum value of lead time demand, the procurement cost, the holding cost, and the shortage cost.

The minimum cost procurement level may be found by substituting Equation (16.15) into Equation (16.14), giving

$$L = q - q\sqrt{\frac{C_h}{qC'_s}\left(\frac{C'_s - 2qC_p}{qC_h - C'_s D_m}\right)}. \quad (16.16)$$

As an example of the application of these equations, consider the previous situation and suppose that procurement cost is $6 per procurement. The minimum cost procurement quantity is found from Equation (16.15) as

$$Q = (1)\sqrt{\frac{\$3}{10(\$0.05)}\left[\frac{\$3 - 2(10)(\$6)}{10(\$0.05) - \$3(1)}\right]}$$

$$= \sqrt{280.8} \approx 17 \text{ units.}$$

The minimum cost procurement level is found from Equation (16.16) as

$$L = 10 - 10\sqrt{\frac{\$0.05}{10\$(3)}\left[\frac{\$3 - 2(10)(\$6)}{10(\$0.05) - \$3(1)}\right]}$$

$$= 10 - 10\sqrt{0.078} \approx 7 \text{ units.}$$

16.7 A SINGLE-PERIOD INVENTORY MODEL

The single-period inventory model is a special case in which each time period of the inventory flow process is considered separately. The demand during the period is assumed to follow a known probability distribution. The decision maker can determine the inventory level at the beginning of the time period, but no additional procurement is deemed possible between the beginning and the end of the time period. If the demand during the period exceeds the inventory level, a shortage cost is incurred. On the other hand, if the demand is less than the inventory level, some inventory has to be carried over to the next period and a holding cost is incurred. The problem is to determinine the optimal inventory level which would minimize the expected total cost of shortage and holding. The trade-off would be between the two costs, that of high inventory level (leading to holding cost) and low inventory level (leading to shortage cost). Let

C_h = holding cost per unit
C_s = shortage cost per unit short
x = demand during the period
$f(x)$ = probability distribution function of x (assumed known)
L = inventory level

The shortage cost would be given by

$$SC = (x - L)C_s \quad \text{if } x > L$$
$$= 0 \quad \text{otherwise.}$$

The holding cost would be given by

$$HC = (L - x)C_h \quad \text{if } x < L$$
$$= 0 \quad \text{otherwise.}$$

Obviously, both shortage and holding costs would not be incurred simultaneously, and the expectation of the total cost would be

$$E(TC) = C_s \int_L^\infty (x - L) f(x)\, dx + C_h \int_0^L (L - x) f(x)\, dx.$$

The optimal inventory level resulting in the minimum expected total cost is found by differentiating with respect to L and equating the derivative to zero. Since L appears as one of the limits of integration, it is necessary to apply Leibnitz' rule

$$\frac{d}{da} \int_{\phi_1(a)}^{\phi_2(a)} F(x, a)\, dx = \int_{\phi_1(a)}^{\phi_2(a)} \frac{\partial F}{\partial a}\, dx + F(\phi_1, a) \frac{d\phi_1}{da} - F(\phi_2, a) \frac{d\phi_2}{da}.$$

The optimal inventory level L^* is given by

$$F(L^*) = \int_0^{L^*} f(x)\, dx = \frac{C_s}{C_h + C_s}. \tag{16.17}$$

As an example of a single-period inventory model, consider the following situation. The demand for gasoline at a gas station varies uniformly over the range of 4,000 to 6,000 gallons per week. Gasoline can be procured only once per week, as the schedule for the gasoline tankers would not permit intermediate stops. The operator of the gas station estimates that he loses $0.03 per gallon in profits and goodwill if demand cannot be satisfied. At the same time it costs him an estimated $0.06 per gallon carryover to the next week. In this case

$$f(x) = 1/2{,}000 \quad 4{,}000 \leq x \leq 6{,}000$$
$$= 0 \quad \text{otherwise.}$$

Therefore,
$$F(L) = \int_{4,000}^{L} \frac{1}{2,000} dx$$
$$= \frac{L - 4,000}{2,000}.$$

For optimal inventory level L^*
$$F(L^*) = \frac{C_s}{C_h + C_s}$$
$$\frac{L^* - 4,000}{2,000} = \frac{3}{3 + 0.6} = 0.8333$$
$$L^* = 5,666 \text{ gallons.}$$

The operator should maintain an inventory level of 5,666 gallons at the beginning of each week in order to minimize the expected total system cost.

QUESTIONS

16.1. Explain why it is not possible to keep both the number of periods per cycle and the procurement quantity fixed if the inventory process is probabilistic.

16.2. In the probabilistic inventory process, procurement action is often initiated when the stock on hand is below the procurement level. Explain.

16.3. Give reasons why simulated sampling gives a better description of the probabilistic inventory process than mathematical expressions.

16.4. Name and describe the three expressions for expected values for the probabilistic system and compare with their counterparts for the deterministic system.

16.5. Why is an inventory policy based on the expected minimum total system cost valid?

16.6. Although lead time demand is independent of the procurement level, shortages are dependent on the specific procurement level chosen. Explain.

16.7. Explain why the expected number of unit periods of shortage is a better expression for shortage condition than the probability of one or more shortages.

16.8. Discuss Equation (16.11) in terms of $E = f(x_i, y_j)$.

PROBLEMS

16.1. Use simulated sampling to plot eight cycles of inventory flow for the case where the demand is distributed Poisson with a mean of 0.8 unit per period and the lead time is four periods. Set the procurement level at three units and the procurement quantity at eight units.

16.2. Calculate P_x, I_x, and S_x for each cycle plotted in Problem 16.1. What are the values of P_m, I_m, and S_m for this eight-cycle sample?

16.3. The home plate umpire in the game of baseball must maintain an inventory of baseballs in the many pockets of his baggy suit. This inventory is necessary to meet the demands of play when balls must be replaced after they become dirty or misshapen or are boldly hit into the stands of jeering and cheering spectators. One knowledgeable umpire, affectionately referred to by the players as "old four-eyes," concluded that the technique of simulated sampling analysis might be aptly used to describe this probabilistic inventory system. He found that the pattern of usage followed a Poisson distribution with a mean of 1.2 baseballs per player at bat. A deterministic lead time of 3 players at bat was necessary to catch the eye of the ball boy and receive a replenishment quantity of baseballs. With a procurement level of 4 baseballs and a procurement quantity of 10 balls, use simulation to plot 10 cycles of inventory flow.

16.4. Use Equation (16.3) and the cumulative distributions of Figure 16.2 to develop the distribution of lead time demand by Monte Carlo simulation. Compare the results obtained after 50 cycles with the exact distribution of Figure 16.9.

16.5. Specify the distribution of lead time demand if the demand is distributed normal with a mean of 10 units per period, and a standard deviation of 3 units per period. Lead time is constant and equal to four periods.

16.6. Specify the distribution of lead time demand if demand is constant and equal to 4 units per period and lead time is distributed Poisson with a mean of eight periods.

16.7. Develop the distribution of lead time demand by the exact method if demand is distributed Poisson with a mean of 1 unit per period. Lead time will be one, two, three, or four periods with probabilities of 0.10, 0.30, 0.40, and 0.20, respectively.

16.8. Plot the probability of an empty warehouse and the probability of one or more shortages as a function of the procurement level. (Use the data of Table 16.4.)

16.9. Plot the expected number of shortages per inventory cycle and the expected number of unit periods of shortage per cycle as a function of the procurement level. (Use the data of Table 16.5.)

16.10. If the lead time demand has a Poisson distribution with a mean of 12, if $D_m = 3$, and if the procurement level is set at 10 units, calculate the following: (a) the probability of an empty warehouse, (b) the probability of four or more shortages, (c) the expected number of shortages, and (d) the expected number of unit periods of shortage.

16.11. If the procurement level is set at 12 units, if the lead time demand is distributed Poisson with a mean of 10, and if $D_m = 4$, calculate the following: (a) the probability of an empty warehouse, (b) the probability of two or more shortages, (c) the expected number of shortages, and (d) the expected number of unit periods of shortage.

16.12. If the procurement level is set at 12 units, if $D_m = 2$ units per period, and if lead time demand is distributed uniformly in the range of 1 to 16 units, calculate the following: (a) the probability of an empty warehouse, (b) the probability of one or more shortages, (c) the expected number of shortages, and (d) the expected number of unit periods of shortage. (Use continuous approximations.)

16.13. The lead time demand has an empirical distribution as given in the following table, with a mean of 4.4 and $D_m = 5$. If the procurement level is set at 8 units, calculate the following: (a) the probability of an empty warehouse, (b) the probability of one or more shortages, (c) the expected number of shortages, and (d) the expected number of unit periods of shortage.

Lead Time Demand	Cumulative Probability	Lead Time Demand	Cumulative Probability
2	0.100	7	0.750
3	0.200	8	0.850
4	0.400	9	0.900
5	0.600	10	0.950
6	0.650	11	1.000

16.14. The demand and lead time distributions for a certain inventory process are given by Figure 16.1. The holding cost per unit per period is $0.03 and the shortage cost is $3.00 per unit short. Using the expected number of shortages per cycle given in Table 16.5, plot the expected total cost as a function of the procurement level if the procurement quantity is fixed at 10 units.

16.15. What is the expected total system cost for the conditions of Problem 16.14 if the procurement level is 8 units, the procurement quantity is 12 units, and the procurement cost is $6.50 per procurement?

16.16. The expected demand for a custom-made electronics device is 4 units per period. The expected lead time is eight periods. Lead time demand is uniformly distributed in the range of 0 to 20 units. The holding cost is $0.25 per unit per period and the shortage cost is $45 per unit short. The device is being procured in lots of 30 units. Determine the minimum cost procurement level.

16.17. The procurement cost per procurement in Problem 16.16 is $120. What is the minimum cost procurement level and procurement quantity? What is the expected minimum total system cost?

16.18. The probability distribution of demand for an inventory problem is normal with a mean of 120 and a standard deviation of 25. If the total cost per unit is $80 and the total cost of a shortage is $800 per unit, how many units should be ordered to minimize the expected total cost?

16.19. In Problem 16.18, if the opportunity cost of an overstock of 1 unit is $110 and the opportunity cost of an understock of 1 unit is $700, determine the number of units that should be ordered so as to minimize the expected total cost.

16.20. If the salvage value of our unused item is $20 and the conditions of Problem 16.18 apply, calculate the minimum cost order quantity.

16.21. Show that the optimal inventory level for a single-period inventory system is expressed by $C_s/(C_h + C_s)$.

VI

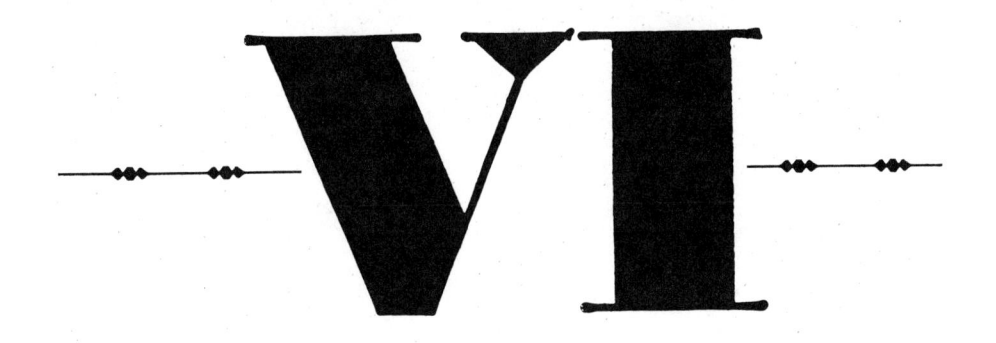

*Models
for
Queuing Operations*

17

Deterministic Queuing Models

The queuing or waiting-line systems presented with in this chapter may be described as follows. A facility or group of facilities is maintained to meet the demand for service created by a population of individuals. These individuals form a waiting line or queue and receive service in accordance with a predetermined waiting-line discipline. In most cases, the serviced units rejoin the population and again become candidates for the service they received. In other cases, the individuals form a waiting line at the next stage of the system. In either case, the flow of individuals through the system is a discrete process analogous to the procurement and inventory process discussed in previous chapters.

Systems having the foregoing characteristics are common in many real-world operations in which people, materials, or vehicles form waiting lines. In public service, waiting lines are formed at cafeterias, theaters, and doctors' offices. In production, the flow of items in process produces a waiting line at each machine center. In transportation, waiting lines form at toll gates, traffic signals, docks, and landing strips. In each case, the objective is to determine the capacity of the service facility in the light of the relevant costs and the characteristics of the arrival pattern so that the sum of all costs associated with the queuing system will be minimized. This chapter describes the queuing system in general terms and presents several deterministic queuing models.

17.1 THE QUEUING SYSTEM

A multiple-channel queuing system is illustrated schematically in Figure 17.1. It exists because the population shown demands service. In satisfying the demand on the system, the decision maker must establish the level of service capacity to provide. This will involve increasing or decreasing the service capacity by altering the service rate at existing channels or, by adding or deleting channels. The following paragraphs describe the components of the waiting-line system and indicate their importance in the decision-making process.

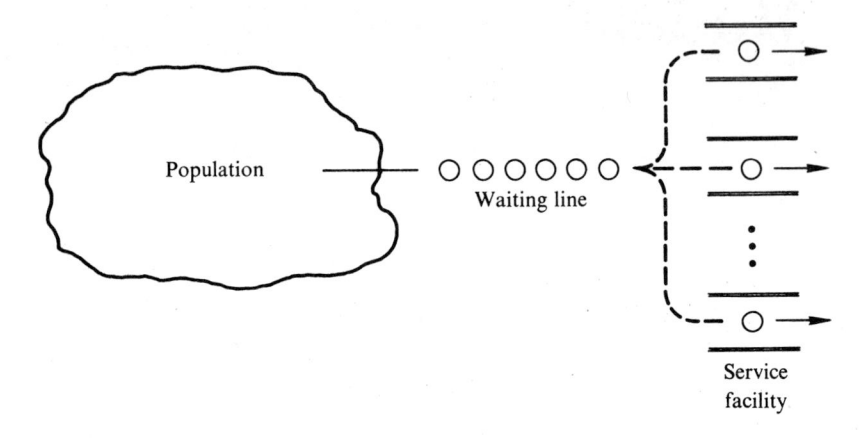

Figure 17.1 Multiple-channel queuing system.

The Arrival Population. Waiting-line systems come into being because there exists a population of individuals requiring service from time to time. Usually, the arrival population is best thought of as a group of items, some of which depart and join the waiting line. For example, if the population is composed of all airborne aircraft, flight schedules and random occurrences will determine the number of aircraft that will join the landing pattern of a given airport during a given time interval. If the population is composed of telephone subscribers, the time of day and the day of the week, as well as many other factors, will determine the number of calls placed on an exchange. If the population consists of production machines the deterioration wearout and use rates will determine the departure mechanism causing the machines to join a waiting line of machines requiring repair service.

The arrival population, although always finite in size, may be considered infinite under certain conditions. If the departure rate is small relative to the size of the population, the number of units that potentially may require service will not be seriously depleted. Under this condition, the population may be considered infinite. Models used to explain the behavior of such systems are much easier to formulate than models for the finite population. Examples of populations that may usually be treated as infinite are automobiles that may require passage over a bridge, customers who may potentially patronize a theater, telephone subscribers who may place a call, and production orders that may require processing at a specific machine center.

In some cases the proportion of the population requiring service may be fairly large when compared with the population itself. In these cases, the population is seriously depleted by the departure of individuals to the extent that the departure rate will not remain stable. Since models used to explain waiting-line systems depend on the stability of the arrival rate, finite cases must be given special treatment. Examples of waiting-line operations that might be classified as finite are production machines that may require repair, semiautomatic production facilities that require operator attention, and company cafeterias that serve a captive population. Waiting-line systems for the case where the infinite population assumption does not hold will be treated in the next chapter.

The Waiting Line. In any waiting-line system, a departure mechanism exists which governs the rate at which individuals leave the population and join the queue. This departure mechanism is responsible for the formation of the waiting line and the need to provide service. Formation of the queue is a discrete process. Individuals or items joining the waiting line do so as integer values. The number of units in the waiting line at any point in time is an integer value. Rarely, if ever, is the queuing process continuous.

Individuals or items becoming a part of the waiting line take a position in the queue in accordance with a certain waiting-line discipline. The most common discipline is that of first come, first served. Other priority rules that may exist are the random selection process, the head-of-the-line rule, first come last served, and disciplines involving a combination of these. In addition, individuals may remain in the queue for a period of time and rejoin the population. This behavior is called *reneging*.

In an ideal sense, the waiting line may be thought of as a number of items which is increased by arrivals and decreased by services. As such, it is analogous to a stock of items on hand in inventory. The arrivals represent additions to stock and the services represent demands on the system.

The Service Facility. Service may be thought of as the process of providing the activities required by the units in the waiting line. It may consist of collecting a toll, filling an order, providing a necessary repair, or completing a manufacturing operation. In each case, the act of providing the service causes a unit decrease in the waiting line. The service mechanism, like the arrival mechanism, is discrete, since items are processed on a unit basis.

The service facility may consist of a single channel, or it may consist of several channels in parallel, as in Figure 17.1. If it consists of only a single channel, all arrivals must eventually pass through it. If several channels are provided, items may move from the waiting line into the first channel that becomes empty. The rate at which individuals are processed depends on the service capacity provided at the individual channels and on the number of channels in the system.

The service may be provided by human beings only, by human beings aided by tools and equipment, or by equipment alone. For example, collecting a toll is essentially a clerk's task which requires no tools or equipment. Repairing a vehicle, on the other hand, requires a mechanic aided by tools and equipment. Processing a phone call dialed by the subscriber seldom requires human intervention and is usually paced by the automatic equipment. These examples indicate that service facilities can vary widely with respect to the human–machine mix utilized to provide the required service.

17.2 THE DECISION ENVIRONMENT

The waiting-line system described in Section 17.1 exists in a decision environment composed of an arrival mechanism, a service mechanism, waiting cost, and service facility cost. This section describes each of these. The total system cost depends on the level of service capacity provided. Therefore, this section also establishes the basic structure of decision models that may be used to establish the service capacity so that the sum of all costs associated with the waiting-line system is minimized.

The Arrival Mechanism. The demand for service is the primary stimulus on the waiting-line system and the justification for its existence. As previously indicated, the waiting-line system may exist to meet the service demand created by people, materials, vehicles, or machines. The characteristics of the arrival pattern depend on the nature of the population giving rise to the demand for service.

The simplest arrival pattern may be classified as deterministic. In this special case, the future demand for service can be predicted with certainty. The arrival mechanism considered in this restricted sense is only an approximation of reality. All models developed in this chapter are based on the assumption that the arrival mechanism is deterministic.

In the general case, the arrival pattern may be described as a random variable that takes on values in accordance with a specific probability distribution. If the characteristics of the population remain stable over time, the parameters and the form of the distribution will not change. Such steady-state processes are an exception, however, rather than the rule. The probabilistic steady-state waiting-line process will be treated in Chapter 18.

The Service Mechanism. The rate at which units requiring service are serviced is assumed to be a variable directly under the control of the decision maker. This parameter can be assigned a specific value to create a minimum cost waiting-line system. For each channel, then, the characteristics of the service mechanism may be established.

In the simplest case, service time may be classified as deterministic. Under this assumption the duration of each service is known with certainty. As with the arrival rate, however, the service duration considered in this restricted sense is only an approximation of reality. All models developed in this chapter are based on the assumption of a deterministic service rate.

Most real-world service facilities incorporate a service duration that is a random variable, taking on values in accordance with a specific probability distribution. If the characteristics of the service facility remain constant over time, the parameters and the form of the distribution will not change. Those service facilities utilizing a human–machine service element may exhibit learning. In this case the service rate will increase, causing a probabilistic nonsteady-state waiting line process. Models based on probabilistic steady-state distributions for service are treated in the next chapter.

Waiting Cost. When a unit joins the waiting line, or is being serviced, a waiting cost is incurred. Waiting cost per unit per period will depend on the units in question. If expensive production machinery waits for operator attention, the loss of profit may be sizable. Vehicles waiting in queue at a toll gate incur a waiting cost due to interruption of trip progress. Customers waiting at a checkout counter become irritated and the proprietor suffers a loss of goodwill.

Increasing the level of service capacity will cause a decrease in both the length of the waiting line and the time for each service. As a result, the waiting time will be decreased. Since waiting cost to the system is a product of the number of units waiting and the time duration involved, this action will decrease this cost component. But since increasing the service facility capacity increases the service cost, it is appropriate to seek a reduction in waiting cost for the system only up to the point where the saving exceeds the added facility cost.

Service Facility Cost. Each channel of the service facility represents a capital investment plus operating and maintenance costs. In addition, wages for personnel may be involved, together with associated overhead rates. The capability of the channel to process units requiring service is a function of the resources expended at the channel. For example, the channel may consist of a single repairperson with modest tools, or it may be a crew of workers with complex tools and equipment. The cost of providing such a facility will depend on the characteristics of the personnel and equipment employed.

Since increasing the service capacity will result in a reduction in the waiting line, it is appropriate to adjust service capacity so that the sum of waiting cost and service cost is a minimum. This chapter and the following one consider models useful in establishing the minimum cost service level. The general structure of decision models directed to this objective will be presented next.

The Decision Model. The primary objective of the waiting-line system is to meet the demand for service at minimum cost. This requires the establishment of an appropriate level of service capacity by constructing and optimizing a mathematical model of the form[1]

$$E = f(x_i, y_j),$$

where E = measure of effectiveness sought (minimize total system cost)
x_i = policy variable concerning the level of service capacity to provide
y_j = system parameters of the arrival pattern, the waiting cost, and the service facility cost.

The following sections are devoted to developing deterministic decision models with the preceding characteristics. The following symbolism will be used:

TC = total system cost per period
A = number of periods between arrivals
S = number of periods to complete one service
C_w = cost of waiting per unit per period
C_f = service facility cost for servicing 1 unit

Additional notation will be adopted and defined as required for deriving specific decision models.

17.3 MODELS FOR NO INITIAL WAITING LINE

In this section, assume that a queuing situation begins with no units in the system and that arrivals occur at regular intervals of length A periods. The first arrival occurs at the beginning of the process. Service time is constant and equal to S periods. Since each unit serviced will require S periods, it is essential that S be less than or equal to A periods if a single channel is employed. If M channels are to be used, it is required that S be less than or equal to MA periods. If these restrictions are violated, a waiting line will form which will grow beyond bound. This section treats the simple cases described as an introduction to deterministic waiting-line operations.

A Single-Channel Model. A single-channel waiting-line system may be represented schematically as shown in Figure 17.2. The heavy dot represents an

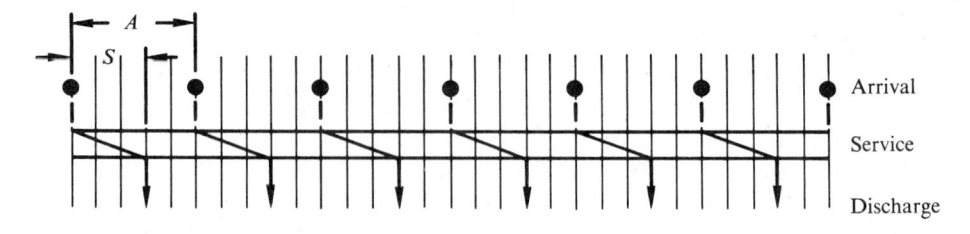

Figure 17.2 Single-channel system with no initial queue.

[1] Some optimization techniques used in this chapter require a familiarity with Appendix B.

arrival every five periods. The slanting path represents a service operation requiring three periods. Since S is less than A, no waiting line will ever form.

The total system cost per period will be the sum of the waiting cost for the period and the service facility cost for the period; that is,

$$TC = WC + FC.$$

The waiting cost per period will be the product of the cost of waiting per unit per period and the number of units waiting each period, or

$$WC = C_w\left(\frac{S}{A}\right).$$

The service facility cost for the period will be the product of the number of units serviced during the period and the cost of servicing 1 unit, or

$$FC = C_f\left(\frac{1}{S}\right).$$

Expressing the service facility cost per period as a linear function of the number of units serviced per period may be somewhat unrealistic. It is, however, a convenient means for relating the cost of providing service to the capacity of the service facility. Most of the models derived in this and the following chapter use this expression for service facility cost per period.

The total system cost per period will be the sum of the waiting cost per period and the facility cost per period, or

$$TC = C_w\left(\frac{S}{A}\right) + C_f\left(\frac{1}{S}\right). \tag{17.1}$$

A minimum cost service interval may be found by differentiating with respect to S, setting the result equal to zero, and solving for S as follows:

$$\frac{dTC}{dS} = \frac{C_w}{A} - \frac{C_f}{S^2} = 0$$

$$S^2 = \frac{C_f A}{C_w} \tag{17.2}$$

$$S = \sqrt{\frac{C_f A}{C_w}}, \quad S \leq A.$$

As an application of the foregoing model, consider the following example. A unit will arrive every five periods. The cost of waiting is \$5 per unit per period. One unit can be serviced at a cost of \$9. Waiting cost per period, facility cost per period, and total cost per period may be tabulated as a function of S to illustrate the nature of the cost components. The results shown in Table 17.1 were developed from Equation (17.1). Inspection of the tabulated values indicates that waiting cost per period is directly proportional and that facility cost per period is inversely proportional to S. The minimum cost service interval is three periods and may be provided at a facility cost of \$3 per period.

Table 17.1. COST COMPONENTS FOR SINGLE-CHANNEL MODEL

S	WC	FC	TC
0	$0.00	∞	∞
1	1.00	$ 9.00	$10.00
2	2.00	4.50	6.50
3	3.00	3.00	6.00
4	4.00	2.25	6.25
5	5.00	1.80	6.80

The minimum cost service interval may be found directly by substituting into Equation (17.2) as follows:

$$S = \sqrt{\frac{\$9(5)}{\$5}} = 3 \text{ periods.}$$

Under the conditions assumed, the decision maker would provide a single service channel capable of serving one unit every three periods, as shown in Figure 17.2.

In this example, the service interval resulting in a minimum total system cost is a whole number of periods. This occurred because of the cost values assigned. Normally, the minimum service interval will not be an integer. The decision maker will strive to establish a service interval as close to the minimum cost value as possible.

A Multiple-Channel Model. A two-channel waiting-line system may be represented schematically as shown in Figure 17.3. As for Figure 17.2, the heavy dot represents an arrival and the slanting path represents a service operation. The second arrival finds the first service channel busy and goes immediately into the second. The third arrival finds the second channel busy and goes immediately into the first. Since S is less than MA, no waiting line will ever form.

The total system cost for the period will be the sum of the waiting cost for the period and the facility cost for the period; that is,

$$TC = WC + FC.$$

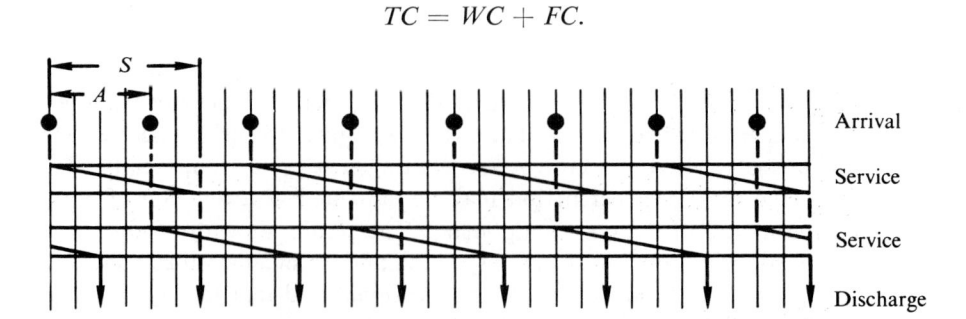

Figure 17.3 Multiple-channel system with no initial queue.

The waiting cost per period will be the product of the cost of waiting per unit per period and the number of units waiting per period, or

$$WC = C_w\left(\frac{S}{A}\right).$$

The facility cost for the period will be the product of the number of units served during the period, the cost of serving 1 unit, and the number of channels in operation, or

$$FC = C_f\left(\frac{1}{S}\right)M.$$

The total system cost per period will be the sum of the waiting cost per period and the facility cost per period, or

$$TC = C_w\left(\frac{S}{A}\right) + C_f\left(\frac{1}{S}\right)M. \tag{17.3}$$

A minimum cost service interval may be found by differentiating with respect to S, setting the result equal to zero, and solving for S as follows:

$$\frac{dTC}{dS} = \frac{C_w}{A} - \frac{C_f M}{S^2} = 0$$

$$S^2 = \frac{C_f M A}{C_w} \tag{17.4}$$

$$S = \sqrt{\frac{C_f M A}{C_w}}, \quad S \leq MA.$$

Equation (17.4) reduces to Equation (17.2) for the single-channel case; $M = 1$.

To illustrate the application of the foregoing model, consider the following example. A unit will arrive every four periods. The cost of waiting is $2 per unit per period. A unit can be serviced for a cost of $9. Two channels are to be used. The minimum cost service interval may be found by substituting into Equation (17.4) as follows:

$$S = \sqrt{\frac{\$9(2)(4)}{\$2}} = 6 \text{ periods.}$$

Under the conditions assumed, the decision maker would provide two service channels, each with the capability of serving one unit every six periods as was shown in Figure 17.3.

17.4 A MODEL WITH AN INITIAL WAITING LINE[2]

Suppose that a queuing situation made up of repetitive cycles begins with a finite number of units in the system and that arrivals occur at regular intervals of length A periods. The first arrival occurs at the beginning of the process.

---

[2] This derivation was adapted from a Technical Note by A. A. B. Pritsker, "A Deterministic Queuing Situation," *Journal of Industrial Engineering*, Vol. IV, No. 5 (September–October 1963).

Service time is constant and equal to S periods. Since each unit serviced will require S periods, it is essential that S be sufficiently less than A so that the initial units plus those which arrive will be serviced before the end of the cycle. If the cycle ends with units waiting, there will be a carryover to the next cycle and the waiting line will grow beyond bound. This section will present an exact deterministic model for the preceding situation involving a single service channel.

General System Relationships. The waiting-line system under consideration may be represented schematically as shown in Figure 17.4. The small circles represent initial units in the system, designated k. Assume that these units accumulated since the termination of the previous cycle. A dot represents an arrival every five periods and the initial arrival occurs at the beginning of the cycle. The service operation is of duration two periods. The cycle is composed of P periods, where $P = 40$ for this example. The final arrival occurs at the beginning of the forty-first period and becomes part of the initial queue for the next cycle.

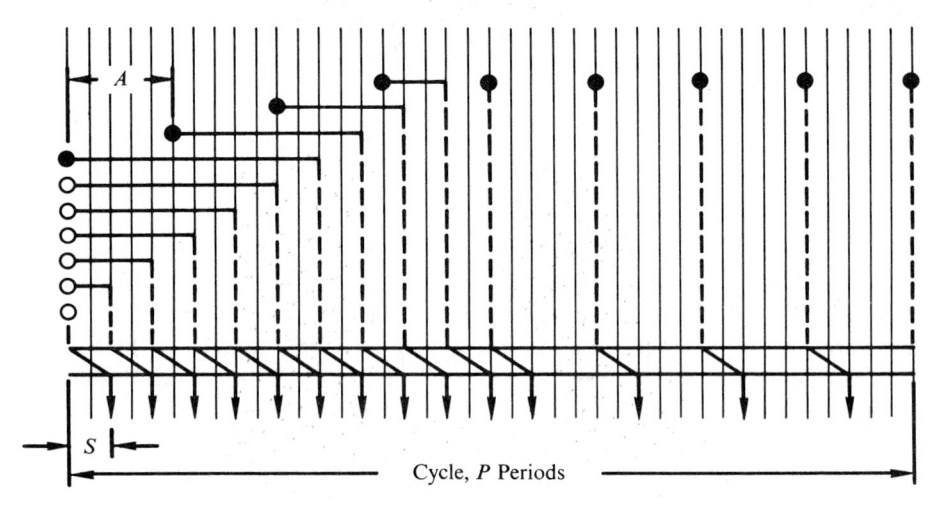

Figure 17.4 Waiting-line process with an initial queue.

Under the conditions assumed in Figure 17.4, the first units to be serviced are the initial units in the system. The first of these goes immediately into service and the others follow in turn, because of a first-come, first-served queue discipline. The first arrival faces 6 units in the system and must wait 12 periods before it can enter the service channel. The second arrival faces 4 units in the waiting line and 1 unit in service. It must wait nine periods before entering the service channel. The fifth arrival finds no units in the system and may move immediately into service. From this point on, each arrival may move directly into the service channel. The service facility will not be fully utilized beyond

Chap. 17   Deterministic Queuing Models   405

this point. The total number of unit periods of waiting for the cycle may be found by observing the length of the horizontal paths.

The number of arrivals up to and including t periods will be the largest integer contained in the ratio t/A plus the unit that arrived at $t = 0$. This may be expressed as

$$\text{number of arrivals} = \left[\frac{t}{A} + 1\right].$$

Therefore, for a cycle of P periods, the total number of arrivals will be

$$\text{total number of arrivals} = \left[\frac{P}{A} + 1\right].$$

The brackets indicate a rounding operation downward to $[x] < x \leq [x + 1]$, where x is an integer expressing the number of arrivals up to and including t periods.

The arrival time in periods for the ith arrival may be expressed as $(i - 1)A$. The service completion time in periods for the ith arrival is $(k + i)S$ if the unit waits. If the unit does not wait, the service completion time in periods is $S + (i - 1)A$. These relationships may be verified by reference to Figure 17.4.

Total Waiting Time.   The total time in periods that the ith unit spends in the queue and in service is given by

$$\max\{(k + i)S - (i - 1)A;\, S\},$$

which may be written as

$$\max\{kS + A - i(A - S);\, S\}.$$

There is a number, i^*, such that for every $i \leq i^*$ the first term within the brackets will be larger than the second, and for every $i > i^*$ the second term will be larger. Therefore,

$$kS + A - i^*(A - S) > S$$

$$i^* < \frac{kS + A - S}{A - S}$$

or

$$i^* = \left[\frac{kS}{A - S} + 1\right]. \tag{17.5}$$

The brackets indicate a rounding operation downward as previously specified. In effect, i^* is the last unit that arrives during the cycle that must wait before entering the service channel. The next unit, $i^* + 1$, is the first unit that arrives during the cycle that may be serviced immediately after arrival. The use of Equation (17.5) may be demonstrated for the situation illustrated in Figure 17.4 as

$$i^* = \left[\frac{6(2) + 5 - 2}{5 - 2}\right] = [5] = 4 \text{ units.}$$

The waiting time may be expressed as iS if the item is a member of the initial queue, or as $kS + A - i(A - S)$ if $0 \leq i \leq i^*$, or S if $i > i^*$ and if the item is a new arrival. The total number of unit periods of delay incurred during the cycle by all units is then

$$D = \sum_{i=1}^{k} iS + \sum_{i=1}^{i^*} \{kS + A - i(A - S)\} + \sum_{i=i^*+1}^{[(P/A)+1]} S. \qquad (17.6)$$

The use of Equation (17.6) may also be demonstrated for the situation illustrated in Figure 17.4 as

$$D = \sum_{i=1}^{6} 2i + \sum_{i=1}^{4} \{6(2) + 5 - i(5-2)\} + \sum_{i=5}^{8} 2$$

$$= 42 + 38 + 8 = 88 \text{ unit periods.}$$

A general expression for the total number of unit periods of delay may be derived from Equation (17.6) as

$$D = \frac{k(k+1)S}{2} + (kS + A)i^* - \frac{A-S}{2}i^*(i^* + 1) + S\left\{\left[\frac{P}{A} + 1\right] - i^*\right\}$$

$$= \frac{k(k+1)S}{2} + S\left[\frac{P}{A} + 1\right] + (kS + A - S)i^* - \frac{A-S}{2}i^*(i^* + 1)$$

$$= \frac{k(k+1)S}{2} + S\left[\frac{P}{A} + 1\right] + i^*\left\{kS + A - S - \frac{A-S}{2}(i^* + 1)\right\}$$

$$= \frac{k(k+1)S}{2} + S\left[\frac{P}{A} + 1\right] + i^*\left\{kS - \frac{A-S}{2}(i^* - 1)\right\}.$$

Substituting Equation (17.5) for i^* gives

$$D = \frac{k(k+1)S}{2} + S\left[\frac{P}{A} + 1\right] + \left[\frac{kS + A - S}{A - S}\right]\left\{kS - \frac{A-S}{2}\left[\frac{kS}{A-S}\right]\right\}. \qquad (17.7)$$

Total System Cost. Total system cost for the period will be the sum of the cost of delay including the waiting cost and the facility cost per period. Substituting Equation (17.7) gives

$$TC = \frac{C_w}{P}\left(\frac{k(k+1)S}{2} + S\left[\frac{P}{A} + 1\right] + \left[\frac{kS + A - S}{A - S}\right]\right.$$

$$\left. \times \left\{kS - \frac{A-S}{2}\left[\frac{kS}{A-S}\right]\right\}\right) + C_f\left(\frac{1}{S}\right). \qquad (17.8)$$

For the case where there is no initial queue, $k = 0$, Equation (17.8) reduces to

$$TC = \frac{C_w}{P}\left(S\left[\frac{P}{A} + 1\right]\right) + C_f\left(\frac{1}{S}\right).$$

By considering the rounding operation, this becomes

$$TC = C_w\left(\frac{S}{A}\right) + C_f\left(\frac{1}{S}\right)$$

which was shown previously to be the total system cost when there is no initial queue.

An Example Application. Mathematical minimization of Equation (17.8) to find the least cost service interval, S, is not possible. The quantities in brackets are not differentiable, making a numerical procedure necessary.

Consider the following example: A waiting-line process begins with 6 units in the system at the beginning of a cycle 40 periods long. A unit will arrive every 5 periods, with the first arrival occurring at the beginning of the cycle. The cost of waiting is $5 per unit per period. A unit can be serviced for a facility cost of $40. The objective is to determine the minimum cost service interval.

Substituting each system and cost parameter into Equation (17.8) gives

$$TC = \frac{\$5}{40}\left(\frac{6(7)S}{2}\right) + S\left[\frac{40}{5} + 1\right] + \left[\frac{6S + 5 - S}{5 - S}\right]\left\{6S - \frac{5 - S}{2}\left[\frac{6S}{5 - S}\right]\right\} + \frac{\$40}{S}.$$

Waiting cost per period, facility cost per period, and total cost per period may be tabulated as a function of S. By performing the rounding operations specified by the brackets, the values given in Table 17.2 may be found. The minimum cost

Table 17.2. COST COMPONENTS FOR INITIAL QUEUE MODEL

S	WC	FC	TC
0	0	∞	∞
1	$ 4.63	$40.00	$44.63
2	11.00	20.00	31.00
3	22.13	13.33	35.46
4	52.00	10.00	62.00
5	∞	8.00	∞

service interval is two periods and may be provided at a cost of $20 per period. Under the conditions assumed, the decision maker would provide a single service channel capable of serving 1 unit every two periods, as was shown in Figure 17.4.

17.5 AN APPROXIMATION FOR TOTAL WAITING TIME

The number of units in the waiting-line system is an integer value at any point in time. This occurs because both the formation of the waiting line and the completion of service are normally discrete processes. Only if the system involves the flow of a fluid material can continuous analysis be accurately applied. Nevertheless, use of continuous analysis for discrete processes often leads to a simplification resulting in more complete understanding. This section, for comparison with earlier results, treats the queuing situation described in Section 17.4 as though it were continuous.

Approximate Total Waiting Time. In addition to the notation already presented, let n be the total number of units in the system at any point in time and let λ and μ be defined as the arrival rate $(1/A)$ and service rate $(1/S)$, respectively. The number of units in the system at any time t will be the sum of the initial units in the system and the cumulative arrivals up to the time t, minus the cumulative service completions up to time t:

$$n = k + 1 + \lambda t - \mu t.$$

When $n = 0$, waiting in queue ceases and utilization of the service facility becomes intermittent. This occurs after 22 periods in Figure 17.5 and is approximated by

$$0 = k + 1 - (\mu - \lambda)t$$

$$t = \frac{k+1}{\mu - \lambda}.$$

This approximation gives 23.33 periods for the condition assumed.

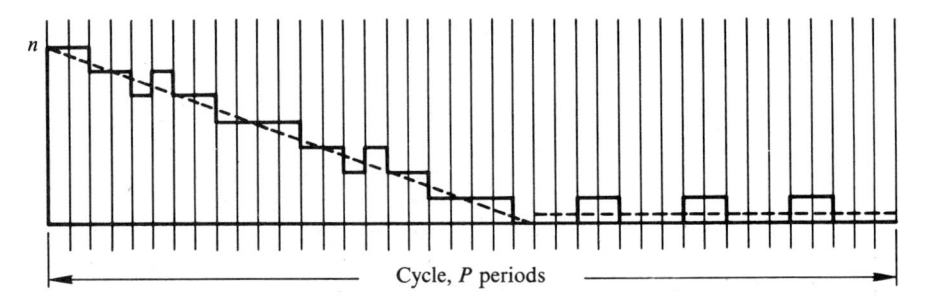

Figure 17.5 Actual and approximate number in the system.

Cumulative waiting time up to the point where waiting in queue ceases is approximated by the area of the triangle under the dashed line in Figure 17.5.

$$W_1 = \frac{1}{2}(k+1)\left(\frac{k+1}{\mu - \lambda}\right)$$

$$= \frac{(k+1)^2}{2(\mu - \lambda)}.$$

And the cumulative waiting time from this point to the end of the cycle is approximated by the area under the horizontal dashed line.

$$W_2 = \left(P - \frac{k+1}{\mu - \lambda}\right)\left(\frac{\lambda}{\mu}\right).$$

Total cumulative waiting time for the cycle is approximated by

$$W = W_1 + W_2$$

$$= \frac{(k+1)^2}{2(\mu - \lambda)} + \frac{P\lambda}{\mu} - \frac{\lambda(k+1)}{\mu(\mu - \lambda)}. \tag{17.9}$$

This result is an approximation for Equation (17.7) but is much easier to work with.

Comparison of Exact and Approximate Expressions. Figure 17.5 is a plot of the number of units in the system at any point in time for the queuing situation described in the preceding section. The solid line represents the actual number in the system resulting from the waiting-line process illustrated in Figure 17.4. The dashed line represents the approximate number in the system based on the continuous approximation of this section.

The total number of unit periods of waiting during the cycle may be found exactly from Equation (17.7) as

$$W = \frac{6(6+1)2}{2} + 2\left[\frac{40}{5} + 1\right] + \left[\frac{6(2)+5-2}{5-2}\right]\left\{6(2) - \frac{5-2}{2}\left[\frac{6(2)}{5-2}\right]\right\}$$

$$= 42 + 16 + 30 = 88 \text{ unit periods.}$$

The approximate number of unit periods of waiting for the cycle may be found from Equation (17.9) as

$$W = \frac{(6+1)^2}{2(0.5-0.2)} + \frac{40(0.2)}{0.5} - \frac{0.2(6+1)}{0.5(0.5-0.2)}$$

$$= 88.34 \text{ unit periods.}$$

The discrepancy between the actual and the approximate total waiting time is only 0.34 unit periods for this example. This discrepancy will be even less for cycles of longer duration. Therefore, Equation (17.9) may be substituted for W into Equation (17.8) in place of Equation (17.7). It is unlikely that this simplification will affect the minimum cost service interval significantly.

17.6 A GENERAL NUMERICAL SOLUTION METHOD

The waiting-line situations presented in previous sections assumed that arrivals occur at regular intervals. A more general system is allowed if it is assumed that arrivals occur in some irregular pattern during the cycle. The deterministic assumption of this chapter requires, however, that this pattern be known with certainty. Nevertheless, the ability to analyze waiting-line operations with deterministic non-steady-state arrivals adds considerable generality. As before, the queuing system will be viewed in terms of a cycle made up of P periods. Instead of an arrival occurring every A periods, the system will be viewed as accepting a number of arrivals per period with the number depending on the period. It is assumed that the cycle repeats itself and that no carryover is permitted from one cycle to the next. The objective will be to determine the minimum cost service capacity.

Total Waiting Time. Suppose that a waiting-line system is to be subjected to the arrival pattern shown in Figure 17.6. It is anticipated that this pattern will repeat itself for the cycles that follow. The number of units that can

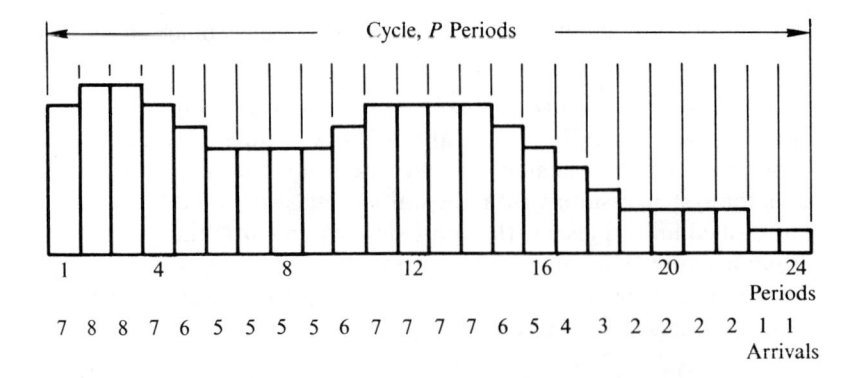

Figure 17.6 Deterministic non-steady-state arrival pattern.

be serviced per period may vary in increments of 1 unit with a cost of $1 per unit serviced. Waiting cost is $0.30 per unit per period.

The total number of unit periods of waiting for the cycle will be a function of the number of units serviced per period. The "no carryover" restriction requires that the service rate be sufficiently large to process all units before the end of the cycle. Table 17.3 gives the computations necessary to establish the total number of unit periods of waiting in the queue. It begins with the case where $\mu = 7$, providing a cumulative service capacity sufficient to process all arrivals for the cycle. The number of units in the queue for each period is found by subtracting the cumulative services from the cumulative arrivals. Any error introduced because of services and arrivals occurring during the period is neglected.

The total waiting time in the queue is found by adding the number in queue for all periods. This was found to be 284, 69, and 6 unit periods, respectively for $\mu = 5$, 6, and 7. The total waiting time in queue and in service (in the system) may be found by adding the service time incurred by all units in each case. For $\mu = 5$ the total waiting time is $284 + 118/5$ or approximately 308 unit periods. For $\mu = 6$ it is approximately $69 + 118/6$ or 89 unit periods. And for $\mu = 7$ the total number of unit periods of waiting is approximately $6 + 118/7$ or 23. The result of increasing the service rate is a reduction in the total number of unit periods of waiting for the cycle.

The Minimum Cost Service Rate. The total system cost per period given by the expression

$$TC = C_w\left(\frac{W}{P}\right) + C_f\left(\frac{1}{S}\right)$$

may be used to determine a minimum cost service rate, μ. With the costs given and the total number of unit periods calculated, the total cost per period for a service rate of five units per period is

Chap. 17 Deterministic Queuing Models

Table 17.3. CALCULATING TOTAL WAITING TIME IN QUEUE

Period	Arrivals	Σ Arrivals	$\mu = 5$ Services	$\mu = 5$ Σ Services	$\mu = 5$ Queue	$\mu = 6$ Services	$\mu = 6$ Σ Services	$\mu = 6$ Queue	$\mu = 7$ Services	$\mu = 7$ Σ Services	$\mu = 7$ Queue
1	7	7	5	5	2	6	6	1	7	7	0
2	8	15	5	10	5	6	12	3	7	14	1
3	8	23	5	15	8	6	18	5	7	21	2
4	7	30	5	20	10	6	24	6	7	28	2
5	6	36	5	25	11	6	30	6	7	35	1
6	5	41	5	30	11	6	36	5	6	41	0
7	5	46	5	35	11	6	42	4	5	46	0
8	5	51	5	40	11	6	48	3	5	51	0
9	5	56	5	45	11	6	54	2	5	56	0
10	6	62	5	50	12	6	60	2	6	62	0
11	7	69	5	55	14	6	66	3	7	69	0
12	7	76	5	60	16	6	72	4	7	76	0
13	7	83	5	65	18	6	78	5	7	83	0
14	7	90	5	70	20	6	84	6	7	90	0
15	6	96	5	75	21	6	90	6	6	96	0
16	5	101	5	80	21	6	96	5	5	101	0
17	4	105	5	85	20	6	102	3	4	105	0
18	3	108	5	90	18	6	108	0	3	108	0
19	2	110	5	95	15	2	110	0	2	110	0
20	2	112	5	100	12	2	112	0	2	112	0
21	2	114	5	105	9	2	114	0	2	114	0
22	2	116	5	110	6	2	116	0	2	116	0
23	1	117	5	115	2	1	117	0	1	117	0
24	1	118	3	118	0	1	118	0	1	118	0
Unit periods of waiting					284			69			6

$$TC = \$0.30\left(\frac{308}{24}\right) + \$1(5) = \$8.85.$$

For a service rate of 6 units per period,

$$TC = \$0.30\left(\frac{89}{24}\right) + \$1(6) = \$7.11.$$

For a service rate of 7 units per period,

$$TC = \$0.30\left(\frac{23}{24}\right) + \$1(7) = \$7.29.$$

Therefore, the minimum cost service rate for this situation is 6 units per period. If the service rate can be established as a continuous variable, the minimum cost might be found to be between 6 and 7 units per period.

QUESTIONS

17.1. Name and briefly describe the components of the waiting-line system.

17.2. Describe the essential facets of the decision environment relative to waiting-line operations.

17.3. Name and describe (a) a parallel channel service facility, and (b) a random queue discipline.

17.4. Contrast a deterministic and a probabilistic arrival mechanism. Give an example of each.

17.5. Contrast a deterministic and a probabilistic service mechanism. Give an example of each.

17.6. Describe how learning would cause the service interval to be a non-steady-state process.

17.7. Explain how the cost of a service facility is related to its capacity.

17.8. Explain how an increased resource expenditure on the service facility reduces the cost of waiting.

17.9. Describe the general effectiveness function for the waiting-line system, $E = f(x_i, y_j)$.

17.10. Explain the conditions under which a deterministic waiting-line system might become explosive.

PROBLEMS

17.1. A single-channel waiting-line system receives a unit every 10 periods. The waiting cost is $3.00 per unit period and the cost to service 1 unit is $12.
  (a) Plot total system cost as a function of the service interval.
  (b) Calculate the minimum cost service interval.

17.2. Suppose that the waiting cost for the system described in Problem 17.1 drops to $1 per unit per period.
  (a) Plot the total system cost as a function of the service interval.
  (b) Indicate the zone of explosive condition.
  (c) What is the minimum cost service interval under this condition?

17.3. Suppose that two channels are provided for the waiting-line system described in Problem 17.1.
  (a) Calculate the minimum cost service interval.
  (b) Calculate the minimum total system cost and compare with the minimum total system cost for one channel.

17.4. Use Equation (17.4) to calculate the minimum number of channels for which the minimum cost service interval lies outside the explosive zone. Express M in terms of C_f, C_w, and A. If $C_f = \$60$, $C_w = \$2.50$, and $A = 8$ periods, calculate the minimum number of channels required.

17.5. A waiting-line system starts with 20 units in the system at the beginning of a 1-hour-long cycle. A unit arrives every 8 minutes, with the first arrival occurring at the beginning of the hour. Each unit can be inspected at a cost of $0.25. The waiting cost is $0.04 per unit per minute due to spoilage. Determine the number of units that should be inspected per minute so as to minimize the total cost.

17.6. Waiting-line models have recently received widespread attention in a number of leading popular medical journals. This theory has been found to be useful in studying and minimizing patient waiting time which has always been of great concern to the medical fraternity. One such enterprising physician, Thaddeus Quack, M.D., D.V.M., specialist in pediatrics, pathology, and small animals, reported a startling breakthrough in the study of patient waiting time. He found that by adding nursing assistants, he could reduce patient service time and thus reduce total patient waiting time. With no nurses, he found it took him exactly 12 minutes to process each animal or human patient. Adding two nurses reduced this service time to 8 minutes, adding two more nurses reduced the service time to 6 minutes. The doctor worked a 10-hour day and found there were always 20 patients, evenly divided between people and animals, waiting to be treated at the start of the day. He treated these patients on a democratic first-come, first-served basis. Patients arrived during the work day at the rate of one every 30 minutes. The doctor estimated that patient waiting time was worth $2.00 per patient-hour. Nurses must be paid at the rate of $9.00 per hour.
(a) What is the average patient waiting time under the three conditions described?
(b) Which operational policy will result in a minimum total system cost?

17.7. A stenographic pool receives 120 letters during the day from the various offices. Thirty more letters are awaiting each morning which were dictated the previous evening. Each hour of delay in typing the letters costs the company $20. A typist can type a letter in 15 minutes. If a typist costs $110 per 8-hour day, how many typists will be needed? Use the approximate expression for W.

17.8. A waiting-line process begins with 8 units in the system and a unit will arrive every six periods. The first arrival occurs at the beginning of the cycle. It takes three periods to service 1 unit. Calculate the minimum value of P required to avoid an explosive condition.

17.9. Under the condition assumed in Problem 17.8, calculate the cumulative waiting time up to the point where waiting in queue ceases. Plot the number of units in the system as a function of time. Use approximate expressions.

17.10. Using the approximate expression, Equation (17.9), plot the cumulative waiting time as a function of S for a waiting-line process with 24 units at the beginning of the system. The first arrival occurs at the beginning of the cycle, and 1 unit arrives at every 8 periods. The cycle length is 80 periods.

17.11. Suppose that 11 arrivals occur per hour during the first 8 hours of a 24-hour cycle. During the next 6 hours, 7 arrivals occur per hour. During the remaining 10 hours, the arrival pattern is as follows: 6, 5, 4, 3, 3, 2, 2, 2, 1, 1. This cycle will repeat itself exactly each day. Waiting cost is $0.12 per unit per hour and it costs $0.60 per unit serviced. Determine the minimum cost per number of units to service per hour.

17.12. Rework the example of Section 17.4 by the method of Section 17.6. Compare the results obtained with those given in Table 17.2.

18

Probabilistic Queuing Models

In this chapter the deterministic restriction on arrival time and service time does not apply. Ordinarily, both the arrival rate and the service rate are expected values from specified probability distributions. A probabilistic queuing system will result, however, if either the arrival time and/or the service time is a random variable. For simplicity, the arrival rate is often assumed to be an expected value from a Poisson distribution. This assumption is mathematically convenient and has a sound practical basis in many situations. Most models presented in this chapter assume that the number of arrivals per period obey the Poisson distribution.

Two types of waiting-line systems are presented in the sections that follow. The first is based on the assumption of an infinite population, in that the size of the population is large relative to the arrival rate. In this case, individuals leaving the population do not significantly affect the arrival potential of the remaining units. The second involves a finite population, in that the population is small relative to the arrival rate. In this system, individuals leaving the population significantly change the characteristics of the population and the arrival pattern. This chapter presents probabilistic queuing models for each of these systems.

18.1 SIMULATION OF WAITING LINES[1]

Decision models for probabilistic waiting-line systems are usually based on certain assumptions regarding the mathematical forms of the arrival and service time distributions. Simulated sampling or Monte Carlo analysis, however, does not require that the arrival and service time distributions obey certain theoretical forms. Waiting-line data are produced as the system is simulated over time. Conclusions can be reached from the output statistics whatever the form of the distributions assumed. In addition, the detailed numerical description which results from simulated sampling analysis assists greatly in understanding the probabilistic queuing process. This section illustrates the application of Monte Carlo analysis to an infinite population, single-channel waiting-line system.

Arrival and Service Time Distributions. The probabilistic waiting-line system usually involves both an arrival time and a service time distribution. Monte Carlo analysis requires that the form and parameters of these distributions be specified. The cumulative distributions may then be developed and used as a means for generating arrival and service time data.

For the example under consideration, assume that the time between arrivals, A_x, has an empirical distribution with a mean of 6.325 periods. Service time, S_x, will be assumed to have a normal distribution with a mean of 5.000 periods and a standard deviation of 1 period. These distributions are exhibited in Figure 18.1. The probabilities associated with each value of A_x and S_x are indicated. By summing these individual probabilities from left to right, the cumulative distributions of Figure 18.2 result. These distributions may be used with a table of random rectangular variates to generate arrival and service time random variables.

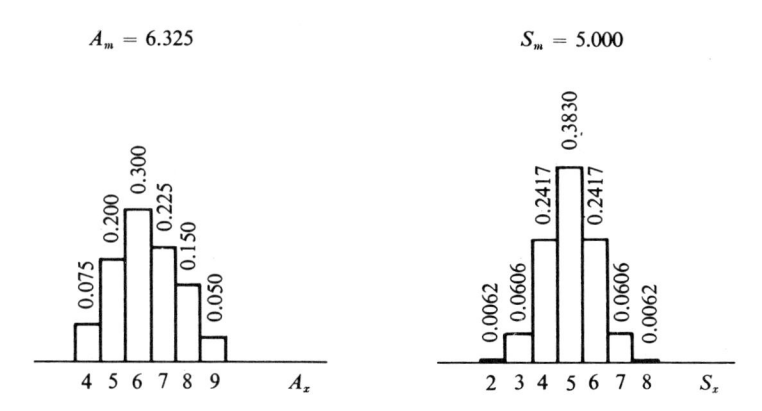

Figure 18.1 Arrival and service time distributions.

[1] It is suggested that Appendix C, Section C.5, be reviewed as a prerequisite to this section.

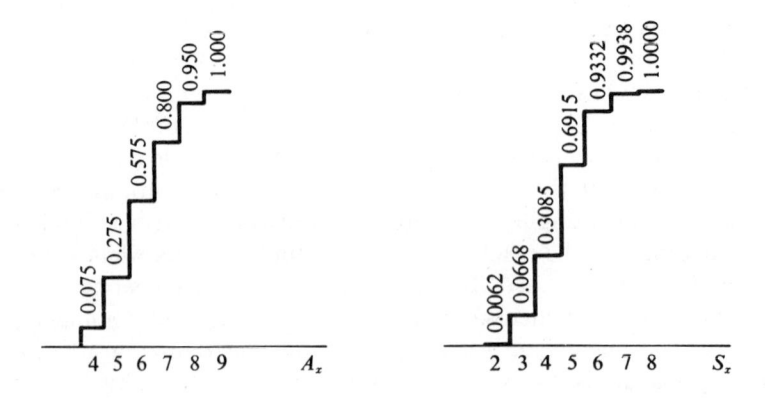

Figure 18.2 Cumulative arrival and service time distributions.

The Simulated Sampling Analysis. The queuing process under study is assumed to begin when the first arrival occurs. A unit will move immediately into the service facility if it is empty. If the service facility is not empty, the unit will wait in the queue. Units in the waiting line will enter the service facility on a first-come, first-served basis. The objective of the simulated sampling is to simulate this process over time. The number of unit periods of waiting in the queue and in service may be observed for each of several service rates. The service rate resulting in a minimum cost system may then be adopted.

The waiting-line process resulting from the arrival and service time distributions of Figure 18.1 is shown in Figure 18.3. The illustration reads from left to right, with the second line being a continuation of the first, and so forth. The interval between vertical lines represents two periods, the heavy dots represent arrivals, the slanting path a unit in service, and the arrows a service completion. When a unit cannot move directly into the service channel, it waits in the queue which is represented by a horizontal path. This graphical representation is identical to that used for the deterministic process in Figure 17.2.

The probabilistic waiting-line process of Figure 18.3 involves 400 periods and was developed in the following manner. First, the sequence of arrivals was established by the use of random rectangular variates and the cumulative arrival distribution of Figure 18.2. Next, each arrival was moved into the service channel if it was available. This availability is a function of the arrival pattern and the service durations selected with the aid of random rectangular variates and the cumulative service time distribution of Figure 18.2.

Specifically, the simulated sampling analysis proceeded as follows. Random rectangular variates from Appendix A, Table A.2, were chosen as 5668, 3513, 2060, 7804, 0815, 2639, 9845, 6549, 6353, 7941, and so on. These correspond to arrival intervals of 6, 6, 5, 7, 5, 5, 9, 7, 7, 7, and so forth. Next, random rectangular variates were chosen as 323, 249, 404, 275, 879, 404, 740, 779, 441, 384, and so on. These correspond to service durations of 5, 4, 5, 4, 6, 5, 6, 6, 5, 5, and so forth. These service times determine the time an arrival

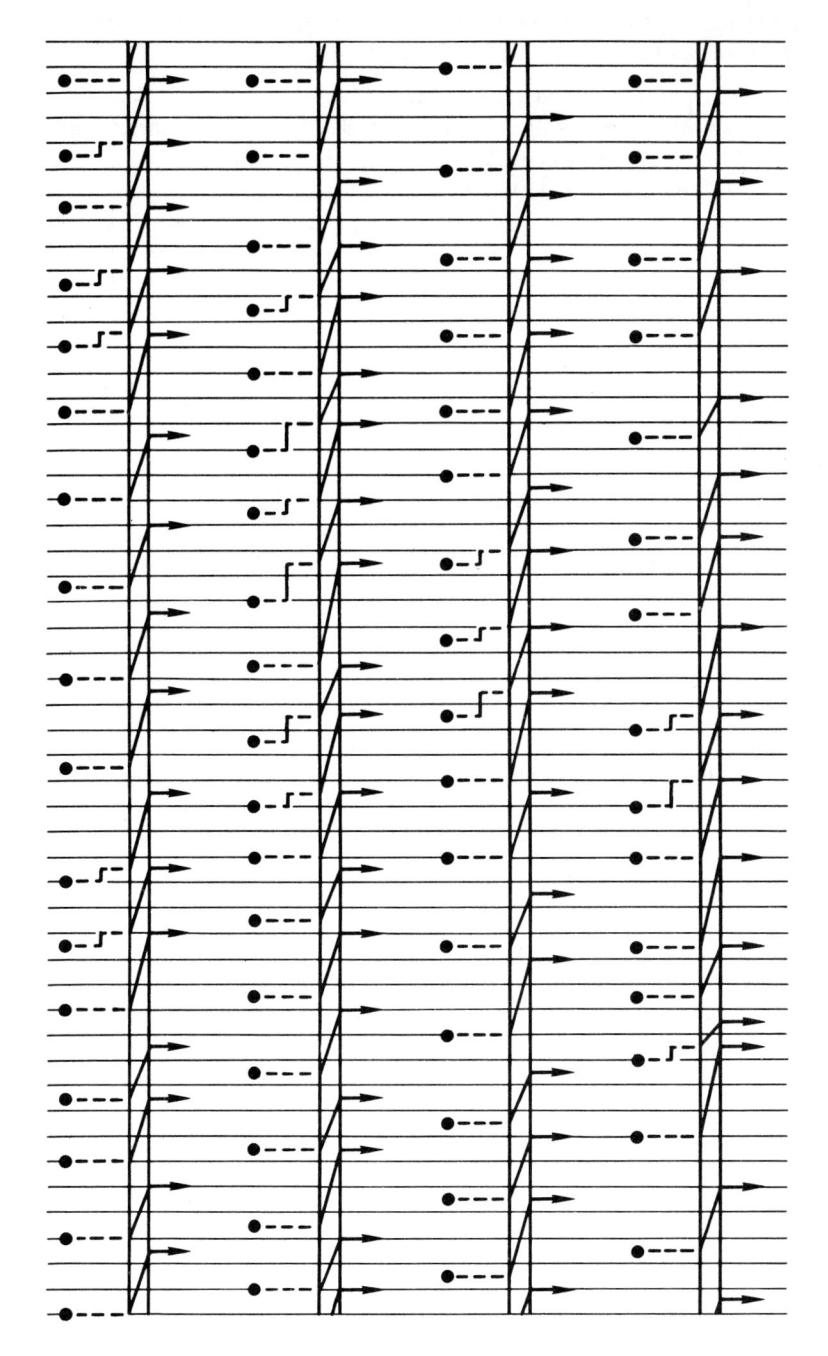

Figure 18.3 Single-channel probabilistic queuing process.

enters the service channel and the time it is discharged. By proceeding in this manner, the results of Figure 18.3 are obtained.

Economic Analysis of Output Results. The 400 periods simulated produced a waiting pattern involving 337 unit periods of waiting in service and 23 unit periods of waiting in the queue. The total number of unit periods of waiting for the 400-period sample was 360.

Suppose that waiting cost per unit per period is $0.04 and that it costs $0.065 to provide the service capability indicated by the service time distribution of Figure 18.1. The total system cost for the study period is therefore $0.04(360) + $0.065(400) = $40.40. This total system cost may be compared with the total system cost for alternate service policies by performing a simulation for the alternative policies. Although this process is time consuming, it is applicable to many situations that cannot be treated by mathematical means.

18.2 SINGLE-CHANNEL QUEUING DERIVATIONS

In this section, assume that the number of arrivals per period to the queue is a random variable with a Poisson distribution, and the time required to service each unit is a random variable with an exponential distribution. Events are recognized to have occurred at the time of arrival of a unit or at the time of completion of a service. Under the assumption of Poisson arrivals and exponential service, it can be shown that the probability of the occurrence of an event (arrival or service completion) during a specific time interval does not depend on the time of the occurrence of the immediately preceding event of the same kind. The expected number of arrivals per period may be expressed as $1/A_m$, or λ, and the expected number of service completions per period may be expressed as $1/S_m$ or μ. The population of units that may demand service is assumed to be infinite.

The Probability of n Units in the System. Under the foregoing assumptions the propability that an arrival occurs between the time t and time $t + \Delta t$ is $\lambda \Delta t$. Similarly, the probability that a service completion occurs between time t and time $t + \Delta t$, given that a unit is being serviced at time t, is $\mu \Delta t$. Let

n = number of units in the system at time t including the unit being served, if any

$P_n(t)$ = probability of n units in the system at time t

Since the time interval Δt is small, it can be assumed that the probability of more than one arrival or service completion during the interval is negligible. Consider the event that there are n units in the system at time $t + \Delta t$ with $n \geq 1$.

Event $\{n$ units in the system at time $t + \Delta t\}$
    = Event $\{n$ units in the system at time t, no arrivals during interval Δt, and no service completions during interval $\Delta t\}$

Chap. 18   Probabilistic Queuing Models   419

or Event $\{n + 1$ units in the system at time t, no arrivals during interval Δt, and one service completion during interval $\Delta t\}$

or Event $\{n - 1$ units in the system at time t, one arrival during interval Δt, and no service completion during interval $\Delta t\}$.

The probability of the event n units in the system at time $t + \Delta t$ can be written as the sum of the probabilities of the three mutually exclusive events described above.

$$\begin{aligned} P_n(t + \Delta t) &= \{P_n(t)[1 - \lambda\,\Delta t][1 - \mu\,\Delta t]\} \\ &\quad + \{P_{n+1}(t)[1 - \lambda\,\Delta t]\mu\,\Delta t + \{P_{n-1}(t)\lambda\,\Delta t[1 - \mu\,\Delta t]\} \\ &= P_n(t) - (\lambda + \mu)P_n(t)\,\Delta t + \lambda\mu P_n(t)(\Delta t)^2 + \mu P_{n+1}(t)\,\Delta t \\ &\quad - \lambda\mu P_{n+1}(t)(\Delta t)^2 + \lambda P_{n-1}(t)\,\Delta t - \lambda\mu P_{n-1}(t)(\Delta t)^2. \end{aligned} \quad (18.1)$$

Terms involving $(\Delta t)^2$ can be neglected. Subtracting $P_n(t)$ from both sides and dividing by Δt,

$$\frac{P_n(t + \Delta t) - P_n(t)}{\Delta t} = -(\lambda + \mu)P_n(t) + \mu P_{n+1}(t) + \lambda P_{n-1}(t).$$

In the limit

$$\lim_{\Delta t \to 0} \frac{P_n(t + \Delta t) - P_n(t)}{\Delta t} = \frac{d}{dt}P_n(t) \\ = -(\lambda + \mu)P_n(t) + \mu P_{n+1}(t) + \lambda P_{n-1}(t). \quad (18.2)$$

For the special case $n = 0$,

Event $\{0$ units in the system at time $t + \Delta t\}$

= Event $\{0$ units in the system at time t and no arrivals during the interval $\Delta t\}$

or Event $\{1$ unit in the system at time t, no arrivals during the interval Δt, and one service completion during the interval $\Delta t\}$.

Hence,

$$\begin{aligned} P_0(t + \Delta t) &= \{P_0(t)[1 - \lambda\,\Delta t]\} + \{P_1(t)[1 - \lambda\,\Delta t]\mu\,\Delta t\} \\ &= P_0(t) - \lambda P_0(t)\,\Delta t + \mu P_1(t)\,\Delta t - \lambda\mu P_1(t)(\Delta t)^2. \end{aligned} \quad (18.3)$$

Again neglecting terms involving $(\Delta t)^2$, subtracting $P_0(t)$ from both sides, and dividing by Δt gives

$$\frac{P_0(t + \Delta t) - P_0(t)}{\Delta t} = -\lambda P_0(t) + \mu P_1(t).$$

In the limit

$$\frac{d}{dt}P_n(t) = \lim_{\Delta t \to 0} \frac{P_0(t + \Delta t) - P_0(t)}{\Delta t} = -\lambda P_0(t) + \mu P_1(t). \quad (18.4)$$

Equations (18.3) and (18.4) are called as the governing equations of a Poisson arrival and exponential service single-channel queue. These differential equations constitute an infinite system. The general solution of this system is rather difficult to obtain and is considered beyond the scope of this book. However, Figure 18.4 shows an example of the nature of the solution for a particular case.

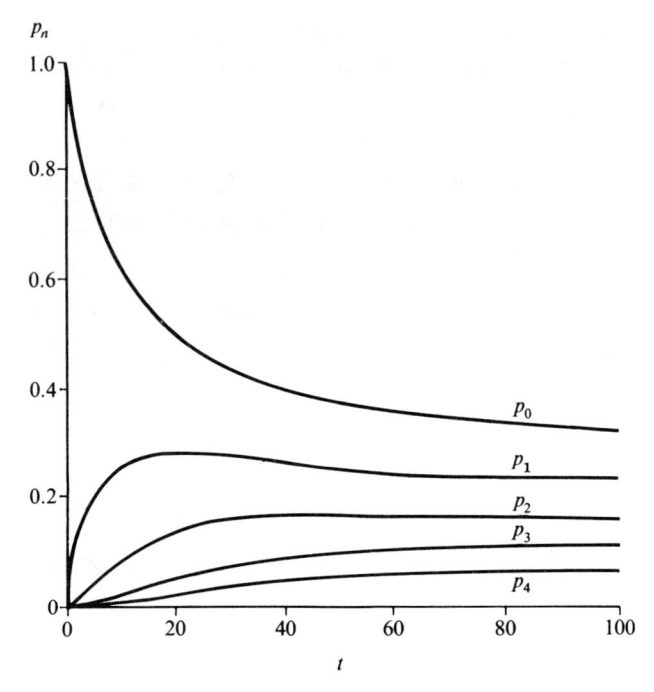

Figure 18.4 Transient solution to governing equations of a Poisson-exponential queue.

As long as the probabilities $P_n(t)$ are changing with time, the queue is considered to be in a transient state. From Figure 18.4 it should be noted that this change in $P_n(t)$ becomes smaller and smaller as the time increases. After a long time there will be hardly any change in $P_n(t)$, and the queue can be considered to have reached a steady state. In the steady state the rate of change $dP_n(t)/dt$ can be considered to be zero and the probabilities written as P_n independent of time. The steady-state governing equations can be written as

$$(\lambda + \mu)P_n = \mu P_{n+1} + \lambda P_{n-1} \qquad (18.5)$$

and

$$\lambda P_0 = \mu P_1. \qquad (18.6)$$

Equations (18.5) and (18.6) constitute an infinite system of algebraic equations which can be solved by substituting $P_{n+1} = P_n \cdot \rho$ into Equation (18.5), giving

$$(\lambda + \mu)\rho P_{n-1} = (\rho^2 \mu + \lambda)P_{n-1}$$

or
$$(\lambda + \mu)\rho = \rho^2\mu + \lambda$$
or
$$\rho = \frac{\lambda}{\mu}.$$

A substitution in Equation (18.6) gives the same result. Using this substitution, the general solution can be written as
$$P_1 = \rho P_0$$
and
$$P_n = \rho P_{n-1}$$
$$= \rho^n P_0. \qquad (18.7)$$

However, since $\sum_{n=0}^{\infty} P_n = 1$,
$$1 = \sum_{n=0}^{\infty} P_0 \rho^n = P_0 \sum_{n=0}^{\infty} \rho^n$$
$$= P_0 \left(\frac{1}{1-\rho}\right). \qquad (18.8)$$

Hence,
$$P_0 = 1 - \frac{\lambda}{\mu}$$
and
$$P_n = \left(1 - \frac{\lambda}{\mu}\right)\left(\frac{\lambda}{\mu}\right)^n. \qquad (18.9)$$

The requirement for the convergence of the sum $\sum_{n=0}^{\infty} (\lambda/\mu)^n$ is that λ/μ be less than 1. This implies that the arrival rate λ must be less than the service rate μ for the queue to reach steady state.

As an example of the significance of Equation (18.9) in waiting-line operations, suppose that a queue is experiencing Poisson arrivals with a mean rate of 1/10 unit per period and that the service duration is distributed exponentially with a mean of four periods. The service rate is, therefore, 1/4, or 0.25 unit per period. Probabilities associated with each value of n may be calculated as follows:

$$P_0 = (0.6)(0.4)^0 = 0.600$$
$$P_1 = (0.6)(0.4)^1 = 0.240$$
$$P_2 = (0.6)(0.4)^2 = 0.096$$
$$P_3 = (0.6)(0.4)^3 = 0.039$$
$$P_4 = (0.6)(0.4)^4 = 0.015$$
$$P_5 = (0.6)(0.4)^5 = 0.006$$
$$P_6 = (0.6)(0.4)^6 = 0.003$$
$$P_7 = (0.6)(0.4)^7 = 0.001.$$

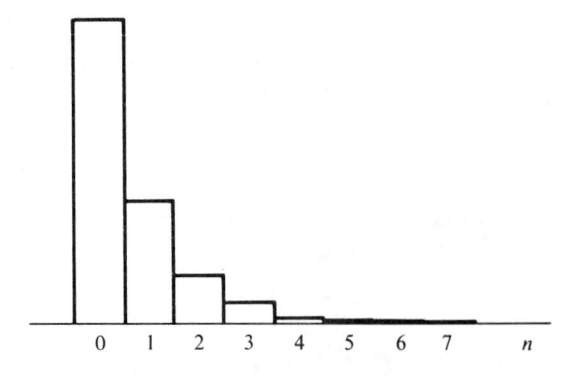

Figure 18.5 Probability distribution of *n* units in the system.

Figure 18.5 exhibits the probability distribution of *n* units in the system. Certain important characteristics of the waiting-line system can be extracted from this distribution. For example, the probability of one or more units in the system is 0.4, the probability of no units in the system is 0.6, the probability of more than 4 units in the system is 0.01, and so forth. Such information as this is useful when there is a restriction on the number of units in the system. By altering the arrival population or the service rate or both, the probability of the number of units in the system exceeding a specified value may be controlled.

The Mean Number of Units in the System. The mean number of units in the system may be expressed as

$$n_m = \sum_{n=0}^{\infty} nP_n = \sum_{n=0}^{\infty} n(1-\rho)\rho^n$$

$$= (1-\rho)\sum_{n=0}^{\infty} n\rho^n.$$

Let $g = \sum_{n=0}^{\infty} n\rho^n$; then

$$\rho g = \sum_{n=0}^{\infty} n\rho^{n+1} = \sum_{n=1}^{\infty} (n-1)\rho^n.$$

Subtracting ρg from g yields

$$(1-\rho)g = \sum_{n=0}^{\infty} n\rho^n - \sum_{n=1}^{\infty} (n-1)\rho^n$$

$$= \sum_{n=1}^{\infty} n\rho^n - \sum_{n=1}^{\infty} n\rho^n + \sum_{n=1}^{\infty} \rho^n$$

$$= \sum_{n=1}^{\infty} \rho^n = \rho \sum_{n=0}^{\infty} \rho^n = \frac{\rho}{1-\rho}.$$

Hence,

$$n_m = (1-\rho)g = \frac{\rho}{1-\rho}.$$

Substituting $\rho = \lambda/\mu$ gives

$$n_m = \frac{\lambda}{\mu - \lambda}. \tag{18.10}$$

For the example given previously, the mean number of units in the system is

$$n_m = \frac{0.10}{0.25 - 0.10} = 0.667.$$

The Average Length of the Waiting Line. The average length of the queue, m_m, can be expressed as the average number of units in the system less the average number of units being serviced or

$$\begin{aligned} m_m &= \frac{\lambda}{\mu - \lambda} - \frac{\lambda}{\mu} \\ &= \frac{\lambda^2}{\mu(\mu - \lambda)}. \end{aligned} \tag{18.11}$$

For the preceding example the average length of queue is

$$m_m = \frac{(0.10)^2}{0.25(0.25 - 0.10)} = 0.267,$$

the average length of a nonempty waiting line. The probability that the queue is nonempty is given by

$$\begin{aligned} P(m > 0) &= 1 - P_0 - P_1 \\ &= 1 - (1 - \rho) - (1 - \rho)\rho = \rho^2. \end{aligned} \tag{18.12}$$

The average length of the nonempty queue is

$$\begin{aligned} (m \mid m > 0)_m &= \frac{m_m}{P(m > 0)} \\ &= \frac{\lambda^2/\mu(\mu - \lambda)}{\rho^2} \\ &= \frac{\mu}{\mu - \lambda}. \end{aligned} \tag{18.13}$$

For the preceding numerical example, the probability that the queue is nonempty is

$$P(m > 0) = \rho^2 = \frac{(0.10)^2}{(0.25)^2} = 0.16.$$

The average length of the nonempty queue is

$$\frac{0.25}{0.25 - 0.10} = 1.667.$$

18.3 THE DISTRIBUTION OF WAITING TIME

In deterministic waiting-line systems such as those described in Chapter 17, it is possible to compute exactly the waiting time spent by a unit before it goes into service. However, in a probabilistic queuing situation, this waiting time is a random variable which depends on the status of the system at the time of the arrival and also on the times required to service the units already waiting for service. In the case of a single-channel system, an arriving unit can go immediately into service only if there are no other units in the system. In all other cases the arriving unit will have to wait.

Two different events can be identified under the Poisson arrival and exponential service assumption for the waiting time, w:

1. Event $\{w = 0\}$ is identical to Event $\{0$ units in the system$\}$.
2. Event $\{$waiting time is in the interval w and $w + \Delta w\}$ is a composite event of there being n units in the system at the time of the arrival, $n - 1$ services being completed during the time w, and the last service being completed within the interval w and $w + \Delta w$.

The probability of the first event occurring is given by

$$P(w = 0) = 1 - P_0$$
$$= 1 - \frac{\lambda}{\mu}. \qquad (18.14)$$

The second event is illustrated in Figure 18.6. There will be one such event for every n. Furthermore,

$$P(w \leq \text{waiting time} \leq w + \Delta w) = f(w)\,\Delta w$$

$$= \sum_{n=1}^{\infty} [P_n \cdot P\{(n-1) \text{ services in time } w\}]$$

$$\cdot P\{\text{one service completion in time } \Delta w\}$$

$$= \sum_{n=1}^{\infty} \left(1 - \frac{\lambda}{\mu}\right)\left(\frac{\lambda}{\mu}\right)^n \left[\frac{(\mu w)^{n-1} e^{-\mu w}}{(n-1)!}\right] \mu\,\Delta w$$

$$= \sum_{n=1}^{\infty} \left(\frac{\lambda}{\mu}\right)^n \left[\frac{(\mu w)^{n-1}}{(n-1)!}\right] e^{-\mu w} \left(1 - \frac{\lambda}{\mu}\right) \mu\,\Delta w.$$

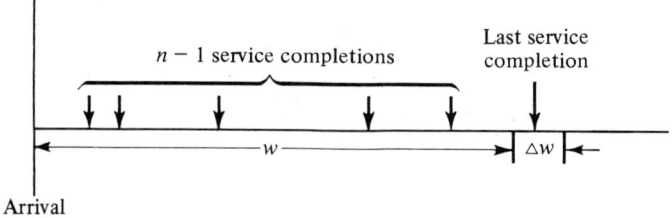

Figure 18.6 Waiting time for an arriving unit when there are n units in the system.

Let $k = n - 1$. Then

$$f(w) \, \Delta w = \sum_{k=0}^{\infty} \left(\frac{\lambda}{\mu}\right)^k \frac{\mu^k w^k}{k!} \left(\frac{\lambda}{\mu}\right) e^{-\mu w} \left(1 - \frac{\lambda}{\mu}\right) \mu \, \Delta w. \qquad (18.15)$$

However,

$$\sum_{k=0}^{\infty} \left(\frac{\lambda}{\mu}\right)^k \frac{\mu^k w^k}{k!} = \sum_{k=0}^{\infty} \frac{(\lambda w)^k}{k!} = e^{\lambda w}. \qquad (18.16)$$

Substituting Equation (18.16) into Equation (18.15) gives

$$f(w) \, \Delta w = e^{\lambda w} \left(\frac{\lambda}{\mu} e^{-\mu w}\right) \mu \, \Delta w \left(1 - \frac{\lambda}{\mu}\right)$$

$$= \lambda \left(1 - \frac{\lambda}{\mu}\right) e^{-(\mu-\lambda)w} \, \Delta w$$

or

$$f(w) = \lambda \left(1 - \frac{\lambda}{\mu}\right) e^{-(\mu-\lambda)w}. \qquad (18.17)$$

Equations (18.14) and (18.17) describe the waiting time distribution for a single-channel queue with Poisson arrivals and exponential service. Note that this distribution is partly discrete and partly continuous.

The Mean Waiting Time. The mean time an arrival spends waiting for service can be obtained from the waiting time distribution as

$$w_m = 0 \cdot P(w = 0) + \int_{w>0} w\lambda \left(1 - \frac{\lambda}{\mu}\right) e^{-(\mu-\lambda)w} \, dw.$$

After several steps,

$$w_m = \frac{\lambda}{\mu(\mu - \lambda)}. \qquad (18.18)$$

For the numerical example presented previously,

$$w_m = \frac{0.10}{0.25(0.25 - 0.10)}$$

$$= 2.667 \text{ periods.}$$

The Average Time in the System. The average time that a unit spends in the waiting-line system is composed of the average waiting time and the average time required for service, or

$$t_m = \frac{\lambda}{\mu(\mu - \lambda)} + \frac{1}{\mu}$$

$$= \frac{\lambda + \mu - \lambda}{\mu(\mu - \lambda)} = \frac{1}{\mu - \lambda}. \qquad (18.19)$$

For the example above the average time spent in the system will be

$$t_m = \frac{1}{0.25 - 0.10} = 6.667 \text{ periods.}$$

The Minimum Cost Service Rate. The expected total system cost per period is the sum of the expected waiting cost per period and the expected facility cost per period; that is,

$$TC_m = WC_m + FC_m.$$

The expected waiting cost per period is obtained as the product of cost of waiting per period, the expected number of units arriving per period, and the average time each unit spends in the system, or

$$WC_m = C_w(\lambda)\frac{1}{\mu - \lambda}$$
$$= \frac{C_w \lambda}{\mu - \lambda}. \qquad (18.20)$$

Alternatively, the expected waiting cost per period can be obtained as the product of cost of waiting per period and the mean number of units in the system during the period, or

$$WC_m = C_w(n_m)$$
$$= \frac{C_w \lambda}{\mu - \lambda}.$$

The expected service cost per period is the product of the cost of servicing one unit and the service rate in units per period, or

$$FC_m = C_f(\mu).$$

The expected total system cost per period is the sum of these cost components and may be expressed as

$$TC_m = \frac{C_w \lambda}{\mu - \lambda} + C_f(\mu). \qquad (18.21)$$

A minimum cost service rate may be found by differentiating with respect to μ, setting the result equal to zero, and solving for μ as follows:

$$\frac{dTC_m}{d\mu} = -C_w \lambda (\mu - \lambda)^{-2} + C_f = 0$$

$$(\mu - \lambda)^2 C_f = \lambda C_w \qquad (18.22)$$

$$\mu = \lambda + \sqrt{\frac{\lambda C_w}{C_f}}.$$

As an application of the preceding model, consider the following Poisson arrival and exponential service time illustration. The mean time between arrivals is eight periods, the cost of waiting is $0.10 per unit per period, and the facility cost for serving 1 unit is $0.165. The expected waiting cost per period, the expected facility cost per period, and the expected total system cost per period is exhibited as a function of μ in Table 18.1. The expected waiting cost per period is infinite when $\mu = \lambda$ and decreases as μ increases. The expected

Table 18.1. COST COMPONENTS FOR EXPONENTIAL SERVICE DURATION

μ	WC_m	FC_m	TC_m
0.125	∞	$0.0206	∞
0.150	$0.5000	0.0248	$0.5248
0.200	0.1667	0.0330	0.1997
0.250	0.1000	0.0413	0.1413
0.300	0.0714	0.0495	0.1209
0.400	0.0455	0.0660	0.1115
0.500	0.0333	0.0825	0.1158
0.600	0.0263	0.0990	0.1253
0.800	0.0185	0.1320	0.1505
1.000	0.0143	0.1650	0.1793

facility cost per period increases with increasing values of μ. The minimum expected total system cost occurs when μ is 0.4 unit per period.

The minimum cost service rate may be found directly by substituting into Equation (18.22) as follows:

$$\mu = 0.125 + \sqrt{\frac{(0.125)(\$0.10)}{\$0.165}}$$

$$= 0.125 + 0.275 = 0.400 \text{ unit per period.}$$

18.4 MULTIPLE-CHANNEL WAITING-LINE DERIVATIONS

In previous sections the arriving units were assumed to have been serviced through a single service facility. In many practical situations, however, there are several alternative service facilities. One example is the toll plaza on a turnpike where several toll booths may serve the arriving traffic.

In the multiple-channel case the service facility will have c service channels, each capable of serving one unit at a time. An arriving unit will go to the first available service channel that is not busy. If all channels are busy, additional arrivals will form a single queue. As soon as any busy channel completes service and becomes available, it accepts the first unit in the queue for service. The steady-state probabilities in such a system are defined as

$P_{m,n}(t)$ = probability that there are n units waiting in queue and m channels are busy at time t

It must be noted that m can only be an integer between 0 and c, and n is zero unless $m = c$.

The determination of the steady-state probabilities follows the logic used in the single-channel case, although the solution becomes quite involved. The results are given below for the Poisson arrival and exponential service situation. Define

$$\rho = \frac{\lambda}{c\mu}$$

$$P_{c,n} = P_{0,0}\left(\frac{\lambda}{\mu}\right)^c \frac{1}{c!}\rho^n$$

$$P_{m,0} = P_{0,0}\left(\frac{\lambda}{\mu}\right)^m \frac{1}{m!}. \quad (18.23)$$

$$P_{0,0} = \frac{1}{(\lambda/\mu)^c(1/c!)[1/(1-\rho)] + \sum_{r=0}^{c-1}(\lambda/\mu)^r(1/r!)}$$

As an example, consider a three-channel system with Poisson arrivals at a mean rate of 0.50 unit per period and exponential service at each channel with a mean service rate of 0.25 unit per period. Under these conditions ρ is equal to $(0.50/3 \times 0.25) = 2/3$.

$$P_{0,0} = \frac{1}{(0.50/0.25)^3(1/3!)[1/(1-2/3)] + \sum_{r=0}^{2}(0.50/0.25)^r(1/r!)}$$

$$= \frac{1}{4+1+2+2} = \frac{1}{9} = 0.11.$$

Average Length of the Queue. The average queue length is obtained from the expression

$$m_m = P_{0,0}\frac{(\lambda/\mu)^{c+1}}{(c-1)!(c-\lambda/\mu)^2}. \quad (18.24)$$

For the example considered

$$m_m = \frac{1}{9}\left[\frac{(0.50/0.25)^4}{2!(3-0.50/0.25)^2}\right]$$

$$= \frac{1}{9}\left[\frac{(2)^4}{2}\right] = \frac{8}{9} = 0.89 \text{ unit.}$$

Average Number of Units in the System. The average number of units in the system is

$$n_m = m_m + \frac{\lambda}{\mu}. \quad (18.25)$$

For the example considered

$$n_m = 0.89 + \frac{0.50}{0.25} = 2.89 \text{ units.}$$

Average Waiting Time. The average waiting time can be obtained from the expression for m_m as

$$w_m = \frac{m_m}{\lambda}. \quad (18.26)$$

In the illustrative example $w_m = 0.89/0.50$ or 1.78 periods.

Average Delay or Holding Time. The average delay is obtained as the sum of waiting and service times as

$$d_m = w_m + \frac{1}{\mu}. \tag{18.27}$$

In the example average delay is $1.78 + 4$ or 5.78 periods.

The Probability that an Arriving Unit Has to Wait. The probability of a delay is the same as the probability that all channels are occupied.

$$P(w > 0) = \sum_0^\infty P_{c,n}$$

$$= P_{0,0} \left(\frac{\lambda}{\mu}\right)^c \frac{1}{c!(1-\rho)}. \tag{18.28}$$

In the example the probability that an arriving unit has to wait is

$$P(w > 0) = \frac{1}{9}\left(\frac{0.50}{0.25}\right)^3 \frac{1}{3!(1-2/3)}$$

$$= \frac{1}{9}(8)\frac{1}{2} = \frac{4}{9} = 0.444.$$

18.5 POISSON ARRIVALS WITH NONEXPONENTIAL SERVICE

The assumption that the number of arrivals per period obeys a Poisson distribution has a sound practical basis. Although it cannot be said that the Poisson distribution always adequately describes the distribution of the number of arrivals per period, much evidence exists to indicate that this is often the case. Intuitive considerations add support to this assumption, since arrival rates are usually independent of time, queue length, or any other property of the waiting-line system. Evidence in support of the exponential distribution of service durations is not as strong. Often this distribution is assumed for mathematical convenience, as in previous sections. When the service time distribution is nonexponential, the development of decision models is quite difficult. Therefore, this section will present models with nonexponential service without proof. The assumptions that μ is greater than λ and that the population is infinite are retained.

Poisson Arrivals with Constant Service Times. When service is provided automatically by mechanical means, or when the service operation is mechanically paced, the service duration might be a constant. Under these conditions, the service time distribution has a variance of zero. The mean number of units in the system is given by

$$n_m = \frac{(\lambda/\mu)^2}{2[1-(\lambda/\mu)]} + \frac{\lambda}{\mu}. \tag{18.29}$$

The mean waiting time is

$$w_m = \frac{\lambda/\mu}{2\mu[1 - (\lambda/\mu)]} + \frac{1}{\mu}. \qquad (18.30)$$

The expected total system cost per period is the sum of the expected waiting cost per period and the expected facility cost per period; that is,

$$TC_m = WC_m + FC_m.$$

The expected waiting cost per period is the product of the cost of waiting per unit per period and the mean number of units in the system during the period, or

$$WC_m = C_w(n_m)$$
$$= C_w \left\{ \frac{(\lambda/\mu)^2}{2[1 - (\lambda/\mu)]} + \frac{\lambda}{\mu} \right\}.$$

The expected facility cost per period is the product of the cost of servicing one unit and the service rate units per period, or

$$FC_m = C_f(\mu).$$

The expected total system cost per period is the sum of these cost components and may be expressed as

$$TC_m = C_w \left\{ \frac{(\lambda/\mu)^2}{2[1 - (\lambda/\mu)]} + \frac{\lambda}{\mu} \right\} + C_f(\mu). \qquad (18.31)$$

As an application of the foregoing model, consider the example of the preceding section. Instead of the parameter μ being the expected value from an exponential distribution, however, assume that it is a constant. The expected waiting cost per period, the expected service cost per period, and the expected total system cost per period is exhibited as a function of μ in Table 18.2. Although the expected waiting cost function differs from the previous example, the minimum cost service interval is still 0.4 unit per period.

Table 18.2. COST COMPONENTS FOR CONSTANT SERVICE DURATION

μ	WC_m	FC_m	TC_m
0.1250	∞	$0.0206	∞
0.1500	$0.2913	0.0248	$0.3161
0.2000	0.1145	0.0330	0.1475
0.2500	0.0750	0.0413	0.1163
0.3000	0.0566	0.0495	0.1061
0.4000	0.0383	0.0660	0.1043
0.5000	0.0292	0.0825	0.1117
0.6000	0.0236	0.0990	0.1226
0.8000	0.0170	0.1320	0.1490
1.0000	0.0134	0.1650	0.1784

The examples may be more easily compared by graphing the expected total cost functions as shown in Figure 18.7. The upper curve is the expected total system cost function when μ is an expected value from an exponential distribution. The lower curve is the expected total system cost when μ is a constant. No significant difference in the minimum cost policy is evident for the example considered.

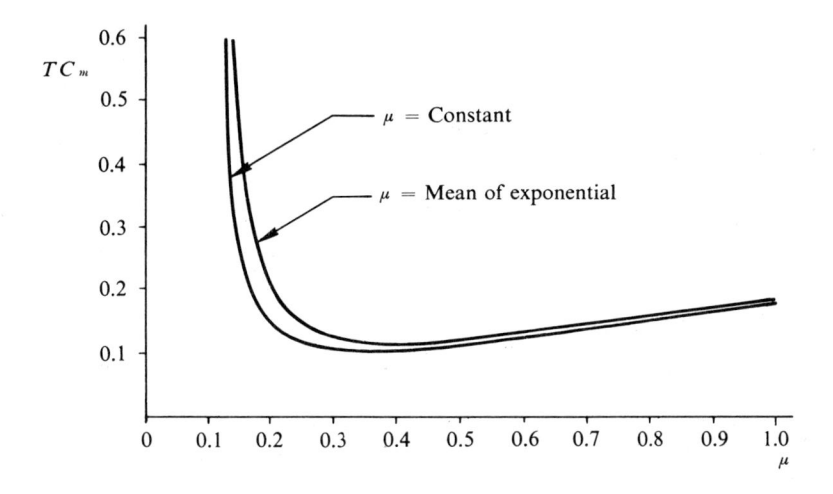

Figure 18.7 TC_m as a function of the service rate.

Poisson Arrivals with Any Service Time Distribution. For further generality, it is desirable to have expressions for pertinent system characteristics regardless of the form of the service time distribution. If σ^2 is the variance of the service time distribution, the mean number of units in the system is given by

$$n_m = \frac{(\lambda/\mu)^2 + \lambda^2\sigma^2}{2[1 - (\lambda/\mu)]} + \frac{\lambda}{\mu}. \tag{18.32}$$

The mean waiting time is

$$w_m = \frac{(\lambda/\mu^2) + \lambda\sigma^2}{2[1 - (\lambda/\mu)]} + \frac{1}{\mu}. \tag{18.33}$$

Equation (18.32) reduces to Equation (18.29) and Equation (18.33) reduces to Equation (18.30) when $\sigma^2 = 0$. In addition, since the variance of an exponential distribution is $(1/\mu)^2$, Equation (18.32) reduces to Equation (18.10) and Equation (18.33) reduces to Equation (18.21) when this substitution is made.

The expected total system cost per period is the sum of the expected waiting cost per period and the expected facility cost per period; that is,

$$TC_m = WC_m + FC_m.$$

The expected waiting cost per period is the product of the cost of waiting per unit per period and the mean number of units in the system during the period. The expected facility cost per period may be taken as the product of the cost of serving one unit and the service rate in units per period. Therefore, the expected total system cost per period is

$$TC_m = C_w \left\{ \frac{(\lambda/\mu)^2 + \lambda^2\sigma^2}{2[1 - (\lambda/\mu)]} + \frac{\lambda}{\mu} \right\} + C_f(\mu). \qquad (18.34)$$

As an example of the application of this model, consider the following situation. The number of arrivals per hour has a Poisson distribution with a mean of 0.2 unit per hour. The cost of waiting per unit per hour is $2.10 and the cost of servicing one unit is $4.05. The decision maker may choose one of two service policies. The first will result in a service rate of 0.4 unit per hour with a service time variance of 3 hours. The second will result in a service rate of 0.5 unit per hour with a service time variance of 4 hours. The first policy will result in an expected total system cost of

$$TC_m = \$2.10 \left\{ \frac{(0.2/0.4)^2 + (0.2)^2(3)}{2[1 - (0.2/0.4)]} + \frac{0.2}{0.4} \right\} + \$4.05(0.4)$$

$$= \$1.83 + \$1.62 = \$3.45.$$

The second policy will result in an expected total system cost of

$$TC_m = \$2.10 \left\{ \frac{(0.2/0.5)^2 + (0.2)^2(4)}{2[1 - (0.2/0.5)]} + \frac{0.2}{0.5} \right\} + \$4.05(0.5)$$

$$= \$1.40 + \$2.03 = \$3.43.$$

From these results, it is evident that it makes little difference which policy is adopted.

18.6 FINITE POPULATION MODELS

Finite waiting-line models must be applied to those waiting-line systems where the population is small relative to the arrival rate. In these systems, units leaving the population significantly affect the characteristics of the population and the arrival probabilities. It is assumed that both the time between calls for service for a unit of the population and the service times are distributed exponentially.

An analysis similar to the infinite population case yields the following expressions for steady-state behavior when the population is finite, size m, and the arrival rate is specified as $m\lambda$.

$$P_{n,0} = P_{0,0} \left(\frac{\lambda}{\mu}\right)^n \left(\frac{m}{n}\right)$$

$$P_{c,n} = P_{0,0} \left(\frac{\lambda}{\mu}\right)^n \left(\frac{m}{n}\right) \frac{(c+n)!}{c!\,c^n}. \qquad (18.35)$$

As the expressions involve computations of factorials, it becomes cumbersome to obtain expressions for the average number in the system or the mean waiting time. Tables describing important facets of the finite waiting line systems are, however, available.[2] The use of these tables for systems having the characteristics described above will be presented in this and the following section.

The Finite Queuing Tables. For convenience, the notation used in the tables will be adopted. Let

N = number of units in the population

M = number of service channels

T = mean service time

U = mean time between calls for service

H = mean number of units being serviced

L = mean number of units waiting for service

J = mean number of units running or productive

Appendix D gives a portion of the finite queuing tables (for populations of 10, 20, and 30 units). Each set of values is indexed by N, the number of units in the population. Within each set, data are classified by X, the service factor, and M, the number of service channels. Two values are listed for each value of N, X, and M. The first is D, the probability of a delay, expressing the probability that an arrival will have to wait. The second is F, an efficiency factor needed in the calculation of H, L, and J.

The service factor is a function of the mean service time and the mean time between calls for service,

$$X = \frac{T}{T + U}. \tag{18.36}$$

The mean number of units being serviced is a function of the efficiency factor, the number of units in the population, and the service factor,

$$H = FNX. \tag{18.37}$$

The mean number of units waiting for service is a function of the number of units in the population and the efficiency factor,

$$L = N(1 - F). \tag{18.38}$$

Finally, the mean number of units running or productive is a function of the number of units in the population, the efficiency factor, and the service factor,

$$J = NF(1 - X). \tag{18.39}$$

[2]L. G. Peck and R. N. Hazelwood, *Finite Queuing Tables* (New York: John Wiley & Sons, Inc., 1958).

A knowledge of N, T, and U for the waiting-line system under study, together with a set of tabular values and these expressions, makes possible the derivation of optimum waiting-line policies. This will be illustrated by several examples.

Number of Service Channels Under Control. As a first example, assume that a population of 20 units exists, with each unit having a mean time between required service of 32 minutes. Each service channel provided will have a mean service time of 8 minutes. Both the time between arrivals and the service interval are distributed exponentially. The number of channels to be provided is under management control. The cost of providing one channel with a mean service time capacity of 8 minutes is $10 per hour. The cost of waiting is $5 per unit per hour. The service factor for this system is

$$X = \frac{T}{T+U} = \frac{8}{8+32} = 0.200.$$

Table 18.3 provides a systematic means for finding the minimum cost number of service channels. The values in columns A and B are entered from Appendix D, Table D.2, with $N = 20$ and $X = 0.200$. The mean number of units being serviced is found from Equation (18.37) and entered in column C. The mean number of units waiting for service is found from Equation (18.38) and is entered in column D. The mean number of units waiting in queue and in service is given in column E. The data of columns A and E may be multiplied by their respective costs to give the total system cost.

Table 18.3. COST AS A FUNCTION OF THE NUMBER OF SERVICE CHANNELS

M (A)	F (B)	H (C)	L (D)	H+L (E)	Waiting Cost (F)	Service Cost (G)	Total Cost (H)
8	0.999	4.00	0.02	4.02	$20.10	$80	$100.10
7	0.997	3.99	0.06	4.05	20.25	70	90.25
6	0.988	3.95	0.24	4.19	20.95	60	80.95
5	0.963	3.85	0.74	4.59	22.95	50	72.95
4	0.895	3.58	2.10	5.68	28.40	40	68.40
3	0.736	2.94	5.28	8.22	41.10	30	71.10
2	0.500	2.00	10.00	12.00	60.00	20	80.00

First, multiplying $5 per unit per hour by the mean number of units waiting gives the waiting cost per hour in column F. Second, multiplying $10 per channel per hour by the number of channels gives the service cost per hour in column G. Finally, adding the expected waiting cost and the service cost gives the expected total system cost in column H. The minimum cost number of channels is found to be four.

In this example, the cost of waiting was taken to be $5 per unit per hour. If this is due to lost profit, resulting from unproductive units, the same solution may be obtained by maximizing profit. As before, the values in columns A and

Chap. 18 Probabilistic Queuing Models

Table 18.4. PROFIT AS A FUNCTION OF THE NUMBER OF SERVICE CHANNELS

M (A)	F (B)	J (C)	Gross Profit (D)	Service Cost (E)	Net Profit (F)
8	0.999	15.98	$79.90	$80	$−0.10
7	0.997	15.95	79.75	70	9.75
6	0.988	15.81	79.05	60	19.05
5	0.963	15.41	77.05	50	27.05
4	0.895	14.32	71.60	40	31.60
3	0.736	11.78	58.90	30	28.90
2	0.500	8.00	40.00	20	20.00

B of Table 18.4 are entered from Appendix D, Table D.2, with $N = 20$ and $X = 0.200$. The mean number of units running or productive is found from Equation (18.39) and entered in column C.

The profit per hour in column D is found by multiplying the mean number of productive units by $5 profit per productive unit per hour. The cost of service per hour in column E is obtained by multiplying the number of channels by $10 per channel per hour. Finally, the net profit in column F is found by subtracting the service cost per hour from the profit per hour. As before, the number of channels that should be used is four. This example illustrates that either the minimum cost or the maximum profit approach may be used with equivalent results.

Mean Service Time Under Control. Assume that a population of 10 units is to be served by a single service channel. The mean time between calls for service is 30 minutes. If the mean service rate is 60 units per hour, the service cost will be $100 per hour. The service cost per hour is inversely proportional to the time in minutes to service one unit, expressed as $100/T$. Both the time between calls for service and the service duration are distributed exponentially. Lost profit due to units waiting in the system is $15 per hour.

Column A in Table 18.5 gives the capacity of the channel expressed as the mean service time in minutes per unit processed. The service factor for each service time is found from Equation (18.36) and entered in column B. The

Table 18.5. PROFIT AS A FUNCTION OF THE MEAN SERVICE TIME

T (A)	X (B)	F (C)	J (D)	Gross Profit (E)	Service Cost (F)	Net Profit (G)
1	0.032	0.988	9.56	$143.20	$100.00	$43.20
2	0.062	0.945	8.86	132.90	50.00	82.90
3	0.091	0.864	7.85	117.75	33.33	84.42
4	0.118	0.763	6.73	101.00	25.00	76.00
5	0.143	0.674	5.77	86.51	20.00	66.51

efficiency factors in column C are found by interpolation in Appendix D, Table D.1, for $N = 10$ and the respective service factors of column B. The mean number of units running is found from Equation (18.39) and entered in column D. The data given in column A and column D may now be used to find the service capacity that results in a maximum net profit.

The expected profit per hour in column E is found by multiplying the mean number of units running by $15 per hour. The cost of service per hour is found by dividing $100 by the value for T in column A. These costs are entered in column F. By subtracting the cost of service per hour from the expected gross profit per hour, the expected net profit per hour in column G is found. The mean service time resulting in an expected maximum profit is three periods.

18.7 FINITE POPULATION MODELS AND MAINTENANCE

Suppose that a population of production equipment is under study with the objective of deriving minimum cost maintenance policy. It is assumed that both the time between calls for maintenance for a unit of the population and the service times are distributed exponentially. Two parameters of the system are subject to management control: First, by increasing the repair capability (reducing T) the average machine downtime will be reduced. Second, alternative policies of preventive maintenance will alter the mean time between breakdowns, U. Therefore, the problem of machine maintenance reduces to one of determining the service factor, X, that will result in a minimum cost system. This section presents methods for establishing and controlling the service factor in maintenance operations.

Machine Downtime as a Function of the Service Factor. As machines break down, they become unproductive with a resulting economic loss. This loss may be reduced by reducing the service factor. But a decrease in the service factor requires either a reduction in the repair time or a more expensive policy of preventive maintenance, or both. Therefore, the objective is to find an economic balance between the cost of unproductive machines and the cost of maintaining a specific service factor.

The analysis of this situation is facilitated by developing curves giving the percentage of machines not running as a function of the service factor. Figure 18.8 gives curves for selected populations when one service channel is provided. Each curve is developed from Equation (18.39) and the finite queuing tables. As was expected, the percentage of machines not running increases as the service factor increases.

As an example of the determination of the minimum cost service factor, consider the following situation. Eight machines are maintained by a mechanic and his helper. Each machine produces a profit of $22 per hour while it is running. The mechanic and his assistant cost the company $48 per hour.

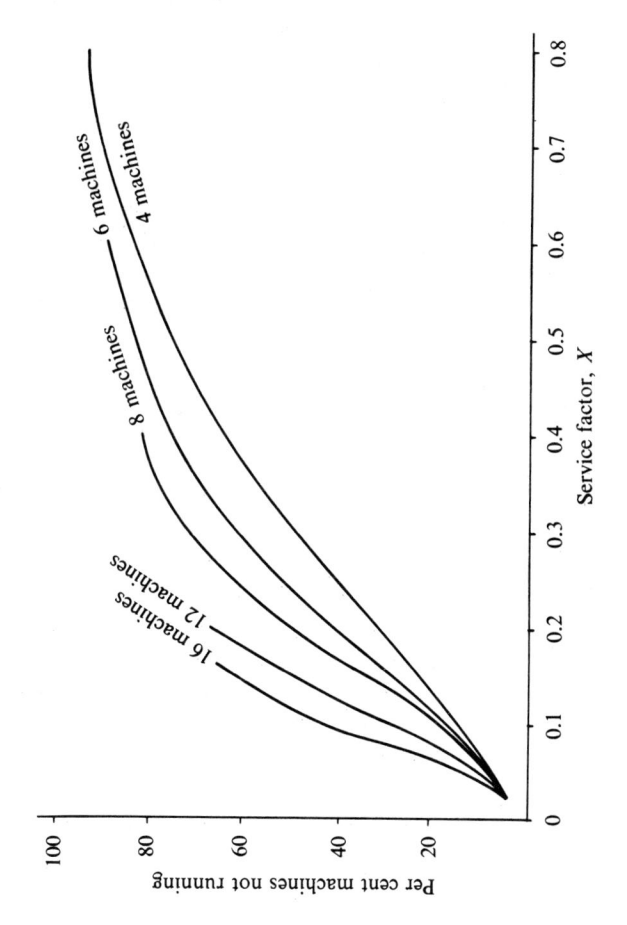

Figure 18.8 Percentage of machines not running as a function of the service factor.

Three policies of preventive maintenance are under consideration. The first will cost $80 per hour. After considering the increase in the mean time between breakdowns and the effect on service time, it is estimated that the resulting service factor will be 0.04. The second policy of preventive maintenance will cost only $18 per hour, but will result in a service factor of 0.10. The third alternative involves no preventive maintenance at all; hence, it will cost nothing, but a service factor in excess of 0.2 will result. The time between calls for service and the service times are distributed exponentially. By reference to Figure 18.8, the results of Table 18.6 are developed. From the results of the last column, it is evident that the second alternative should be adopted.

Table 18.6. THREE POLICIES OF PREVENTIVE MAINTENANCE

Maintenance Policy	Service Factor, X	Machines not Running	Cost of Lost Profit	Cost of Maintenance	Cost of Mechanic	Total Cost
1	0.04	0.5	$11	$80	$48	$139
2	0.10	1.6	35	18	48	101
3	0.20	4.1	90	0	48	138

Service Factor Control by Chart. Once the service factor resulting in a minimum cost system has been established, it may be desirable to implement a control model for detecting the effects of a shift in the arrival rate or the service rate or both. This may be accomplished by constructing a control chart for the number of machines not running. The statistical control models presented in Chapter 10 cannot be applied directly to this variable, since its distribution is badly skewed. The expected form of the distribution is known in advance, however, a factor usually missing in other control applications.

As an example of the application of control charts in waiting-line operations, consider a one-person N-machine situation.[3] Suppose that 20 automatic machines are to be run by one person, and that the minimum cost service factor is found to be 0.03. It is assumed that the machines require service at randomly distributed times, that the service times are distributed exponentially, and that machines are serviced on a first come, first served basis. The probability of n machines in the queue and in service (not running) is given by

$$P_n = \frac{N!}{(N-n)!} \rho^n P_0, \qquad (18.40)$$

where P_n = probability that n machines are not running at any point in time
P_0 = probability that all machines are running at any point in time
ρ = ratio of λ/μ
N = number of machines assigned
n = number of machines not running at any point in time.

[3] Adapted from R. W. Llewellyn, "Control Charts for Queueing Applications," *Journal of Industrial Engineering*, XI, No. 4 (July–August 1960).

Table 18.7. CALCULATION OF P_n AND $\sum P_n$

n (A)	$\dfrac{P_n}{P_0}$ (B)	P_n (C)	$\sum P_n$ (D)
0	1.000000000	0.434772422	0.434772422
1	0.600000000	0.260863453	0.695635875
2	0.342000000	0.148692168	0.844328043
3	0.184680000	0.080293771	0.924621814
4	0.094186800	0.040949823	0.965571637
5	0.045209664	0.019655915	0.985227552
6	0.020344349	0.008845162	0.994072714
7	0.008544627	0.003714968	0.997787682
8	0.003332405	0.001448838	0.999236520
9	0.001199666	0.000521582	0.999758102
10	0.000395890	0.000172122	0.999930224
11	0.000118767	0.000051637	0.999981861
12	0.000032067	0.000013942	0.999995803
13	0.000007696	0.000003346	0.999999149
14	0.000001616	0.000000703	0.999999852
15	0.000000291	0.000000127	0.999999979
16	0.000000044	0.000000019	0.999999998
17	0.000000005	0.000000002	1.000000000
18	0.000000000	0.000000000	1.000000000
19	0.000000000	0.000000000	1.000000000
20	0.000000000	0.000000000	1.000000000
	2.300053887		

Values for P_n are given in column C of Table 18.7 for $0 \leq n \leq N$. The first entry is found by dividing the first entry in column B by 2.30005387. The second results from dividing the second entry in column B by the same value, and so on. The results for P_n are plotted in Figure 18.9. The distribution of n is seen to be extremely skewed, being completely convex. Unlike some control chart applications, the distribution of the variable to be controlled is known. It may be used to determine the control limits.

Since the probability that all machines are running is approximately 0.435, the lower control limit is obviously zero. The upper control limit is all that needs to be determined, since the variable n can go out of control only at the top. Thus, the entire critical range will be at the upper end of the distribution. It will be desirable to set this limit so that it will not be violated too frequently. Since n is an integer, the magnitude of the critical range can be observed as a function of n from column D in Table 18.7. If six machines not running is chosen as a point in control and seven is a point out of control, the probability of designating the system out of control when it is really in control is

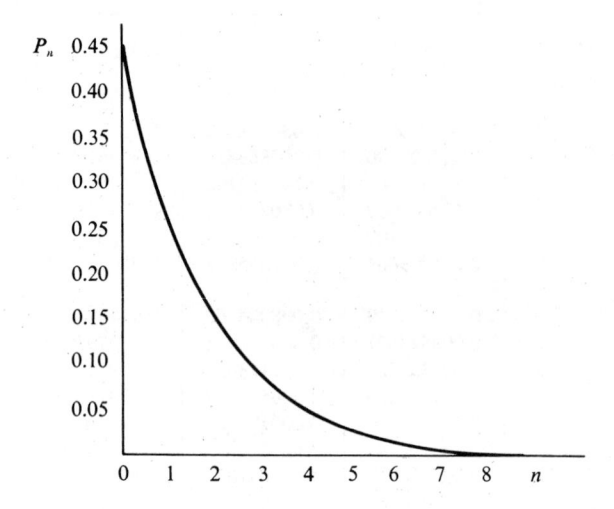

Figure 18.9 Probability distribution of the number of machines not running.

$$1 - \sum_{n=0}^{6} P_n = 0.0059.$$

Therefore, a control limit set at 6.5 should be satisfactory. The control chart applied to a period of operation might appear as in Figure 18.10. It would be concluded that the service factor has not changed during this period of observation.

In order for the application of this control model to be valid, two conditions must be met. First, the observation must be made at random times. Second, the observations must be spaced far enough apart, so that the results

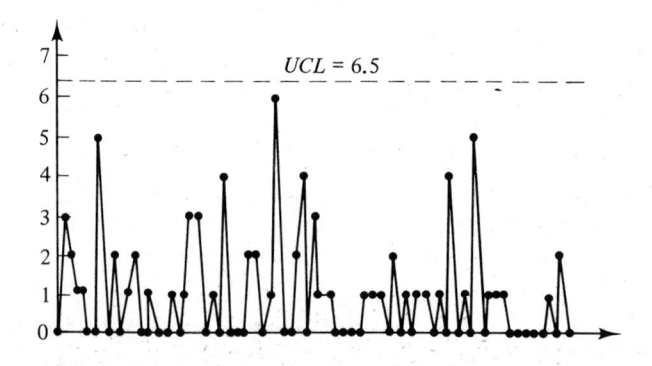

Figure 18.10 Control chart for the number of machines not running.

are independent. For example, if the service time averages 5 minutes, and if six machines are idle in an observation, then an observation taken 10 minutes later would probably indicate at least four idle machines. The readings should be far enough apart for a waiting line to be dissipated. To ensure both randomness and spacing, all numbers from 45 to 90 could be taken from a random number table with their order preserved; numbers from 00 to 44 and from 91 to 99 would be dropped. These numbers can then be used to space the observations. This would yield an average of eight random observations per day with a minimum spacing of 45 minutes and a maximum spacing of 90 minutes.

If the control chart indicates that n is no longer in control, corrective action must be taken. This will require investigation to determine whether the service factor has changed because of a change in the mean time between calls or a change in the mean service time, or both. Specific items that might be studied are the policy of preventive maintenance, the age of the machines, the capability of the operator, or material characteristics. Once the assignable cause for the out-of-control condition is located, it may be corrected so that the system will return to minimum cost operation.

QUESTIONS

18.1. Contrast the deterministic waiting-line system and the probabilistic waiting-line system.

18.2. Name and describe (a) an infinite population, and (b) a finite population.

18.3. Under what conditions is it mandatory that Monte Carlo analysis be used in the study of a waiting-line system?

18.4. Why is it essential that μ be greater than λ in a probabilistic waiting-line process?

18.5. What conditions must be met for the Poisson distribution to describe adequately the number of arrivals per period?

18.6. Name and describe a situation in which the assumption of a constant service rate would be valid.

18.7. Describe a situation in which it is possible to alter the service rate and the service factor.

18.8. Why might it be desirable to apply a control chart to the number of machines not running?

PROBLEMS

18.1. Suppose that the time between arrivals is distributed exponentially with a mean of 4 minutes and that service time is constant and equal to 3 minutes. Service is provided on a first come, first served basis. No units are in the system at 8:00 A.M. Use Monte Carlo analysis to estimate the total number of unit minutes of waiting between 8:00 A.M. and 12:00 noon.

18.2. Rework the example of Section 18.1 if the service time distribution of Figure 18.1 has a mean of six periods with the same standard deviation. Compare the total system cost with that found in the text if the cost of providing this service capacity is $0.06 per period and the waiting cost per unit per period remains the same.

18.3. Use Monte Carlo analysis to verify Equation (18.9) if the number of arrivals per period has a Poisson distribution with a mean of 0.10 and if the service duration is distributed exponentially with a mean of four periods. Plot the histogram of the number of units in the system and compare with Figure 18.5.

18.4. Suppose that arrivals are distributed according to the Poisson distribution with a mean of 0.125 unit per period and that the service duration is distributed exponentially with a mean of four periods. Develop the probability distribution of n units in the system. What is the probability of there being more than 6 units in the system?

18.5. The arrival rate for a certain waiting-line system obeys a Poisson distribution with a mean of 0.5 unit per period. It is required that the probability of one or more units in the system not exceed 0.25. What is the minimum service rate that must be provided if the service duration will be distributed exponentially?

18.6. What is the expected number of units in the system and the expected waiting time for the conditions of Problem 18.4?

18.7. The expected number of units in a waiting-line system experiencing Poisson arrivals with a rate of 0.4 unit per period must not exceed 8. What is the minimum service rate that must be provided if the service duration will be distributed exponentially? What will be the expected waiting time?

18.8. Plot the mean number of units in the system, and the mean waiting time, as a function of λ/μ, if the number of arrivals per period obey the Poisson distribution and if the service duration is distributed exponentially. What is the significance of this illustration?

18.9. The number of arrivals per period is distributed according to the Poisson with an expected value of 0.8 unit per period. The cost of waiting per unit per period is $3.20. The facility cost for serving one unit per period is $5.15. What expected service rate should be established if the service duration will be distributed exponentially? What is the expected total system cost?

18.10. The expected waiting time in a waiting-line system with Poisson arrivals at a rate of 1.5 units per day must not exceed 5 days. What is the minimum constant service rate that must be provided? What is the expected number in the system?

18.11. Trucks arrive at a loading dock in a Poisson manner at the rate of 3.5 per day. The cost of waiting per truck per day is $420. A three-person crew that can load at a constant rate of four trucks per day costs $560 per day. Compute the total system cost for the operation.

18.12. Enrolling and advising new students at Sharecropper State University is currently accomplished through the services of a graduate assistant who is paid $3.90 per hour. Each student requires an average of 5 minutes, but there is a variance of 12 minutes in the distribution of advisement times. An associate professor can be hired to accomplish this same task at $8 per hour. He will spend all of 6 minutes with each student, but because of the rigor of his academic preparation, there will be no variance in this time. Students arrive for enrollment and advice in a Poisson manner with an average interval of 8 minutes. The cost of student waiting is estimated at $3.80 per student per hour. Is there an economic advantage in using the associate professor?

18.13. Cars arrive at a toll plaza at the rate of 60 cars per hour. There are four booths each capable of servicing 30 cars per hour. Assuming a Poisson distribution for arrivals and an exponential distribution for the service time, determine (a) the probability of no cars in the toll plaza, (b) the average length of the queue, and (c) the average time spent by a car in the plaza.

18.14. Derive a total cost expression, similar to Equation (18.21), for a multiple-channel queue.

18.15. In Problem 18.13, if it costs $18 per hour to operate a toll booth and the waiting cost per car is $0.25 per minute spent at the plaza, how many booths should be operated to minimize total cost?

18.16. In a three-channel queuing system the arrival rate is 1 unit per time period and the service rate is 0.6 unit per time period. Determine the probability that an arriving unit does not have to wait.

18.17. Plot the waiting cost, service cost, and total cost given in Table 18.3. Also, plot the gross profit, service cost, and net profit given in Table 18.4.

18.18. Each truck in a fleet of 30 delivery trucks will return to a warehouse for reloading at an average interval of 160 minutes. An average of 20 minutes is required by the driver and one warehouseman to load the next shipment. If the warehouse personnel are busy loading previous arrivals, the driver and his unit must wait in queue. Both the time between arrivals and the loading time are distributed exponentially. The cost of waiting in the system is $30 per hour per truck and the total cost per warehouseman is $12 per hour. Find the minimum cost number of warehousemen to employ.

18.19. A population of 10 cargo ships each produces a profit of $3,000 per 24-hour period when not waiting to be unloaded. The time between arrivals is distributed exponentially with a mean of 144 hours. The unloading time at the dock is distributed exponentially with a mean of 21 hours. It costs $100 per hour to lease a dock with this unloading capacity. How many docks should be leased?

18.20. Each machine in a semiautomatic group of 20 machines requires operator attention at an average interval of 18 minutes. Each operator assigned can service the machine in an average of 4 minutes. Both the time between calls for service and the service duration approximate the exponential distribution. Each minute a machine is idle produces a lost profit of $0.20. Operators cost the firm $0.40 per operator per minute, which includes overhead. How many operators should be assigned for maximum profit?

18.21. A population of 30 chemical processing units is to be unloaded and loaded by a single crew. The mean time between calls for this operation is 68 minutes. If the mean service rate is 1 unit per minute, the cost of the crew and equipment will be $1.60 per minute. This cost will decrease to $1.20, $0.90, and $0.70 for service intervals of 2, 3, and 4 minutes, respectively. The time between calls for service and the service duration are distributed exponentially. If it costs $28 per hour for each unit that is idle, find the minimum cost service interval.

18.22. A cab company has 20 vehicles in service, each of which produces a profit of $120 per 8-hour day. Each vehicle requires service on the average of every 23.5 hours. This service is provided by a mechanic who is paid $6.70 per hour including benefits. The mean service time is 1.5 hours. Assuming exponential arrival and service time distributions, what is the number of mechanics that will provide a maximum profit?

18.23. Plot the percentage of machines not running as a function of the service factor for a population of 20 machines with exponential arrivals and services (a) if a single channel is employed, and (b) if two channels are employed.

18.24. A group of 12 machines are repaired by a single repairperson when they break down. Each machine yields a profit of $4.60 per hour while running. The mechanic costs the firm $8.20 per hour, including overhead. At the present time no preventive maintenance is utilized. It is proposed that one mechanic be employed to perform certain routine maintenance and adjustment tasks. This will cost $7.50 per hour, but will reduce the service factor from 0.12 to 0.08. What is the economic advantage of implementing preventive maintenance?

18.25. One operator is assigned to run 14 automatic machines. The minimum cost service factor is 0.2. The machines require attention at random, and the service duration is distributed exponentially. Machines receive service on a first come, first served basis. Specify the upper control limit if the probability of designating the system out of control when it is really in control must not exceed 0.05.

Appendices

A

Linear and Matrix Algebra

Linear and matrix algebra are mathematical tools of considerable importance in OR/MS. Linear relationships are used to represent operations in linear programming models, linear game models, linear break-even models, and others. In this appendix, the fundamental algebra useful in dealing with linear equations is presented.

A.1 SOLVING LINEAR EQUATIONS

Linear equations often appear simultaneously. The solution of these "systems" of equations falls into two broad categories which depend on the number of equations and the number of unknowns. Each of these will be treated by the *elimination substitution technique* in the paragraphs that follow.

Unknowns and Equations Equal in Number. When the number of unknowns in a system of linear equations equals the number of equations in the system, one unique solution can be found. The approach begins with the original $n \times n$ system of equations and forms $n - 1$ linear combinations of equation pairs, with each linear combination eliminating the same variable. This process results in the reduction of the $n \times n$ system to one that has $n - 1$ equations and $n - 1$ variables. The elimination procedure is continued, using each successive equation pair, until there is one equation and one variable remaining. If this occurs, a unique solution to the original $n \times n$ system exists. The values of the other $n - 1$ variables can be found by substituting backward through the subsystems of equations comprising the linear combinations.

As an example of the procedure described above, consider a simple system of two linear equations with two unknowns:

$$x_1 + 5x_2 = 20 \tag{A.1}$$
$$3x_1 + 3x_2 = 12. \tag{A.2}$$

Multiplying Equation (A.1) by -3 and adding it to Equation (A.2) gives

$$-12x_2 = -48$$
$$x_2 = 4.$$

Substituting x_2 into Equation (A.1) gives

$$x_1 + 5(4) = 20$$
$$x_1 = 0.$$

Thus, a unique solution with $x_1 = 0$ and $x_2 = 4$ exists for this system of linear equations.

As a second example, consider a system of three linear equations with three unknowns:

$$x_1 + x_2 + x_3 = 6 \tag{A.3}$$
$$4x_1 - x_2 + 2x_3 = 9 \tag{A.4}$$
$$5x_1 + 3x_2 - x_3 = -2. \tag{A.5}$$

Eliminate x_2 from Equations (A.3) and (A.4) by adding them to give

$$5x_1 + 3x_3 = 15.$$

Next, eliminate x_2 from Equations (A.3) and (A.4) by multiplying Equation (A.3) by -3 and adding it to Equation (A.5) to give

$$2x_1 - 4x_3 = -20.$$

The resulting system of equations is now

$$5x_1 + 3x_3 = 15 \quad (A.6)$$
$$2x_1 - 4x_3 = -20. \quad (A.7)$$

In this 2×2 system, x_1 can be eliminated by multiplying Equation (A.6) by -2 and Equation (A.7) by 5 and adding them together to give

$$-26x_3 = -130$$
$$x_3 = 5.$$

Substituting x_3 into Equation (A.6) gives

$$5x_1 + 3(5) = 15$$
$$x_1 = 0.$$

Finally, substituting x_1 and x_3 into Equation (A.3) gives

$$0 + x_2 + 5 = 6$$
$$x_2 = 1.$$

Thus, a unique solution with $x_1 = 0$, $x_2 = 1$, and $x_3 = 5$ exists for this system of linear equations.

The elimination substitution technique illustrated above may be used for the general $n \times n$ case by forming $n - 1$ linear combinations of equation pairs. In so doing, care must be exercised to be sure that each of the n equations was used at least once in forming the combinations.

Unknowns Exceed Number of Equations. When the number of unknowns exceeds the number of equations, a unique solution generally does not exist. In such cases, several solutions may exist for the system of equations. The solution procedure is to set one or more of the variables equal to zero so that the remaining variables are equal in numbers to the number of equations. Thus, if there are n variables and m equations with $n > m$, then $m - n$ variables are set equal to zero. A solution is then sought for the remaining m variables.

Consider the following system of two equations and three unknowns:

$$x_1 + 5x_2 + x_3 = 20 \quad (A.8)$$
$$3x_1 + 3x_2 + 2x_3 = 12. \quad (A.9)$$

Set $x_1 = 0$, multiply Equation (A.8) by -2, and add it to Equation (A.9) to give

$$-7x_2 = -28$$
$$x_2 = 4.$$

Substituting into Equation (A.8) gives

$$0 + 5(4) + x_3 = 20$$
$$x_3 = 0.$$

This is one solution to this system of equations.

Next, set $x_2 = 0$, multiply Equation (A.8) by -3, and add it to Equation (A.9) to give
$$-x_3 = -48$$
$$x_3 = 48.$$
Substituting into Equation (A.8) gives
$$x_1 + 5(0) + 48 = 20$$
$$x_1 = -28.$$
This is a second solution to the system of equations.

Finally, set $x_3 = 0$, multiply Equation (A.8) by -3, and add it to Equation (A.9) to give
$$-12x_2 = -48$$
$$x_2 = 4.$$
Substituting into Equation (A.8) gives
$$3x_1 + 3(4) = 12$$
$$x_1 = 0.$$
This is a third solution to the system of equations.

A.2 MATRIX DEFINITIONS

A *matrix* is an $m \times n$ array of numbers with m rows and n columns. The numbers are called elements and the matrix itself is often referred to by a capital letter. For example,

$$A = \begin{bmatrix} a_{11} & a_{12} & \cdots & a_{1n} \\ a_{21} & a_{22} & \cdots & a_{zn} \\ \vdots & \vdots & & \vdots \\ a_{m1} & a_{m2} & \cdots & a_{mn} \end{bmatrix}$$

may be referred to as matrix A with elements a_{ij}.

The notation of matrix algebra may be used to represent a system of linear equations. For example, the left-hand side of the system of Equations (A.1) and (A.2) may be represented by the 2×2 matrix

$$A = \begin{bmatrix} 1 & 5 \\ 3 & 3 \end{bmatrix}.$$

if the coefficients are designated a_{mn}. Also, the variables of the system and the right-hand side can be represented in matrix form as

$$X = \begin{bmatrix} X_1 \\ X_2 \end{bmatrix} \quad \text{and} \quad B = \begin{bmatrix} 20 \\ 12 \end{bmatrix}.$$

App. A Linear and Matrix Algebra   451

Following the laws of matrix algebra, the system of linear equations can be written as

$$\begin{bmatrix} 1 & 5 \\ 3 & 3 \end{bmatrix} \begin{bmatrix} X_1 \\ X_2 \end{bmatrix} = \begin{bmatrix} 20 \\ 12 \end{bmatrix} \quad (A.10)$$

or as

$$A \cdot X = B.$$

Matrices may appear in rectangular form (when $m \neq n$), in square form (when $m = n$), or in vector form (when m or $n = 1$). The *order* of a matrix is important in matrix operations and is established by m and n. In general, the order of a matrix is $m \times n$. Matrix A above is of order 2×2 or, since $m = n$, simply of order 2. Both matrix X and matrix B are of order 2×1.

An important special matrix is known as the *identity matrix*. Normally denoted by the letter I, the identity matrix is square with ones on its main diagonal and zeros elsewhere. An identity matrix of order 3 is

$$I = \begin{bmatrix} 1 & 0 & 0 \\ 0 & 1 & 0 \\ 0 & 0 & 1 \end{bmatrix}. \quad (A.11)$$

Another special matrix of importance is the *transpose*. The transpose of matrix A is denoted by A^T. It has the rows of A as its columns and the columns of A as its rows as follows:

$$\begin{bmatrix} 3 & 2 & -1 \\ 6 & 3 & 8 \end{bmatrix}^T = \begin{bmatrix} 3 & 6 \\ 2 & 3 \\ -1 & 8 \end{bmatrix}.$$

A.3 MATRIX OPERATIONS

Matrices may be subjected to certain algebraic operations. These are addition, subtraction, and multiplication. The operation of division is not applicable to matrices. Generally, the resultant of operations with matrices will be another matrix.

Addition or Subtraction. When matrix A is added or subtracted from matrix B, matrix C results; that is, $A + B = C$. Matrices cannot be added or subtracted if they are not conformable, or of the same order. If C results from $A + B$, then it is required that

$$C_{ij} = A_{ij} + B_{ij}.$$

The element of row i and column j of matrix C is obtained from the corresponding elements in matrices A and B by addition. For example:

$$\begin{bmatrix} 3 & 2 \\ -1 & 4 \\ 5 & 0 \end{bmatrix} + \begin{bmatrix} 4 & 3 \\ 7 & 0 \\ 2 & 5 \end{bmatrix} = \begin{bmatrix} 3+4 & 2+3 \\ -1+7 & 4+0 \\ 5+2 & 0+5 \end{bmatrix} = \begin{bmatrix} 7 & 5 \\ 6 & 4 \\ 7 & 5 \end{bmatrix}.$$

The same procedure is used for subtraction.

Matrix Multiplication. The order in which matrices are multiplied is important since the cummutative law of algebra ($ab = ba$) does not hold in matrix multiplication; that is, $AB \neq BA$. Conformability is required for multiplication, but with a different meaning than for addition or subtraction. For the product AB to be conformable for multiplication, the number of columns in matrix A must be equal to the number of rows in matrix B. In general, if the order of matrix A is $m \times p$ and the order of matrix B is $p \times n$, the matrices are conformable for multiplication and the product matrix C will be of order $m \times n$.

In multiplying matrix A by matrix B, each row of matrix A must be multiplied by each column of matrix B. The product of the ith row of A times the jth column of B becomes the entry in the ith row and jth column of A times B or C. For example, suppose that

$$A = \begin{bmatrix} 1 & 3 \\ 2 & 0 \\ -1 & 4 \end{bmatrix} \quad \text{and} \quad B = \begin{bmatrix} 2 & -1 & 0 \\ 1 & 4 & 3 \end{bmatrix}.$$

The first element, C_{11}, in matrix C, where $C = AB$, is found by multiplying the first row of A by the first column of B as follows:

$$(1)(2) + (3)(1) = 5.$$

Similarly, a_{12} in matrix C is found by multiplying the first row of A by the second column of B as follows:

$$(1)(-1) + (3)(4) = 11.$$

Continuing in this manner for all C_{ij} gives

$$C = AB = \begin{bmatrix} 5 & 11 & 9 \\ 4 & -2 & 0 \\ 2 & 17 & 12 \end{bmatrix}.$$

As another example of matrix multiplication, consider the system of linear equations represented in matrix form by Equation (A.10) as

$$\begin{bmatrix} 1 & 5 \\ 3 & 3 \end{bmatrix} \begin{bmatrix} X_1 \\ X_2 \end{bmatrix} = \begin{bmatrix} 20 \\ 12 \end{bmatrix}.$$

Multiplying the coefficient matrix by the X vector recreates the statement for this sytem as given by Equations (A.1) and (A.2):

$$1X_1 + 5X_2 = 20$$
$$3X_1 + 3X_2 = 12.$$

Matrix Inversion. The inverse of matrix A is denoted by A^{-1}. It has the following meaning:

$$AA^{-1} = A^{-1}A = I,$$

where I is an identity matrix of the form given by Equation (A.11).

App. A   Linear and Matrix Algebra

Not all matrices have inverses. Two requirements must be met for a matrix to have an inverse. First, the matrix must be *square*. Second, the matrix must contain linearly independent rows and columns. If it does not, the inverse is not possible to complete.

Three rules apply in seeking the inverse of a matrix. They may be utilized without changing the equivalence of the matrix being inverted. These rules are:

1. Rows may be interchanged.
2. Elements in the rows may be multiplied by a nonzero scalar.
3. A linear multiple of one row may be added to another row.

Consider the inverse for the A matrix from the system of linear equations given by Equations (A.1) and (A.2). It is found by the following procedure. First, an identity matrix of the same order is attached to the matrix being inverted

$$\begin{bmatrix} 1 & 5 \\ 3 & 3 \end{bmatrix} \begin{bmatrix} 1 & 0 \\ 0 & 1 \end{bmatrix}.$$

The objective is to reduce the A matrix to an identity matrix by performing operations on both the A matrix and the I matrix in accordance with the rules above. This will convert the I matrix to the desired inverse, A^{-1}.

In this example, element a_{11} in the A matrix is already 1, so no operation is required at this point. Element a_{12} is considered next. To reduce it to zero as required for an identity matrix, multiply row one by -3 and add it to row two [rule (3)], which gives

$$\begin{bmatrix} -3 & -15 \\ 3 & 3 \end{bmatrix} \begin{bmatrix} -3 & 0 \\ 0 & 1 \end{bmatrix}$$

$$\begin{bmatrix} -3 & -15 \\ 0 & -12 \end{bmatrix} \begin{bmatrix} -3 & 0 \\ -3 & 1 \end{bmatrix}.$$

Multiply row 1 by $-1/3$ [rule (2)]:

$$\begin{bmatrix} 1 & 5 \\ 0 & -12 \end{bmatrix} \begin{bmatrix} 1 & 0 \\ -3 & 1 \end{bmatrix}.$$

Element a_{22} is considered next. To reduce it to 1 as required for an identity matrix, multiply row two by $-1/12$ [rule (2)]. The result is

$$\begin{bmatrix} 1 & 5 \\ 0 & 1 \end{bmatrix} \begin{bmatrix} 1 & 0 \\ 1/4 & -1/12 \end{bmatrix}.$$

Finally, consider element a_{12}. To reduce it to 0 as required for an identity matrix, multiply row two by -5 and add it to row one [rule (3)]. The result is

$$\begin{bmatrix} 1 & 0 \\ 0 & 1 \end{bmatrix} \begin{bmatrix} -1/4 & 5/12 \\ 1/4 & -1/12 \end{bmatrix}.$$

To verify that A^{-1} has been found, the following can be demonstrated to be true:
$$\begin{bmatrix} 1 & 5 \\ 3 & 3 \end{bmatrix} \begin{bmatrix} -1/4 & 5/12 \\ 1/4 & -1/12 \end{bmatrix} = \begin{bmatrix} 1 & 0 \\ 0 & 1 \end{bmatrix}.$$

The inverse can be used to solve the system of linear equations by utilizing the following derivation:
$$AX = B$$
$$A^{-1}AX = A^{-1}B$$
$$IX = A^{-1}B$$
$$X = A^{-1}B.$$

For the inverse just found,
$$X = \begin{bmatrix} -1/4 & 5/12 \\ 1/4 & -1/12 \end{bmatrix} \begin{bmatrix} 20 \\ 12 \end{bmatrix}$$
$$X = \begin{bmatrix} 0 \\ 4 \end{bmatrix}.$$

This is the solution to the system of linear equations given by Equations (A.1) and (A.2) as utilized in this example.

B

Classical Optimization Methods

Optimization is the process of seeking the best. In OR/MS, optimization is utilized to find the maximum (or the minimum) of an effectiveness function of one or more decision variables. This appendix presents some calculus-based optimization methods which are applicable to continuous effectiveness functions, or to continuous approximations for discrete effectiveness functions.

B.1 SLOPE OF A FUNCTION

The slope of a function $y = f(x)$ is defined as the rate of change of the dependent variable, y, divided by the rate of change of the independent variable, x. If a positive change in x results in a positive change in y, the slope is positive. Conversely, a positive change in x resulting in a negative change in y indicates a negative slope.

If $y = f(x)$ defines a straight line, the difference between any two points x_1 and x_2 represents the change in x and the difference between any two points y_1 and y_2 represents the change in y. Thus, the rate of change of y with respect to x is $(y_1 - y_2)/(x_1 - x_2)$; the slope of the straight line. This slope is constant for all points on the straight line; $\Delta y / \Delta x =$ constant. For a nonlinear function, the rate of change of y with respect to changes in x is not constant, but changes with changes in x. The slope must be evaluated at each point on the curve. This can be done by assuming an arbitrary point on the function p, for which the x and y values are x_0 and $f(x_0)$, as shown in Figure B.1. The rate of change of y with respect to x at point p is equal to the slope of a line tangent to the function at that point. It is observed that the rate of change of y with respect to x differs from that at p at other points on the curve.

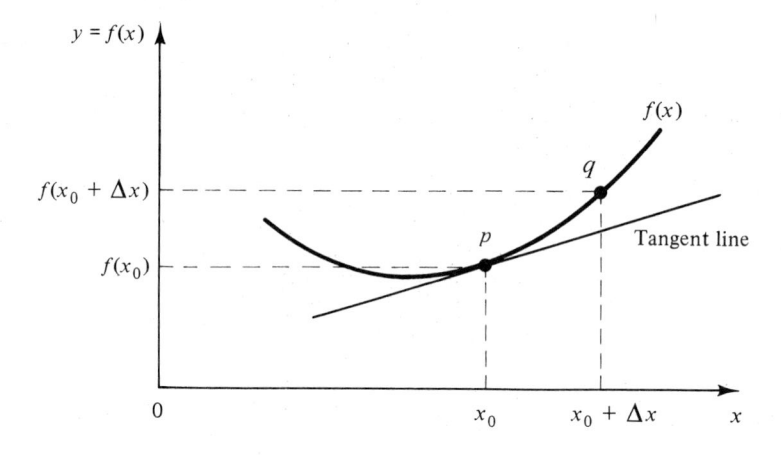

Figure B.1 Slope of a function.

B.2 DIFFERENTIAL CALCULUS

Differential calculus is a mathematical tool for finding successively better and better approximations for the slope of the tangent line shown in Figure B.1. Consider another point on $f(x)$ designated q, situated at an x distance from point p equal to Δx and situated at a y distance from point p equal to Δy. Then the slope of a line segment through points p and q would have a slope $\Delta x / \Delta y$. But this is the average slope of $f(x)$ between the designated points. In classical optimization, it is the instantaneous rate of change at a given point that is sought.

The instantaneous rate of change in $f(x)$ at $x = x_0$ can be found by letting $\Delta x \to 0$. Referring to Figure B.1, this can be stated as

$$\lim_{\Delta x \to 0} \frac{f(x_0 + \Delta x) - f(x_0)}{\Delta x}. \tag{B.1}$$

It is noted that as Δx becomes smaller and smaller, the line segment passing through points p and q approaches the tangent line to point p. Thus, the slope of the function at x_0 is given by Equation (B.1) when Δx is infinitesimally small.

Equation (B.1) is an expression for slope of general applicability. It is called a *derivative*, and its appliatcion is a process known as *differentiation*. For the function $y = f(x)$, the symbolism dy/dx or $f'(x)$ is most often used to denote the derivative.

As an example of the process of differentiation utilizing Equation (B.1), consider the function $y = f(x) = 8x - x^2$. Substituting into Equation (B.1) gives

$$\lim_{\Delta x \to 0} = \frac{[8(x + \Delta x) - (x + \Delta x)^2] - [8x - x^2]}{\Delta x}$$

$$= \frac{8x + 8\Delta x - x^2 - 2x\,\Delta x - \Delta x^2 - 8x + x^2}{\Delta x}$$

$$= \frac{8\Delta x - 2x\,\Delta x - \Delta x^2}{\Delta x}$$

$$= 8 - 2x - \Delta x.$$

As $\Delta x \to 0$ the derivative, $dy/dx = 8 - 2x$, the slope at any point on the function. For example, at $x = 4$, $dy/dx = 0$, indicating that the slope of the function is zero at $x = 4$.

An alternative example of the process of differentiation, not tied to Equation (B.1), might be useful to consider. Begin with a function of some form such as $y = f(x) = 3x^2 + x + 2$. Let x increase by an amount Δx. Then y will increase by an amount Δy as shown in Figure B.2, giving

$$y + \Delta y = 3(x + \Delta x)^2 + (x + \Delta x) + 2$$
$$= 3[x^2 + 2x\,(\Delta x) + (\Delta x)^2] + (x + \Delta x) + 2$$
$$\Delta y = 3[x^2 + 2x\,(\Delta x) + (\Delta x)^2] + (x + \Delta x) + 2 - y$$

but $y = 3x^2 + x + 2$, giving

$$\Delta y = 3x^2 + 6x(\Delta x) + 3(\Delta x)^2 + x + \Delta x + 2 - 3x^2 - x - 2$$
$$= 6x(\Delta x) + 3(\Delta x)^2 + \Delta x.$$

The average rate of change of Δy with respect to Δx is

$$\frac{\Delta y}{\Delta x} = \frac{6x(\Delta x)}{\Delta x} + \frac{3(\Delta x)^2}{\Delta x} + \frac{\Delta x}{\Delta x}$$
$$= 6x + 3(\Delta x) + 1.$$

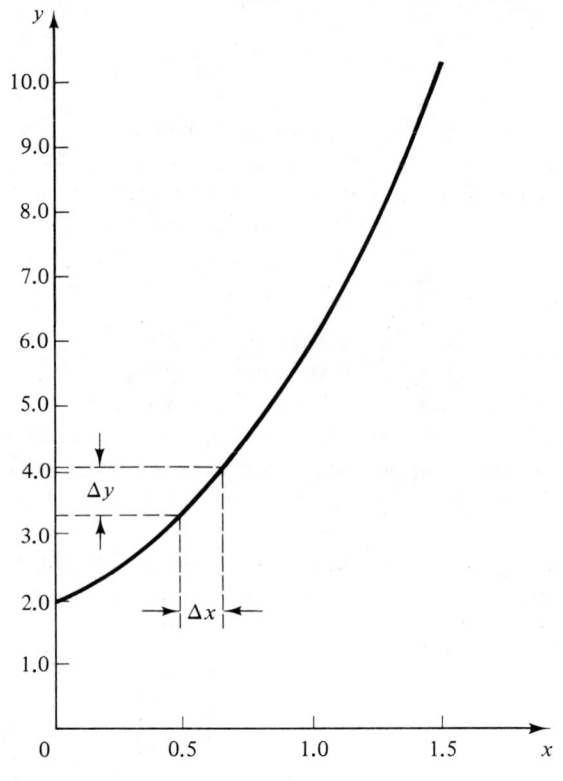

Figure B.2 Function $3x^2 + x + 2$.

But since

$$\lim_{\Delta x \to 0} \frac{\Delta y}{\Delta x} = \frac{dy}{dx} = f'(x),$$

the instantaneous rate of change is $6x + 1$.

Instead of proceeding as above for each case encountered, certain rules of differentiation have been developed for a range of common functional forms. Some of these are:

1. Derivative of a constant: If $f(x) = k$, a constant, then $dy/dx = 0$.
2. Derivative of a variable: If $f(x) = x$, a variable, then $dy/dx = 1$.
3. Derivative of a straight line: If $f(x) = ax + b$, a straight line, then $dy/dx = a$.
4. Derivative of a variable raised to a power: If $f(x) = x^n$, a variable raised to a power, then $dy/dx = nx^{n-1}$.
5. Derivative of a constant times a function: If $f(x) = k[g(x)]$, a constant times a function, then

$$\frac{dy}{dx} = k\left[\frac{dg(x)}{dx}\right].$$

App. B   Classical Optimization Methods   **459**

6. Derivative of the sum or difference of two functions: If $f(x) = g(x) \pm h(x)$, a sum or difference of two functions, then

$$\frac{dy}{dx} = \frac{dg(x)}{dx} \pm \frac{dh(x)}{dx}.$$

7. Derivative of the product of two functions: If $f(x) = g(x)h(x)$, a product of two functions, then

$$\frac{dy}{dx} = g(x)\frac{dh(x)}{dx} + h(x)\frac{dg(x)}{dx}.$$

8. Derivative of an exponential function: If $f(x) = e^x$, an exponent of e, then

$$\frac{dy}{dx} = e^x.$$

9. Derivative of the natural logarithm: If $f(x) = \ln x$, natural log of x, then

$$\frac{dy}{dx} = \frac{1}{x}.$$

The methods presented above may be used to find *higher-order* derivatives. When a function is differentiated, another function results which may also be differentiated if desired. For example, the derivative of $8x - x^2$ was $8 - 2x$. This was the slope of the function. If the slope is differentiated, the higher-order derivative is found to be -2. This is the rate of change in dy/dx and is designated d^2y/dx^2, of $f''(x)$. The process of differentiation can be extended to even higher orders as long as there remains some function to differentiate.

B.3 PARTIAL DIFFERENTIATION

Partial differentiation is the process of finding the rate of change whenever the dependent variable is a function of more than one independent variable. In the process of partial differentiation, all variables except the dependent variable, y, and the chosen independent variable are treated as constants and differentiated as such. The symbolism $\partial y/\partial x_1$ is used to represent the partial derivative of y with respect to x_1.

As an example, consider the following function of two independent variables, x_1 and x_2:

$$4x_1^2 + 6x_1 x_2 - 3x_2.$$

The partial derivative of y with respect to x_1 is

$$\frac{\partial y}{\partial x_1} = 8x_1 + 6x_2 - 0.$$

The partial derivative of y with respect to x_2 is

$$\frac{\partial y}{\partial x_2} = 0 + 6x_1 - 3.$$

Partial differentiation permits a view of slope along one dimension at a time of an n-dimensional function. By combining this information from such a function, the slope at any point on the function can be found.

B.4 UNCONSTRAINED OPTIMIZATION

Unconstrained optimization simply requires that no constraints be placed on the function under consideration. Under this assumption, a *necessary* condition for x^* to be an optimum point on $f(x)$ is that the first derivative be equal to zero. This is stated as

$$\left.\frac{df(x)}{dx}\right|_{x=x^*} = 0. \tag{B.2}$$

The first derivative being zero at the stationary point x^* is not *sufficient*, since it is possible for the derivative to be zero at a point of inflection on $f(x)$. It is sufficient for x^* to be an optimum point if the second derivative at x^* is positive or negative; x^* being a minimum if the second derivative is positive and a maximum if the second derivative is negative.

If the second derivative is also zero, a higher-order derivative is sought until the first nonzero one is found at the nth derivative as

$$\left.\frac{d^n f(x)}{dx^n}\right|_{x=x^*} = 0. \tag{B.3}$$

If n is odd, then x^* is a point of inflection. If n is even and if

$$\left.\frac{d^n f(x)}{dx^n}\right|_{x=x^*} < 0 \tag{B.4}$$

then x^* is a local maximum. But if

$$\left.\frac{d^n f(x)}{dx^n}\right|_{x=x^*} > 0 \tag{B.5}$$

then x^* is a local minimum.

As an example, suppose that the minimum value of x is sought for the function $f(x) = 2x^3 - 3x^2 + 1$ exhibited in Figure B.3. The necessary condition for a minimum to exist is

$$\frac{df(x)}{dx} = 6x^2 - 6x = 0.$$

Both $x = 0$ and $x = 1$ satisfy the condition above. Accordingly, the second derivative is taken as

$$\frac{d^2 f(x)}{dx^2} = 12x - 6$$

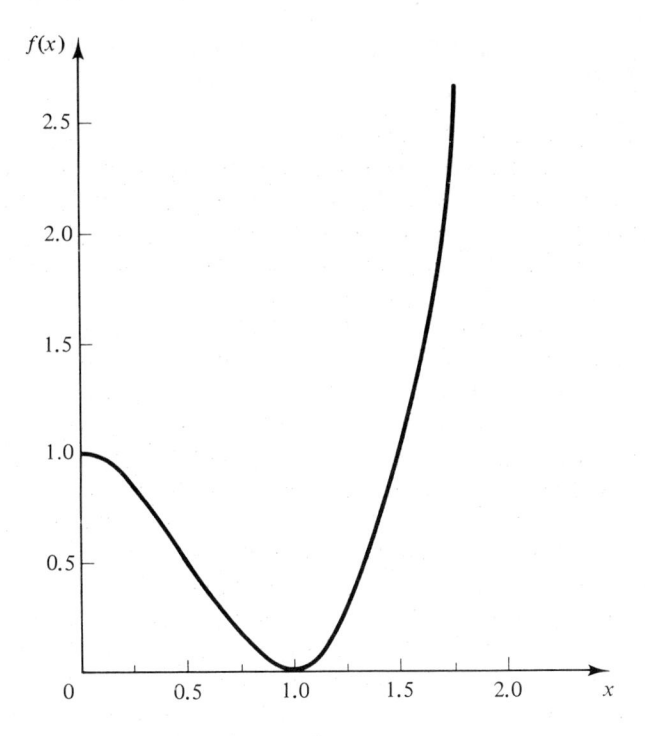

Figure B.3 Function $2x^3 - 3x^2 + 1$.

and evaluated at $x = 0$ and $x = 1$. At $x = 0$ the second derivative is -6, indicating that this is a maximum point. At $x = 1$ the second derivative is 6, indicating that this is the minimum sought. These points are shown on Figure B.2.

For functions of more than one independent variable, the vector $x^* = [x_1, x_2, \ldots, x_n]$ will have a stationary point on a function $f(x)$ if all elements of the vector of first partial derivatives evaluated at x^* are zero. Symbolically,

$$F(x) = \left[\frac{\partial F(x)}{\partial x_1}, \frac{\partial F(x)}{\partial x_2}, \ldots, \frac{\partial F(x)}{\partial x_n} \right] = 0. \tag{B.6}$$

Consider a function in two variables, x_1 and x_2, given as

$$f(x_1, x_2) = x_1^2 - 8x_2 + 2x_2^2 - 6x_1 + 30.$$

The necessary condition requires that

$$\frac{\partial f(x_1, x_2)}{\partial x_1} = 2x_1 - 6 = 0$$

and

$$\frac{\partial f(x_1, x_2)}{\partial x_2} = 4x_2 - 8 = 0.$$

The optimal value x_1^* is found to be 3 and the optimal value x_2^* is found to be 2. These may be substituted into $f(x_1, x_2)$ to give the optimal value.

$$f(x_1, x_2) = (3)^2 - 8(2) + 2(2)^2 - 6(3) + 30 = 13.$$

To determine whether this value for $f(x_1, x_2)$ is a maximum or a minimum, the second partials are required. These are

$$\frac{\partial(2x_1 - 6)}{\partial x_1} = 2 \quad \text{and} \quad \frac{\partial(4x_2 - 8)}{\partial x_2} = 4.$$

Each is greater than zero, indicating that a minimum may have been found. To verify this, the following relationship must be satisfied:

$$\left(\frac{\partial^2 y}{\partial x_1^2}\right)\left(\frac{\partial^2 y}{\partial x_2^2}\right) - \left(\frac{\partial^2 y}{\partial x_1 \, \partial x_2}\right)^2 > 0, \tag{B.7}$$

where

$$\frac{\partial^2 y}{\partial x_1 \, \partial y_2} = \frac{\partial(\partial y/\partial x_1)}{\partial x_2}.$$

Since

$$\frac{\partial y}{\partial x_1} = 2x_1 - 6$$

$$\frac{\partial^2 y}{\partial x_1 \, \partial x_2} = \frac{\partial(2x_1 - 6)}{\partial x_2} = 0.$$

Substituting back into Equation (B.7) gives $(2)(4) - 0 = 8$, verifying that the value found for $f(x_1, x_2)$ is a minimum.

C

Probability and Simulated Sampling

Some decision models formulated and optimized to evaluate operational systems will give satisfactory results if random variation is not incorporated. However, most models must incorporate probabilistic elements if meaningful results are to be obtained. This appendix presents some basic probability concepts, probability distribution theory, and the fundamentals of simulated sampling.

C.1 PROBABILITY CONCEPTS

The consequence of an experiment is not likely to be known until after its completion. If one tosses a coin, the outcome will not be known with certainty until either the head or the tail is observed. Experiments such as tossing a coin will lead to an occurrence that can be considered a *random event*. Most events in the decision environment are random in nature. Probability theory provides a means for quantifying such events.

The Universe and the Sample. The terms *universe* and *population* are used interchangeably. A universe consists of all possible objects, states, and events within an arbitrarily defined boundary. A universe may be finite or it may be infinite. If it is finite, the universe may be very large or very small. If the universe is large, it may sometimes be assumed to be infinite for computational purposes. A universe need not always be large; it may be defined as a dozen events or as only one object. The relative usefulness of the universe as an entity will be paramount in its definition.

All able-bodied men in the United States make up a universe. The children in a specific town may be a second population. Automobile accidents occurring in a given state during a given year are another population. The preceding populations are finite. They constitute items which can be counted. In some cases, they may be so large in number—for example, pebbles on a beach—that they are treated as if they are infinite. Other populations are actually infinite. The points on a line are infinite. The times required for a worker to complete a workpiece are infinite. Possible diameters of a bar constitute an infinite universe. The universe cannot be enumerated completely when it is infinite.

A *sample* is a part or portion of a universe. It may range in size from one to one less than the size of the universe. A sample is drawn from the population, and observations are made. This is done either because the universe is infinite in size or scope or because the population is large and/or inaccessible as a whole. The sample is used because it is smaller, more accessible, and more economical, and because it suggests certain characteristics of the population. It is usually assumed that the sample is typical of the population, at least in regard to the characteristic under consideration. The sample is then assessed, and inferences are made in regard to the population as a whole. To the extent that the sample is representative of the population, these inferences may be correct. The problem of selecting a representative sample from a population is an area in statistics to which one might easily devote an entire textbook.

Subsequent discussion assumes that the sample is a *random sample*, that is, one in which each object or state or event that constitutes the population has an equally likely chance or probability of being selected and represented in the sample. It is rather simple to make this definition; it may be much more difficult to implement it in a sampling operation.

The Probability of an Event. A measure of the relative certainty of an event, before the occurrence of the event, is its probability. The usual representation of a probability is a number $P(A)$ assigned to the outcome A. This number has the following property: $0 \leq P(A) \leq 1$, with $P(A) = 0$ if the event is certain not to occur, and $P(A) = 1$ if the event will occur.

Since probability is only a measure of the certainty (or uncertainty) associated with an event, its definition is rather tenuous. The concept of relative ferquency is sometimes employed to establish the number $P(A)$. Sometimes probabilities are established a priori. Other times they are simply a subjective estimate. Consider again the example of tossing a fair coin. In a lengthy series of tosses, the coin may have come up heads as often as tails. Then, the limiting value of the relative ferquency of a head will be 0.5 and will be stated as $P(H) = 0.5$.

Two definitions pertaining to events are needed in the development of probability theorems. These are:

1. Events A and B are said to be *mutually exclusive* if both cannot occur at the same time.
2. Event A is said to be *independent* of event B if the probability of the occurrence of A is the same regardless of whether or not B has occurred.

The Addition Theorem. The probability of the occurrence of either one or another of a series of mutually exclusive events is the sum of the probabilities of their separate occurrences. If a fair coin is tossed, and success is defined as the occurrence of either a head or a tail, then the probability of a head or a tail is

$$P(H + T) = P(H) + P(T)$$
$$= 0.5 + 0.5 = 1.0.$$

The key to use of the addition theorem is the proper definition of mutually exclusive events. Such events must be distinct one from another. If one event occurs, it must be impossible for the second to occur at the same time. For example, assume that the probability of having a flat tire during a given year, on each of four tires on an automobile, is 0.3. Then the probability of having a flat tire on any of the four tires during this time period is not given up by the addition of these four probabilities. If $P(T_1) = P(T_2) = P(T_3) = P(T_4) = 0.3$ are the respective probabilities of failure for each of the four tires, then

$$P(T_1 + T_2 + T_3 + T_4) \neq P(T_1) + P(T_2) + P(T_3) + P(T_4)$$
$$\neq 0.3 + 0.3 + 0.3 + 0.3 = 1.2.$$

This is not true because the failure of tires is not mutually exclusive. During the time period established, two or more tires may fail, whereas in the example of the coin tossing, it is not possible to obtain a head and a tail on the same toss.

The Multiplication Theorem. The probability of occurrence of independent events is the product of the probabilities of their separate events. Implicit in this theorem is the successful occurrence of two events simultaneously or in succession. Thus, the probability of the occurrence of two heads in two tosses of a coin is

$$P(H \cdot H) = P(H)P(H)$$
$$= (0.5)(0.5) = 0.25.$$

The tire failure example can now be resolved by considering the probabilities of each tire not failing. The probability of tire one not failing is given by $P(\bar{T}_1) = 0.7$. The probability of no tire failing is then given by

$$P[(\bar{T}_1)(\bar{T}_2)(\bar{T}_3)(\bar{T}_4)] = P(\bar{T}_1)P(\bar{T}_2)P(\bar{T}_3)P(\bar{T}_4)$$
$$= (0.7)(0.7)(0.7)(0.7) = 0.2401.$$

The probability of a tire failing, or of one or more tires failing, is

$$P(T_1 + T_2 + T_3 + T_4) = 1 - 0.2401 = 0.7599.$$

This approach is valid, since the probability of one tire not failing is independent of the success or failure of the other three tires.

The Conditional Theorem. The probability of the occurrence of two dependent events is the probability of the first event times the probability of the second event, given that the first has occurred. This may be expressed as

$$P(W_1 \cdot W_2) = P(W_1)P(W_2 | W_1).$$

This theorem is similar to the multiplication theorem, except that consideration is given to the lack of independence between events.

As an example, consider the probability of selecting two successive white balls from an urn containing three white and two black balls. This problem reduces to a calculation of the product of the probability of selecting a white ball times the probability of selecting a second white ball, given that the first attempt has been successful.

$$P(W_1 \cdot W_2) = \left(\frac{3}{5}\right)\left(\frac{2}{4}\right) = \frac{3}{10}.$$

The conditional theorem makes allowances for a change in probabilities between two successive events. This theorem will be helpful in constructing finite discrete probability distributions.

Probability Distributions. The pattern of the distribution of probabilties over all possible outcomes is called a probability distribution. *Probability distributions* provide a means for assigning the likelihood of occurrence of all possible values. Variables described in terms of a probability distribution are conveniently called *random variables*. The specific value of a random variable is determined by the distribution. The occurrence of that value is then governed by the associated probability.

A probability distribution is completely defined when the probability associated with every possible outcome is defined. In most instances the outcomes themselves are represented by numbers or different values of a variable, such as the lengths of maple leaves. When the pattern of the probability distribution is expressed as a function of this variable, the resulting function is called a *probability distribution function*.

An example probability distribution function may be developed as follows. A maintenance mechanic attends four machines and his services are needed only when a machine fails. He would like to estimate how many machines will fail each shift. From previous experience, and using the relative frequency concept of probability, the mechanic knows that 40 percent of the time only one machine will fail at least once during the shift. Further, 30 percent of the time two machines will fail, three machines will fail 20 percent of the time, and all four will fail 10 percent of the time.

The probability distribution of the number of failed machines may be expressed as $P(1) = 0.4$, $P(2) = 0.3$, $P(3) = 0.2$, and $P(4) = 0.1$. This probability distribution is exhibited in Figure C.1.

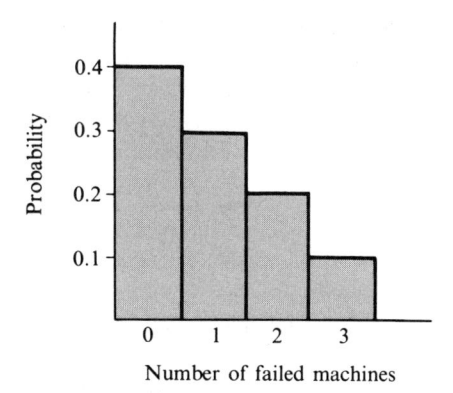

Figure C.1 Probability distribution of the number of failed machines.

The probability distribution function for this case may be defined as

$$P(x) = \frac{5 - x}{10} \quad \text{if } x = 1, 2, 3, 4$$

and

$$P(x) = 0$$

otherwise. Although the function $P(x) = (5 - x)/10$ uniquely represents the probability distribution pattern for the number of failed machines, the function itself belongs to a wider class of functions of the type $P(x) = (a - x)/b$. All functions of this type indicate similar patterns; yet each pair of numbers (a, b) uniquely defines a specific probability distribution. These numbers (a, b) are called *parameters*.

In the sense that they serve to define the probability distribution function, it is possible to look upon parameters as properties of the distribution function.

The choice of representation of parameters is not unique, and the most desirable representation would reflect a measure of the properties of the universe under study. Two most commonly sought measures are the *mean*, an indication of central tendency, and the *variance*, a measure of dispersion.

The *standard deviation*, defined as the positive square root of the variance, is sometimes used as a measure of dispersion. The standard deviation is usually represented as σ (where σ^2 implies the variance) and is dimensionally compatible with the random variable it describes. For example, if the variable is in centimeters of length, then the standard deviation will be expressed in centimeters of length as well.

C.2 DISCRETE PROBABILITY DISTRIBUTIONS

In this and the next section, some discrete and some continuous probability distributions are presented. When appropriate, the mean and the variance for each will be given. Formal definitions of these parameters, together with a summary table, are given in Section C.4.

The Hypergeometric Distribution. The hypergeometric is the most fundamental discrete probability distribution. It describes the case of sampling without replacement and is a simple extension of the conditional probability theorem. This distribution can be developed from the theory of combinations, where the number of combinations of n things taken x at a time is given by the expression

$$C_x^n = \frac{n!}{x!(n-x)!}.$$

For example, suppose that there are four items labeled *A*, *B*, *C*, and *D*. The number of possible pairs which can be made up of these four items can be enumerated as *A-B*, *A-C*, *A-D*, *B-C*, *B-D*, and *C-D*, for a total of six such pairs. Alternatively, this same solution is

$$C_2^4 = \frac{4!}{2!\,2!} = \frac{(4)(3)(2)(1)}{(2)(1)(2)(1)} = 6.$$

Similarly, the number of combinations of four units taken three at a time is

$$C_3^4 = \frac{4!}{3!\,1!} = 4.$$

The number of combinations of four units taken four at a time is

$$C_4^4 \frac{4!}{4!\,0!} = 1.$$

Note that $0! = 1$. At the other extreme, where very large factorials are encountered, it is convenient to work with logarithms of factorials.

Combinations are used in the construction of the hypergeometric distribution by defining the probability of each occurrence as a fraction consisting of

App. C   Probability and Simulated Sampling

all favorable combinations divided by the total number of combinations. As an example, consider an urn containing two black balls and one white ball. Two balls are selected at random from this urn. The probability that one is white and one is black is sought. The denominator of the fraction is the total number of combinations of three balls taken two at a time. The numerator is the number of combinations which will satisfy the requirement of selecting exactly one white and one black ball. This is the product of the number of combinations of one white ball selected from the one which is available times the number of combinations of one black ball selected from the two black balls which are available. The probability of drawing exactly one white and one black ball is

$$\frac{C_1^1 C_1^2}{C_2^3} = \frac{(1!2!)/0!\,1!\,1!\,1!}{3!/2!\,1!} = \frac{2/1}{6/2} = \frac{2}{3}.$$

The only remaining alternative is that of drawing exactly two black balls. The probability of so doing is given by

$$\frac{C_2^2 C_0^1}{C_2^3} = \frac{(2!\,1!)/2!\,0!\,0!\,1!}{3!/2!\,1!} = \frac{2/2}{6/2} = \frac{1}{3}.$$

These two probabilities represent the relative frequencies for a hypergeometric probability distribution.

Another example can be used to illustrate this distribution. Assume a container of 50 items includes 3 which are defective. A sample of 5 is selected from the 50. The probability is desired that exactly 0, 1, 2, or all 3 defectives will be contained in the sample of 5. These probabilities may be calculated as

$$P(0) = \frac{C_0^3 C_5^{47}}{C_5^{50}} = \frac{(3!\,47!)/0!\,3!\,5!\,42!}{50!/5!\,45!} = 0.7240$$

$$P(1) = \frac{C_1^3 C_4^{47}}{C_5^{50}} = \frac{(3!\,47!)/1!\,2!\,4!\,43!}{50!/5!\,45!} = 0.2525$$

$$P(2) = \frac{C_2^3 C_3^{47}}{C_5^{50}} = \frac{(3!\,47!)/2!\,1!\,3!\,44!}{50!/5!\,45!} = 0.0230$$

$$P(3) = \frac{C_3^3 C_2^{47}}{C_5^{50}} = \frac{(3!\,47!)/3!\,0!\,2!\,45!}{50!/5!\,45!} = 0.0005$$

$$P(0) + P(1) + P(2) + P(3) = 1.0000.$$

Note that the probability distribution is skewed and that the area it encompasses totals unity, since the sum of the probabilities of drawing zero, one, two, or three defectives is 1.0000. Hypergeometric distributions have no typical form. They may be symmetrical or they may be skewed either to the right or to the left. They are representative of sampling distributions where the population is finite and replacement between items is not effected.

The Binomial Distribution. The binomial probability distribution is also a sampling distribution. It is applicable where the probability is sought of exactly x occurrences in n trials of an event that has a constant probability of occurrence p. The requirement of a constant probability of occurrence is satisfied when the population being sampled is infinite in size, or where replacement of the sampled unit is affected. This distribution is used as an approximation to the hypergeometric distribution when the population is relatively large when compared to the sample which is drawn. Under these conditions, the constant probability of occurrence is approximated.

The probability of exactly x occurrences in n trials of an event that has a constant probability of occurrence p is given as

$$P(x) = C_x^n p^x q^{n-x} = \frac{n!}{x!(n-x)!} p^x q^{n-x} \qquad 0 \leq x \leq n, \qquad (C.1)$$

where $q = 1 - p$. The mean and variance of this distribution are given by np and npq, respectively.

As an example of the application of the binomial distribution, assume that a fair coin is to be tossed five times. The probability of obtaining exactly two heads is

$$P(2) = C_2^5 (p)^2 (1-p)^3$$

$$= \frac{5!}{3!\,2!} (0.5)^5$$

$$= 10(0.03125) = 0.3125.$$

A probability distribution may be constructed by solving for the probability of exactly zero, one, two, three, four, and five heads in five tosses. If $p = 0.5$, as in this example, the resulting distribution is symmetrical. If $p < 0.5$, the distribution is skewed to the right; if $p > 0.5$, the distribution is skewed to the left.

The binomial distribution finds frequent use as an approximation to the hypergeometric distribution because of the relative ease with which the individual probabilities may be found. It will serve as a good approximation to the extent that the lot or population is large relative to the sample size. This may be illustrated by reworking the example used to demonstrate the hypergeometric distribution. Since the container of 50 items contained three defectives, $p = 0.06$ and $q = 0.94$, the respective probabilities are

$$P(0) = \frac{5!}{0!\,5!} (0.06)^0 (0.94)^5 = (1)(0.94)^5 \qquad = 0.7339$$

$$P(1) = \frac{5!}{1!\,4!} (0.06)^1 (0.94)^4 = (5)(0.06)(0.94)^4 \qquad = 0.2343$$

$$P(2) = \frac{5!}{2!\,3!} (0.06)^2 (0.96)^3 = (10)(0.06)^2 (0.94)^3 = 0.0299$$

$$P(3) = \frac{5!}{3!\,2!} (0.06)^3 (0.94)^2 = (10)(0.06)^3 (0.94)^2 = 0.0019$$

$$P(0) + P(1) + P(2) + P(3) = 1.0000.$$

The Poisson Distribution. The Poisson distribution is useful as a distribution in its own right and as an approximation to the binomial. It is applicable when the opportunity for the occurrence of an event is large, but when the actual occurrence is extremely unlikely. The probability of exactly x occurrences of an event of probability p in a sample n is

$$P(x) = \frac{(\mu)^x e^{-\mu}}{x!} \qquad 0 \leq x \leq \infty. \tag{C.2}$$

The mean and variance of this distribution are equal and given by μ, where $\mu = np$.

As an example of the application of the Poisson distribution, assume that a sample of 100 items is selected from a population of items which are 1 percent defective. The probability of obtaining exactly three defectives in the sample is found from Equation (C.2) as

$$P(3) = \frac{(1)^3 (2.72)^{-1}}{3!} = 0.062.$$

Cumulative Poisson probabilities are tabulated for values of μ ranging up to 24 in Appendix D, Table D.1. Less precise values for these cumulative probabilities may be found from the modified Thorndike chart illustrated in Table D.2. This graph gives the cumulative probability for the occurrence of x or fewer items in a sample of n, from a population containing a proportion, p, of such items. Either Table D.1 on Table D.2 could be used to find $P(x)$ in Equation (C.2).

The Poisson distribution may be used as an approximation to the binomial distribution. Such an approximation is good when n is relatively large, p is relatively small, and in general, $pn < 5$. These conditions were satisfied in the previous example.

C.3 CONTINUOUS PROBABILITY DISTRIBUTIONS

Continuous probability distributions are used to define the probability of the occurrence of an event that may take on values over a continuum. Under certain conditions, it may be desirable to use a continuous probability distribution to approximate a discrete probability distribution. By so doing, tedious summations may be replaced by integrals. In other instances, it may be desirable to make a continuous distribution discrete. This operation is necessary where a numerical solution is to be performed on a digital computer. This section deals with continuous probability distributions.

The Rectangular Distribution. The rectangular or uniform probability distribution may be either discrete or continuous. The continuous form of this simple distribution is given by

$$f(x) = \frac{1}{a} \qquad 0 \leq x \leq a. \tag{C.3}$$

The discrete form divides the interval 0 to a into $n + 1$ cells over the range 0 to n with $1/(n + 1)$ as the unit probabilities. The mean and variance of the rectangular probability distribution are given as $a/2$ and $a^2/12$ for the continuous case, and as $n/2$ and $n^2/12 + n/6$ for the discrete case.

The general form of the rectangular probability distribution is shown in Figure C.2. The probability that a value of x will fall between 0 and a is the area under the function $1/a$ between the limits 0 and a. This is equal to unity. One may determine the probability associated with a specific value of x, or a range of x, by integration for the continuous case. The probability associated with a specific value of x for the discrete distributions of the previous section was found from the functions given. Determination of the probability associated with a range of x required a summation of individual probabilities. This is a fundamental difference in dealing with discrete and continuous probability distributions.

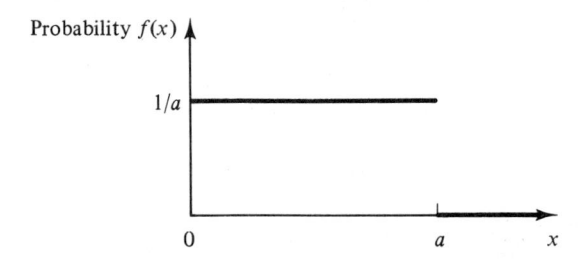

Figure C.2 General form of the rectangular distribution.

Values drawn at random from the rectangular distribution with x allowed to take on values ranging from 0 through 9 are given in Appendix D, Table D.3. These random rectangular variates may be used to randomize a sample or to develop values drawn at random from other probability distributions. As such, they are a useful tool in statistical analysis.

The Exponential Distribution. The exponential probability distribution is given by

$$f(x) = \frac{1}{a} e^{-x/a} \qquad 0 \leq x \leq \infty. \tag{C.4}$$

The mean and variance of this distribution are given by a and a^2, respectively. Its form is illustrated in Figure C.3.

As an example of the exponential probability distribution, consider the selection of a light bulb from a population of light bulbs whose life is known to be exponentially distributed with a mean $\mu = 1{,}000$ hours. The probability of the life of this sample bulb not exceeding 1,000 hours would be expressed as $P(x \leq 1{,}000)$. This would be the proportional area under the exponential function over the range $x = 0$ to $x = 1{,}000$, or

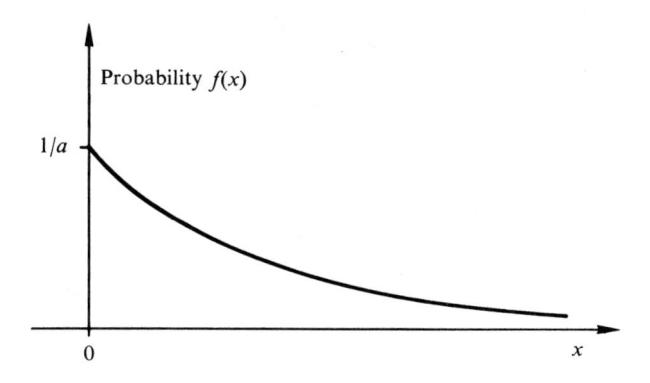

Figure C.3 General form of the exponential distribution.

$$P(x \le 1{,}000) = \int_0^{1{,}000} f(x)\,dx$$

$$= \int_0^{1{,}000} \frac{1}{1{,}000} e^{-x/1{,}000}\,dx$$

$$= -e^{-x/1{,}000}\big|_0^{1{,}000}$$

$$= 1 - e^{-1} = 0.632.$$

Note that 0.632 is that proportion of the area of an exponential distribution to the left of the mean. This implies that the probability of the occurrence of an event exceeding the mean value is only $1 - 0.632 = 0.368$.

The Normal Distribution. This normal or Gaussian probability distribution is one of the most important of all distributions. It is defined by

$$f(x) = \frac{1}{\sigma\sqrt{2\pi}} e^{[-(x-\mu)^2/2\sigma^2]} \qquad -\infty \le x \le +\infty. \tag{C.5}$$

The mean and variance are μ and σ^2, respectively. Variation is inherent in nature, and much of this variation appears to follow the normal distribution, the form of which is given in Figure C.4.

The normal distribution is symmetrical about the mean and possesses some interesting and useful properties in regard to its shape. Where distances from the mean are expressed in terms of standard deviations, σ, the relative areas defined between two such distances will be constant from one distribution to another. In effect, all normal distributions, when defined in terms of a common value of μ and σ, will be identical in form, and corresponding probabilities may be tabulated. Normally, cumulative probabilities are given from $-\infty$ to any value expressed as standard deviation units. Such probabilities are given in Appendix D, Table D.4. The table gives the probability from $-\infty$ to Z, where

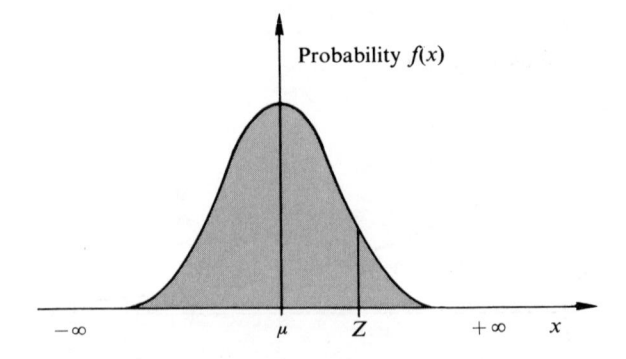

Figure C.4 Normal probability distribution.

Z is a standard normal variate defined as

$$Z = \frac{x - \mu}{\sigma}.$$

This is shown as the shaded area in Figure C.5.

The area from $-\infty$ to -1σ is indicated as the shaded area in Figure C.5. From Table D.4, the probability of x falling in this range is 0.1587. Similarly, the area from $-\infty$ to $+2\sigma$ is 0.9773. If the probability of a value falling in the

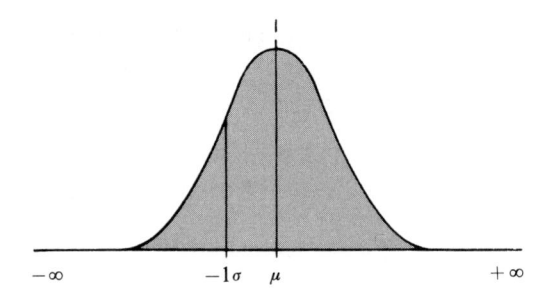

Figure C.5 Area from $-\infty$ to -1σ under the normal distribution.

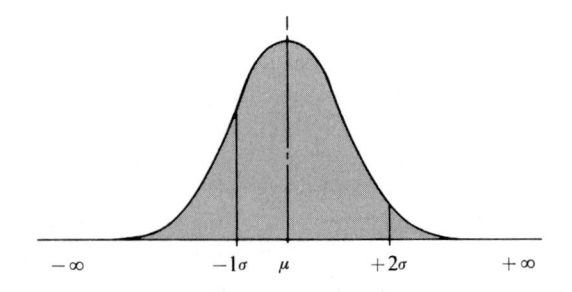

Figure C.6 Area from -1σ to $+2\sigma$ under the normal distribution.

interval -1σ to $+2\sigma$ is required, the following computations may be made:

$$P(\text{area } -\infty \text{ to } +2\sigma) = 0.9773$$
$$- P(\text{area } -\infty \text{ to } -1\sigma) = 0.1587$$
$$\overline{P(\text{area } -1\sigma \text{ to } +2\sigma) = 0.8186.}$$

This situation is shown in Figure C.6. The probabilities associated with any normal probability distribution can be calculated by the use of Table D.4.

C.4 SUMMARY OF PROBABILITY DISTRIBUTIONS

The mean, variance, and distribution function for each probability distribution presented previously is summarized in Table C.1. In most cases the hypergeometric probability distribution would be appropriately used to describe

Table C.1. SUMMARY OF PROBABILITY DISTRIBUTIONS

Probability Distribution	Function	Mean	Variance
Hypergeometric	$P(x) = \dfrac{C_x^{N_p} C_{n-x}^{N-N_p}}{C_n^N}$	np	$npq\left(\dfrac{N-n}{N-1}\right)$
Binomial	$P(x) = \dfrac{n!}{x!(n-x)!} p^x q^{n-x}$	np	npq
Poisson	$P(x) = \dfrac{\mu^x e^{-\mu}}{x!}$	μ	μ
Uniform (discrete)	$P(x) = \dfrac{1}{a+1}$	$\dfrac{a}{2}$	$\dfrac{a^2}{12} + \dfrac{a}{6}$
Uniform (continuous)	$f(x) = \dfrac{1}{a}$	$\dfrac{a}{2}$	$\dfrac{a^2}{12}$
Exponential	$f(x) = \dfrac{1}{a} e^{-x/a}$	a	a^2
Normal	$f(x) = \dfrac{1}{\sigma\sqrt{2\pi}} e^{-(x-\mu)^2/2\sigma^2}$	μ	σ^2

sampling from finite populations. As an alternative, we may use the binomial distribution as an approximation if the population is relatively large. In this case the value of p does not change appreciably as items are taken from the population. The Poisson distribution may be used as an approximation to the binomial when n is relatively large, p is relatively small, and $pn < 5$. These approximations are shown in Figure C.7.

The normal distribution may also be used as an approximation to the binomial. This approximation will usually be satisfactory if p is close to 0.5 or if n is large. If $n \geq 50$, p may be as small as 0.20 or as large as 0.80 before the approximation ceases to be reasonably good. The ease with which the Poisson

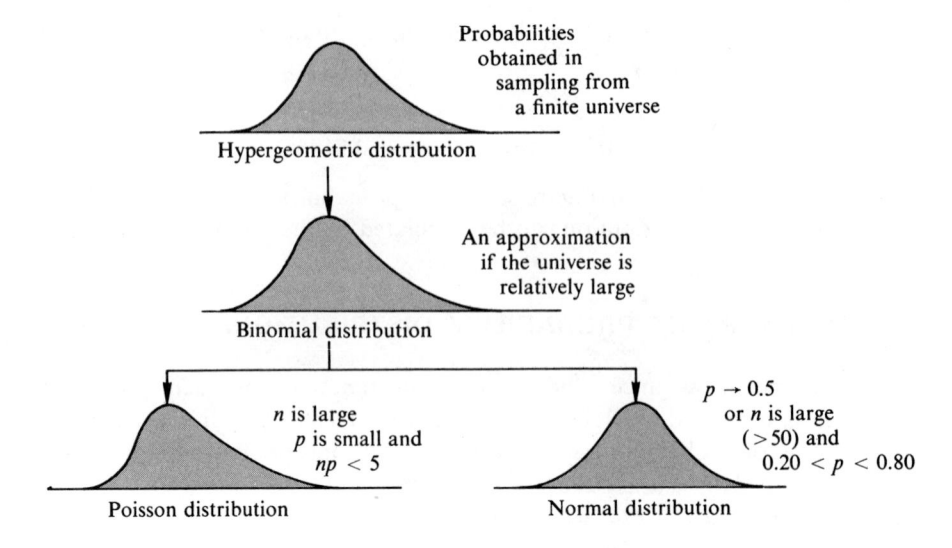

Figure C.7 Poisson and normal distributions as approximations.

and the normal distributions may be used justifies their application in many instances.

Derivations leading to the parameters of probability distributions follow a common pattern. The expectation or expected value of a function $h(x)$ of a random variable x is defined as

$$E[h(x)] = \sum_R h(x)P(x) \tag{C.6}$$

if x is discrete, and

$$E[h(x)] = \int_R h(x)f(x)\,dx \tag{C.7}$$

if x is continuous. In each, $\sum_R$ or $\int_R$ denotes the summation or integration over the entire range of possible values of the outcome x.

The mean of the random variable x is defined as $\mu = E(x)$, and the variance of the random variable x is defined as $\sigma^2 = E[(x - \mu)^2]$. For computational ease it is sometimes desirable to express the variance in an alternative manner as

$$\sigma^2 = E(x^2) - [E(x)]^2.$$

The derivations for the mean and the variance can be illustrated using the Poisson distribution as an example. If a random variable x exhibits a Poisson distribution function,

$$P(x) = \frac{\mu^x e^{-\mu}}{x!}$$

where $x > 0$ and is an integer.

$$\text{Mean of } x = E[x]$$
$$= \sum_R xP(x) \quad \text{since } x \text{ is discrete}$$
$$= \sum_0^\infty x \frac{\mu^x e^{-\mu}}{x!}$$
$$= e^{-\mu} \sum_0^\infty \frac{\mu^x}{(x-1)!}.$$

Letting $k = x - 1$,
$$\text{mean} = e^{-\mu} \sum_0^\infty \mu \frac{\mu^k}{k!} = \mu$$

since
$$\sum_0^\infty \frac{\mu^k}{k!} = e^\mu.$$

$$\text{Variance of } x = E(x^2) - [E(x)]^2$$
$$= \sum_0^\infty x^2 \frac{\mu^x e^{-\mu}}{x!} - \mu^2$$
$$= e^{-\mu} \sum_0^\infty \left[\frac{\mu^x}{(x-2)!} + \frac{\mu^x}{(x-1)!} \right] - \mu^2$$
$$= e^{-\mu}(\mu^2 e^\mu + \mu e^\mu) - \mu^2$$
$$= \mu^2 + \mu - \mu^2 = \mu.$$

Thus, both the mean and the variance of the Poisson distribution have the value μ as given in Table C.1.

C.5 SIMULATED SAMPLING

Models used to explain operational systems often incorporate probabilistic elements. This may be necessary, since the decision environment is made up of a multitude of random variables. In some cases, formal mathematical solutions are difficult or impossible to obtain from these models. Under these conditions it may be necessary to use a method known as *simulated sampling* or *Monte Carlo analysis*. The step-by-step procedure used in simulated sampling is presented in this section.

Step 1—Formalize the System Logic. The system under study is usually assumed to operate in accordance with a certain logical pattern. Before beginning the actual simulated sampling process, it is necessary to formalize the operational procedure by the construction of a model. This may require the development of a step-by-step flow diagram outlining the logic. If the actual simulation process is to be performed on a digital computer, it is mandatory to prepare an accurate logic diagram. From this, the computer can be programmed to pattern the process under study.

Consider the evaluation of the random variable *A* which is the result of a ratio formed by the random variable *B* and the random variable *C*. Although this may not conform to any real-world situation, the model describing the process is $A = B/C$. This expression formalizes the system under study. It establishes the computational procedure required to evaluate the variable of interest.

Step 2—Determine the Distributions. Each random variable in the model refers to an event in the system being studied. Therefore, an important step in simulated sampling is determining the behavior of these random variables. This involves the development of empirical frequency distributions to describe the relevant variables by the collection of historical data. Once this is done, the frequency distribution for each variable may be studied statistically to ascertain whether it conforms to a known theoretical distribution.

For the example under consideration, assume that data for random variable B have been collected and studied. It is concluded that this random variable conforms to the exponential distribution with a mean of 4. This is a theoretical distribution with the functional form

$$f(x) = \tfrac{1}{4}e^{-x/4}.$$

Similarly, assume that data for random variable *C* have been collected. Suppose that the resulting frequency distribution is as shown in Figure C.8. It is decided that no theoretical distribution adequately describes these data. Therefore, the empirical distribution will be used in the analysis.

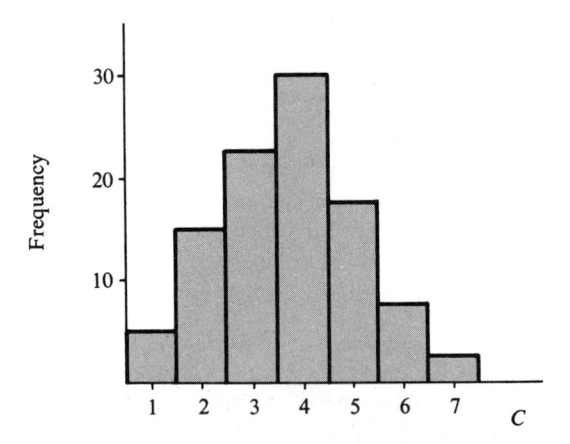

Figure C.8   Distribution of the random variable *C*.

Step 3—Develop the Cumulative Distributions. The probability distributions describing the random variables will be theoretical or empirical or both. Those expressed theoretically may be manipulated mathematically in order to obtain the required cumulative probability distributions. The cumulative distribution for random variable B may be expressed as

$$F(x) = \int_0^x f(x)\,dx$$
$$= \int_0^x \tfrac{1}{4} e^{-x/4}\,dx$$
$$= -e^{-x/4}\big|_0^x$$
$$= 1 - e^{-x/4}. \tag{C.8}$$

This cumulative exponential distribution is shown in Figure C.9.

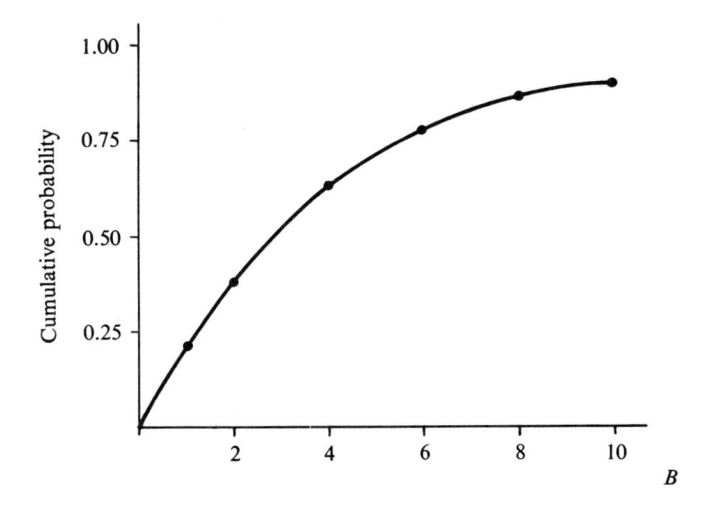

Figure C.9 Cumulative exponential distribution of mean $a = 4$.

Those distributions expressed empirically cannot be converted to cumulative distributions by mathematical means. This is the case for random variable C shown in Figure C.8. The simulated sampling, however, requires a cumulative distribution for each random variable. Therefore, graphical means must be used. Figure C.10 exhibits the cumulative distribution corresponding to the distribution of Figure C.8. It is developed by summing the probabilities from left to right and plotting the results. This is the same as the mathematical process used for the exponential distribution.

The cumulative distributions of Figures C.9 and C.10 may be used to transform random rectangular variates, such as those given in Appendix D, Table D.3, to values drawn at random from the basic distributions. By this means, specific values are determined for random variable B and random variable C. Thus, a random rectangular variate with a value of 681 gives a value for the random variable B of 4.572, as shown in Figure C.9. Similarly, a random rectangular variate with a value of 654 gives a value for the random variable C of 4, as is shown in Figure C.10. Use of Figure C.9 may be bypassed

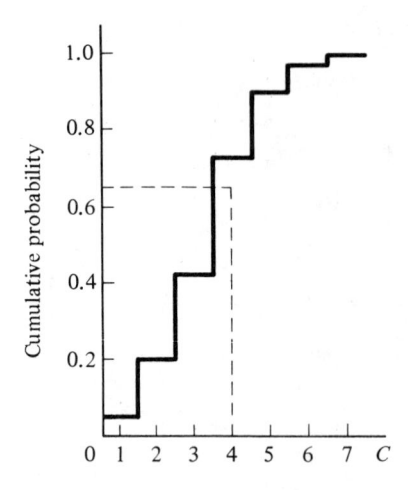

Figure C.10 Cumulative distribution of the random variable C.

since its mathematical equivalent is available. Equation (C.8) may be used to transform the random rectangular variate 681 to a random exponential variable directly. The result is

$$0.681 = 1 - e^{-x/4}$$
$$x = 4.572.$$

Table C.2. SIMULATED SAMPLING ANALYSIS

Trial (A)	Random Number (B)	B (C)	Random Number (D)	C (E)	$A = \dfrac{B}{C}$ (F)
1	0.681	4.572	0.654	4.0	1.143
2	0.425	2.220	0.695	4.0	0.555
3	0.469	2.540	0.126	2.0	1.270
4	0.392	1.996	0.206	3.0	0.665
5	0.104	0.440	0.020	1.0	0.440
6	0.990	18.420	0.766	5.0	3.684
7	0.833	8.260	0.391	3.0	2.753
8	0.953	12.240	0.407	3.0	4.080
9	0.657	4.280	0.313	3.0	1.427
10	0.604	3.732	0.213	3.0	1.244
11	0.925	10.380	0.748	5.0	2.076
12	0.808	6.600	0.509	4.0	1.650
13	0.730	5.240	0.888	5.0	1.048
14	0.754	5.640	0.585	4.0	1.410
15	0.511	2.868	0.033	1.0	2.868
16	0.851	7.628	0.131	2.0	3.814
17	0.746	5.480	0.344	3.0	1.827
18	0.899	9.180	0.384	3.0	3.060
19	0.092	0.386	0.802	5.0	0.077
20	0.807	6.580	0.874	5.0	1.316

Step 4—Perform the Sampling Analysis. The example under consideration requires that random variable B be divided by random variable C. This requirement is established by the model of the system under study. The result of one outcome is the random variable A. For the two values previously obtained, A is found to be $4.572/4 = 1.143$. This is the first entry in Table C.2.

Repeated application of this process gives values for the random variable A. Twenty trials are exhibited in Table C.2. Column A identified the trial. Column B is a three-digit random rectangular variate taken from Appendix D, Table D.3. This random rectangular variate is converted to a value drawn at random from distribution B by the use of Figure C.9. The result is entered in column C. Column D is the next random rectangular variate in sequence from Appendix D, Table D.3. It is converted to a value drawn at random from distribution C by the use of Figure C.10. The result is entered in column E. Finally, column F is the value in column C divided by the value in column E. It is the random variable A.

The analysis shown in Table C.2 was continued through 100 trials. A frequency distribution of the values in column F is shown in Figure C.11. It describes the nature of random variable A within sampling variation. There is no mathematical method for deriving the distribution of random variable A from the distributions assumed for random variables B and C. Therefore, the need and value of simulated sampling should be evident.

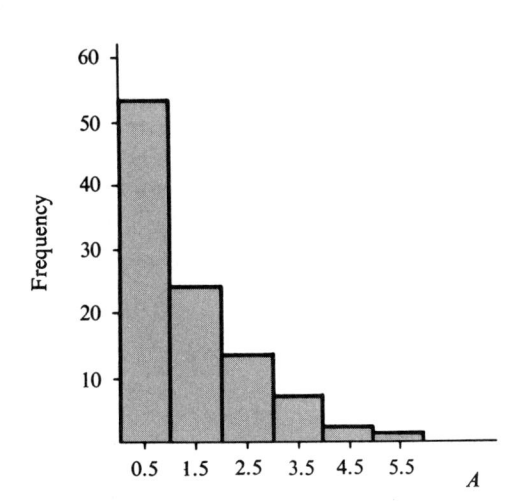

Figure C.11 Frequency distribution of the random variable A.

D

Statistical Tables

TABLE D.1 CUMULATIVE POISSON PROBABILITIES

Cumulative probabilities $\times$ 1,000 for the Poisson distribution are given for μ up to 24. The tabular values were computed from $\sum (\mu^x e^{-\mu}/x!)$.

TABLE D.2 CUMULATIVE POISSON PROBABILITY CURVES

Cumulative Poisson curves (modified Thorndike chart). (Reproduced with permission from H.F. Dodge and H.G. Roming, *Sampling Inspection Tables*. New York: John Wiley & Sons, Inc., 1959.)

TABLE D.3 RANDOM RECTANGULAR VARIATES

Random variates from the rectangular distribution, $f(x) = 1/10$, are presented. (Reproduced with permission from the Rand Corporation, *A Million Random Digits with 100,000 Normal Deviates*. New York: The Free Press, 1955, pp. 130–131.)

TABLE D.4 CUMULATIVE NORMAL PROBABILITIES

Cumulative probabilities are given from $-\infty$ to $Z = (x - \mu)/\sigma$ for the standard normal distribution. (Tabular values adapted with permission from E. L. Grant, *Statistical Quality Control*, 3rd ed. New York: McGraw-Hill Book Company, 1964.)

Table D.1. CUMULATIVE POISSON PROBABILITIES × 1,000

μ \ x	0	1	2	3	4	5	6	7	8	9
0.1	905	995	1,000							
0.2	819	982	999	1,000						
0.3	741	963	996	1,000						
0.4	670	938	992	999	1,000					
0.5	607	910	986	998	1,000					
0.6	549	878	977	997	1,000					
0.7	497	844	966	994	999	1,000				
0.8	449	809	953	991	999	1,000				
0.9	407	772	937	987	998	1,000				
1.0	368	736	920	981	996	999	1,000			
1.1	333	699	900	974	995	999	1,000			
1.2	301	663	879	966	992	998	1,000			
1.3	273	627	857	957	989	998	1,000			
1.4	247	592	833	946	986	997	999	1,000		
1.5	223	558	809	934	981	996	999	1,000		
1.6	202	525	783	921	976	994	999	1,000		
1.7	183	493	757	907	970	992	998	1,000		
1.8	165	463	731	891	964	990	997	999	1,000	
1.9	150	434	704	875	956	987	997	999	1,000	
2.0	135	406	677	857	947	983	995	999	1,000	
2.2	111	355	623	819	928	975	993	998	1,000	
2.4	091	308	570	779	904	964	988	997	999	1,000
2.6	074	267	518	736	877	951	983	995	999	1,000

Table D.1. CUMULATIVE POISSON PROBABILITIES × 1,000 (Continued)

μ \ x	0	1	2	3	4	5	6	7	8	9	10	11	12	13	14
2.8	061	231	469	692	848	935	976	992	998	999	1,000				
3.0	050	199	423	647	815	916	966	988	996	999	1,000				
3.2	041	171	380	603	781	895	955	983	994	998	1,000				
3.4	033	147	340	558	744	871	942	977	992	997	999	1,000			
3.6	027	126	303	515	706	844	927	969	988	996	999	1,000			
3.8	022	107	269	473	668	816	909	960	984	994	998	999	1,000		
4.0	018	092	238	433	629	785	889	949	979	992	997	999	1,000		
4.2	015	078	210	395	590	753	867	936	972	989	996	999	1,000		
4.4	012	066	185	359	551	720	844	921	964	985	994	998	999	1,000	
4.6	010	056	163	326	513	686	818	905	955	980	992	997	999	1,000	
4.8	008	048	143	294	476	651	791	887	944	975	990	996	999	1,000	
5	007	040	125	265	440	616	762	867	932	968	986	995	998	999	1,000
6	002	017	062	151	285	446	606	744	847	916	957	980	991	996	999
7	001	007	030	082	173	301	450	599	729	830	901	947	973	987	994
8	000	003	014	042	100	191	313	453	593	717	816	888	936	966	983
9	000	001	006	021	055	116	207	324	456	587	706	803	876	926	959
10		000	003	010	029	067	130	220	333	458	583	697	792	864	917
11		000	001	005	015	038	079	143	232	341	460	579	689	781	854
12		000	001	002	008	020	046	090	155	242	347	462	576	682	772
13			000	001	004	011	026	054	100	166	252	353	463	573	675
14			000	000	002	006	014	032	062	109	176	260	358	464	570
15				000	001	003	008	018	037	070	118	185	268	363	466

485

Table D.1. CUMULATIVE POISSON PROBABILITIES × 1,000 (*Continued*)

μ \ x	15	16	17	18	19	20	21	22	23	24	25	26	27	28	29
7	998	999	1,000												
8	992	996	998	999	1,000										
9	978	989	995	998	999	1,000									
10	951	973	986	993	997	998	999	1,000							
11	907	944	968	982	991	995	998	999	1,000						
12	844	899	937	963	979	988	994	997	999	999	1,000				
13	764	835	890	930	957	975	986	992	996	998	999	1,000			
14	669	756	827	883	923	952	971	983	991	995	997	999	999	1,000	
15	568	664	749	819	875	917	947	967	981	989	994	997	998	999	1,000

μ \ x	0	1	2	3	4	5	6	7	8	9	10	11	12	13	14
16					000	001	004	010	022	043	077	127	193	275	368
17					000	001	002	005	013	026	049	085	135	201	281
18						000	001	003	015	015	030	055	092	143	208
19						000	001	002	004	009	018	035	061	098	150
20							000	001	002	005	011	021	039	066	105
21								000	001	003	006	013	025	043	072
22								000	001	002	004	008	015	028	048
23									000	001	002	004	009	017	031
24										000	001	003	005	011	020

Table D.2. CUMULATIVE POISSON PROBABILITY CURVES

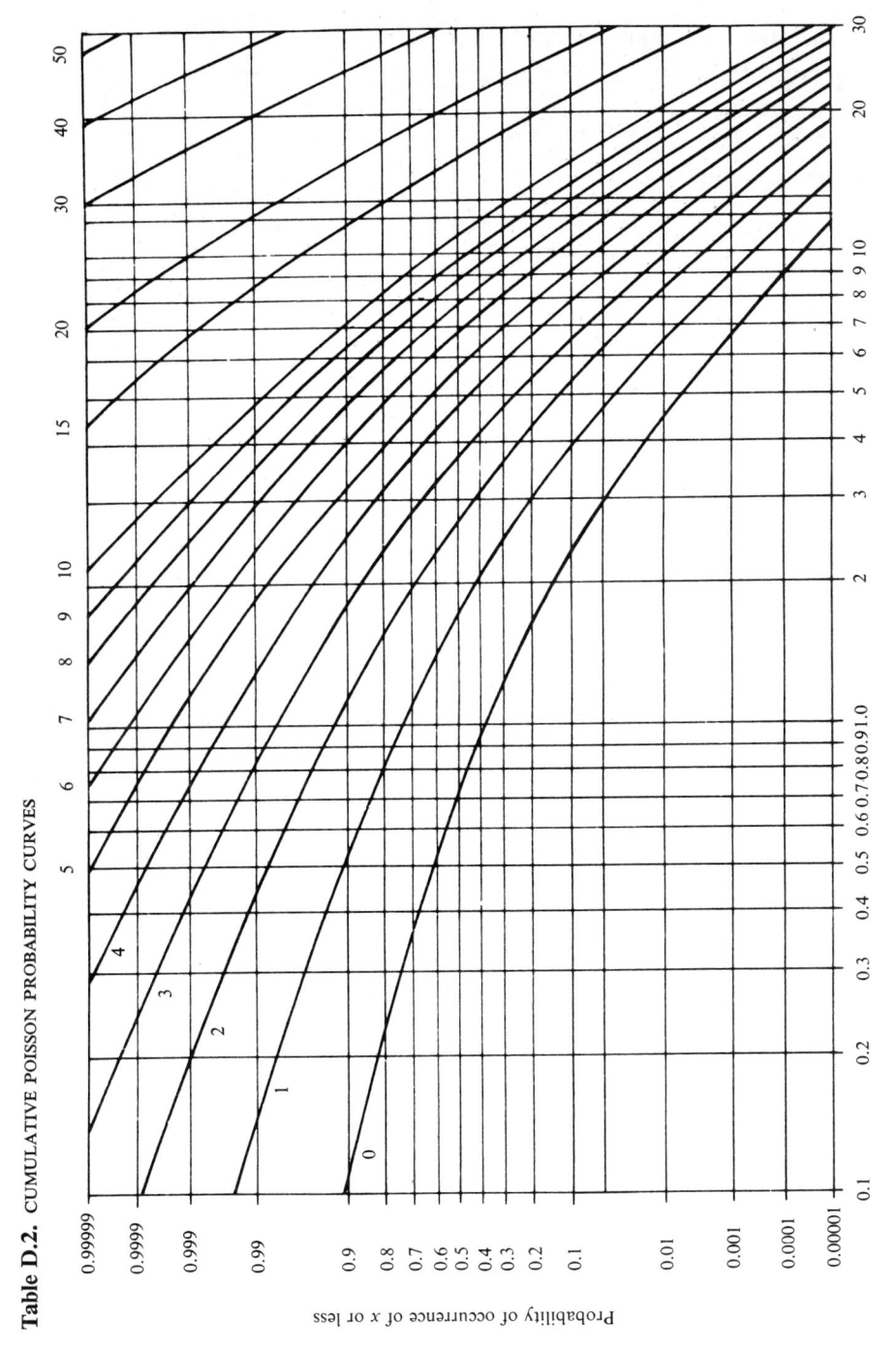

Table D.3. RANDOM RECTANGULAR VARIATES

14541	36678	54343	94932	25238	84928	30668	34992	69955	06633
88626	98899	01337	48085	83315	33563	78656	99440	55584	54178
31466	87268	62975	19310	28192	06654	06720	64938	67111	55091
52738	52893	51373	43430	95885	93795	20129	54847	68674	21040
17444	35560	35348	75467	26026	89118	51810	06389	02391	96061
62596	56854	76099	38469	26285	86175	65468	32354	02675	24070
38338	83917	50232	29164	07461	25385	84838	07405	38303	55635
29163	61006	98106	47538	99122	36242	90365	15581	89597	03327
59049	95306	31227	75288	10122	92687	99971	97105	37597	91673
67447	52922	58657	67601	96148	97263	39110	95111	04682	64873
57082	55108	26992	19196	08044	57300	75095	84330	92314	11370
00179	04358	95645	91751	56618	73782	38575	17401	38686	98435
65420	87257	44374	54312	94692	81776	24422	99198	51432	63943
52450	75445	40002	69727	29775	32572	79980	67902	97260	21050
82767	26273	02192	88536	08191	91750	46993	02245	38659	28026
17066	64286	35972	32550	82167	53177	32396	34014	20993	03031
86168	32643	23668	92038	03096	51029	09693	45454	89854	70103
33632	69631	70537	06464	83543	48297	67693	63137	62675	56572
77915	56481	43065	24231	43011	40505	90386	13870	84603	73101
90000	92887	92668	93521	44072	01785	27003	01851	40232	25842
55809	70237	10368	58664	39521	11137	20461	53081	07150	11832
50948	64026	03350	03153	75913	72651	28651	94299	67706	92507
27138	59012	27872	90522	69791	85482	80337	12252	83388	48909
03534	58643	75913	63557	25527	47131	72295	55801	44847	48019
48895	34733	58057	00195	79496	93453	07813	66038	55245	43168
57585	23710	77321	70662	82884	80132	42281	17032	96737	93284
95913	24669	42050	92757	68677	75567	99777	49246	93049	79863
12981	37145	95773	92475	43700	85253	33214	87656	13295	09721
62349	64163	57369	65773	86217	00135	33762	72398	16343	02263
68193	37564	56257	50030	53951	84887	34590	22038	40629	29562
56203	82226	83294	60361	29924	09353	87021	08149	11167	81744
31945	23224	08211	02562	20299	85836	94714	50278	99818	62489
68726	52274	59535	80873	35423	05166	06911	25916	90728	20431
79557	25747	55585	93461	44360	18359	20493	54287	43693	88568
05764	29803	01819	51972	91641	03524	18381	65427	11394	37447
30187	66931	01972	48438	90716	21847	35114	91839	26913	68893
30858	43646	96984	80412	91973	81339	05548	49812	40775	14263
85117	38268	18921	29519	33359	80642	95362	22133	40322	37826
59422	12752	56798	31954	19859	32451	04433	62116	14899	38825
73479	91833	91122	45524	73871	77931	67822	95602	23325	37718
83648	66882	15327	89748	76685	76282	98624	71547	49089	33105
19454	91265	09051	94410	06418	34484	37929	61070	62346	79970
49327	97807	61390	08005	71795	49290	52285	82119	59348	55986
54482	51025	12382	35719	66721	84890	38106	44136	95164	92935
30487	19459	25693	09427	10967	36164	33893	07087	16141	12734
42998	68627	66295	59360	44041	76909	56321	12978	31304	97444
03668	61096	26292	79688	05625	52198	74844	69815	76591	35398
45074	91457	28311	56499	60403	13658	81838	54729	12365	24082
58444	99255	14960	02275	37925	03852	81235	91628	72136	53070
82912	91185	89612	02362	93360	20158	24796	38284	55328	96041

Table D.3. RANDOM RECTANGULAR VARIATES (*Continued*)

44553	29642	20317	69470	57789	27631	68040	73201	51302	66497
01914	36106	71351	69176	53353	57353	42430	68050	47862	61922
00768	37958	69915	17709	31629	49587	07136	42959	56207	03625
29742	67676	62608	54215	97167	07008	77130	15806	53081	14297
07721	20143	56131	56112	23451	48773	38121	74419	11696	42614
99158	07133	04325	43936	83619	77182	55459	28808	38034	01054
97168	13859	78155	55361	04871	78433	58538	78437	14058	79510
07508	63835	83056	74942	70117	91928	10383	93793	31015	60839
68400	66460	67212	28690	66913	90798	71714	07698	31581	31086
88512	62908	65455	64015	00821	23970	58118	93174	02201	16771
94549	31145	62897	91582	94064	14687	47570	83714	45928	32685
02307	86181	44897	60884	68072	77693	83413	61680	55872	12111
28922	89390	66771	39185	04266	55216	91537	36500	48154	04517
73898	85742	97914	74170	10383	16366	37404	73282	20524	85004
66220	81596	18533	84825	43509	16009	00830	13177	54961	31140
64452	91627	21897	31830	62051	00760	43702	22305	79009	15065
26748	19441	87908	06086	62879	99865	50739	98540	54002	98337
61328	52330	17850	53204	29955	48425	84694	11280	70661	27303
89134	85791	73207	93578	62563	37205	97667	61453	01067	31982
91365	23327	81658	56441	01480	09677	86053	11505	30898	82143
54576	02572	60501	98257	40475	81401	31624	27951	60172	21382
39870	60476	02934	39857	06430	59325	84345	62302	98616	13452
82288	29758	35692	21268	35101	77554	35201	22795	84532	29927
57404	93848	87288	30246	34990	50575	49485	60474	17377	46550
22043	17104	49653	79082	45099	24889	04829	49097	58065	23492
61981	00340	43594	22386	41782	94104	08867	68590	61716	36120
96056	16227	74598	28155	23304	66923	07918	15303	44988	79076
64013	74715	31525	62676	75435	93055	37086	52737	89455	83016
59515	37354	55422	79471	23150	79170	74043	49340	61320	50390
38534	33169	40448	21683	82153	23411	53057	26069	86906	49708
41422	50502	40570	59748	59499	70322	62416	71408	06429	70123
38633	80107	10241	30880	13914	09228	68929	06438	17749	81149
48214	75994	31689	25257	28641	14854	72571	78189	35508	26381
54799	37862	06714	55885	07481	16966	04797	57846	69080	49631
25848	27142	63477	33416	60961	19781	65457	23981	90348	24499
27576	47298	47163	69614	29372	24859	62090	81667	50635	08295
52970	93916	81350	81057	16962	56039	27739	59574	79617	45698
69516	87573	13313	69388	32020	66294	99126	50474	04258	03084
94504	41733	55936	77595	55959	90727	61367	83645	80997	62103
67935	14568	27992	09784	81917	79303	08616	83509	64932	34764
63345	09579	40232	51061	09455	36491	04810	06040	78959	41435
87119	21605	86917	97715	91250	79587	80967	39872	52512	78444
02612	97319	10487	68923	58607	38261	67119	36351	48521	69965
69860	16526	41420	01514	46902	03399	12286	52467	80387	10561
27669	67730	53932	38578	25746	00025	98917	18790	51091	24920
59705	91472	01302	33123	35274	88433	55491	27609	02824	05245
36508	74042	44014	36243	12724	06092	23742	90436	33419	12301
13612	24554	73326	61445	77198	43360	62006	31038	54756	88137
82893	11961	19656	71181	63201	44946	14169	72755	47883	24119
97914	61228	42903	71187	54964	14945	20809	33937	13257	66387

Table D.4. CUMULATIVE NORMAL PROBABILITIES

Z	0.09	0.08	0.07	0.06	0.05	0.04	0.03	0.02	0.01	0.00
−3.5	0.00017	0.00017	0.00018	0.00019	0.00019	0.00020	0.00021	0.00022	0.00022	0.00023
−3.4	0.00024	0.00025	0.00026	0.00027	0.00028	0.00029	0.00030	0.00031	0.00033	0.00034
−3.3	0.00035	0.00036	0.00038	0.00039	0.00040	0.00042	0.00043	0.00045	0.00047	0.00048
−3.2	0.00050	0.00052	0.00054	0.00056	0.00058	0.00060	0.00062	0.00064	0.00066	0.00069
−3.1	0.00071	0.00074	0.00076	0.00079	0.00082	0.00085	0.00087	0.00090	0.00094	0.00097
−3.0	0.00100	0.00104	0.00107	0.00111	0.00114	0.00118	0.00122	0.00126	0.00131	0.00135
−2.9	0.0014	0.0014	0.0015	0.0015	0.0016	0.0016	0.0017	0.0017	0.0018	0.0019
−2.8	0.0019	0.0020	0.0021	0.0021	0.0022	0.0023	0.0023	0.0024	0.0025	0.0026
−2.7	0.0026	0.0027	0.0028	0.0029	0.0030	0.0031	0.0032	0.0033	0.0034	0.0035
−2.6	0.0036	0.0037	0.0038	0.0039	0.0040	0.0041	0.0043	0.0044	0.0045	0.0047
−2.5	0.0048	0.0049	0.0051	0.0052	0.0054	0.0055	0.0057	0.0059	0.0060	0.0062
−2.4	0.0064	0.0066	0.0068	0.0069	0.0071	0.0073	0.0075	0.0078	0.0080	0.0082
−2.3	0.0084	0.0087	0.0089	0.0091	0.0094	0.0096	0.0099	0.0102	0.0104	0.0107
−2.2	0.0110	0.0113	0.0116	0.0119	0.0122	0.0125	0.0129	0.0132	0.0136	0.0139
−2.1	0.0143	0.0146	0.0150	0.0154	0.0158	0.0162	0.0166	0.0170	0.0174	0.0179
−2.0	0.0183	0.0188	0.0192	0.0197	0.0202	0.0207	0.0212	0.0217	0.0222	0.0228
−1.9	0.0233	0.0239	0.0244	0.0250	0.0256	0.0262	0.0268	0.0274	0.0281	0.0287
−1.8	0.0294	0.0301	0.0307	0.0314	0.0322	0.0329	0.0336	0.0344	0.0351	0.0359
−1.7	0.0367	0.0375	0.0384	0.0392	0.0401	0.0409	0.0418	0.0427	0.0436	0.0446
−1.6	0.0455	0.0465	0.0475	0.0485	0.0495	0.0505	0.0516	0.0526	0.0537	0.0548
−1.5	0.0559	0.0571	0.0582	0.0594	0.0606	0.0618	0.0630	0.0643	0.0655	0.0668
−1.4	0.0681	0.0694	0.0708	0.0721	0.0735	0.0749	0.0764	0.0778	0.0793	0.0808
−1.3	0.0823	0.0838	0.0853	0.0869	0.0885	0.0901	0.0918	0.0934	0.0951	0.0968
−1.2	0.0985	0.1003	0.1020	0.1038	0.1057	0.1075	0.1093	0.1112	0.1131	0.1151
−1.1	0.1170	0.1190	0.1210	0.1230	0.1251	0.1271	0.1292	0.1314	0.1335	0.1357
−1.0	0.1379	0.1401	0.1423	0.1446	0.1469	0.1492	0.1515	0.1539	0.1562	0.1587
−0.9	0.1611	0.1635	0.1660	0.1685	0.1711	0.1736	0.1762	0.1788	0.1814	0.1841
−0.8	0.1867	0.1894	0.1922	0.1949	0.1977	0.2005	0.2033	0.2061	0.2090	0.2119
−0.7	0.2148	0.2177	0.2207	0.2236	0.2266	0.2297	0.2327	0.2358	0.2389	0.2420
−0.6	0.2451	0.2483	0.2514	0.2546	0.2578	0.2611	0.2643	0.2676	0.2709	0.2743
−0.5	0.2776	0.2810	0.2843	0.2877	0.2912	0.2946	0.2981	0.3015	0.3050	0.3085
−0.4	0.3121	0.3156	0.3192	0.3228	0.3264	0.3300	0.3336	0.3372	0.3409	0.3446
−0.3	0.3483	0.3520	0.3557	0.3594	0.3632	0.3669	0.3707	0.3745	0.3783	0.3821
−0.2	0.3859	0.3897	0.3936	0.3974	0.4013	0.4052	0.4090	0.4129	0.4168	0.4207
−0.1	0.4247	0.4286	0.4325	0.4364	0.4404	0.4443	0.4483	0.4522	0.4562	0.4602
−0.0	0.4641	0.4681	0.4721	0.4761	0.4801	0.4840	0.4880	0.4920	0.4960	0.5000

Table D.4. CUMULATIVE NORMAL PROBABILITIES (*Continued*)

Z	0.00	0.01	0.02	0.03	0.04	0.05	0.06	0.07	0.08	0.09
+0.0	0.5000	0.5040	0.5080	0.5120	0.5160	0.5199	0.5239	0.5279	0.5319	0.5359
+0.1	0.5398	0.5438	0.5478	0.5517	0.5557	0.5596	0.5636	0.5675	0.5714	0.5753
+0.2	0.5793	0.5832	0.5871	0.5910	0.5948	0.5987	0.6026	0.6064	0.6103	0.6141
+0.3	0.6179	0.6217	0.6255	0.6293	0.6331	0.6368	0.6406	0.6443	0.6480	0.6517
+0.4	0.6554	0.6591	0.6628	0.6664	0.6700	0.6736	0.6772	0.6808	0.6844	0.6879
+0.5	0.6915	0.6950	0.6985	0.7019	0.7054	0.7088	0.7123	0.7157	0.7190	0.7224
+0.6	0.7257	0.7291	0.7324	0.7357	0.7389	0.7422	0.7454	0.7486	0.7517	0.7549
+0.7	0.7580	0.7611	0.7642	0.7673	0.7704	0.7734	0.7764	0.7794	0.7823	0.7852
+0.8	0.7881	0.7910	0.7939	0.7967	0.7995	0.8023	0.8051	0.8079	0.8106	0.8133
+0.9	0.8159	0.8186	0.8212	0.8238	0.8264	0.8289	0.8315	0.8340	0.8365	0.8389
+1.0	0.8413	0.8438	0.8461	0.8485	0.8508	0.8531	0.8554	0.8577	0.8599	0.8621
+1.1	0.8643	0.8665	0.8686	0.8708	0.8729	0.8749	0.8770	0.8790	0.8810	0.8830
+1.2	0.8849	0.8869	0.8888	0.8907	0.8925	0.8944	0.8962	0.8980	0.8997	0.9015
+1.3	0.9032	0.9049	0.9066	0.9082	0.9099	0.9115	0.9131	0.9147	0.9162	0.9177
+1.4	0.9192	0.9207	0.9222	0.9236	0.9251	0.9265	0.9279	0.9292	0.9306	0.9319
+1.5	0.9332	0.9345	0.9357	0.9370	0.9382	0.9394	0.9406	0.9418	0.9429	0.9441
+1.6	0.9452	0.9463	0.9474	0.9484	0.9495	0.9505	0.9515	0.9525	0.9535	0.9545
+1.7	0.9554	0.9564	0.9573	0.9582	0.9591	0.9599	0.9608	0.9616	0.9625	0.9633
+1.8	0.9641	0.9649	0.9656	0.9664	0.9671	0.9678	0.9686	0.9693	0.9699	0.9706
+1.9	0.9713	0.9719	0.9726	0.9732	0.9738	0.9744	0.9750	0.9756	0.9761	0.9767
+2.0	0.9773	0.9778	0.9783	0.9788	0.9793	0.9798	0.9803	0.9808	0.9812	0.9817
+2.1	0.9821	0.9826	0.9830	0.9834	0.9838	0.9842	0.9846	0.9850	0.9854	0.9857
+2.2	0.9861	0.9864	0.9868	0.9871	0.9875	0.9878	0.9881	0.9884	0.9887	0.9890
+2.3	0.9893	0.9896	0.9898	0.9901	0.9904	0.9906	0.9909	0.9911	0.9913	0.9916
+2.4	0.9918	0.9920	0.9922	0.9925	0.9927	0.9929	0.9931	0.9932	0.9934	0.9936
+2.5	0.9938	0.9940	0.9941	0.9943	0.9945	0.9946	0.9948	0.9949	0.9951	0.9952
+2.6	0.9953	0.9955	0.9956	0.9957	0.9959	0.9960	0.9961	0.9962	0.9963	0.9964
+2.7	0.9965	0.9966	0.9967	0.9968	0.9969	0.9970	0.9971	0.9972	0.9973	0.9974
+2.8	0.9974	0.9975	0.9976	0.9977	0.9977	0.9978	0.9979	0.9979	0.9980	0.9981
+2.9	0.9981	0.9982	0.9983	0.9983	0.9984	0.9984	0.9985	0.9985	0.9986	0.9986
+3.0	0.99865	0.99869	0.99874	0.99878	0.99882	0.99886	0.99889	0.99893	0.99896	0.99900
+3.1	0.99903	0.99906	0.99910	0.99913	0.99915	0.99918	0.99921	0.99924	0.99926	0.99929
+3.2	0.99931	0.99934	0.99936	0.99938	0.99940	0.99942	0.99944	0.99946	0.99948	0.99950
+3.3	0.99952	0.99953	0.99955	0.99957	0.99958	0.99960	0.99961	0.99962	0.99964	0.99965
+3.4	0.99966	0.99967	0.99969	0.99970	0.99971	0.99972	0.99973	0.99974	0.99975	0.99976
+3.5	0.99977	0.99978	0.99978	0.99979	0.99980	0.99981	0.99981	0.99982	0.99983	0.99983

Interest Factor Tables

TABLES E.1–E.13 INTEREST FACTORS FOR ANNUAL COMPOUNDING

Values for each of the six interest formulas derived in Chapter 9 are given for interest rates from 6–30 percent. (Reproduced with permission from W. J. Fabrycky and G. J. Thuesen, *Economic Decision Analysis*, 2nd ed. Englewood Cliffs, N.J.: Prentice-Hall, Inc., 1980.)

Table E.1. 6% INTEREST FACTORS FOR ANNUAL COMPOUNDING

	Single Payment		Equal Payment Series			
	Compound-amount factor	Present-worth factor	Compound-amount factor	Sinking-fund factor	Present-worth factor	Capital-recovery factor
n	To find F Given P F/P i,n	To find P Given F P/F i,n	To find F Given A F/A i,n	To find A Given F A/F i,n	To find P Given A P/A i,n	To find A Given P A/P i,n
1	1.060	0.9434	1.000	1.0000	0.9434	1.0600
2	1.124	0.8900	2.060	0.4854	1.8334	0.5454
3	1.191	0.8396	3.184	0.3141	2.6730	0.3741
4	1.262	0.7921	4.375	0.2286	3.4651	0.2886
5	1.338	0.7473	5.637	0.1774	4.2124	0.2374
6	1.419	0.7050	6.975	0.1434	4.9173	0.2034
7	1.504	0.6651	8.394	0.1191	5.5824	0.1791
8	1.594	0.6274	9.897	0.1010	6.2098	0.1610
9	1.689	0.5919	11.491	0.0870	6.8017	0.1470
10	1.791	0.5584	13.181	0.0759	7.3601	0.1359
11	1.898	0.5268	14.972	0.0668	7.8869	0.1268
12	2.012	0.4970	16.870	0.0593	8.3839	0.1193
13	2.133	0.4688	18.882	0.0530	8.8527	0.1130
14	2.261	0.4423	21.015	0.0476	9.2950	0.1076
15	2.397	0.4173	23.276	0.0430	9.7123	0.1030
16	2.540	0.3937	25.673	0.0390	10.1059	0.0990
17	2.693	0.3714	28.213	0.0355	10.4773	0.0955
18	2.854	0.3504	30.906	0.0324	10.8276	0.0924
19	3.026	0.3305	33.760	0.0296	11.1581	0.0896
20	3.207	0.3118	36.786	0.0272	11.4699	0.0872
21	3.400	0.2942	39.993	0.0250	11.7641	0.0850
22	3.604	0.2775	43.392	0.0231	12.0416	0.0831
23	3.820	0.2618	46.996	0.0213	12.3034	0.0813
24	4.049	0.2470	50.816	0.0197	12.5504	0.0797
25	4.292	0.2330	54.865	0.0182	12.7834	0.0782
26	4.549	0.2198	59.156	0.0169	13.0032	0.0769
27	4.822	0.2074	63.706	0.0157	13.2105	0.0757
28	5.112	0.1956	68.528	0.0146	13.4062	0.0746
29	5.418	0.1846	73.640	0.0136	13.5907	0.0736
30	5.744	0.1741	79.058	0.0127	13.7648	0.0727
31	6.088	0.1643	84.802	0.0118	13.9291	0.0718
32	6.453	0.1550	90.890	0.0110	14.0841	0.0710
33	6.841	0.1462	97.343	0.0103	14.2302	0.0703
34	7.251	0.1379	104.184	0.0096	14.3682	0.0696
35	7.686	0.1301	111.435	0.0090	14.4983	0.0690
40	10.286	0.0972	154.762	0.0065	15.0463	0.0665
45	13.765	0.0727	212.744	0.0047	15.4558	0.0647
50	18.420	0.0543	290.336	0.0035	15.7619	0.0635
55	24.650	0.0406	394.172	0.0025	15.9906	0.0625
60	32.988	0.0303	533.128	0.0019	16.1614	0.0619
65	44.145	0.0227	719.083	0.0014	16.2891	0.0614
70	59.076	0.0169	967.932	0.0010	16.3846	0.0610
75	79.057	0.0127	1300.949	0.0008	16.4559	0.0608
80	105.796	0.0095	1746.600	0.0006	16.5091	0.0606
85	141.579	0.0071	2342.982	0.0004	16.5490	0.0604
90	189.465	0.0053	3141.075	0.0003	16.5787	0.0603
95	253.546	0.0040	4209.104	0.0002	16.6009	0.0602
100	339.302	0.0030	5638.368	0.0002	16.6176	0.0602

Table E.2. 7% INTEREST FACTORS FOR ANNUAL COMPOUNDING

	Single Payment		Equal Payment Series			
	Compound-amount factor	Present-worth factor	Compound-amount factor	Sinking-fund factor	Present-worth factor	Capital-recovery factor
n	To find F Given P F/P i,n	To find P Given F P/F i,n	To find F Given A F/A i,n	To find A Given F A/F i,n	To find P Given A P/A i,n	To find A Given P A/P i,n
1	1.070	0.9346	1.000	1.0000	0.9346	1.0700
2	1.145	0.8734	2.070	0.4831	1.8080	0.5531
3	1.225	0.8163	3.215	0.3111	2.6243	0.3811
4	1.311	0.7629	4.440	0.2252	3.3872	0.2952
5	1.403	0.7130	5.751	0.1739	4.1002	0.2439
6	1.501	0.6664	7.153	0.1398	4.7665	0.2098
7	1.606	0.6228	8.654	0.1156	5.3893	0.1856
8	1.718	0.5820	10.260	0.0975	5.9713	0.1675
9	1.838	0.5439	11.978	0.0835	6.5152	0.1535
10	1.967	0.5084	13.816	0.0724	7.0236	0.1424
11	2.105	0.4751	15.784	0.0634	7.4987	0.1334
12	2.252	0.4440	17.888	0.0559	7.9427	0.1259
13	2.410	0.4150	20.141	0.0497	8.3577	0.1197
14	2.579	0.3878	22.550	0.0444	8.7455	0.1144
15	2.759	0.3625	25.129	0.0398	9.1079	0.1098
16	2.952	0.3387	27.888	0.0359	9.4467	0.1059
17	3.159	0.3166	30.840	0.0324	9.7632	0.1024
18	3.380	0.2959	33.999	0.0294	10.0591	0.0994
19	3.617	0.2765	37.379	0.0268	10.3356	0.0968
20	3.870	0.2584	40.996	0.0244	10.5940	0.0944
21	4.141	0.2415	44.865	0.0223	10.8355	0.0923
22	4.430	0.2257	49.006	0.0204	11.0613	0.0904
23	4.741	0.2110	53.436	0.0187	11.2722	0.0887
24	5.072	0.1972	58.177	0.0172	11.4693	o.0872
25	5.427	0.1843	63.249	0.0158	11.6536	0.0858
26	5.807	0.1722	68.676	0.0146	11.8258	0.0846
27	6.214	0.1609	74.484	0.0134	11.9867	0.0834
28	6.649	0.1504	80.698	0.0124	12.1371	0.0824
29	7.114	0.1406	87.347	0.0115	12.2777	0.0815
30	7.612	0.1314	94.461	0.0106	12.4091	0.0806
31	8.145	0.1228	102.073	0.0098	12.5318	0.0798
32	8.715	0.1148	110.218	0.0091	12.6466	0.0791
33	9.325	0.1072	118.933	0.0084	12.7538	0.0784
34	9.978	0.1002	128.259	0.0078	12.8540	0.0778
35	10.677	0.0937	138.237	0.0072	12.9477	0.0772
40	14.974	0.0668	199.635	0.0050	13.3317	0.0750
45	21.002	0.0476	285.749	0.0035	13.6055	0.0735
50	29.457	0.0340	406.529	0.0025	13.8008	0 0725
55	41.315	0.0242	575.929	0.0017	13.9399	0.0717
60	57.946	0.0173	813.520	0.0012	14.0392	0.0712
65	81.273	0.0123	1146.755	0.0009	14.1099	0.0709
70	113.989	0.0088	1614.134	0.0006	14.1604	0.0706
75	159.876	0.0063	2269.657	0.0005	14.1964	0.0705
80	224.234	0.0045	3189.063	0.0003	14.2220	0.0703
85	314.500	0.0032	4478.576	0.0002	14.2403	0.0702
90	441.103	0.0023	6287.185	0.0002	14.2533	0.0702
95	618.670	0.0016	8823.854	0.0001	14.2626	0.0701
100	867.716	0.0012	12381.662	0.0001	14.2693	0.0701

Table E.3. 8% INTEREST FACTORS FOR ANNUAL COMPOUNDING

	Single Payment		Equal Payment Series			
	Compound-amount factor	Present-worth factor	Compound-amount factor	Sinking-fund factor	Present-worth factor	Capital-recovery factor
n	To find F Given P $F/P\ i,n$	To find P Given F $P/F\ i,n$	To find F Given A $F/A\ i,n$	To find A Given F $A/F\ i,n$	To find P Given A $P/A\ i,n$	To find A Given P $A/P\ i,n$
1	1.080	0.9259	1.000	1.0000	0.9259	1.0800
2	1.166	0.8573	2.080	0.4808	1.7833	0.5608
3	1.260	0.7938	3.246	0.3080	2.5771	0.3880
4	1.360	0.7350	4.506	0.2219	3.3121	0.3019
5	1.469	0.6806	5.867	0.1705	3.9927	0.2505
6	1.587	0.6302	7.336	0.1363	4.6229	0.2163
7	1.714	0.5835	8.923	0.1121	5.2064	0.1921
8	1.851	0.5403	10.637	0.0940	5.7466	0.1740
9	1.999	0.5003	12.488	0.0801	6.2469	0.1601
10	2.159	0.4632	14.487	0.0690	6.7101	0.1490
11	2.332	0.4289	16.645	0.0601	7.1390	0.1401
12	2.518	0.3971	18.977	0.0527	7.5361	0.1327
13	2.720	0.3677	21.495	0.0465	7.9038	0.1265
14	2.937	0.3405	24.215	0.0413	8.2442	0.1213
15	3.172	0.3153	27.152	0.0368	8.5595	0.1168
16	3.426	0.2919	30.324	0.0330	8.8514	0.1130
17	3.700	0.2703	33.750	0.0296	9.1216	0.1096
18	3.996	0.2503	37.450	0.0267	9.3719	0.1067
19	4.316	0.2317	41.446	0.0241	9.6036	0.1041
20	4.661	0.2146	45.762	0.0219	9.8182	0.1019
21	5.034	0.1987	50.423	0.0198	10.0168	0.0998
22	5.437	0.1840	55.457	0.0180	10.2008	0.0980
23	5.871	0.1703	60.893	0.0164	10.3711	0.0964
24	6.341	0.1577	66.765	0.0150	10.5288	0.0950
25	6.848	0.1460	73.106	0.0137	10.6748	0.0937
26	7.396	0.1352	79.954	0.0125	10.8100	0.0925
27	7.988	0.1252	87.351	0.0115	10.9352	0.0915
28	8.627	0.1159	95.339	0.0105	11.0511	0.0905
29	9.317	0.1073	103.966	0.0096	11.1584	0.0896
30	10.063	0.0994	113.283	0.0088	11.2578	0.0888
31	10.868	0.0920	123.346	0.0081	11.3498	0.0881
32	11.737	0.0852	134.214	0.0075	11.4350	0.0875
33	12.676	0.0789	145.951	0.0069	11.5139	0.0869
34	13.690	0.0731	158.627	0.0063	11.5869	0.0863
35	14.785	0.0676	172.317	0.0058	11.6546	0.0858
40	21.725	0.0460	259.057	0.0039	11.9246	0.0839
45	31.920	0.0313	386.506	0.0026	12.1084	0.0826
50	46.902	0.0213	573.770	0.0018	12.2335	0.0818
55	68.914	0.0145	848.923	0.0012	12.3186	0.0812
60	101.257	0.0099	1253.213	0.0008	12.3766	0.0808
65	148.780	0.0067	1847.248	0.0006	12.4160	0.0806
70	218.606	0.0046	2720.080	0.0004	12.4428	0.0804
75	321.205	0.0031	4002.557	0.0003	12.4611	0.0803
80	471.955	0.0021	5886.935	0.0002	12.4735	0.0802
85	693.456	0.0015	8655.706	0.0001	12.4820	0.0801
90	1018.915	0.0010	12723.939	0.0001	12.4877	0.0801
95	1497.121	0.0007	18701.507	0.0001	12.4917	0.0801
100	2199.761	0.0005	27484.516	0.0001	12.4943	0.0800

Table E.4. 9% INTEREST FACTORS FOR ANNUAL COMPOUNDING

	Single Payment		Equal-Payment Series			
	Compound-Amount Factor	Present-Worth Factor	Compound-Amount Factor	Sinking-Fund Factor	Present-Worth Factor	Capital-Recovery Factor
n	To Find F Given P $F/P, i, n$	To Find P Given F $P/F, i, n$	To Find F Given A $F/A, i, n$	To Find A Given F $A/F, i, n$	To Find P Given A $P/A, i, n$	To Find A Given P $A/P, i, n$
1	1.090	0.9174	1.000	1.0000	0.9174	1.0900
2	1.188	0.8417	2.090	0.4785	1.7591	0.5685
3	1.295	0.7722	3.278	0.3051	2.5313	0.3951
4	1.412	0.7084	4.573	0.2187	3.2397	0.3087
5	1.539	0.6499	5.985	0.1671	3.8897	0.2571
6	1.677	0.5963	7.523	0.1329	4.4859	0.2229
7	1.828	0.5470	9.200	0.1087	5.0330	0.1987
8	1.993	0.5019	11.028	0.0907	5.5348	0.1807
9	2.172	0.4604	13.021	0.0768	5.9953	0.1668
10	2.367	0.4224	15.193	0.0658	6.4177	0.1558
11	2.580	0.3875	17.560	0.0570	6.8052	0.1470
12	2.813	0.3555	20.141	0.0497	7.1607	0.1397
13	3.066	0.3262	22.953	0.0436	7.4869	0.1336
14	3.342	0.2993	26.019	0.0384	7.7862	0.1284
15	3.642	0.2745	29.361	0.0341	8.0607	0.1241
16	3.970	0.2519	33.003	0.0303	8.3126	0.1203
17	4.328	0.2311	36.974	0.0271	8.5436	0.1171
18	4.717	0.2120	41.301	0.0242	8.7556	0.1142
19	5.142	0.1945	46.018	0.0217	8.9501	0.1117
20	5.604	0.1784	51.160	0.0196	9.1286	0.1096
21	6.109	0.1637	56.765	0.0176	9.2923	0.1076
22	6.659	0.1502	62.873	0.0159	9.4424	0.1059
23	7.258	0.1378	69.532	0.0144	9.5802	0.1044
24	7.911	0.1264	76.790	0.0130	9.7066	0.1030
25	8.623	0.1160	84.701	0.0118	9.8226	0.1018
26	9.399	0.1064	93.324	0.0107	9.9290	0.1007
27	10.245	0.0976	102.723	0.0097	10.0266	0.0997
28	11.167	0.0896	112.968	0.0089	10.1161	0.0989
29	12.172	0.0822	124.135	0.0081	10.1983	0.0981
30	13.268	0.0754	136.308	0.0073	10.2737	0.0973
31	14.462	0.0692	149.575	0.0067	10.3428	0.0967
32	15.763	0.0634	164.037	0.0061	10.4063	0.0961
33	17.182	0.0582	179.800	0.0056	10.4645	0.0956
34	18.728	0.0534	196.982	0.0051	10.5178	0.0951
35	20.414	0.0490	215.711	0.0046	10.5668	0.0946
40	31.409	0.0318	337.882	0.0030	10.7574	0.0930
45	48.327	0.0207	525.859	0.0019	10.8812	0.0919
50	74.358	0.0135	815.084	0.0012	10.9617	0.0912
55	114.408	0.0088	1260.092	0.0008	11.0140	0.0908
60	176.031	0.0057	1944.792	0.0005	11.0480	0.0905
65	270.846	0.0037	2998.288	0.0003	11.0701	0.0903
70	416.730	0.0024	4619.223	0.0002	11.0845	0.0902
75	641.191	0.0016	7113.232	0.0002	11.0938	0.0902
80	986.552	0.0010	10950.574	0.0001	11.0999	0.0901
85	1517.932	0.0007	16854.800	0.0001	11.1038	0.0901
90	2335.527	0.0004	25939.184	0.0001	11.1064	0.0900
95	3593.497	0.0003	39916.635	0.0000	11.1080	0.0900
100	5529.041	0.0002	61422.675	0.0000	11.1091	0.0900

Table E.5. 10% INTEREST FACTORS FOR ANNUAL COMPOUNDING

	Single Payment		Equal Payment Series			
	Compound-amount factor	Present-worth factor	Compound-amount factor	Sinking-fund factor	Present-worth factor	Capital-recovery factor
n	To find F Given P F/P i,n	To find P Given F P/F i,n	To find F Given A F/A i,n	To find A Given F A/F i,n	To find P Given A P/A i,n	To find A Given P A/P i,n
1	1.100	0.9091	1.000	1.0000	0.9091	1.1000
2	1.210	0.8265	2.100	0.4762	1.7355	0.5762
3	1.331	0.7513	3.310	0.3021	2.4869	0.4021
4	1.464	0.6830	4.641	0.2155	3.1699	0.3155
5	1.611	0.6209	6.105	0.1638	3.7908	0.2638
6	1.772	0.5645	7.716	0.1296	4.3553	0.2296
7	1.949	0.5132	9.487	0.1054	4.8684	0.2054
8	2.144	0.4665	11.436	0.0875	5.3349	0.1875
9	2.358	0.4241	13.579	0.0737	5.7590	0.1737
10	2.594	0.3856	15.937	0.0628	6.1446	0.1628
11	2.853	0.3505	18.531	0.0540	6.4951	0.1540
12	3.138	0.3186	21.384	0.0468	6.8137	0.1468
13	3.452	0.2897	24.523	0.0408	7.1034	0.1408
14	3.798	0.2633	27.975	0.0358	7.3667	0.1358
15	4.177	0.2394	31.772	0.0315	7.6061	0.1315
16	4.595	0.2176	35.950	0.0278	7.8237	0.1278
17	5.054	0.1979	40.545	0.0247	8.0216	0.1247
18	5.560	0.1799	45.599	0.0219	8.2014	0.1219
19	6.116	0.1635	51.159	0.0196	8.3649	0.1196
20	6.728	0.1487	57.275	0.0175	8.5136	0.1175
21	7.400	0.1351	64.003	0.0156	8.6487	0.1156
22	8.140	0.1229	71.403	0.0140	8.7716	0.1140
23	8.954	0.1117	79.543	0.0126	8.8832	0.1126
24	9.850	0.1015	88.497	0.0113	8.9848	0.1113
25	10.835	0.0923	98.347	0.0102	9.0771	0.1102
26	11.918	0.0839	109.182	0.0092	9.1610	0.1092
27	13.110	0.0763	121.100	0.0083	9.2372	0.1083
28	14.421	0.0694	134.210	0.0075	9.3066	0.1075
29	15.863	0.0630	148.631	0.0067	9.3696	0.1067
30	17.449	0.0573	164.494	0.0061	9.4269	0.1061
31	19.194	0.0521	181.943	0.0055	9.4790	0.1055
32	21.114	0.0474	201.138	0.0050	9.5264	0.1050
33	23.225	0.0431	222.252	0.0045	9.5694	0.1045
34	25.548	0.0392	245.477	0.0041	9.6086	0.1041
35	28.102	0.0356	271.024	0.0037	9.6442	0.1037
40	45.259	0.0221	442.593	0.0023	9.7791	0.1023
45	72.890	0.0137	718.905	0.0014	9.8628	0.1014
50	117.391	0.0085	1163.909	0.0009	9.9148	0.1009
55	189.059	0.0053	1880.591	0.0005	9.9471	0.1005
60	304.482	0.0033	3034.816	0.0003	9.9672	0.1003
65	490.371	0.0020	4893.707	0.0002	9.9796	0.1002
70	789.747	0.0013	7887.470	0.0001	9.9873	0.1001
75	1271.895	0.0008	12708.954	0.0001	9.9921	0.1001
80	2048.400	0.0005	20474.002	0.0001	9.9951	0.1001
85	3298.969	0.0003	32979.690	0.0000	9.9970	0.1000
90	5313.023	0.0002	53120.226	0.0000	9.9981	0.1000
95	8556.676	0.0001	85556.760	0.0000	9.9988	0.1000
100	13780.612	0.0001	137796.123	0.0000	9.9993	0.1000

Table E.6. 11% INTEREST FACTORS FOR ANNUAL COMPOUNDING

	Single Payment		Equal-Payment Series			
	Compound-Amount Factor	Present-Worth Factor	Compound-Amount Factor	Sinking-Fund Factor	Present-Worth Factor	Capital-Recovery Factor
n	To Find F Given P $F/P, i,n$	To Find P Given F $P/F, i,n$	To Find F Given A $F/A, i,n$	To Find A Given F $A/F, i,n$	To Find P Given A $P/A, i,n$	To Find A Given P $A/P, i,n$
1	1.110	0.9009	1.000	1.0000	0.9009	1.1100
2	1.232	0.8116	2.110	0.4739	1.7125	0.5839
3	1.368	0.7312	3.342	0.2992	2.4437	0.4092
4	1.518	0.6587	4.710	0.2123	3.1024	0.3223
5	1.685	0.5935	6.228	0.1606	3.6959	0.2706
6	1.870	0.5346	7.913	0.1264	4.2305	0.2364
7	2.076	0.4817	9.783	0.1022	4.7121	0.2122
8	2.305	0.4339	11.859	0.0843	5.1462	0.1943
9	2.558	0.3909	14.164	0.0706	5.5371	0.1806
10	2.839	0.3522	16.722	0.0598	5.8893	0.1698
11	3.152	0.3173	19.561	0.0511	6.2066	0.1611
12	3.498	0.2858	22.713	0.0440	6.4922	0.1540
13	3.883	0.2575	26.212	0.0382	6.7499	0.1482
14	4.310	0.2320	30.095	0.0332	6.9818	0.1432
15	4.785	0.2090	34.405	0.0291	7.1906	0.1391
16	5.311	0.1883	39.190	0.0255	7.3790	0.1355
17	5.895	0.1696	44.501	0.0225	7.5489	0.1325
18	6.544	0.1528	50.396	0.0198	7.7018	0.1298
19	7.263	0.1377	56.939	0.0176	7.8394	0.1276
20	8.062	0.1240	64.203	0.0156	7.9631	0.1256
21	8.949	0.1117	72.265	0.0138	8.0749	0.1238
22	9.934	0.1007	81.214	0.0123	8.1759	0.1223
23	11.026	0.0907	91.148	0.0110	8.2665	0.1210
24	12.239	0.0817	102.174	0.0098	8.3479	0.1198
25	13.586	0.0736	114.413	0.0087	8.4218	0.1187
26	15.080	0.0663	127.999	0.0078	8.4882	0.1178
27	16.739	0.0597	143.079	0.0070	8.5477	0.1170
28	18.580	0.0538	159.817	0.0063	8.6014	0.1163
29	20.624	0.0485	178.397	0.0056	8.6498	0.1156
30	22.892	0.0437	199.021	0.0050	8.6941	0.1150
31	25.410	0.0394	221.913	0.0045	8.7329	0.1145
32	28.206	0.0355	247.324	0.0040	8.7689	0.1140
33	31.308	0.0319	275.529	0.0036	8.8005	0.1136
34	34.752	0.0288	306.837	0.0033	8.8292	0.1133
35	38.575	0.0259	341.590	0.0029	8.8550	0.1129
40	65.001	0.0154	581.826	0.0017	8.9509	0.1117
45	109.530	0.0091	986.639	0.0010	9.0082	0.1110
50	184.565	0.0054	1688.771	0.0006	9.0416	0.1106

Table E.7. 12% INTEREST FACTORS FOR ANNUAL COMPOUNDING

	Single Payment		Equal Payment Series			
	Compound-amount factor	Present-worth factor	Compound-amount factor	Sinking-fund factor	Present-worth factor	Capital-recovery factor
n	To find F Given P F/P i,n	To find P Given F P/F i,n	To find F Given A F/A i,n	To find A Given F A/F i,n	To find P Given A P/A i,n	To find A Given P A/P i,n
1	1.120	0.8929	1.000	1.0000	0.8929	1.1200
2	1.254	0.7972	2.120	0.4717	1.6901	0.5917
3	1.405	0.7118	3.374	0.2964	2.4018	0.4164
4	1.574	0.6355	4.779	0.2092	3.0374	0.3292
5	1.762	0.5674	6.353	0.1574	3.6048	0.2774
6	1.974	0.5066	8.115	0.1232	4.1114	0.2432
7	2.211	0.4524	10.089	0.0991	4.5638	0.2191
8	2.476	0.4039	12.300	0.0813	4.9676	0.2013
9	2.773	0.3606	14.776	0.0677	5.3283	0.1877
10	3.106	0.3220	17.549	0.0570	5.6502	0.1770
11	3.479	0.2875	20.655	0.0484	5.9377	0.1684
12	3.896	0.2567	24.133	0.0414	6.1944	0.1614
13	4.364	0.2292	28.029	0.0357	6.4236	0.1557
14	4.887	0.2046	32.393	0.0309	6.6282	0.1509
15	5.474	0.1827	37.280	0.0268	6.8109	0.1468
16	6.130	0.1631	42.753	0.0234	6.9740	0.1434
17	6.866	0.1457	48.884	0.0205	7.1196	0.1405
18	7.690	0.1300	55.750	0.0179	7.2497	0.1379
19	8.613	0.1161	63.440	0.0158	7.3658	0.1358
20	9.646	0.1037	72.052	0.0139	7.4695	0.1339
21	10.804	0.0926	81.699	0.0123	7.5620	0.1323
22	12.100	0.0827	92.503	0.0108	7.6447	0.1308
23	13.552	0.0738	104.603	0.0096	7.7184	0.1296
24	15.179	0.0659	118.155	0.0085	7.7843	0.1285
25	17.000	0.0588	133.334	0.0075	7.8431	0.1275
26	19.040	0.0525	150.334	0.0067	7.8957	0.1267
27	21.325	0.0469	169.374	0.0059	7.9426	0.1259
28	23.884	0.0419	190.699	0.0053	7.9844	0.1253
29	26.750	0.0374	214.583	0.0047	8.0218	0.1247
30	29.960	0.0334	241.333	0.0042	8.0552	0.1242
31	33.555	0.0298	271.293	0.0037	8.0850	0.1237
32	37.582	0.0266	304.848	0.0033	8.1116	0.1233
33	42.092	0.0238	342.429	0.0029	8.1354	0.1229
34	47.143	0.0212	384.521	0.0026	8.1566	0.1226
35	52.800	0.0189	431.664	0.0023	8.1755	0.1223
40	93.051	0.0108	767.091	0.0013	8.2438	0.1213
45	163.988	0.0061	1358.230	0.0007	8.2825	0.1207
50	289.002	0.0035	2400.018	0.0004	8.3045	0.1204

Table E.8. 13% INTEREST FACTORS FOR ANNUAL COMPOUNDING

	Single Payment		Equal-Payment Series			
	Compound-Amount Factor	Present-Worth Factor	Compound-Amount Factor	Sinking-Fund Factor	Present-Worth Factor	Capital-Recovery Factor
n	To Find F Given P $F/P, i,n$	To Find P Given F $P/F, i,n$	To Find F Given A $F/A, i,n$	To Find A Given F $A/F, i,n$	To Find P Given A $P/A, i,n$	To Find A Given P $A/P, i,n$
1	1.130	0.8850	1.000	1.0000	0.8850	1.1300
2	1.277	0.7831	2.130	0.4695	1.6681	0.5995
3	1.443	0.6931	3.407	0.2935	2.3612	0.4235
4	1.631	0.6133	4.850	0.2062	2.9745	0.3362
5	1.842	0.5428	6.480	0.1543	3.5173	0.2843
6	2.082	0.4803	8.323	0.1202	3.9976	0.2502
7	2.353	0.4251	10.405	0.0961	4.4226	0.2261
8	2.658	0.3762	12.757	0.0784	4.7987	0.2084
9	3.004	0.3329	15.416	0.0649	5.1316	0.1949
10	3.395	0.2946	18.420	0.0543	5.4262	0.1843
11	3.836	0.2607	21.814	0.0458	5.6870	0.1758
12	4.335	0.2307	25.650	0.0390	5.9175	0.1690
13	4.898	0.2042	29.985	0.0334	6.1218	0.1634
14	5.535	0.1807	34.883	0.0287	6.3024	0.1587
15	6.254	0.1599	40.417	0.0247	6.4625	0.1547
16	7.067	0.1415	46.672	0.0214	6.6037	0.1514
17	7.986	0.1252	53.739	0.0186	6.7290	0.1486
18	9.024	0.1108	61.725	0.0162	6.8399	0.1462
19	10.197	0.0981	70.749	0.0141	6.9382	0.1441
20	11.523	0.0868	80.947	0.0124	7.0249	0.1424
21	13.021	0.0768	92.470	0.0108	7.1018	0.1408
22	14.714	0.0680	105.491	0.0095	7.1695	0.1395
23	16.627	0.0601	120.205	0.0083	7.2296	0.1383
24	18.788	0.0532	136.831	0.0073	7.2828	0.1373
25	21.231	0.0471	155.620	0.0064	7.3298	0.1364
26	23.991	0.0417	176.850	0.0057	7.3719	0.1357
27	27.109	0.0369	200.841	0.0050	7.4085	0.1350
28	30.634	0.0326	227.950	0.0044	7.4410	0.1344
29	34.616	0.0289	258.583	0.0039	7.4699	0.1339
30	39.116	0.0256	293.199	0.0034	7.4957	0.1334
31	44.201	0.0226	332.315	0.0030	7.5182	0.1330
32	49.947	0.0200	376.516	0.0027	7.5381	0.1327
33	56.440	0.0177	426.463	0.0023	7.5563	0.1323
34	63.777	0.0157	482.903	0.0021	7.5717	0.1321
35	72.069	0.0139	546.681	0.0018	7.5855	0.1318
40	132.782	0.0075	1013.704	0.0010	7.6342	0.1310
45	244.641	0.0041	1874.165	0.0005	7.6611	0.1305
50	450.736	0.0022	3459.507	0.0003	7.6752	0.1303

Table E.9. 14% INTEREST FACTORS FOR ANNUAL COMPOUNDING

	Single Payment		Equal-Payment Series			
	Compound-Amount Factor	Present-Worth Factor	Compound-Amount Factor	Sinking-Fund Factor	Present-Worth Factor	Capital-Recovery Factor
n	To Find F Given P $F/P, i,n$	To Find P Given F $P/F, i,n$	To Find F Given A $F/A, i,n$	To Find A Given F $A/F, i,n$	To Find P Given A $P/A, i,n$	To Find A Given P $A/P, i,n$
1	1.140	0.8772	1.000	1.0000	0.8772	1.1400
2	1.300	0.7695	2.140	0.4673	1.6467	0.6073
3	1.482	0.6750	3.440	0.2907	2.3216	0.4307
4	1.689	0.5921	4.921	0.2032	2.9138	0.3432
5	1.925	0.5194	6.610	0.1513	3.4331	0.2913
6	2.195	0.4556	8.536	0.1172	3.8886	0.2572
7	2.502	0.3996	10.730	0.0932	4.2883	0.2332
8	2.853	0.3506	13.233	0.0756	4.6389	0.2156
9	3.252	0.3075	16.085	0.0622	4.9463	0.2022
10	3.707	0.2697	19.337	0.0517	5.2162	0.1917
11	4.226	0.2366	23.045	0.0434	5.4529	0.1834
12	4.818	0.2076	27.271	0.0367	5.6603	0.1767
13	5.492	0.1821	32.089	0.0312	5.8425	0.1712
14	6.261	0.1597	37.581	0.0266	6.0020	0.1666
15	7.138	0.1401	43.842	0.0228	6.1421	0.1628
16	8.137	0.1229	50.980	0.0196	6.2649	0.1596
17	9.277	0.1078	59.118	0.0169	6.3727	0.1569
18	10.575	0.0946	68.394	0.0146	6.4675	0.1546
19	12.056	0.0829	78.969	0.0127	6.5505	0.1527
20	13.744	0.0728	91.025	0.0110	6.6230	0.1510
21	15.668	0.0638	104.768	0.0095	6.6872	0.1495
22	17.861	0.0560	120.436	0.0083	6.7431	0.1483
23	20.362	0.0491	138.297	0.0072	6.7921	0.1472
24	23.212	0.0431	158.659	0.0063	6.8353	0.1463
25	26.462	0.0378	181.871	0.0055	6.8729	0.1455
26	30.167	0.0331	208.333	0.0048	6.9061	0.1448
27	34.390	0.0291	238.499	0.0042	6.9353	0.1442
28	39.205	0.0255	272.889	0.0037	6.9609	0.1437
29	44.693	0.0224	312.094	0.0032	6.9832	0.1432
30	50.950	0.0196	356.787	0.0028	7.0028	0.1428
31	58.083	0.0172	407.737	0.0025	7.0200	0.1425
32	66.215	0.0151	465.820	0.0022	7.0348	0.1422
33	75.485	0.0132	532.035	0.0019	7.0482	0.1419
34	86.053	0.0116	607.520	0.0017	7.0597	0.1417
35	98.100	0.0102	693.573	0.0014	7.0701	0.1414
40	188.884	0.0053	1342.025	0.0008	7.1048	0.1408
45	363.679	0.0027	2590.565	0.0004	7.1230	0.1404
50	700.233	0.0014	4994.521	0.0002	7.1327	0.1402

Table E.10. 15% INTEREST FACTORS FOR ANNUAL COMPOUNDING

	Single Payment		Equal Payment Series			
	Compound-amount factor	Present-worth factor	Compound-amount factor	Sinking-fund factor	Present-worth factor	Capital-recovery factor
n	To find F Given P F/P i,n	To find P Given F P/F i,n	To find F Given A F/A i,n	To find A Given F A/F i,n	To find P Given A P/A i,n	To find A Given P A/P i,n
1	1.150	0.8696	1.000	1.0000	0.8696	1.1500
2	1.323	0.7562	2.150	0.4651	1.6257	0.6151
3	1.521	0.6575	3.473	0.2880	2.2832	0.4380
4	1.749	0.5718	4.993	0.2003	2.8550	0.3503
5	2.011	0.4972	6.742	0.1483	3.3522	0.2983
6	2.313	0.4323	8.754	0.1142	3.7845	0.2642
7	2.660	0.3759	11.067	0.0904	4.1604	0.2404
8	3.059	0.3269	13.727	0.0729	4.4873	0.2229
9	3.518	0.2843	16.786	0.0596	4.7716	0.2096
10	4.046	0.2472	20.304	0.0493	5.0188	0.1993
11	4.652	0.2150	24.349	0.0411	5.2337	0.1911
12	5.350	0.1869	29.002	0.0345	5.4206	0.1845
13	6.153	0.1625	34.352	0.0291	5.5832	0.1791
14	7.076	0.1413	40.505	0.0247	5.7245	0.1747
15	8.137	0.1229	47.580	0.0210	5.8474	0.1710
16	9.358	0.1069	55.717	0.0180	5.9542	0.1680
17	10.761	0.0929	65.075	0.0154	6.0472	0.1654
18	12.375	0.0808	75.836	0.0132	6.1280	0.1632
19	14.232	0.0703	88.212	0.0113	6.1982	0.1613
20	16.367	0.0611	102.444	0.0098	6.2593	0.1598
21	18.822	0.0531	118.810	0.0084	6.3125	0.1584
22	21.645	0.0462	137.632	0.0073	6.3587	0.1573
23	24.891	0.0402	159.276	0.0063	6.3988	0.1563
24	28.625	0.0349	184.168	0.0054	6.4338	0.1554
25	32.919	0.0304	212.793	0.0047	6.4642	0.1547
26	37.857	0.0264	245.712	0.0041	6.4906	0.1541
27	43.535	0.0230	283.569	0.0035	6.5135	0.1535
28	50.066	0.0200	327.104	0.0031	6.5335	0.1531
29	57.575	0.0174	377.170	0.0027	6.5509	0.1527
30	66.212	0.0151	434.745	0.0023	6.5660	0.1523
31	76.144	0.0131	500.957	0.0020	6.5791	0.1520
32	87.565	0.0114	577.100	0.0017	6.5905	0.1517
33	100.700	0.0099	664.666	0.0015	6.6005	0.1515
34	115.805	0.0086	765.365	0.0013	6.6091	0.1513
35	133.176	0.0075	881.170	0.0011	6.6166	0.1511
40	267.864	0.0037	1779.090	0.0006	6.6418	0.1506
45	538.769	0.0019	3585.128	0.0003	6.6543	0.1503
50	1083.657	0.0009	7217.716	0.0002	6.6605	0.1501

Table E.11. 20% INTEREST FACTORS FOR ANNUAL COMPOUNDING

	Single Payment		Equal Payment Series			
	Compound-amount factor	Present-worth factor	Compound-amount factor	Sinking-fund factor	Present-worth factor	Capital-recovery factor
n	To find F Given P $F/P\ i,n$	To find P Given F $P/F\ i,n$	To find F Given A $F/A\ i,n$	To find A Given F $A/F\ i,n$	To find P Given A $P/A\ i,n$	To find A Given P $A/P\ i,n$
1	1.200	0.8333	1.000	1.0000	0.8333	1.2000
2	1.440	0.6945	2.200	0.4546	1.5278	0.6546
3	1.728	0.5787	3.640	0.2747	2.1065	0.4747
4	2.074	0.4823	5.368	0.1863	2.5887	0.3863
5	2.488	0.4019	7.442	0.1344	2.9906	0.3344
6	2.986	0.3349	9.930	0.1007	3.3255	0.3007
7	3.583	0.2791	12.916	0.0774	3.6046	0.2774
8	4.300	0.2326	16.499	0.0606	3.8372	0.2606
9	5.160	0.1938	20.799	0.0481	4.0310	0.2481
10	6.192	0.1615	25.959	0.0385	4.1925	0.2385
11	7.430	0.1346	32.150	0.0311	4.3271	0.2311
12	8.916	0.1122	39.581	0.0253	4.4392	0.2253
13	10.699	0.0935	48.497	0.0206	4.5327	0.2206
14	12.839	0.0779	59.196	0.0169	4.6106	0.2169
15	15.407	0.0649	72.035	0.0139	4.6755	0.2139
16	18.488	0.0541	87.442	0.0114	4.7296	0.2114
17	22.186	0.0451	105.931	0.0095	4.7746	0.2095
18	26.623	0.0376	128.117	0.0078	4.8122	0.2078
19	31.948	0.0313	154.740	0.0065	4.8435	0.2065
20	38.338	0.0261	186.688	0.0054	4.8696	0.2054
21	46.005	0.0217	225.026	0.0045	4.8913	0.2045
22	55.206	0.0181	271.031	0.0037	4.9094	0.2037
23	66.247	0.0151	326.237	0.0031	4.9245	0.2031
24	79.497	0.0126	392.484	0.0026	4.9371	0.2026
25	95.396	0.0105	471.981	0.0021	4.9476	0.2021
26	114.475	0.0087	567.377	0.0018	4.9563	0.2018
27	137.371	0.0073	681.853	0.0015	4.9636	0.2015
28	164.845	0.0061	819.223	0.0012	4.9697	0.2012
29	197.814	0.0051	984.068	0.0010	4.9747	0.2010
30	237.376	0.0042	1181.882	0.0009	4.9789	0.2009
31	284.852	0.0035	1419.258	0.0007	4.9825	0.2007
32	341.822	0.0029	1704.109	0.0006	4.9854	0.2006
33	410.186	0.0024	2045.931	0.0005	4.9878	0.2005
34	492.224	0.0020	2456.118	0.0004	4.9899	0.2004
35	590.668	0.0017	2948.341	0.0003	4.9915	0.2003
40	1469.772	0.0007	7343.858	0.0002	4.9966	0.2001
45	3657.262	0.0003	18281.310	0.0001	4.9986	0.2001
50	9100.438	0.0001	45497.191	0.0000	4.9995	0.2000

Table E.12. 25% INTEREST FACTORS FOR ANNUAL COMPOUNDING

	Single Payment		Equal-Payment Series			
	Compound-Amount Factor	Present-Worth Factor	Compound-Amount Factor	Sinking-Fund Factor	Present-Worth Factor	Capital-Recovery Factor
n	To Find F Given P $F/P, i, n$	To Find P Given F $P/F, i, n$	To Find F Given A $F/A, i, n$	To Find A Given F $A/F, i, n$	To Find P Given A $P/A, i, n$	To Find A Given P $A/P, i, n$
1	1.250	0.8000	1.000	1.0000	0.8000	1.2500
2	1.563	0.6400	2.250	0.4445	1.4400	0.6945
3	1.953	0.5120	3.813	0.2623	1.9520	0.5123
4	2.441	0.4096	5.766	0.1735	2.3616	0.4235
5	3.052	0.3277	8.207	0.1219	2.6893	0.3719
6	3.815	0.2622	11.259	0.0888	2.9514	0.3388
7	4.768	0.2097	15.073	0.0664	3.1611	0.3164
8	5.960	0.1678	19.842	0.0504	3.3289	0.3004
9	7.451	0.1342	25.802	0.0388	3.4631	0.2888
10	9.313	0.1074	33.253	0.0301	3.5705	0.2801
11	11.642	0.0859	42.566	0.0235	3.6564	0.2735
12	14.552	0.0687	54.208	0.0185	3.7251	0.2685
13	18.190	0.0550	68.760	0.0146	3.7801	0.2646
14	22.737	0.0440	86.949	0.0115	3.8241	0.2615
15	28.422	0.0352	109.687	0.0091	3.8593	0.2591
16	35.527	0.0282	138.109	0.0073	3.8874	0.2573
17	44.409	0.0225	173.636	0.0058	3.9099	0.2558
18	55.511	0.0180	218.045	0.0046	3.9280	0.2546
19	69.389	0.0144	273.556	0.0037	3.9424	0.2537
20	86.736	0.0115	342.945	0.0029	3.9539	0.2529
21	108.420	0.0092	429.681	0.0023	3.9631	0.2523
22	135.525	0.0074	538.101	0.0019	3.9705	0.2519
23	169.407	0.0059	673.626	0.0015	3.9764	0.2515
24	211.758	0.0047	843.033	0.0012	3.9811	0.2512
25	264.698	0.0038	1054.791	0.0010	3.9849	0.2510
26	330.872	0.0030	1319.489	0.0008	3.9879	0.2508
27	413.590	0.0024	1650.361	0.0006	3.9903	0.2506
28	516.988	0.0019	2063.952	0.0005	3.9923	0.2505
29	646.235	0.0016	2580.939	0.0004	3.9938	0.2504
30	807.794	0.0012	3227.174	0.0003	3.9951	0.2503
31	1009.742	0.0010	4034.968	0.0003	3.9960	0.2503
32	1262.177	0.0008	5044.710	0.0002	3.9968	0.2502
33	1577.722	0.0006	6306.887	0.0002	3.9975	0.2502
34	1972.152	0.0005	7884.609	0.0001	3.9980	0.2501
35	2465.190	0.0004	9856.761	0.0001	3.9984	0.2501

Table E.13. 30% INTEREST FACTORS FOR ANNUAL COMPOUNDING

	Single Payment		Equal-Payment Series			
	Compound-Amount Factor	Present-Worth Factor	Compound-Amount Factor	Sinking-Fund Factor	Present-Worth Factor	Capital-Recovery Factor
n	To Find F Given P $F/P, i, n$	To Find P Given F $P/F, i, n$	To Find F Given A $F/A, i, n$	To Find A Given F $A/F, i, n$	To Find P Given A $P/A, i, n$	To Find A Given P $A/P, i, n$
1	1.300	0.7692	1.000	1.0000	0.7692	1.3000
2	1.690	0.5917	2.300	0.4348	1.3610	0.7348
3	2.197	0.4552	3.990	0.2506	1.8161	0.5506
4	2.856	0.3501	6.187	0.1616	2.1663	0.4616
5	3.713	0.2693	9.043	0.1106	2.4356	0.4106
6	4.827	0.2072	12.756	0.0784	2.6428	0.3784
7	6.275	0.1594	17.583	0.0569	2.8021	0.3569
8	8.157	0.1226	23.858	0.0419	2.9247	0.3419
9	10.605	0.0943	32.015	0.0312	3.0190	0.3312
10	13.786	0.0725	42.620	0.0235	3.0915	0.3235
11	17.922	0.0558	56.405	0.0177	3.1473	0.3177
12	23.298	0.0429	74.327	0.0135	3.1903	0.3135
13	30.288	0.0330	97.625	0.0103	3.2233	0.3103
14	39.374	0.0254	127.913	0.0078	3.2487	0.3078
15	51.186	0.0195	167.286	0.0060	3.2682	0.3060
16	66.542	0.0150	218.472	0.0046	3.2832	0.3046
17	86.504	0.0116	285.014	0.0035	3.2948	0.3035
18	112.455	0.0089	371.518	0.0027	3.3037	0.3027
19	146.192	0.0069	483.973	0.0021	3.3105	0.3021
20	190.050	0.0053	630.165	0.0016	3.3158	0.3016
21	247.065	0.0041	820.215	0.0012	3.3199	0.3012
22	321.184	0.0031	1067.280	0.0009	3.3230	0.3009
23	417.539	0.0024	1388.464	0.0007	3.3254	0.3007
24	542.801	0.0019	1806.003	0.0006	3.3272	0.3006
25	705.641	0.0014	2348.803	0.0004	3.3286	0.3004
26	917.333	0.0011	3054.444	0.0003	3.3297	0.3003
27	1192.533	0.0008	3971.778	0.0003	3.3305	0.3003
28	1550.293	0.0007	5164.311	0.0002	3.3312	0.3002
29	2015.381	0.0005	6714.604	0.0002	3.3317	0.3002
30	2619.996	0.0004	8729.985	0.0001	3.3321	0.3001
31	3405.994	0.0003	11349.981	0.0001	3.3324	0.3001
32	4427.793	0.0002	14755.975	0.0001	3.3326	0.3001
33	5756.130	0.0002	19183.768	0.0001	3.3328	0.3001
34	7482.970	0.0001	24939.899	0.0001	3.3329	0.3001
35	9727.860	0.0001	32422.868	0.0000	3.3330	0.3000

F

Progress Function Tables

TABLE F.1 MANUFACTURING PROGRESS FACTORS—UNIT VALUES

Unit values computed from Kx^n are given for slope parameters of 70, 75, 80, 85, and 90 percent for selected values of x up to 500.

TABLE F.2 MANUFACTURING PROGRESS FACTORS—CUMULATIVE VALUES

Cumulative values computed as $\sum Kx^n$ are given for slope parameters of 70, 75, 80, 85, and 90 percent for selected values of x up to 500.

Table F.1. MANUFACTURING PROGRESS FACTORS—UNIT VALUES

Unit Number	Slope Parameter, ϕ					
	0.70	0.75	0.80	0.85	0.90
1	1.0000	1.0000	1.0000	1.0000	1.0000
2	0.7000	0.7500	0.8000	0.8500	0.9000
3	0.5682	0.6338	0.7021	0.7729	0.8462
4	0.4900	0.5625	0.6400	0.7225	0.8100
5	0.4368	0.5127	0.5956	0.6857	0.7830
6	0.3977	0.4754	0.5617	0.6570	0.7616
7	0.3674	0.4459	0.5345	0.6337	0.7439
8	0.3430	0.4219	0.5120	0.6141	0.7290
9	0.3228	0.4017	0.4929	0.5974	0.7161
10	0.3058	0.3846	0.4765	0.5828	0.7047
11	0.2912	0.3696	0.4621	0.5699	0.6945
12	0.2784	0.3565	0.4493	0.5584	0.6854
13	0.2672	0.3449	0.4379	0.5481	0.6771
14	0.2572	0.3344	0.4276	0.5386	0.6695
15	0.2482	0.3250	0.4182	0.5300	0.6626
16	0.2401	0.3164	0.4096	0.5220	0.6561
17	0.2327	0.3085	0.4017	0.5146	0.6501
18	0.2260	0.3013	0.3944	0.5078	0.6444
19	0.2198	0.2946	0.3876	0.5014	0.6392
20	0.2141	0.2884	0.3812	0.4954	0.6342
21	0.2088	0.2826	0.3753	0.4898	0.6295
22	0.2038	0.2772	0.3697	0.4845	0.6251
23	0.1992	0.2722	0.3644	0.4794	0.6209
24	0.1949	0.2674	0.3595	0.4747	0.6169
25	0.1908	0.2629	0.3548	0.4702	0.6131
26	0.1870	0.2587	0.3503	0.4658	0.6094
27	0.1834	0.2546	0.3461	0.4617	0.6059
28	0.1800	0.2508	0.3421	0.4578	0.6026
29	0.1768	0.2472	0.3382	0.4541	0.5994
30	0.1738	0.2437	0.3346	0.4505	0.5963
31	0.1708	0.2405	0.3310	0.4470	0.5933
32	0.1681	0.2373	0.3277	0.4437	0.5905
33	0.1654	0.2343	0.3244	0.4405	0.5877
34	0.1629	0.2314	0.3213	0.4375	0.5851
35	0.1605	0.2286	0.3184	0.4345	0.5825
36	0.1582	0.2260	0.3155	0.4316	0.5800
37	0.1560	0.2234	0.3127	0.4289	0.5776
38	0.1539	0.2210	0.3100	0.4262	0.5753
39	0.1518	0.2186	0.3075	0.4236	0.5730
40	0.1498	0.2163	0.3050	0.4211	0.5708
41	0.1480	0.2141	0.3026	0.4187	0.5686
42	0.1461	0.2120	0.3002	0.4163	0.5666
43	0.1444	0.2099	0.2979	0.4140	0.5645
44	0.1427	0.2079	0.2958	0.4118	0.5626
45	0.1410	0.2060	0.2936	0.4096	0.5607

Table F.1. MANUFACTURING PROGRESS FACTORS—UNIT VALUES (*Continued*)

Unit Number	Slope Parameter, ϕ				
	0.70	0.75	0.80	0.85	0.90
46	0.1394	0.2041	0.2915	0.4075	0.5588
47	0.1379	0.2023	0.2895	0.4055	0.5570
48	0.1364	0.2005	0.2876	0.4035	0.5552
49	0.1350	0.1988	0.2857	0.4015	0.5534
50	0.1336	0.1972	0.2838	0.3996	0.5517
55	0.1272	0.1895	0.2753	0.3908	0.5438
60	0.1216	0.1828	0.2676	0.3829	0.5367
65	0.1167	0.1768	0.2608	0.3758	0.5302
70	0.1124	0.1715	0.2547	0.3693	0.5242
75	0.1084	0.1666	0.2491	0.3634	0.5188
80	0.1049	0.1622	0.2440	0.3579	0.5137
85	0.1017	0.1582	0.2393	0.3529	0.5090
90	0.0987	0.1545	0.2349	0.3482	0.5046
95	0.0960	0.1511	0.2308	0.3438	0.5005
100	0.0935	0.1479	0.2271	0.3397	0.4966
105	0.0912	0.1449	0.2235	0.3358	0.4929
110	0.0890	0.1421	0.2202	0.3322	0.4894
115	0.0870	0.1395	0.2171	0.3287	0.4861
120	0.0851	0.1371	0.2141	0.3255	0.4830
125	0.0834	0.1348	0.2113	0.3224	0.4800
130	0.0817	0.1326	0.2087	0.3194	0.4772
135	0.0801	0.1306	0.2062	0.3166	0.4744
140	0.0787	0.1286	0.2038	0.3139	0.4718
145	0.0772	0.1267	0.2015	0.3113	0.4693
150	0.0759	0.1250	0.1993	0.3089	0.4669
155	0.0746	0.1233	0.1972	0.3065	0.4646
160	0.0734	0.1217	0.1952	0.3042	0.4623
165	0.0723	0.1201	0.1933	0.3021	0.4602
170	0.0712	0.1184	0.1914	0.3000	0.4581
175	0.0701	0.1172	0.1896	0.2979	0.4561
180	0.0691	0.1159	0.1879	0.2960	0.4541
185	0.0681	0.1146	0.1863	0.2941	0.4522
190	0.0672	0.1133	0.1847	0.2922	0.4504
195	0.0663	0.1121	0.1831	0.2905	0.4486
200	0.0655	0.1109	0.1817	0.2887	0.4469
225	0.0616	0.1056	0.1749	0.2809	0.4390
250	0.0584	0.1011	0.1691	0.2740	0.4320
275	0.0556	0.0972	0.1640	0.2680	0.4258
300	0.0531	0.0937	0.1594	0.2626	0.4202
325	0.0510	0.0907	0.1554	0.2577	0.4151
350	0.0491	0.0879	0.1517	0.2532	0.4105
375	0.0474	0.0854	0.1484	0.2492	0.4062
400	0.0458	0.0832	0.1453	0.2454	0.4022
450	0.0431	0.0792	0.1399	0.2387	0.3951
500	0.0409	0.0758	0.1353	0.2329	0.3888

App. F   Progress Function Tables

Table F.2. MANUFACTURING PROGRESS FACTORS—CUMULATIVE VALUES

Unit Number	Slope Parameter, ϕ				
	0.70	0.75	0.80	0.85	0.90
1	1.0000	1.0000	1.0000	1.0000	1.0000
2	1.7000	1.7500	1.8000	1.8500	1.9000
3	2.2682	2.3838	2.5021	2.6229	2.7462
4	2.7582	2.9463	3.1421	3.3454	3.5562
5	3.1950	3.4590	3.7377	4.0311	4.3392
6	3.5927	3.9344	4.2994	4.6881	5.1008
7	3.9601	4.3803	4.8339	5.3218	5.8447
8	4.3031	4.8022	5.3459	5.9359	6.5737
9	4.6259	5.2039	5.8388	6.5333	7.2898
10	4.9317	5.5885	6.3153	7.1161	7.9945
11	5.2229	5.9581	6.7774	7.6860	8.6890
12	5.5013	6.3146	7.2267	8.2444	9.3744
13	5.7685	6.6595	7.6646	8.7925	10.0515
14	6.0257	6.9939	8.0922	9.3311	10.7210
15	6.2739	7.3189	8.5104	9.8611	11.3836
16	6.5140	7.6353	8.9200	10.3831	12.0397
17	6.7467	7.9438	9.3217	10.8977	12.6898
18	6.9727	8.2451	9.7161	11.4055	13.3342
19	7.1925	8.5397	10.1037	11.9069	13.9734
20	7.4066	8.8281	10.4849	12.4023	14.6076
21	7.6154	9.1107	10.8602	12.8921	15.2371
22	7.8192	9.3879	11.2299	13.3766	15.8622
23	8.0184	9.6601	11.5943	13.8560	16.4831
24	8.2133	9.9275	11.9538	14.3307	17.1000
25	8.4041	10.1904	12.3086	14.8009	17.7131
30	9.3051	11.4454	14.0199	17.0908	20.7267
35	10.1328	12.6175	15.6427	19.2940	23.6658
40	10.9025	13.7228	17.1934	21.4254	26.5425
45	11.6247	14.7727	18.6835	23.4958	29.3655
50	12.3070	15.7756	20.1216	25.5134	32.1416
55	12.9553	16.7382	21.5147	27.4847	34.8762
60	13.5743	17.6653	22.8678	29.4147	37.5735
65	14.1675	18.5611	24.1852	31.3077	40.2371
70	14.7378	19.4290	25.4708	33.1669	42.8699
75	15.2876	20.2717	26.7273	34.9955	45.4745
80	15.8191	21.0914	27.9573	36.7960	48.0530
85	16.3338	21.8904	29.1629	38.5705	50.6072
90	16.8333	22.6701	30.3460	40.3207	53.1388
95	17.3187	23.2811	31.5081	42.0484	55.1488
100	17.7912	24.1779	32.6509	43.7550	58.1399
150	21.9730	30.9338	43.2338	59.8901	82.1539
200	25.4833	36.8000	52.7203	74.7908	104.9614
300	31.3452	46.9418	69.6637	102.2341	148.1968
400	36.2640	55.7464	84.8495	127.5737	189.2588
500	40.5822	63.6741	98.8480	151.4560	228.7746

G

Finite Queuing Tables

TABLES G.1–G.3 FINITE QUEUING FACTORS

The probability of a delay, D, and the efficiency factor, F, are given for populations of 10, 20, and 30 units. Each set of values is keyed to the service factor, X, and the number of channels, M. (Tabular values adapted with permission from L. G. Peck and R. N. Hazelwood, *Finite Queuing Tables*. New York: John Wiley & Sons, Inc., 1958.)

Table G.1. FINITE QUEUING FACTORS—POPULATION 10

X	M	D	F	X	M	D	F	X	M	D	F
0.008	1	0.072	0.999		2	0.177	0.990		3	0.182	0.986
0.013	1	0.117	0.998		1	0.660	0.899		2	0.528	0.921
0.016	1	0.144	0.997	0.085	3	0.037	0.999		1	0.954	0.610
0.019	1	0.170	0.996		2	0.196	0.988	0.165	4	0.049	0.997
0.021	1	0.188	0.995		1	0.692	0.883		3	0.195	0.984
0.023	1	0.206	0.994	0.090	3	0.043	0.998		2	0.550	0.914
0.025	1	0.224	0.993		2	0.216	0.986		1	0.961	0.594
0.026	1	0.232	0.992		1	0.722	0.867	0.170	4	0.054	0.997
0.028	1	0.250	0.991	0.095	3	0.049	0.998		3	0.209	0.982
0.030	1	0.268	0.990		2	0.237	0.984		2	0.571	0.906
0.032	2	0.033	0.999		1	0.750	0.850		1	0.966	0.579
	1	0.285	0.988	0.100	3	0.056	0.998	0.180	5	0.013	0.999
0.034	2	0.037	0.999		2	0.258	0.981		4	0.066	0.996
	1	0.302	0.986		1	0.776	0.832		3	0.238	0.978
0.036	2	0.041	0.999	0.105	3	0.064	0.997		2	0.614	0.890
	1	0.320	0.984		2	0.279	0.978		1	0.975	0.549
0.038	2	0.046	0.999		1	0.800	0.814	0.190	5	0.016	0.999
	1	0.337	0.982	0.110	3	0.072	0.997		4	0.078	0.995
0.040	2	0.050	0.999		2	0.301	0.974		3	0.269	0.973
	1	0.354	0.980		1	0.822	0.795		2	0.654	0.873
0.042	2	0.055	0.999	0.115	3	0.081	0.996		1	0.982	0.522
	1	0.371	0.978		2	0.324	0.971	0.200	5	0.020	0.999
0.044	2	0.060	0.998		1	0.843	0.776		4	0.092	0.994
	1	0.388	0.975	0.120	4	0.016	0.999		3	0.300	0.968
0.046	2	0.065	0.998		3	0.090	0.995		2	0.692	0.854
	1	0.404	0.973		2	0.346	0.967		1	0.987	0.497
0.048	2	0.071	0.998		1	0.861	0.756	0.210	5	0.025	0.999
	1	0.421	0.970	0.125	4	0.019	0.999		4	0.108	0.992
0.050	2	0.076	0.998		3	0.100	0.994		3	0.333	0.961
	1	0.437	0.967		2	0.369	0.962		2	0.728	0.835
0.052	2	0.082	0.997		1	0.878	0.737		1	0.990	0.474
	1	0.454	0.963	0.130	4	0.022	0.999	0.220	5	0.030	0.998
0.054	2	0.088	0.997		3	0.110	0.994		4	0.124	0.990
	1	0.470	0.960		2	0.392	0.958		3	0.366	0.954
0.056	2	0.094	0.997		1	0.893	0.718		2	0.761	0.815
	1	0.486	0.956	0.135	4	0.025	0.999		1	0.993	0.453
0.058	2	0.100	0.996		3	0.121	0.993	0.230	5	0.037	0.998
	1	0.501	0.953		2	0.415	0.952		4	0.142	0.988
0.060	2	0.106	0.996		1	0.907	0.699		3	0.400	0.947
	1	0.517	0.949	0.140	4	0.028	0.999		2	0.791	0.794
0.062	2	0.113	0.996		3	0.132	0.991		1	0.995	0.434
	1	0.532	0.945		2	0.437	0.947	0.240	5	0.044	0.997
0.064	2	0.119	0.995		1	0.919	0.680		4	0.162	0.986
	1	0.547	0.940	0.145	4	0.032	0.999		3	0.434	0.938
0.066	2	0.126	0.995		3	0.144	0.990		2	0.819	0.774
	1	0.562	0.936		2	0.460	0.941		1	0.996	0.416
0.068	3	0.020	0.999		1	0.929	0.662	0.250	6	0.010	0.999
	2	0.133	0.994	0.150	4	0.036	0.998		5	0.052	0.997
	1	0.577	0.931		3	0.156	0.989		4	0.183	0.983
0.070	3	0.022	0.999		2	0.483	0.935		3	0.469	0.929
	2	0.140	0.994		1	0.939	0.644		2	0.844	0.753
	1	0.591	0.926	0.155	4	0.040	0.998		1	0.997	0.400
0.075	3	0.026	0.999		3	0.169	0.987	0.260	6	0.013	0.999
	2	0.158	0.992		2	0.505	0.928		5	0.060	0.996
	1	0.627	0.913		1	0.947	0.627		4	0.205	0.980
0.080	3	0.031	0.999	0.160	4	0.044	0.998		3	0.503	0.919

Table G.1. FINITE QUEUING FACTORS—POPULATION 10 (*Continued*)

X	M	D	F	X	M	D	F	X	M	D	F
	2	0.866	0.732		4	0.533	0.906		7	0.171	0.982
	1	0.998	0.384		3	0.840	0.758		6	0.413	0.939
0.270	6	0.015	0.999		2	0.986	0.525		5	0.707	0.848
	5	0.070	0.995	0.400	7	0.026	0.998		4	0.917	0.706
	4	0.228	0.976		6	0.105	0.991		3	0.991	0.535
	3	0.537	0.908		5	0.292	0.963	0.580	8	0.057	0.995
	2	0.886	0.712		4	0.591	0.887		7	0.204	0.977
	1	0.999	0.370		3	0.875	0.728		6	0.465	0.927
0.280	6	0.018	0.999		2	0.991	0.499		5	0.753	0.829
	5	0.081	0.994	0.420	7	0.034	0.998		4	0.937	0.684
	4	0.252	0.972		6	0.130	0.987		3	0.994	0.517
	3	0.571	0.896		5	0.341	0.954	0.600	9	0.010	0.999
	2	0.903	0.692		4	0.646	0.866		8	0.072	0.994
	1	0.999	0.357		3	0.905	0.700		7	0.242	0.972
0.290	6	0.022	0.999		2	0.994	0.476		6	0.518	0.915
	5	0.093	0.993	0.440	7	0.045	0.997		5	0.795	0.809
	4	0.278	0.968		6	0.160	0.984		4	0.953	0.663
	3	0.603	0.884		5	0.392	0.943		3	0.996	0.500
	2	0.918	0.672		4	0.698	0.845	0.650	9	0.021	0.999
	1	0.999	0.345		3	0.928	0.672		8	0.123	0.988
0.300	6	0.026	0.998		2	0.996	0.454		7	0.353	0.954
	5	0.106	0.991	0.460	8	0.011	0.999		6	0.651	0.878
	4	0.304	0.963		7	0.058	0.995		5	0.882	0.759
	3	0.635	0.872		6	0.193	0.979		4	0.980	0.614
	2	0.932	0.653		5	0.445	0.930		3	0.999	0.461
	1	0.999	0.333		4	0.747	0.822	0.700	9	0.040	0.997
0.310	6	0.031	0.998		3	0.947	0.646		8	0.200	0.979
	5	0.120	0.990		2	0.998	0.435		7	0.484	0.929
	4	0.331	0.957	0.480	8	0.015	0.999		6	0.772	0.836
	3	0.666	0.858		7	0.074	0.994		5	0.940	0.711
	2	0.943	0.635		6	0.230	0.973		4	0.992	0.571
0.320	6	0.036	0.998		5	0.499	0.916	0.750	9	0.075	0.994
	5	0.135	0.988		4	0.791	0.799		8	0.307	0.965
	4	0.359	0.952		3	0.961	0.621		7	0.626	0.897
	3	0.695	0.845		2	0.998	0.417		6	0.870	0.792
	2	0.952	0.617	0.500	8	0.020	0.999		5	0.975	0.666
0.330	6	0.042	0.997		7	0.093	0.992		4	0.998	0.533
	5	0.151	0.986		6	0.271	0.966	0.800	9	0.134	0.988
	4	0.387	0.945		5	0.553	0.901		8	0.446	0.944
	3	0.723	0.831		4	0.830	0.775		7	0.763	0.859
	2	0.961	0.600		3	0.972	0.598		6	0.939	0.747
0.340	7	0.010	0.999		2	0.999	0.400		5	0.991	0.625
	6	0.049	0.997	0.520	8	0.026	0.998		4	0.999	0.500
	5	0.168	0.983		7	0.115	0.989	0.850	9	0.232	0.979
	4	0.416	0.938		6	0.316	0.958		8	0.611	0.916
	3	0.750	0.816		5	0.606	0.884		7	0.879	0.818
	2	0.968	0.584		4	0.864	0.752		6	0.978	0.705
0.360	7	0.014	0.999		3	0.980	0.575		5	0.998	0.588
	6	0.064	0.995		2	0.999	0.385	0.900	9	0.387	0.963
	5	0.205	0.978	0.540	8	0.034	0.997		8	0.785	0.881
	4	0.474	0.923		7	0.141	0.986		7	0.957	0.777
	3	0.798	0.787		6	0.363	0.949		6	0.995	0.667
	2	0.978	0.553		5	0.658	0.867	0.950	9	0.630	0.938
0.380	7	0.019	0.999		4	0.893	0.729		8	0.934	0.841
	6	0.083	0.993		3	0.986	0.555		7	0.994	0.737
	5	0.247	0.971	0.560	8	0.044	0.996				

Table G.2. FINITE QUEUING FACTORS—POPULATION 20

X	M	D	F	X	M	D	F	X	M	D	F
0.005	1	0.095	0.999		1	0.837	0.866		3	0.326	0.980
0.009	1	0.171	0.998	0.052	3	0.080	0.998		2	0.733	0.896
0.011	1	0.208	0.997		2	0.312	0.986		1	0.998	0.526
0.013	1	0.246	0.996		1	0.858	0.851	0.100	5	0.038	0.999
0.014	1	0.265	0.995	0.054	3	0.088	0.998		4	0.131	0.995
0.015	1	0.283	0.994		2	0.332	0.984		3	0.363	0.975
0.016	1	0.302	0.993		1	0.876	0.835		2	0.773	0.878
0.017	1	0.321	0.992	0.056	3	0.097	0.997		1	0.999	0.500
0.018	2	0.048	0.999		2	0.352	0.982	0.110	5	0.055	0.998
	1	0.339	0.991		1	0.893	0.819		4	0.172	0.992
0.019	2	0.053	0.999	0.058	3	0.105	0.997		3	0.438	0.964
	1	0.358	0.990		2	0.372	0.980		2	0.842	0.837
0.020	2	0.058	0.999		1	0.908	0.802	0.120	6	0.022	0.999
	1	0.376	0.989	0.060	4	0.026	0.999		5	0.076	0.997
0.021	2	0.064	0.999		3	0.115	0.997		4	0.219	0.988
	1	0.394	0.987		2	0.392	0.978		3	0.514	0.950
0.022	2	0.070	0.999		1	0.922	0.785		2	0.895	0.793
	1	0.412	0.986	0.062	4	0.029	0.999	0.130	6	0.031	0.999
0.023	2	0.075	0.999		3	0.124	0.996		5	0.101	0.996
	1	0.431	0.984		2	0.413	0.975		4	0.271	0.983
0.024	2	0.082	0.999		1	0.934	0.768		3	0.589	0.933
	1	0.449	0.982	0.064	4	0.032	0.999		2	0.934	0.748
0.025	2	0.088	0.999		3	0.134	0.996	0.140	6	0.043	0.998
	1	0.466	0.980		2	0.433	0.972		5	0.131	0.994
0.026	2	0.094	0.998		1	0.944	0.751		4	0.328	0.976
	1	0.484	0.978	0.066	4	0.036	0.999		3	0.661	0.912
0.028	2	0.108	0.998		3	0.144	0.995		2	0.960	0.703
	1	0.519	0.973		2	0.454	0.969	0.150	7	0.017	0.999
0.030	2	0.122	0.998		1	0.953	0.733		6	0.059	0.998
	1	0.553	0.968	0.068	4	0.039	0.999		5	0.166	0.991
0.032	2	0.137	0.997		3	0.155	0.995		4	0.388	0.968
	1	0.587	0.962		2	0.474	0.966		3	0.728	0.887
0.034	2	0.152	0.996		1	0.961	0.716		2	0.976	0.661
	1	0.620	0.955	0.070	4	0.043	0.999	0.160	7	0.024	0.999
0.036	2	0.168	0.995		3	0.165	0.994		6	0.077	0.997
	1	0.651	0.947		2	0.495	0.962		5	0.205	0.988
0.038	3	0.036	0.999		1	0.967	0.699		4	0.450	0.957
	2	0.185	0.995	0.075	4	0.054	0.999		3	0.787	0.860
	1	0.682	0.938		3	0.194	0.992		2	0.987	0.622
0.040	3	0.041	0.999		2	0.545	0.953	0.180	7	0.044	0.998
	2	0.202	0.994		1	0.980	0.659		6	0.125	0.994
	1	0.712	0.929	0.080	4	0.066	0.998		5	0.295	0.978
0.042	3	0.047	0.999		3	0.225	0.990		4	0.575	0.930
	2	0.219	0.993		2	0.595	0.941		3	0.879	0.799
	1	0.740	0.918		1	0.988	0.621		2	0.996	0.555
0.044	3	0.053	0.999	0.085	4	0.080	0.997	0.200	8	0.025	0.999
	2	0.237	0.992		3	0.257	0.987		7	0.074	0.997
	1	0.767	0.906		2	0.643	0.928		6	0.187	0.988
0.046	3	0.059	0.999		1	0.993	0.586		5	0.397	0.963
	2	0.255	0.991	0.090	5	0.025	0.999		4	0.693	0.895
	1	0.792	0.894		4	0.095	0.997		3	0.938	0.736
0.048	3	0.066	0.999		3	0.291	0.984		2	0.999	0.500
	2	0.274	0.989		2	0.689	0.913	0.220	8	0.043	0.998
	1	0.815	0.881		1	0.996	0.554		7	0.115	0.994
0.050	3	0.073	0.998	0.095	5	0.031	0.999		6	0.263	0.980
	2	0.293	0.988		4	0.112	0.996		5	0.505	0.943

Table G.2. FINITE QUEUING FACTORS—POPULATION 20 (*Continued*)

X	M	D	F	X	M	D	F	X	M	D	F
0.240	4	0.793	0.852	0.380	4	0.998	0.555	0.500	14	0.033	0.998
	3	0.971	0.677		12	0.024	0.999		13	0.088	0.995
	9	0.024	0.999		11	0.067	0.996		12	0.194	0.985
	8	0.068	0.997		10	0.154	0.989		11	0.358	0.965
	7	0.168	0.989		9	0.305	0.973		10	0.563	0.929
	6	0.351	0.969		8	0.513	0.938		9	0.764	0.870
	5	0.613	0.917		7	0.739	0.874		8	0.908	0.791
	4	0.870	0.804		6	0.909	0.777		7	0.977	0.698
	3	0.988	0.623		5	0.984	0.656		6	0.997	0.600
0.260	9	0.039	0.998		4	0.999	0.526	0.540	15	0.023	0.999
	8	0.104	0.994	0.400	13	0.012	0.999		14	0.069	0.996
	7	0.233	0.983		12	0.037	0.998		13	0.161	0.988
	6	0.446	0.953		11	0.095	0.994		12	0.311	0.972
	5	0.712	0.884		10	0.205	0.984		11	0.509	0.941
	4	0.924	0.755		9	0.379	0.962		10	0.713	0.891
	3	0.995	0.576		8	0.598	0.918		9	0.873	0.821
0.280	10	0.021	0.999		7	0.807	0.845		8	0.961	0.738
	9	0.061	0.997		6	0.942	0.744		7	0.993	0.648
	8	0.149	0.990		5	0.992	0.624		6	0.999	0.556
	7	0.309	0.973	0.420	13	0.019	0.999	0.600	16	0.023	0.999
	6	0.544	0.932		12	0.055	0.997		15	0.072	0.996
	5	0.797	0.848		11	0.131	0.991		14	0.171	0.988
	4	0.958	0.708		10	0.265	0.977		13	0.331	0.970
	3	0.998	0.536		9	0.458	0.949		12	0.532	0.938
0.300	10	0.034	0.998		8	0.678	0.896		11	0.732	0.889
	9	0.091	0.995		7	0.863	0.815		10	0.882	0.824
	8	0.205	0.985		6	0.965	0.711		9	0.962	0.748
	7	0.394	0.961		5	0.996	0.595		8	0.992	0.666
	6	0.639	0.907	0.440	13	0.029	0.999		7	0.999	0.583
	5	0.865	0.808		12	0.078	0.995	0.700	17	0.047	0.998
	4	0.978	0.664		11	0.175	0.987		16	0.137	0.991
	3	0.999	0.500		10	0.333	0.969		15	0.295	0.976
0.320	11	0.018	0.999		9	0.540	0.933		14	0.503	0.948
	10	0.053	0.997		8	0.751	0.872		13	0.710	0.905
	9	0.130	0.992		7	0.907	0.785		12	0.866	0.849
	8	0.272	0.977		6	0.980	0.680		11	0.953	0.783
	7	0.483	0.944		5	0.998	0.568		10	0.988	0.714
	6	0.727	0.878	0.460	14	0.014	0.999		9	0.998	0.643
	5	0.915	0.768		13	0.043	0.998	0.800	19	0.014	0.999
	4	0.989	0.624		12	0.109	0.993		18	0.084	0.996
0.340	11	0.029	0.999		11	0.228	0.982		17	0.242	0.984
	10	0.079	0.996		10	0.407	0.958		16	0.470	0.959
	9	0.179	0.987		9	0.620	0.914		15	0.700	0.920
	8	0.347	0.967		8	0.815	0.846		14	0.867	0.869
	7	0.573	0.924		7	0.939	0.755		13	0.955	0.811
	6	0.802	0.846		6	0.989	0.651		12	0.989	0.750
	5	0.949	0.729		5	0.999	0.543		11	0.998	0.687
	4	0.995	0.588	0.480	14	0.022	0.999	0.900	19	0.135	0.994
0.360	12	0.015	0.999		13	0.063	0.996		18	0.425	0.972
	11	0.045	0.998		12	0.147	0.990		17	0.717	0.935
	10	0.112	0.993		11	0.289	0.974		16	0.898	0.886
	9	0.237	0.981		10	0.484	0.944		15	0.973	0.833
	8	0.429	0.954		9	0.695	0.893		14	0.995	0.778
	7	0.660	0.901		8	0.867	0.819		13	0.999	0.722
	6	0.863	0.812		7	0.962	0.726	0.950	19	0.377	0.981
	5	0.971	0.691		6	0.994	0.625		18	0.760	0.943

Table G.3. FINITE QUEUING FACTORS—POPULATION 30

X	M	D	F	X	M	D	F	X	M	D	F
0.004	1	0.116	0.999		1	0.963	0.772		3	0.426	0.976
0.007	1	0.203	0.998	0.044	4	0.040	0.999		2	0.847	0.873
0.009	1	0.260	0.997		3	0.154	0.996	0.075	5	0.069	0.998
0.010	1	0.289	0.996		2	0.474	0.977		4	0.201	0.993
0.011	1	0.317	0.995		1	0.974	0.744		3	0.486	0.969
0.012	1	0.346	0.994	0.046	4	0.046	0.999		2	0.893	0.840
0.013	1	0.374	0.993		3	0.171	0.996	0.080	6	0.027	0.999
0.014	2	0.067	0.999		2	0.506	0.972		5	0.088	0.998
	1	0.403	0.991		1	0.982	0.716		4	0.240	0.990
0.015	2	0.076	0.999	0.048	4	0.053	0.999		3	0.547	0.959
	1	0.431	0.989		3	0.189	0.995		2	0.929	0.805
0.016	2	0.085	0.999		2	0.539	0.968	0.085	6	0.036	0.999
	1	0.458	0.987		1	0.988	0.689		5	0.108	0.997
0.017	2	0.095	0.999	0.050	4	0.060	0.999		4	0.282	0.987
	1	0.486	0.985		3	0.208	0.994		3	0.607	0.948
0.018	2	0.105	0.999		2	0.571	0.963		2	0.955	0.768
	1	0.513	0.983		1	0.992	0.663	0.090	6	0.046	0.999
0.019	2	0.116	0.999	0.052	4	0.068	0.999		5	0.132	0.996
	1	0.541	0.980		3	0.227	0.993		4	0.326	0.984
0.020	2	0.127	0.998		2	0.603	0.957		3	0.665	0.934
	1	0.567	0.976		1	0.995	0.639		2	0.972	0.732
0.021	2	0.139	0.998	0.054	4	0.077	0.998	0.095	6	0.057	0.999
	1	0.594	0.973		3	0.247	0.992		5	0.158	0.994
0.022	2	0.151	0.998		2	0.634	0.951		4	0.372	0.979
	1	0.620	0.969		1	0.997	0.616		3	0.720	0.918
0.023	2	0.163	0.997	0.056	4	0.086	0.998		2	0.984	0.697
	1	0.645	0.965		3	0.267	0.991	0.100	6	0.071	0.998
0.024	2	0.175	0.997		2	0.665	0.944		5	0.187	0.993
	1	0.670	0.960		1	0.998	0.595		4	0.421	0.973
0.025	2	0.188	0.996	0.058	4	0.096	0.998		3	0.771	0.899
	1	0.694	0.954		3	0.288	0.989		2	0.991	0.664
0.026	2	0.201	0.996		2	0.695	0.936	0.110	7	0.038	0.999
	1	0.718	0.948		1	0.999	0.574		6	0.105	0.997
0.028	3	0.051	0.999	0.060	5	0.030	0.999		5	0.253	0.988
	2	0.229	0.995		4	0.106	0.997		4	0.520	0.959
	1	0.763	0.935		3	0.310	0.987		3	0.856	0.857
0.030	3	0.060	0.999		2	0.723	0.927		2	0.997	0.605
	2	0.257	0.994		1	0.999	0.555	0.120	7	0.057	0.998
	1	0.805	0.918	0.062	5	0.034	0.999		6	0.147	0.994
0.032	3	0.071	0.999		4	0.117	0.997		5	0.327	0.981
	2	0.286	0.992		3	0.332	0.986		4	0.619	0.939
	1	0.843	0.899		2	0.751	0.918		3	0.918	0.808
0.034	3	0.083	0.999	0.064	5	0.038	0.999		2	0.999	0.555
	2	0.316	0.990		4	0.128	0.997	0.130	8	0.030	0.999
	1	0.876	0.877		3	0.355	0.984		7	0.083	0.997
0.036	3	0.095	0.998		2	0.777	0.908		6	0.197	0.991
	2	0.347	0.988	0.066	5	0.043	0.999		5	0.409	0.972
	1	0.905	0.853		4	0.140	0.996		4	0.712	0.914
0.038	3	0.109	0.998		3	0.378	0.982		3	0.957	0.758
	2	0.378	0.986		2	0.802	0.897	0.140	8	0.045	0.999
	1	0.929	0.827	0.068	5	0.048	0.999		7	0.115	0.996
0.040	3	0.123	0.997		4	0.153	0.995		6	0.256	0.987
	2	0.410	0.983		3	0.402	0.979		5	0.494	0.960
	1	0.948	0.800		2	0.825	0.885		4	0.793	0.884
0.042	3	0.138	0.997	0.070	5	0.054	0.999		3	0.979	0.710
	2	0.442	0.980		4	0.166	0.995	0.150	9	0.024	0.999

Table G.3. FINITE QUEUING FACTORS—POPULATION 30 (*Continued*)

X	M	D	F	X	M	D	F	X	M	D	F
	8	0.065	0.998		7	0.585	0.938		7	0.901	0.818
	7	0.155	0.993		6	0.816	0.868		6	0.981	0.712
	6	0.322	0.980		5	0.961	0.751		5	0.999	0.595
	5	0.580	0.944		4	0.998	0.606	0.290	14	0.023	0.999
	4	0.860	0.849	0.230	12	0.023	0.999		13	0.055	0.998
	3	0.991	0.665		11	0.056	0.998		12	0.117	0.994
0.160	9	0.036	0.999		10	0.123	0.994		11	0.223	0.986
	8	0.090	0.997		9	0.242	0.985		10	0.382	0.969
	7	0.201	0.990		8	0.423	0.965		9	0.582	0.937
	6	0.394	0.972		7	0.652	0.923		8	0.785	0.880
	5	0.663	0.924		6	0.864	0.842		7	0.929	0.795
	4	0.910	0.811		5	0.976	0.721		6	0.988	0.688
	3	0.996	0.624		4	0.999	0.580		5	0.999	0.575
0.170	10	0.019	0.999	0.240	12	0.031	0.999	0.300	14	0.031	0.999
	9	0.051	0.998		11	0.074	0.997		13	0.071	0.997
	8	0.121	0.995		10	0.155	0.992		12	0.145	0.992
	7	0.254	0.986		9	0.291	0.981		11	0.266	0.982
	6	0.469	0.961		8	0.487	0.955		10	0.437	0.962
	5	0.739	0.901		7	0.715	0.905		9	0.641	0.924
	4	0.946	0.773		6	0.902	0.816		8	0.830	0.861
	3	0.998	0.588		5	0.986	0.693		7	0.950	0.771
0.180	10	0.028	0.999		4	0.999	0.556		6	0.993	0.666
	9	0.070	0.997	0.250	13	0.017	0.999	0.320	15	0.023	0.999
	8	0.158	0.993		12	0.042	0.998		14	0.054	0.998
	7	0.313	0.980		11	0.095	0.996		13	0.113	0.994
	6	0.546	0.948		10	0.192	0.989		12	0.213	0.987
	5	0.806	0.874		9	0.345	0.975		11	0.362	0.971
	4	0.969	0.735		8	0.552	0.944		10	0.552	0.943
	3	0.999	0.555		7	0.773	0.885		9	0.748	0.893
0.190	10	0.039	0.999		6	0.932	0.789		8	0.901	0.820
	9	0.094	0.996		5	0.992	0.666		7	0.977	0.727
	8	0.200	0.990	0.260	13	0.023	0.999		6	0.997	0.625
	7	0.378	0.973		12	0.056	0.998	0.340	16	0.016	0.999
	6	0.621	0.932		11	0.124	0.994		15	0.040	0.998
	5	0.862	0.845		10	0.233	0.986		14	0.086	0.996
	4	0.983	0.699		9	0.402	0.967		13	0.169	0.990
0.200	11	0.021	0.999		8	0.616	0.930		12	0.296	0.979
	10	0.054	0.998		7	0.823	0.864		11	0.468	0.957
	9	0.123	0.995		6	0.954	0.763		10	0.663	0.918
	8	0.249	0.985		5	0.995	0.641		9	0.836	0.858
	7	0.446	0.963	0.270	13	0.032	0.999		8	0.947	0.778
	6	0.693	0.913		12	0.073	0.997		7	0.990	0.685
	5	0.905	0.814		11	0.151	0.992		6	0.999	0.588
	4	0.991	0.665		10	0.279	0.981	0.360	16	0.029	0.999
0.210	11	0.030	0.999		9	0.462	0.959		15	0.065	0.997
	10	0.073	0.997		8	0.676	0.915		14	0.132	0.993
	9	0.157	0.992		7	0.866	0.841		13	0.240	0.984
	8	0.303	0.980		6	0.970	0.737		12	0.392	0.967
	7	0.515	0.952		5	0.997	0.617		11	0.578	0.937
	6	0.758	0.892	0.280	14	0.017	0.999		10	0.762	0.889
	5	0.938	0.782		13	0.042	0.998		9	0.902	0.821
	4	0.995	0.634		12	0.093	0.996		8	0.974	0.738
0.220	11	0.041	0.999		11	0.185	0.989		7	0.996	0.648
	10	0.095	0.996		10	0.329	0.976	0.380	17	0.020	0.999
	9	0.197	0.989		9	0.522	0.949		16	0.048	0.998
	8	0.361	0.974		8	0.733	0.898		15	0.101	0.995

Table G.3. FINITE QUEUING FACTORS—POPULATION 30 (*Continued*)

X	M	D	F	X	M	D	F	X	M	D	F
	14	0.191	0.988		16	0.310	0.977		22	0.038	0.998
	13	0.324	0.975		15	0.470	0.957		21	0.085	0.996
	12	0.496	0.952		14	0.643	0.926		20	0.167	0.990
	11	0.682	0.914		13	0.799	0.881		19	0.288	0.980
	10	0.843	0.857		12	0.910	0.826		18	0.443	0.963
	9	0.945	0.784		11	0.970	0.762		17	0.612	0.936
	8	0.988	0.701		10	0.993	0.694		16	0.766	0.899
	7	0.999	0.614		9	0.999	0.625		15	0.883	0.854
0.400	17	0.035	0.999	0.500	20	0.032	0.999		14	0.953	0.802
	16	0.076	0.996		19	0.072	0.997		13	0.985	0.746
	15	0.150	0.992		18	0.143	0.992		12	0.997	0.690
	14	0.264	0.982		17	0.252	0.983		11	0.999	0.632
	13	0.420	0.964		16	0.398	0.967	0.600	23	0.024	0.999
	12	0.601	0.933		15	0.568	0.941		22	0.059	0.997
	11	0.775	0.886		14	0.733	0.904		21	0.125	0.993
	10	0.903	0.823		13	0.865	0.854		20	0.230	0.986
	9	0.972	0.748		12	0.947	0.796		19	0.372	0.972
	8	0.995	0.666		11	0.985	0.732		18	0.538	0.949
0.420	18	0.024	0.999		10	0.997	0.667		17	0.702	0.918
	17	0.056	0.997	0.520	21	0.021	0.999		16	0.837	0.877
	16	0.116	0.994		20	0.051	0.998		15	0.927	0.829
	15	0.212	0.986		19	0.108	0.994		14	0.974	0.776
	14	0.350	0.972		18	0.200	0.988		13	0.993	0.722
	13	0.521	0.948		17	0.331	0.975		12	0.999	0.667
	12	0.700	0.910		16	0.493	0.954	0.700	25	0.039	0.998
	11	0.850	0.856		15	0.663	0.923		24	0.096	0.995
	10	0.945	0.789		14	0.811	0.880		23	0.196	0.989
	9	0.986	0.713		13	0.915	0.827		22	0.339	0.977
	8	0.998	0.635		12	0.971	0.767		21	0.511	0.958
0.440	19	0.017	0.999		11	0.993	0.705		20	0.681	0.930
	18	0.041	0.998		10	0.999	0.641		19	0.821	0.894
	17	0.087	0.996	0.540	21	0.035	0.999		18	0.916	0.853
	16	0.167	0.990		20	0.079	0.996		17	0.967	0.808
	15	0.288	0.979		19	0.155	0.991		16	0.990	0.762
	14	0.446	0.960		18	0.270	0.981		15	0.997	0.714
	13	0.623	0.929		17	0.421	0.965	0.800	27	0.053	0.998
	12	0.787	0.883		16	0.590	0.938		26	0.143	0.993
	11	0.906	0.824		15	0.750	0.901		25	0.292	0.984
	10	0.970	0.755		14	0.874	0.854		24	0.481	0.966
	9	0.994	0.681		13	0.949	0.799		23	0.670	0.941
	8	0.999	0.606		12	0.985	0.740		22	0.822	0.909
0.460	19	0.028	0.999		11	0.997	0.679		21	0.919	0.872
	18	0.064	0.997		10	0.999	0.617		20	0.970	0.832
	17	0.129	0.993	0.560	22	0.023	0.999		19	0.991	0.791
	16	0.232	0.985		21	0.056	0.997		18	0.998	0.750
	15	0.375	0.970		20	0.117	0.994	0.900	29	0.047	0.999
	14	0.545	0.944		19	0.215	0.986		28	0.200	0.992
	13	0.717	0.906		18	0.352	0.973		27	0.441	0.977
	12	0.857	0.855		17	0.516	0.952		26	0.683	0.953
	11	0.945	0.793		16	0.683	0.920		25	0.856	0.923
	10	0.985	0.724		15	0.824	0.878		24	0.947	0.888
	9	0.997	0.652		14	0.920	0.828		23	0.985	0.852
0.480	20	0.019	0.999		13	0.972	0.772		22	0.996	0.815
	19	0.046	0.998		12	0.993	0.714		21	0.999	0.778
	18	0.098	0.995		11	0.999	0.655	0.950	29	0.226	0.993
	17	0.184	0.989	0.580	23	0.014	0.999		28	0.574	0.973

Selected References

ACKOFF, R. L., *Scientific Method: Optimizing Applied Research Decisions.* New York: John Wiley & Sons, Inc., 1962.

ADAM, E. E., JR., and B. J. EBERT, *Production and Operations Management: Concepts, Models, and Behavior.* Englewood Cliffs, N.J.: Prentice-Hall, Inc., 1982.

ANDERSON, D. R., D. W. SWEENEY, and T. A. WILLIAMS, *An Introduction to Management Science: Quantitative Approaches to Decision Making.* St. Paul, Minn.: West Publishing Co., Inc., 1982.

BARNARD, C. I., *The Functions of the Executive.* Cambridge, Mass.: Harvard University Press, 1938.

BAUMOL, W. J., *Economic Theory and Operations Analysis.* Englewood Cliffs, N.J.: Prentice-Hall, Inc., 1977.

BELLMAN, R. E., and S. E. DREYFUS, *Applied Dynamic Programming.* Princeton, N.J.: Princeton University Press, 1962.

BOWKER, A. H., and G. J. LIEBERMAN, *Engineering Statistics.* Englewood Cliffs, N.J.: Prentice-Hall, Inc., 1972.

BUDNICK, F. S., R. WOJENA, and T. E. VOLLMANN, *Principles of Operations Research for Management.* Homewood, Ill.: Richard D. Irwin, Inc., 1977.

Selected References

BUFFA, E. S., and J. S. DYER, *Essentials of Management Science/Operations Research.* New York: John Wiley & Sons, Inc., 1978.

CABOT, A. V., and D. L. HARNETT, *An Introduction to Management Science.* Reading, Mass.: Addison-Wesley Publishing Co., Inc., 1977.

CONWAY, R. W., W. L. MAXWELL, and L. W. MILLER, *Theory of Scheduling.* Reading, Mass.: Addison-Wesley Publishing Co., Inc., 1977.

DENARDO, E. V., *Dynamic Programming: Models and Applications.* Englewood Cliffs, N.J.: Prentice-Hall, Inc., 1982.

FABRYCKY, W. J., and G. J. THUESEN, *Economic Decision Analysis.* Englewood Cliffs, N.J.: Prentice-Hall, Inc., 1980.

GASS, S. I., *Linear Programming.* New York: McGraw-Hill Book Company, 1969.

GRANT, E. L., and R. S. LEAVENWORTH, *Statistical Quality Control.* New York: McGraw-Hill Book Company, 1972.

HADLEY, G., *Linear Programming.* Reading, Mass.: Addison Wesley Publishing Co., Inc. 1962.

HARTLEY, R. V., *Operations Research: A Managerial Emphasis.* Pacific Palisades, Calif.: Goodyear Publishing Co., Inc., 1976.

HILLIER, F. S., and G. J. LIEBERMAN, *Introduction to Operations Research.* San Francisco: Holden-Day, Inc., 1980.

IGNIZIO, J. P., *Linear Programming in Single and Multiple Objective Systems.* Englewood Cliffs, N.J., Prentice-Hall, Inc., 1982.

LEE, S. M., *Goal Programming for Decision Analysis.* Philadelphia, Pa.: Auerback Publishers, 1972.

PECK, L. G., and R. N. HAZELWOOD, *Finite Queuing Tables.* New York: John Wiley & Sons, Inc., 1958.

RIGGS, J. L., and M. S. INOUE, *Introduction to Operations Research and Management Science.* New York: McGraw-Hill Book Company, 1975.

SCHMIDT, J. W., and R. E. TAYLOR, *Simulation and Analysis of Industrial Systems.* Homewood, Ill.: Richard D. Irwin, Inc., 1970.

SHAMBLIN, J. E., and G. T. STEVENS, *Operations Research: A Fundamental Approach.* New York: McGraw-Hill Book Company, 1974.

SHANNON, R. E., *Systems Simulation: The Art and Science.* Englewood Cliffs, N.J.: Prentice-Hall, Inc., 1975.

TAHA, H. A., *Operations Research.* New York: Macmillan Publishing Co., Inc., 1982.

THUESEN, G. J., and W. J. FABRYCKY, *Engineering Economy.* Englewood Cliffs, N.J.: Prentice-Hall, Inc., 1984.

TORGERSEN, P. E., *A Concept of Organization.* New York: Van Nostrand Reinhold Company, 1969.

———, and I. T. WEINSTOCK, *Management: An Integrated Approach.* Englewood Cliffs, N.J.: Prentice-Hall, Inc., 1972.

WAGNER, H. M., *Principles of Operations Research.* Englewood Cliffs, N.J.: Prentice-Hall, Inc., 1969.

———, *Principles of Management Science.* Englewood Cliffs, N.J.: Prentice-Hall, Inc., 1970.

Index

A

Acceptable quality level, 318
Acceptance sampling models, 316-24
  average outgoing quality, 322-24
  concept of, 316-17
  deriving a plan, 319-22
  operating characteristics curve, 317-19
Addition, of matrices, 451
Addition theorem, 465
Algebra:
  linear, 448-50
  matrix, 450-53
Allocation:
  of capital, 113-16
  maximum profit, 73-75
  of resources, 112-13
Alternatives:
  comparing multiple, 190-92
  considerations in problem definition, 15
  evaluating singly, 187-90
  for procurement, 332-34, 344-45
  and pursuit of objectives, 10, 11-12
Arc, 280-81
Arrival mechanism, 398
Arrival population, 396-97
Arrival time, 415, 429-32
Aspiration level criterion, 131
Assets:
  depreciation of, 196-98 (*see also* Depreciation)
  equivalent annual cost, 186-87, 191
  payout evaluation, 189-90
  replacement of, 207-12
Assignment model, 77-84
  iteration toward optimal assignment, 80-82

matrix, 78-80
maximum profit assignment, 82-84
traveling salesman problem, 84-90
Attributes, control models for, 310-15
Automation, of management process, 28
Average inspection load, 322-24
Average outgoing quality, 322-24

B

Bellman, Richard, 108
Binomial distributions, 469-71
  approximation to, 471, 475
  p chart, 311
Blackett, P. M. S., 4
Boeing modified progress curve, 245
Branch-and-bound procedure:
  for flow-shop sequencing, 256-60
  in traveling salesman problem, 84-86
Break-even models, 158-63
  effect of dumping, 161-63
  finding the break-even point, 159-61
  production above normal capacity, 161

C

Capital:
  allocation problem, 113-16
  as production cost, 149
  and production function, 164
  recovery:
    through depreciation, 197-98
    interest formulas, 181-82
c chart, 313-15
Certainty, assumed, 127-29
Charts, with schematic models, 20-21
  (*see also* Control charts)
Circuit, 280
Compound interest, 177
Computers:
  output statistics for simulated sampling analysis, 370-73
  role in operations research/management science, 6-7
  role in optimizing model, 16
  type of effectiveness functions requiring, 25
Conditional theorem, 466
Connected graph, 280
Consumer risk, 318
Continuous probability distributions, 471-75
  exponential, 472-73

  normal, 473-75
  rectangular, 471-72
  summary, 475-76
Control:
  of functional relationships, 26-27
  of input parameters, 26
Control charts:
  application of, 299-301
  for attributes, 310-15
  power of, 308-10
  for service factor control, 438-41
  for variables, 301-6
Control limits:
  effectiveness, 13
  and specification limits, 307-8
  use of, 298, 299
Costs:
  equivalent annual, 186-87, 188-89, 191
  holding, 355, 389
  input combinations to minimize, 166-67
  inventory policy to minimize, 382-88
  of labor, 152
  of procurement alternatives, 333-43
  of production (*see* Production costs)
  and project control, 290-92
  of service facility, 399, 401, 403, 426
  of shortage, 335, 348-55, 388-89
  sunk, 209-10
  of waiting, 399, 401, 403, 426
Counteractions, effect of, 12
Critical path:
  defined, 281
  determination of, 284-86
  and PERT, 286
Critical path method (CPM), 280-86
  basic definitions, 280
  distinguished from PERT, 281, 286
  economic aspects, 290-92
  principal relationships, 280-81
  project control example, 282-86
  reasons for acceptance of, 279
Cumulative average formula, 240-42
Cumulative formula, 240-42
Cumulative normal probabilities, 490-91 *tab*.
Cumulative Poisson probabilities, 484-86 *tab*.
Cumulative Poisson probability curves, 487 *tab*.
Cycle:
  in critical path method, 280

Index

in deterministic procurement and inventory model, 336
expected number of periods per, 374

D

Dantzig, George, 33
Data:
  for comparison of job-shop sequencing rules, 267-68
  reliability of, in production progress models, 249-50
Decision and game models, 27, 125-44
  control chart monitoring, 300-301
  decisions under assumed certainty, 127-29
  decisions under risk, 129-32
    aspiration level criterion, 131
    elimination of dominance, 130
    expected future criterion, 131-32
    most probable future criterion, 131
  decisions under uncertainty, 132-38
    Hurwicz criterion, 134-36
    Laplace criterion, 133
    maximin and maximax rules, 133-34
    minimax regret criterion, 136-37
  game decision models, 138-44 (*see also* Game decision models)
  for inventory and procurement, 336-37
  payoff matrix model, 126-27
Decision environment:
  and control of model, 26-27
  with deterministic queuing models, 398-400
  with procurement models, 334-37
  static, assumption of, 25
Decision maker, 15
Decision making:
  and scientific method, 4, 6
  use and limitations of models, 16-17
  value of models, 27-28
Decision models (*see* Decision and game models)
Degeneracy:
  in the simplex method, 60
  in transportation model, 73
Demand:
  probability distributions, 367-68, 375-77
  and procurement and inventory models, 335, 388-89
  variable, 355-58
Departure mechanism, 397

Depreciation:
  capital recovery plus return, 197-98
  and classification of costs, 152
  classifications, 196
  and equivalent annual cost, 186-87
  value-time function, 196-97
Depreciation models:
  equivalence of, 205-7
  fixed-percentage, 201-3
  sinking-fund, 201
  straight-line, 198-201
  sum-of-the-years, 203-5
Derivatives:
  defined, 457
  higher-order, 459
Deterioration (*see* Depreciation)
Deterministic models, 21
Deterministic procurement and inventory models (*see* Procurement and inventory, deterministic models)
Deterministic project control, 280-86 (*see also* Critical path method)
Deterministic queuing models, 395-411
  approximation for total waiting time, 407-9
  decision environment, 398-400
    arrival mechanism, 398
    decision model, 399-400
    service facility cost, 399
    service mechanism, 398-99
    waiting cost, 399
  general numerical solution method, 409-11
    minimum cost service rate, 410-11
    total waiting time, 409-10
  with initial waiting line, 403-7
    example application, 407
    general system relationships, 404-5
    total system cost, 406-7
    total waiting time, 405-6
  with no initial waiting line, 400-403
    multiple-channel, 402-3
    single-channel, 400-401
  queuing system, 396-98
    arrival population, 396-97
    service facility, 397-98
    waiting line, 397
Differential calculus, 456-59
Differentiation, 457
  partial, 459-60
  rules of, 458-59
Direct experimentation, 22
Discrete probability distributions, 468-71

Discrete probability distributions *(cont.)*
   binomial, 469-71
   hypergeometric, 468-69
   Poisson, 471 (*see also* Poisson
      distributions)
   summary, 475-77
Distribution models (*see* Linear
      programming, distribution models)
Distributions (*see* Probability
      distributions)
Dominance:
   elimination of, 130-31
   in games with saddle points, 139
Duality:
   fundamental relationship of, 58
   in linear programming, 58-60
Dumping, 161-63
Dynamic programming models, 108-20
   capital allocation problem, 113-16
   computational procedures, 110-13
      network flow procedure, 110-12
      resource allocation procedure,
         112-13
   formulation, 109-10
   shipping or "knapsack" problem,
      117-20
Dynamic replacement models, 215-19

E

Economic efficiency (*see* Efficiency)
Economic equivalence models, 175-92
   calculation of equivalence, 183-87
   comparing multiple alternatives,
      190-92
   evaluating a single alternative, 187-90
   interest and interest formulas, 178-83
   time value of money, 176-78
Effectiveness, 12-14, 16
Effectiveness function:
   construction of, 23-24
   and decision model, 27
   for minimum cost inventory policies,
      378, 382-83, 386
   and optimization of model, 25
   in terms of profit, 82
Efficiency, 12-13, 14
   economic vs. physical, 150-51
   of production operations, 148
   reduction in, as replacement
      consideration, 208
Elements:
   in critical path method, 280

   of matrix, 450
Elimination substitution technique, 448
Empty warehouse condition, 378
Environment, 15 (*see also* Decision
      environment)
Equality constraints, 60-62
Equivalence, of depreciation models,
   205-7
Equivalence function diagrams, 185-86
Equivalent annual cost, 186-87
   comparison of multiple alternatives,
      191
   evaluation of single alternative, 188-89
Events, in probability theory, 465
Expected value criterion, 131-32
Expected values, expressions for, 373-75
Experience curve (*see* Production
      progress models)
Experimentation, 22
Exponential distributions, 472-73

F

Feedback, 17
Finite population models, 432-36
Finite queuing tables, 433-34, 510-17
Finite shortage cost, 348-55
First-come, first-served (FCFS) rule, 267,
   268-69, 271-74
Fixed costs, 151-52
Fixed-percentage depreciation models,
   201-3
Flow-process chart, 21
Flow-shop sequencing, 254-62
   for n machines, 260-62
   for three machines, 256-60
   for two machines, 254-56
Functional depreciation, 196

G

Game decision models, 138-44
   for games without saddle points,
      140-44
   for games with saddle points, 139-40
   payoff matrix, 138-39
Gantt, Henry, 6
Gaussian distribution, 473
Gilbreth, Frank, 6
Gilbreth, Lillian, 6
Goal programming models (*see* Linear
      programming, goal programming
      models)
Graph, in critical path method, 280

Index

Graphical optimization methods, 34-42
  with goal programming model, 100-101
  maximization for three activities, 37-40
  maximization for two activities, 35-37
  minimization for two activities, 40-42
Graphical production progress function, 235-39
  on arithmetic paper, 235-36
  on log-log paper, 236-39
Graph theory, 280

H

Higher-order derivatives, 459
Holding cost, 335, 389
Holding time, 429
Human-machine chart, 21
Human want satisfaction, 8-10
  concept of utilities, 8-9
  and development of models, 28
  and efficiency, 14
  organization for, 9-10
Hurwicz criterion, 134-36, 137
Hypergeometric distribution, 468-69
  approximation of, 470, 475

I

Identity matrix, 451
Improvement curve (see Production progress models)
Incremental costs, 152-54
Indirect experimentation, 22
Industrial engineering, 6
Industrial Revolution, 11
Inflation, and interest rates, 176
Input-output functions, 163-66
Input parameters, control of, 26
Inputs, 149
  combinations to maximize profit, 167-70
  combinations to minimize cost, 166-67
Inspection programs:
  nonrectifying, 316
  rectifying, 316, 322
Institute of Management Science, The (TIMS), 5 and *fn*.
Interest:
  comparing multiple alternatives, 190-92
  compound, 177
  and depreciation, 196
  effective rates, 178
  equal payment series:
    capital-recovery factor, 181-82
    compound-amount factor, 180-81
    present-worth factor, 182-83
    sinking-fund factor, 181
  equivalence calculations, 184-87
  evaluating a single alternative, 187-90
  formulas, 178-83
  nominal annual rate, 178
  as production cost, 149
  simple, 177
  single-payment factors:
    compound-amount, 178-79
    present-worth, 179-80
  tables, 492-505
International Federation of Operational Research Societies, 5
Intrafirm transfer, 333
Inventory management:
  decision environment, 334-37
  effectiveness, 13
  and production time improvements, 234
Inventory models (see Procurement and inventory)
Inventory system, 332-34
Inversion, of matrices, 452-53
Item cost, in procurement models, 333-34, 345-48, 359-61

J

Job-shop sequencing problem, 262-66
  comparison of rules, 266-74
  example of completion performance, 265-66
  urgency factor algorithm, 264-65
  urgency factor model, 263-64

K

"Knapsack" problem, 117-20

L

Labor:
  cost of, 152
  as input, 149
  and production function, 164
Laplace criterion, 133, 137
Lead time:
  probability distributions, 367-68, 375-77
  in procurement alternatives, 332-34
Learning curve, 233

Linear break-even models (see Break-even models)
Linear equations:
  in matrix form, 450-51
  solving, 448-50
Linear programming:
  definition and applications, 33
  distribution models, 66-90
    assignment model, 77-84
    transportation model, 67-75
    traveling salesman problem, 84-90
    Vogel's approximation method, 75-77
  and effectiveness function, 25
  general models, 34-62
    degeneracy, 60
    dual problems, 58-60
    equality constraints, 60-62
    extensions, 62
    graphical optimization methods, 34-42
    mathematical formulation, 34
    matrix formulation, 47-52
    maximizing by simplex method, 42
    minimizing by simplex method, 46-47
    revised simplex method, 52-57
  goal programming models, 95-106
    formulation, 96
    graphical optimization method, 100-101
    modified simplex optimization method, 102-6
    for multiple goals, 97-100
Logic diagrams, 25
Lot tolerance percent defective, 318

M

Machine maintenance, and service factor, 436-38
Maintenance costs:
  patterns of, 212-13
  and replacement decision, 208
Maintenance rate, 221
Major objectives, 10-11
Management process, automation of, 28
Management science:
  history, 5-6
  relation to operations research, 5, 7-8
  and scientific management movement, 6-7
  simulation in, 23
  systematic plan for application of, 14-17
Manufacture alternative:
  considerations, 333-34
  decision model, 340-43
  with finite shortage costs, 352-55
  vs. purchase alternative, 343-44
  with variable item cost, 347-48
Manufacturing progress function tables, 505-9 (see also Production progress models)
Material input, 149
Mathematical models, 21-22
Matrix:
  defined, 450
  elements, 450
  forms, 451
  operations, 451-53
    addition, 451
    inversion, 452-53
    multiplication, 452
    subtraction, 451
  order, 451
  special types, 451
Maximax rules, 133-34, 137
Maximin rules, 133-34, 137
Maximization:
  graphical, 35-40
  simplex method, 42-46
Maximum profit–input rate combination, 167-70
Mean, 468
Minimax regret criterion, 136-37
Minimization:
  graphical, 40-42
  simplex method, 46-47
Minimum cost:
  input rate combination, 166-67
  inventory policies, 382-88
  service rate, 410-11, 426-27
Mixed strategy, 139, 140-44
Models, 19-28
  application of, 27-28
  classification of, 20-22
    mathematical, 21-22
    physical, 20
    schematic, 20-21
  experimentation with, 22-23
  formulation of, 15-16, 23-25
  optimization of, 16, 25
  review and control of, 26-27
  role in operations research/management science, 5, 6

Index

Models *(cont.)*
  and simulation, 22-23
  use and limitations, 16-17
Money:
  earning power of, 177
  equivalence factors, 183
  time value of, 176-78
Monte Carlo analysis, 477
  of inventory flow, 367, 375, 385
Most probable future criterion, 131
Multiple-channel queuing models:
  deterministic, 402-3
  probabilistic, 427-29
Multiplication, of matrices, 452
Multiplication theorem, 466

N

Network, in critical path method, 280-81
Network analysis, in PERT, 288-89
Network flow procedure, 110-12
Network theory, 280
Nominal annual interest rate, 178
Nonrectifying inspection program, 316
Non-zero-sum game, 138
Normal distributions, 473-76

O

Objectives, 10-12
  alternative means of achieving, 11-12
  conflict of, 11
  considerations in problem definition, 15
  effect of counteractions, 12
  major and subordinate, 10-11
Obsolescence, 196
Operating characteristics curve, 317-19
Operations analysis, 6
Operations research:
  history, 4-5
  and management science, 5, 7-8
  and scientific management movement, 6-7
  simulation in, 23
  systematic plan for application of, 14-17
Operations Research Society (U.K.), 5
Operations Research Society of America (ORSA), 5 and *fn*.
Optimality:
  principle of, 108
  testing for:
    in modified simplex method, 102-3
    in simplex method, 43-44
  in transportation model, 70-71
Optimization methods, 456-62
  differential calculus, 456-59
    partial differentiation, 459-60
    slope of a function, 456
  graphical, 34-42
  modified simplex method, 102-6
  simplex method, 42-46
  unconstrained, 460-62
Optimum replacement interval, 212-15
Organization chart, 21
Organizations, 9-10
Oriented arc, 280
Outcomes:
  effect of counteractions on, 12
  evaluation of, 17
  nonquantifiable, 128-29
  in payoff matrix model, 126-27
Outputs, 149-50

P

Parameters, 467-68
  input, control of, 26
Partial differentiation, 459-60
Path, 280 *(see also* Critical path)
Payoff matrix model, 126-27
  structure and assumptions, 126-27
  for two-person zero-sum game, 138-39
Payout, evaluation of, 189-90
p chart, 311-13
Periods:
  in deterministic procurement and inventory model, 336-37
  expected number per cycle, 374
PERT *(see* Program evaluation and review technique)
Physical depreciation, 196
Physical models, 20
Poisson distributions, 471, 475-77
  arrivals, 418-27, 429-32
  and c chart, 314
  for demand, 367, 377
  operating characteristics curve, 317-18, 319
Population:
  defined, 464
  finite, 432-41
  in queuing system, 396-97
Present worth:
  comparison of multiple alternatives, 190

Present worth *(cont.)*
  equivalence function diagrams, 185-86
  evaluation of single alternative, 188
  factor in interest formulas:
    equal-payment series, 179-80
    single-payment, 182-83
Price, 157-58
Probabilistic models, 21
  and effectiveness function, 25
  for inventory and procurement *(see* Procurement and inventory, probabilistic models)
Probabilistic project control, 286-90 *(see also* Program evaluation and review technique)
Probabilistic queuing models, 414-41
  distribution of waiting time, 424-27
    average time in system, 425
    mean waiting time, 425
    minimum cost service rate, 426-27
  finite population models, 433-41
    finite queuing tables, 433-34
    and maintenance, 436-41
    mean service time under control, 435-36
    number of service channels under control, 434-35
  multiple-channel waiting-line derivations, 427-29
    average delay or holding time, 429
    average length of queue, 428
    average number of units in system, 428
    average waiting time, 428
    probability that an arriving unit has to wait, 429
  Poisson arrivals with nonexponential service, 429-32
    with any service time distribution, 431-32
    with constant service time, 429-31
  simulation of waiting lines, 415-18
    arrival and service time distributions, 415
    economic analysis of output results, 418
    simulated sampling analysis, 416-18
  single-channel queuing derivations, 418-23
    average length of waiting line, 423
    mean number of units in system, 422-23
    probability of n units in system, 418-22
Probability distribution function, 467, 475 *tab.*
Probability distributions, 466-68
  arrival and service time, 415
  continuous, 471-75
    exponential, 472-73
    normal, 473-75
    rectangular, 471-72
  cumulative, 478-80
  for demand and lead time, 367-68
  determination of, 478
  discrete, 468-71
    binomial, 469-71
    hypergeometric, 468-69
    Poisson, 471 *(see also* Poisson distributions)
  lead time demand, 375-77
  summary, 475-77
  of waiting time, 424-27
Probability sequencing (PS):
  observations, 271-74
  as rule, 267
  and urgency factor, 264-65
Probability theory, 464-77
  addition theorem, 465
  conditional theorem, 466
  multiplication theorem, 466
  probability of an event, 465
  the universe and the sample, 464 *(see also* Probability distributions)
Problem, components of, 15
Procurement and inventory:
  applications of production progress models, 246
  deterministic models, 331-61
    based only on item cost, 359-61
    decision environment, 334-37
    for finite shortage cost, 348-55
    making the source decision, 343-45
    manufacture alternative, 333-34, 340-43
    to meet variable demand, 355-58
    purchase alternative, 332-33, 337-40
    for variable item cost, 345-48
  effectiveness of operations, 13
  probabilistic models, 366-90
    distribution of lead time demand, 375-78
    expressions for expected values, 373-75

Index

expressions for shortage conditions, 378-82
minimum cost policies, 382-85, 386-88
simplified system, 386-88
simulation of inventory flow, 367-73
single-period, 388-90
system, 332-34
Producer goods:
depreciation of (*see* Depreciation)
as input to production, 149
Producer risk, 318
Production:
effectiveness, 13
above normal capacity, 161
procurement alternative (*see* Manufacture alternative)
time improvements, 232-35 (*see also* Production progress models)
Production costs, 151-54
depreciation as, 197
fixed, 151-52
incremental, 152-54
interest as, 176-77
variable, 152
Production function, 163-70
input-output function, 163-66
maximum profit–input rate combination, 167-70
minimum cost–input rate combination, 166-67
Production operations models, 148-70
classification of production costs, 151-54
linear break-even models, 158-63
and production function, 163-70
and production system, 149-51
Production progress models, 231-50
applications, 245-50
financial, 248-49
procurement, 246-47
production, 247-48
reliability of data, 249-50
defining, 242-45
determining progress function from production standards, 243
fitting progress function to more than two points, 242-44
refinement of progress function, 245
graphical progress function, 235-39
on arithmetic paper, 235-36
on log-log paper, 236-39

mathematical models, 239-42
cumulative and cumulative average formulas, 240-42
tabular values, 242
unit formula, 239-40
time improvements, 232-35
and learning, 233-34
rate of, 232-33
shape of function, 234-35
Production quantity:
model, 154-58
and production time improvements, 232-33
Production sequencing, 253-74
comparison of job-shop rules, 266-74
job-shop simulation, 267-69
observations, 271-74
simulated outputs, 269-71
flow-shop sequencing, 254-62
for n machines, 260-62
for several machines, 256-60
for two machines, 254-56
job-shop sequencing problem, 262-66
example of complete performance, 265-66
urgency factor algorithm, 264-65
urgency factor model, 263-64
Production standards, 243
Production surface, 164
Production system, 149-51
defined, 149
economic efficiency, 150-51
inputs, 149
outputs, 149-50
Production time improvements, 232-35 (*see also* Production progress models)
Profit:
input combinations to maximize, 167-70
maximum allocation, 73-75
maximum assignment, 82-84
related to production quantity, 154-57
related to production quantity and price, 157-58
Program evaluation and review technique (PERT), 286-90
distinguished from critical path method, 281, 286
economic aspects, 290-92
project control example, 287-90
reasons for acceptance of, 279

Project, defined, 279
Project end, 280-81, 284
Project planning and control models, 279-92
  deterministic, 280-86 (*see also* Critical path method)
  economic aspects, 290-92
  probabilistic, 286-92 (*see also* Program evaluation and review technique)
  two conditions, 279
Project start, 280-81
Purchase alternative:
  considerations, 332-33
  decision model, 337-40
  with finite shortage cost, 349-52
  vs. manufacture alternative, 343-44
  with variable item cost, 345-47
Pure strategy, 138-39

Q

Quality control:
  and acceptance sampling, 316
  and production time improvements, 234
Queue (*see* Waiting line)
Queuing models:
  deterministic, 395-411 (*see also* Deterministic queuing models)
  probabilistic, 414-41 (*see also* Probabilistic queuing models)
Queuing system, 396-98
  arrival population, 396-97
  average time in, 425
  decision environment, 398-400
  service facility, 397-98
  waiting line, 397

R

RAND modified progress curve, 249
Random event, 464
Random rectangular variates, 488-89 *tab.*
Random sample, 464
Random variable:
  arrival patterns as, 398
  defined, 466
  demand and lead time as, 367-68
Rate of return:
  comparison of multiple alternatives, 191
  and depreciation, 198
  evaluation of single alternative, 189
R charts:
  applications, 303-6
  construction, 303
Rectangular distributions, 471-72
Rectifying inspection programs, 316, 322
Remanufacture alternative, 334, 340-43
Reneging, 397
Rent, 176
Replacement models, 207-24
  considerations leading to replacement, 207-9
  dynamic, 215-19
  optimum replacement interval, 212-15
  replacement of units that fail, 219-24
  treatment of sunk costs, 209-10
  treatment of unequal service life, 210-12
Replenishment rate, 333-34
Resource allocation:
  with dynamic programming model, 112-13
  and time needed for completion, 290-91
Return on investment (*see* Rate of return)
Revised simplex method, 52-57
Risk:
  decisions under, 129-32
  and inspection sampling, 318
  and interest rates, 176

S

Saddle points, 139-140
Sample, defined, 464
Sampling:
  acceptance (*see* Acceptance sampling models)
  simulated, 477-81
    inventory models, 367-73
Schematic models, 20-21, 25
Scientific management movement, 6-8
Scientific method, 4, 6
Service channels, 434-35
Service facility, 397-98
Service facility cost, 399, 426
  with multiple-channel model, 401
  with single-channel model, 403
Service factor:
  control by chart, 438-41
  machine downtime as function of, 436-38
Service life:
  comparison of multiple alternatives, 191-92
  unequal, 210-12

Index

Service mechanism, 398-99
Service rate, minimum cost, 410-11
Service time:
    mean, under control, 435-36
    with Poisson arrivals, 429-32
    probability distributions, 415
Shipping problem, 117-20
Shortage conditions, 378-82
    empty warehouse, 378-79
    expected number of shortages, 379-82
    expected number of unit period shortages, 382
    one or more shortages, 379
Shortage cost, 335
    finite, 348-55
    in single-period model, 388-89
Shortest processing time (SPT) rule, 267, 271-74
Simple interest, 177
Simplex method, 25
    degeneracy in, 60
    development of, 33
    with goal programming models, 102-6
    maximizing by, 42-46
    minimizing by, 46-47
    revised, 52-57
    treating equality constraints, 60-62
Simulated sampling, 477-81
Simulation:
    for comparison of job-shop sequencing rules, 267-71
    and experimentation, 22-23
    of inventory flow, 367-73
    of waiting lines, 415-18
Single-channel queuing model:
    deterministic, 400-402
    probabilistic, 418-23
Single-payment compound-amount factor, 178-79
Single-payment present-worth factor, 178-80
Single-period inventory model, 388-89
Sinking fund:
    depreciation model, 201
    interest formulas, 181
Specification limits, 307-8
Square matrix, 451, 453
Standard deviation, 468
Stanford progress curves, 249
Statistical control models, 297-324
    acceptance sampling, 316-24
    for attributes, 310-15
    concept of, 298-301

    control by control chart, 299-301
    patterns of statistical variation, 298-99
    operating characteristics of $\bar{X}$ charts, 306-10
    for variables, 301-6
Statistical tables, 482-91
    cumulative normal probabilities, 490-91
    cumulative Poisson probabilities, 484-86
    cumulative Poisson probability curves, 487
    random rectangular variates, 488-89
Straight-line depreciation, 198-201
Strategy, 138-39
Subordinate objectives, 10-11
Sum-of-the-years depreciation model, 203-5
Sunk costs, in replacement model, 209-10
Systems:
    formalizing logic of, 477-78
    procurement and inventory, 332-34
    production, 149-51
    queuing, 396-98, 404-5

T

Tabular values, use of, 242
Taylor, Frederick, 6
Tolerance limit, 307
Transportation model, 67-75
    and assignment model, 77
Transpose matrix, 451
Traveling salesman problem, 84-90

U

Uncertainty, 132-38
Unconstrained optimization, 460-62
Universe, 464
Urgency factor:
    algorithm, 264-65
    model, 263-64
Utilities:
    creating and exchanging, 9-10
    and human want satisfaction, 8-9

V

Value-time function, 196-97
Variable costs, 152
    in probabilistic inventory model, 384-85, 386-88
Variable demand, 355-58

Variable item cost, 345-48
  production decision, 347-48
  purchase decision, 345-47
Variables:
  control models for, 301-6
  in mathematical models, 21, 23
  random, 466
Variance, 468
Vendors, evaluating alternative, 344
Vertex, 280
Vogel's approximation method, 75-77

W

Waiting cost, 399
  with multiple-channel model, 403
  with probabilistic model, 426
  with single-channel model, 401
Waiting line, 397
  average length, 423
  models with initial, 403-7
  models without initial, 400-403
  simulation of, 415-18

Waiting-line models (see Deterministic queuing models; Probabilistic queuing models)
Waiting-line operations, effectiveness, 13
Waiting time:
  average, in multiple-channel system, 428
  mean, in single-channel system, 425
  probability distribution, 424-27
  total:
    approximation for, 407-9
    with initial waiting line, 405-7
    with irregular arrivals, 409-10
Work-sampling study, 311-13

X

$\bar{X}$ charts:
  applications, 303-6
  construction, 301-3
  operating characteristics, 306-10

Z

Zero-sum game, 138